FINANCIAL MANAGEMENT
FOR DECISION MAKERS

SEVENTH EDITION

FINANCIAL MANAGEMENT

FOR DECISION MAKERS

Peter Atrill

PEARSON

Harlow, England • London • New York • Boston • San Francisco • Toronto • Sydney
Auckland • Singapore • Hong Kong • Tokyo • Seoul • Taipei • New Delhi
Cape Town • São Paulo • Mexico City • Madrid • Amsterdam • Munich • Paris • Milan

Pearson Education Limited
Edinburgh Gate
Harlow CM20 2JE
United Kingdom
Tel: +44 (0)1279 623623
Web: www.pearson.com/uk

First published 1997 (print)
Second edition published 2000 (print)
Third edition published 2003 (print)
Fourth edition published 2006 (print)
Fifth edition published 2009 (print)
Sixth edition published (print) 2012
Seventh edition published 2014 (print and electronic)

© Pearson Education Limited 2014 (print and electronic)

The Financial Times. With a worldwide network of highly respected journalists, *The Financial Times* provides global business news, insightful opinion and expert analysis of business, finance and politics. With over 500 journalists reporting from 50 countries worldwide, our in-depth coverage of international news is objectively reported and analysed from an independent, global perspective. To find out more, visit www.ft.com/pearsonoffer.

ISBN: 978-1-292-01606-1 (print)
       978-1-292-01609-2 (PDF)
       978-1-292-01607-8 (eText)

British Library Cataloguing-in-Publication Data
A catalogue record for the print edition is available from the British Library

Library of Congress Cataloguing-in-Publication Data
A catalogue record for the print edition is available from the Library of Congress

10 9 8 7 6 5 4 3 2 1
16 15 14 13 12

Front cover image: Getty Image

Print edition typeset in 9.25/13pt Helvetica Neue LT Pro by 35
Print edition printed and bound by L.E.G.O. S.p.A., Italy

NOTE THAT ANY PAGE CROSS REFERENCES REFER TO THE PRINT EDITION

Contents

10 Managing working capital 407

11 Measuring and managing for shareholder value 455

Preface

This book has been written for those wishing to achieve a broad understanding of financial management at either undergraduate or postgraduate/post-experience level. It is aimed primarily at students who are studying financial management as part of their course in business, management, accounting, economics, computing, or some other area. The book should also be suitable for those who are not following a particular course but nevertheless need an understanding of financial management to help them manage their business.

As there are several excellent books on financial management already published, you may wonder why another book is needed in this area. Many of the available books are too detailed and demanding to provide a suitable introduction to the subject. They are often around 1,000 pages in length and contain mathematical formulae that many students find daunting. This book assumes no previous knowledge of financial management (although a basic understanding of financial statements is required) and is written in an accessible style. Each topic is introduced carefully and there is a gradual building of knowledge. In addition, mathematical formulae have been kept to a minimum.

The book rests on a solid foundation of theory, but the main focus throughout is its practical value. It is assumed that readers are primarily concerned with understanding financial management in order to make better financial decisions. The title of the book reflects this decision-making focus.

The book is written in an 'open learning' style; that is, it tries to involve you in a way not traditionally found in textbooks. Throughout each chapter there are activities and self-assessment questions for you to attempt. The purpose of these is to help check understanding of the points that are being made and to encourage you to think around particular topics. More detail concerning the nature and use of these activities and self-assessment questions is given in the 'How to use this book' section following this preface. The open learning style has been adopted because, I believe, it is more user friendly. Irrespective of whether you are using the book as part of a taught course or for independent study, the interactive approach employed makes it easier for you to learn.

As it is likely that most of you will not have studied financial management before, the use of technical jargon has been kept to a minimum. Where technical terminology is unavoidable, I try to provide clear explanations. To help you further, all the key terms are highlighted in the book and then listed at the end of each chapter with a page reference to help you rapidly revise the main concepts. All these key terms are listed alphabetically with a short definition in the glossary, which can be found towards the end of the book.

In writing the seventh edition, I have taken account of helpful comments and suggestions made by lecturers, students and other readers. Many areas have been revised to improve the clarity of the writing and I have introduced new topics such as directors' share options. I have also expanded certain areas such as the measurement of shareholder value and the problem of short termism. Finally, I have introduced more activities throughout to enhance the interactive nature of the text.

I do hope that you will find the book readable and helpful.

Peter Atrill
June 2013

Acknowledgements

We are grateful to the following for permission to reproduce copyright material:

Figures

Figure 1.5 adapted from Ownership of UK quoted shares 2012, based on information from the Office of National Statistics, www.ons.gov.uk, Crown copyright, source: Office for National Statistics licensed under the Open Government Licence v.2.0; Figure 3.3 from *Accounting and Finance for Non-specialists*, 7 edn, (Atrill, P. and McLaney, E., 2010) p. 206, FT/Prentice Hall, Pearson Education Ltd; Figures 4.1, 4.2, 4.4 from *Accounting An Introduction*, 5 edn, (Atrill, P. and McLaney, E., 2009) FT/Prentice Hall, Pearson Education Ltd; Figure 4.6 from *Accounting and Finance for Non-specialists*, 8 edn, (Atrill, P. and McLaney, E., 2013) Pearson Education, Pearson Education Ltd; Figure 7.3 from 'Reading the signs', *The Independent*, 27/03/2004, reproduced with permission from *The Independent*; Figures 8.6, 8.7 from '"Practitioners" perspectives on the UK cost of capital', *European Journal of Finance*, 10, 123–38 (McLaney, E., Pointon, J., Thomas, M. and Tucker, J., 2004).

Tables

Table 7.14 from *Angel Investing: Matching Start-up Funds with Start-up Companies – A Guide for Entrepreneurs and Individual Investors*, Jossey-Bass Inc. (Van Osnabrugge, M. and Robinson, R.J., 2000) Copyright © 2000, John Wiley and Sons.

Text

Box 1.1 from 'Assessing the rate of return', *Financial Times Mastering Management Series*, 1, 13 (Dimson, E., 1995), Financial Times; Box 1.3 from 'Forget how the crow flies', *The Financial Times*, 17/01/2004 (Kay, J.), copyright © The Financial Times Limited, All Rights Reserved; Box 1.5 adapted from Extracts from Code of Ethics, Sage Group www.sage.com, Sage Group plc; Box 1.10 from 'Sly Bailey to leave Trinity Mirror', *Financial Times*, 03/05/2102 (Fenton, B., Davoudi, S. and Burgess, K.), copyright © The Financial Times Limited, All Rights Reserved; Box 1.12 from UK Stewardship Code, July 2012, www.frc.org.uk, Financial Reporting Council, © The Financial Reporting Council – adapted and reproduced with the kind permission of the FRC, all rights reserved; Box 2.2 from 'Companies need to learn to care for cash', *Financial Times*, 02/10/2009 (Sakoui, A.) © The Financial Times Limited, All Rights Reserved; Box 2.3 from 'Vanco's shares fall on profit warning', *Financial Times*, 21/08/2007 (Stafforr, P.), © The Financial Times Limited, All Rights Reserved; Box 2.4 from 'Funding plans a key matter in annual reports', *Financial Times*, 25/01/2009 (Hughes, J.), © The Financial Times Limited, All Rights Reserved; Box 2.6 from Analysts' consensus, J. Sainsbury plc, www.j-sainsbury.co.uk; Box 3.4 adapted from 'Costs vibrate as VW accelerates', *Financial Times*, 29/03/2010 (Schäfer, D.), © The Financial Times Limited, All Rights Reserved; Box 3.5 adapted from

'Companies monitor companies credit scores', *Financial Times*, 26/01/2012 (Moules, J.), © The Financial Times Limited, All Rights Reserved; Box 3.6 from 'Gearing levels set to plummet', *Financial Times*, 10/02/2009 (Grant, J.) © The Financial Times Limited, All Rights Reserved; Box 3.10 from 'New study re-writes the A to Z of value investing', *Financial Times*, 14/08/2009 (Mathurin, P.), © The Financial Times Limited, All Rights Reserved; Box 3.12 from *Arnold Weinstock and the Making of GEC* (Aris, S., 1998) Aurum Press; Box 4.6 from 'Deutsche Telekom backs MetroPCS takeover', *Financial Times*, 03/10/2012 (Taylor, P. and Gelles, D.), © The Financial Times Limited, All Rights Reserved; Box 4.11 from 'Easy ride', *Financial Times*, 26/10/2007 (Hughes, C.), © The Financial Times Limited, All Rights Reserved; Box 5.4 from 'Positive scoping study at 100% owned Azuca project in southern Peru', news release, Hochschild Mining plc, phx.corporate-ir.netphx.corporate-ir.net; Box 5.5 from 'A story can be more useful than maths', *Financial Times*, 26/02/2013 (Kay, J.), © The Financial Times Limited, All Rights Reserved; Box 5.6 from South Hampshire Rapid Transit Fareham–Gosport–Portsmouth Investment Appraisal, 2005, www.hants.gov.uk Hampshire County Council, contains public sector information licensed under the Open Government Licence v2.0. http://www.nationalarchives.gov.uk/doc/open-government-licence/version/2/; Box 5.7 from 'Mace set to grow in all directions', *Financial Times*, 01/08/2010 (Hammond, E.), © The Financial Times Limited, All Rights Reserved; Box 6.1 from 'St Modwen to launch unsecured bonds', *Financial Times*, 17/10/2102 (Eley, J.), © The Financial Times Limited, All Rights Reserved; Box 6.2 from Shareholder letter, Berkshire Hathaway Inc., www.berkshirehathaway.com, Warren Buffett, the material is copyrighted and used with permission of the author; Box 6.3 from 'Man Utd's first bond suffers from lack of support', *Financial Times*, 03/02/2010 (Sakoui, A. and Blitz, R.), © The Financial Times Limited, All Rights Reserved; Box 6.5 from Lex column, 'Sony – group bonding', 15 November 2012 www.FT.com, © The Financial Times Limited, All Rights Reserved; Box 6.9 from Wolseley plc Annual Report 2012, p. 148 www.wolseley.com, Wolseley Group plc; Box 6.9 from Barratt Developments plc, Annual Report and Accounts 2012, www.barrattdevelopments.co.uk Barratt Developments plc; Box 6.12 from 'Seeds of Woolworths' demise sown long ago', *Financial Times*, 29/11/2008 (Rigby, E.), © The Financial Times Limited, All Rights Reserved; Box 7.4 from 'Esure moves closer to bumper valuation', *Financial Times*, 13/03/2013 (Gray, A.), © The Financial Times Limited, All Rights Reserved; Box 7.5 from 'Dell to go private in $24.4bn deal', *Daily Telegraph*, 06/02/2013 (Blackden, R.), copyright © Telegraph Media Group Limited 2013; Box 7.7 from Tempure Pedic: Hard Landing Lex column, 08/06/2012, www.ft.com, © The Financial Times Limited, All Rights Reserved; Box 7.9 from 'Abramovich invests in "gas-to-liquids" in UK', *Financial Times*, 04/01/2013 (Chazan, G.), © The Financial Times Limited, All Rights Reserved; Box 7.12 from 'Does tax relief tempt angels?', *Financial Times*, 20/04/2012 (Mason, C.); Box 9.4 from Shareholder letter, www.berkshirehathaway.com, Warren Buffett, the material is copyrighted and used with permission of the author; Box 9.5 from 'BP raises dividend after Russian deal', *Financial Times*, 30/10/2012 (Chazan, G.), © The Financial Times Limited, All Rights Reserved; Box 9.6 from 'Companies in Europe see dividend rises', *Financial Times*, 22/02/2010 (Milne, R.), © The Financial Times Limited, All Rights Reserved; Box 9.7 from R. Wall, 'Aer Lingus profit falls as dividend raised in Ryanair bid battle', www.bloomberg.com, Bloomberg; Box 9.13 from 'The value of share buybacks', *Financial Director* (Goddard, M.), copyright Incisive Media Investments Ltd 2010, reproduced with permission; Box 10.4 from 'Wal-Mart aims for further inventory cuts', *Financial Times*, 19/04/2006 (Birchall, J.), © The Financial Times Limited, All Rights Reserved; Box 10.5 from 'Inventory control in retail', *Financial Times*, 13/02/2012 (Bird, J.), © The Financial Times Limited, All Rights Reserved; Box 10.9 from www.atradius.us/news/press-releases; Box 10.11 from 'Dash for Cash', Karaian, J., *CFO Europe Magazine*, 8 July 2008, www.cfo.com, CFO.com; Box 10.12 from 'Big companies resist prompt payment code', *Financial Times*, 09/01/2013 (Rigby, E. and Parker, G.), © The Financial Times Limited. All Rights Reserved.; Box 10.13 from 'Dash for Cash', Karaian, J. *CFO Europe Magazine*, 8 July 2008, www.CFO.com, CFO.com; General displayed texts 11 from Annual Report to shareholders, Berkshire Hathaway Inc 1985, www.berkshirehathaway.com, Warren Buffett, the material is copyrighted and used with permission of the author; Box 11.1 from 'Siemens chief finds himself in a difficult balancing act', *Financial Times*, 06/05/2006 (Milne, R.), © The Financial Times Limited, All Rights Reserved; Box 11.9 from Boston Consulting Group, 'The 2012 value creators rankings', www.bcgperspectives.com, Boston Consulting Group; Box 11.13 from 'Ebay seeks to alter terms of stock options', *Financial Times*, 11/03/2009 (Gelles, D.), © The Financial Times Limited, All Rights Reserved; Box 12.2 adapted from 'Computing the future for Yahoo and Microsoft', *Financial Times*, 04/05/2007 (Nuttall, C. and Waters, R.), © The Financial Times Limited, All Rights Reserved; Box 12.3 from 'Dear Mickey: open letter to Disney', *Financial Times*, 11/02/2004, © The Financial Times Limited, All Rights Reserved; Box 12.4 from 'Decline of the conglomerates', *Financial Times*, 04/02/2007 (Guerrera, F.), © The Financial Times Limited, All Rights Reserved; Boxes 12.5, 12.9 from Letter to shareholders, www.berkshirehathaway.com, Warren Buffett, the material is copyrighted and used with permission of the author; Box 12.6 adapted from Shareholders letter, Berkshire Hathaway Inc, www.berkshirehathaway.com 26 February 2010, Warren Buffett, the material is copyrighted and used with permission of the author; Box 12.8 from 'Merger to provide $100m boost for advisers,' *Financial Times*, 02/02/2012 (Sakoui, A. and Blas, J.), © The Financial Times Limited, All Rights Reserved; Box 12.11 from 'Logic of corporate shrinkage asserts itself', *Financial Times*, 04/09/2011 (Jackson, T.), © The Financial Times Limited, All Rights Reserved.

In some instances we have been unable to trace the owners of copyright material and we would appreciate any information that would enable us to do so.

How to use this book

The contents of the book have been ordered in what I believe is a logical sequence and, for this reason, I suggest that you work through the book in the order in which it is presented. Every effort has been made to ensure that earlier chapters do not refer to concepts or terms that are not explained until a later chapter. If you work through the chapters in the 'wrong' order, you will probably encounter concepts and points that were explained previously but which you have missed.

Irrespective of whether you are using the book as part of a lecture/tutorial-based course or as the basis for a more independent form of study, I recommend you follow broadly the same approach.

Integrated assessment material

Interspersed throughout each chapter are numerous **Activities**. You are strongly advised to attempt all these questions. They are designed to stimulate the sort of 'quick-fire' questions that a good lecturer might throw at you during a lecture or tutorial. Activities seek to serve two purposes:

- To give you the opportunity to check that you understand what has been covered so far.
- To encourage you to think about the topic just covered, either to see a link between that topic and others with which you are already familiar, or to link the topic just covered to the next.

The answer to each Activity is provided immediately after the question. This answer should be covered up until you have deduced your solution, which can then be compared to the one given.

Towards the end of most chapters, there is a **Self-assessment question**. This is rather more demanding and comprehensive than any of the Activities and is designed to give you an opportunity to see whether you understand the core material in the chapter. The solution to each of the Self-assessment questions is provided at the end of the book. As with the Activities, it is very important that you attempt each question thoroughly before referring to the solution. If you have difficulty with a Self-assessment question, you should go over the relevant chapter again.

End-of-chapter assessment material

At the end of each chapter, there are four **Review questions**. These are short questions requiring a narrative answer or discussion within a tutorial group. They are intended to enable you to assess how well you can recall and critically evaluate the core terms and concepts covered in each chapter. Suggested answers to these questions are included at the end of the book. Again, a real attempt should be made to answer these questions before referring to the solutions.

At the end of a chapter, there are normally seven Exercises. (However, Chapter 1 has none, and Chapters 9 and 11 have six.) These are mostly computational and are designed to reinforce your knowledge and understanding. Exercises are of varying complexity, with the more advanced ones clearly identified. Although the less advanced Exercises are fairly straightforward, the more advanced ones can be quite demanding. Nevertheless, they are capable of being successfully completed if you have worked conscientiously through the chapter and have attempted the less advanced Exercises beforehand.

Answers to those Exercises marked with a coloured number are provided at the end of the book. Three of the Exercises in each chapter are marked with a coloured number to enable you to check progress. The marked Exercises are a mixture of less advanced and more advanced Exercises. Solutions to the Exercises that are not marked with a coloured number are given in a separate lecturer's Solutions Manual. Yet again, a thorough attempt should be made to answer these Exercises before referring to the solutions.

Guided tour of the book

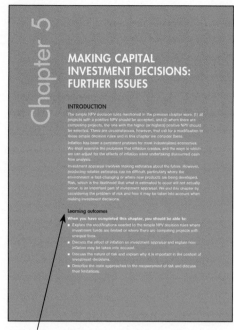

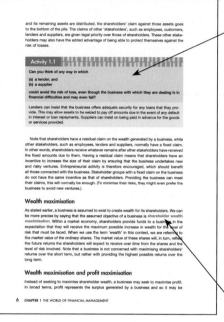

Activities These short questions, integrated throughout each chapter, allow you to check your understanding as you progress through the text. They comprise either a narrative question requiring you to review or critically consider topics, or a numerical problem requiring you to deduce a solution. A suggested answer is given immediately after each activity.

Key terms The key concepts and techniques in each chapter are highlighted in colour where they are first introduced.

Learning outcomes Bullet points at the start of each chapter show what you can expect to learn from that chapter, and highlight the core coverage.

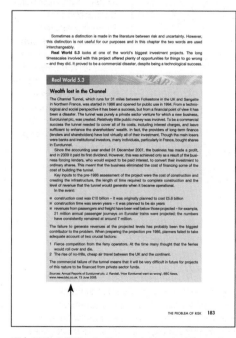

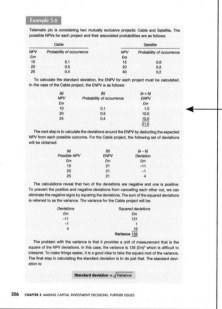

Examples At frequent intervals throughout most chapters, there are numerical examples that give you step-by-step workings to follow through to the solution.

'Real World' illustrations Integrated throughout the text, these illustrative examples highlight the practical application of accounting concepts and techniques by real businesses, including extracts from company reports and financial statements, survey data and other insights from business.

Self-assessment questions   Towards the end of most chapters you will encounter one of these questions, allowing you to attempt a comprehensive question before tackling the end-of-chapter assessment material. To check your understanding and progress, solutions are provided at the end of the book.

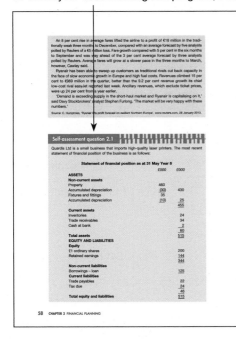

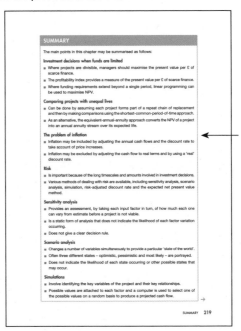

Bullet point chapter summary   Each chapter ends with a 'bullet-point' summary. This highlights the material covered in the chapter and can be used as a quick reminder of the main issues.

Key terms summary   At the end of each chapter, there is a listing (with page references) of all the key terms introduced in that chapter, allowing you to refer back easily to the most important points.

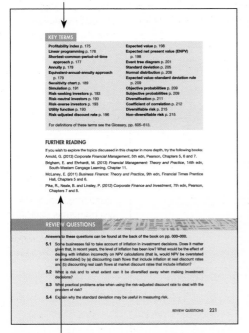

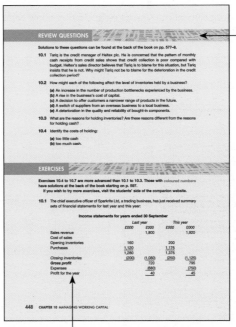

Review questions
These short questions encourage you to review and/or critically discuss your understanding of the main topics covered in each chapter, either individually or in a group. Solutions to these questions can be found at the back of the book.

Further reading   This section comprises a listing of relevant chapters in other textbooks that you might refer to in order to pursue a topic in more depth or gain an alternative perspective.

Exercises   These comprehensive questions at the end of most chapters. The more advanced questions are separately identified. Solutions to five of the questions (those with coloured numbers) are provided at the end of the book, enabling you to assess your progress. Solutions to the remaining questions are available online for lecturers only. Additional exercises can be found on the companion website at **www.pearsoned.co.uk/atrill**.

THE WORLD OF FINANCIAL MANAGEMENT

INTRODUCTION

In this first chapter, we shall look at the role of the finance function within a business and the context within which financial decisions are made. This should help to set the scene for subsequent chapters. We begin by identifying the tasks of the finance function and their relation to the tasks of managers. We then go on to consider the objectives that a business may pursue.

Modern financial management theory assumes that the primary objective of a business is to maximise the wealth of its shareholders. We shall examine this and other possible objectives for a business to understand why shareholder wealth maximisation is considered the most appropriate. There is, however, a danger that businesses will adopt too narrow a focus in pursuit of this objective. For a business to survive and prosper over the long term, it must be pursued in a way that takes account of the business environment. We shall see that managers therefore must act in an ethical manner and must be sensitive to the interests of other groups with a stake in the business.

Simply stating that a business's primary objective is shareholder wealth maximisation will not automatically cause this to happen. There is always a risk that managers will pursue their own interests at the expense of shareholders' interests. This is often referred to as the 'agency problem'. We end the chapter by considering how this problem may be managed through such methods as regulation and through the active involvement of shareholders.

Learning outcomes

When you have completed this chapter, you should be able to:

- Discuss the role of the finance function within a business.

- Identify and discuss possible objectives for a business and explain the advantages of the shareholder wealth maximisation objective.

- Explain how risk, ethical considerations and the needs of other stakeholders influence the pursuit of shareholder wealth maximisation.

- Describe the agency problem and explain how it may be managed.

THE FINANCE FUNCTION

Put simply, the finance function within a business exists to help managers to manage. To understand how the finance function can achieve this, we must first be clear about what managers do. One way of describing the role of managers is to classify their activities into the following categories:

- *Strategic management*. This involves developing objectives for a business and then formulating a strategy (long-term plan) to achieve them. Deciding on an appropriate strategy will involve identifying and evaluating the various options available. The option chosen should be the one that offers the greatest potential for achieving the objectives developed.
- *Operations management*. To ensure that things go according to plan, managers must exert day-to-day control over the various business functions. Where events do not conform to earlier plans, appropriate decisions and actions must be taken.
- *Risk management*. The risks faced by a business must be identified and properly managed. These risks, which may be many and varied, arise from the nature of business operations and from the way in which the business is financed.

As we can see from Figure 1.1, these three management activities are not separate and distinct. They are interrelated, and overlaps arise between them. When considering a particular strategy, for example, managers must also make a careful assessment of the risks involved and how these risks may be managed. Similarly, when making operational decisions, managers must try to ensure they fit within the strategic (long-term) plan that has been formulated.

The figure shows the three overlapping roles of management.

Figure 1.1 The role of managers

The finance function is concerned with helping managers in each of the three areas identified. This is achieved by undertaking various key tasks, which are set out in Figure 1.2 and described below.

- *Financial planning.* It is vital for managers to assess the potential impact of proposals on future financial performance and position. They can more readily evaluate the implications of their decisions if they are provided with projected financial statements (such as projected cash flow statements and projected income statements) and with other estimates of financial outcomes.
- *Investment project appraisal*. Investment in new long-term projects can have a profound effect on the future prospects of a business. By carrying out appraisals of the profitability

and riskiness of investment project proposals, managers can make informed decisions about whether to accept or reject them. Financial appraisals can also help to prioritise those investment projects that have been accepted.

■ *Financing decisions*. Investment projects and other business activities have to be financed. Various sources of finance are available, each with their own characteristics and costs, which need to be identified and evaluated. When selecting an appropriate source, consideration must be given to the overall financial structure of a business. An appropriate balance must be struck between long-term and short-term sources of finance and between the financing contribution of shareholders and that of lenders. Not all of the finance required may come from external sources: some may be internally generated. An important source of internally generated finance is profits, and the extent to which these are reinvested by a business, rather than distributed to the owners, requires careful consideration.

■ *Capital market operations*. New finance may be raised through the capital markets, such as through a stock exchange or banks. Managers will often need advice on how finance can be raised through these markets, how securities (shares and loan capital) are priced, and how the markets may react to proposed investment and financing plans.

■ *Financial control*. Once plans are implemented, managers must ensure that things stay on course. Regular reporting of information on actual outcomes, such as the profitability of investment projects, levels of working capital and cash flows, is required as a basis for monitoring performance and, where necessary, taking corrective action.

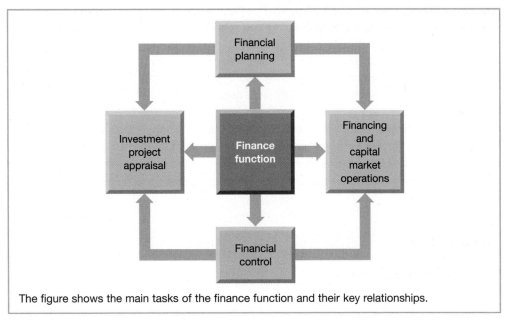

The figure shows the main tasks of the finance function and their key relationships.

Figure 1.2 The tasks of the finance function

The links between the tasks of managers, which were identified earlier, and the tasks of the finance function are many and varied. Strategic management decisions, for example, may require an input from the finance function on issues relating to financial planning, investment project appraisal, financing and capital market operations. Operations management may require an input on issues relating to financial planning, investment project appraisal, financing and financial control. Risk management may require an input from the finance function on issues relating to all of the tasks identified above.

STRUCTURE OF THE BOOK

In this book, each of the tasks of the finance function will be considered in some detail. We begin, in Chapter 2, by examining the way in which financial plans are prepared and the role of projected financial statements in helping managers to assess likely future outcomes.

In Chapter 3, we go on to consider how financial statements can be analysed and interpreted. The financial techniques examined in this chapter are important for financial planning, including the control of working capital and the evaluation of projected financial statements, as well as for long-term financing decisions, which are discussed in later chapters.

Chapters 4 and 5 are concerned with investment project appraisal. In these two chapters, we take a look at the methods used to assess the profitability of investment proposals. We also consider how risk may be taken into account and how investment projects, once implemented, may be monitored and controlled.

Chapters 6 to 9 are concerned with various aspects of the financing decision. We first discuss the various sources of finance available and the role and efficiency of capital markets. We then go on to consider the mix of finance that a business might have within its capital structure and how the level of borrowing can affect future risks and returns. Finally, we consider the dividend decision and the factors to be taken into account when deciding upon the appropriate balance between the retention and distribution of profits.

In Chapter 10, we look at the ways in which managers can exert financial control over the working capital of a business. We examine the key elements of working capital (inventories, receivables, cash and payables) and discuss the various techniques available for controlling each element.

In Chapter 11, we consider some of the main methods for measuring and managing shareholder wealth. We shall evaluate their usefulness and explore the reasons why new methods of measuring shareholder wealth were necessary.

Finally, in Chapter 12, we take a look at mergers and takeovers. This will involve drawing on our understanding of a number of topics covered earlier, in particular investment appraisal, financing and capital market operations. We consider the effect of mergers on shareholder wealth and the ways in which merger proposals may be financed. We end the chapter by seeing how the shares of a business may be valued for mergers and for other purposes.

MODERN FINANCIAL MANAGEMENT

In the early years of its development, financial management was really an offshoot of accounting. Much of the early work was descriptive, and arguments were based on casual observation rather than on any clear theoretical framework. However, over the years, financial management became increasingly influenced by economic theories and the reasoning applied to particular issues has become more rigorous and analytical. Indeed, such is the influence of economic theory that modern financial management is often viewed as a branch of applied economics.

Economic theories concerning the efficient allocation of scarce resources have been taken and developed into decision-making tools for management. This development of economic theories for practical business use has usually involved taking account of both the time dimension and the risks associated with management decision making. An investment decision, for example, must look at both the time period over which the investment extends and the degree of risk associated with the investment. This fact has led to financial management being described as the *economics of time and risk*. Certainly time and risk will be recurring themes throughout this text.

Economic theories have also helped us to understand the importance of capital markets, such as stock exchanges and banks, to a business. Capital markets have a vital role to play in bringing together borrowers and lenders, in allowing investors to select the type of investment that best meets their risk requirements, and in helping to evaluate the performance of businesses through the prices assigned to their shares.

Real World 1.1 is an extract from an article by Professor Dimson of London Business School. It neatly sums up how time, risk and capital markets are at the centre of modern financial management.

Real World 1.1

Finance on the back of a postage stamp

The leading textbooks in finance are nearly 1,000 pages long. Many students learn by making notes on each topic. They then summarise their notes. Here is one student's summary of his Finance course: Time is money . . . Don't put all your eggs in one basket . . . You can't fool all the people all of the time.

- The idea that time is money refers to the fact that a sum of money received now is worth more than the same sum paid in the future. This gives rise to the principle that future cash flows should be discounted, in order to calculate their present value.
- You can reduce the risk of an investment if you don't put all your eggs in one basket. In other words, a diversified portfolio of investments is less risky than putting all your money in a single asset. Risks that cannot be diversified away should be accepted only if they are offset by a higher expected return.
- The idea that you can't fool all of the people all of the time refers to the efficiency of financial markets. An efficient market is one in which information is widely and cheaply available to everyone and relevant information is therefore incorporated into security prices. Because new information is reflected in prices immediately, investors should expect to receive only a normal rate of return. Possession of information about a company will not enable an investor to outperform. The only way to expect a higher expected return is to be exposed to greater risk.

These three themes of discounted cash flow, risk and diversification, and market efficiency lie at the very heart of most introductory finance courses. Each of these themes will be considered in this book.

FT *Source*: Dimson, E. (1995), *Assessing the Rate of Return*, Financial Times Mastering Management series, supplement issue no. 1, p. 13.
© The Financial Times Limited 2012. All Rights Reserved.

WHY DO BUSINESSES EXIST?

A key assumption underpinning modern financial management is that businesses exist to create wealth for their shareholders. This has provoked much debate and so is worth exploring in some detail. Shareholders are considered of paramount importance because they effectively own the business and therefore bear the residual risk. During the good times they benefit, but during the bad times they must bear any losses. Furthermore, if the business fails and its remaining assets are distributed, the shareholders' claim against those assets goes to the bottom of the pile. The claims of other 'stakeholders', such as employees, customers, lenders and suppliers, are given legal priority over those of shareholders. These other stakeholders may also have the added advantage of being able to protect themselves against the risk of losses.

Activity 1.1

Can you think of any way in which

(a) a lender, and
(b) a supplier

could avoid the risk of loss, even though the business with which they are dealing is in financial difficulties and may even fail?

Lenders can insist that the business offers adequate security for any loans that they provide. This may allow assets to be seized to pay off amounts due in the event of any default in interest or loan repayments. Suppliers can insist on being paid in advance for the goods or services provided.

Note that shareholders have a residual claim on the wealth generated by a business, while other stakeholders, such as employees, lenders and suppliers, normally have a fixed claim. In other words, shareholders receive whatever remains after other stakeholders have received the fixed amounts due to them. Having a residual claim means that shareholders have an incentive to increase the size of their claim by ensuring that the business undertakes new and risky ventures. Entrepreneurial activity is therefore encouraged, which should benefit all those connected with the business. Stakeholder groups with a fixed claim on the business do not have the same incentive as that of shareholders. Providing the business can meet their claims, this will normally be enough. (To minimise their risks, they might even prefer the business to avoid new ventures.)

Wealth maximisation

As stated earlier, a business is assumed to exist to create wealth for its shareholders. We can be more precise by saying that the assumed objective of a business is shareholder wealth maximisation. Within a market economy, shareholders provide funds to a business in the expectation that they will receive the maximum possible increase in wealth for the level of risk that must be faced. When we use the term 'wealth' in this context, we are referring to the *market value of the ordinary shares.* The market value of these shares will, in turn, reflect the future returns the shareholders will expect to receive *over time* from the shares and the level of risk involved. Note that a business is not concerned with maximising shareholders' returns over the short term, but rather with providing the highest possible returns over the long term.

Wealth maximisation and profit maximisation

Instead of seeking to maximise shareholder wealth, a business may seek to maximise profit. In broad terms, profit represents the surplus generated by a business and so it may be tempting to conclude that the maximisation of profit will ultimately lead to the maximisation of shareholder wealth. Unfortunately, things aren't so straightforward.

Profit maximisation is a vague concept that does not adequately capture all aspects of shareholder wealth. The following difficulties lay in the path of attempts to implement profit maximisation as a business objective:

Lack of precision: the term 'profit' is imprecise and different measures of both profit and profitability exist. They include:

- operating profit (that is, profit before interest and tax)
- profit before tax
- profit after tax
- profit available to shareholders per ordinary share
- profit available to shareholders as a percentage of ordinary shareholders' funds invested.

These measures do not all move in lockstep. An injection of new share capital, for example, may result in an increase in profit after tax whereas the profit available to shareholders per ordinary share may decrease. It is quite possible, therefore, for different profit measures to offer a different narrative of financial performance.

Lack of objectivity: the profit measures mentioned cannot be objectively determined. They are all influenced by the particular accounting policies and estimates employed, such as those relating to depreciation, inventories and bad debts. They are also susceptible to manipulation by managers who may wish to present a particular picture of financial health to investors.

Time period: the period over which profit should be maximised is uncertain. This is a serious flaw as conflict can occur between short-term and long-term profit maximisation. It is possible, for example, to maximise short-term profits at the expense of long-term profits.

Activity 1.2

How might the managers of a business increase short-term profits at the expense of long-term profits?

Managers may reduce operating expenses, and so increase short-term profits, by:

- cutting research and development expenditure
- cutting staff training and development
- buying lower-quality materials
- cutting quality control mechanisms.

The methods identified, however, may well injure the long-term competitiveness and performance of the business.

Risk: the goal of profit maximisation takes no account of the risks involved. Shareholders, however, are normally very concerned with risk. To protect their investment, they may shy away from high-risk projects even where there is the potential to generate large profits.

Opportunity cost: suppose that managers decide to reinvest current profits in order to boost future profits. This policy may well be consistent with the goal of profit maximisation, but what if the returns on profits reinvested were lower than those that shareholders could achieve from investing in a similar business with similar levels of risk? It would mean that, by reinvesting the profits, shareholders are effectively impeded from maximising their wealth.

The weaknesses of the profit maximisation objective are not shared by the shareholder wealth maximisation objective. The latter is more precise and, as we shall discuss in some detail in later chapters, takes account of both risk and the opportunity cost of shareholders' funds.

Do managers really have a choice?

Within a market economy there are strong competitive forces at work to ensure that failure to maximise shareholder wealth will not be tolerated for long. Competition for the funds provided by shareholders and competition for managers' jobs should ensure that the interests of the shareholders prevail. If the managers of a business do not provide the expected increase in shareholder wealth, the shareholders have the power to replace the existing management team with a new team that is more responsive to their needs. Alternatively, the shareholders may decide to sell their shares in the business (and reinvest in other businesses that provide better returns in relation to the risks involved). The sale of shares in the business is likely to depress the market price of the shares, which management will have to rectify in order to avoid the risk of takeover. This can be done only by pursuing policies that are consistent with the needs of shareholders.

It should also be mentioned that managers are usually encouraged to maximise shareholder wealth through their remuneration arrangements. Financial incentives are normally on offer to help align the interests of the managers with those of the shareholders. These incentives, which are often linked to share price performance, may take the form of bonus payments and options to buy shares in the business.

Criticisms of shareholder wealth maximisation

Critics of the shareholder wealth maximisation objective believe that a number of the problems of modern business can be laid at its door. It has been argued, for example, that the relentless pursuit of this objective has led businesses to implement measures such as cost cutting, redundancies and forcing suppliers to lower prices. These are sometimes carried to a point which results in serious conflict between various stakeholder groups and leaves businesses too weak to exploit profitable opportunities. It is difficult to see, however, how this kind of behaviour is consistent with the objective of maximising shareholder wealth. As mentioned earlier, shareholder wealth maximisation is a long-term goal and the sort of behaviour described will only undermine the achievement of this goal.

A further criticism is that, by making shareholders the dominant group, other stakeholders will feel like second-class citizens and will not become fully engaged with the business. Shareholder wealth maximisation cannot be achieved if other stakeholders are unhappy with their lot. Discontented staff can lead to low productivity and strikes. Discontented suppliers can lead to the business being given lower ordering priority and receiving slower deliveries in the future. In both cases, the wealth of shareholders will be adversely affected. At the very least this means that the needs of other stakeholders must somehow be satisfied if shareholder wealth maximisation is to be successfully pursued.

A final criticism is that shareholder wealth maximisation encourages unethical behaviour. In a highly competitive environment, managers are under huge pressure to produce the returns that shareholders require. To achieve these returns, they may be tempted to act in unethical ways.

To survive and prosper over the longer term, a business needs the approval of the society in which it operates. Increasingly, society expects high standards of business behaviour, and so ethical behaviour may be a necessary condition for maximising shareholder wealth. This point will be considered in more detail a little later in the chapter.

The stakeholder approach

Those who are uncomfortable with the idea that a business should be run for the principal benefit of shareholders often propose a **stakeholder approach** as an alternative. This approach is not very clearly defined and varying views exist as to what it is and what it entails. In broad terms, however, it embodies the idea that a business should serve those groups which may benefit from, or which may be harmed by, its operations.

According to the stakeholder approach, each group with a legitimate stake in the business should have its interests reflected in the objectives that the business pursues. Thus, managers should not simply serve the interests of shareholders but should promote the interests of, and mediate between, various stakeholder groups.

This alternative approach acknowledges the interest of the shareholders in a business but does not accept that this particular interest should dominate. This may seem strange given the fact that shareholders are effectively the owners of a business. Supporters of the stakeholder approach, however, tend to view things from a different perspective. They argue that a business corporation is a separate legal entity, which no one really owns. They also argue that the business is essentially a web of contracts. That is, contracts exist between the business, which is at the centre of the web, and its various stakeholder groups such as suppliers, employees, managers, lenders and so on. The contract between the business and its shareholders forms just one part of this web.

Other arguments can be used to diminish the relative importance of shareholders within a business. These are often based on the view that shareholders are more remote and less engaged than other stakeholders. Thus, it is claimed that shareholders can, by having a diversified share portfolio, diversify away risks associated with their investment in the business whereas employees, for example, cannot diversify away their employment risks. Furthermore, shareholders can sell their shares within seconds whereas other stakeholder groups, such as employees, suppliers and lenders, cannot usually exit from the business so easily.

Activity 1.5

Is it always possible for shareholders to exit from a business easily? Can you think of an example where it may be difficult for a shareholder to sell shares in a business?

One important example is a shareholder wishing to sell shares in a small business that does not have its shares traded on a stock exchange. Many family-owned businesses would fit into this category. It may be difficult to find a buyer and there may also be restrictions on the right to sell shares. It is worth pointing out that small businesses are far more numerous than large businesses that have shares listed on a stock exchange.

Problems with the stakeholder approach

A major difficulty with the stakeholder approach is that it does not offer a simple, clear-cut objective for managers to pursue and for which to account. Considering the needs of the various stakeholder groups will inevitably lead a business to having multiple objectives. It has been pointed out, however, that this means no objectives at all. To implement this approach, the managers must consider the competing needs of all the various stakeholder groups and then carefully weigh these before embarking on any course of action. An obvious question that arises is, 'How is this done?' In the absence of a well-reasoned method of doing this, there really is no effective objective to pursue.

Adopting this approach will add to the problems of accountability for two reasons. The first is that there is no clear way in which we can determine whether there has been an improvement or deterioration in performance during a particular period. The fact that, say, profit is lower than in previous periods may be caused by the pursuit of other legitimate objectives. The second reason is that multiple objectives can be used by managers as a convenient smokescreen behind which they can pursue their own objectives. It can, therefore, provide an incentive for them to promote the stakeholder approach at the expense of shareholder wealth maximisation.

A final problem with the stakeholder approach is that it raises many thorny questions concerning the identification and treatment of the various stakeholder groups. Who are the stakeholders? Should a broad view be taken so that many stakeholder groups are included or should a narrow view be taken so as to include only those with close links to the business? Are competitors considered to be stakeholders of the business? Should all stakeholder groups benefit equally from the business or should those that contribute more receive more? If it is the latter, how will the benefits attributable to each group be determined? Should stakeholder groups that contribute nothing to the business, but are affected by its actions, receive any benefits, and if so, how will these benefits be determined? Although such questions may create endless happy hours of debate for academics, there seems little chance that they will be resolved in a way that provides clear decision rules for managing a business.

Shareholders versus stakeholders

When comparing the shareholder and stakeholder approaches, a few points are worth making. First, the gulf between the two may not be as wide as is sometimes portrayed. We saw earlier that, in pursuit of shareholder wealth maximisation, managers must take account of the needs of other stakeholders. Factors such as customer satisfaction, employee morale and status within the community will determine the degree of success in achieving their ultimate objective. Balancing the needs of the various stakeholder groups must feature, therefore, in management decisions. Second, shareholders are not an exclusive group. Other stakeholders may become shareholders if they so wish. They may acquire shares directly through the market or indirectly through, for example, membership of an employee share purchase scheme. By widening share ownership, the potential for conflict between shareholders and other stakeholders may be reduced.

Perhaps we can sum up the discussion concerning the two approaches by saying that, within a competitive market economy, the shareholder approach has more to commend it. The quest for shareholder wealth maximisation provides a convincing business objective. It is, however, by no means perfect. The potential for conflict between shareholders and other stakeholders undoubtedly exists.

Wealth maximisation in practice

There is evidence that businesses pursue shareholder wealth maximisation as their main objective, or at least claim to do so. Their commitment is often expressed in proclamations adorning their annual reports and websites. **Real World 1.2** provides examples where a commitment to maximising shareholder wealth (or value, as it is often called) is declared.

Real World 1.2

Something of value

BP plc is a large energy business. Its stated purpose is to:

> maximise long-term shareholder value through the allocation of its resources to activities in the oil, natural gas, petrochemicals and energy businesses.

GKN plc is a global engineering business that aims to:

> maximise shareholder value whilst safeguarding shareholders' investment by combining high standards of business performance with high standards of corporate governance and risk management.

Lloyds Banking Group plc has a governing objective of:

> maximising shareholder value over time.

Diamond Corp plc is a diamond producer focused on:

> maximising shareholder value through the development of high margin diamond production assets.

Sources: Board Governance Principles, www.bp.com; The GKN Values, www.gkn.com; www.lloydsbankinggroup.com; www.diamondcorp.plc.uk; accessed 29 January 2013.

A paradox

How should a business go about maximising shareholder wealth? It is often argued that it involves concentrating on controlling costs, increasing revenues and ensuring that only opportunities offering clear, wealth-maximising outcomes are undertaken. An interesting counterargument, however, is that such a narrow focus may prove to be self-defeating and that shareholder wealth maximisation is more likely to be achieved when pursued indirectly. It has been claimed that those who are most successful in generating wealth are often seized by a passion to develop the best possible product or to provide the best possible service for their customers. If a business concentrates its efforts on the challenges that this entails, financial rewards will usually follow. Thus, to maximise shareholder wealth, it may be best for the business to concentrate on something else.

Real World 1.3 is an extract from an article written by John Kay in which he points out that the richest individuals are often not driven by cravings for wealth or material gain.

Real World 1.3

How to make real money

Sam Walton, founder and principal shareholder of Wal-Mart, the world's largest retailer, drove himself around in a pick-up truck. 'I have concentrated all along on building the finest retailing company that we possibly could. Period. Creating a huge personal fortune was never particularly a goal of mine,' Walton said. Still, five of the top ten places in the Forbes rich list are occupied by members of the Walton family . . .

Warren Buffett, the most successful investor in history, still lives in the Omaha bungalow he bought almost fifty years ago and continues to take pleasure in a Nebraskan steak washed down with cherry Coke. For Buffett, 'It's not that I want money. It's the fun of making money and watching it grow.'

The individuals who are most successful in making money are not those who are most interested in making money. This is not surprising: the principal route to great wealth is the creation of a successful business, and building a successful business demands exceptional talents and hard work. There is no reason to think that these characteristics are associated with greed and materialism: rather the opposite. People who are obsessively interested in money are drawn to get-rich-quick schemes rather than to business opportunities, and when these schemes come off, as occasionally they do, they retire to their villas in the sun . . .

 Source: Kay, J. (2004) Forget how the crow flies, *Financial Times*, 17 January, p. 21.
© The Financial Times Limited 2012. All Rights Reserved.

BALANCING RISK AND RETURN

All decisions attempt to influence future outcomes and financial decisions are no exception. The only thing certain about the future, however, is that we cannot be sure what is going to happen. There is a risk that things will not turn out as planned, and this should be taken into account when making financial decisions.

As in other aspects of life, risk and return tend to be related. Evidence shows that returns often relate to risk in the way shown in Figure 1.3.

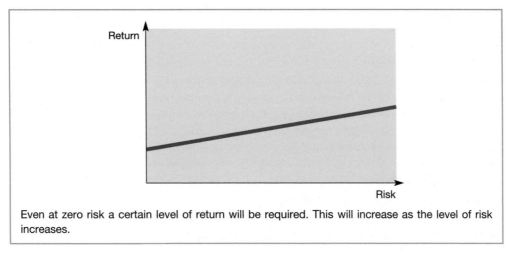

Even at zero risk a certain level of return will be required. This will increase as the level of risk increases.

Figure 1.3 Relationship between risk and return

Activity 1.6

Look at Figure 1.3 and state, in broad terms, where an investment in:

(a) a government savings account, and
(b) a lottery ticket

should be placed on the risk–return line.

A government savings account is normally a very safe investment. Even if a government is in financial difficulties, it can always print more money to repay investors. Returns from this form of investment, however, are normally very low. Investing in a lottery ticket runs a very high risk of losing the whole amount invested. This is because the probability of winning is normally very low. However, a winning ticket can produce enormous returns.

Thus, the government savings account should be placed towards the far left of the risk–return line and the lottery ticket towards the far right.

This relationship between risk and return has important implications for the shareholders of a business. They will require a minimum return to induce them to invest at all, but will require an additional return to compensate for taking risks; the higher the risk, the higher the required return. Thus, future returns from an investment must be assessed in relation to the likely risks involved. As stated earlier, managers who pursue the shareholder wealth-maximisation objective will choose investments that provide the highest returns in relation to the risks involved.

The recent turmoil in the banking industry has shown that the right balance between risk and return is not always struck. Some banks have taken excessive risks in pursuit of higher returns, with disastrous consequences. **Real World 1.4** discusses the implications of this for the future of banking.

Banking on change

The taxpayer has become the majority shareholder in the Royal Bank of Scotland (RBS). This change in ownership, resulting from the huge losses sustained by the bank, will shape the future decisions made by its managers. This does not simply mean that it will affect the amount that the bank lends to homeowners and businesses; rather, it is about the amount of risk that it will be prepared to take in pursuit of higher returns.

In the past, those managing banks such as RBS saw themselves as producers of financial products that enabled banks to grow faster than the economy as a whole. They didn't want to be seen as simply part of the infrastructure of the economy. It was too dull. It was far more exciting to be seen as creators of financial products that generated huge profits and, at the same time, benefited us all through unlimited credit at low rates of interest. These financial products, with exotic names such as 'collateralised debt obligations' and 'credit default swaps', ultimately led to huge losses that taxpayers had to absorb in order to prevent the banks from collapse.

Now that many banks throughout the world are in taxpayers' hands, they are destined to lead a much quieter life. They will have to focus more on the basics such as taking deposits, transferring funds and making simple loans to customers. Is that such a bad thing?

The history of banking has reflected a tension between carrying out their core functions and the quest for high returns through high-risk strategies. It seems, however, that for some time to come they will have to concentrate on the former and will be unable to speculate with depositors' cash.

Source: Based on information in R. Peston, 'We own Royal Bank', BBC News, www.bbc.co.uk, accessed 28 November 2008.

BEHAVING ETHICALLY

The pursuit of shareholder wealth maximisation has gained impetus in recent years. One of the effects of the global deregulation of markets and of technological change has been to provide investors with greater opportunities to increase their returns. They are now able to move their funds around the world with comparative ease. This has increased competition among businesses for investment funds and has put managers under greater pressure to produce returns that are attractive in international, rather than merely national, terms.

Given these pressures, there is a risk that shareholder wealth maximisation may be pursued by managers using methods that are generally regarded as unethical. Examples of such behaviour were considered earlier in the chapter. Nevertheless, some managers may feel that even unethical behaviour can be justified because 'all is fair in business'. Professor Rose, however, points out that responsibility to maximise the wealth of shareholders 'does not mean that managers are being asked to act in a manner which absolves them from the considerations of morality and simple decency that they would readily acknowledge in other walks of life' (see reference 1 at the end of the chapter). When considering a particular course of action, managers should therefore ask themselves whether it conforms to accepted moral standards, whether it treats people unfairly and whether it has the potential for harm.

Large businesses often declare their commitment to high standards of ethical and social behaviour. This may be set out in a statement of corporate philosophy or reflected in a code of business practice. **Real World 1.5** provides an example of how one large business seeks to be a good corporate citizen.

The only way is ethics

The Sage Group plc is a global provider of business management software. It has a code of ethics which states that the business:

> will operate responsibly and in accordance with all relevant laws and regulations. Specifically we will:

- promote ethical business practice
- ensure equal opportunities
- provide a safe and healthy work environment
- value diversity in the workplace
- trade ethically
- provide a safe route for people to highlight non-compliance.

> These practices sit alongside our principles of trust, integrity, simplicity, agility and innovation and together act at the heart of all our dealings and drive the way we work for the benefit of our people, customers, suppliers, shareholders and other stakeholders.

Source: Extracts from Code of Ethics, Sage Group plc, www.sage.com, accessed 28 January 2013.

Ethical behaviour and the pursuit of shareholder wealth maximisation need not conflict. Indeed, some believe that high ethical standards may be a necessary condition for wealth maximisation.

Can you think why this may be the case?

It can be argued that a business that treats customers, suppliers and employees fairly and with integrity is more likely to flourish over the longer term.

In recent years, attempts have been made to demonstrate a link between high ethical standards and superior financial performance over time. **Real World 1.6** briefly describes two of these.

Profiting from ethics?

In 2003 the Institute of Business Ethics produced a report which suggested that businesses with a code of ethics produced financial performance superior to those without a code. It compared a group of companies in the FTSE 250 index over a period of four years, divided into those that had codes of ethics for five years or more and those that explicitly said they did not. It found that on three measures – economic value added, market value added and stability of price/earnings ratios – the ethical companies outperformed, though on a fourth measure – return on capital employed – the figures were more mixed.*

Some caveats are perhaps in order. The time period for the study is not that long. And taking the existence of ethical codes as a proxy for ethical behaviour could be stretching reality. After all, even Enron had a code of ethical behaviour. So while indicative, this is not likely to be the last word. As the study admits, it is not clear why an ethical stance should mean better results. Maybe it is simply that good managers, who produce good results, tend to view ethical codes as part of good business.[1]

In 2007 the Institute of Business Ethics published a follow-up research study. The majority of large businesses now have a code of ethics and so it is not really possible to use the existence of a code as evidence that a business is 'more ethical'. Instead, 'more ethical' businesses were identified as those that attempted to embed ethical business practice through staff training programmes. A group of 50 large businesses, selected from the FTSE 350 index, was divided into two equal-size groups based on this criterion. Using four measures (return on capital employed, return on assets, total return and market value added*) over a five-year period, the study found that those with training programmes had significantly better financial performance than those without.[2]

Again, the results are not conclusive. It is not clear why there should be a link between ethical training and financial performance. It may be that ethical training of employees instils confidence among stakeholders and this makes the business more able to deal with setbacks and change. Or it may simply be that profitable businesses can afford to spend money on ethical training programmes.

* Each of these measures is discussed later in the book.

Sources: (1) Adapted from Martin Dickson, 'Ethics', *Financial Times*, 3 April 2003; (2) K. Ugoji, N. Dando and L. Moir, *Does Business Ethics Pay? – Revisited: The value of ethics training*, Institute of Business Ethics, 2007.

Ethics and the finance function

Integrity and ethical behaviour are particularly important within the finance function, where many opportunities for sharp practice exist. To demonstrate their commitment to integrity and ethical behaviour, some businesses provide a code of standards for their finance staff. **Real World 1.7** provides an example of one such code.

Real World 1.7

Code calling

Vodafone plc, the communications business, has a code of ethics for its senior financial officers. The key elements of this code are that they should:

■ act with integrity, including being honest and candid while maintaining the confidentiality of company information where required or in the company's interests;

■ observe, fully, applicable governmental laws, rules and regulations;

■ comply with the requirements of applicable accounting and auditing standards and company policies in the maintenance of a high standard of accuracy and completeness in the company's financial records;

■ adhere to a high standard of business ethics and not seek competitive advantage through unlawful or unethical business practices;

■ avoid conflicts of interest wherever possible. Anything that would be a conflict for a senior financial officer will also be a conflict if it is related to a member of his or her family or a close relative;

■ not knowingly misrepresent, or cause others to misrepresent, facts about the company to others, whether within or outside the company, including to the company's independent auditors, governmental regulators, self-regulating organisations and other governmental officials, as appropriate;

- properly review and critically analyse proposed disclosure for accuracy and completeness in relation to his or her area of responsibility;
- adhere to the standards and restrictions imposed by laws, rules and regulations, including those relating to accounting and auditing matters;
- notify the group general counsel and company secretary promptly of any existing or potential violation of this code;
- not retaliate against any employee for reports of potential violations that are made in good faith.

Source: Adapted from Code of Ethics, www.vodafone.com, accessed 28 January 2013.

Although there may be rules in place to try to prevent sharp practice, these will provide only a partial answer. The finance staff themselves must appreciate the importance of fair play in building long-term relationships for the benefit of all those connected with the business.

PROTECTING SHAREHOLDERS' INTERESTS

In recent years, the issue of **corporate governance** has generated much debate. The term is used to describe the ways in which businesses are directed and controlled. The issue of corporate governance is important because in businesses of any size, those who own the company (that is, the shareholders) are usually divorced from the day-to-day control of the business. The shareholders employ professional managers (known as directors) to manage the business for them. These directors may, therefore, be viewed as *agents* of the shareholders (who are the *principals*).

Given this agent–principal relationship, it may seem reasonable to assume that the best interests of shareholders will guide the directors' decisions. In other words, the directors will seek to maximise the wealth of the shareholders. However, in practice this does not always occur. The directors may be more concerned with pursuing their own interests, such as increasing their pay and perks (such as expensive cars, overseas visits and so on) and improving their job security and status. As a result, a conflict can occur between the interests of shareholders and the interests of directors.

It can be argued that in a competitive market economy, this **agency problem**, as it is termed, should not persist over time. The competition for the funds provided by shareholders, and competition for directors' jobs, should ensure that the interests of the shareholders will prevail. However, if competitive forces are weak, or if information concerning the directors' activities is not available to shareholders, the risk of agency problems will be increased. Shareholders must be alert to such risks and should take steps to ensure that the directors operate the business in a manner that is consistent with shareholder needs.

Protecting through rules

Where directors pursue their own interests at the expense of the shareholders, it is clearly a problem for the shareholders. However, it may also be a problem for society as a whole. Where investors feel that their funds are likely to be mismanaged, they will be reluctant to invest. A shortage of funds will mean that businesses can make fewer investments. Furthermore, the costs of funds will increase as businesses compete for what funds are available. Thus, a lack of concern for shareholders can have a profound effect on the performance of individual businesses and, with this, the health of the economy. To avoid these problems, most competitive market economies have a framework of rules to help monitor and control the behaviour of directors. These rules are usually based around three guiding principles:

- *Disclosure*. This lies at the heart of good corporate governance. An OECD report (see reference 2 at the end of the chapter) summed up the benefits of disclosure as follows:

  > Adequate and timely information about corporate performance enables investors to make informed buy-and-sell decisions and thereby helps the market reflect the value of a corporation under present management. If the market determines that present management is not performing, a decrease in stock [share] price will sanction management's failure and open the way to management change.

- *Accountability*. This involves defining the roles and duties of the directors and establishing an adequate monitoring process. In the UK, the law requires that the directors of a business act in the best interests of the shareholders. This means, among other things, that they must not try to use their position and knowledge to make gains at the expense of the shareholders. The law also requires larger businesses to have their annual financial statements independently audited. The purpose of an independent audit is to lend credibility to the financial statements prepared by the directors.

- *Fairness*. Directors should not be able to benefit from access to 'inside' information that is not available to shareholders. As a result, both the law and the London Stock Exchange place restrictions on the ability of directors to buy and sell the shares of the business. One example of these restrictions is that the directors cannot buy or sell shares immediately before the announcement of the annual trading results of the business or before the announcement of a significant event, such as a planned merger or the loss of the chief executive.

Activity 1.8

What market consequences may arise from a failure to ensure that directors do not benefit from inside information?

Buying and selling shares must be seen as a 'fair game' where all investors have access to the same information. Where the dice are loaded and directors can benefit from inside information, investors are unlikely to invest.

The guiding principles are set out in Figure 1.4.

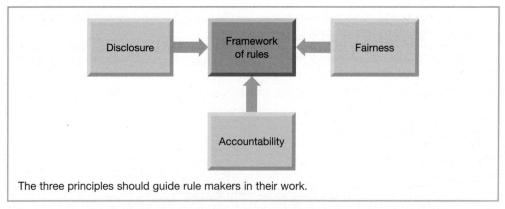

The three principles should guide rule makers in their work.

Figure 1.4 Principles underpinning a framework of rules

Source: P. Atrill and E. McLaney, *Financial Accounting for Decision Makers*, 6th edn, Financial Times Prentice Hall, 2010, p. 392.

Strengthening the framework of rules

The number of rules designed to safeguard shareholders has increased considerably over the years. This has been in response to weaknesses in corporate governance procedures, which have been exposed through well-publicised business failures and frauds, excessive pay increases to directors, and evidence that some financial reports were being 'massaged' so as to mislead shareholders.

The most important development has been the introduction of the **UK Corporate Governance Code** (formerly known as the Combined Code), which sets out best practice on corporate governance matters for large businesses. The UK Corporate Governance Code has the backing of the London Stock Exchange, which means that all businesses listed on this exchange must 'comply or explain'. That is, they must comply with the requirements of the Code or must give their shareholders a good reason why they do not. Failure to do one or other of these can lead to the business's shares being suspended from listing.

Activity 1.9

Why might this be an important sanction against a non-compliant business?

A major advantage of a stock exchange listing is that it enables investors to sell their shares whenever they wish. A business that is suspended from listing would find it hard, and therefore expensive, to issue shares because there would be no ready market for them.

The UK Corporate Governance Code sets out a number of principles relating to such matters as the role and remuneration of directors, their relations with shareholders, and their accountability. **Real World 1.8** outlines some of the more important of these.

Real World 1.8

The UK Corporate Governance Code

Key principles of the UK Code are as follows:

Leadership

- Every listed company should have a board of directors that is led by a chairman and is collectively responsible for its success.
- There should be a clear division of responsibilities between the chairman and the chief executive officer of the company to try to ensure that a single person does not have unbridled power.
- As part of their role as board members, non-executive directors should constructively challenge and help develop proposals on strategy.

Effectiveness

- There should be an appropriate balance of skills, experience, independence and knowledge to enable the board to carry out its duties effectively.
- Appointments to the board should be the subject of rigorous, formal and transparent procedures.
- All directors should allocate sufficient time to discharge their responsibilities.

→

- All board members should refresh their skills regularly and new board members should receive induction.
- The board should receive timely information that is of sufficient quality to enable them to carry out their duties.
- The board should undertake a formal and rigorous examination of its own performance each year, which will include its committees and individual directors.
- All directors should submit themselves for re-election at regular intervals, subject to satisfactory performance.

Accountability

- The board should present a balanced and understandable assessment of the company's position and future prospects.
- The board should define the company's risk appetite and tolerance and should maintain sound risk management and internal control systems.
- The board should establish formal and transparent arrangements for corporate reporting, risk management and internal control and for maintaining an appropriate relationship with the company's auditors.

Remuneration

- Remuneration levels should be sufficient to attract, retain and motivate directors of the appropriate quality and should take account of both individual and company performance.
- There should be formal and transparent procedures for developing policy on directors' remuneration. No director should determine his or her own level of remuneration.

Relations with shareholders

- The board should try to ensure that a satisfactory dialogue with shareholders occurs.
- Boards should use the annual general meeting to communicate with investors and encourage their participation.

Source: Adapted from the UK Corporate Governance Code, Financial Reporting Council, September 2012, pp. 6–7, www.frc.org.uk.

Strengthening the framework of rules in this way has been generally agreed to have improved the quality of information available to shareholders, resulted in better checks on the powers of directors, and provided greater transparency in corporate affairs. However, rules can only be a partial answer. A balance must be struck between the need to protect shareholders and the need to encourage the entrepreneurial spirit of directors – which could be stifled under a welter of rules. This implies that rules should not be too tight and so unscrupulous directors may still find ways around them.

SHAREHOLDER INVOLVEMENT

Improving corporate governance has focused mainly on developing a framework of rules for managing businesses listed on the London Stock Exchange. While rules are important, there are many who take the view that it is also important for those who own the businesses to play their part by actively monitoring and controlling the behaviour of directors. In this section, we identify the main shareholders of listed businesses and discuss their role in establishing good corporate governance. We also consider why there has been greater shareholder activism in recent years.

Who are the main shareholders?

Real World 1.9 provides an analysis of the ownership of shares in UK-listed businesses at the end of 2010.

Going overseas

The breakdown of ownership of UK listed shares as at 31 December 2010 is as shown in Figure 1.5.

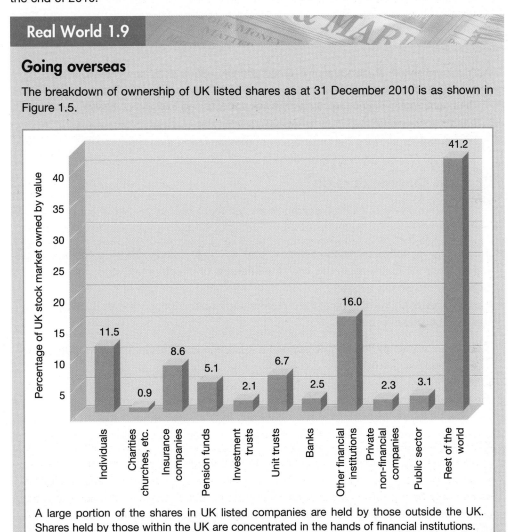

A large portion of the shares in UK listed companies are held by those outside the UK. Shares held by those within the UK are concentrated in the hands of financial institutions.

Figure 1.5 Ownership of UK listed shares, end of 2010

Looking at the changes in the ownership of listed shares in recent years shows two striking features:

1 The value of listed shares owned by overseas residents has gone up progressively from 30.7 per cent in 1998 to 41.2 per cent in 2010.
2 The value of listed shares held by UK individuals has fallen from 16.7 per cent in 1998 to 11.5 per cent in 2010. Share ownership is becoming increasingly concentrated in the hands of large financial institutions.

Source: Ownership of UK Quoted Shares 2010, Office for National Statistics, 28 February 2012.

The rise of financial institutions means that private individuals have less direct investment in listed shares than in the past. Does that mean they have less financial interest in listed shares?

No. It means that individuals are tending to invest through the institutions, for example by making pension contributions rather than buying shares directly. Ultimately, all of the investment finance must come from individuals.

The concentration of ownership of listed shares means that financial institutions have enormous voting power and, as a result, the potential to exercise significant influence over the way in which stock exchange listed businesses are directed and controlled. In the past, however, they have been reluctant to exercise this power and have been criticised for being too passive and for allowing the directors of businesses too much independence.

What can shareholders do?

There are two main ways in which shareholders can try to control the behaviour of directors. These are by:

■ introducing incentive plans for directors that link their remuneration to the share performance of the business. In this way, the interests of directors and shareholders should become more closely aligned
■ closely monitoring the actions of the directors and exerting influence over the way in which they use business resources.

The first issue will be picked up in Chapter 10. It is the second issue to which we now turn.

Getting active

In the past, financial institutions have chosen to take a non-interventionist approach to the affairs of a business. Instead, they have confined their investment activities to determining whether to buy, hold or sell shares in a particular business. They appear to have taken the view that the costs of actively engaging with directors and trying to influence their decisions are too high in relation to the likely benefits. It is also worth pointing out that these costs are borne by the particular financial institution that becomes actively involved, whereas the benefits are spread across all shareholders. (This phenomenon is often referred to as the 'free-rider' problem.)

Waking the sleeping giants

In recent years, financial institutions have begun to play a more active role in corporate governance. More time is being invested in monitoring the actions of directors and in engaging with the directors over key decisions. This change of heart has occurred for a variety of reasons. One important reason is that the increasing concentration of share ownership has made it more difficult for financial institutions to simply walk away from an investment in a poorly performing business by selling its shares.

Why might it be a problem for a financial institution that holds a substantial number of shares in a poorly performing business to simply sell the shares?

Where a substantial number of shares are held, a decision to sell can have a significant impact on the market price, perhaps leading to heavy losses.

A further reason why it may be difficult to disinvest is that a business's shares may be included in a stock market index (such as the FTSE 100 or FTSE 250). Certain types of financial institution, such as investment trusts or unit trusts, may offer investments that are designed to 'track' the particular index and so they become locked into a business's shares in order to reflect the index. In both situations outlined, therefore, a financial institution may have little choice but to stick with the shares held and try to improve performance by seeking to influence the actions and decisions of the directors.

It is also worth mentioning that financial institutions have experienced much greater competitive pressures in recent years. There have been increasing demands from clients for them to demonstrate their investment skills, and thereby justify their fees, by either outperforming benchmarks or beating the performance of similar financial institutions. These increased competitive pressures may be due, at least in part, to the fact that economic conditions have not favoured investors in the recent past; they have experienced a period of relatively low stock market returns. Whatever the reason, the increased pressure to enhance the wealth of their clients has led financial institutions, in turn, to become less tolerant towards underperforming boards of directors.

The regulatory environment has also favoured greater activism on the part of financial institutions. This point will be considered in more detail a little later.

Forms of activism

It is important to be clear about what is meant by the term 'shareholder activism' as it can take various forms. In its simplest form it involves taking a more active role in voting for or against the resolutions put before the annual general meeting or any extraordinary general meeting of the business. This form of activism is seen by the UK government as being vital to good corporate governance. The government is keen to see much higher levels of participation than currently exist, and expects institutional shareholders to exercise their right to vote. In the past, financial institutions have often indicated their dissent by abstaining from a vote rather than by outright opposition to a resolution. There is some evidence, however, that they are now more prepared to use their vote to oppose resolutions of the board of directors. Much of the evidence available remains anecdotal rather than based on systematic research.

A particularly rich source of contention between shareholders and directors concerns payments made to directors and there have been several shareholder revolts over this issue. **Real World 1.10** provides an example of a fairly recent falling-out.

Revolting shareholders

Sly Bailey, the chief executive of Trinity Mirror who was facing a shareholder revolt about her £1.7m pay package, unexpectedly handed in her notice to the board on Thursday. A statement from the company said that Ms Bailey, who has held the job for 10 years, would leave by the end of the year.

Ms Bailey's departure followed a meeting of directors, who had held talks with investors earlier on Thursday. Aviva Global Investors, a top three shareholder with 11.9 per cent, had threatened to make public its opposition before the weekend. On Wednesday, the *Financial Times* reported that investors were unhappy about her pay package and were planning a revolt at the company's annual meeting next week.

One investor said the board had been involved in discussions for several weeks about concerns over her pay package, but talks broke down when it became clear that Ms Bailey was unhappy with any real changes proposed to her pay. One investor said: 'She helped to bring everything to a head and wrote her own exit.' The next question is what exit terms she gets, he added.

Investors in the publisher of the *Daily Mirror* and *The People* have repeatedly demanded a substantial cut in Ms Bailey's pay in the light of the group's market capitalisation, which has dwindled from £1.1bn when she joined in 2003 to £83.7m currently. Trinity has paid no dividend since 2008.

The board has been in discussions with a number of leading institutions in recent weeks over limiting the size of Ms Bailey's potential bonus, ensuring it is reinvested in Trinity shares as well as aligning her long-term incentives more closely to the share price. However, the board's proposals have so far failed to appease angry shareholders.

Although shareholder revolts are widely reported and catch the newspaper headlines, they do not happen very often. Nevertheless, the benefits for shareholders of flexing their muscles and voting against resolutions put forward by the directors may go beyond their immediate, intended objective: other boards of directors may take note of shareholder dissatisfaction and adjust their behaviour in order to avoid a similar fate. The cost of voting need not be high as there are specialist agencies that offer research and advice to financial institutions on how their votes should be cast.

Another form of activism involves meetings and discussions between representatives of a particular financial institution and the board of directors of a business. At such meetings, a wide range of issues affecting the business may be discussed.

Activity 1.12

What might financial institutions wish to discuss with the directors of a business? Try to think of at least two financial and two non-financial aspects of the business.

Some of the more important aspects that are likely to attract their attention include:

- objectives and strategies adopted
- trading performance
- internal controls

- policies regarding mergers and acquisitions
- major investments and disinvestments
- adherence to the recommendations of the UK Corporate Governance Code
- corporate social responsibility
- directors' incentive schemes and remuneration.

This is not an exhaustive list. For shareholders, and therefore owners, of a business, anything that might have an impact on their wealth should be a matter of concern.

This form of activism requires a fairly high degree of involvement with the business and some of the larger financial institutions have dedicated teams for this purpose. Therefore, this can be a costly exercise. **Real World 1.11** reveals the approach taken by one major financial institution.

Real World 1.11

Getting active

Fidelity (FIL Ltd) is one of the UK's largest investment fund managers. Its approach to engaging with investee companies is as follows:

> We hold regular meetings with companies to discuss specific results or events as well as a more informal dialogue incorporating site visits and other research initiatives. Regular access to executive management is a key part of FIL's investment process and we encourage managers to provide regular trading updates to the market in order to enhance this dialogue as much as possible.
>
> On occasion our views will differ from those of management and where this is accompanied by a failure to achieve our reasonable expectations for shareholder return we will consider promoting change. Our specific response will be determined on a case-by-case basis and we will weigh up the relative merit of intervention or a sale of the shares. Typically we will choose to intervene to promote change when the expected benefits of intervention (through increased returns to our investors) outweigh the anticipated cost.

Source: Extracts taken from 'Stewardship, corporate governance, fidelity', www.fidelity.co.uk, accessed 29 January 2013.

Meetings between financial institutions and the managers of investee companies can be a useful mechanism for exchanging views and for gaining a greater understanding of the needs and motivations of each party. This may help to pre-empt public arguments between the board of directors and financial institutions, which is rarely the best way to resolve issues.

The final form of activism involves intervention in the affairs of the business. This can be very costly, however, depending on the nature of the problem. Where strategic and operational issues raise concerns, intervention can be very costly indeed. Identifying the weaknesses and problems relating to these issues requires a detailed understanding of the nature of the business. This implies close monitoring by relevant experts who are able to analyse the issues and then propose feasible solutions. The costs associated with such an exercise would normally be prohibitive, although the costs may be mitigated through some kind of collective action by financial institutions.

Not all forms of intervention in the affairs of a business need be costly, however. Where there are corporate governance issues to be addressed, for example, such as a failure to adhere to the recommendations of the UK Corporate Governance Code, a financial institution may nominate individuals for appointment as non-executive directors who can be relied upon to ensure that necessary changes are made. This should involve relatively little cost for the financial institution.

The main forms of shareholder activism are summarised in Figure 1.6.

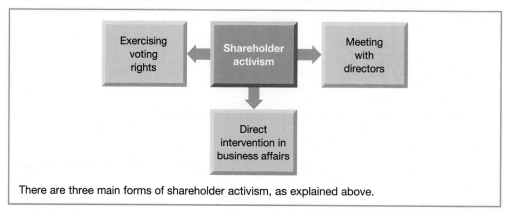

There are three main forms of shareholder activism, as explained above.

Figure 1.6 The main forms of shareholder activism

To improve the quality of engagement between financial institutions and investee businesses, the Financial Reporting Council has issued the **UK Stewardship Code**. **Real World 1.12** sets out the main principles of this code.

The future of shareholder activism

The rise of shareholder activism raises two important questions that have yet to be answered. First, is it simply a passing phenomenon? It is no coincidence that shareholder activism took root during a period when stock market returns were fairly low. There is a risk that financial institutions will become less active and less vigilant in monitoring businesses when stock market returns improve. Second, does shareholder activism really make a difference to corporate performance? Early research in the US was not encouraging for those who urge financial institutions to take a more active approach. However, a recent study of 2,000 interventions by active investors found that operating performance of US businesses was improved for a five-year period following the interventions (see reference 3 at the end of the chapter). Further research is required and some time may elapse before a clear picture emerges.

SUMMARY

The main points in this chapter may be summarised as follows:

The finance function

■ Helps managers in carrying out their tasks of strategic management, operations management and risk management.

■ Helps managers in each of these tasks through financial planning, investment appraisal, financing decisions, capital market operations and financial control.

Modern financial management

■ Is influenced by economic theory.

■ Has been described as the economics of time and risk.

Shareholders

■ Are assumed to be the most important stakeholder group because they effectively own the business and bear the residual risk.

Shareholder wealth maximisation

■ Is assumed to be the primary objective of a business.

■ Is a long-term rather than a short-term objective.

■ Takes account of both risk and the long-term returns that shareholders expect to receive.

■ Must take account of the needs of other stakeholders.

■ May be best achieved indirectly through a commitment to developing the best possible product or service.

Profit maximisation

■ Does not automatically lead to shareholder wealth maximisation.

■ Is a vague concept that can be interpreted in different ways.

■ Cannot be objectively measured and may be manipulated by managers.

■ Fails to take account of risk and the opportunity cost of shareholders' funds.

The stakeholder approach

■ Reflects the idea that a business should serve those groups that benefit from, or are harmed by, its operations.

■ Will lead to a business having multiple objectives, which adds to the problems of accountability.

■ Raises many questions about the identification and treatment of stakeholder groups.

Risk and return

- Are related.

- Shareholders normally require additional return to compensate for additional risk.

- Shareholder wealth maximisation involves selecting investments that provide the highest returns in relation to the risks involved.

Behaving ethically

- Need not conflict with the maximisation of shareholder wealth.

- May be set out in policies and codes.

- Is particularly important in the finance function.

Protecting shareholders

- An agency problem may exist between shareholders and directors.

- This has led to rules, set out in the UK Corporate Governance Code, to help monitor and control the behaviour of directors.

Shareholder involvement

- Financial institutions are now the most important group of UK shareholders in London Stock Exchange listed businesses.

- Shareholder involvement may take the form of providing incentives for directors and/or monitoring and controlling their actions.

- Shareholder activism may involve taking a more active role in voting, meetings and discussions with directors and direct intervention in the affairs of the business.

KEY TERMS

Capital markets p. 5
Shareholder wealth maximisation p. 6
Stakeholder approach p. 9
Corporate governance p. 17

Agency problem p. 17
UK Corporate Governance Code p. 19
UK Stewardship Code p. 26

For definitions of these terms, see the Glossary, pp. 605–613.

REFERENCES

1 Rose, H. (1995) *Tasks of the Finance Function*, Financial Times Mastering Management Series, supplement issue no. 1, p. 11.

2 *Corporate Governance: Improving Competitiveness and Access to Capital In Global Markets*, OECD Report by Business Sector Advisory Group on Corporate Governance, Organisation for Economic Co-operation and Development, 1998.

3 Bebchuk, L., Brav, A. and Jiang, W. (2013) 'The long-term effect of hedge fund activism', Working paper ssrn.com.

FURTHER READING

If you wish to explore the topics discussed in this chapter in more depth, try the following books:

Arnold, G. (2013) *Corporate Financial Management*, 5th edn, Financial Times Pearson, Chapter 1.

Mallin, C. (2010) *Corporate Governance*, 3rd edn, Oxford University Press, Chapters 2, 4 and 6.

Pike, R., Neale, B. and Linsley, P. (2012) *Corporate Finance and Investment*, 7th edn, Pearson, Chapters 1 and 2.

Tricker, B. (2012) *Corporate Governance: Principles, policies and practices*, 2nd edn, Oxford University Press, Chapters 1, 4 and 5.

Reading the *Financial Times* and *Investors Chronicle* on a regular basis can help you to keep up to date on financial management topics.

REVIEW QUESTIONS

Answers to these questions can be found at the back of the book on p. 571.

1.1 What are the main tasks of the finance function within a business?

1.2 Why is wealth maximisation viewed as superior to profit maximisation as a business objective?

1.3 Some managers, if asked what the main objective of their business is, may simply state: 'To survive!' What do you think of this as a primary objective?

1.4 What are the main drawbacks of adopting the stakeholder approach as the basis for setting the objectives of a business?

Chapter 2

FINANCIAL PLANNING

INTRODUCTION

In this chapter, we take a look at financial planning and the role that projected (forecast) financial statements play in this process. We shall see how these statements help in assessing the likely impact of management decisions on the financial performance and position of a business. We shall also examine the way in which these statements are prepared and the issues involved in their preparation.

This chapter and the one that follows assume some understanding of the three major financial statements: the cash flow statement, the income statement and the statement of financial position (balance sheet). If you need to brush up on these statements, please take a look at Chapters 2–6 of *Financial Accounting for Decision Makers* by Atrill and McLaney (7th edition, Pearson, 2013).

Learning outcomes

When you have completed this chapter, you should be able to:

- Explain how business plans are developed and the role that projected financial statements play in this process.

- Prepare projected financial statements for a business and interpret their significance for decision-making purposes.

- Discuss the strengths and weaknesses of each of the main methods of preparing projected financial statements.

- Describe the ways in which projected financial statements may take account of risk and uncertainty.

PLANNING FOR THE FUTURE

It is vital that a business develops plans for the future. Whatever a business is trying to achieve, it is unlikely to succeed unless the future is mapped out in a systematic way. Finance lies at the heart of the planning process. To ensure that the limited resources of a business are used as effectively as possible, managers must carefully evaluate the financial implications of each possible course of action.

Developing plans for a business involves the following key steps:

1 *Setting the aims and objectives of the business.* The starting point is to establish the long-term aims and objectives of the business. These will set out what the business is trying to achieve and should provide managers with a clear sense of direction. We saw in Chapter 1 that the primary objective of a business is assumed to be the maximisation of shareholder wealth.

2 *Identifying the options available.* To achieve the long-term aims and objectives that are set, a number of possible options (strategies) may be available to the business. Each option must be clearly identified, which will involve collecting a wide range of information. This can be extremely time-consuming, particularly when the business is considering entering new markets or investing in new technology.

3 *Select option and develop long-term plans.* Each option (strategy) must be examined within the context of the long-term objectives that have been set and the resources available. This step will include an assessment of the impact of each option on future financial performance and position. Management must then select the most suitable option so as to provide the long-term (strategic) plan for the business. The plan will usually cover a period of 3–5 years.

4 *Developing short-term plans.* Within the framework of the long-term (strategic) plan, detailed short-term (tactical) plans will normally be prepared for the forthcoming year. These help to ensure that day-to-day management decisions and actions are consistent with the long-term plans.

Figure 2.1 sets out this process diagrammatically.

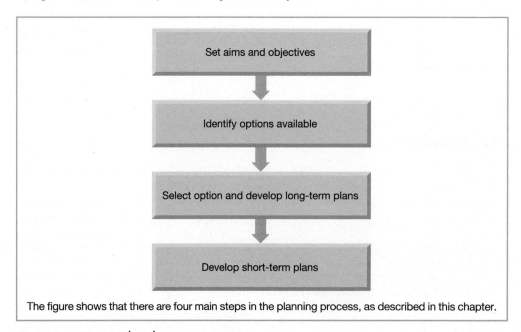

The figure shows that there are four main steps in the planning process, as described in this chapter.

Figure 2.1 Steps in the planning process

THE ROLE OF PROJECTED FINANCIAL STATEMENTS

Projected (forecast) financial statements can play a vital role in the final two steps of the planning process – that is, the evaluation of long-term strategic options and the development of short-term plans. They can be prepared for both long and short time horizons. However, the length of the time horizon will influence the amount of detail that can be provided and the extent to which simplifying assumptions will be relied upon when preparing these statements.

The main financial statements used for planning purposes are:

- a projected cash flow statement
- a projected income statement
- a projected statement of financial position (balance sheet).

When taken together, they provide a comprehensive picture of likely future performance and position. Where different options are being considered, they enable comparisons to be made of the impact of each option on future profitability, liquidity and financial position. This should help managers in identifying the most suitable way forward.

Activity 2.1

Assume that the managers of a business are considering only one option. Could projected financial statements still help them?

Where only one course of action is being considered, a comparison can still be made with the option to do nothing. Once the course of action has been adopted, projected financial statements can also provide targets against which to compare actual performance.

We mentioned earlier that, for long-term planning, projected financial statements for each year may be prepared to cover a period of 3–5 years. For short-term planning, they may be prepared for a period of one year. However, quarterly, monthly or weekly projections may also be prepared to help assess likely progress towards achieving the short-term plan. **Real World 2.1** describes the projected, or forecast, financial statements prepared for one large business on a routine basis.

Real World 2.1

Read all about it

Trinity Mirror plc, which owns a number of national and regional newspapers, including the Daily Mirror, states:

> Weekly revenue and profit forecasts are received from all operating units followed by monthly management accounts, which are prepared promptly and reported against the approved budget (that is, short-term financial plan). Consolidated monthly accounts, including detailed profit analysis with comparisons to budget, latest forecasts and prior year together with a treasury report, are prepared, providing relevant, reliable and up-to-date financial and other information to the Board. Profit and cash flow forecasts for the current year are prepared and submitted to the Board at quarterly intervals during the year.

Source: Adapted from Internal Financial Control, Trinity Mirror plc, www.trinitymirror.com, accessed 13 February 2013.

Preparing projected financial statements usually means collecting and processing large amounts of information. This can be a costly and time-consuming exercise, which must be weighed against likely benefits. To help strike the right balance, a trade-off may be made between the reliability of the projected information produced and the cost and time involved. Sometimes, this trade-off is achieved by employing simplifying assumptions in the preparation process. We shall see a little later how this may be done.

PREPARING PROJECTED FINANCIAL STATEMENTS

To prepare projected financial statements, the key variables affecting performance and position must be identified. These variables fall into two broad categories: external and internal.

External variables usually relate to government policies and to economic conditions, and include:

- rate of taxation
- interest rates for borrowings
- rate of inflation.

There is often a great deal of published information available to help identify future rates for each of the variables mentioned. Care must be taken, however, to ensure that their particular impact on the business is properly assessed. When estimating the likely rate of inflation, for example, each major category of item affected by inflation should be considered separately. Using an average rate of inflation for all items is often inappropriate as levels of inflation can vary significantly between items.

Internal variables cover the policies and agreements to which the business is committed. Examples include:

- capital expenditure commitments
- financing agreements
- inventories holding policies
- credit period allowed to customers
- payment policies for trade payables
- accounting policies (for example, depreciation rates and methods)
- dividend policy.

The last item may require some clarification. For large businesses at least, a target level of dividends is often established and managers are usually reluctant to deviate from this target. The target may be linked to the level of profits for the particular year and/or to dividends paid in previous years. (This issue is discussed in more detail in Chapter 9.)

Once the key variables influencing future performance and position have been identified, we can begin to forecast the items included in the projected financial statements. We have to make a start somewhere and the usual starting point is to forecast sales. It is sales that normally sets a limit to business growth and determines the level of operating activity. The influence of sales on other items appearing in the financial statements, such as cost of goods sold, overheads, inventories, trade receivables and so on, makes a reliable sales forecast essential. If this forecast is wrong, other forecasts will also be wrong. Producing a reliable sales forecast requires an understanding of general economic conditions, industry conditions and the threat posed by major competitors.

Two main approaches to forecasting sales can be found in practice. The first approach relies on the views of the sales force or sales managers. It is a 'bottom-up' approach that involves aggregating forecasts from those with specialist knowledge of particular products, services or market segments. This approach tends to be most useful for fairly short forecasting horizons. However, care must be taken to ensure that there is no bias, particularly towards optimism, in the forecasts developed. The second approach relies on statistical techniques or, in the case of very large businesses, such as multinational motor-car manufacturers, econometric models. These techniques and models can range from simple extrapolation of past trends to extremely sophisticated models, which incorporate a large number of variables with complex interrelationships. There are no hard and fast rules concerning which approach to use. Managers must assess the benefits of each approach in terms of reliability and then weigh these benefits against the associated costs. Where they wish to carry out a cross-check on the reliability of forecast figures, both of the main approaches may be used.

PREPARING THE PROJECTED STATEMENTS: A WORKED EXAMPLE

We shall now take a look at how projected financial statements are put together. It was mentioned earlier that these financial statements consist of a:

- projected cash flow statement
- projected income statement
- projected statement of financial position (balance sheet).

For short forecast horizons, these statements are usually prepared in some detail. Where the forecast horizon is fairly long, however, or the costs of preparation prohibitive, simpler, less detailed statements are often provided. We shall look first at how to prepare detailed projected financial statements, and then look at simpler statements a little later in the chapter.

If you already have some background in accounting, the following sections, which deal with the detailed approach, should pose few problems. This is because projected financial statements employ the same methods and principles as those for conventional financial statements. The key difference is that projected financial statements rely on forecast, rather than actual, information.

To illustrate the preparation of projected financial statements, let us consider Example 2.1.

Example 2.1

Designer Dresses Ltd is a small business to be formed by James and William Clark to sell an exclusive range of dresses from a small boutique. On 1 January, they plan to invest £50,000 cash to acquire 25,000 £1 shares each in the business. Of this, £30,000 is to be invested in new fittings in January. These fittings are to be depreciated over three years on the straight-line basis (their scrap value is assumed to be zero at the end of their lives). The straight-line basis of depreciation allocates the total amount to be depreciated evenly over the life of the asset. In this case, a half-year's depreciation is to be charged in the first six months. The sales and purchases projections for the business are as follows:

	Jan	Feb	Mar	Apr	May	June	Total
Sales revenue (£000)	10.2	30.6	30.6	40.8	40.8	51.0	204.0
Purchases (£000)	20.0	30.0	25.0	25.0	30.0	30.0	160.0
Other costs* (£000)	9.0	9.0	9.0	9.0	9.0	9.0	54.0

* 'Other costs' includes wages but excludes depreciation.

The sales will all be made by credit card. The credit card business will take one month to pay and will deduct its fee of 2 per cent of gross sales before paying amounts due to Designer Dresses. One month's credit is allowed by suppliers. Other costs shown above do not include rent and rates of £10,000 per quarter, payable on 1 January and 1 April. All other costs will be paid in cash. The value of closing inventories at the end of June is expected to be £58,000.

Having set up the example, we shall now go on to prepare a projected cash flow statement and income statement for the six months to 30 June, and a projected statement of financial position as at that date (ignoring taxation and working to the nearest thousand pounds).

PROJECTED CASH FLOW STATEMENT

The projected cash flow statement monitors future changes in liquidity and helps managers to assess the impact of expected future events on the cash balance. Cash has been described as the 'lifeblood' of a business and so managers keep a close eye on forecast cash flows.

Activity 2.2

Can you think why cash is so important to a business?

To survive, a business must have sufficient cash resources to meet its maturing obligations. Ultimately, all businesses that fail do so because they do not have the cash to pay for the goods and services needed to continue operations.

The projected cash flow statement helps to identify when cash surpluses and cash deficits are likely to occur. Managers can then plan for these events. Where there is a cash surplus, they should consider the profitable investment of the cash. Where there is a cash deficit, they should consider ways in which it can be financed.

The cash flow statement is fairly easy to prepare. It simply records the cash inflows and outflows of the business. The main sources of cash inflows and outflows are:

- issue and redemption of long-term funds (for example, shares and loans)
- purchase and sale of non-current assets
- operating activities (sales revenue and operating expenses)
- tax and dividends.

These are set out in Figure 2.2.

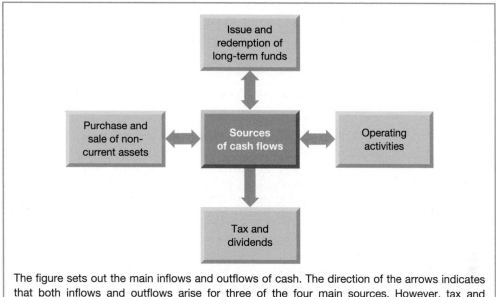

The figure sets out the main inflows and outflows of cash. The direction of the arrows indicates that both inflows and outflows arise for three of the four main sources. However, tax and dividends are usually cash outflows only.

Figure 2.2 Sources of cash inflows and outflows

When preparing the cash flow statement for a short period, such as six months or a year, it is often useful to provide a monthly breakdown of all cash inflows and outflows. This helps managers to monitor closely changes in the cash position of the business. There is no set format for this statement as it is normally used for internal purposes only. Managers are free to decide on the form of presentation that best suits their needs.

Set out below is an outline projected cash flow statement for Designer Dresses Ltd for the six months to 30 June. This format seems to be widely used and we shall use it throughout the chapter.

Projected cash flow statement for the year to 30 June

	Jan £000	Feb £000	Mar £000	Apr £000	May £000	June £000
Cash inflows						
Issue of shares						
Credit sales	—	—	—	—	—	—
	—	—	—	—	—	—
Cash outflows						
Credit purchases						
Other costs						
Rent and rates	—	—	—	—	—	—
	—	—	—	—	—	—
Net cash flow						
Opening balance	—	—	—	—	—	—
Closing balance	—	—	—	—	—	—

We can see from this outline that:

- each column represents a monthly period
- at the top of each column the cash inflows are set out and a total for each month's inflows is shown

- immediately below the monthly total for cash inflows, the cash outflows are set out and a monthly total for these is also shown
- the difference between the monthly totals of cash inflows and outflows is the net cash flow for the month
- if we add this net cash flow to the opening cash balance, which has been brought forward from the previous month, we derive the closing cash balance. (This will become the opening cash balance in the next month.)

In preparing a projected cash flow statement, we should ask two questions when examining a particular item of financial information. The first question is: *Does it involve a cash inflow or cash outflow?* If the answer is no, then it should be ignored when preparing the statement. Various items of information relating to a financial period, such as depreciation charges and bad debts, do not involve cash movements. If the answer is yes, we must ask the second question: *When did the cash inflow or outflow take place?* Where there is a monthly breakdown of cash flows, it is important to identify the particular month in which the cash movement occurred. Where sales and purchases are made on credit, the cash movement will often take place a month or two after the sale or purchase. (We return to this point later when discussing the projected income statement.)

Problems in preparing cash flow statements usually arise because the two questions above have not been properly addressed.

Activity 2.3

Fill in the outline cash flow statement for Designer Dresses Ltd for the six months to 30 June using the information contained in Example 2.1.

The completed statement will be as follows:

Projected cash flow statement for the six months to 30 June

	Jan £000	Feb £000	Mar £000	Apr £000	May £000	June £000
Cash inflows						
Issue of shares	50					
Credit sales	–	10	30	30	40	40
	50	10	30	30	40	40
Cash outflows						
Credit purchases	–	20	30	25	25	30
Other costs	9	9	9	9	9	9
Rent and rates	10			10		
Fittings	30	–	–	–	–	–
	49	29	39	44	34	39
Net cash flow	1	(19)	(9)	(14)	6	1
Opening balance	–	1	(18)	(27)	(41)	(35)
Closing balance	1	(18)	(27)	(41)	(35)	(34)

Notes:

1 The receipts from credit sales will arise one month after the sale has taken place. Hence, January's sales will be received in February, and so on. Similarly, trade payables are paid one month after the goods have been purchased.

2 The closing cash balance for each month is deduced by adding to (or subtracting from) the opening balance, the cash flow for the month.

Some further points

In the above example, the projected cash flow statement is broken down into monthly periods. Some businesses, however, carry out a weekly, or even daily, breakdown of future cash flows. Feasibility and cost/benefit considerations will determine whether more detailed analysis should be carried out.

Cash flow projections are normally prepared for a particular period and towards the end of that period, a new cash flow projection is prepared. This means that, as time passes, the forecast horizon becomes shorter and shorter. To overcome this problem, it is possible to produce a **rolling cash flow projection**. Let us use Example 2.1 to explain how this works. To begin with, a cash flow projection for the six months to 30 June will be prepared as before. At the end of January, however, a cash flow projection is prepared for the month of July. As a result, a full six months' forecast horizon is then restored. At the end of February, a cash flow projection is prepared for the month of August – and so on. A problem with this approach, however, is the need for constant forecasting, which may encourage a rather mechanical attitude to the whole process.

Real World 2.2 emphasises the importance of projected cash flow statements in difficult economic times.

Real World 2.2

Cash is king

As the number of corporate failures has risen, there is one line that bankers continue to echo: it is not a fall in profits that leads to failure but a lack of cash. In too many situations, companies and their investors have been focused on profits, but in an environment where liquidity is tight and confidence thin, cash is king. 'Cash management is incredibly important and even very large and stable businesses are taking it very seriously. Those that don't are doing so at their peril, as their customers and suppliers will be taking [cash] more seriously than they are,' says David Sage, working capital management partner at Ernst & Young. 'Poor cash management is one of the key reasons why nine out of ten companies fail when they do.'

While credit market conditions have improved in recent months, the retrenchment in bank lending is still a big challenge for many businesses. 'Banks are adopting more cautious lending policies and placing greater pressure on companies to mitigate cash needs through their own self-help measures,' says Ian Devlin, an associate partner in Deloitte's reorganisation services team. 'Overdrafts are on demand, so a critical issue for companies is to ensure that sufficient committed facilities are in place and to maintain a strong and proactive dialogue with providers of uncommitted lines.'

Mr Devlin says there are a number of such steps that a business can take to improve its cash position: 'Rigorous and focused attention to robust short-term forecasting and management of cash can yield rapid improvements, for example through freeing up trapped or blocked cash in parts of the group, selling surplus assets, embedding delegated purchase authority levels, negotiating with suppliers and, most importantly, instilling a strong cash culture throughout the organisation.'

David Sage recommends that companies adopt 13-week rolling cash flow forecasts. 'It is one of the best risk management tools and even more relevant in these times. I find it surprising how few companies do this,' he says. 'Most successful entrepreneurs will have their finger on the cash button daily and then they have the maximum amount of time to plan for any opportunities, as well as any problems.'

Accurate cash flow projections are also important for businesses that are growing rapidly. Failure to generate sufficient cash to meet growing commitments can have dire consequences. Where a growing business publishes cash flow projections which it then fails to meet, there is a risk that shareholders will view this as a sign of weakness and react by selling shares. **Real World 2.3** provides an example of one growing business that suffered from this problem.

PROJECTED INCOME STATEMENT

A projected income statement provides an insight into likely future profits (or losses), which represent the difference between the predicted level of revenue and expenses for a period. Revenue is reported when it is reasonably certain of being received and can be reliably measured. This means that revenue from the sale of goods or services will normally be recorded *before* the cash is actually received. Expenses are matched to the revenues they help to generate, which means they are included in the same income statement. Expenses may be reported in an income statement for a period occurring either before or after they are actually paid. This may seem odd at first sight. We should bear in mind, however, that the purpose of the income statement is to show the profits (or losses) during a particular period, which is the difference between revenue and expenses. The timing of the cash inflows from revenues and cash outflows for expenses is irrelevant for this statement.

The format of the projected income statement for Designer Dresses Ltd is as follows:

Projected income statement for the six months to 30 June

	£000	£000
Credit sales revenue		
Less Cost of sales		
Opening inventories		
Add Purchases	—	
Less Closing inventories	—	—
Gross profit		
Less		
Credit card discounts		
Rent and rates		
Other costs		
Depreciation of fittings		—
Profit for the period		—

Activity 2.4

Fill in the outline projected income statement for Designer Dresses Ltd for the six months to 30 June, using the information contained in Example 2.1 above.

The statement will be as follows:

Projected income statement for the six months to 30 June

	£000	£000
Credit sales revenue		204
Cost of sales		
Opening inventories	–	
Purchases	(160)	
	(160)	
Closing inventories	58	(102)
Gross profit		102
Credit card discounts		(4)
Rent and rates		(20)
Other costs		(54)
Depreciation of fittings		(5)
Profit for the period		19

Notes:
1 There were no opening inventories in this case.
2 The credit card discount is shown as a separate expense and not deducted from the sales figure. This approach is more informative than simply netting off the amount of the discount against sales.

PROJECTED STATEMENT OF FINANCIAL POSITION (BALANCE SHEET)

The projected statement of financial position reveals the end-of-period balances for assets, liabilities and equity. It is the last statement to be prepared as the other two statements produce information needed for this statement. The projected cash flow statement provides the end-of-period cash balance for inclusion under 'current assets' (or where there is a negative balance, for inclusion under 'current liabilities'). The projected income statement provides the projected profit (or loss) for the period for inclusion under the 'equity' section of the statement of financial position (after adjustment for dividends). The projected income statement also provides the depreciation charge for the period, which is used to adjust non-current assets.

The format of the projected statement of financial position for Designer Dresses Ltd will be as follows:

Projected statement of financial position as at 30 June

	£000
ASSETS	
Non-current assets	
Fittings	
Accumulated depreciation	___
	___
Current assets	
Inventories	
Trade receivables	___
	___
Total assets	___
EQUITY AND LIABILITIES	
Equity	
Share capital	
Retained earnings	___
	___
Current liabilities	
Trade payables	
Bank overdraft	___
	___
Total equity and liabilities	___

Fill in the outline projected statement of financial position for Designer Dresses Ltd as at 30 June using the information contained in Example 2.1 and in the answers to Activities 2.3 and 2.4.

The completed statement will be as follows:

Projected statement of financial position as at 30 June

	£000
ASSETS	
Non-current assets	
Fittings	30
Accumulated depreciation	(5)
	25
Current assets	
Inventories	58
Trade receivables	50
	108
Total assets	133
EQUITY AND LIABILITIES	
Equity	
Share capital	50
Retained earnings	19
	69
Current liabilities	
Trade payables	30
Bank overdraft	34
	64
Total equity and liabilities	133

Note: The trade receivables figure represents June credit sales (less the credit card discount). Similarly, the trade payables figure represents June purchases.

PROJECTED FINANCIAL STATEMENTS AND DECISION MAKING

The performance and position revealed by the projected financial statements should be examined with a critical eye. There is always a danger that the figures will be too readily accepted. Forecast figures are rarely completely accurate and some assessment must be made of the extent to which they can be relied upon. Thus, managers should ask questions such as:

- How were the projections developed?
- What underlying assumptions have been made and are they valid?
- Have all relevant items been included?

Only when satisfactory answers to these questions have been received should the statements be used for making decisions.

Projected financial statements do not come with clear decision rules to indicate whether a proposed course of action should go ahead. Managers must use their judgement when examining the information before them. To help form a judgement, the following questions should be asked:

- Are the cash flows satisfactory? Can they be improved by changing policies or plans (for example, delaying capital expenditure decisions, requiring receivables to pay more quickly and so on)?
- Is there a need for additional financing? Is it feasible to obtain the amount required?
- Can any surplus funds be profitably reinvested?
- Is the level of projected profit satisfactory in relation to the risks involved? If not, what could be done to improve matters?
- Are the sales and individual expense items at a satisfactory level?
- Is the financial position at the end of the period acceptable?
- Is the level of borrowing acceptable? Is the business too dependent on borrowing?

Activity 2.6

Evaluate the performance and position of Designer Dresses Ltd as set out in the projected financial statements. Pay particular attention to the projected profitability and liquidity of the business.

The projected cash flow statement reveals that the business will have a bank overdraft throughout most of the period under review. The maximum overdraft requirement will be £41,000 in April. Although the business will be heavily dependent on bank finance in the early months, this situation should not last for too long. This is provided that the business achieves, and then maintains, the level of projected profit and provided it does not invest heavily in further assets.

The business is expected to generate a profit of 9.3p for every £1 of sales (that is, £19,000/£204,000). The profit of £19,000 on the original outlay of £50,000 by the owners seems high. However, the business may be of a high-risk nature and therefore the owners will be looking to make high returns. It is not clear from the question whether the wages (under 'other costs' in the income statement) include any remuneration for James and William Clark. If no remuneration for their efforts has been included, the level of returns (after wages) may not be so high.

When evaluating performance and position of Designer Dresses Ltd, two points are worth making. First, this is a new business and so it may be very difficult to project into the future with any accuracy. The bases upon which the projections have been made must, therefore, be carefully investigated. Second, we must avoid the temptation to make a simple extrapolation of projected revenues and expenses for the six-month period in order to obtain a projected profit for the year. It is unlikely, for example, to be double the profit for the first six months.

Activity 2.7

Can you think why it would be unlikely to be double the profit for the first six months?

Two possible reasons are:

- the business is seasonal in nature
- a clear pattern of revenue is unlikely to emerge until the business becomes more established.

PER-CENT-OF-SALES METHOD

An alternative approach to preparing a projected income statement and statement of financial position is the **per-cent-of-sales method**. This is a simpler approach to forecasting, which assumes that most items appearing in the income statement and statement of financial position vary with the level of sales. Hence, these statements can be prepared by expressing most items as a percentage of the sales revenue that is forecast for the period.

To use this method, an examination of past records needs to be undertaken to see by how much items vary with sales. It may be found, for example, that inventories levels have been around 30 per cent of sales in previous periods. If the sales for the forecast period are, say, £10 million, the level of inventories will be forecast as £3 million (that is, 30% × £10 million). The same approach will be used for other items.

Below is a summary of how key items appearing in the income statement and statement of financial position are derived.

Income statement

The per-cent-of-sales method assumes that the following income statement items can be expressed as a percentage of sales:

- expenses
- profit before tax, which is the difference between sales revenues and expenses.

Tax is assumed to vary with the level of profit before tax and so is expressed as a percentage of this figure. It has, therefore, an indirect relationship with sales.

Statement of financial position

The per-cent-of-sales method assumes that the following items in the statement of financial position can be expressed as a percentage of sales:

- current assets that increase spontaneously with sales, such as inventories and trade receivables
- current liabilities that increase spontaneously with sales, such as trade payables and accrued expenses
- cash (as a projected cash flow statement is not prepared to provide a more accurate measure of cash).

However:

- non-current assets will be expressed as a percentage of sales only if they are already operating at full capacity – otherwise they will not usually change
- non-current liabilities and equity will not be expressed as a percentage of sales but will be based on figures at the beginning of the forecast period (unless changes are made as a result of management decisions)
- dividends (which will affect the retained earnings figure for the year) are normally expressed as a percentage of profit for the year.

Identifying the financing gap

Where sales revenue increases, a business may outgrow the finance that has been committed. The increase in assets needed to sustain the increased sales may exceed the increase in equity (in the form of retained earnings) and liabilities. When this occurs there will be a financing gap. Any future financing gap is easily identified under the per-cent-of-sales method because the projected statement of financial position will not balance: total assets will exceed total equity and liabilities. The additional finance required by the business will be the amount needed to make the statement of financial position balance.

The way in which a business decides to fill the financing gap is referred to as the plug. Various forms of finance may be used as a plug, including borrowings and share capital, and these will be discussed in detail in Chapter 6.

A worked example

Let us go through a simple example to show how the per-cent-of-sales method works.

Example 2.2

The financial statements of Burrator plc for the year that has just ended are as follows:

Income statement for Year 8

	£000
Credit sales revenue	800
Cost of sales	(600)
Gross profit	200
Selling expenses	(80)
Distribution expenses	(20)
Other expenses	(20)
Profit before taxation	80
Tax (25%)	(20)
Profit for the year	60

Statement of financial position as at the end of Year 8

	£000
ASSETS	
Non-current assets	160
Current assets	
Inventories	320
Trade receivables	200
Cash	20
	540
Total assets	700
EQUITY AND LIABILITIES	
Equity	
Share capital – 25p ordinary shares	60
Retained earnings	380
	440
Current liabilities	
Trade payables	240
Tax due	20
	260
Total equity and liabilities	700

In line with previous years, a dividend of 50 per cent of the profit for the year was proposed and paid during the year.

The following information is relevant for Year 9:

1 Sales revenue is expected to be 10 per cent higher than in Year 8.
2 The non-current assets of the business are currently operating at full capacity.
3 The tax rate will be the same as in Year 8 and 50 per cent of the tax due will be outstanding at the year end.
4 The business intends to maintain the same dividend policy as for Year 8.
5 Half of the tax relating to Year 9 will be outstanding at the year end. Tax due at the end of Year 8 will be paid during Year 9.
6 Any financing gap will be filled by an issue of long-term loan notes.

We shall prepare a projected income statement and statement of financial position for Year 9 using the per-cent-of-sales method (assuming that Year 8 provides a useful guide to past experience).

To prepare the projected income statement, we calculate each expense as a percentage of sales for Year 8 and then use this percentage to forecast the equivalent expense in Year 9. Tax is calculated as a percentage of the profit before tax for Year 9, using percentages from Year 8.

The statement is therefore as follows:

Projected income statement for the year ended 31 December Year 9

	£000
Credit sales revenue (800 + (10% × 800))	880
Cost of sales (75% of sales)	(660)
Gross profit (25% of sales)	220
Selling expenses (10% of sales)	(88)
Distribution expenses (2.5% of sales)	(22)
Other expenses (2.5% of sales)	(22)
Profit before taxation (10% of sales)	88
Tax (25% of profit before tax)	(22)
Profit for the year	66

We apply the same broad principles when preparing the projected statement of financial position for Year 9.

Prepare a projected statement of financial position for Burrator plc as at the end of Year 9.

This will be as follows:

Projected statement of financial position as at 31 December Year 9

	£000
ASSETS	
Non-current assets (20% of sales)	
	176
Current assets	
Inventories (40% of sales)	352
Trade receivables (25% of sales)	220
Cash (2.5% of sales)	22
	594
Total assets	770
EQUITY AND LIABILITIES	
Equity	
Share capital – 25p ordinary shares	60
Retained earnings [380 + (66 – 33*)]	413
	473
Non-current liabilities	
Loan notes (balancing figure)	22
Current liabilities	
Trade payables (30% of sales)	264
Tax due (50% of tax due)	11
	275
Total equity and liabilities	770

* The dividend is 50 per cent of the profit for the year (as in previous years) and is deducted in deriving the retained earnings for the year.

Evaluating the per-cent-of-sales method

The main advantage of the per-cent-of-sales method is that the task of preparing the projected financial statements becomes much more manageable. It can provide an approximate figure for any future financing requirements without the need to prepare a projected cash flow statement. It can also reduce the time and cost of forecasting every single item appearing in the projected income statement and statement of financial position. This can be of particular benefit for large businesses.

The per-cent-of-sales method suffers from two main drawbacks, however. First, it employs relationships between individual items and sales that are based on the past. These relationships may change over time because of changes in strategic direction (for example, launching completely new products) or because of changes in management policies (for example, allowing longer credit periods to customers). Second, it fails to recognise that many expenses are fixed over time and do not vary with the level of sales.

Activity 2.9

Can you think of three examples of fixed expenses that a business may incur?

They may include:

- salaries
- rent payable
- insurance
- interest payable.

You may have thought of others.

Where sales are increasing, the per-cent-of-sales method will increase fixed expenses in line with the increase in sales. The effect will be to overstate expenses and to understate profits for the period. Where sales are decreasing, the opposite will be true. The higher the level of fixed expenses incurred by the business, the greater will be the resulting overstatement or understatement.

Activity 2.10

The above suggests that the per-cent-of-sales method is best suited to a business with at least one of two possible characteristics. What might these be?

It is probably best suited to a business where:

- sales remain stable over time, and/or
- expenses are not fixed but variable (that is, they vary directly with sales).

Note: The second characteristic mentioned would be a very rare occurrence. For most businesses, fixed expenses account for the greater part of total expenses incurred.

LONG-TERM CASH FLOW PROJECTIONS

The projected cash flow statement prepared in Activity 2.3 required a detailed analysis of each element of the cash flows of the business. This may be fine when dealing with a short forecast horizon. However, as the forecasting horizon increases, forecasting difficulties start to mount. A point may soon be reached where it is simply not possible to undertake such detailed analysis.

To prepare projected cash flow statements for the longer term, a method that uses simplifying assumptions rather than detailed analysis may be used. The starting point is to identify the sales revenue for each year of the planning horizon. The operating profit (that is, profit before interest and taxation) for each year is then calculated as a percentage of the sales revenue figure. (The particular percentage is often determined by reference to past experience.) A few simple adjustments are then made to the annual operating profits in order to derive annual operating cash flows.

These adjustments rely on the fact that, broadly, sales revenue gives rise to cash inflows and expenses give rise to outflows. As a result, operating profit will be closely linked to the operating cash flows. This does not mean that operating profit for the year will be equal to operating cash flows. An important reason for this is timing differences. When sales are made on credit, the cash receipt occurs some time after the sale. Thus, sales revenue made towards the end of a particular year will be included in that year's income statement. Most of the cash from those sales, however, will flow into the business and should be included in the cash flows for the following year. Fortunately it is easy to deduce the cash received, as we see in Example 2.3.

Example 2.3

The sales revenue figure for a business for the year was £34 million. The trade receivables totalled £4 million at the beginning of the year, but had increased to £5 million by the end of the year.

Basically, the trade receivables figure is dictated by sales revenue and cash receipts. It is increased when a sale is made and decreased when cash is received from a credit customer. If, over the year, the sales revenue and the cash receipts had been equal, the beginning-of-year and end-of-year trade receivables figures would have been equal. Since the trade receivables figure increased, it must mean that less cash was received than sales revenues were made. This means that the cash receipts from sales must be £33 million (that is, 34 − (5 − 4)).

Put slightly differently, we can say that as a result of sales, assets of £34 million flowed into the business during the year. If £1 million of this went to increasing the asset of trade receivables, this leaves only £33 million that went to increase cash.

Other important adjustments for timing differences relate to cash payments for purchases (by adjusting for opening and closing trade payables) and cost of goods sold (by adjusting for opening and closing inventories). The same general point, however, is true in respect of most other items that are taken into account in deducing the operating profit figure. An important exception is depreciation, which is not normally associated with any movement in cash; it is simply an accounting entry.

All of this means that we can take the operating profit (profit before interest and taxation) for the year, add back the depreciation charged in arriving at that profit, and adjust this total for movements in trade (and other) receivables and payables and for inventories. This will provide us with a measure of the operating cash flows. If we then go on to deduct payments made during the year for taxation, interest on borrowings and dividends, we have the net cash flows from operations.

The method of deducing the net cash flows from operations is summarised in Figure 2.3.

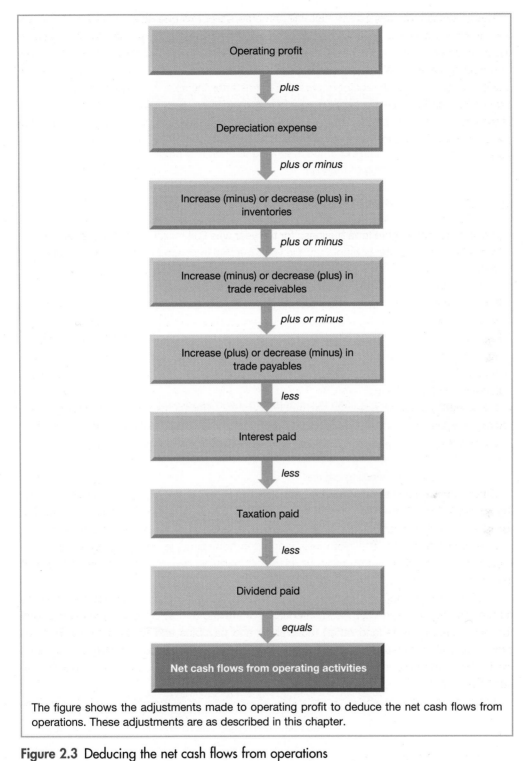

The figure shows the adjustments made to operating profit to deduce the net cash flows from operations. These adjustments are as described in this chapter.

Figure 2.3 Deducing the net cash flows from operations

The following example should make all of the above points clearer.

Example 2.4

Relevant forecast information for Drago plc for next year is as follows:

	£m
Operating profit	128
Depreciation to be charged in arriving at operating profit	34
At the beginning of the year:	
Inventories	15
Trade receivables	24
Trade payables	18
At the end of the year:	
Inventories	17
Trade receivables	21
Trade payables	19

The following further information is available about forecast payments during next year:

	£m
Taxation paid	32
Interest paid	5
Dividends paid	9

The projected operating cash flows can be derived as follows:

	£m	£m
Operating profit		128
Depreciation		34
*Decrease in working capital**		
Increase in inventories (17 – 15)	(2)	
Decrease in trade receivables (21 – 24)	3	
Increase in trade payables (19 – 18)	1	2
Operating cash flows		164
Interest paid		(5)
Taxation paid		(32)
Dividends paid		(9)
Net cash flows from operations		118

* Working capital is a term widely used in accounting and finance, not just in the context of projected financial statements. We shall encounter it several times in later chapters.

As we can see, there will be a decrease in working capital (that is, current assets less current liabilities) as a result of trading operations. We saw that an additional £2 million will go into increased inventories and that this will have an adverse effect on cash. However, more cash will be received from trade receivables than sales revenue generated. Similarly, less cash will be paid to trade payables than purchases of goods and services on credit. Both of these will have a favourable effect on cash. The net effect, therefore, is a projected decrease in working capital investment leading to an increase in cash of £2 million.

Example 2.4 illustrates how the various elements of working capital affect cash flows. When preparing long-term cash flow projections, however, detailed adjustments to each element of working capital may be avoided. Instead, a simplifying assumption may be adopted that takes working capital investment as a fixed percentage of sales revenue. Changes in working capital are then measured according to changes in sales revenue.

Activity 2.11

Why might calculating working capital as a fixed percentage of sales be a reasonable simplifying assumption?

Key elements of working capital, such as trade receivables, inventories and trade payables, tend to increase, or decrease, in line with increases, or decreases, in sales.

Let us now consider a further example, to see how we prepare projected cash flow statements using the approach outlined.

Example 2.5

Santos Engineering Ltd started operations on 1 January Year 1 and has produced the following forecasts for annual sales revenue:

Year to 31 December	Year 1	Year 2	Year 3	Year 4
Forecast sales revenue (£)	500,000	550,000	640,000	720,000

The following additional information has been provided:

1. The operating profit of the business is expected to be 20 per cent of the sales revenue throughout the four-year period.
2. The company has issued £400,000 5 per cent loan notes, which are redeemable at the end of Year 4.
3. The tax rate is expected to be 25 per cent throughout the four-year period. Tax is paid in the year following the year in which the relevant profits were made.
4. An initial investment in working capital of £50,000 is required. Thereafter, investment in working capital is expected to represent 10 per cent of sales revenue for the relevant year.
5. Depreciation of £40,000 per year must be charged for the non-current assets currently held.
6. Land costing £490,000 will be acquired during Year 2. This will not be depreciated as it has an infinite life.
7. Dividends of £30,000 per year will be announced for Year 1. Thereafter, dividends will rise by £6,000 each year. Dividends are paid in the year following the period to which they relate.
8. The business has a current cash balance of £85,000.

We shall now prepare projected cash flow statements showing the financing requirements of the business for each of the next four years. The starting point is to calculate the projected operating profit for the period and then to make the depreciation and the working capital adjustments as described earlier. This will provide us with a figure of operating cash flows. We then simply adjust for the interest, tax and dividends to deduce the net cash flows from operations each year.

The financing requirements for Santos Engineering Ltd are calculated as follows:

Projected cash flow statements

	Year 1 £	Year 2 £	Year 3 £	Year 4 £
Sales revenue	500,000	560,000	640,000	700,000
Operating profit (20%)	100,000	112,000	128,000	140,000
Depreciation	40,000	40,000	40,000	40,000
Working capital*	(50,000)	(6,000)	(8,000)	(6,000)
Operating cash flows	90,000	146,000	160,000	174,000
Interest	(20,000)	(20,000)	(20,000)	(20,000)
Tax**		(20,000)	(23,000)	(27,000)
Dividends		(30,000)	(36,000)	(42,000)
Non-current assets		(490,000)		
Loan repayment				(400,000)
Net cash flows from operations	70,000	(414,000)	81,000	(315,000)
Opening balance	85,000	155,000	(259,000)	(178,000)
Closing balance	155,000	(259,000)	(178,000)	(493,000)

* The initial investment in working capital will be charged in the first year. Thereafter only increases (or decreases) in the level of working capital will be shown as an adjustment.

** The tax charge for each year is shown below.

	Year 1 £	Year 2 £	Year 3 £	Year 4 £
Operating profit (as above)	100,000	112,000	128,000	140,000
Interest	(20,000)	(20,000)	(20,000)	(20,000)
Profit before tax	80,000	92,000	108,000	120,000
Tax (25%)	(20,000)	(23,000)	(27,000)	(30,000)
Profit after tax	60,000	69,000	81,000	90,000

Note: Tax will be paid in the year after the relevant profit is made.

TAKING ACCOUNT OF RISK

When making estimates concerning the future, there is always a chance that things will not turn out as expected. The likelihood that what is estimated to occur will not actually occur is referred to as **risk** and this will be considered in some detail in Chapter 5. However, it is worth taking a little time at this point to consider the ways in which managers may deal with the problem of risk in the context of projected financial statements. In practice, there are various methods available to help managers deal with any uncertainty surrounding the reliability of the projected financial statements. Below we consider two possible methods.

Sensitivity analysis

Sensitivity analysis is a useful technique to employ when evaluating the contents of projected financial statements. This involves taking a single variable (for example, volume of sales) and examining the effect of changes in the chosen variable on the likely performance and position of the business. By examining the shifts that occur, it is possible to arrive at some assessment of how sensitive changes are for the projected outcomes. Although only one variable is examined at a time, a number of variables that are considered to be important to the performance of a business may be examined consecutively.

One form of sensitivity analysis is to pose a series of 'what if?' questions. If we take sales as an example, the following 'what if?' questions may be asked:

■ What if sales volume is 5 per cent higher than expected?
■ What if sales volume is 10 per cent lower than expected?
■ What if sales price is reduced by 15 per cent?
■ What if sales price could be increased by 20 per cent?

In answering these questions, it is possible to develop a better 'feel' for the effect of forecast inaccuracies and possible changes on the final outcomes. However, this technique does not assign probabilities to each possible change, nor does it consider the effect on projected outcomes of more than one variable at a time.

Real World 2.4 describes how the auditors of a business may use sensitivity analysis.

Real World 2.4

Sensitive issue

When reviewing the financial statements of a business, auditors may use sensitivity analysis to see whether the business is likely to encounter financial difficulties, such as breaching the conditions of a loan agreement. (Loan conditions may include a requirement not to exceed certain borrowing levels or to generate operating profits that exceed interest charges.) Where there is a serious risk of such an event occurring, the auditors must mention it in their report to shareholders, which accompanies the annual report. This is often done through an 'emphasis of matter' paragraph in the auditors' report, which attempts to direct the attention of shareholders to important issues.

The auditors will normally comb through managers' forecasts for the forthcoming year and examine the underlying assumptions used. Andrew Buchanan, technical partner of accountancy firm BDO Stoy Hayward, says: 'If you've got a company close to breaching covenants (loan conditions) if markets deteriorate further, I'd want that to be set out very clearly. If a sensitivity analysis on forecasts shows that you're in danger of breaching covenants, auditors are more likely to consider adding an emphasis paragraph to their report.'

 Source: Based on J. Hughes (2009) 'Funding plans a key matter in annual reports', www.ft.com, 25 January.
© The Financial Times Limited 2012. All Rights Reserved.

Scenario analysis

Another approach to helping managers gain a feel for the effect of forecast inaccuracies is to prepare projected financial statements according to different possible 'states of the world'. For example, managers may wish to examine projected financial statements prepared on the following bases:

■ an optimistic view of likely future events
■ a pessimistic view of likely future events
■ a 'most likely' view of future events.

This approach is referred to as scenario analysis and, unlike sensitivity analysis, it will involve changing a number of variables simultaneously in order to portray a possible state of the world. It does not, however, identify the likelihood of each state of the world occurring. This information would also be useful in assessing the level of risk involved.

Real World 2.5 describes how one large business employs this technique in its risk assessment.

Real World 2.5

Making a scene

Cairn Energy plc, a leading energy business, uses scenario analysis when assessing the risk of a shortfall in operational cash flows. In its 2011 annual report, the business states:

> The Group's liquidity is carefully and routinely monitored through cash forecasts, which are prepared using a number of different scenarios. These forecasts show that the Group will be able to operate with significant financial headroom for the 12 months from the date of approval of the 2011 Annual Report and Accounts.

Source: Cairn Energy plc, *Annual Report and Accounts 2011*, p. 35.

What about investors?

Projected financial statements are prepared for internal purposes and managers are normally reluctant to make these statements more widely available. Only on rare occasions, such as when a company is seeking new finance or resisting a hostile takeover bid, will investors and other external parties be given access to them.

Activity 2.12

Why do you think managers are normally reluctant to make projected financial statements publicly available? Try to think of at least one reason.

One reason is the fear that it may damage future business performance. Competitors will gain access to the information and may use details of future sales, profits and so on to their advantage. Another reason is the fear that investors will not fully appreciate the risk of forecasting error when using the statements for decision making. A final, less charitable, reason is that managers may not wish to be held accountable for any divergence between projected and actual figures. Where projected figures turn out to be incorrect, particularly where they prove to be over-optimistic, investors are likely to be critical.

To fill the void, investment analysts often produce their own profit projections for large businesses. Investors may, therefore, gain access to these to help guide their decisions. **Real World 2.6** sets out the profit projections from analysts for one well-known business.

Real World 2.6

Reaching a consensus

J. Sainsbury plc, the supermarket chain, publishes on its website profit projections produced by independent investment analysts. These are updated from time to time as revisions are often made in the light of new information. The following extracts from the website, which were taken in February 2013, set out analysts' consensus projections, as well as the range of their projections, relating to profit before tax.

	2012/13 Profit before tax £m	2013/14 Profit before tax £m
Consensus	742	784
Minimum	721	757
Maximum	754	833

Source: Analysts' consensus J. Sainsbury plc, www.j-sainsbury.co.uk, accessed 13 February 2013.

Note that the range of projected profits is narrower for the financial year 2012/13 (which ended 16 March 2013) than for the financial year 2013/14. This is, perhaps, not surprising. The 2012/13 financial year was near to completion and analysts would already have received much information from the business about trading performance in the form of interim financial reports, trading announcements and so on. They would also have information about the trading performance of similar businesses. This should all help to eliminate areas of uncertainty.

However, the business finally reported profit before tax for 2012/13 of £788 million, which fell outside the range of projections. Its profit performance, therefore, appears to have caught analysts by surprise.

Although businesses shy away from publishing detailed projections, some large businesses publish key figures, such as projected sales and profit, for the current financial year. This is often done at a fairly late point in the year so that the size of any forecasting error is likely to be small.

Real World 2.7 reveals how the projected profit, or forecast, figure of one well-known business was upgraded in the light of changing conditions.

Real World 2.7

Flying higher

Dublin-based Ryanair, Europe's top low-cost airline, which has used its size and low costs to undercut struggling flag carriers, hiked its profit forecast to €540 million ($728 million) for the year to March, up from an earlier €490–520 million range. 'We saw strong demand out of the UK, out of Germany and out of Scandinavia and that has gone straight to our bottom line,' Chief Operating Officer Michael Cawley told Reuters.

Strong demand in the run-up to Christmas and a high uptake of reserved seating options helped to lift ticket prices in northern Europe well above the company's forecasts, he said. Sales were not as buoyant in Southern Europe, with Spain in particular 'very weak', and fare growth in Italy flat, he said.

→

An 8 per cent rise in average fares lifted the airline to a profit of €18 million in the traditionally weak three months to December, compared with an average forecast by five analysts polled by Reuters of a €5 million loss. Fare growth compared with 5 per cent in the six months to September and was way ahead of the 3 per cent average forecast by three analysts polled by Reuters. Average fares will grow at a slower pace in the three months to March, however, Cawley said.

Ryanair has been able to sweep up customers as traditional rivals cut back capacity in the face of slow economic growth in Europe and high fuel costs. Revenues climbed 15 per cent to €969 million in the quarter, better than the 9.2 per cent revenue growth its chief low-cost rival easyJet reported last week. Ancillary revenues, which exclude ticket prices, were up 24 per cent from a year earlier.

'Demand is exceeding supply in the short-haul market and Ryanair is capitalising on it,' said Davy Stockbrokers' analyst Stephen Furlong. 'The market will be very happy with these numbers.'

Source: C. Humphries, 'Ryanair lifts profit forecast on resilient Northern Europe', www.reuters.com, 28 January 2013.

Self-assessment question 2.1

Quardis Ltd is a small business that imports high-quality laser printers. The most recent statement of financial position of the business is as follows:

Statement of financial position as at 31 May Year 8

	£000	£000
ASSETS		
Non-current assets		
Property	460	
Accumulated depreciation	(30)	430
Fixtures and fittings	35	
Accumulated depreciation	(10)	25
		455
Current assets		
Inventories		24
Trade receivables		34
Cash at bank		2
		60
Total assets		515
EQUITY AND LIABILITIES		
Equity		
£1 ordinary shares		200
Retained earnings		144
		344
Non-current liabilities		
Borrowings – loan		125
Current liabilities		
Trade payables		22
Tax due		24
		46
Total equity and liabilities		515

The following forecast information is available for the year ending 31 May Year 9:

1 Sales are expected to be £280,000 for the year. Sixty per cent of sales are on credit and it is expected that, at the year end, three months' credit sales will be outstanding. Sales revenues accrue evenly over the year.
2 Purchases of inventories during the year will be £186,000 and will accrue evenly over the year. All purchases are on credit and at the year end it is expected that two months' purchases will remain unpaid.
3 Fixtures and fittings costing £25,000 will be purchased and paid for during the year. Depreciation is charged at 10 per cent on the cost of fixtures and fittings held at the year end.
4 Depreciation is charged on property at 2 per cent on cost.
5 On 1 June Year 8, £30,000 of the loan from the Highland Bank is to be repaid. Interest is at the rate of 13 per cent per year and all interest accrued to 31 May Year 9 will be paid on that day.
6 Inventories at the year end are expected to be 25 per cent higher than at the beginning of the year.
7 Wages for the year will be £34,000. It is estimated that £4,000 of this total will remain unpaid at the year end.
8 Other overhead expenses for the year (excluding those mentioned above) are expected to be £21,000. It is expected that £3,000 of this total will still be unpaid at the year end.
9 A dividend of 5p per share will be announced and paid during the year.
10 Tax is payable at the rate of 35 per cent. Tax outstanding at the beginning of the year will be paid during the year. Half of the tax relating to the year will also be paid during the year.

Required:
(a) Prepare a projected income statement for the year ending 31 May Year 9.
(b) Prepare a projected statement of financial position as at 31 May Year 9.
(c) Comment on the significant features revealed by these statements.

All workings should be shown to the nearest £000.

Note: A projected cash flow statement is not required. The cash figure in the projected statement of financial position will be a balancing figure.

The answer to this question can be found at the back of the book on pp. 559–560.

SUMMARY

The main points in this chapter may be summarised as follows:

Planning for the future
- Developing plans for a business involves:
  - setting aims and objectives
  - identifying the options available
  - selecting options and developing long-term plans
  - developing short-term plans.

The role of projected financial statements

- They help in evaluating the impact of plans on financial performance and position.
- They can be prepared for long or short time horizons.

Preparing projected financial statements

- Involves:
  - identifying the key variables that affect future financial performance
  - forecasting sales for the period, as many other items vary in relation to sales.
- Financial statements that can be prepared for planning purposes are:
  - a projected cash flow statement
  - a projected income statement
  - a projected statement of financial position.

Projected financial statements and decision making

- Projected statements should be checked for reliability before being used for decision making.
- They do not provide clear decision rules for managers, who must employ judgement.

Per-cent-of-sales method

- Assumes that most items on the income statement and statement of financial position vary with sales.
- Calculates any financing gap by reference to the amount required to make the statement of financial position balance.
- Makes the preparation of projected statements easier and less costly.
- Assumes that past relationships between particular items and sales will also hold and that all expenses vary with sales.

Long-term cash projections

- When making long-term cash projections, a method using simplifying assumptions is often employed. It involves:
  - forecasting sales revenue and calculating operating profit as a percentage of this figure
  - adjusting operating profit for depreciation, and working capital to derive operating cash flows
  - deducting interest, dividends and tax paid from the operating cash flows to derive the net cash flow from operations.

Taking account of risk

- Two methods of dealing with risk are:
  - sensitivity analysis
  - scenario analysis.
- These techniques can be applied to projected financial statements to help managers gain a 'feel' for the risks involved.

Projected financial statements and investors

- They are not normally made available to investors.
- Investors may gain access to profit projections prepared by investment analysts.

KEY TERMS

Projected financial statements p. 33
Rolling cash flow projections p. 39
Per-cent-of-sales method p. 45
Plug p. 46

Working capital p. 52
Risk p. 54
Sensitivity analysis p. 54
Scenario analysis p. 56

For definitions of these terms, see the Glossary, pp. 605–613.

FURTHER READING

If you wish to explore the topics discussed in this chapter in more depth, try the following books:

Allman, K. (2010) *Corporate Valuation Modelling: A step-by-step guide*, 2nd edn, John Wiley & Sons.

Brealey, R., Myers, S. and Allen, F. (2011) *Principles of Corporate Finance*, 10th edn, McGraw-Hill, Chapter 29.

Brigham, E. and Ehrhardt, M. (2013) *Financial Management: Theory & Practice*, 14th edn, South-Western Cengage Learning, Chapter 12.

Fight, A. (2005) *Cash Flow Forecasting (Essential Capital Markets)*, Butterworths, Chapters 1–4.

REVIEW QUESTIONS

Answers to these questions can be found at the back of the book on p. 571.

2.1 In what ways might projected financial statements help a business that is growing fast?

2.2 'The future is uncertain and so projected financial statements will almost certainly prove to be inaccurate. It is, therefore, a waste of time to prepare them.' Comment.

2.3 Why would it normally be easier for an established business than for a new business to prepare projected financial statements?

2.4 Why is the sales forecast normally critical to the preparation of projected financial statements?

EXERCISES

Exercises 2.5 to 2.7 are more advanced than 2.1 to 2.4. Those with a coloured number have solutions at the back of the book, starting on p. 581.

If you wish to try more exercises, visit the students' side of this book's companion website.

2.1 Choice Designs Ltd operates a small group of wholesale/retail carpet stores in the north of England. The statement of financial position of the business as at 31 May Year 8 is as follows:

Statement of financial position as at 31 May Year 8

	£000	£000
ASSETS		
Non-current assets		
Property	600	
Accumulated depreciation	(100)	500
Fixtures and fittings	140	
Accumulated depreciation	(80)	60
		560
Current assets		
Inventories		240
Trade receivables		220
Bank		165
		625
Total assets		1,185
EQUITY AND LIABILITIES		
Equity		
£1 ordinary shares		500
Retained earnings		251
		751
Current liabilities		
Trade payables		268
Tax due		166
		434
Total equity and liabilities		1,185

As a result of falling profits the directors of the business would like to completely refurbish each store during June Year 8 at a total cost of £300,000. However, before making such a large capital expenditure commitment, they require projections of performance and position for the forthcoming year.

The following information is available concerning the year to 31 May Year 9:

■ The forecast sales for the year are £1,400,000 and the gross profit is expected to be 30 per cent of sales. Eighty per cent of all sales are on credit. At present the average credit period is six weeks, but it is likely that this will change to eight weeks in the forthcoming year.

■ At the year end, inventories are expected to be 25 per cent higher than at the beginning of the year.

■ During the year, the directors intend to pay £40,000 for a fleet of delivery vans.

■ Administration expenses for the year are expected to be £225,000 (including £12,000 for depreciation of property and £38,000 for depreciation of fixtures and fittings). Selling expenses are expected to be £85,000 (including £10,000 for depreciation of motor vans).

■ All purchases are on credit. It has been estimated that the average credit period taken will be 12 weeks during the forthcoming year.

■ Tax for the year is expected to be £34,000. Half of this will be paid during the year and the remaining half will be outstanding at the year end.

■ Dividends proposed and paid for the year are expected to be 6.0p per share.

Required:
(a) Prepare a projected income statement for the year ending 31 May Year 9.
(b) Prepare a projected statement of financial position as at 31 May Year 9.

All workings should be made to the nearest £000.

Note: The cash balance will be the balancing figure.

2.2 Forecast information for Saturn plc for next year is as follows:

	£m
Projected profit before taxation (after interest)	165
Depreciation charged in arriving at operating profit	41
Interest expense	21
At the beginning of the year:	
Inventories	22
Trade receivables	18
Trade payables	15
At the end of the year:	
Inventories	23
Trade receivables	21
Trade payables	17

The following further information is available about forecast payments during next year:

	£m
Taxation paid	49
Interest paid	25
Dividends paid	28

Required:
What will be the projected net cash from operating activities for next year?

2.3 Davis Travel Ltd specialises in the provision of weekend winter breaks but also organises weekend summer breaks. You are given the following information:

Statement of financial position as at 30 September Year 4

	£000
ASSETS	
Non-current assets	
Property, plant and equipment	560
Current assets	
Cash	30
Total assets	590
EQUITY AND LIABILITIES	
Equity	
Share capital	100
Retained earnings	200
	300
Non-current liabilities	
Borrowings – loans	110
Current liabilities	
Trade payables	180
Total equity and liabilities	590

Its sales estimates for the next six months are:

	Number of bookings received	Number of holidays taken	Promotion expenditure (£000)
October	1,000		100
November	3,000		150
December	3,000	1,000	150
January	3,000	4,000	50
February		3,000	
March		2,000	
Total	10,000	10,000	450

1 Holiday breaks sell for £300 each. Ten per cent is payable when the holiday is booked and the remainder after two months.
2 Travel agents are paid a commission of 10 per cent of the price of the holiday break one month after the booking is made.
3 The cost of a flight is £50 per holiday and that of a hotel £100 per holiday. Flights and hotels must be paid for in the month when the holiday breaks are taken.
4 Other variable costs are £20 per holiday and are paid in the month of the holiday break.
5 Administration costs, including depreciation of non-current assets of £42,000, amount to £402,000 for the six months. Administration costs can be spread evenly over the period.
6 Loan interest of £10,000 is payable on 31 March Year 5 and a loan repayment of £20,000 is due on that date. For your calculations you should ignore any interest on the overdraft.
7 The trade payables of £180,000 at 30 September are to be paid in October.
8 A payment of £50,000 for non-current assets is to be made in March Year 5.
9 The airline and the hotel chain base their charges on Davis Travel's forecast requirements and hold capacity to meet those requirements. If Davis is unable to fill this reserved capacity, a charge of 50 per cent of those published above is made.

Required:
(a) Prepare:
   (i)   A projected cash flow statement for the six months to 31 March Year 5.
   (ii) A projected income statement for the six months ending on that date.
   (iii) A projected statement of financial position at 31 March Year 5.
(b) Discuss the main financial problems confronting Davis Travel Ltd.
Ignore taxation in your calculations.

2.4 Changes Ltd owns five shops selling fashion goods. In the past the business maintained a healthy cash balance. However, this has fallen in recent months and at the end of September Year 10 the company had an overdraft of £70,000. In view of this, Changes Ltd's chief executive has asked you to prepare a cash flow projection for the next six months. You have collected the following data:

	Oct £000	Nov £000	Dec £000	Jan £000	Feb £000	Mar £000
Sales forecast	140	180	260	60	100	120
Purchases	160	180	140	50	50	50
Wages and salaries	30	30	40	30	30	32
Rent			60			
Insurance						40
Other expenses	20	20	20	20	20	20
Refurbishing shops				80		

Inventories at 1 October amounted to £170,000 and payables were £70,000. The purchases in October, November and December are contractually committed, and those in January, February and March are the minimum necessary to replenish inventories with spring fashions. Cost of sales is 50 per cent of sales and suppliers allow one month's credit on purchases. Tax of £90,000 is due on 1 January. The insurance payment is a charge for a whole year and other expenses include depreciation of £10,000 per month.

Required:

(a) Compute the projected cash balance at the end of each month, for the six months to 31 March Year 11.

(b) Compute the projected inventories levels at the end of each month for the six months to 31 March Year 11.

(c) Prepare a projected income statement for the six months ending 31 March Year 11.

(d) What problems might Changes Ltd face in the next six months and how would you attempt to overcome them?

(*Hint*: A forecast of inventories flows is required to answer part (b). This will be based on the same principles as a cash flow statement – that is, inflows and outflows with opening and closing balances.)

2.5 The financial statements of Danube Engineering plc for the year that has just ended are as follows:

Income statement for the year ending 31 March Year 5

	£m
Sales revenue	500
Cost of sales	(350)
Gross profit	150
Selling expenses	(30)
Distribution expenses	(40)
Other expenses	(25)
Profit before taxation	55
Tax (20%)	(11)
Profit for the year	44

Statement of financial position as at the end of Year 5

	£m
ASSETS	
Non-current assets	700
Current assets	
Inventories	175
Trade receivables	125
Cash	40
	340
Total assets	1,040
EQUITY AND LIABILITIES	
Equity	
Share capital – 50p ordinary shares	80
Retained earnings	249
	329
Non-current liabilities	
Loan notes	500
Current liabilities	
Trade payables	200
Tax due	11
	211
Total equity and liabilities	1,040

As in previous years, a dividend of 25 per cent of the profit for the year was proposed and paid during the year.

The following information is relevant for Year 6:

1 Sales revenue is expected to be 20 per cent higher than in Year 5.
2 All sales are on credit.
3 Non-current assets of the business have plenty of spare capacity.
4 The tax rate will be the same as in Year 5 and all of the tax due will be outstanding at the year end.
5 The business intends to maintain the same dividend policy as for Year 5.
6 Tax due at the end of Year 5 will be paid during Year 6.
7 Half of the loan notes in issue will be redeemed at the end of Year 6.
8 Any financing gap will be filled by an issue of shares at nominal value. The new shares will not, however, rank for dividend during Year 6.

Required:

Prepare a projected income statement and statement of financial position for Year 6 using the per-cent-of-sales method. (All workings should be to the nearest £ million.)

2.6 Newtake Records Ltd owns a small chain of shops selling rare jazz and classical recordings to serious collectors. At the beginning of June, the business had an overdraft of £35,000 and the bank has asked for this to be eliminated by the end of November of the same year. As a result, the directors of the business have recently decided to review their plans for the next six months in order to comply with this requirement.

The following forecast information was prepared for the business some months earlier:

	May £000	June £000	July £000	Aug £000	Sept £000	Oct £000	Nov £000
Expected sales	180	230	320	250	140	120	110
Purchases	135	180	142	94	75	66	57
Admin. expenses	52	55	56	53	48	46	45
Selling expenses	22	24	28	26	21	19	18
Tax payment				22			
Finance payments	5	5	5	5	5	5	5
Shop refurbishment	–	–	14	18	6	–	–

Notes:

1 Inventories held at 1 June were £112,000. The business believes it is necessary to maintain a minimum inventories level of £40,000 over the period to 30 November of the same year.
2 Suppliers allow one month's credit. The first three months' purchases are subject to a contractual agreement that must be honoured.
3 The gross profit margin is 40 per cent.
4 All sales income is received in the month of sale. However, 50 per cent of customers pay with a credit card. The charge made by the credit card business to Newtake Records Ltd is 3 per cent of the sales value. These charges are in addition to the selling expenses identified above. The credit card business pays Newtake Records Ltd in the month of sale.
5 The business has a bank loan that it is paying off in instalments of £5,000 per month. The interest element represents 20 per cent of each instalment.
6 Administration expenses are paid when incurred. This item includes a charge of £15,000 each month in respect of depreciation.
7 Selling expenses are payable in the following month.

Required:

(a) Prepare a projected cash flow statement for the six months ending 30 November that shows the cash balance at the end of each month.

(b) Compute the projected inventories levels at the end of each month for the six months to 30 November.

(c) Prepare a projected income statement for the six months ending 30 November. (A monthly breakdown of profit is not required.)

(d) What problems is Newtake Records Ltd likely to face in the next six months? Can you suggest how the business might deal with these problems?

2.7 Eco-Energy Appliances Ltd started operations on 1 January and has produced the following forecasts for annual sales revenue:

Year to 31 December	Year 1	Year 2	Year 3	Year 4
Forecast sales revenue (£)	1,200,000	1,440,000	1,500,000	1,400,000

The following additional information is also available:

1 Operating profit is expected to be 15 per cent of sales revenue throughout the four-year period.

2 The company has an £800,000 10 per cent bank loan, half of which is redeemable at the end of Year 3.

3 The tax rate is expected to be 20 per cent throughout the four-year period. Tax is paid in the year following the year in which the relevant profits are made.

4 An initial investment in net working capital of £140,000 is required. Thereafter, investment in net working capital is expected to represent 10 per cent of sales revenue for the relevant year.

5 Depreciation of £70,000 per year must be charged for the non-current assets currently held.

6 Equipment costing £100,000 will be acquired at the beginning of Year 4. This will be depreciated at the rate of 10 per cent per year.

7 Dividends equal to 50 per cent of the profit for the year will be announced each year. These dividends are paid in the year following the period to which they relate.

8 The business has a current cash balance of £125,000.

Required:

Prepare projected cash flow statements of the business for each of the next four years. (Note: All workings should be to the nearest £000.)

ANALYSING AND INTERPRETING FINANCIAL STATEMENTS

INTRODUCTION

In this chapter we shall consider the analysis and interpretation of financial statements. We shall see how the use of financial (or accounting) ratios can help to assess the financial performance and position of a business. We shall also take a look at the problems encountered when applying these ratios.

Financial ratios can be used to examine various aspects of financial health and are widely used for planning and control purposes. They can be very helpful to managers in a wide variety of decision areas, such as profit planning, working capital management, financial structure and dividend policy.

Learning outcomes

When you have completed this chapter, you should be able to:

- Identify the major categories of ratios that can be used for analysing financial statements.
- Calculate key ratios for assessing the financial performance and position of a business and explain their significance.
- Discuss the use of ratios in helping to predict financial failure.
- Discuss the limitations of ratios as a tool of financial analysis.

FINANCIAL RATIOS

Financial ratios provide a quick and relatively simple means of assessing the financial health of a business. A ratio simply relates one figure appearing in the financial statements to another figure appearing there (for example, operating profit in relation to sales revenue) or, perhaps, to some resource of the business (for example, operating profit per employee).

Ratios can be very helpful when comparing the financial health of different businesses. Differences may exist between businesses in the scale of operations. As a result a direct comparison of, say, the operating profit generated by each business may be misleading. By expressing operating profit in relation to some other measure (for example, capital employed), the problem of scale is eliminated. This means that a business with an operating profit of £10,000 and capital employed of £100,000 can be compared with a much larger business with an operating profit of £80,000 and capital employed of £1,000,000 by the use of a simple ratio. The operating profit to capital employed ratio for the smaller business is 10 per cent (that is, (10,000/100,000) × 100%) and the same ratio for the larger business is 8 per cent (that is, (80,000/1,000,000) × 100%). These ratios can be directly compared whereas comparison of the absolute operating profit figures would be much less meaningful. The need to eliminate differences in scale through the use of ratios can also apply when comparing the performance of the same business from one time period to another.

By calculating a small number of ratios it is often possible to build up a revealing picture of the position and performance of a business. It is not surprising, therefore, that ratios are widely used by those who have an interest in businesses and business performance. Ratios are not difficult to calculate; however, they can be difficult to interpret.

Ratios help us to identify which questions to ask rather than provide the answers. They help to highlight the financial strengths and weaknesses of a business, but cannot explain why those strengths and weaknesses exist or why certain changes have occurred. They provide a starting point for further analysis. Only a detailed investigation will reveal the underlying reasons.

Ratios can be expressed in various forms, for example as a percentage or as a proportion. The way that a particular ratio is presented will depend on the needs of those who will use the information. Although it is possible to calculate a large number of ratios, only a few, based on key relationships, may be helpful to a particular user. Many ratios that could be calculated from the financial statements (for example, rent payable in relation to current assets) may not be considered because there is not usually any clear or meaningful relationship between the two items.

There is no generally accepted list of ratios that can be applied to the financial statements, nor is there a standard method of calculating many ratios. Variations in both the choice of ratios and their calculation will be found in practice. It is important, therefore, to be consistent in the way in which ratios are calculated for comparison purposes. The ratios that we shall discuss are very popular – presumably because they are seen as useful for decision-making purposes.

FINANCIAL RATIO CLASSIFICATIONS

Ratios can be grouped into categories, with each category relating to a particular aspect of financial performance or position. The following five broad categories provide a useful basis for explaining the nature of the financial ratios to be dealt with.

- *Profitability*. Businesses generally exist with the primary purpose of creating wealth for their owners. Profitability ratios provide some indication of the degree of success in achieving this purpose. They normally express the profit made in relation to other key figures in the financial statements or to some business resource.
- *Efficiency*. Ratios may be used to measure the efficiency with which particular resources, such as inventories or employees, have been used within the business. These ratios are also referred to as *activity* ratios.
- *Liquidity*. It is vital to the survival of a business that there are sufficient liquid resources available to meet maturing obligations (that is, amounts due for payment in the near future). Liquidity ratios examine the relationship between the liquid resources held and maturing obligations.
- *Financial gearing*. This is the relationship between the contribution to financing the business made by its owners and the contribution made by others, in the form of loans. This relationship is important because the level of gearing has a significant effect on the level of risk associated with a business. Gearing ratios help to reveal the extent to which loan finance is utilised and the consequent effect on the level of risk borne by a business.
- *Investment*. These ratios are concerned with assessing the returns and performance of shares in a particular business from the perspective of shareholders who are not involved with the management of the business.

These five key aspects of financial health that ratios seek to examine are summarised in Figure 3.1.

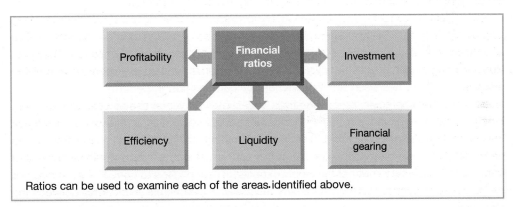

Ratios can be used to examine each of the areas identified above.

Figure 3.1 The key aspects of financial health

Before analysing the financial statements, we need to be clear *who* the target users are and *why* they need the information. Different users are likely to have different information needs. This, in turn, will determine the ratios that they find useful. Shareholders, for example, are likely to be interested in their returns in relation to the level of risk associated with their investment. Profitability, investment and gearing ratios should therefore be of particular interest. Long-term lenders are likely to be concerned with the long-term viability of the business and, to assess this, profitability and gearing ratios should, once again, be of interest. Short-term lenders, such as suppliers of goods and services on credit, are likely to be interested in the ability of the business to repay amounts owing in the short term. Liquidity ratios should thus be of interest.

THE NEED FOR COMPARISON

Merely calculating a ratio will not tell us very much about the position or performance of a business. If, for example, a ratio revealed that a retail business was generating £100 in sales revenue per square metre of floor space, it would not be possible to deduce from this information alone whether this particular level of performance was good, bad or indifferent. It is only when we compare this ratio with some 'benchmark' that the information can be interpreted and evaluated.

Activity 3.1

Can you think of any bases that could be used to compare a ratio you have calculated from the financial statements of a business for a particular period?

Hint: There are three main possibilities.

You may have thought of the following bases:

- past periods for the same business
- similar businesses for the same or past periods
- planned performance for the business.

We shall now take a closer look at these three in turn.

Past periods

By comparing a particular ratio with the same ratio for a previous period, it is possible to see whether there has been an improvement or deterioration in performance. It can often be useful to track particular ratios over time (say, five or ten years) to see whether any trends emerge. The comparison of ratios from different periods, however, brings certain problems. There is always the possibility that trading conditions were quite different in the periods being compared. Furthermore, when comparing the performance of a single business over time, operating inefficiencies may not be clearly exposed. The fact, for example, that sales revenue per employee has risen by 10 per cent over the previous period may seem satisfactory at first sight. This may not be the case, however, if similar businesses have shown an improvement of 30 per cent for the same period, or had much better sales revenue per employee ratios to begin with. Finally, there is the problem that inflation may have distorted the figures on which the ratios are based. Inflation can lead to an overstatement of profit and an understatement of asset values, as we will discuss later in the chapter.

Similar businesses

In a competitive environment, a business must consider its performance in relation to that of other businesses operating in the same industry. Survival may depend on its ability to achieve comparable levels of performance. A useful basis for comparing a particular ratio, therefore, is the ratio achieved by similar businesses during the same period. This basis is not without its problems, however. Competitors may have different year ends and so trading conditions may not be identical. They may also have different accounting policies (for example, different methods of calculating depreciation or valuing inventories), which can have a significant effect on reported profits and asset values. Finally, it may be difficult to obtain the financial statements of competitor businesses. Sole proprietorships and partnerships, for example, are not obliged to make their financial statements available to the public. In the case of limited companies, there is a legal obligation to do so. However, a diversified business may not provide a sufficiently detailed breakdown of activities to enable comparisons with other businesses.

Planned performance

Ratios may be compared with the targets that managers developed before the start of the period under review. The comparison of actual performance with planned performance can be a useful way of assessing the level of achievement attained. Indeed, planned performance is likely to be the most valuable benchmark against which managers may assess their own business. Planned performance, however, must be based on realistic assumptions in order to be worthwhile for comparison purposes.

Planned, or target, ratios may be prepared for each aspect of the business's activities. When developing these ratios, account should normally be taken of past performance and the performance of other businesses. This does not mean, however, that a business should seek to achieve either of these levels of performance; neither may provide an appropriate target.

We should bear in mind that those outside the business do not normally have access to the business's plans. For them, past performance and the performances of other, similar, businesses may provide the only practical benchmarks.

CALCULATING THE RATIOS

Probably the best way to explain financial ratios is through an example. Example 3.1 provides a set of financial statements from which we can calculate important ratios.

Example 3.1

The following financial statements relate to Alexis plc, which operates a wholesale carpet business.

Statements of financial position (balance sheets) as at 31 March

	2013 £m	2014 £m
ASSETS		
Non-current assets		
Property, plant and equipment (at cost less depreciation)		
Land and buildings	381	427
Fixtures and fittings	129	160
	510	587
Current assets		
Inventories	300	406
Trade receivables	240	273
Cash at bank	4	–
	544	679
Total assets	1,054	1,266

	2013 £m	2014 £m
EQUITY AND LIABILITIES		
Equity		
£0.50 ordinary shares (Note 1)	300	300
Retained earnings	263	234
	563	534
Non-current liabilities		
Borrowings – 9% loan notes (secured)	200	300
Current liabilities		
Trade payables	261	354
Taxation	30	2
Short-term borrowings (all bank overdraft)	–	76
	291	432
Total equity and liabilities	1,054	1,266

Income statements for the year ended 31 March

	2013 £m	2014 £m
Revenue (Note 2)	2,240	2,681
Cost of sales (Note 3)	(1,745)	(2,272)
Gross profit	495	409
Operating expenses	(252)	(362)
Operating profit	243	47
Interest payable	(18)	(32)
Profit before taxation	225	15
Taxation	(60)	(4)
Profit for the year	165	11

Notes:

1 The market value of the shares of the business at the end of the year was £2.50 for 2013 and £1.50 for 2014.
2 All sales and purchases are made on credit.
3 The cost of sales figure can be analysed as follows:

	2013 £m	2014 £m
Opening inventories	241	300
Purchases (Note 2)	1,804	2,378
	2,045	2,678
Closing inventories	(300)	(406)
Cost of sales	1,745	2,272

4 At 31 March 2012, the trade receivables stood at £223 million and the trade payables at £183 million.
5 A dividend of £40 million had been paid to the shareholders in respect of each of the years.
6 The business employed 13,995 staff at 31 March 2013 and 18,623 at 31 March 2014.
7 The business expanded its capacity during 2014 by setting up a new warehouse and distribution centre in the north of England.
8 At 1 April 2012, the total of equity stood at £438 million and the total of equity and non-current liabilities stood at £638 million.

Before we start our detailed look at the ratios for Alexis plc (see Example 3.1), it is helpful to take a quick look at what information is obvious from the financial statements. This will usually pick up some issues that ratios may not be able to identify. It may also highlight some points that could help us in our interpretation of the ratios. Starting at the top of the statement of financial position, the following points can be noted:

■ *Expansion of non-current assets*. These have increased by about 15 per cent (from £510 million to £587 million). Note 7 mentions a new warehouse and distribution centre, which may account for much of the additional investment in non-current assets. We are not told when this new facility was established, but it is quite possible that it was well into the year. This could mean that not much benefit was reflected in terms of additional sales revenue or cost saving during 2014. Sales revenue, in fact, expanded by about 20 per cent (from £2,240 million to £2,681 million): greater than the expansion in non-current assets.

■ *Major expansion in the elements of working capital*. Inventories increased by about 35 per cent, trade receivables by about 14 per cent and trade payables by about 36 per cent between 2013 and 2014. These are major increases, particularly in inventories and payables (which are linked because the inventories are all bought on credit – see Note 2).

■ *Reduction in the cash balance*. The cash balance fell from £4 million (in funds) to a £76 million overdraft between 2013 and 2014. The bank may be putting the business under pressure to reverse this, which could create difficulties.

■ *Apparent debt capacity*. Comparing the non-current assets with the long-term borrowings indicates that the business may well be able to offer security on further borrowing. Potential lenders usually look at the value of assets, particularly land and buildings, which can be offered as security when assessing loan requests. At 31 March 2014, for example, non-current assets had a carrying amount (the value at which they appeared in the statement of financial position) of £587 million, but long-term borrowing was only £300 million (although there was also an overdraft of £76 million). Carrying amounts do not normally reflect market values. However, land and buildings tend to be shown in the statement of financial position below their market value. This is due to a general tendency to inflation in property values.

■ *Lower operating profit*. Though sales revenue expanded by 20 per cent between 2013 and 2014, the cost of sales and operating expenses rose by a greater percentage, leaving both gross profit and operating profit massively reduced. The level of staffing, which increased by about 33 per cent (from 13,995 to 18,623 employees – see Note 6), may have greatly affected the operating expenses. (Without knowing when the additional employees were recruited during 2014, we cannot be sure of the effect on operating expenses.) Increasing staffing by 33 per cent must put an enormous strain on management, at least in the short term. It is not surprising, therefore, that 2014 was not successful for the business – at least, not in profit terms.

Having had a quick look at what is fairly obvious, without calculating any financial ratios, we shall now go on to calculate and interpret some.

The following ratios may be used to evaluate the profitability of the business:

- return on ordinary shareholders' funds
- return on capital employed
- operating profit margin
- gross profit margin.

We shall look at each of these in turn.

Return on ordinary shareholders' funds (ROSF)

The **return on ordinary shareholders' funds** ratio compares the amount of profit for the period available to the owners with the owners' average stake in the business during that same period. The ratio (which is normally expressed in percentage terms) is as follows:

$$\text{ROSF} = \frac{\text{Profit for the year less any preference dividend}}{\text{Ordinary share capital} + \text{Reserves}} \times 100$$

The profit for the year (less any preference dividend) is used in the ratio, as it represents the profit attributable to the owners.

In the case of Alexis plc, the ratio for the year ended 31 March 2013 is:

$$\text{ROSF} = \frac{165}{(438 + 563)/2} \times 100 = 33.0\%$$

Note that, when calculating the ROSF, the average of the figures for ordinary shareholders' funds as at the beginning and at the end of the year has been used. This is because an average figure is normally more representative. The amount of shareholders' funds was not constant throughout the year, yet we want to compare it with the profit earned during the whole period. We know, from Note 8, that the amount of shareholders' funds at 1 April 2012 was £438 million. By a year later, however, it had risen to £563 million, according to the statement of financial position as at 31 March 2013.

The easiest approach to calculating the average amount of shareholders' funds is to take a simple average based on the opening and closing figures for the year. This is often the only information available, as is the case with Example 3.1. Averaging is normally appropriate for all ratios that combine a figure for a period (such as profit for the year) with one taken at a single point in time (such as shareholders' funds).

Where the beginning-of-year figure is not available, it will be necessary to rely on just the year-end figure. This is not ideal, but when this approach is applied consistently, it can still produce useful ratios.

Activity 3.2

Calculate the ROSF for Alexis plc for the year to 31 March 2014.

The ratio for 2014 is:

$$\text{ROSF} = \frac{11}{(563 + 534)/2} \times 100 = 2.0\%$$

Broadly, businesses seek to generate as high a value as possible for this ratio. This is provided that it is not achieved at the expense of potential future returns, for example by taking on more risky activities. The 2014 ratio is very poor by any standards; a bank deposit account will normally yield a better return. We need to try to find out why things went so badly wrong in 2014. As we look at other ratios, we should find some clues.

Return on capital employed (ROCE)

The return on capital employed ratio is a fundamental measure of business performance. This ratio expresses the relationship between the operating profit generated during a period and the average long-term capital invested in the business.

The ratio is expressed in percentage terms and is as follows:

$$\text{ROCE} = \frac{\text{Operating profit}}{\text{Share capital} + \text{Reserves} + \text{Non-current liabilities}} \times 100$$

Note that, in this case, the profit figure used is the operating profit (that is, the profit *before* interest and taxation). This is because the ratio attempts to measure the returns to all suppliers of long-term finance before any deductions for financing costs (interest payable on borrowings and payments of dividends to shareholders).

ROCE is considered by many to be a primary measure of profitability. It compares inputs (capital invested) with outputs (operating profit) so as to reveal the effectiveness with which funds have been deployed. Once again, an average figure for capital employed should be used where the information is available.

For the year to 31 March 2013, the ratio for Alexis plc is:

$$\text{ROCE} = \frac{243}{(638 + 763)/2} \times 100 = 34.7\%$$

(The capital employed figure, which is the total equity + non-current liabilities, at 1 April 2012 is given in Note 8 to Example 3.1.)

Activity 3.3

Calculate the ROCE for Alexis plc for the year to 31 March 2014.

The ratio for 2014 is:

$$\text{ROCE} = \frac{47}{(763 + 834)/2} \times 100 = 5.9\%$$

This ratio tells much the same story as ROSF: a poor performance, with the return on the assets being less than the rate that the business has to pay for most of its borrowed funds (that is, 10 per cent for the loan notes).

Real World 3.1 shows how financial ratios are used by businesses as a basis for setting profitability targets.

Targeting profitability

The ROCE ratio is widely used by businesses when establishing targets for profitability. These targets are sometimes made public. Here are some examples:

- Air France–KLM, the world's largest airline (on the basis of sales revenue), has set itself the target of achieving a ROCE of 7 per cent.
- BMW, the car-maker, has a long-term target ROCE in excess of 26 per cent.
- Marks and Spencer plc, the retailer, announced in June 2011 a target return on capital employed for new capital invested of 12–15 per cent over three years.
- Tesco plc, the supermarket chain, aims to increase ROCE to 14.6 per cent by 2015. So far this has not been achieved – in 2012, ROCE was 13.3 per cent.
- 'EasyJet, the budget airline has a target ROCE of 12 per cent.'
- AkzoNobel, the textiles, paints and chemicals business, aims to achieve a 14 per cent ROCE by 2015, from less than 9 per cent in 2012.

Sources: Information taken from Air France–KLM, Press Release, 14 February 2008; 'BMW adds to carmakers' gloom', www.ft.com, 1 August 2008; 'M&S to shake up executive pay to reflect Bolland plan', www.ft.com, 8 June 2011; 'Tesco looking afar for growth', www.ft.com, 19 April 2011; 'EasyJet faces debate on capital return', www.ft.com, 19 February 2012; 'AkzoNobel: Painting by numbers', www.ft.com, 20 February 2013. © The Financial Times Limited 2012. All Rights Reserved.

Real World 3.2 provides some indication of the levels of ROCE achieved by UK businesses.

Achieving profitability

Quarterly ROCE ratios for UK manufacturing and service companies for each of the six years ending in 2012 are shown in Figure 3.2.

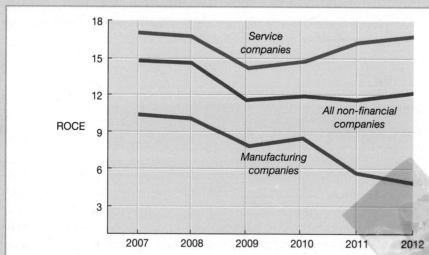

ROCE of manufacturing businesses has been consistently lower than that of service businesses over the period.

Figure 3.2 ROCE of UK companies

According to the Office for National Statistics, the difference in ROCE between the two sectors is accounted for by the higher capital intensity of manufacturing.

Source: 'Profitability of UK companies Q4 2012', Office for National Statistics, www.statistics.gov.uk/, 10 April 2013.

Operating profit margin

The **operating profit margin** ratio relates the operating profit for the period to the sales revenue. The ratio is expressed as follows:

$$\text{Operating profit margin} = \frac{\text{Operating profit}}{\text{Sales revenue}} \times 100$$

Operating profit (that is, profit before interest and taxation) is used in this ratio as it represents the profit from trading operations before the interest payable expense is taken into account. It is normally the most appropriate measure of operational performance when making comparisons. This is because differences arising from the way in which the business is financed will not influence the measure.

For the year ended 31 March 2013, Alexis plc's operating profit margin ratio is:

$$\text{Operating profit margin} = \frac{243}{2,240} \times 100 = 10.8\%$$

This ratio compares one output of the business (operating profit) with another output (sales revenue). The ratio can vary considerably between different types of business. Supermarkets, for example, tend to operate on low prices and, therefore, low operating profit margins. This is done in an attempt to stimulate sales and thereby increase the total amount of operating profit generated. Jewellers, meanwhile, tend to have high operating profit margins but have much lower levels of sales volume. Factors such as the degree of competition, the type of customer, the economic climate and industry characteristics (such as the level of risk) will influence the operating profit margin of a business. This point is picked up again later in the chapter.

Activity 3.4

Calculate the operating profit margin for Alexis plc for the year to 31 March 2014.

The ratio for 2014 is:

$$\text{Operating profit margin} = \frac{47}{2,681} \times 100 = 1.8\%$$

Once again, this is a very weak performance compared with that of 2013. In 2013, for every £1 of sales revenue an average of 10.8p (that is, 10.8 per cent) was left as operating profit, after paying the cost of the carpets sold and other expenses of operating the business. By 2014, however, this had fallen to only 1.8p for every £1. The reason for the poor ROSF and ROCE ratios appears to have been partially, if not wholly, due to a high level of expenses relative to sales revenue. The next ratio should provide us with a clue as to how the sharp decline in this ratio occurred.

Real World 3.3 sets out the target operating profit margins for some well-known car manufacturers.

Profit driven

- BMW has a long-term target operating profit margin of between 8 per cent and 10 per cent.
- Daimler had a target operating profit margin for its Mercedes unit of 10 per cent for 2013. However, this target was abandoned in the face of tough market conditions.
- Nissan has a target operating profit margin of 8 per cent and a target global market share of 8 per cent to be achieved by 2017.
- Toyota announced a medium-term target operating profit margin of 5 per cent in March 2011.
- Renault was committed to a target operating profit margin in excess of 5 per cent for 2013.
- Opel, the European arm of General Motors, aimed to achieve an operating profit margin of 4–5 per cent by 2013.

Premium car manufacturers, such as BMW and Mercedes, appear to have higher targets for their operating profit margin than mass-market car manufacturers, although the target periods often differ.

FT *Sources*: 'BMW brings forward 2m car sales target', www.ft.com, 13 March 2012; 'Daimler has grand aims for small cars', www.ft.com, 14 June 2010; 'Daimler cuts full year earnings target', www.ft.com, 24 October 2012; 'Nissan: Ghosn for broke', www.ft.com, 28 June 2011; 'Nissan: More China please', www.ft.com, 27 June 2011; 'Nissan £Q3 operating profit sneaks up 3.5%', www.just-auto.com; 'Snap news', www.ft.com, 10 February 2011; 'Opel handed ambitious profit target', www.ft.com, 17 December 2009.
© The Financial Times Limited 2012. All Rights Reserved.

Gross profit margin

The **gross profit margin** ratio relates the gross profit of the business to the sales revenue generated for the same period. Gross profit represents the difference between sales revenue and the cost of sales. The ratio is therefore a measure of profitability in buying (or producing) and selling goods or services before any other expenses are taken into account. As cost of sales represents a major expense for many businesses, a change in this ratio can have a significant effect on the 'bottom line' (that is, the profit for the year). The gross profit margin ratio is calculated as follows:

$$\text{Gross profit margin} = \frac{\text{Gross profit}}{\text{Sales revenue}} \times 100$$

For the year to 31 March 2013, the ratio for Alexis plc is:

$$\text{Gross profit margin} = \frac{495}{2,240} \times 100 = 22.1\%$$

Calculate the gross profit margin for Alexis plc for the year to 31 March 2014.

The ratio for 2014 is:

$$\text{Gross profit margin} = \frac{409}{2,681} \times 100 = 15.3\%$$

The decline in this ratio means that gross profit was lower *relative* to sales revenue in 2014 than it had been in 2013. Bearing in mind that

Gross profit = Sales revenue − Cost of sales (or cost of goods sold)

this means that cost of sales was higher *relative* to sales revenue in 2014 than in 2013. This may indicate that sales prices were lower and/or that the purchase cost of carpets sold had increased. It is possible that both sales prices and purchase costs had reduced, but the former at a greater rate than the latter. Similarly, they may both have increased, but with sales prices having increased at a lesser rate than the cost of the carpets.

Clearly, part of the decline in the operating profit margin ratio is linked to the dramatic decline in the gross profit margin ratio. While after paying for the carpets sold, for each £1 of sales revenue 22.1p was left to cover other operating expenses in 2013, this was only 15.3p in 2014.

The profitability ratios for the business over the two years can be set out as follows:

	2013 %	2014 %
ROSF	33.0	2.0
ROCE	34.7	5.9
Operating profit margin	10.8	1.8
Gross profit margin	22.1	15.3

What do you deduce from a comparison of the declines in the operating profit and gross profit margin ratios?

We can see that the decline in the operating profit margin was 9 percentage points (that is, 10.8 per cent to 1.8 per cent), whereas that of the gross profit margin was only 6.8 percentage points (that is, from 22.1 per cent to 15.3 per cent). This can only mean that operating expenses were greater, compared with sales revenue in 2014, than they had been in 2013. The decline in both ROSF and ROCE was therefore caused partly by the business incurring higher inventories purchasing costs relative to sales revenue and partly through higher operating expenses compared with sales revenue. We need to compare each of these ratios with their planned level, however, before we can usefully assess the business's success.

An investigation is needed to discover what caused the increases in both cost of sales and operating expenses, relative to sales revenue, from 2013 to 2014. This will involve checking to see what happened with sales prices and inventories costs over the two years. It will also involve looking at each of the individual operating expenses to discover which were responsible for the increase, relative to sales revenue. Here, further ratios, such as employee expenses (wages and salaries) to sales revenue, should be calculated to isolate the cause of the change from 2013 to 2014. As mentioned earlier, the increase in employee numbers may well account for most of the increase in operating expenses.

Real World 3.4 discusses how high operating costs may adversely affect the future profitability of a leading car-maker.

Real World 3.4

VW accelerates but costs vibrate

Volkswagen's fervent quest to overtake Japanese rival Toyota by 2018 threatens to exacerbate its already high cost structure and to hamper profitability in the coming years, analysts and industry executives have warned. The industry executives and analysts argue that VW's growth initiative – which involves a huge investment of €26.6 billion ($35.7 billion) in the next three years, the €16 billion takeovers of Porsche and its Salzburg dealership and a €1.7 billion stake in Japanese small car specialist Suzuki – will put the car-maker back on a low-profit-margin track.

So far, Europe's largest car-maker has been one of the most successful during the crisis. The Wolfsburg-based manufacturer posted a €911 million profit after tax and a 1.2 per cent profit margin in 2009 at a time when many others were making losses. VW is now aiming for an industry-leading pre-tax profit margin of more than 8 per cent in 2018, by which time it wants to become the world's leading car producer 'economically as well as ecologically', Martin Winterkorn, VW's chief executive, has said. The car-maker wants to lift its sales from 6.3 million cars in the past year to more than 10 million by 2018.

While few dispute that VW could overtake Toyota – which sold almost 9 million cars in 2009 – in terms of sales, the profitability target remains in doubt. 'There should be more doubt in the market about the sustainability of VW's profits,' says Philippe Houchois, analyst at UBS.

In spite of its success, VW's cost structure is still in dire straits, particularly in Germany. With its 370,000 global workforce, the partly state-owned car-maker trails almost all global rivals when it comes to statistics such as revenues or vehicles per employee. 'People forget that despite their large scale, VW has some of the worst cost structures in the industry. They have abysmal labour productivity and high plant costs,' says Max Warburton, analyst at research firm Sanford Bernstein.

Mr Warburton says high margins have been the exception at VW, and that '2007–2008 represented a brief period of temporary profit maximisation delivered by a [now departed] temporary management team who made temporary, emergency cost cuts'. He says VW disputes that it has taken its eye off cost-cutting. Hans Dieter Pötsch, the car-maker's chief financial officer, says that 'by optimising our purchasing and increasing productivity . . . we have reached cost cuts of €1 billion throughout 2009'. In addition, he points to the car-maker's ongoing productivity improvement target of 10 per cent each year.

VW's profit figures for last year paint a dark picture of the car-maker's cost structures. At least three of its nine brands – Seat, Bentley and Lamborghini – and probably also Bugatti, whose results are not disclosed, were lossmaking, and are not expected to return to profit this year. VW's light truck operations only posted a profit after a one-off gain from the sale of its Brazil operations. Operating profit at the group's core brand, VW, was crimped by 79 per cent to €561 million, in spite of the marque benefiting hugely from European scrapping incentive programmes.

Efficiency ratios are used to try to assess how successfully the various resources of the business are managed. The following ratios examine some of the more important aspects of resource management:

- average inventories turnover period
- average settlement period for trade receivables
- average settlement period for trade payables
- sales revenue to capital employed
- sales revenue per employee.

We shall look at each of these in turn.

Average inventories turnover period

Inventories often represent a significant investment for a business. For some types of business (for example, manufacturers and certain retailers), inventories may account for a substantial proportion of the total assets held (see Real World 10.1, p. 410). The **average inventories turnover period** ratio measures the average period for which inventories are being held. The ratio is calculated as follows:

$$\text{Average inventories turnover period} = \frac{\text{Average inventories held}}{\text{Cost of sales}} \times 365$$

The average inventories for the period can be calculated as a simple average of the opening and closing inventories levels for the year. In the case of a highly seasonal business, however, where inventories levels may vary considerably over the year, a monthly average would be better, assuming the information is available. Monthly averaging is equally relevant to other assets or claims that vary over the reporting period, such as trade receivables and payables.

In the case of Alexis plc, the inventories turnover period for the year ending 31 March 2013 is:

$$\text{Average inventories turnover period} = \frac{(241 + 300)/2}{1,745} \times 365 = 56.6 \text{ days}$$

(The opening inventories figure was taken from Note 3 to the financial statements.)

This means that, on average, the inventories held are being 'turned over' every 56.6 days. So, a carpet bought by the business on a particular day would, on average, have been sold about eight weeks later. A business will normally prefer a short inventories turnover period to a long one, because holding inventories incurs costs, such as the opportunity cost of the funds. When judging the amount of inventories to carry, the business must consider such things as likely sales demand, the possibility of supply shortages, the likelihood of price rises, the storage space available and their perishability and/or susceptibility to obsolescence.

This ratio is sometimes expressed in terms of weeks or months rather than days: multiplying by 52 or 12, rather than 365, will achieve this.

Calculate the average inventories turnover period for Alexis plc for the year ended 31 March 2014.

The ratio for 2014 is:

$$\text{Average inventories turnover period} = \frac{(300 + 406)/2}{2{,}272} \times 365 = 56.7 \text{ days}$$

The inventories turnover period is virtually the same in both years.

Average settlement period for trade receivables

With the exception of retailers, selling on credit is the custom for most businesses. Thus, trade receivables must be accepted as a necessary evil. The average settlement period for trade receivables ratio calculates how long, on average, credit customers take to pay the amounts owing. The ratio is as follows:

$$\textbf{Average settlement period for trade receivables} = \frac{\textbf{Average trade receivables}}{\textbf{Credit sales revenue}} \times \textbf{365}$$

A business will normally prefer a shorter average settlement period to a longer one as, once again, funds are tied up that may be used for more profitable purposes. Furthermore, the shorter the settlement period, the better will be the business's cash flow.

Although this ratio can be useful, it is important to remember that it produces an *average* figure for the number of days for which debts are outstanding. This average may be badly distorted by, for example, a few large customers who are very slow or very fast payers.

Since all sales made by Alexis plc are on credit, the average settlement period for trade receivables for the year ended 31 March 2013 is:

$$\text{Average settlement period for trade receivables} = \frac{(223 + 240)/2}{2{,}240} \times 365 = 37.7 \text{ days}$$

(The opening trade receivables figure was taken from Note 4 to the financial statements.)

Calculate the average settlement period for Alexis plc's trade receivables for the year ended 31 March 2014.

The ratio for 2014 is:

$$\text{Average settlement period for trade receivables} = \frac{(240 + 273)/2}{2{,}681} \times 365 = 34.9 \text{ days}$$

On the face of it, this reduction in the settlement period is welcome. It means that less cash was tied up in trade receivables for each £1 of sales revenue in 2014 than in 2013. This reduction may not be so welcome, however, if it was achieved at a high cost. This may arise where customers are chased too vigorously, leading to a loss of goodwill, or where large discounts are awarded for prompt payment.

Average settlement period for trade payables

The average settlement period for trade payables ratio measures how long, on average, the business takes to pay those who have supplied goods and services on credit. The ratio is calculated as follows:

$$\text{Average settlement period for trade payables} = \frac{\text{Average trade payables}}{\text{Credit purchases}} \times 365$$

This ratio provides an average figure, which, like the average settlement period for trade receivables ratio, can be distorted by the payment period for one or two large suppliers.

As trade payables provide a free source of finance for a business, it is not surprising that some businesses attempt to increase their average settlement period for trade payables. Such a policy can be taken too far, however, and result in a loss of supplier goodwill.

For the year ended 31 March 2013, Alexis plc's average settlement period for trade payables is:

$$\text{Average settlement period for trade payables} = \frac{(183 + 261)/2}{1,804} \times 365 = 44.9 \text{ days}$$

(The opening trade payables figure was taken from Note 4 to the financial statements and the purchases figure from Note 3.)

Activity 3.9

Calculate the average settlement period for trade payables for Alexis plc for the year ended 31 March 2014.

The ratio for 2014 is:

$$\text{Average settlement period for trade payables} = \frac{(261 + 354)/2}{2,378} \times 365 = 47.2 \text{ days}$$

There was an increase, between 2013 and 2014, in the average length of time that elapsed between buying goods and services and paying for them. Providing there is no loss of goodwill, this is beneficial as the business is using free finance provided by suppliers.

Real World 3.5 reveals that paying promptly may also be desirable in order to keep small suppliers in business.

Real World 3.5

Feeling the squeeze

Large companies are increasingly monitoring the creditworthiness of their suppliers for fear that some of the smaller businesses may be at risk of collapse, according to Experian, the credit rating agency. Its claim, based on data and client feedback, suggests that large companies, previously criticised for unfairly squeezing smaller businesses by delaying payment to them, may now be realising that it is in their interests to look after these often vital elements of their supply chain.

→

This view is backed up by Experian's latest late payment figures, published on Thursday. They show that the time companies took to settle supplier bills in the fourth quarter of 2012 shrank slightly compared with the previous three months despite the economy taking a turn for the worse. On average, companies took 25.84 days beyond the agreed date set out in their terms to pay their suppliers, compared with 26.17 in the third quarter of 2012, with the biggest improvements coming from the largest companies. This runs counter to previous experience, when economic downturns have led to companies stretching out the time they take to pay suppliers in order to preserve some of the cash in their coffers.

Phil McCabe, FPB spokesman, said: 'Perhaps large companies are finally waking up to the fact that paying their suppliers late or imposing unfair changes to payment terms is damaging to their own businesses as well as small firms and the economy. Late payment forces businesses to close. Clearly, a smaller supplier base means less choice for these companies and, ultimately, their customers. Embracing prompt payment is simple commercial common sense.'

The improving payment times are not solely down to improved behaviour among large companies, because smaller businesses are also better at getting in money owed to them on time, according to Gareth Rumsey, research director at Experian. 'It is easy to bash the larger businesses that are paying late, but you cannot ignore the need for smaller businesses to get their own house in order,' he said.

FT   Source: Adapted from Moules, J. (2012) 'Companies monitor companies credit scores', www.ft.com, 26 January.
© The Financial Times Limited 2012. All Rights Reserved.

Sales revenue to capital employed

The **sales revenue to capital employed** ratio (or net asset turnover ratio) examines how effectively the assets of the business are being used to generate sales revenue. It is calculated as follows:

$$\text{Sales revenue to capital employed ratio} = \frac{\text{Sales revenue}}{\text{Share capital} + \text{Reserves} + \text{Non-current liabilities}}$$

Generally speaking, a higher sales revenue to capital employed ratio is preferred to a lower one. A higher ratio will normally suggest that assets are being used more productively in the generation of revenue. A very high ratio, however, may suggest that the business is 'overtrading on its assets'; in other words, it has insufficient assets to sustain the level of sales revenue achieved. We shall take a longer look at overtrading later in the chapter. When comparing this ratio for different businesses, factors such as the age and condition of assets held, the valuation bases for assets and whether assets are leased or owned outright can complicate interpretation.

A variation of this formula is to use the total assets less current liabilities (which is equivalent to long-term capital employed) in the denominator (lower part of the fraction). The identical result is obtained.

For the year ended 31 March 2013, this ratio for Alexis plc is:

$$\text{Sales revenue to capital employed} = \frac{2,240}{(638 + 763)/2} = 3.20 \text{ times}$$

Activity 3.10

Calculate the sales revenue to capital employed ratio for Alexis plc for the year ended 31 March 2014.

The ratio for 2014 is:

$$\text{Sales revenue to capital employed} = \frac{2,681}{(763 + 834)/2} = 3.36 \text{ times}$$

This seems to be an improvement, since in 2014 more sales revenue was being generated for each £1 of capital employed (£3.36) than was the case in 2013 (£3.20). Provided that overtrading is not an issue, and that the additional sales generate an acceptable profit, this is to be welcomed.

Sales revenue per employee

The **sales revenue per employee** ratio relates sales revenue generated during a reporting period to a particular business resource, that is, labour. It provides a measure of the productivity of the workforce. The ratio is:

$$\textbf{Sales revenue per employee} = \frac{\textbf{Sales revenue}}{\textbf{Number of employees}}$$

Generally, businesses would prefer a high value for this ratio, implying that they are deploying their workforce efficiently.

For the year ended 31 March 2013, the ratio for Alexis plc is:

$$\text{Sales revenue per employee} = \frac{£2,240m}{13,995} = £160,057$$

Activity 3.11

Calculate the sales revenue per employee for Alexis plc for the year ended 31 March 2014.

The ratio for 2014 is:

$$\text{Sales revenue per employee} = \frac{£2,681m}{18,623} = £143,962$$

This represents a fairly significant decline, which merits further investigation. As mentioned previously, the number of employees increased significantly (by about 33 per cent) during 2014. We need to know why this has not generated sufficient additional sales revenue to maintain the ratio at its 2013 level. It may be because the extra employees were not appointed until late in the year ended 31 March 2014.

The efficiency, or activity, ratios may be summarised as follows:

	2013	2014
Average inventories turnover period	56.6 days	56.7 days
Average settlement period for trade receivables	37.7 days	34.9 days
Average settlement period for trade payables	44.9 days	47.2 days
Sales revenue to capital employed (net asset turnover)	3.20 times	3.36 times
Sales revenue per employee	£160,057	£143,962

Activity 3.12

What do you deduce from a comparison of the efficiency ratios over the two years?

Maintaining the inventories turnover period at the 2013 level might be reasonable, although we need to know the planned inventories period to make a proper assessment. The inventories turnover period for other businesses operating in carpet retailing, particularly those regarded as the market leaders, may have been helpful in formulating the plans. On the face of it, a shorter trade receivables settlement period and a longer trade payables settlement period are both desirable. However, this may have been achieved at the cost of a loss of goodwill among customers and suppliers. The increased sales revenue to capital employed ratio seems beneficial, provided that the business can manage this increase. The decline in the sales revenue per employee ratio is undesirable but is probably related to the dramatic increase in the number of employees. As with the inventories turnover period, these other ratios need to be compared with planned, or target, ratios.

RELATIONSHIP BETWEEN PROFITABILITY AND EFFICIENCY

In our earlier discussions concerning profitability ratios, we saw that return on capital employed is regarded as a key ratio by many businesses. The ratio is:

$$\text{ROCE} = \frac{\text{Operating profit}}{\text{Long-term capital employed}} \times 100$$

where long-term capital comprises share capital plus reserves plus non-current liabilities. This ratio can be broken down into two elements, as shown in Figure 3.3. The first ratio is the operating profit margin ratio and the second is the sales revenue to capital employed (net asset turnover) ratio, both of which we discussed earlier.

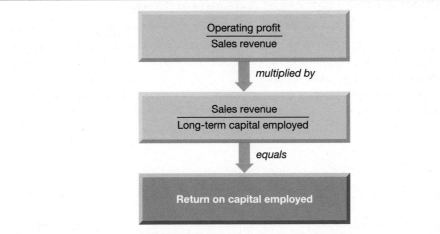

The ROCE ratio can be divided into two elements: operating profit to sales revenue and sales revenue to capital employed. By analysing ROCE in this way, we can see the influence of both profitability and efficiency on this important ratio.

Figure 3.3 The main elements of the ROCE ratio

Source: P. Atrill and E. McLaney, *Accounting and Finance for Non-Specialists*, 7th edn, Financial Times Prentice Hall, 2010, p. 206.

By breaking down the ROCE ratio in this way, we highlight the fact that the overall return on funds employed will be determined both by the profitability of sales and by efficiency in the use of capital.

Example 3.2

Consider the following information, for last year, concerning two different businesses operating in the same industry:

	Antler plc £m	Baker plc £m
Operating profit	20	15
Average long-term capital employed	100	75
Sales revenue	200	300

The ROCE for each business is identical (20 per cent). However, the manner in which that return was achieved by each business was quite different. In the case of Antler plc, the operating profit margin is 10 per cent and the sales revenue to capital employed ratio is 2 times (so ROCE = 10% × 2 = 20%). In the case of Baker plc, the operating profit margin is 5 per cent and the sales revenue to capital employed ratio is 4 times (and so ROCE = 5% × 4 = 20%).

Example 3.2 demonstrates that a relatively high sales revenue to capital employed ratio can compensate for a relatively low operating profit margin. Similarly, a relatively low sales revenue to capital employed ratio can be overcome by a relatively high operating profit margin. In many areas of retail and distribution (for example, supermarkets and delivery services), operating profit margins are quite low but the ROCE can be high, provided that the assets are used productively (that is, low margin, high sales revenue to capital employed).

Activity 3.13

Show how the ROCE ratio for Alexis plc can be analysed into the two elements for each of the years 2013 and 2014. What conclusions can you draw from your figures?

	ROCE	=	Operating profit margin	×	Sales revenue to capital employed
2013	34.7%		10.8%		3.20
2014	5.9%		1.8%		3.36

As we can see, the relationship between the three ratios holds for Alexis plc for both years. (The small apparent differences are simply because the three ratios are stated here only to one or two decimal places.)

In 2014, the business was more effective at generating sales revenue (sales revenue to capital employed ratio increased). However, it fell below the level needed to compensate for the sharp decline in the profitability of sales (operating profit margin). As a result, the 2014 ROCE was well below the 2013 value.

LIQUIDITY

Liquidity ratios are concerned with the ability of the business to meet its short-term financial obligations. The following ratios are widely used:

- current ratio
- acid test ratio.

We will now consider these two ratios.

Current ratio

The current ratio compares the 'liquid' assets (that is, cash and those assets held that will soon be turned into cash) with the current liabilities. The ratio is calculated as follows:

$$\text{Current ratio} = \frac{\text{Current assets}}{\text{Current liabilities}}$$

There seems to be a belief that there is an 'ideal' current ratio (usually 2 times or 2:1) for all businesses. However, this is not the case. Different types of business require different current ratios. A manufacturing business, for example, will often have a relatively high current ratio because it has to hold inventories of finished goods, raw materials and work in progress. It will also sell goods on credit, thereby giving rise to trade receivables. A supermarket chain, meanwhile, will have a relatively low ratio, as it will hold only fast-moving inventories of finished goods and its sales will be for cash rather than on credit.

The higher the current ratio, the more liquid the business is considered to be. As liquidity is vital to the survival of a business, a higher current ratio might be thought to be preferable to a lower one. If a business has a very high ratio, however, it may indicate that excessive funds are tied up in cash, or other liquid assets, rather than being employed more productively.

As at 31 March 2013, the current ratio of Alexis plc is:

$$\text{Current ratio} = \frac{544}{291} = 1.9 \text{ times (or 1.9:1)}$$

Although there is a decline from 2013 to 2014, this need not be cause for concern. The next ratio may provide a clue as to whether there seems to be a problem.

Acid test ratio

The acid test ratio is similar to the current ratio but provides a more stringent test of liquidity. For many businesses, inventories cannot be converted into cash quickly. (Note that in the case of Alexis plc, the inventories turnover period was about 57 days in both years (see p. 83).) As a result, this particular asset may be excluded when measuring liquidity.

The acid test ratio is calculated as follows:

$$\text{Acid test ratio} = \frac{\textbf{Current assets (excluding inventories)}}{\textbf{Current liabilities}}$$

The acid test ratio for Alexis plc as at 31 March 2013 is:

$$\text{Acid test ratio} = \frac{544 - 300}{291} = 0.8 \text{ times (or 0.8:1)}$$

We can see that the 'liquid' current assets do not quite cover the current liabilities, so the business may be experiencing some liquidity problems.

The 2014 ratio is significantly below that for 2013. The 2014 level may well be a source of concern. The rapid decline in this ratio should be investigated and, if necessary, corrective action taken. The minimum level for this ratio is often stated as 1.0 times (or 1:1). For many highly successful businesses, however, it is not unusual for the acid test ratio to be below 1.0 without causing liquidity problems.

The liquidity ratios for the two-year period may be summarised as follows:

	2013	2014
Current ratio	1.9	1.6
Acid test ratio	0.8	0.6

Activity 3.16

What do you deduce from the liquidity ratios set out above?

Both ratios indicate a decline in liquidity from 2013 to 2014. This decline, however, may be planned, short-term and linked to the increase in non-current assets and the number of employees. When the benefits of the expansion come on stream, liquidity may improve. On the other hand, short-term claimants may become anxious when they see signs of weak liquidity. This could lead them to press for payment, which could cause problems for Alexis plc.

FINANCIAL GEARING

Financial gearing occurs when a business is financed, at least in part, by borrowing instead of by finance provided by the owners as equity. The extent to which a business is geared (that is, financed from borrowing) is an important factor in assessing risk. Borrowing involves taking on a commitment to pay interest charges and to make capital repayments. Where the borrowing is heavy, this can be a significant financial burden; it can increase the risk of the business becoming insolvent. Nevertheless, most businesses are geared to some extent.

Given the risks involved, we may wonder why a business would want to take on gearing. One reason is that the owners have insufficient funds, so the only way to finance the business adequately is to borrow. Another reason is that gearing can be used to increase the returns to owners. This is possible provided that the returns generated from borrowed funds exceed the cost of paying interest. The issue of gearing is important and we shall leave a detailed discussion of this topic until Chapter 8.

Two ratios are widely used to assess gearing:

- gearing ratio
- interest cover ratio.

Gearing ratio

The **gearing ratio** measures the contribution of long-term lenders to the long-term capital structure of a business.

$$\text{Gearing ratio} = \frac{\text{Long-term (non-current) liabilities}}{\text{Share capital} + \text{Reserves} + \text{Long-term (non-current) liabilities}} \times 100$$

The gearing ratio for Alexis plc, as at 31 March 2013, is:

$$\text{Gearing ratio} = \frac{200}{(563 + 200)} \times 100 = 26.2\%$$

This is a level of gearing that would not normally be considered to be very high.

Activity 3.17

Calculate the gearing ratio of Alexis plc as at 31 March 2014.

The ratio as at 31 March 2014 is:

$$\text{Gearing ratio} = \frac{300}{(534 + 300)} \times 100 = 36.0\%$$

This is a substantial increase in the level of gearing over the year.

Interest cover ratio

The interest cover ratio measures the amount of operating profit available to cover interest payable. The ratio may be calculated as follows:

$$\text{Interest cover ratio} = \frac{\text{Operating profit}}{\text{Interest payable}}$$

The ratio for Alexis plc for the year ended 31 March 2013 is:

$$\text{Interest cover ratio} = \frac{243}{18} = 13.5 \text{ times}$$

This ratio shows that the level of operating profit is considerably higher than the level of interest payable. This means that a large fall in operating profit could occur before operating profit levels failed to cover interest payable. The lower the level of operating profit coverage, the greater the risk to lenders that interest payments will not be met. There will also be a greater risk to the shareholders that lenders will take action to recover the interest due.

Activity 3.18

Calculate the interest cover ratio of Alexis plc for the year ended 31 March 2014.

The ratio for the year ended 31 March 2014 is:

$$\text{Interest cover ratio} = \frac{47}{32} = 1.5 \text{ times}$$

Alexis plc's gearing ratios are:

	2013	2014
Gearing ratio	26.2%	36.0%
Interest cover ratio	13.5 times	1.5 times

What do you deduce from a comparison of Alexis plc's gearing ratios over the two years?

The gearing ratio has changed significantly. This is mainly due to the substantial increase in the contribution of long-term lenders to financing the business. The gearing ratio at 31 March 2014 would not necessarily be considered to be very high for a business that was trading successfully. It is the low profitability that is the problem.

The interest cover ratio has declined dramatically from 13.5 times in 2013 to 1.5 times in 2014. This was partly caused by the increase in borrowings in 2014, but was mainly caused by the dramatic decline in profitability in that year. The situation in 2014 looks hazardous. Only a small decline in future operating profit would leave the business unable to cover its interest payments.

Without knowing the planned ratios, it is not possible to reach a firm conclusion on Alexis plc's gearing.

Real World 3.6 contains extracts from an article that discusses the likely lowering of gearing levels as a result of the poor economic climate. It explains that many businesses are likely to issue additional ordinary shares to reduce borrowing as a means of reducing gearing. Note that the gearing ratio mentioned in the article differs slightly from the one discussed above.

Real World 3.6

Changing gear

With a wave of share issues now expected from the UK's non-financial companies – and with funds from these being used to pay down debt – the pendulum is rapidly swinging back in favour of more conservative balance sheet management. Gearing levels are set to fall dramatically, analysts say. 'There is going to be an appreciable and material drop in gearing, by about a quarter or a third over the next three years,' predicts Mr Siddall, chief executive of the Association of Corporate Treasurers.

Historically, gearing levels – as measured by net debt as a proportion of shareholders' funds – have run at an average of about 30 per cent over the past 20 years. Peak levels (around 45 per cent) were reached in the past few years as companies took advantage of cheap credit. Current predictions see it coming down to about 20 per cent – and staying there for a good while to come. Graham Secker, managing director of equity research at Morgan Stanley, says, 'This is going to be a relatively long-term phenomenon.'

One of the most immediate concerns to heavily indebted companies is whether, in a recessionary environment, they will be able to generate the profit and cash flows to service their debts.

Gearing levels vary from sector to sector as well. Oil companies prefer low levels given their exposure to the volatility of oil prices. BP's net debt to shareholders' funds ratio of 21 per cent is at the low end of a 20 to 30 per cent range it considers prudent. Miners' gearing is on a clear downward trend already. Xstrata, the mining group, stressed last month that its £4.1 billion share issue would cut gearing from 40 per cent to less than 30 per cent. A week later, BHP said its $13 billion of first-half cash flows had cut gearing to less than 10 per cent. Rio Tinto, which had gearing of 130 per cent at the last count in August 2008, is desperately trying to cut it by raising fresh equity.

Utilities tend to be highly geared because they can afford to borrow more against their typically reliable cash flows. But even here the trend is downwards. Severn Trent, the UK water group, says its appropriate long-term gearing level is 60 per cent. But 'given ongoing uncertainties . . . it is prudent in the near term to retain as much liquidity and flexibility as possible'. It does not expect to pursue that target until credit markets improve.

Reducing gearing is not easy, especially for the most indebted companies that need to reduce it the most: shareholders will be more reluctant to finance replacement equity in companies with highly leveraged balance sheets. The supply of fresh equity will also be constrained, not only by a glut of demand from companies but by the squeeze on investor money from a wave of government bond issuance.

Richard Jeffrey, chief investment officer at Cazenove Capital Management, says there is a risk of the government making it more difficult to raise money to improve balance sheets. 'That is of extreme concern because that could become a limitation, longer term, in the capital that companies have to fund investment.'

FT *Source*: Grant, J. (2009) 'Gearing levels set to plummet', *Financial Times*, 10 February. © The Financial Times Limited 2012. All Rights Reserved.

INVESTMENT RATIOS

Various ratios are available to help shareholders assess the returns on their investment. The following are widely used:

- dividend payout ratio
- dividend yield ratio
- earnings per share
- price/earnings ratio.

Dividend payout ratio

The dividend payout ratio measures the proportion of earnings that a business pays out to shareholders in the form of dividends. The ratio is calculated as follows:

$$\text{Dividend payout ratio} = \frac{\text{Dividends announced for the year}}{\text{Earnings for the year available for dividends}} \times 100$$

In the case of ordinary shares, the earnings available for dividend will normally be the profit for the year (that is, the profit after taxation) less any preference dividends relating to the year. This ratio is normally expressed as a percentage.

The dividend payout ratio for Alexis plc for the year ended 31 March 2013 is:

$$\text{Dividend payout ratio} = \frac{40}{165} \times 100 = 24.2\%$$

Activity 3.20

Calculate the dividend payout ratio of Alexis plc for the year ended 31 March 2014.

The ratio for 2014 is:

$$\text{Dividend payout ratio} = \frac{40}{11} \times 100 = 363.6\%$$

This reveals an alarming increase in the ratio over the two years. Paying a dividend of £40 million in 2014 appears to be very imprudent.

The information provided by the above ratio is often expressed slightly differently as the dividend cover ratio. Here the calculation is:

$$\text{Dividend cover ratio} = \frac{\text{Earnings for the year available for dividends}}{\text{Dividends announced for the year}}$$

For 2013, the ratio for Alexis plc would be 165/40 = 4.1 times. That is to say, the earnings available for dividend cover the actual dividend paid by just over four times. For 2014, the ratio is 11/40 = 0.3 times.

Dividend yield ratio

The dividend yield ratio relates the cash return from a share to its current market value. This can help investors to assess the cash return on their investment in the business. The ratio, expressed as a percentage, is:

$$\text{Dividend yield} = \frac{\text{Dividend per share}/(1 - t)}{\text{Market value per share}} \times 100$$

where t is the 'dividend tax credit' rate of income tax. This requires some explanation. In the UK, investors who receive a dividend from a business also receive a tax credit. As this tax credit can be offset against any tax liability arising from the dividends received, the dividends are effectively issued net of income tax, at the dividend tax credit rate.

Investors may wish to compare the returns from shares with the returns from other forms of investment, say a building society deposit. As these other forms of investment are usually quoted on a 'gross' (that is, pre-tax) basis it is useful to 'gross up' the dividend to make comparison easier. We can achieve this by dividing the dividend per share by $(1 - t)$, where t is the 'dividend tax credit' rate of income tax.

Using the 2012/13 (and the 2013/14) dividend tax credit rate of 10 per cent, the dividend yield for Alexis plc for the year ended 31 March 2013 is:

$$\text{Dividend yield} = \frac{0.067^*/(1 - 0.10)}{2.50} \times 100 = 3.0\%$$

The shares' market value is given in Note 1 to Example 3.1 (p. 73).

* Dividend proposed/number of shares = 40/(300 × 2) = £0.067 dividend per share (the 300 is multiplied by 2 because they are £0.50 shares).

Activity 3.21

Calculate the dividend yield for Alexis plc for the year ended 31 March 2014.

The ratio for 2014 is:

$$\text{Dividend yield} = \frac{0.067^*/(1 - 0.10)}{1.50} \times 100 = 5.0\%$$

* 40/(300 × 2) = £0.067.

Earnings per share

The **earnings per share** (EPS) ratio relates the earnings generated, which are available to shareholders for a period, to the number of shares in issue. For equity (ordinary) shareholders, this amount will be the profit for the year (that is, profit after taxation) less any preference dividend. The ratio for equity shareholders is calculated as follows:

$$\text{Earnings per share} = \frac{\text{Earnings available to ordinary shareholders}}{\text{Number of ordinary shares in issue}}$$

In the case of Alexis plc, the earnings per share for the year ended 31 March 2013 is as follows:

$$\text{EPS} = \frac{£165m}{600m} = 27.5p$$

Many investment analysts regard the EPS ratio as a fundamental measure of share performance. The trend in earnings per share over time is used to help assess the investment potential of a business's shares. Although it is possible to make total profit increase through ordinary shareholders investing more in the business, this will not necessarily lead to an increase in the profitability *per share*.

It is not usually very helpful to compare the EPS of one business with that of another. Differences in financing arrangements (for example, in the nominal value of shares issued) can render any such comparison meaningless. However, it can be very useful to monitor the changes that occur in this ratio for a particular business over time.

Activity 3.22

Calculate the earnings per share of Alexis plc for the year ended 31 March 2014.

The ratio for 2014 is:

$$\text{EPS} = \frac{£11m}{600m} = 1.8p$$

Price/earnings (P/E) ratio

The **price/earnings ratio** relates the market value of a share to the earnings per share. This ratio can be calculated as follows:

$$\text{P/E ratio} = \frac{\text{Market value per share}}{\text{Earnings per share}}$$

The P/E ratio for Alexis plc as at 31 March 2013 is:

$$\text{P/E ratio} = \frac{£2.50}{27.5p^*} = 9.1 \text{ times}$$

* The EPS figure (27.5p) was calculated above.

This ratio indicates that the market value of the share is 9.1 times higher than its current level of earnings. It is a measure of market confidence in the future of a business. The higher the P/E ratio, the greater the confidence in the future earning power of the business and, consequently, the more investors are prepared to pay in relation to that current earning power.

Activity 3.23

Calculate the P/E ratio of Alexis plc as at 31 March 2014.

The ratio as of 31 March 2014 is:

$$\text{P/E ratio} = \frac{£1.50}{1.8p} = 83.3 \text{ times}$$

As P/E ratios provide a useful guide to market confidence about the future, they can be helpful when comparing different businesses. However, differences in accounting policies between businesses can lead to different profit and earnings per share figures. This can distort comparisons.

The investment ratios for Alexis plc over the two-year period are as follows:

	2013	2014
Dividend payout ratio	24.2%	363.6%
Dividend yield ratio	3.0%	5.0%
Earnings per share	27.5p	1.8p
Price/earnings ratio	9.1 times	83.3 times

Activity 3.24

What do you deduce from the investment ratios set out above? Can you explain why the share price has not fallen as much as it might have done, bearing in mind the much poorer trading performance in 2014?

Although the EPS has fallen dramatically and the dividend payment for 2014 seems very imprudent, the share price has held up reasonably well (fallen from £2.50 to £1.50). Moreover, the dividend yield and P/E ratios have improved in 2014. This is an anomaly of these two ratios, which stems from using a forward-looking value (the share price) in conjunction with historic data (dividends and earnings). Share prices are based on investors' assessments of the business's future. It seems that 'the market' was less happy with Alexis plc at the end of 2014 than at the end of 2013. This is evidenced by the fact that the share price had fallen by £1 a share. The decline in share price, however, was less dramatic than the decline in profit for the year. This suggests that investors believe that the business will perform better in the future. Perhaps they are confident that the large increase in assets and employee numbers occurring in 2014 will yield benefits in the future: benefits that the business was not able to generate during 2014.

Real World 3.7 provides information about the share performance of a selection of large, well-known UK businesses. This type of information is provided on a daily basis by several newspapers, notably the *Financial Times*.

Market statistics for some well-known businesses

The following data was extracted from the *Financial Times* of 3 January 2013, relating to the previous day's trading of the shares of some well-known businesses on the London Stock Exchange:

Share	Price	Chng	52 Week High/Low		Yld	P/E	Volume 000s
Marks and Spencer	382.70	+0.40	399.69	303.80	4.4	11.5	9,926
JD Wetherspoon	530.50	−2.50	554	366.90	2.3	12.1	94
National Express	210	+5.90	256.20	162.90	4.6	11.9	1,037
Tesco	342.75	+6.75	412	294.50	4.3	11.5	29,161
Rolls-Royce	910.50	+37	922.14	713.66	1.7	14	6,106
TUI Travel	287.70	+5.20	293.60	156.50	4.1	13.9	3,009

The column headings are as follows:

Mid-market price in pence (that is, the price midway between buying and selling price) of the shares at the end of trading on 2 January 2013

Chng — Gain or loss in the mid-market price during 2 January 2013

High/Low — Highest and lowest prices reached by the share during the 52 weeks ended on 2 January 2013

Yld — Gross dividend yield, based on the most recent year's dividend and the current share price

P/E — Price/earnings ratio, based on the most recent year's (after-tax) profit for the year and the current share price

Volume — The number of shares (in thousands) that were bought/sold on 2 January 2013

So, for example for Marks and Spencer plc, the retail business:

- the shares had a mid-market price of 382.70 each at the close of Stock Exchange trading on 2 January 2013
- the shares had increased in price by 0.40 pence during trading on 2 January 2013
- the shares had highest and lowest prices during the previous 52 weeks of 399.69p and 303.80p, respectively
- the shares had a dividend yield, based on the 2 January 2013 price (and the dividend for the most recent year) of 4.4 per cent
- the shares had a P/E ratio, based on the 2 January 2013 price (and the after-taxation earnings per share for the most recent year), of 11.5
- during trading on 2 January 2013, 9,926,000 of the business's shares had changed hands between buyers and sellers.

FT Source: *Financial Times*, 3 January 2013, p. 26.
© The Financial Times Limited 2012. All Rights Reserved.

Real World 3.8 shows how investment ratios can vary between different industry sectors.

Yielding dividends

Investment ratios can vary significantly between businesses and between industries. To give some indication of the range of variations that occurs, the average dividend yield ratios and average P/E ratios for listed businesses in 12 different industries are shown in Figures 3.4 and 3.5, respectively.

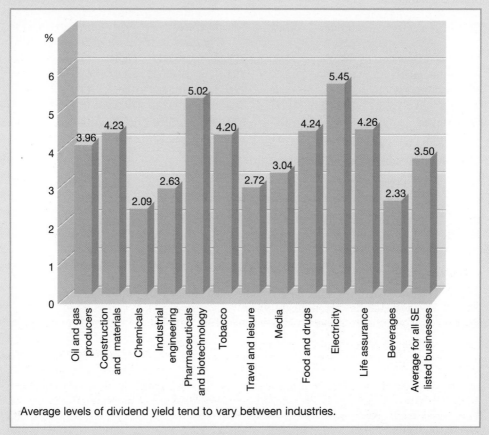

Average levels of dividend yield tend to vary between industries.

Figure 3.4 Average dividend yield ratios for businesses in a range of industries

Source: Constructed from data appearing in the *Financial Times*, 3 January 2013.

These dividend yield ratios are calculated from the current market value of the shares and the most recent year's dividend paid.

Some industries tend to pay out lower dividends than others, leading to lower dividend yield ratios. The average for all Stock Exchange listed businesses was 3.50 per cent (as shown in Figure 3.4), but there is a wide variation with Chemicals at 2.09 per cent and Electricity at 5.45 per cent.

Some types of businesses tend to invest heavily in developing new products, hence their tendency to pay low dividends compared with their share prices. Some of the inter-industry differences in the dividend yield ratio can be explained by the nature of the calculation of the ratio. The prices of shares at any given moment are based on expectations of their economic futures; dividends are actual past events. A business that had a good trading year recently may have paid a dividend that, in the light of investors' assessment of the business's economic future, may be high (a high dividend yield).

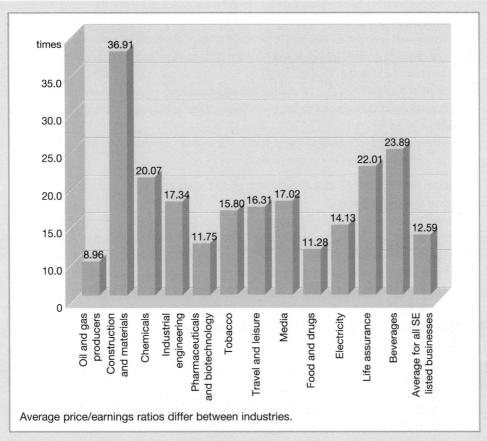

times

Average price/earnings ratios differ between industries.

Figure 3.5 Average price/earnings ratios for businesses in a range of industries

Source: Constructed from data appearing in the *Financial Times*, 3 January 2013.

These P/E ratios are calculated from the current market value of the shares and the most recent year's EPS.

Businesses that have a high share price relative to their recent historic earnings have high P/E ratios. This may be because their future is regarded as economically bright, which may be the result of investing heavily in the future at the expense of recent profits (earnings). High P/Es also arise where businesses have recent low earnings but investors believe that their future is brighter. The average P/E for all Stock Exchange listed businesses was 12.59 times, but oil and gas producers was as low as 8.96 times and Construction and materials as high as 36.91 times.

FINANCIAL RATIOS AND THE PROBLEM OF OVERTRADING

Overtrading occurs where a business is operating at a level of activity that cannot be supported by the amount of finance that has been committed. This situation is usually due to poor financial control over the business by its managers. The underlying reasons for overtrading are varied. It may occur:

- in young, expanding businesses that fail to prepare adequately for the rapid increase in demand for their goods or services. This often leads to insufficient finance to fund the trade receivables and inventories needed to support the additional sales generated
- in businesses where the managers may have misjudged the level of sales demand or have failed to control escalating project costs
- as a result of a fall in the value of money (inflation), causing more finance to be committed to inventories and trade receivables, even where there is no expansion in the real volume of trade
- where the owners are unable to inject further funds into the business and/or they cannot persuade others to invest in the business.

Whatever the reason, the problems that it brings must be resolved if the business is to survive over the longer term.

Overtrading results in liquidity problems such as exceeding borrowing limits, or slow repayment of borrowings and trade payables. The last of these can result in suppliers withholding supplies, thereby making it difficult to meet customer needs. The managers of the business may be forced to direct all of their efforts to dealing with immediate and pressing problems, such as finding cash to meet interest charges due or paying wages. Their time may be spent lurching from crisis to crisis rather than engaging in longer-term planning. Ultimately, the business may fail because it cannot meet its maturing obligations.

Activity 3.25

If a business is overtrading, do you think the following ratios would be higher or lower than normally expected?

1 Current ratio
2 Average inventories turnover period
3 Average settlement period for trade receivables
4 Average settlement period for trade payables

Your answers should be as follows:

1 The current ratio would be lower than normally expected. This ratio is a measure of liquidity and lack of liquidity is a symptom of overtrading.
2 The average inventories turnover period would be lower than normally expected. Where a business is overtrading, the level of inventories held will be low because of the problems of financing them. In the short term, sales revenue may not be badly affected by the low inventories levels and therefore inventories will be turned over more quickly.
3 The average settlement period for trade receivables may be lower than normally expected. Where a business is suffering from liquidity problems, it may chase credit customers more vigorously in an attempt to improve cash flows.
4 The average settlement period for trade payables may be higher than normally expected. The business may delay payments to its suppliers because of the liquidity problems arising.

To deal with the overtrading problem, a business must ensure that the finance available is consistent with the level of operations. Thus, if a business that is overtrading is unable to raise new finance, it should cut back its level of operations in line with the finance available. Although this may lead to lost sales and lost profits in the short term, cutting back may be necessary to ensure survival over the longer term.

It is often helpful to see whether ratios are indicating trends. Key ratios can be plotted on a graph to provide a simple visual display of changes occurring over time. The trends occurring within a business may be plotted against trends for rival businesses or for the industry as a whole for comparison purposes. An example of trend analysis is shown in **Real World 3.9**.

Real World 3.9

Trend setting

In Figure 3.6, the current ratio of three of the UK's leading supermarkets is plotted over time. We can see that the current ratios of the three businesses have tended to move closer. Tesco plc was lower than that of its main rivals until 2005, when it overtook Morrison, and 2009, when it overtook Sainsbury. The current ratio of Sainsbury shows a fairly consistent downward path until 2010. Morrison has tended to maintain the lowest current ratio over time. With well-managed businesses like these, it is highly likely that any changes are the result of deliberate policy.

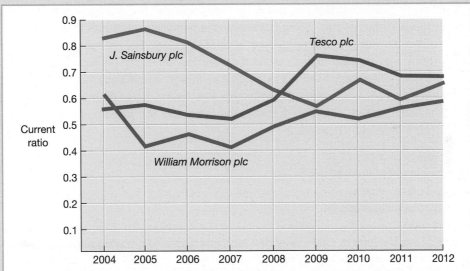

The current ratio for three leading UK supermarket businesses is plotted for the financial years ended during 2004 to 2012. This enables comparison to be made regarding the ratio, both for each of the three businesses over time and between the businesses.

Figure 3.6 Graph plotting current ratio against time

Source: Ratios calculated from information in the annual reports of the three businesses for each of the years 2004 to 2012.

Source: Annual reports of the three businesses 2004 to 2012.

USING RATIOS TO PREDICT FINANCIAL FAILURE

Financial ratios, based on current or past performance, are often used to help predict the future. Normally, both the choice of ratios and the interpretation of results are dependent on the judgement and opinion of the analyst. However, there have been attempts to develop a more rigorous and systematic approach to the use of ratios for prediction purposes. These attempts have often focused on the ability of ratios to predict the financial failure of a business. By financial failure, we mean a business either being forced out of business or being severely adversely affected by its inability to meet its financial obligations. It is often referred to as 'going bust' or 'going bankrupt'. This, of course, is an area of concern for all those connected with the business.

Using single ratios

Various methods of using ratios to predict future financial failure have been developed. Early research looked at whether a single ratio was a good or bad predictor of financial failure. It involved tracking a particular ratio (for example, the current ratio) for a business over several years leading up to the date of the failure. This was to see whether the ratio exhibited a trend that could be taken as a warning sign.

Beaver (see reference 1 at the end of the chapter) carried out the first research in this area. He identified 79 businesses that had failed. He then calculated the average (mean) of various ratios for these 79 businesses, going back over the financial statements of each business for each of the ten years leading up to each business's failure. Beaver then compared these average ratios with similarly derived ratios for a sample of 79 businesses that did not fail over this period. (The research used a matched-pair design, where each failed business was matched with a non-failed business of similar size and industry type.) Beaver found that some ratios exhibited a marked difference between the failed and non-failed businesses for up to five years prior to failure. These were:

- cash flow/total debt
- net income (profit)/total assets
- total debt/total assets
- working capital/total assets
- current ratio
- no credit interval (that is, cash generated from operations to maturing obligations).

To illustrate Beaver's findings, the average current ratio of failed businesses for five years prior to failure, along with the average current ratio of non-failed businesses for the same period, is shown in Figure 3.7.

Research by Zmijewski (see reference 2), using a sample of 72 failed and 3,573 non-failed businesses over a six-year period, found that businesses that ultimately went on to fail were characterised by lower rates of return, higher levels of gearing, lower levels of coverage for their fixed interest payments and more variable returns on shares. While we may not find these results very surprising, it is interesting to note that Zmijewski did not find liquidity ratios particularly useful in predicting financial failure. We saw earlier, however, that Beaver did find the current ratio to be a useful predictor.

The approach adopted by Beaver and Zmijewski is referred to as **univariate analysis** because it looks at one ratio at a time. It can produce interesting results but there are practical problems associated with its use.

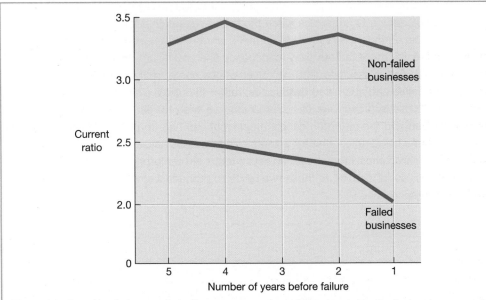

The vertical scale of the graph is the average value of the current ratio for each group of businesses (failed and non-failed). The horizontal axis is the number of years before failure. Thus, Year 1 is the most recent year and Year 5 the least recent year. We can see that a clear difference between the average for the failed and non-failed businesses can be detected five years prior to the failure of the former group.

Figure 3.7 Average (mean) current ratio of failed and non-failed businesses

---

Activity 3.26

Let us assume that research indicates that a particular ratio is shown to be a good predictor of failure. Can you think of a practical problem that may arise when using this ratio to predict financial failure for a particular business?

Where a particular ratio for a business differs from the mean ratios of non-failed businesses, the analyst must rely on judgement to interpret whether it is significant. There is no clear decision rule that can be applied. Different analysts may therefore come to different conclusions about the likelihood of failure.

A further problem arises where more than one ratio is used to predict failure. Let us say, for example, that past research has identified two ratios as being good predictors of financial failure. When applied to a particular business, however, it may be that one ratio predicts financial failure, whereas the other does not. Given these conflicting signals, how should the analyst interpret the results?

Using combinations of ratios

The weaknesses of univariate analysis have led to the development of models that combine ratios so as to produce a single index that can be interpreted more clearly. One approach to model development, much favoured by researchers, uses multiple discriminate analysis

(MDA). This is, in essence, a statistical technique that is similar to regression analysis and which can be used to draw a boundary between those businesses that fail and those businesses that do not. This boundary is referred to as the **discriminate function**. In this context, MDA attempts to identify those factors likely to influence financial failure. MDA differs from regression analysis in that it assumes that the observations come from two different populations (for example, failed and non-failed businesses) rather than from a single population.

To illustrate this approach, let us assume that we wish to test whether two ratios (say, the current ratio and the return on capital employed) can help to predict failure. To do this, we can calculate these ratios, first for a sample of failed businesses and then for a matched sample of non-failed ones. From these two sets of data, we can produce a scatter diagram that plots each business according to these two ratios to produce a single coordinate. Figure 3.8 illustrates this approach.

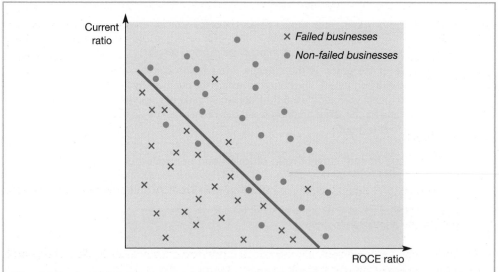

The distribution of failed and non-failed businesses is based on two ratios. The line represents a boundary between the samples of failed and non-failed businesses. Although there is some crossing of the boundary, the boundary represents the line that minimises the problem of mis-classifying particular businesses.

Figure 3.8 Scatter diagram showing the distribution of failed and non-failed businesses

Source: P. Atrill and E. McLaney, *Accounting: An Introduction*, 7th edn, Financial Times Prentice Hall, 2009.

Using the observations plotted on the diagram, we try to identify the boundary between the failed and the non-failed businesses. This is the diagonal line in Figure 3.8. We can see that those businesses that fall below and to the left of the line are predominantly failed and those that fall to the right are predominantly non-failed ones. Note that there is some overlap between the two populations. In practice, the boundary produced is unlikely to eliminate all errors. Some businesses that fail may fall on the non-failed side of the boundary. The opposite also happens. However, the analysis will *minimise* the misclassification errors.

The boundary shown in Figure 3.8 can be expressed in the form:

$$Z = a + (b \times \text{Current ratio}) + (c \times \text{ROCE})$$

where *a*, *b* and *c* are all constants and *b* and *c* are weights to be attached to each ratio. A weighted average or total score (*Z*) is then derived. By 'constants' we mean that the same values are used for assessing each individual business. The weights given to the two ratios will depend on the slope of the line and its absolute position (that is, they will depend on the values of *a*, *b* and *c*). Using this model to assess a particular business's health involves calculating the current and ROCE ratios for that business and using them in the equation above. If the resulting Z score were to come out below a certain value, we should view that business as being at risk.

Note that this example, using the current and ROCE ratios, is purely hypothetical and intended only to illustrate the approach.

Z-score models

Altman (see reference 3 at the end of the chapter) was the first to develop a model (in 1968), using financial ratios, that was able to predict financial failure. In 2000, he revised this model. The revisions needed to make the model effective for present times, however, were quite minor. Altman's revised model, the Z-score model, is based on five financial ratios and is as follows:

$$Z = 0.717a + 0.847b + 3.107c + 0.420d + 0.998e$$

where *a* = Working capital/Total assets
  b = Accumulated retained profits/Total assets
  c = Operating profit/Total assets
  d = Book (statement of financial position) value of ordinary and preference shares/Total liabilities at book (statement of financial position) value
  e = Sales revenue/Total assets.

The weightings (or coefficients) in the above model are constants that reflect the importance to the Z-score of each of the ingredients (*a* to *e*).

In developing and revising this model, Altman carried out experiments using a paired sample of failed businesses and non-failed businesses and collected relevant data for each business for five years prior to failure. He found that the model represented by the formula above was able to predict failure for up to two years before it occurred. However, the predictive accuracy of the model became weaker the longer the time before the date of the actual failure.

The ratios used in this model were identified by Altman through a process of trial and error, as there is no underlying theory of financial failure to help guide researchers in selecting appropriate ratios. According to Altman, those businesses with a Z-score of less than 1.23 tend to fail. The lower the score, the greater is the probability of failure. Those with a Z-score greater than 4.14 tend not to fail. Those businesses with a Z-score between 1.23 and 4.14 occupied a 'zone of ignorance' and were difficult to classify. However, the model was able overall to classify 91 per cent of the businesses correctly; only 9 per cent fell into the 'zone of ignorance'. Altman based his model on US businesses.

Real World 3.10 discusses some research that showed that investing in shares in businesses with very low Z-scores is unsuccessful compared with investing in businesses with higher Z-scores. This is what we might expect to happen and provides support for the use of Z-scores in assessing the health of businesses. The research did not show, however, that the higher the Z-score, the more successful the investment.

From A to Z

Investors looking to profit during a recession should be targeting stocks with strong fundamentals, according to research by Morgan Stanley. This 'value investing' approach – buying into companies where fundamental measures, such as book value and earnings, are not yet reflected in their share prices – is not new. But Morgan Stanley's analysis has found that the ability of this approach to deliver returns in downturns depends on the financial strength of the companies – in particular, the importance attached to the balance sheet (statement of financial position) by investors.

'If a stock's balance sheet is weak, the valuation multiple will be of little importance at this stage in the economic cycle,' says Graham Secker, Morgan Stanley strategy analyst. He ranked a basket of European companies by their Altman Z-score – a measure of financial strength devised by US academic Edward Altman. A Z-score can be calculated for all non-financial companies and the lower the score, the greater the risk of the company falling into financial distress. When Secker compared the companies' Z-scores with their share price movements, he discovered that the companies with weaker balance sheets underperformed the market more than two-thirds of the time.

Morgan Stanley also found that a company with an Altman Z-score of less than 1 tends to underperform the wider market by more than 4 per cent over the year with an associated probability of 72 per cent. 'Given the poor performance over the last year by stocks with a low Altman Z-score, the results of our backtest are now even more compelling than they were 12 months ago,' argues Secker. 'We calculate that the median stock with an Altman Z-score of 1 or less has underperformed the wider market by 5–6 per cent per annum between 1990 and 2008.'

Secker sees this as logical. In a recession, companies with balance sheets that are perceived to be weak are deemed a higher risk by lenders and face a higher cost of capital. This turns market sentiment against them and will generally lead to their share prices falling below those of their peers.

In 2008, the share price performance for stocks with an Altman Z-score of less than 1 was the worst since Morgan Stanley's analysis began in 1991. Under the Morgan Stanley methodology, the 2008 score is calculated using 2007 company financials. Of all the companies with a 2008 Z-score of less than 1, the median share price performance was a loss of 49 per cent, compared with a wider market fall of 42 per cent.

When compound annual growth rates since 1991 are analysed, the results are more dramatic. On average, companies with Z-scores of less than 1 saw their shares fall 4.4 per cent, compared with an average rise of 1.3 per cent for their peers. In only five of the last 18 years has a stock with an Altman score of 1 or less outperformed the market. These were generally years of strong economic growth. However, companies with the highest Z-scores aren't necessarily the best performers. During the bear market of 2000 to 2002, companies that had a Z-score above 3 fell almost twice as much as the market.

Analysts say the 2009 Z-scores, based on 2008 balance sheets, are far lower than in previous years as companies absorb the strain of the downturn in their accounts. 'There's been a lot of change between 2007 and 2008 [accounting years], tightening of credit and a vast deterioration in corporate balance sheets,' says Secker. 'I'd expect 2009 [Z-scores] to be much worse.'

Analysis by the *Financial Times* and Capital IQ, the data provider, corroborates this – showing that the 2009 scores have been badly affected by the crisis. Some 8 per cent of global companies with a market capitalisation of more than $500 million have Altman scores below 1 for 2009 – based on 2008 company financials. This is the highest percentage since 2002 and the largest annual increase since 2001 – showing the impact of the recession on the balance sheets of even the largest companies. If smaller companies were included, the results would be worse – as their earnings and market capitalisations have been affected far more.

European balance sheets were hit the hardest, with companies averaging a Z-score of 2.8, compared with 4.0 for Asia and the US, according to Capital IQ. This suggests the scores are not due to chance. A similar differential was recorded in 2001 during the last recession. On this evidence, US companies appear more resilient than their global peers in a down-turn. On a sector basis, healthcare and IT companies have the highest Z-scores. In 2008, their scores were more than three times higher than the average for the lowest scoring sector: utilities. A similar pattern was found in 2001 – suggesting that investors may want to think twice before buying into 'defensive' utilities in a downturn.

FT *Source*: P. Mathurin, 'New study re-writes the A to Z of value investing', www.ft.com, 14 August 2009.
© The Financial Times Limited 2012. All Rights Reserved.

Development of the Z-score model

In recent years, other models, using a similar approach to Altman, have been developed throughout the world. In the UK, Taffler has developed separate multivariate models for different types of business. (See reference 4 for a discussion of the work of Taffler and others.)

The prediction of financial failure is not the only area where research into the predictive ability of ratios has taken place. Researchers have also developed ratio-based, multivariate models that claim to assess the vulnerability of a business to takeover by another. This is another area that is vital to all those connected with the business.

Recently, a Z-Metrics model has been developed by RiskMetrics Group, in conjunction with Altman. This model includes market-based and macroeconomic measures as well as financial ratios. The Z-Metrics model is claimed to be superior to the Z-score model in two important respects. First, it possesses better predictive accuracy, and second, it is capable of providing a credit rating for businesses based on the probability of default. (See reference 5 at the end of the chapter.) The model is used for commercial purposes and so its precise nature is not disclosed.

LIMITATIONS OF RATIO ANALYSIS

Although ratios offer a quick and useful method of analysing the position and performance of a business, they are not without their problems and limitations. We shall now review some of their shortcomings.

Quality of financial statements

It must always be remembered that ratios are based on financial statements. They will, therefore, inherit the limitations of the financial statements on which they are based. One important limitation of financial statements is their failure to include all resources controlled by the business. Internally generated goodwill and brands, for example, are excluded from the statement of financial position because they fail to meet the strict definition of an asset. This means that even though these resources may be of considerable value, key ratios such as ROSF, ROCE and the gearing ratio will fail to acknowledge their presence.

Creative accounting

There is also the problem of deliberate attempts to make the financial statements misleading. Despite the proliferation of accounting rules and the independent checks that are imposed, there is evidence that the directors of some businesses have employed particular accounting policies or structured particular transactions in such a way as to portray a picture of financial health that is in line with what they would like users to see rather than what is a true and fair view of financial position and performance. This practice is referred to as creative accounting and it can pose a major problem for those seeking to gain an impression of the financial health of a business.

The particular methods that unscrupulous directors use to manipulate the financial statements are many and varied. They can involve overstatement of revenues, manipulation of expenses, concealing losses and liabilities and overstating asset values.

Overstating revenues has been a particularly popular target for creative accounting. The methods used often involve the early recognition of sales income or the reporting of sales transactions that have no real substance. **Real World 3.11** is based on an article in *The Times* that provides examples of both types of revenue manipulation.

Overstating revenue

Channel stuffing: a business, usually with considerable market power, may pressurise its distributors to accept more goods than are needed to meet normal sales demand. In this way, the business can record additional sales for a period even though there has effectively been only a transfer of inventories from the business to its distributors. This method of artificially increasing sales is also known as 'trade loading'.

Pre-dispatching: normally, revenue for credit sales is recognised when goods have been passed to, and accepted by, the customer. To boost sales and profits for a period, however, some businesses have been known to recognise revenue as soon as the order for goods has been received.

Hollow swaps: telecom businesses may agree to sell unused fibre optic capacity to each other – usually at the same price. Although this will not increase profits, it will increase revenues and give an impression that the business is growing.

Round tripping: energy businesses may agree to buy and sell energy between each other. Again this is normally for the same price and so no additional profits will be made. It will, however, boost revenues to give a false impression of business growth. This method is also known as 'in and out trading'.

Source: Based on information in 'Dirty laundry: how companies fudge the numbers', *The Times*, Business Section, 22 September 2002.

When examining the financial statements of a business, a number of checks may be carried out to help gain a 'feel' for their reliability. These can include checks to see whether:

- the reported profits are significantly higher than the operating cash flows for the period, which may suggest that profits have been overstated
- the tax charge is low in relation to reported profits, which may suggest, again, that profits are overstated, although there may be other, more innocent, explanations
- the valuation methods used for assets held are based on historic cost or current values, and if the latter approach has been used why and how the current values were determined
- there have been any changes in accounting policies over the period, particularly in key areas such as revenue recognition, inventory valuation and depreciation
- the accounting policies adopted are in line with those adopted by the rest of the industry
- the auditors' report gives a 'clean bill of health' to the financial statements
- the 'small print', that is, the notes to the financial statements, is not being used to hide significant events or changes.

Although such checks are useful, they are not guaranteed to identify creative accounting practices, some of which may be very deeply seated.

Inflation

A persistent, though recently less severe, problem in most countries is that the financial results of businesses can be distorted as a result of inflation. One effect of inflation is that the reported value of assets held for any length of time may bear little relation to current values. Generally speaking, the reported values of assets will be understated in current terms during a period of inflation as they are usually reported at the original cost (less any amounts written off for depreciation). This means that comparisons, either between businesses or between periods, will be hindered. A difference in, say, ROCE may simply be owing to the fact that assets shown in one of the statements of financial position being compared were acquired more recently (ignoring the effect of depreciation on the asset values). Another effect of inflation is to distort the measurement of profit. In the calculation of profit, sales revenue is often matched with costs incurred at an earlier time. This is because there is often a time lag between acquiring a particular resource and using it to help generate sales revenue. For example, inventories may well be acquired several months before they are sold. During a period of inflation, this will mean that the expense does not reflect prices that are current at the time of the sale. The cost of sales figure is usually based on the historic cost of the inventories concerned. As a result, expenses will be understated in the income statement and this, in turn, means that profit will be overstated. One effect of this will be to distort the profitability ratios discussed earlier.

Over-reliance on ratios

It is important not to rely exclusively on ratios, thereby losing sight of information contained in the underlying financial statements. As we saw earlier in the chapter, some items reported in these statements can be vital in assessing position and performance. For example, the total sales revenue, capital employed and profit figures may be useful in assessing changes in absolute size that occur over time, or in assessing differences in scale between businesses. Ratios do not provide such information. When comparing one figure with another, ratios measure relative performance and position and therefore provide only part of the picture. When comparing two businesses, therefore, it will often be useful to assess the absolute size of profits, as well as the relative profitability of each business. For example, Business A may generate £1 million operating profit and have a ROCE of 15 per cent and Business B may generate £100,000 operating profit and have a ROCE of 20 per cent. Although Business B has a higher level of profitability, as measured by ROCE, it generates lower total operating profits.

The basis for comparison

We saw earlier that if ratios are to be useful, they require a basis for comparison. Moreover, it is important that we compare like with like. Where the comparison is with another business, there can be difficulties. No two businesses are identical: the greater the differences between the businesses being compared, the greater the limitations of ratio analysis. Furthermore, any differences in accounting policies, financing methods (gearing levels) and financial year ends will add to the problems of making comparisons between businesses.

Statement of financial position ratios

Because the statement of financial position is only a 'snapshot' of the business at a particular moment in time, any ratios based on statement of financial position figures, such as the liquidity ratios, may not be representative of the financial position of the business for the year as a whole. It is common for a seasonal business, for example, to have a financial year end that coincides with a low point in business activity. As a result, inventories and trade receivables may be low at the year end. This means that the liquidity ratios may also be low. A more representative picture of liquidity can only really be gained by taking additional measurements at other points in the year.

Real World 3.12 points out another way in which ratios are limited.

Remember, it's people that really count . . .

Lord Weinstock (1924–2002) was an influential industrialist whose management style and philosophy helped to shape management practice in many UK businesses. During his long and successful reign at GEC plc, a major engineering business, Lord Weinstock relied heavily on financial ratios to assess performance and to exercise control. In particular, he relied on ratios relating to sales revenue, expenses, trade receivables, profit margins and inventories turnover. However, he was keenly aware of the limitations of ratios and recognised that, ultimately, people produce profits.

In a memo written to GEC managers he pointed out that ratios are an aid to good management rather than a substitute for it. He wrote:

> The operating ratios are of great value as measures of efficiency but they are only the measures and not efficiency itself. Statistics will not design a product better, make it for a lower cost or increase sales. If ill-used, they may so guide action as to diminish resources for the sake of apparent but false signs of improvement.
>
> Management remains a matter of judgement, of knowledge of products and processes and of understanding and skill in dealing with people. The ratios will indicate how well all these things are being done and will show comparison with how they are done elsewhere. But they will tell us nothing about how to do them. That is what you are meant to do.

Source: Extract from S. Aris, *Arnold Weinstock and the Making of GEC*, Aurum Press, 1998, published in *The Sunday Times*, 22 February 1998, p. 3.

Self-assessment question 3.1

Both Ali plc and Bhaskar plc operate wholesale electrical stores throughout the UK. The financial statements of each business for the year ended 30 June 2014 are as follows:

Statements of financial position as at 30 June 2014

	Ali plc £m	Bhaskar plc £m
ASSETS		
Non-current assets		
Property, plant and equipment		
(cost less depreciation)		
Land and buildings	360.0	510.0
Fixtures and fittings	87.0	91.2
	447.0	601.2
Current assets		
Inventories	592.0	403.0
Trade receivables	176.4	321.9
Cash at bank	84.6	91.6
	853.0	816.5
Total assets	1,300.0	1,417.7

→

	Ali plc £m	Bhaskar plc £m
EQUITY AND LIABILITIES		
Equity		
£1 ordinary shares	320.0	250.0
Retained earnings	367.6	624.6
	687.6	874.6
Non-current liabilities		
Borrowings – loan notes	190.0	250.0
Current liabilities		
Trade payables	406.4	275.7
Taxation	16.0	17.4
	422.4	293.1
Total equity and liabilities	1,300.0	1,417.7

Income statements for the year ended 30 June 2014

	Ali plc £m	Bhaskar plc £m
Revenue	1,478.1	1,790.4
Cost of sales	(1,018.3)	(1,214.9)
Gross profit	459.8	575.5
Operating expenses	(308.5)	(408.6)
Operating profit	151.3	166.9
Interest payable	(19.4)	(27.5)
Profit before taxation	131.9	139.4
Taxation	(32.0)	(34.8)
Profit for the year	99.9	104.6

All purchases and sales were on credit. Ali plc had announced its intention to pay a dividend of £135 million and Bhaskar plc £95 million in respect of the year. The market values of a share in Ali plc and Bhaskar plc at the end of the year were £6.50 and £8.20 respectively.

Required:

For each business, calculate two ratios that are concerned with each of the following aspects:

- profitability
- efficiency
- liquidity
- gearing
- investment (ten ratios in total).

Required:

(a) What can you conclude from the ratios that you have calculated?
(b) Calculate the Z-scores for each business using the Altman model.
(c) Comment on the Z-scores for each business and on the validity of applying the Altman model to these particular businesses.

The answer to this question can be found at the back of the book on pp. 560–561.

SUMMARY

The main points of this chapter may be summarised as follows:

Ratio analysis

- Compares two related figures, usually both from the same set of financial statements.
- Is an aid to understanding what the financial statements really mean.
- Is an inexact science so results must be interpreted cautiously.
- Past periods, the performance of similar businesses and planned performance are often used to provide benchmark ratios.
- A brief review of the financial statements may provide insights not revealed by ratios and/or may help in their interpretation.

Profitability ratios

- Are concerned with effectiveness at generating profit.
- Include the return on ordinary shareholders' funds (ROSF), return on capital employed (ROCE), operating profit margin and gross profit margin.

Efficiency ratios

- Are concerned with efficiency of using assets/resources.
- Include the average inventories turnover period, average settlement period for trade receivables, average settlement period for trade payables, sales revenue to capital employed and sales revenue per employee.

Liquidity ratios

- Are concerned with the ability to meet short-term obligations.
- Include the current ratio and the acid test ratio.

Gearing ratios

- Are concerned with relationship between equity and debt financing.
- Include the gearing ratio and the interest cover ratio.

Investment ratios

- Are concerned with returns to shareholders.
- Include the dividend payout ratio, dividend yield ratio, earnings per share and price/earnings ratio.

Uses of ratios

- Can be used to identify signs of overtrading.
- Individual ratios can be tracked (by plotting on a graph, for example) to detect trends.
- Can be used to help predict financial distress. Univariate analysis employs one ratio at a time, whereas multiple discriminate analysis combines various ratios within a model.

→

Limitations of ratio analysis

■ Ratios are only as reliable as the financial statements from which they derive.

■ Creative accounting can deliberately distort the portrayal of financial health.

■ Inflation can also distort financial information.

■ Ratios provide only part of the picture and there should not be over-reliance on them.

■ It can be difficult to find a suitable benchmark (for example, another business) to compare with.

■ Some ratios could mislead due to the 'snapshot' nature of the statement of financial position.

KEY TERMS

Return on ordinary shareholders' funds ratio (ROSF) p. 76

Return on capital employed ratio (ROCE) p. 77

Operating profit margin ratio p. 79

Gross profit margin ratio p. 80

Average inventories turnover period ratio p. 83

Average settlement period for trade receivables ratio p. 84

Average settlement period for trade payables ratio p. 85

Sales revenue to capital employed ratio p. 86

Sales revenue per employee ratio p. 87

Current ratio p. 90

Acid test ratio p. 91

Financial gearing p. 92

Gearing ratio p. 92

Interest cover ratio p. 93

Dividend payout ratio p. 95

Dividend cover ratio p. 96

Dividend yield ratio p. 96

Dividend per share p. 96

Earnings per share p. 97

Price/earnings ratio p. 97

Overtrading p. 101

Univariate analysis p. 104

Multiple discriminate analysis p. 105

Discriminate function p. 106

Creative accounting p. 110

For definitions of these terms see the Glossary, pp. 605–613.

REFERENCES

1 Beaver, W.H. (1966) 'Financial ratios as predictors of failure', in *Empirical Research in Accounting: Selected Studies*, pp. 71–111.

2 Zmijewski, M.E. (1983) 'Predicting corporate bankruptcy: An empirical comparison of the extent of financial distress models', Research Paper, State University of New York.

3 Altman, E.I. (2000) 'Predicting financial distress of companies: Revisiting the Z-score and Zeta models', New York University Working Paper, June.

4 Neophytou, E., Charitou, A. and Charalamnous, C. (2001) 'Predicting corporate failure: Empirical evidence for the UK', University of Southampton Department of Accounting and Management Science Working Paper 01-173.

5 Altman, E. (ed.) (2010) 'The Z-Metrics™ methodology for estimating company credit ratings and default risk probabilities', Risk Metrics Group, March.

FURTHER READING

If you would like to explore the topics covered in this chapter in more depth, try the following books:

Elliott, B. and Elliott, J. (2012) *Financial Accounting and Reporting*, 15th edn, Financial Times Prentice Hall, Chapters 28 and 29.

Fridson, M. and Alvarez, F. (2011) *Financial Statement Analysis: A practitioner's guide*, 4th edn, Wiley Finance, Chapters 13 and 14.

Penman, S. (2012) *Financial Statement Analysis and Security Valuation*, 3rd edn, McGraw-Hill Irwin, Chapters 7 to 12.

Schoenebeck, K. and Holtzman, M. (2012) *Interpreting and Analysing Financial Statements*, 6th edn, Prentice Hall, Chapters 2 to 5.

REVIEW QUESTIONS

Answers to these questions can be found at the back of the book on pp. 572–3.

3.1 Some businesses operate on a low operating profit margin (an example might be a super-market chain). Does this mean that the return on capital employed from the business will also be low?

3.2 What potential problems arise for the external analyst from the use of statement of financial position figures in the calculation of financial ratios?

3.3 Is it responsible to publish Z-scores of businesses that are in financial difficulties? What are the potential problems of doing this?

3.4 Identify and discuss three reasons why the P/E ratio of two businesses operating in the same industry may differ.

EXERCISES

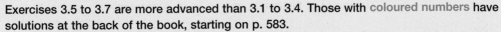

Exercises 3.5 to 3.7 are more advanced than 3.1 to 3.4. Those with coloured numbers have solutions at the back of the book, starting on p. 583.

If you wish to try more exercises, visit the students' side of this book's companion website.

3.1 Set out below are ratios relating to three different businesses. Each business operates within a different industrial sector.

Ratio	A plc	B plc	C plc
Operating profit margin	3.6%	9.7%	6.8%
Sales to capital employed	2.4 times	3.1 times	1.7 times
Average inventories turnover period	18 days	N/A	44 days
Average settlement period for trade receivables	2 days	12 days	26 days
Current ratio	0.8 times	0.6 times	1.5 times

Required:
State, with reasons, which one of the above is:

(a) a holiday tour operator
(b) a supermarket chain
(c) a food manufacturer.

3.2 Amsterdam Ltd and Berlin Ltd are both engaged in wholesaling, but they seem to take a different approach to it according to the following information:

Ratio	Amsterdam Ltd	Berlin Ltd
Return on capital employed (ROCE)	20%	17%
Return on ordinary shareholders' funds (ROSF)	30%	18%
Average settlement period for trade receivables	63 days	21 days
Average settlement period for trade payables	50 days	45 days
Gross profit margin	40%	15%
Operating profit margin	10%	10%
Average inventories turnover period	52 days	25 days

Required:

Describe what this information indicates about the differences in approach between the two businesses. If one of them prides itself on personal service and one of them on competitive prices, which do you think is which and why?

3.3 Conday and Co. Ltd has been in operation for three years and produces antique reproduction furniture for the export market. The most recent set of financial statements for the business is set out as follows:

Income statement for the year ended 30 November

	£000
Revenue	2,600
Cost of sales	(1,620)
Gross profit	980
Selling and distribution expenses (Note 1)	(408)
Administration expenses	(194)
Operating profit	378
Finance expenses	(58)
Profit before taxation	320
Taxation	(95)
Profit for the year	225

Statement of financial position as at 30 November

	£000
ASSETS	
Non-current assets	
Property, plant and equipment (cost less depreciation)	
Land and buildings	228
Plant and machinery	762
	990
Current assets	
Inventories	600
Trade receivables	820
	1,420
Total assets	2,410

	£000
EQUITY AND LIABILITIES	
Equity	
Ordinary shares of £1 each	700
Retained earnings	365
	1,065
Non-current liabilities	
Borrowings – 9% loan notes (Note 2)	200
Current liabilities	
Trade payables	665
Taxation	48
Short-term borrowings (all bank overdraft)	432
	1,145
Total equity and liabilities	2,410

Notes:

1   Selling and distribution expenses include £170,000 in respect of bad debts.
2   The loan notes are secured on the land and buildings.
3   A dividend of £160,000 was paid on the ordinary shares during the year.
4   The directors have invited an investor to take up a new issue of ordinary shares in the business at £6.40 each, making a total investment of £200,000. The directors wish to use the funds to finance a programme of further expansion.

Required:

(a) Analyse the financial position and performance of the business and comment on any features that you consider to be significant.

(b) State, with reasons, whether or not the investor should invest in the business on the terms outlined.

3.4 The directors of Helena Beauty Products Ltd have been presented with the following abridged financial statements:

Income statement for the year ended 30 September

	2013 £000	2013 £000	2014 £000	2014 £000
Sales revenue		3,600		3,840
Cost of sales				
Opening inventories	320		400	
Purchases	2,240		2,350	
	2,560		2,750	
Closing inventories	(400)	(2,160)	(500)	(2,250)
Gross profit		1,440		1,590
Expenses		(1,360)		(1,500)
Profit		80		90

Statement of financial position as at 30 September

	2013 £000	2014 £000
ASSETS		
Non-current assets		
Property, plant and equipment	1,900	1,860
Current assets		
Inventories	400	500
Trade receivables	750	960
Cash at bank	8	4
	1,158	1,464
Total assets	3,058	3,324
EQUITY AND LIABILITIES		
Equity		
£1 ordinary shares	1,650	1,766
Retained earnings	1,018	1,108
	2,668	2,874
Current liabilities	390	450
Total equity and liabilities	3,058	3,324

Required:

Using six ratios, comment on the profitability (three ratios) and efficiency (three ratios) of the business as revealed by the statements shown above.

3.5 Threads Limited manufactures nuts and bolts, which are sold to industrial users. The abbreviated financial statements for 2013 and 2014 are as follows:

Income statements for the year ended 30 June

	2013 £000	2014 £000
Revenue	1,180	1,200
Cost of sales	(680)	(750)
Gross profit	500	450
Operating expenses	(200)	(208)
Depreciation	(66)	(75)
Operating profit	234	167
Interest	(–)	(8)
Profit before taxation	234	159
Taxation	(80)	(48)
Profit for the year	154	111

Statements of financial position as at 30 June

	2013 £000	2014 £000
ASSETS		
Non-current assets		
Property, plant and equipment	702	687
Current assets		
Inventories	148	236
Trade receivables	102	156
Cash	3	4
	253	396
Total assets	955	1,083
EQUITY AND LIABILITIES		
Equity		
Ordinary share capital (£1 shares, fully paid)	500	500
Retained earnings	256	295
	756	795
Non-current liabilities		
Borrowings – bank loan	–	50
Current liabilities		
Trade payables	60	76
Other payables and accruals	18	16
Taxation	40	24
Short-term borrowings (all bank overdraft)	81	122
	199	238
Total equity and liabilities	955	1,083

Dividends were paid on ordinary shares of £70,000 and £72,000 in respect of 2013 and 2014, respectively.

Required:

(a) Calculate the following financial ratios for *both* 2013 and 2014 (using year-end figures for statement of financial position items):

1 return on capital employed
2 operating profit margin
3 gross profit margin
4 current ratio
5 acid test ratio
6 settlement period for trade receivables
7 settlement period for trade payables
8 inventories turnover period.

(b) Comment on the performance of Threads Limited from the viewpoint of a business considering supplying a substantial amount of goods to Threads Limited on usual trade credit terms.

3.6 Genesis Ltd was incorporated three years ago and has grown rapidly since then. The rapid rate of growth has created problems for the business, which the directors have found difficult to deal with. Recently, a firm of management consultants has been asked to help the directors to overcome these problems.

In a preliminary report to the board of directors, the management consultants state: 'Most of the difficulties faced by the business are symptoms of an underlying problem of overtrading.'

The most recent financial statements of the business are set out below.

Income statement for the year ended 31 October

	£000	£000
Revenue		1,640
Cost of sales		
Opening inventories	116	
Purchases	1,260	
	1,376	
Closing inventories	(128)	(1,248)
Gross profit		392
Selling and distribution expenses		(204)
Administration expenses		(92)
Operating profit		96
Interest payable		(44)
Profit before taxation		52
Taxation		(16)
Profit for the year		36

Statement of financial position as at 31 October

	£000
ASSETS	
Non-current assets	
Property, plant and equipment at cost less depreciation	
Land and buildings	442
Fixtures and fittings at cost	116
Motor vans at cost	64
	622
Current assets	
Inventories	128
Trade receivables	104
	232
Total assets	854
EQUITY AND LIABILITIES	
Equity	
Ordinary £0.50 shares	60
General reserve	50
Retained earnings	74
	184
Non-current liabilities	
Borrowings – 10% loan notes (secured)	120
Current liabilities	
Trade payables	184
Taxation	8
Short-term borrowings (all bank overdraft)	358
	550
Total equity and liabilities	854

Notes:

1 All purchases and sales were on credit.
2 A dividend was paid during the year on ordinary shares of £4,000.

Required:

(a) Calculate and discuss five financial ratios that might be used to establish whether the business is overtrading. Do these five ratios suggest that the business is overtrading?

(b) State the ways in which a business may overcome the problem of overtrading.

3.7 The financial statements for Clarrods Ltd are given below for the two years ending 30 June 2013 and 30 June 2014. Clarrods Ltd operates a department store in the centre of a small town.

Income statement for the years ending 30 June

	2013 £000	2014 £000
Sales revenue	2,600	3,500
Cost of sales	(1,560)	(2,350)
Gross profit	1,040	1,150
Wages and salaries	(320)	(350)
Overheads	(260)	(200)
Depreciation	(150)	(250)
Operating profit	310	350
Interest payable	(50)	(50)
Profit before taxation	260	300
Taxation	(105)	(125)
Profit for the year	155	175

Statement of financial position as at 30 June

	2013 £000	2014 £000
ASSETS		
Non-current assets		
Property, plant and equipment	1,265	1,525
Current assets		
Inventories	250	400
Trade receivables	105	145
Cash at bank	380	115
	735	660
Total assets	2,000	2,185
EQUITY AND LIABILITIES		
Equity		
Share capital: £1 shares fully paid	490	490
Share premium	260	260
Retained earnings	350	450
	1,100	1,200
Non-current liabilities		
Borrowings – 10% loan notes	500	500
Current liabilities		
Trade payables	300	375
Other payables	100	110
	400	485
Total equity and liabilities	2,000	2,185

Dividends were paid on ordinary shares of £65,000 and £75,000 in respect of 2013 and 2014, respectively.

Required:

(a) Choose and calculate eight ratios that would be helpful in assessing the performance of Clarrods Ltd. Use end-of-year values and calculate ratios for both 2013 and 2014.

(b) Using the ratios calculated in (a) and any others you consider helpful, comment on the business's performance from the viewpoint of a prospective purchaser of a majority of shares.

Chapter 4

MAKING CAPITAL INVESTMENT DECISIONS

INTRODUCTION

In this chapter we shall look at how businesses can make decisions involving investments in new plant, machinery, buildings and other long-term assets. When making these decisions, businesses should be trying to pursue their key financial objective, which is to maximise the wealth of the owners (shareholders).

Investment appraisal is a very important area for businesses: expensive and far-reaching consequences can flow from bad investment decisions.

Learning outcomes

When you have completed this chapter, you should be able to:

■ Explain the nature and importance of investment decision making.

■ Identify and discuss the four main investment appraisal methods found in practice.

■ Use each method to reach a decision on a particular investment opportunity.

■ Explain the key stages in the investment decision-making process.

THE NATURE OF INVESTMENT DECISIONS

The essential feature of investment decisions is *time*. Investment involves making an outlay of something of economic value, usually cash, at one point in time, which is expected to yield economic benefits to the investor at some other point in time. Usually, the outlay precedes the benefits. Furthermore, the outlay is typically a single large amount while the benefits arrive as a series of smaller amounts over a fairly protracted period.

Investment decisions tend to be of profound importance to the business for the following reasons:

- *Large amounts of resources are often involved*. Many investments made by businesses involve laying out a significant proportion of their total resources. If mistakes are made with the decision, the effects on the business could be significant, if not catastrophic.
- *It is often difficult and/or expensive to bale out of an investment once it has been undertaken.* Investments made by a business are often specific to its needs. A manufacturing business, for example, may invest in a new, custom-designed factory. However, the specialist nature of the factory may lead to it having a limited resale value. If the business found, after having made the investment, that goods produced from the factory had no real market, the only course of action might be to sell it. This could mean that the amount recouped from the investment is much less than its original cost.

Real World 4.1 gives an illustration of a major investment decision by a well-known airline business.

Real World 4.1

Plane common sense?

In July 2011, American Airlines announced the purchase of 200 Boeing 737s and 260 Airbus 320 aircraft. This represents the largest order in aviation history and the new aircraft will be delivered to the business over the period 2013 to 2022. Although the precise cost of the new aircraft was not revealed, it has been estimated to be more than £12 billion.

This level of investment is quite extraordinary, even though American Airlines is the fourth largest airline in the world. The business clearly believes that acquiring the new aircraft will be a profitable move, but how would it have reached this conclusion? Presumably, the likely future benefits from passenger fares and likely future operating costs will have been major inputs to the decision.

Source: Based on information at www.bbc.co.uk, 20 July 2011, and www.telegraph.co.uk, 20 July 2011.

The issues raised by American Airlines' investment will be the main subject of this chapter.

Real World 4.2 indicates the level of annual net investment for a number of randomly selected, well-known UK businesses. We can see that the scale of investment varies from one business to another. (It also tends to vary from one year to another for a particular business.) In nearly all of these businesses the scale of investment was significant, despite the fact that many businesses were cutting back on investment during the economic recession.

The scale of investment by UK businesses

| | Expenditure on additional non-current assets as a percentage of: | |
	Annual sales revenue	End-of-year non-current assets
British Sky Broadcasting plc (television)	10.7	22.4
easyJet plc (airline)	10.3	13.1
Go-Ahead Group plc (transport)	4.3	18.0
J D Wetherspoon plc (pub operator)	10.0	12.1
Marks and Spencer plc (stores)	7.6	13.0
Severn Trent Water plc (water and sewerage)	19.4	5.0
Tate and Lyle plc (sugar and allied products)	3.8	3.3
Wm Morrison Supermarkets plc (supermarkets)	5.0	10.4

Source: Annual Reports of the businesses concerned for the financial year ending in 2012.

Real World 4.2 considers only non-current asset investment. This type of investment, however, often requires significant current asset investment to support it (additional inventories, for example). Thus, the real scale of investment is even greater than indicated above.

When managers are making decisions involving capital investments, what should the decision seek to achieve?

Investment decisions must be consistent with the objectives of the particular organisation. For a private sector business, maximising the wealth of the owners (shareholders) is normally assumed to be the key financial objective.

INVESTMENT APPRAISAL METHODS

Given the importance of investment decisions, it is essential that proper screening of investment proposals takes place. An important part of this screening process is to ensure that appropriate methods of evaluation are used. Research shows that there are basically four methods used by businesses to evaluate investment opportunities:

- accounting rate of return (ARR)
- payback period (PP)
- net present value (NPV)
- internal rate of return (IRR).

It is possible to find businesses that use variants of these four methods. It is also possible to find businesses, particularly smaller ones, that do not use any formal appraisal method but rely instead on the 'gut feeling' of their managers. Most businesses, however, seem to use one (or more) of these four methods.

We will examine each of the four methods but we shall see that only one of them (NPV) offers a wholly logical approach; the other three all have flaws. To help in examining these methods, it would be helpful to see how each would cope with a particular investment opportunity. Let us consider the following example.

Example 4.1

Billingsgate Battery Company has carried out some research that shows that the business could provide a standard service that it has recently developed.

Provision of the service would require investment in a machine that would cost £100,000, payable immediately. Sales of the service would take place throughout the next five years. At the end of that time, it is estimated that the machine could be sold for £20,000.

Inflows and outflows from sales of the service would be expected to be as follows:

Time		£000
Immediately	Cost of machine	(100)
1 year's time	Operating profit before depreciation	20
2 years' time	Operating profit before depreciation	40
3 years' time	Operating profit before depreciation	60
4 years' time	Operating profit before depreciation	60
5 years' time	Operating profit before depreciation	20
5 years' time	Disposal proceeds from the machine	20

Note that, broadly speaking, the operating profit before deducting depreciation (that is, before non-cash items) equals the net amount of cash flowing into the business. Broadly, apart from depreciation, all of this business's expenses cause cash to flow out of the business. Sales revenues tend to lead to cash flowing in. Expenses tend to lead to it flowing out. For the time being, we shall assume that working capital – which is made up of inventories, trade receivables and trade payables – remains constant. This means that operating profit before depreciation will tend to equal the net cash inflow.

To simplify matters, we shall assume that the cash from sales and for the expenses of providing the service is received and paid, respectively, at the end of each year. This is clearly unlikely to be true in real life. Money will have to be paid to employees (for salaries and wages) on a weekly or a monthly basis. Customers will pay within a month or two of buying the service. Yet making the assumption probably does not lead to a serious distortion. It is a simplifying assumption, that is often made in real life, and it will make things more straightforward for us now. We should be clear, however, that there is nothing about any of the four methods that *demands* that this assumption is made.

Having set up the example, we shall now go on to consider how each of the appraisal methods works.

ACCOUNTING RATE OF RETURN (ARR)

The first method that we shall consider is the **accounting rate of return (ARR)**. This method takes the average accounting operating profit that the investment will generate and expresses it as a percentage of the average investment made over the life of the project. Thus:

$$ARR = \frac{\text{Average annual operating profit}}{\text{Average investment to earn that profit}} \times 100\%$$

We can see from the equation that, to calculate the ARR, we need to deduce two pieces of information about the particular project:

- the annual average operating profit, and
- the average investment.

In our example, the average annual operating profit *before depreciation* over the five years is £40,000 (that is, £(20 + 40 + 60 + 60 + 20)000 ÷ 5). Assuming 'straight-line' depreciation (that is, equal annual amounts), the annual depreciation charge will be £16,000 (that is, £(100,000 − 20,000)/5). Thus, the average annual operating profit *after depreciation* is £24,000 (that is, £40,000 − £16,000).

The average investment over the five years can be calculated as follows:

$$\text{Average investment} = \frac{\text{Cost of machine} + \text{Disposal value*}}{2}$$

$$= \frac{\text{£}100,000 + \text{£}20,000}{2}$$

$$= \text{£}60,000$$

*Note: To find the average investment, we are simply adding together the value of the amount invested at the beginning and end of the investment period and dividing by two.

Thus, the ARR of the investment is:

$$ARR = \frac{\text{£}24,000}{\text{£}60,000} \times 100\% = 40\%$$

The following decision rules apply when using ARR:

- For a project to be acceptable, it must achieve a target ARR as a minimum.
- Where a choice must be made between two or more competing projects, which all achieve the target ARR minimum rate, the one with the higher (or highest) ARR should be selected.

Thus, to decide whether the 40 per cent return is acceptable, we need to compare this percentage return with the minimum rate required by the business.

Activity 4.2

Chaotic Industries is considering an investment in a fleet of ten delivery vans to take its products to customers. The vans will cost £15,000 each to buy, payable immediately. The annual running costs are expected to total £50,000 for each van (including the driver's salary). The vans are expected to operate successfully for six years, at the end of which period they will all have to be sold, with disposal proceeds expected to be about £3,000 a van. At present, the business outsources transport, for all of its deliveries, to a commercial carrier. It is expected that this carrier will charge a total of £530,000 each year for the next six years to undertake the deliveries.

What is the ARR of buying the vans? (Note that cost savings are as relevant a benefit from an investment as are net cash inflows.)

→

The vans will save the business £30,000 a year (that is, £530,000 − (£50,000 × 10)), before depreciation, in total. Thus, the inflows and outflows will be:

Time		£000
Immediately	Cost of vans (10 × £15,000)	(150)
1 year's time	Saving before depreciation	30
2 years' time	Saving before depreciation	30
3 years' time	Saving before depreciation	30
4 years' time	Saving before depreciation	30
5 years' time	Saving before depreciation	30
6 years' time	Saving before depreciation	30
6 years' time	Disposal proceeds from the vans (10 × £3,000)	30

The total annual depreciation expense (assuming a straight-line method) will be £20,000 (that is, (£150,000 − £30,000)/6). Thus, the average annual saving, *after depreciation*, is £10,000 (that is, £30,000 − £20,000).

The average investment will be:

$$\text{Average investment} = \frac{£150,000 + £30,000}{2} = £90,000$$

and the ARR of the investment is:

$$\text{ARR} = \frac{£10,000}{£90,000} \times 100\% = 11.1\%$$

ARR and ROCE

In essence, ARR and the return on capital employed (ROCE) ratio take the same approach to measuring business performance. Both relate operating profit to the investment required to generate that profit. However, ROCE assesses the overall performance of the business *after* it has performed, while ARR assesses the potential performance of a particular investment *before* it has performed.

We saw that investments must achieve a minimum target ARR. Given the link between ARR and ROCE, this target could be based on some measure of ROCE. It could be based on the industry-average ROCE or the past ROCE of the business, for example.

The link between ARR and ROCE strengthens the case for adopting ARR as the appropriate method of investment appraisal. ROCE is a widely used measure of profitability and some businesses express their financial objective in terms of a target ROCE. It may seem logical, therefore, to use a method of investment appraisal that is consistent with this overall measure of business performance. A secondary point in favour of ARR is that it provides a result expressed in percentage terms, which many managers seem to prefer.

Problems with ARR

ARR suffers from a major defect as a means of assessing investment opportunities. To illustrate this defect, consider three competing projects whose profits are shown below. All three involve investment in a machine that is expected to have no residual value at the end of the five years. Note that all the projects have the same total operating profits after depreciation over the five years.

Time		Project A £000	Project B £000	Project C £000
Immediately	Cost of machine	(160)	(160)	(160)
1 year's time	Operating profit after depreciation	20	10	160
2 years' time	Operating profit after depreciation	40	10	10
3 years' time	Operating profit after depreciation	60	10	10
4 years' time	Operating profit after depreciation	60	10	10
5 years' time	Operating profit after depreciation	20	160	10

Activity 4.3

Can you figure out what the major defect is? (*Hint*: It is not concerned with the ability of the decision maker to forecast future events, though this too can be a problem. Try to remember the essential feature of investment decisions, which we identified at the beginning of this chapter.)

The problem with ARR is that it ignores the time factor. In the example mentioned above, exactly the same ARR would have been computed for each of the three projects.

Since the same total operating profit over the five years (£200,000) arises in all three of these projects, and the average investment in each project is £80,000 (that is, £160,000/2), each project will give rise to the same ARR of 50 per cent (that is, £40,000/£80,000).

To maximise the wealth of the owners, a manager faced with a choice between the three projects set out in Activity 4.3 should select Project C. This is because most of the benefits arise within 12 months of making the initial investment. Project A would rank second and Project B would finish a poor third. Any appraisal technique that is incapable of distinguishing between these three situations must be seriously flawed. We will look at why timing is so important later in the chapter.

The ARR method suffers from further problems, which are discussed below.

Use of average investment

Using the average investment in calculating ARR can lead to daft results. Example 4.2 below illustrates the kind of problem that can arise.

Example 4.2

George put forward an investment proposal to his boss. The business uses ARR to assess investment proposals using a minimum 'hurdle' rate of 27 per cent. Details of the proposal were as follows:

Cost of equipment	£200,000
Estimated residual value of equipment	£40,000
Average annual operating profit before depreciation	£48,000
Estimated life of project	10 years
Annual straight-line depreciation charge	£16,000 (that is, (£200,000 – £40,000)/10)

The ARR of the project will be:

$$ARR = \frac{£48,000 - £16,000}{(£200,000 + £40,000)/2} \times 100\% = 26.7\%$$

The boss rejected George's proposal because it failed to achieve an ARR of at least 27 per cent. Although George was disappointed, he realised that there was still hope. In fact, all the business had to do was to give away the piece of equipment at the end of its useful life rather than sell it. The residual value of the equipment then became zero and the annual depreciation charge became $((£200,000 - £0)/10) = £20,000$ a year. The revised ARR calculation was then as follows:

$$ARR = \frac{£48,000 - £20,000}{(£200,000 + 0)/2} \times 100\% = 28\%$$

Use of accounting profit

We have seen that ARR is based on the use of accounting profit. When measuring performance over the whole life of a project, however, it is cash flows rather than accounting profits that are important. Cash is the ultimate measure of the economic wealth generated by an investment. This is because it is cash that is used to acquire resources and for distribution to owners. Accounting profit is more appropriate for reporting achievement on a periodic basis. It is a useful measure of productive effort for a relatively short period, such as a year or half-year. Thus, it is a question of 'horses for courses'.

Target ARR

We saw earlier a target ARR against which to assess investment opportunities that must be chosen. This cannot be objectively determined and so will depend on the judgement of managers. The target ARR may therefore vary over time and may vary between businesses.

Competing investments

The ARR method can create problems when considering competing investments of different size. Consider Activity 4.4 below.

Activity 4.4

Sinclair Wholesalers plc is considering opening a new sales outlet in Coventry. Two possible sites have been identified for the new outlet. Site A has an area of 30,000 sq m. It will require an average investment of £6 million and will produce an average operating profit of £600,000 a year. Site B has an area of 20,000 sq m. It will require an average investment of £4 million and will produce an average operating profit of £500,000 a year.

What is the ARR of each investment opportunity? Which site would you select and why?

The ARR of Site A is £600,000/£6m = 10 per cent. The ARR of Site B is £500,000/£4m = 12.5 per cent. Thus, Site B has the higher ARR. In terms of the absolute operating profit generated, however, Site A is the more attractive. If the ultimate objective is to increase the wealth of the shareholders of Sinclair Wholesalers plc, it would be better to choose Site A even though the percentage return is lower. It is the absolute size of the return rather than the relative (percentage) size that is important. This is a general problem of using comparative measures, such as percentages, when the objective is measured in absolute terms, such as an amount of money.

Real World 4.3 illustrates how using percentage measures can lead to confusion.

Increasing road capacity by sleight of hand

During the 1970s, the Mexican government wanted to increase the capacity of a major four-lane road. It came up with the idea of repainting the lane markings so that there were six narrower lanes occupying the same space as four wider ones had previously done. This increased the capacity of the road by 50 per cent (that is, $^2/_4 \times 100$). A tragic outcome of the narrower lanes was an increase in deaths from road accidents. A year later the Mexican government had the six narrower lanes changed back to the original four wider ones. This reduced the capacity of the road by 33 per cent (that is, $^2/_6 \times 100$). The Mexican government reported that, overall, it had increased the capacity of the road by 17 per cent (that is, 50% – 33%), despite the fact that its real capacity was identical to that which it had been originally. The confusion arose because each of the two percentages (50 per cent and 33 per cent) is based on different bases (four and six).

Source: G. Gigerenzer, *Reckoning with Risk*, Penguin, 2002.

PAYBACK PERIOD (PP)

The second approach to appraising possible investments is the **payback period (PP)**. This is the time taken for an initial investment to be repaid out of the net cash inflows from a project. As the PP method takes time into account, it appears at first glance to overcome a key weakness of the ARR method.

Let us consider PP in the context of the Billingsgate Battery example. We should recall that the project's cash flows are:

Time		£000
Immediately	Cost of machine	(100)
1 year's time	Operating profit before depreciation	20
2 years' time	Operating profit before depreciation	40
3 years' time	Operating profit before depreciation	60
4 years' time	Operating profit before depreciation	60
5 years' time	Operating profit before depreciation	20
5 years' time	Disposal proceeds	20

Note that all of these figures are amounts of cash to be paid or received (we saw earlier that operating profit before depreciation is a rough measure of the cash flows from the project).

The payback period can be derived by calculating the cumulative cash flows as follows:

Time		Net cash flows £000	Cumulative cash flows £000	
Immediately	Cost of machine	(100)	(100)	
1 year's time	Operating profit before depreciation	20	(80)	(−100 + 20)
2 years' time	Operating profit before depreciation	40	(40)	(−80 + 40)
3 years' time	Operating profit before depreciation	60	20	(−40 + 60)
4 years' time	Operating profit before depreciation	60	80	(20 + 60)
5 years' time	Operating profit before depreciation	20	100	(80 + 20)
5 years' time	Disposal proceeds	20	120	(100 + 20)

We can see that the cumulative cash flows become positive at the end of the third year. Thus, if we assume that cash flows occur at the year ends, the investment will take three years for the initial outlay to be paid back. If, however, we assume that cash flows occur evenly over the year, the payback period will be:

$$2 \text{ years} + (^{40}/_{60}) \text{ years} = 2^2/_3 \text{ years}$$

where the top part of the fraction (40) represents the cash flow needed at the beginning of the third year to repay the initial outlay and the bottom part (60) represents the projected cash flow during the third year.

The following decision rules apply when using PP:

■ For a project to be acceptable, it should have a payback period shorter than a maximum payback period set by the business.
■ If there are two (or more) competing projects with payback periods that are shorter than the maximum payback period, the project with the shorter (or shortest) payback period should be selected.

Thus, if Billingsgate Battery project had a maximum payback period requirement of four years, it should be undertaken, while if it had a maximum payback period requirement of two years it should not.

Activity 4.5

What is the payback period of the Chaotic Industries project from Activity 4.2?

The inflows and outflows are expected to be:

Time		Net cash flows £000	Cumulative net cash flows £000	
Immediately	Cost of vans	(150)	(150)	
1 year's time	Saving before depreciation	30	(120)	(−150 + 30)
2 years' time	Saving before depreciation	30	(90)	(−120 + 30)
3 years' time	Saving before depreciation	30	(60)	(−90 + 30)
4 years' time	Saving before depreciation	30	(30)	(−60 + 30)
5 years' time	Saving before depreciation	30	0	(−30 + 30)
6 years' time	Saving before depreciation	30	30	(0 + 30)
6 years' time	Disposal proceeds from the vans	30	60	(30 + 30)

The payback period here is five years. It is not until the end of the fifth year that the vans will pay for themselves out of the savings that they are expected to generate.

The PP method views projects that recoup their investment quickly as preferable to those that do not. In other words, it emphasises liquidity. Where a business has liquidity problems, a short payback period for a project may seem attractive.

Problems with PP

The PP method takes more account of the timing of the cash flows than the ARR method. It is not, however, a complete answer to the problem. To understand why this is the case, consider the following cash flows arising from three competing projects.

Time		Project 1 £000	Project 2 £000	Project 3 £000
Immediately	Cost of machine	(200)	(200)	(200)
1 year's time	Operating profit before depreciation	70	20	70
2 years' time	Operating profit before depreciation	60	20	100
3 years' time	Operating profit before depreciation	70	160	30
4 years' time	Operating profit before depreciation	80	30	200
5 years' time	Operating profit before depreciation	50	20	440
5 years' time	Disposal proceeds	40	10	20

Activity 4.6

Can you see from the above why the PP method is not a complete answer to the problem concerning the timing of cash flows?

The PP for each project is three years and so all three projects would be regarded as equally acceptable. This conclusion, however, does not take full account of the timing of cash flows. It does not distinguish between those projects that pay back significant amounts early within the three-year payback period and those that do not.

The PP method also ignores cash flows after the payback period. Managers concerned with increasing owners' wealth would prefer Project 3 because the cash inflows will be received earlier. Most of the initial cost of making the investment will be repaid by the end of the second year. Furthermore, the cash inflows are greater in total.

The cumulative cash flows of each project in Activity 4.6 are set out in Figure 4.1.

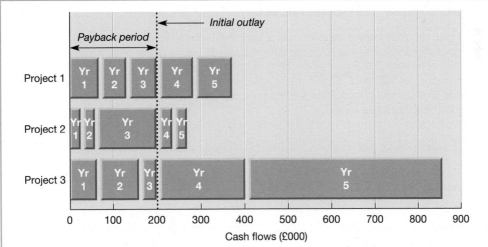

The payback method of investment appraisal would view Projects 1, 2 and 3 as being equally attractive. In doing so, the method completely ignores the fact that Project 3 provides most of the payback cash earlier in the three-year period and goes on to generate large benefits in later years.

Figure 4.1 Cumulative cash flows for each project in Activity 4.6

Source: P. Atrill and E. McLaney, *Accounting: An Introduction*, 5th edn, Financial Times Prentice Hall, 2009.

There are further problems with the PP method, which are considered below.

Relevant information

We saw earlier that the PP method is simply concerned with how quickly the initial investment can be recouped. While this neatly avoids the practical problems of forecasting cash flows over a long period, it means that not all relevant information will be taken into account. Cash flows arising beyond the payback period will be ignored.

Risk

By favouring projects with a short payback period, the PP method provides a way of dealing with risk. However, it offers a fairly crude approach to the problem. It deals only with the risk that the project will end earlier than expected. There are many other risk areas. For example, what about the risk that product demand will be less than expected? More systematic approaches to dealing with risk are available and we will look at these in the next chapter.

Wealth maximisation

Although the PP method takes some note of the timing of project costs and benefits, it is not concerned with maximising the wealth of the business owners. Rather, it favours projects that pay for themselves quickly.

Target payback period

Managers must decide upon a maximum acceptable payback period. When doing so, they confront a similar problem to the one arising when setting a target ARR. No objective basis can be used to determine this period: it is simply a matter of judgement.

Real World 4.4 describes the payback period relating to the opening of a new store.

Real World 4.4

The Next investment

Next plc, the well-known retailer, has a thriving homeware division. Since 2001, it has grown at a steady compound average rate of about 20 per cent and now accounts for about one-fifth of its sales. To capitalise on the trend, Next plc opened its first dedicated Home and Garden store in July 2011. This is an experiment with a new store format and so management is wise to take it slow. The payback period will be 25 months, one-third longer than that of a clothing store.

Source: Adapted from Lex column (2011) 'Next: Cyber shopping', www.ft.com, 16 December.
© The Financial Times Limited 2012. All Rights Reserved.

NET PRESENT VALUE (NPV)

From what we have seen so far, it seems that to make sensible investment decisions, we need a method of appraisal that both:

- considers *all* of the cash flows for each investment opportunity, and
- makes a logical allowance for the *timing* of those cash flows.

The third of the four methods of investment appraisal, the **net present value (NPV)** method, provides us with exactly this.

Consider the Billingsgate Battery example's cash flows, which we should recall are as follows:

Time		£000
Immediately	Cost of machine	(100)
1 year's time	Operating profit before depreciation	20
2 years' time	Operating profit before depreciation	40
3 years' time	Operating profit before depreciation	60
4 years' time	Operating profit before depreciation	60
5 years' time	Operating profit before depreciation	20
5 years' time	Disposal proceeds	20

Given a financial objective of maximising owners' wealth, it would be easy to assess this investment if all cash inflows and outflows were to occur immediately. It would then simply be a matter of adding up the cash inflows (total £220,000) and comparing them with the cash outflows (£100,000). This would lead us to conclude that the project should go ahead because the owners would be better off by £120,000. It is, of course, not as easy as this because time is involved. The cash outflow will occur immediately, whereas the cash inflows will arise at different points in the future.

Why does time matter?

Time is an important issue because people do not normally see an amount paid out now as equivalent in value to the same amount being received in a year's time. Thus, if we were offered £100 in one year's time in exchange for paying out £100 now, we would not be interested, unless we wished to do someone a favour.

Activity 4.7

Why would we see £100 to be received in a year's time as not equal in value to £100 to be paid immediately? (There are basically three reasons.)

The reasons are:

- interest lost
- risk
- inflation.

We shall now take a closer look at these three reasons in turn.

Interest lost

If we are to be deprived of the opportunity to spend our money for a year, we could equally well be deprived of its use by placing it on deposit in a bank or building society. By doing this, we could have our money back at the end of the year along with some interest earned. This interest, which is forgone by not placing our money on deposit, represents an *opportunity cost*. It arises where one course of action deprives us of the opportunity to derive benefit from an alternative course of action.

An investment must exceed the opportunity cost of the funds invested if it is to be worthwhile. Thus, if Billingsgate Battery Company sees putting the money in the bank on deposit as the alternative to investment in the machine, the return from investing in the machine must exceed the return from investing in the bank. If this is not the case, there is no reason to make the investment.

Risk

All investments expose their investors to risk. Thus, when Billingsgate Battery Company buys a machine on the strength of estimates made before its purchase, it must accept that things may not turn out as expected.

It is important to remember that the purchase decision must be taken *before* any of these things are known. Thus it is only after the machine has been purchased that we find out whether, say, the forecast level of sales is going to be achieved. We can study reports and analyses of the market. We can commission sophisticated market surveys and advertise widely to promote sales. All these may give us more confidence in the likely outcome. Ultimately, however, we must decide whether to accept the risk that things will not turn out as expected in exchange for the opportunity to generate profits.

Real World 4.5 gives some impression of the extent to which businesses believe that investment outcomes turn out as expected.

Real World 4.5

Size matters

Senior finance managers of 99 Cambridgeshire manufacturing businesses were asked how their investments were performing compared with expectations at the time of making the investment decision. The results, broken down according to business size, are set out below.

Actual performance relative to expectations	Size of business			
	Large %	Medium %	Small %	All %
Underperformed	8	14	32	14
Performed as expected	82	72	68	77
Overperformed	10	14	0	9

It seems that smaller businesses are much more likely to get it wrong than medium-size or larger businesses. This may be because small businesses are often younger and therefore less experienced both in the techniques of forecasting and in managing investment projects. They are also likely to have less financial expertise. It also seems that small businesses have a distinct bias towards over-optimism and do not take full account of the possibility that things will turn out worse than expected.

Source: M. Baddeley, 'Unpacking the black box: An econometric analysis of investment strategies in real world firms', CEPP Working Paper No. 08/05, University of Cambridge, 2005, p. 14.

We saw in Chapter 1 that people normally expect greater returns in exchange for taking on greater risk. So, when considering the Billingsgate Battery Company's investment opportunity, it is not enough to say that this business should buy the machine providing the expected returns are higher than those from investing in a bank deposit. It should expect much greater returns than the bank deposit interest rate because of the much greater risk involved. The logical equivalent of investing in the machine would be an investment of similar risk. Determining how risky a particular project is, and therefore how large the risk premium should be, is a difficult task. We will consider this in more detail in the next chapter.

Inflation

If we are to be deprived of £100 for a year, when we come to spend that money it will not buy the same amount of goods and services as it would have done a year earlier. Generally, we shall not be able to buy as many tins of baked beans or loaves of bread or bus tickets as before. This is because of the loss in the purchasing power of money, or inflation, which occurs over time. Investors will expect to be compensated for this loss of purchasing power. This will be on top of a return that takes account of what could be gained from an alternative investment of similar risk.

In practice, interest rates observable in the market tend to take inflation into account. Thus, rates offered to building society and bank depositors include an allowance for the expected rate of inflation.

What will logical investors do?

To summarise, logical investors seeking to increase their wealth will invest only when they believe they will be adequately compensated for the loss of interest, for the loss in the purchasing power of money invested and for the risk that the expected returns may not materialise. This normally involves checking to see whether the proposed investment will yield a return greater than the basic rate of interest (which will include an allowance for inflation) plus an appropriate risk premium.

These three factors (interest lost, risk and inflation) are set out in Figure 4.2.

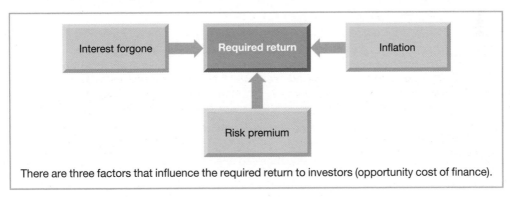

There are three factors that influence the required return to investors (opportunity cost of finance).

Figure 4.2 Factors influencing the return required by investors from a project
Source: P. Atrill and E. McLaney, *Accounting: An Introduction*, 5th edn, Financial Times Prentice Hall, 2009.

Dealing with the time value of money

We saw above that money has a *time value*: that is, £100 received today is not regarded as equivalent in value to £100 received at some future date. We cannot, therefore, simply compare the cash inflows with cash outflows for an investment where they arise at different points in time. Each of these cash flows must be expressed in similar terms. Only then can a direct comparison can be made.

To illustrate how this can be done, let us return to the Billingsgate Battery Company example. We should recall that the cash flows expected from this investment are:

Time		£000
Immediately	Cost of machine	(100)
1 year's time	Operating profit before depreciation	20
2 years' time	Operating profit before depreciation	40
3 years' time	Operating profit before depreciation	60
4 years' time	Operating profit before depreciation	60
5 years' time	Operating profit before depreciation	20
5 years' time	Disposal proceeds	20

Let us assume that the business could make an alternative investment with similar risk and obtain a return of 20 per cent a year.

Activity 4.9

Given that the Billingsgate Battery Company could invest its money at a rate of 20 per cent a year, what is the present (immediate) value of the expected first-year receipt of £20,000? In other words, if instead of having to wait a year for the £20,000, and therefore be deprived of the opportunity to invest it at 20 per cent, the business could have some money now, what sum would be equivalent to getting £20,000 in one year's time?

The business should be happy to accept a lower amount immediately than if it had to wait a year. This is because it could invest this amount at 20 per cent (in the alternative project). Logically, the business should be prepared to accept the amount that, with a year's income, will grow to £20,000. If we call this amount PV (for present value) we can say:

$$PV + (PV \times 20\%) = £20,000$$

– that is, the amount plus income from investing the amount for the year equals the £20,000. If we rearrange this equation we find:

$$PV \times (1 + 0.2) = £20,000$$

(Note that 0.2 is the same as 20 per cent, but expressed as a decimal.) Further rearranging gives:

$$PV = £20,000/(1 + 0.2) = £16,667$$

Thus, logical investors who have the opportunity to invest at 20 per cent a year would not mind whether they have £16,667 now or £20,000 in a year's time. In other words, £16,667 represents the *present value* of £20,000 received in one year's time.

We can make a more general statement about the PV of a particular cash flow. It is:

PV of the cash flow of year *n* = actual cash flow of year *n* divided by $(1 + r)^n$

where *n* is the year of the cash flow (that is, how many years into the future) and *r* is the opportunity financing cost expressed as a decimal (instead of as a percentage).

If we derive the present value (PV) of each of the cash flows associated with Billingsgate's machine investment, we can easily make the direct comparison between the cost of making the investment (£100,000) and the subsequent benefits to be derived in years 1 to 5. We have already seen how this works for the £20,000 inflow for year 1. For year 2 the calculation would be:

$$\text{PV of year 2 cash flow (that is, £40,000)} = £40,000/(1 + 0.2)^2 = £40,000/(1.2)^2$$
$$= £40,000/1.44 = £27,778$$

Thus the present value of the £40,000 to be received in two years' time is £27,778.

Activity 4.10

See whether you can show that an investor would find £27,778, receivable now, equally acceptable to receiving £40,000 in two years' time, assuming that there is a 20 per cent investment opportunity.

To answer this activity, we simply apply the principles of *compounding*. Income earned is reinvested and then added to the initial investment to derive its future value. Thus:

	£
Amount available for immediate investment	27,778
Income for year 1 (20% × 27,778)	5,556
	33,334
Income for year 2 (20% × 33,334)	6,667
	40,001

(The extra £1 is only a rounding error.)

Since the investor can turn £27,778 into £40,000 in two years, these amounts are equivalent. That is, £27,778 is the present value of £40,000 receivable after two years (given a 20 per cent cost of finance).

Calculating the net present value

Now let us calculate the present values of all of the cash flows associated with the Billingsgate machine project and from them, the *net present value* of the project as a whole.

The relevant cash flows and calculations are as follows:

Time	Cash flow £000	Calculation of PV	PV £000
Immediately (time 0)	(100)	*(100)/(1 + 0.2)^0	(100.00)
1 year's time	20	20/(1 + 0.2)^1	16.67
2 years' time	40	40/(1 + 0.2)^2	27.78
3 years' time	60	60/(1 + 0.2)^3	34.72
4 years' time	60	60/(1 + 0.2)^4	28.94
5 years' time	20	20/(1 + 0.2)^5	8.04
5 years' time	20	20/(1 + 0.2)^5	8.04
Net present value (NPV)			24.19

*Note that $(1 + 0.2)^0 = 1$.

Once again, we must decide whether the machine project is acceptable to the business. To help us, the following decision rules for NPV should be applied:

■ If the NPV is positive, the project should be accepted; if it is negative, the project should be rejected.
■ If there are two (or more) competing projects that have positive NPVs, the project with the higher (or highest) NPV should be selected.

In this case, the NPV is positive, so we should accept the project and buy the machine. The reasoning behind this decision rule is quite straightforward. Investing in the machine will make the business, and its owners, £24,190 better off than they would be by taking up the next best available opportunity. The gross benefits from investing in this machine are worth a total of £124,190 today. Since the business can 'buy' these benefits for just £100,000 today, the investment should be made. If, however, the present value of the gross benefits were below £100,000, it would be less than the cost of 'buying' those benefits and the opportunity should therefore be rejected.

Activity 4.11

What is the *maximum* the Billingsgate Battery Company would be prepared to pay for the machine, given the potential benefits of owning it?

The business would logically be prepared to pay up to £124,190 since the wealth of the owners of the business would be increased up to this price – although the business would prefer to pay as little as possible.

Using present value tables

To deduce each PV in the Billingsgate Battery Company project, we took the relevant cash flow and multiplied it by $1/(1 + r)^n$. There is a slightly different way to do this. Tables exist (called present value tables, or discount tables) that show values of this discount factor for a range of values of r and n. Such a table appears in Appendix A on pp. 555–556. Take a look at it.

Look at the column for 20 per cent and the row for one year. We find that the factor is 0.833. This means that the PV of a cash flow of £1 receivable in one year is £0.833. So the present value of a cash flow of £20,000 receivable in one year's time is £16,660 (that is, 0.833 × £20,000). This is the same result, ignoring rounding errors, as we found earlier by using the equation.

Activity 4.12

What is the NPV of the Chaotic Industries project from Activity 4.2, assuming a 15 per cent opportunity cost of finance (discount rate)? (Use the table in Appendix A.)

Remember that the inflows and outflow are expected to be:

Time		£000
Immediately	Cost of vans	(150)
1 year's time	Saving before depreciation	30
2 years' time	Saving before depreciation	30
3 years' time	Saving before depreciation	30
4 years' time	Saving before depreciation	30
5 years' time	Saving before depreciation	30
6 years' time	Saving before depreciation	30
6 years' time	Disposal proceeds from the vans	30

The calculation of the NPV of the project is as follows:

Time	Cash flows £000	Discount factor (15%)	Present value £000
Immediately	(150)	1.000	(150.00)
1 year's time	30	0.870	26.10
2 years' time	30	0.756	22.68
3 years' time	30	0.658	19.74
4 years' time	30	0.572	17.16
5 years' time	30	0.497	14.91
6 years' time	30	0.432	12.96
6 years' time	30	0.432	12.96
		NPV	(23.49)

Activity 4.13

How would you interpret this result?

The project has a negative NPV. This means that the present values of the benefits from the investment are worth less than the initial outlay. Any amount up to £126,510 (the present value of the benefits) would be worth paying, but not £150,000.

The table in Appendix A shows how the value of £1 diminishes as its receipt goes further into the future. Assuming an opportunity cost of finance of 20 per cent a year, £1 to be received immediately, obviously, has a present value of £1. However, as the time before it is to be received increases, the present value diminishes significantly, as shown in Figure 4.3.

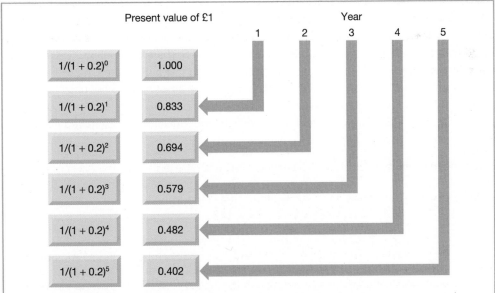

The present value of a future receipt (or payment) of £1 depends on how far in the future it will occur. Those that occur in the near future will have a larger present value than those occurring at a more distant point in time.

Figure 4.3 Present value of £1 receivable at various times in the future, assuming an annual financing cost of 20 per cent

The discount rate and the cost of capital

We have seen that the appropriate discount rate to use in NPV assessments is the opportunity cost of finance. This is, in effect, the cost to the business of the finance needed to fund the investment. It will normally be the cost of a mixture of funds (shareholders' funds and borrowings) employed by the business and is often referred to as the cost of capital. We shall refer to it as cost of capital from now on. The way in which we determine the cost of capital for a business will be considered in detail in Chapter 8.

WHY NPV IS BETTER

From what we have seen, NPV offers a better approach to appraising investment opportunities than either ARR or PP. This is because it fully takes account of each of the following:

■ *The timing of the cash flows*. By discounting the various cash flows associated with each project according to when they arise, NPV takes account of the time value of money. Furthermore, as the discounting process takes account of the opportunity cost of capital, the net benefit *after* financing costs have been met is identified (as the NPV of the project).
■ *The whole of the relevant cash flows*. NPV includes *all* of the relevant cash flows. They are treated differently according to their date of occurrence, but they are all taken into account. Thus, they all have an influence on the decision.
■ *The objectives of the business*. NPV is the only method of appraisal in which the output of the analysis has a direct bearing on the wealth of the owners of the business. Positive NPVs enhance wealth; negative ones reduce it. Since we assume that private sector businesses seek to increase owners' wealth, NPV is superior to the other two methods discussed.

NPV and economic value

NPV can provide the basis for valuing an *economic asset*. This is any asset capable of yielding financial benefits and will include such things as equity shares and loans. The *economic value* of this type of asset will depend on the net benefits that it generates. It can be derived by adding together the discounted (present) values of the asset's future net cash flows.

Real World 4.6 describes a decision by two well-known US mobile phone businesses (MetroPCS and T-Mobile) to merge their operations and identifies the estimated NPV of the financial benefits that are expected to result.

Real World 4.6

On the same wave length

The merger will give T-Mobile USA the scale and spectrum to compete more effectively with its larger US rivals, Verizon Wireless, AT&T Mobility and Sprint Nextel. The combination will also enable the company to build a broader 4G network with greater capacity using LTE technology. The combined company will have nearly $25 billion in annual revenues and projected earnings of $6.3 billion before interest, depreciation and amortisation. In combining the two companies T-Mobile USA is projecting between $6 billion and $7 billion in net present value of savings and synergies.

 Source: Extract from Taylor, P. and Gelles, D. (2012) 'Deutsche Telekom backs MetroPCS takeover', www.ft.com, 3 October.
© The Financial Times Limited 2012. All Rights Reserved.

INTERNAL RATE OF RETURN (IRR)

This is the last of the four major methods of investment appraisal found in practice. It is closely related to the NPV method in that both involve discounting future cash flows. The **internal rate of return (IRR)** of an investment is the discount rate that, when applied to its future cash flows, will produce an NPV of precisely zero. In essence, it represents the yield from an investment opportunity.

Activity 4.14

When we discounted the cash flows of the Billingsgate Battery Company machine project at 20 per cent, we found that the NPV was a positive figure of £24,190 (see p. 141). What does the NPV of the machine project tell us about the rate of return that the investment will yield for the business (that is, the project's IRR)?

As the NPV is positive when discounting at 20 per cent, it implies that the project's rate of return is more than 20 per cent. The fact that the NPV is a pretty large amount implies that the actual rate of return is quite a lot above 20 per cent.

IRR cannot usually be calculated directly. Iteration (trial and error) is the approach normally adopted. Doing this manually can be fairly laborious. Fortunately, computer spreadsheet packages can do this with ease.

Despite it being laborious, we shall now derive the IRR for the Billingsgate project manually. We shall increase the size of the discount rate to reduce NPV, because a higher discount rate gives a lower discounted figure.

Let us try a higher rate, say 30 per cent, and see what happens.

Time	Cash flow £000	Discount factor 30%	PV £000
Immediately (time 0)	(100)	1.000	(100.00)
1 year's time	20	0.769	15.38
2 years' time	40	0.592	23.68
3 years' time	60	0.455	27.30
4 years' time	60	0.350	21.00
5 years' time	20	0.269	5.38
5 years' time	20	0.269	5.38
		NPV	(1.88)

By increasing the discount rate from 20 per cent to 30 per cent, we have reduced the NPV from £24,190 (positive) to £1,880 (negative). Since the IRR is the discount rate that will give us an NPV of exactly zero, we can conclude that the IRR of Billingsgate Battery Company's machine project is very slightly below 30 per cent. Further trials could lead us to the exact rate, but there is probably not much point, given the likely inaccuracy of the cash flow estimates. For most practical purposes, it is good enough to say that the IRR is about 30 per cent.

The relationship between the NPV method discussed earlier and the IRR is shown graphically in Figure 4.4 using the information relating to the Billingsgate Battery Company.

In Figure 4.4, if the discount rate is equal to zero, the NPV will be the sum of the net cash flows. In other words, no account is taken of the time value of money. However, as the discount rate increases there is a corresponding decrease in the NPV of the project. When the NPV line crosses the horizontal axis there will be a zero NPV. That point represents the IRR.

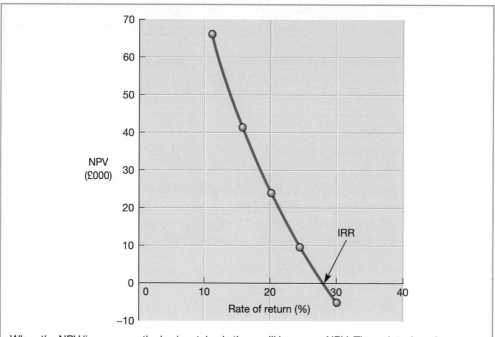

When the NPV line crosses the horizontal axis there will be a zero NPV. The point where it crosses is the IRR.

Figure 4.4 The relationship between the NPV and IRR methods

Source: P. Atrill and E. McLaney, *Accounting: An Introduction*, 5th edn, Financial Times Prentice Hall, 2009.

Activity 4.15

What is the internal rate of return of the Chaotic Industries project from Activity 4.2?

(*Hint*: Remember that you already know the NPV of this project at 15 per cent (from Activity 4.12).)

Since we know that at a 15 per cent discount rate, the NPV is a relatively large negative figure, our next trial is using a lower discount rate, say 10 per cent:

Time	Cash flows £000	Discount factor 10%	Present value £000
Immediately	(150)	1.000	(150.00)
1 year's time	30	0.909	27.27
2 years' time	30	0.826	24.78
3 years' time	30	0.751	22.53
4 years' time	30	0.683	20.49
5 years' time	30	0.621	18.63
6 years' time	30	0.564	16.92
6 years' time	30	0.564	16.92
		NPV	(2.46)

This figure is close to zero NPV. However, the NPV is still negative and so the precise IRR will be a little below 10 per cent.

We could undertake further trials to derive the precise IRR. If done manually, this can be quite time-consuming. We can, however, get an acceptable approximation to the answer fairly quickly by first calculating the change in NPV arising from a 1 per cent change in the discount rate. This is achieved by taking the difference between the two trials (that is, 15 per cent and 10 per cent) that have already been carried out (in Activities 4.12 and 4.15):

Trial	Discount factor %	Net present value £000
1	15	(23.49)
2	10	(2.46)
Difference	5	21.03

The change in NPV for every 1 per cent change in the discount rate will be:

$$(21.03/5) = 4.21$$

The reduction in the 10% discount rate required to achieve a zero NPV would therefore be:

$$(2.46/4.21) \times 1\% = 0.58\%$$

The IRR is therefore:

$$(10.00 - 0.58) = 9.42\%$$

However, to say that the IRR is about 9 per cent or 10 per cent is near enough for most purposes.

Note that this approach assumes a straight-line relationship between the discount rate and NPV. We can see from Figure 4.4 that this assumption is not strictly correct. Over a relatively short range, however, this simplifying assumption is not usually a problem and so we can still arrive at a reasonable approximation using the approach taken. As most businesses have computer software packages to derive a project's IRR, it is not normally necessary to make the calculations just described.

The following decision rules are applied when using IRR:

■ For any project to be acceptable, it must meet a minimum IRR requirement. This is often referred to as the *hurdle rate* and, logically, this should be the opportunity cost of capital.
■ Where there are competing projects, the one with the higher (or highest) IRR should be selected.

Real World 4.7 illustrates how IRR is used to assess the economic effectiveness of research and development activities of pharmaceutical development and manufacturing businesses.

Real World 4.7

IRR from R and D

For most of their history, pharmaceutical companies' core mission has consisted of developing new drugs to advance medical care. But over the past several years, drug companies' return at this central task has steadily declined, which has put pressure on them to reduce research and development funding and enter partnerships that don't require the fixed costs of their own laboratories and employees.

The latest annual study of R&D productivity by Deloitte and Thomson Reuters found that the number of new drug approvals increased by around 30 per cent, yet the expected revenue from these medicines actually fell by a similar amount. In total, the world's top 12 research-based pharmaceutical companies had 41 new drugs approved in 2012, with combined forecast revenues of $211 billion, compared with 32 products with expected revenues of $309 billion a year ago.

With an average internal rate of return (IRR) from R&D in 2012 of 7.2 per cent – against 7.7 per cent and 10.5 per cent in the two preceding years – drug makers are barely covering their average cost of capital, estimated at around 7 per cent. For the 12 companies, the average cost of developing a new medicine between 2010 and 2012 has increased by 4 per cent, from $1,089 million in 2010 to $1,137 million in 2012.

There is wide variation between the 12 companies. The most successful company in the group spent just $315 million to develop a new drug, while at the other extreme one firm spent $2.8 billion.

Industry observers expect market conditions for pharmaceutical companies to continue to be challenging. Dynamics such as the US fiscal cliff, the potential that some countries might exit the euro zone, changing patterns of demand and continuing downward pressure on health care budgets, present the industry with a volatile and highly uncertain economic environment in which to operate, let alone drive productivity improvements.

The companies analysed in the study were Pfizer Inc., Roche Holding Ltd, Novartis AG, Sanofi SA, GlaxoSmithKline plc, Johnson & Johnson, AstraZeneca plc, Merck & Co. Inc., Eli Lilly & Co., Bristol-Myers Squibb Co., Takeda Pharmaceutical Company Limited and Amgen, Inc.

Source: Extracts from M. Zhang, 'Big pharma facing patent cliff and declining R&D returns', *International Business Times*, 5 December 2012.

Real World 4.8 gives some examples of IRRs sought in practice.

Real World 4.8

Rates of return

IRRs for investment projects can vary considerably. Here are a few examples of the expected or target returns from investment projects of large businesses:

- GlaxoSmithKline plc, the leading pharmaceuticals business, is aiming to increase its annual IRR from investments in new products from 11 per cent to 14 per cent.
- Next plc, the fashion retailer, requires an annual IRR of 20 per cent when appraising new stores.
- Apache Capital Partners, a property investment fund, has a target annual IRR of more than 20 per cent.
- Forth Ports plc, a port operator, concentrates on projects that generate an IRR of at least 15 per cent.
- Marks and Spencer plc, the stores chain, has targeted a 'hurdle' internal rate of return of 12–15 per cent on a new investment programme.
- Standard Life, the pensions and life assurance business, requires a 15 per cent internal rate of return from new products.

These values seem surprisingly large. A study of returns made by all of the businesses listed on the London Stock Exchange between 1900 and 2011 showed an average annual return of 5.4 per cent. This figure is the *real* return (that is, ignoring inflation). It would probably be fair to add at least 3 per cent to it to compare it with the targets for the businesses listed above. Also, the targets for the five businesses are probably pre-tax (the businesses do not specify). In that case it is probably reasonable to add about a third to the average Stock Exchange returns. This would give us around 12 per cent per year. This would be roughly in line with the GlaxoSmithKline and Marks and Spencer targets. The targets for the other businesses, however, seem rather ambitious.

Sources: 'UPDATE 1-GSK's R&D engine cranks up investment returns', www.reuters.com, 7 February 2012; Next plc, Results for the half-year to 31 July 2012; D. Thomas, 'Vultures need to pick time to swoop', www.ft.com, 12 June 2009; FAQs, Forth Ports plc, www.forthports.co.uk, accessed 9 February 2010; press release on 2012 annual results, Marks and Spencer plc, 22 May 2012; 'Standard Life flags "step up in performance"', www.ft.com, 10 March 2011; E. Dimson, P. Marsh and M. Staunton, Credit Suisse Global Investments Returns Yearbook, 2012.

Problems with IRR

IRR shares certain key attributes with NPV. All cash flows are taken into account and their timing is logically handled. The main problem of IRR, however, is that it does not directly address the question of wealth generation. It can therefore lead to the wrong decision being made. The IRR approach will always rank a project with an IRR of 25 per cent, for example, above that of a project with an IRR of 20 per cent. Although accepting the project with the higher percentage return will often generate more wealth, this may not always be so. This is because IRR completely ignores the *scale of investment*.

With a 15 per cent cost of capital, £15 million invested at 20 per cent for one year will make us wealthier by £0.75 million (15 × (20 − 15)% = 0.75). With the same cost of capital, £5 million invested at 25 per cent for one year will make us only £0.5 million wealthier (5 × (25 − 15)% = 0.50). IRR does not recognise this point.

Competing projects do not usually possess such large differences in scale and so IRR and NPV normally give the same signal. However, as NPV will always give the correct signal, it is difficult to see why any other method should be used.

A further problem with the IRR method is that it has difficulty handling projects with unconventional cash flows. In the examples studied so far, each project has a negative cash flow arising at the start of its life and then positive cash flows thereafter. In some cases, however, a project may have both positive and negative cash flows at future points in its life. Such a pattern of cash flows can result in there being more than one IRR, or even no IRR at all. This can make the IRR method difficult to use, although it should be said that this problem is also quite rare in practice.

Example 4.3

Let us assume that a project has the following pattern of cash flows:

Time	Cash flows
	£000s
Immediately	(4,000)
One year's time	9,400
Two years' time	(5,500)

These cash flows will give a zero NPV at both 10 per cent and 25 per cent. Thus, we shall have two IRRs, which can be confusing. Let us assume that the minimum acceptable IRR is 15 per cent. Should the project be accepted or rejected?

Figure 4.5 shows the NPV of the above project for different discount rates. Once again, where the NPV touches the horizontal axis, there will be a zero NPV and this will represent the IRR.

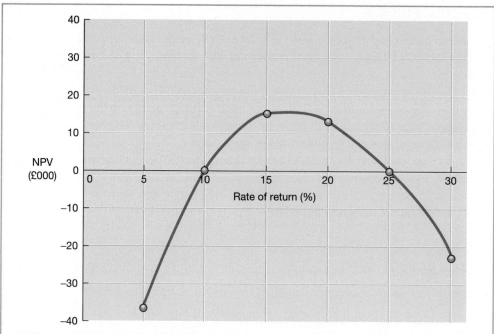

The point at which the NPV line touches the horizontal axis will be the IRR. The figure shows that the NPV of the project is zero at a 10 per cent discount rate and a 25 per cent discount rate. Hence there are two possible IRRs for this project.

Figure 4.5 The IRR method providing more than one solution

SOME PRACTICAL POINTS

When undertaking an investment appraisal, there are several practical points to bear in mind:

■ *Past costs*. As with all decisions, we should take account only of relevant costs in our analysis. This means that only costs that vary with the decision should be considered. Thus, all past costs should be ignored as they cannot vary with the decision. A business may incur costs (such as development costs and market research costs) *before* the evaluation of an opportunity to launch a new product. As those costs have already been incurred, they should be disregarded, even though the amounts may be substantial. Costs that have already been committed but not yet paid should also be disregarded. Where a business has entered into a binding contract to incur a particular cost, it becomes in effect a past cost even though payment may not be due until some point in the future.

■ *Common future costs*. It is not only past costs that do not vary with the decision; some future costs may be the same. For example, the cost of raw materials may not vary with the decision whether to invest in a new piece of manufacturing plant or to continue to use existing plant.

■ *Opportunity costs*. Opportunity costs arising from benefits forgone must be taken into account. Thus, for example, when considering a decision concerning whether or not to continue to use a machine already owned by the business, the realisable value of the machine may be an important opportunity cost.

These points concerning costs are brought together in Activity 4.17.

A garage has an old car that it bought several months ago for £3,000. The car needs a replacement engine before it can be sold. It is possible to buy a reconditioned engine for £300. This would take seven hours to fit by a mechanic who is paid £12 an hour. At present, the garage is short of work, but the owners are reluctant to lay off any mechanics or even cut down their basic working week because skilled labour is difficult to find and an upturn in repair work is expected soon.

Without the engine, the car could be sold for an estimated £3,500. What is the minimum price at which the garage should sell the car, with a reconditioned engine fitted, to avoid making a loss? (Ignore any timing differences in receipts and payments.)

The minimum price is the amount required to cover the relevant costs of the job. At this price, the business will make neither a profit nor a loss. Any price below this amount will result in a reduction in the wealth of the business. Thus, the minimum price is:

	£
Opportunity cost of the car	3,500
Cost of the reconditioned engine	300
Total	3,800

The original cost of the car is a past cost and is therefore irrelevant. However, we are told that without the engine, the car could be sold for £3,500. This is the opportunity cost of the car, which represents the real benefits forgone, and should be taken into account.

The cost of the new engine is relevant because, if the work is done, the garage will have to pay £300 for the engine; it will pay nothing if the job is not done. The £300 is a future cost that varies with the decision and should be taken into account.

The labour cost is irrelevant because the same cost will be incurred whether the mechanic undertakes the work or not. This is because the mechanic is being paid to do nothing if this job is not undertaken; thus the additional labour cost arising from this job is zero.

■ *Taxation*. Owners will be interested in the after-tax returns generated from the business. Profits from the project will be taxed, the capital investment may attract tax relief and so on. As the rate of tax is often significant, taxation becomes an important consideration when making an investment decision. Unless tax is formally taken into account, the wrong decision could easily be made. This means that both the amount and the timing of tax outflows should be reflected in the cash flows for the project.

■ *Cash flows not profit flows*. We have seen that for the NPV, IRR and PP methods, it is cash flows rather than profit flows that are relevant for the assessment of investment proposals. Nevertheless, some proposals may contain only data relating to profits over the investment period. These will need to be adjusted in order to derive the cash flows. As mentioned earlier, operating profit *before* non-cash items (such as depreciation) provides an approximation to the cash flows for a particular period. We should, therefore, work back to this figure.

Where data relating to profit rather than cash flows has been provided, some adjustment for changes in working capital may also be needed. Launching a new product, for example, may give rise to an increase in the net investment made in working capital (trade receivables and inventories less trade payables). This would normally lead to an immediate outlay of cash, which should be shown as a cash outflow in the NPV calculations. However, at the end of the life of the project, the additional working capital will be released. This divestment results in an effective inflow of cash at the end of the project. This should be shown in the NPV calculations at the point at which it is received.

- *Year-end assumption.* In the examples and activities considered so far, we have assumed that cash flows arise at the end of the relevant year. This simplifying assumption is used to make the calculations easier. As already mentioned, this assumption is unrealistic as employees are paid on a weekly or monthly basis, credit customers pay within a month or two of the sale and so on. Nevertheless, it is probably not a serious distortion. If required, it is perfectly possible to deal more precisely with the timing of cash flows.

- *Interest payments.* When using discounted cash flow techniques (NPV and IRR), interest payments should not be taken into account in deriving cash flows for the period. The discount factor already takes account of the costs of financing. To include interest charges in deriving cash flows for the period would, therefore, be double counting.

- *Other factors.* Investment decision making must not be viewed as simply a mechanical exercise. The results derived from a particular investment appraisal method will be only one input to the decision-making process. There may be broader issues connected to the decision that have to be taken into account but may be difficult or impossible to quantify. Nevertheless, they may be critical to the final decision.

The reliability of the forecasts and the validity of the assumptions used in the evaluation will also have a bearing on the final decision.

Activity 4.18

The directors of Manuff (Steel) Ltd are considering closing one of the business's factories. There has been a reduction in the demand for the products made at the factory in recent years. The directors are not optimistic about the long-term prospects for these products. The factory is situated in an area where unemployment is high.

The factory is leased, with four years of the lease remaining. The directors are uncertain whether the factory should be closed immediately or at the end of the period of the lease. Another business has offered to sublease the premises from Manuff (Steel) Ltd at a rental of £40,000 a year for the remainder of the lease period.

The machinery and equipment at the factory cost £1,500,000. The value at which they appear on the statement of financial position is £400,000. In the event of immediate closure, the machinery and equipment could be sold for £220,000. The working capital at the factory is £420,000. It could be liquidated for that amount immediately, if required. Alternatively, the working capital can be liquidated in full at the end of the lease period. Immediate closure would result in redundancy payments to employees of £180,000.

If the factory continues in operation until the end of the lease period, the following operating profits (losses) are expected:

	Year 1 £000	Year 2 £000	Year 3 £000	Year 4 £000
Operating profit (loss)	160	(40)	30	20

The above figures include a charge of £90,000 a year for depreciation of machinery and equipment. The residual value of the machinery and equipment at the end of the lease period is estimated at £40,000.

Redundancy payments are expected to be £150,000 at the end of the lease period if the factory continues in operation. The business has an annual cost of capital of 12 per cent. Ignore taxation.

(a) Determine the relevant cash flows arising from a decision to continue operations until the end of the lease period rather than to close immediately.

(b) Calculate the net present value of continuing operations until the end of the lease period rather than closing immediately.

(c) What other factors might the directors take into account before making a final decision on the timing of the factory closure?

(d) State, with reasons, whether or not the business should continue to operate the factory until the end of the lease period.

Your answer should be as follows:

(a) Relevant cash flows

	Years				
	0	1	2	3	4
	£000	£000	£000	£000	£000
Operating cash flows (Note 1)		250	50	120	110
Sale of machinery (Note 2)	(220)				40
Redundancy costs (Note 3)	180				(150)
Sublease rentals (Note 4)		(40)	(40)	(40)	(40)
Working capital invested (Note 5)	(420)				420
	(460)	210	10	80	380

Notes:

1 Each year's operating cash flows are calculated by adding back the depreciation charge for the year to the operating profit for the year. In the case of the operating loss, the depreciation charge is deducted.

2 In the event of closure, machinery could be sold immediately. Thus an opportunity cost of £220,000 is incurred if operations continue.

3 By continuing operations, there will be a saving in immediate redundancy costs of £180,000. However, redundancy costs of £150,000 will be paid in four years' time.

4 By continuing operations, the opportunity to sublease the factory will be forgone.

5 Immediate closure would mean that working capital could be liquidated. By continuing operations this opportunity is forgone. However, working capital can be liquidated in four years' time.

(b)

	Years				
	0	1	2	3	4
Discount rate 12 per cent	1.000	0.893	0.797	0.712	0.636
Present value	(460)	187.5	8.0	57.0	241.7
Net present value	34.2				

(c) Other factors that may influence the decision include the following:

■ *The overall strategy of the business*. The business may need to set the decision within a broader context. It may be necessary to manufacture the products at the factory because they are an integral part of the business's product range. The business may wish to avoid redundancies in an area of high unemployment for as long as possible.

■ *Flexibility*. A decision to close the factory is probably irreversible. If the factory continues, however, there may be a chance that the prospects for the factory will brighten in the future.

■ *Creditworthiness of sub-lessee*. The business should investigate the creditworthiness of the sub-lessee. Failure to receive the expected sublease payments would make the closure option far less attractive.

■ *Accuracy of forecasts*. The forecasts made by the business should be examined carefully. Inaccuracies in the forecasts or any underlying assumptions may change the expected outcomes.

(d) The NPV of the decision to continue operations rather than close immediately is positive. Hence, shareholders would be better off if the directors took this course of action. The factory should therefore continue in operation rather than close down. This decision is likely to be welcomed by employees and would allow the business to maintain its flexibility.

The main methods of investment appraisal are summarised in Figure 4.6.

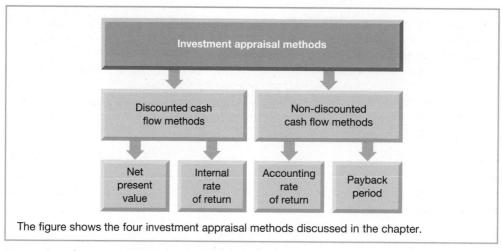

The figure shows the four investment appraisal methods discussed in the chapter.

Figure 4.6 The main investment appraisal methods

INVESTMENT APPRAISAL IN PRACTICE

Many surveys have been conducted in the UK into the methods of investment appraisal used by businesses. They have shown the following features:

■ Businesses tend to use more than one method to assess each investment decision.
■ The discounting methods (NPV and IRR) have become increasingly popular over time. NPV and IRR are now the most popular of the four methods.
■ PP continues to be popular and, to a lesser extent, so does ARR. This is despite the theoretical shortcomings of both methods.
■ Larger businesses tend to rely more heavily on discounting methods than smaller businesses.

Real World 4.9 shows the results of a survey of a number of UK manufacturing businesses concerning their use of investment appraisal methods.

Real World 4.9

A survey of UK business practice

Senior financial managers at 83 of the UK's largest manufacturing businesses were asked about the investment appraisal methods used to evaluate both strategic and non-strategic projects. Strategic projects usually aim to increase or change the competitive capabilities of a business, such as introducing a new manufacturing process.

Method	Non-strategic projects Mean score	Strategic projects Mean score
Net present value	3.6829	3.9759
Payback	3.4268	3.6098
Internal rate of return	3.3293	3.7073
Accounting rate of return	1.9867	2.2667

Response scale: 1 = never, 2 = rarely, 3 = often, 4 = mostly, 5 = always.

We can see that, for both non-strategic and strategic investments, the NPV method is the most popular. As the sample consists of large businesses (nearly all with total sales revenue in excess of £100 million), a fairly sophisticated approach to evaluation might be expected. Nevertheless, for non-strategic investments, the payback method comes second in popularity. It drops to third place for strategic projects.

The survey also found that 98 per cent of respondents used more than one method and 88 per cent used more than three methods of investment appraisal.

Source: Based on information in F. Alkaraan and D. Northcott, 'Strategic capital investment decision-making: A role for emergent analysis tools? A study of practice in large UK manufacturing companies', *The British Accounting Review*, 38, 2006, 159.

A survey of large businesses in five leading industrialised countries, including the UK, also shows considerable support for the NPV and IRR methods. There is less support for the payback method but, nevertheless, it still seems to be fairly widely used. **Real World 4.10** sets out some key findings.

Real World 4.10

A multinational survey of business practice

A survey of investment and financing practices in five different countries was carried out by Cohen and Yagil. This survey, based on a sample of the largest 300 businesses in each country, revealed the following concerning the popularity of three of the investment appraisal methods discussed in this chapter.

Frequency of the use of investment appraisal techniques

	USA	UK	Germany	Canada	Japan	Average
IRR	4.00	4.16	4.08	4.15	3.29	3.93
NPV	3.88	4.00	3.50	4.09	3.57	3.80
PP	3.46	3.89	3.33	3.57	3.52	3.55

Response scale: 1 = never, 5 = always.

Key findings of the survey include the following:

- IRR is more popular than NPV in all countries, except Japan. However, the difference between the two methods is not statistically significant.
- Managers of UK businesses use investment appraisal techniques the most, while managers of Japanese businesses use them the least. This may be related to business traditions within each country.
- There is a positive relationship between business size and the popularity of the IRR and NPV methods. This may be related to the greater experience and understanding of financial theory of managers of larger businesses.

Source: G. Cohen and J. Yagil, 'A multinational survey of corporate financial policies', Working Paper, Haifa University, 2007.

Activity 4.19

Earlier in the chapter, we discussed the limitations of the PP method. Can you explain why it is still a reasonably popular method of investment appraisal among managers?

There are a number of possible reasons:

- PP is easy to understand and use.
- It can avoid the problems of forecasting far into the future.
- It gives emphasis to the early cash flows when there is greater certainty concerning the accuracy of their predicted value.
- It emphasises the importance of liquidity.

The popularity of PP may suggest a lack of sophistication by managers concerning investment appraisal. This criticism is most often made against managers of smaller businesses. This point is borne out by both of the surveys discussed above which have found that smaller businesses are much less likely to use discounted cash flow methods (NPV and IRR) than are larger ones. Other surveys have tended to reach a similar conclusion.

IRR may be popular because it expresses outcomes in percentage terms rather than in absolute terms. This form of expression seems to be preferred by managers, despite the problems of percentage measures that we discussed earlier. This may be because managers are used to using percentage figures as targets (for example, return on capital employed).

INVESTMENT APPRAISAL AND STRATEGIC PLANNING

So far, we have tended to view investment opportunities as unconnected, independent events. In practice, however, successful businesses are those that set out a clear framework for the selection of investment projects. Unless this framework is in place, it may be difficult to identify those projects that are likely to generate a positive NPV. The best investment projects are usually those that match the business's internal strengths (for example, skills, experience, access to finance) with the opportunities available. In areas where this match does not exist, other businesses, for which the match does exist, are likely to have a distinct competitive advantage. This means that they will be able to provide the product or service at a better price and/or quality.

Setting out the framework just described is an essential part of *strategic planning*. In practice, strategic plans often have a time span of around three to five years. It involves asking, 'Where do we want our business to be in (say) five years' time and how can we get there?' It will set the appropriate direction in terms of products, markets, financing and so on, to ensure that the business is best placed to generate profitable investment opportunities.

Real World 4.11 shows how easyJet had made an investment that fitted its strategic objectives.

Real World 4.11

easyFit

The UK budget airline easyJet bought a small rival airline, GB Airways Ltd (GB), in late 2007 for £103 million.

According to an article in the *Financial Times*: GB is a good strategic fit for easyJet. It operates under a British Airways franchise from Gatwick, which happens to be easyJet's biggest base. The deal makes easyJet the single largest passenger carrier at the UK airport. There is plenty of scope for scale economies in purchasing and back-office functions. Moreover, easyJet should be able to boost GB's profitability by switching the carrier to its low-cost business model . . . easyJet makes an estimated £4 a passenger, against GB's £1. Assuming easyJet can drag up GB to its own levels of profitability, the company's value to the low-cost carrier is roughly four times its standalone worth.

The article makes the point that this looks like a good investment for easyJet, because of the strategic fit. For a business other than easyJet, the lack of strategic fit might well have meant that buying GB for exactly the same price of £103 million would not have been a good investment.

FT *Source*: Hughes, C. (2007) 'Easy ride', www.ft.com, 26 October.
© The Financial Times Limited 2012. All Rights Reserved.

THE INVESTMENT APPRAISAL PROCESS

So far, we have been concerned with carrying out calculations to help choose between previously identified investment opportunities. While this is important, it is only *part* of the process of investment decision making. There are other important aspects that must be considered.

The investment appraisal process can be viewed as a sequence of six stages. These are set out in Figure 4.7 and described below.

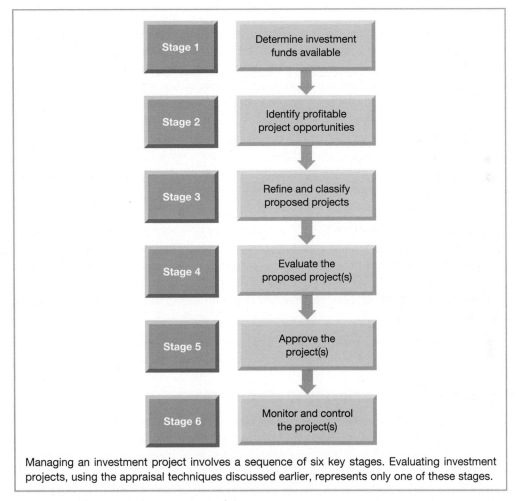

Managing an investment project involves a sequence of six key stages. Evaluating investment projects, using the appraisal techniques discussed earlier, represents only one of these stages.

Figure 4.7 Managing the investment decision

Stage 1: Determine investment funds available

The amount of funds available for investment may be limited by the external market for funds or by internal management. In practice, it is the managers that are more likely to impose limits, perhaps because they lack confidence in the business's ability to handle high levels of investment. In either case, however, there may be insufficient funds to finance all the potentially profitable investment opportunities available. This shortage of investment funds is known as capital rationing. When it arises, managers are faced with the task of deciding on the most profitable use of those funds available. Competing investment opportunities must be prioritised, and in order for this to be done correctly, some modification to the NPV decision rule is necessary. This point is discussed further in the next chapter.

Stage 2: Identify profitable project opportunities

A vital part of the investment process is the search for profitable investment opportunities. The business should carry out methodical routines for identifying feasible projects. To maintain a competitive edge, the search for new investment opportunities should be considered a normal part of the planning process. The range of investment opportunities available to a business may include the development of new products or services, improving existing products or services, entering new markets, and investing to increase capacity or efficiency. The investments pursued should, as already mentioned, fit the strategic plan of the business.

The search for new opportunities will often involve looking outside the business to identify changes in technology, customer demand, market conditions and so on. Information will need to be gathered and this will take some time, particularly for unusual or non-routine investment opportunities. This information gathering may be done through a research and development department or by some other means. Failure to do this is likely to lead to a loss of competitive position with respect to product development, production methods or market penetration.

To help identify good investment opportunities, financial incentives may be offered to employees who come forward with good investment proposals. Even unrefined proposals may be welcome. Resources can then be invested to help develop the proposals to a point where formal submissions can be made.

Activity 4.20

It can be argued that the sequence of these first two stages can be reversed. Can you figure out why?

In theory, finance can always be found for profitable investment opportunities.

Stage 3: Refine and classify proposed projects

Promising ideas need to be converted into full-blown proposals. This means that further information will probably be required, much of it detailed in nature. Collecting information can be time-consuming and costly, however, and so a two-stage process may be adopted. The first stage will involve collecting enough information to allow a preliminary screening. Many proposals fall at this first hurdle because it soon becomes clear that they are unprofitable or unacceptable for other reasons. Proposals considered worthy of further investigation will continue to the second stage. This stage will involve developing the ideas further so that more detailed screening can be carried out.

It can be helpful to classify investment opportunities. The following has been suggested as a possible framework:

- *New product development*. Where a business operates in fast-changing markets (such as computer manufacture), a regular stream of new, innovative products may be needed to survive.
- *Improving existing product sales*. To maintain or enhance competitive position, a business may continually seek to improve the quality or design of existing products.

- *Reducing costs*. New investments may seek to achieve long-term savings. Acquiring a new piece of equipment, for example, may reduce the costs incurred from scrap, equipment maintenance, quality inspection and electrical power.
- *Equipment replacement*. Equipment may have to be replaced to maintain existing levels of output.
- *Regulatory requirements*. Investment may be necessary to adhere to regulations relating to health and safety, environmental pollution, recycling and so on.

Classification can be useful in deciding on the level of information required for a particular proposal. Equipment replacement, for example, may be a routine occurrence and so a replacement proposal may only require evidence that the particular piece of equipment has reached the end of its economic life. New product development, meanwhile, may require market research evidence, a marketing plan and detailed costings to support the proposal.

Classification can also help in deciding on the acceptance criteria to be applied.

Activity 4.21

How might classification help in this way?

The different classes of investment may reflect different levels of risk. Equipment replacement, for example, may be considered to be low-risk and therefore to require only a low rate of return. New product development, however, may be considered to be high-risk and so to require a high rate of return. (The issue of risk and return in relation to investment proposals is considered in some detail in the following chapter.)

Stage 4: Evaluate the proposed project(s)

Once a project has undergone the preliminary screening and a proposal has been fully developed, a detailed evaluation can be carried out. For larger projects, this will involve providing answers to a number of key questions, including:

- What are the nature and purpose of the project?
- Does the project align with the overall strategy and objectives of the business?
- How much finance is required? Does this fit with the funds available?
- What other resources (such as expertise, work space and so on) are required for successful completion of the project?
- How long will the project last and what are its key stages?
- What is the expected pattern of cash flows?
- What are the major problems associated with the project and how can they be overcome?
- What is the NPV of the project? If capital is rationed, how does the NPV of this project compare with that of other opportunities available?
- Have risk and inflation been taken into account in the appraisal process and if so, what are the results?

The ability and commitment of those responsible for proposing and managing the project will be vital to its success. This means that when evaluating a new project, one consideration will be the quality of those proposing it. Senior managers may decide not to support a project that appears profitable on paper if they lack confidence in the ability of key managers to see it through to completion.

Stage 5: Approve the project(s)

Once the managers responsible for investment decision making are satisfied that the project should be undertaken, formal approval can be given. However, a decision on a project may be postponed if senior managers need more information from those proposing the project, or if revisions are required to the proposal. Proposals will normally be rejected if they are considered unprofitable or likely to fail. Before rejecting a proposal, however, the implications of not pursuing the project for such areas as market share, staff morale and existing business operations must be carefully considered.

Approval may be authorised at different levels of the management hierarchy according to the nature of the investment and the amount of finance required. For example, a plant manager may be given authority to invest in new equipment up to a maximum of, say, £300,000. For amounts above this figure, authority may be required from more senior management.

Stage 6: Monitor and control the project(s)

Making a decision to invest does not automatically cause the investment to be made or mean that things will progress smoothly. Managers will need to manage the project actively through to completion. This, in turn, will require further information gathering.

Management should receive progress reports at regular intervals concerning the project. These should provide information relating to the actual cash flows for each stage of the project, which can then be compared against the forecast figures. Reasons for any significant variations should be ascertained and corrective action taken where possible. Any changes in the expected completion date of the project or any expected variations in future cash flows from forecasts should be reported immediately; in extreme cases, managers may even abandon the project if things appear to have changed dramatically for the worse.

Key non-financial measures can also be used to monitor performance. Measures may include wastage rates, physical output, employee satisfaction scores and so on. Certain types of projects, such as civil engineering and construction projects, may have 'milestones' (that is, particular stages of completion) to be reached by certain dates. Progress towards each milestone should be monitored carefully and early warnings should be given of any problems that are likely to prevent their achievement. Project management techniques (for example, critical path analysis) should be employed wherever possible and their effectiveness monitored.

An important part of the control process is a **post-completion audit**. This is, in essence, a review of the project performance to see whether it lived up to expectations and whether any lessons can be learned. In addition to an evaluation of financial costs and benefits, non-financial measures of performance, such as the ability to meet deadlines and levels of quality achieved, will often be examined.

Adopting post-completion audits should encourage the use of more realistic estimates at the initial planning stage. Where over-optimistic estimates are used in an attempt to secure project approval, the managers responsible should be held accountable at the post-completion stage.

The behaviour of managers is likely to be influenced by the way in which a post-completion audit is conducted. If it is simply used as a device to apportion blame, then the problems mentioned in Activity 4.22 may easily occur. But if it is used in a constructive way, these problems need not arise. It should be seen as a tool for learning and should take full account of the degree of risk associated with a project.

Activity 4.22

Can you think of any drawbacks to the use of a post-completion audit? Could it have an adverse effect on management behaviour?

One potential problem is that it will inhibit managers from proposing and supporting high-risk projects. If things go wrong, they could be blamed. This may result in only low-risk projects being submitted for approval. A further potential problem is that managers will feel threatened by the post-completion audit investigation and so will not cooperate fully with the audit team.

Post-completion audits can be costly and time-consuming and so the potential benefits must be weighed against the costs involved. This may result in only larger projects being audited. However, a random sample of smaller projects may also be audited.

Real World 4.12 provides some indication of the extent to which post-completion audits are used by businesses.

Real World 4.12

Looking back

The Chartered Institute of Management Accountants (CIMA) surveyed a wide range of UK businesses. The survey was completed by 439 management accountants. One objective of the survey was to discover the extent to which post-completion audits are used in practice. The results for all businesses surveyed, as well as for very large businesses (with more than 10,000 employees), are set out in Figure 4.8.

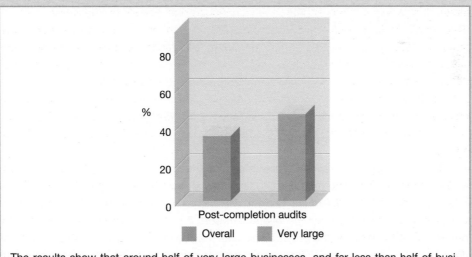

The results show that around half of very large businesses, and far less than half of businesses overall, use post-completion audits.

Figure 4.8 Post-completion audits

We can see that larger businesses are more likely to use this technique. This is not surprising. Larger businesses are likely to undertake more and bigger investment projects and have more finance staff to monitor business performance.

Source: Adapted from figure in 'Management accounting tools for today and tomorrow', CIMA, July 2009, p.18.

Real World 4.13 describes how one large retailer, Kingfisher plc, goes about monitoring and controlling its investment projects. Kingfisher sells do-it-yourself goods, notably through the B&Q chain of stores.

INVESTMENT DECISIONS AND HUMAN BEHAVIOUR

The sequence of stages described earlier may give the impression that investment decision making is an entirely rational process. Studies have shown, however, that this is not always so. In some cases, an investment project will gather support among managers as it is being developed and the greater the level of support, the greater the potential for bias in the information used to evaluate the project. This bias may be reflected in future cash flows being overestimated or the level of risk underestimated. In other cases, project sponsors will seek support among senior managers so that final project approval is simply a formality. These behavioural aspects, though interesting, are beyond the scope of this book. Nevertheless, it is important to recognise that investment decisions are made by individuals who may have their own interests to satisfy.

Beacon Chemicals plc is considering buying some equipment to produce a chemical named X14. The new equipment's capital cost is estimated at £100 million. If its purchase is approved now, the equipment can be bought and production can commence by the end of this year. £50 million has already been spent on research and development work. Estimates of revenues and costs arising from the operation of the new equipment appear below:

	Year 1	Year 2	Year 3	Year 4	Year 5
Sales price (£/litre)	100	120	120	100	80
Sales volume (million litres)	0.8	1.0	1.2	1.0	0.8
Variable cost (£/litre)	50	50	40	30	40
Fixed cost (£000)	30	30	30	30	30

If the equipment is bought, sales of some existing products will be lost, resulting in a loss of contribution of £15 million a year, over the life of the equipment.

The accountant has informed you that the fixed cost includes depreciation of £20 million a year on the new equipment. It also includes an allocation of £10 million for fixed overheads. A separate study has indicated that if the new equipment were bought, additional overheads, excluding depreciation, arising from producing the chemical would be £8 million a year. Production would require additional working capital of £30 million.

For the purposes of your initial calculations, ignore taxation.

Required:
(a) Deduce the relevant annual cash flows associated with buying the equipment.
(b) Deduce the payback period.
(c) Calculate the net present value using a discount rate of 8 per cent.

(*Hint*: You should deal with the investment in working capital by treating it as a cash outflow at the start of the project and an inflow at the end.)

The answer to this question can be found at the back of the book on p. 562.

SUMMARY

The main points of this chapter may be summarised as follows:

Accounting rate of return (ARR) is the average accounting profit from the project expressed as a percentage of the average investment.

- Decision rule – projects with an ARR above a defined minimum are acceptable; the greater the ARR, the more attractive the project becomes.

- Conclusion on ARR:

    - does not relate directly to shareholders' wealth – can lead to illogical conclusions
    - takes almost no account of the timing of cash flows
    - ignores some relevant information and may take account of some that is irrelevant
    - relatively simple to use
    - much inferior to NPV.

Payback period (PP) is the length of time that it takes for the cash outflow for the initial investment to be repaid out of resulting cash inflows.

- Decision rule – projects with a PP up to a defined maximum period are acceptable; the shorter the PP, the more attractive the project.

- Conclusion on PP:
  - does not relate to shareholders' wealth
  - ignores inflows after the payback date
  - takes little account of the timing of cash flows
  - ignores much relevant information
  - does not always provide clear signals and can be impractical to use
  - much inferior to NPV, but it is easy to understand and can offer a liquidity insight, which might be the reason for its widespread use.

Net present value (NPV) is the sum of the discounted values of the net cash flows from the investment.

- Money has a time value.

- Decision rule – all positive NPV investments enhance shareholders' wealth; the greater the NPV, the greater the enhancement and the greater the attractiveness of the project.

- PV of a cash flow = cash flow $\times 1/(1 + r)^n$, assuming a constant cost of capital.

- Discounting brings cash flows at different points in time to a common valuation basis (their present value), which enables them to be directly compared.

- Conclusion on NPV:
  - relates directly to shareholders' wealth objective
  - takes account of the timing of cash flows
  - takes all relevant information into account
  - provides clear signals and is practical to use.

Internal rate of return (IRR) is the discount rate that, when applied to the cash flows of a project, causes it to have a zero NPV.

- Represents the average percentage return on the investment, taking account of the fact that cash may be flowing in and out of the project at various points in its life.

- Decision rule – projects that have an IRR greater than the cost of capital are acceptable; the greater the IRR, the more attractive the project.

- Cannot normally be calculated directly; a trial and error approach is usually necessary.

- Conclusion on IRR:
  - does not relate directly to shareholders' wealth. Usually gives the same signals as NPV but can mislead where there are competing projects of different size
  - takes account of the timing of cash flows
  - takes all relevant information into account
  - problems of multiple IRRs when there are unconventional cash flows
  - inferior to NPV.

Use of appraisal methods in practice:

- All four methods identified are widely used.

- The discounting methods (NPV and IRR) show a steady increase in usage over time.

- Many businesses use more than one method.

- Larger businesses seem to be more sophisticated in their choice and use of appraisal methods than smaller ones.

Managing investment projects

- Determine investment funds available – dealing, if necessary, with capital rationing problems.

- Identify profitable project opportunities.

- Refine and classify the project.

- Evaluate the proposed project.

- Approve the project.

- Monitor and control the project – using a post-completion audit approach.

KEY TERMS

Accounting rate of return (ARR) p. 128	**Cost of capital** p. 144
Payback period (PP) p. 133	**Internal rate of return (IRR)** p. 145
Net present value (NPV) p. 136	**Relevant costs** p. 150
Risk premium p. 139	**Opportunity cost** p. 150
Inflation p. 139	**Capital rationing** p. 157
Discount factor p. 142	**Post-completion audit** p. 160

For definitions of these terms see the Glossary, pp. 605–613.

FURTHER READING

If you would like to explore the topics covered in this chapter in more depth, try the following books:

Arnold, G. (2013) *Corporate Financial Management*, 5th edn, Pearson, Chapters 2, 3 and 4.

Drury, C. (2012) *Management and Cost Accounting*, 8th edn, South Western Cengage Learning, Chapters 13 and 14.

McLaney, E. (2012) *Business Finance: Theory and Practice*, 9th edn, Financial Times Prentice Hall, Chapters 4, 5 and 6.

Pike, R., Neale, B. and Linsley, P. (2012) *Corporate Finance and Investment*, 7th edn, Pearson, Chapters 5, 6 and 7.

Answers to these questions can be found at the back of the book on p. 573.

4.1 Why is the net present value method of investment appraisal considered to be theoretically superior to other methods that are found in practice?

4.2 The payback method has been criticised for not taking into account the time value of money. Could this limitation be overcome? If so, would this method then be preferable to the NPV method?

4.3 Research indicates that the IRR method is extremely popular even though it has short-comings when compared with the NPV method. Why might managers prefer to use IRR rather than NPV when carrying out discounted cash flow evaluations?

4.4 Why are cash flows rather than profit flows used in the IRR, NPV and PP methods of investment appraisal?

Exercises 4.3 to 4.7 are more advanced than 4.1 and 4.2. Those with coloured numbers have solutions at the back of the book, starting on p. 585.

If you wish to try more exercises, visit the students' side of this book's companion website.

4.1 The directors of Mylo Ltd are currently considering two mutually exclusive investment projects. Both projects are concerned with the purchase of new plant. The following data are available for each project:

	Project 1 £000	Project 2 £000
Cost (immediate outlay)	100	60
Expected annual operating profit (loss):		
Year 1	29	18
2	(1)	(2)
3	2	4
Estimated residual value of the plant	7	6

The business has an estimated cost of capital of 10 per cent. It uses the straight-line method of depreciation for all non-current assets, when calculating operating profit. Neither project would increase the working capital of the business. The business has sufficient funds to meet all capital expenditure requirements.

Required:
(a) Calculate for each project:
  (i)   The net present value.
  (ii) The approximate internal rate of return.
  (iii) The payback period.
(b) State which, if either, of the two investment projects the directors of Mylo Ltd should accept and why.

4.2 Arkwright Mills plc is considering expanding its production of a new yarn, code name X15. The plant is expected to cost £1 million and have a life of five years and a nil residual value. It will be bought, paid for and ready for operation on 31 December Year 0. £500,000 has already been spent on development costs of the product, and this has been charged in the income statement in the year it was incurred.

The following results are projected for the new yarn:

	Year 1	Year 2	Year 3	Year 4	Year 5
	£m	£m	£m	£m	£m
Sales revenue	1.2	1.4	1.4	1.4	1.4
Costs, including depreciation	(1.0)	(1.1)	(1.1)	(1.1)	(1.1)
Profit before tax	0.2	0.3	0.3	0.3	0.3

Tax is charged at 50 per cent on annual profits (before tax and after depreciation) and paid one year in arrears. Depreciation of the plant has been calculated on a straight-line basis. Additional working capital of £600,000 will be required at the beginning of the project and released at the end of Year 5. You should assume that all cash flows occur at the end of the year in which they arise.

Required:

(a) Prepare a statement showing the incremental cash flows of the project relevant to a decision concerning whether or not to proceed with the construction of the new plant.

(b) Compute the net present value of the project using a 10 per cent discount rate.

(c) Compute the payback period to the nearest year. Explain the meaning of this term.

4.3 C. George (Controls) Ltd manufactures a thermostat that can be used in a range of kitchen appliances. The manufacturing process is, at present, semi-automated. The equipment used cost £540,000 and has a carrying amount of £300,000. Demand for the product has been fairly stable and output has been maintained at 50,000 units a year in recent years.

The following data, based on the current level of output, have been prepared in respect of the product:

Using existing equipment	Per unit	
	£	£
Selling price		12.40
Labour	(3.30)	
Materials	(3.65)	
Overheads: Variable	(1.58)	
Fixed	(1.60)	
		(10.13)
Operating profit		2.27

Although the existing equipment is expected to last for a further four years before it is sold for an estimated £40,000, the business has recently been considering purchasing new equipment that would completely automate much of the production process. This would give rise to production cost savings. The new equipment would cost £670,000 and would have an expected life of four years, at the end of which it would be sold for an estimated £70,000. If the new equipment is purchased, the old equipment could be sold for £150,000 immediately.

The assistant to the business's accountant has prepared a report to help assess the viability of the proposed change, which includes the following data:

Using new equipment	Per unit	
	£	£
Selling price		12.40
Labour	(1.20)	
Materials	(3.20)	
Overheads: Variable	(1.40)	
Fixed	(3.30)	
		(9.10)
Operating profit		3.30

Depreciation charges will increase by £85,000 a year as a result of purchasing the new machinery; however, other fixed costs are not expected to change.

In the report the assistant wrote:

The figures shown above that relate to the proposed change are based on the current level of output and take account of a depreciation charge of £150,000 a year in respect of the new equipment. The effect of purchasing the new equipment will be to increase the operating profit to sales revenue ratio from 18.3 per cent to 26.6 per cent. In addition, the purchase of the new equipment will enable us to reduce our inventories level immediately by £130,000.

In view of these facts, I recommend purchase of the new equipment.

The business has a cost of capital of 12 per cent.

Required:

(a) Prepare a statement of the incremental cash flows arising from the purchase of the new equipment.

(b) Calculate the net present value of the proposed purchase of new equipment.

(c) State, with reasons, whether the business should purchase the new equipment.

(d) Explain why cash flow projections are used rather than profit projections to assess the viability of proposed capital expenditure projects.

Ignore taxation.

4.4 The accountant of your business has recently been taken ill through overwork. In his absence his assistant has prepared some calculations of the profitability of a project, which are to be discussed soon at the board meeting of your business. His workings, which are set out below, include some errors of principle. You can assume that the statement below includes no arithmetical errors.

	Year 1 £000	Year 2 £000	Year 3 £000	Year 4 £000	Year 5 £000	Year 6 £000
Sales revenue		450	470	470	470	470
Less costs						
Materials		126	132	132	132	132
Labour		90	94	94	94	94
Overheads		45	47	47	47	47
Depreciation		120	120	120	120	120
Working capital	180					
Interest on working capital		27	27	27	27	27
Write-off of development costs		30	30	30		
Total costs	180	438	450	450	420	420
Operating profit/(loss)	(180)	12	20	20	50	50

$$\frac{\text{Total profit (loss)}}{\text{Cost of equipment}} = \frac{(£28,000)}{£600,000} = \text{Return on investment (4.7\%)}$$

You ascertain the following additional information:

■ The cost of equipment contains £100,000, being the carrying amount of an old machine. If it were not used for this project it would be scrapped with a zero net realisable value. New equipment costing £500,000 will be purchased on 31 December Year 0. You should assume that all other cash flows occur at the end of the year to which they relate.

■ The development costs of £90,000 have already been spent.

■ Overheads have been costed at 50 per cent of direct labour, which is the business's normal practice. An independent assessment has suggested that incremental overheads are likely to amount to £30,000 a year.

■ The business's cost of capital is 12 per cent.

Required:

(a) Prepare a corrected statement of the incremental cash flows arising from the project. Where you have altered the assistant's figures you should attach a brief note explaining your alterations.

(b) Calculate:
   (i)   The project's payback period.
   (ii) The project's net present value as at 31 December Year 0.

(c) Write a memo to the board advising on the acceptance or rejection of the project.

Ignore taxation in your answer.

4.5 Newton Electronics Ltd has incurred expenditure of £5 million over the past three years researching and developing a miniature hearing aid. The hearing aid is now fully developed. The directors are considering which of three mutually exclusive options should be taken to exploit the potential of the new product. The options are as follows:

1 Newton Electronics Ltd could manufacture the hearing aid itself. This would be a new departure, since the business has so far concentrated on research and development projects. However, the business has manufacturing space available that it currently rents to another business for £100,000 a year. Newton Electronics Ltd would have to purchase plant and equipment costing £9 million and invest £3 million in working capital immediately for production to begin.

   A market research report, for which the business paid £50,000, indicates that the new product has an expected life of five years. Sales of the product during this period are predicted as follows:

	Year 1	Year 2	Year 3	Year 4	Year 5
Number of units (000s)	800	1,400	1,800	1,200	500

Predicted sales for the year ended 30 November

The selling price per unit will be £30 in the first year but will fall to £22 for the following three years. In the final year of the product's life, the selling price will fall to £20. Variable production costs are predicted to be £14 a unit. Fixed production costs (including depreciation) will be £2.4 million a year. Marketing costs will be £2 million a year.

Newton Electronics Ltd intends to depreciate the plant and equipment using the straight-line method and based on an estimated residual value at the end of the five years of £1 million. The business has a cost of capital of 10 per cent a year.

2 Newton Electronics Ltd could agree to another business manufacturing and marketing the product under licence. A multinational business, Faraday Electricals plc, has offered to undertake the manufacture and marketing of the product and in return will make a royalty payment to Newton Electronics Ltd of £5 per unit. It has been estimated that the annual number of sales of the hearing aid will be 10 per cent higher if the multinational business, rather than Newton Electronics Ltd, manufactures and markets the product.

3 Newton Electronics Ltd could sell the patent rights to Faraday Electricals plc for £24 million, payable in two equal instalments. The first instalment would be payable immediately and the second at the end of two years. This option would give Faraday Electricals the exclusive right to manufacture and market the new product.

Required:

(a) Calculate the net present value (as at 1 January Year 1) of each of the options available to Newton Electronics Ltd.

(b) Identify and discuss any other factors that Newton Electronics Ltd should consider before arriving at a decision.

(c) State what you consider to be the most suitable option and why.

Ignore taxation.

4.6 Chesterfield Wanderers is a professional football club that has enjoyed considerable success in recent years. As a result, the club has accumulated £10 million to spend on its further development. The board of directors is currently considering two mutually exclusive options for spending the funds available.

The first option is to acquire another player. The team manager has expressed a keen interest in acquiring Basil ('Bazza') Ramsey, a central defender, who currently plays for a rival club. The rival club has agreed to release the player immediately for £10 million if required. A decision to acquire 'Bazza' Ramsey would mean that the existing central defender, Vinnie Smith, could be sold to another club. Chesterfield Wanderers has recently received an offer of £2.2 million for this player. This offer is still open but will be accepted only if 'Bazza' Ramsey joins Chesterfield Wanderers. If this does not happen, Vinnie Smith will be expected to stay on with the club until the end of his playing career in five years' time. During this period, Vinnie will receive an annual salary of £400,000 and a loyalty bonus of £200,000 at the end of his five-year period with the club.

Assuming 'Bazza' Ramsey is acquired, the team manager estimates that gate receipts will increase by £2.5 million in the first year and £1.3 million in each of the four following years. There will also be an increase in advertising and sponsorship revenues of £1.2 million for each of the next five years if the player is acquired. At the end of five years, the player can be sold to a club in a lower division and Chesterfield Wanderers will expect to receive £1 million as a transfer fee. 'Bazza' will receive an annual salary of £800,000 during his period at the club and a loyalty bonus of £400,000 after five years.

The second option is for the club to improve its ground facilities. The west stand could be extended and executive boxes could be built for businesses wishing to offer corporate hospitality to clients. These improvements would also cost £10 million and would take one year to complete. During this period, the west stand would be closed, resulting in a reduction in gate receipts of £1.8 million. However, gate receipts for each of the following four years would be £4.4 million higher than current receipts. In five years' time, the club has plans to sell the existing ground and to move to a new stadium nearby. Improving the ground facilities is not expected to affect the ground's value when it comes to be sold. Payment for the improvements will be made when the work has been completed at the end of the first year.

Whichever option is chosen, the board of directors has decided to take on additional ground staff. The additional wages bill is expected to be £350,000 a year over the next five years.

The club has a cost of capital of 10 per cent. Ignore taxation.

Required:

(a) Calculate the incremental cash flows arising from each of the options available to the club, and calculate the net present value of each of the options.

(b) On the basis of the calculations made in (a) above, which of the two options would you choose and why?

(c) Discuss the validity of using the net present value method in making investment decisions for a professional football club.

4.7 Haverhill Engineers Ltd manufactures components for the car industry. It is considering automating its line for producing crankshaft bearings. The automated equipment will cost £700,000. It will replace equipment with a scrap value of £50,000 and a book written-down value of £180,000.

At present, the line has a capacity of 1.25 million units per year but typically it has been run at only 80 per cent of capacity because of the lack of demand for its output. The new line has a capacity of 1.4 million units per year. Its life is expected to be five years and its scrap value at that time £100,000.

The accountant has prepared the following cost estimates based on the expected output of 1 million units per year:

	New line (per unit) pence	Old line (per unit) pence
Materials	40	36
Labour	22	10
Variable overheads	14	14
Fixed overheads	44	20
	120	80
Selling price	150	150
Profit per unit	30	70

Fixed overheads include depreciation on the old machine of £40,000 per year and £120,000 for the new machine. It is considered that, for the business overall, fixed overheads are unlikely to change.

The introduction of the new machine will enable inventories to be reduced by £160,000. The business uses 10 per cent as its cost of capital. You should ignore taxation.

Required:

(a) Prepare a statement of the incremental cash flows arising from the project.

(b) Calculate the project's net present value.

(c) Calculate the project's approximate internal rate of return.

(d) Explain the terms net present value and internal rate of return. State which method you consider to be preferable, giving reasons for your choice.

Chapter 5

MAKING CAPITAL INVESTMENT DECISIONS: FURTHER ISSUES

INTRODUCTION

The simple NPV decision rules mentioned in the previous chapter were: (1) all projects with a positive NPV should be accepted, and (2) where there are competing projects, the one with the higher (or highest) positive NPV should be selected. There are circumstances, however, that call for a modification to these simple decision rules and in this chapter we consider these.

Inflation has been a persistent problem for most industrialised economies. We shall examine the problems that inflation creates, and the ways in which we can adjust for the effects of inflation when undertaking discounted cash flow analysis.

Investment appraisal involves making estimates about the future. However, producing reliable estimates can be difficult, particularly where the environment is fast-changing or where new products are being developed. Risk, which is the likelihood that what is estimated to occur will not actually occur, is an important part of investment appraisal. We end this chapter by considering the problem of risk and how it may be taken into account when making investment decisions.

Learning outcomes

When you have completed this chapter, you should be able to:

■ Explain the modifications needed to the simple NPV decision rules where investment funds are limited or where there are competing projects with unequal lives.

■ Discuss the effect of inflation on investment appraisal and explain how inflation may be taken into account.

■ Discuss the nature of risk and explain why it is important in the context of investment decisions.

■ Describe the main approaches to the measurement of risk and discuss their limitations.

INVESTMENT DECISIONS WHEN FUNDS ARE LIMITED

We saw in the previous chapter that projects with a positive NPV should be undertaken if the business wishes to maximise shareholder wealth. What if, however, there aren't enough funds to undertake all projects with a positive NPV? It may be that investors are not prepared to provide the necessary funds or that managers decide to restrict the funds available for investment projects. Where funds are limited and, as a result, not all projects with a positive NPV can be undertaken, the basic NPV rules require modification. To illustrate the modification required, let us consider Example 5.1.

Example 5.1

Unicorn Engineering Ltd is considering three possible investment projects: X, Y and Z. The expected pattern of cash flows for each project is as follows:

	Project cash flows		
	X	Y	Z
	£m	£m	£m
Initial outlay	(8)	(9)	(11)
1 year's time	5	5	4
2 years' time	2	3	4
3 years' time	3	3	5
4 years' time	4	5	6.5

The business has a cost of capital of 12 per cent and the investment budget for the year that has just begun is restricted to £12 million. Each project is divisible (that is, it is possible to undertake part of a project if required).

Which investment project(s) should the business undertake?

Solution

If the cash flows for each project are discounted using the cost of capital as the appropriate discount rate, the NPVs are:

Project X			Project Y			Project Z		
Cash	Discount rate	PV	Cash	Discount rate	PV	Cash	Discount rate	PV
£m	12%	£m	£m	12%	£m	£m	12%	£m
(8)	1.00	(8.0)	(9)	1.00	(9.0)	(11)	1.00	(11.0)
5	0.89	4.5	5	0.89	4.5	4	0.89	3.6
2	0.80	1.6	3	0.80	2.4	4	0.80	3.2
3	0.71	2.1	3	0.71	2.1	5	0.71	3.6
4	0.64	2.6	5	0.64	3.2	6.5	0.64	4.2
	NPV	**2.8**		**NPV**	**3.2**		**NPV**	**3.6**

It is tempting to think that the best approach to dealing with the limited availability of funds would be to rank the projects according to their NPV. Hence, Project Z would be ranked first, Project Y would be ranked second and Project X would be ranked last. Given that £12 million is available, this would lead to the acceptance of Project Z (£11 million) and part of Project Y (£1 million). Therefore, the total NPV from the £12 million invested would be:

$$£3.6m + \frac{£3.2m}{9} = £4m$$

However, this solution would not represent the most efficient use of the limited funds available.

The best approach, *when projects are divisible*, is to maximise the *present value per £ of scarce finance*. By dividing the present values of the future cash inflows by the outlay for each project, a figure that represents the present value per £ of scarce finance is obtained. This provides the basis for a measure known as the profitability index.

Using the information above, the following figures would be obtained for the profitability index for each project. (In each case, the top part of the fraction represents the future cash flows *before* deducting the investment outlays.)

	Project X	Project Y	Project Z
Profitability index:	$\frac{10.8}{8.0}$	$\frac{12.2}{9.0}$	$\frac{14.6}{11.0}$
	= 1.35	= 1.36	= 1.33

Note that all the projects provide a profitability index of greater than 1. This will always be so where the NPV from a project is positive.

Activity 5.1

What does the profitability index calculated in Example 5.1 suggest about the relative profitability of the projects? What would be the NPV of the £12 million invested, assuming the profitability index approach is used?

The above calculations indicate that Project Y provides the highest present value per £ of scarce finance and so should be ranked first. Project X should be ranked second and Project Z should be ranked third. To maximise the use of the limited funds available (£12 million), the business should, therefore, undertake all of Project Y (£9 million) and part of Project X (£3 million).

The total NPV of the £12 million invested would be £3.2 million + (3/8 × £2.8 million) = £4.3 million. Note that this figure is higher than the total NPV obtained where projects were ranked according to their absolute NPVs.

Real World 5.1 and Figure 5.1 reveal the popularity of the profitability index among large businesses in five major industrialised countries.

A popularity index

The multinational study of financial policies by Cohen and Yagil (see Real World 4.10) revealed the frequency with which the profitability index is used by large businesses, as shown in Figure 5.1.

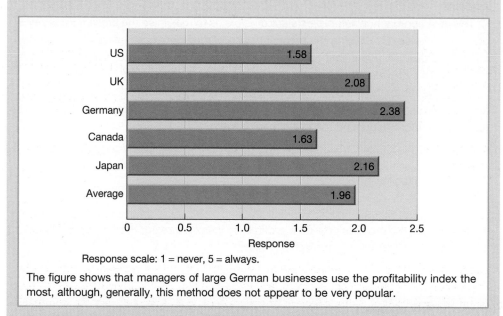

Response scale: 1 = never, 5 = always.

The figure shows that managers of large German businesses use the profitability index the most, although, generally, this method does not appear to be very popular.

Figure 5.1 Frequency of use of profitability index by large businesses

Source: G. Cohen and J. Yagil, 'A multinational survey of corporate financial policies', Working Paper, Haifa University, 2007.

There may be a need for projects to be funded over more than one year and limits may be placed on the availability of funds in each year. In such circumstances, there will be more than one constraint to consider. A mathematical technique known as **linear programming** can be used to maximise the NPV, given that not all projects with a positive NPV can be undertaken. This technique adopts the same approach (that is, it maximises the NPV per £ of scarce finance) as that illustrated above. Computer software is available to undertake the analysis required for this kind of multi-period rationing problem. A detailed consideration of linear programming is beyond the scope of this book. If, however, you are interested in this technique, take a look at the suggested further reading at the end of the chapter.

Non-divisible investment projects

The profitability index approach is suitable only where projects are divisible. Where this is not the case, the problem must be looked at in a different way. The particular investment project, or combination of whole projects, that will produce the highest NPV for the limited finance available should be selected.

Activity 5.2

Recommend a solution for Unicorn Engineering Ltd if the investment projects were not divisible (that is, it was not possible to undertake part of a project) and the finance available was:

(a) £12 million
(b) £18 million
(c) £20 million.

If the capital available was £12 million, only Project Z should be recommended as this would provide the highest NPV (£3.6 million) for the funds available for investment. If the capital available was £18 million, Projects X and Y should be recommended as this would provide the highest NPV (£6 million). If the capital available was £20 million, Projects Y and Z should be recommended as this would provide the highest NPV (£6.8 million).

In the following section, we look at another situation where modification to the simple NPV decision rules is needed to make optimal investment decisions.

COMPARING PROJECTS WITH UNEQUAL LIVES

On occasions, a business may find itself in a position where it has to decide between two (or more) competing investment projects, aimed at meeting a continuous need, which have different life spans. When this situation arises, accepting the project with the shorter life may offer the business the opportunity to reinvest sooner in another project with a positive NPV. The opportunity for earlier reinvestment should be taken into account so that proper comparisons between competing projects can be made. This is not taken into account in the simple form of NPV analysis, however.

To illustrate how direct comparisons between two (or more) competing projects with unequal lives can be made, let us consider Example 5.2.

Example 5.2

Khan Engineering Ltd has the opportunity to invest in two competing machines. Details of each machine are as follows:

	Machine A	Machine B
	£000	£000
Initial outlay	(100)	(140)
Cash flows		
1 year's time	50	60
2 years' time	70	80
3 years' time	–	32

The business has a cost of capital of 10 per cent.

State which of the two machines, if either, should be acquired.

Solution

One way to tackle this problem is to assume that the machines form part of a repeat chain of replacement and to compare the machines using the shortest-common-period-of-time

approach. If we assume that investment in Machine A can be repeated every two years and that investment in Machine B can be repeated every three years, the *shortest common period of time* over which the machines can be compared is six years (that is, 2 × 3).

The first step in this process of comparison is to calculate the NPV for each project over their expected lives. Thus, the NPV for each project will be as follows:

	Cash flows £000	Discount rate 10%	Present value £000
Machine A			
Initial outlay	(100)	1.00	(100.0)
1 year's time	50	0.91	45.5
2 years' time	70	0.83	58.1
		NPV	3.6
Machine B			
Initial outlay	(140)	1.00	(140.0)
1 year's time	60	0.91	54.6
2 years' time	80	0.83	66.4
3 years' time	32	0.75	24.0
		NPV	5.0

The next step is to calculate the NPV arising for each machine, over a six-year period, using the reinvestment assumption discussed above. That is, investment in Machine A will be repeated three times and investment in Machine B will be repeated twice during the six-year period.

This means that, for Machine A, the NPV over the six-year period will be equal to the NPV above (that is, £3,600) plus equivalent amounts two years and four years later. The calculation (in £000s) will be:

$$NPV = £3.6 + \frac{£3.6}{(1 + 0.1)^2} + \frac{£3.6}{(1 + 0.1)^4}$$

$$= £3.6 + £3.0 + £2.5 = £9.1$$

These calculations can be shown in the form of a diagram as in Figure 5.2.

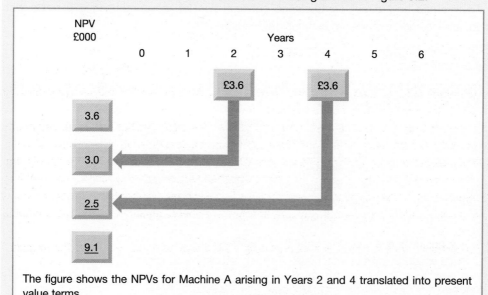

The figure shows the NPVs for Machine A arising in Years 2 and 4 translated into present value terms.

Figure 5.2 NPV for Machine A using a common period of time

Activity 5.3

What is the NPV for Machine B over the six-year period? Which machine is the better buy?

In the case of Machine B, the NPV over the six-year period will be equal to the NPV above plus the equivalent amount three years later. The calculation (in £000s) will be:

$$NPV = £5.0 + \frac{£5.0}{(1 + 0.1)^3} = £8.8$$

The calculations set out above suggest that Machine A is the better buy as it will have the higher NPV over the six-year period.

An alternative approach

When investment projects have a longer life span than those in Example 5.2, the calculations required using this method can be time-consuming. Fortunately, there is another method that can be used which avoids the need for laborious calculations. This approach uses the annuity concept to solve the problem. An annuity is simply an investment that pays a constant sum each year over a period of time. Thus, fixed payments made in respect of a loan or mortgage or a fixed amount of income received from an investment bond would be examples of annuities.

To illustrate the annuity principle, let us assume that we are given a choice of purchasing a new car by paying either £6,000 immediately or by paying three annual instalments of £2,410, commencing at the end of Year 1. Assuming interest rates of 10 per cent, the present value of the annuity payments would be:

	Cash outflows £	Discount rate 10%	Present value £
1 year's time	2,410	0.91	2,193
2 years' time	2,410	0.83	2,000
3 years' time	2,410	0.75	1,807
		NPV	6,000

As the immediate payment required is £6,000, we should be indifferent as to the form of payment. They are equal in present value terms.

In the example provided, a cash sum paid today is the equivalent of making three annuity payments over a three-year period. The second approach to solving the problem of competing projects that have unequal lives is based on this annuity principle. Put simply, the equivalent-annual-annuity approach, as it is referred to, converts the NPV of a project into an annual annuity stream over its expected life. This conversion is carried out for each competing project and the one that provides the highest annual annuity is the most profitable project.

To establish the equivalent annual annuity of the NPV of a project, we apply the formula

$$\text{Annual annuity} = \frac{i}{1 - (1 + i)^{-n}}$$

where i is the interest rate and n is the number of years.

Thus, using the information from the car loan example above, the annual value of an annuity that lasts for three years, which has a present value of £6,000 and where the discount rate is 10 per cent, is:

$$\text{Annual annuity} = £6,000 \times \frac{0.1}{1 - (1 + 0.1)^{-3}}$$

$$= £6,000 \times 0.402$$
$$= £2,412$$

(*Note*: The small difference between this final figure and the one used in the example earlier is due to rounding.)

There are tables that make life easier by providing the annual equivalent factors for a range of possible discount rates. An example of such an annuity table is given as Appendix B at the end of this book.

Activity 5.4

Use the table provided in Appendix B to calculate the equivalent annual annuity for each machine referred to in Example 5.2. Which machine is the better buy?

The equivalent annual annuity for Machine A (in £000s) is:

£3.6 × 0.5762 = £2.07

The equivalent annual annuity for Machine B (in £000s) is:

£5.0 × 0.4021 = £2.01

Machine A is therefore the better buy as it provides the higher annuity value. This is consistent with the finding of the shortest-common-period-of-time approach described earlier.

THE ABILITY TO DELAY

In recent years there has been some criticism of the NPV approach. One important criticism is that conventional theory does not recognise the fact that, in practice, it is often possible to delay making an investment decision. This ability to delay can have a profound effect on the final investment decision.

Activity 5.5

What are the possible benefits of delaying an investment decision?

By delaying, it may be possible to acquire more information concerning the likely outcome of the investment proposal. If a business decides not to delay, the investment decision, once made, may be irreversible. This may lead to losses if conditions prove to be unfavourable.

If managers do not exercise their option to delay, there may be an opportunity cost in the form of the benefits lost from later information. This opportunity cost can be large, and so failure to take it into account could be a serious error. One way of dealing with this problem is to modify the NPV decision rule so that the present value of the future cash flows must exceed the initial outlay *plus* any expected benefits from delaying the decision in order to obtain additional information. While in theory this may be fine, in practice the benefits will often be difficult to quantify.

THE PROBLEM OF INFLATION

Inflation is a problem that affects most modern economies. Although the rate of inflation may change over time, there has been a persistent tendency for the general price level to rise. It is important to recognise this phenomenon when evaluating investment projects, as inflation will affect both the cash flows and the discount rate over the life of the project.

During a period of inflation, the physical monetary amount required to acquire resources will rise over time and the business may seek to pass on any increase to customers in the form of higher prices. Inflation will also have an effect on the cost of financing the business, as investors seek to protect their investment from a decline in purchasing power by demanding higher returns. As a result of these changes, the cash flows and discount rates relating to the investment project will be affected.

To deal with the problem of inflation in the appraisal of investment projects, two possible approaches can be used:

- *Either* include inflation in the calculations by adjusting annual cash flows by the expected rate of inflation and by using a discount rate that is also adjusted for inflation. This will mean estimating the actual monetary cash flows expected from the project and using a market rate of interest that will take inflation into account.
- *Or* exclude inflation from the calculations by adjusting cash flows accordingly and by using a 'real' discount rate that does not include any element to account for inflation.

Both methods, properly applied, will give the same result.

If all cash flows are expected to increase in line with the general rate of inflation, it would be possible to use net cash flows as the basis for any adjustments. However, it is unlikely that the relationship between the various items that go to make up the net cash flows of the business (materials, labour costs and so on) will remain constant over time. In practice, inflation is likely to affect each item of cash flow differently. Separate adjustments for each item will therefore be needed.

Activity 5.6

Why is inflation likely to have a differing effect on the various items making up the net cash flow of a business?

Different costs (such as materials and labour) may increase at different rates due to relative changes in demand. In addition, some costs (such as lease payments) may be fixed over time and therefore unaffected by inflation, at least over the period of the project. In a competitive environment, a business may be unable to pass on all of the increase in costs to customers and so will have to absorb some of the increase by reducing profits. Thus, cash inflows from sales may not fully reflect the rise in the costs of the various inputs such as materials and labour.

To compute the real cash flows from a project, it will be necessary to calculate the monetary cash flows relating to each item and then deflate these amounts by the *general* rate of inflation. This adjustment will provide us with the *current general purchasing power* of the cash flows. This measure of general purchasing power is of more relevance to investors than if the cash flows were deflated by a specific rate of inflation relevant to each type of cash flow. Similarly, the real discount rate will be deduced by deflating the market rate of interest by the *general* rate of inflation.

Real World 5.2 sets out the findings of a survey of UK businesses which reveals how inflation is dealt with in practice.

THE PROBLEM OF RISK

Risk arises where the future is unclear and where a range of possible future outcomes exists. As the future is uncertain, there is a chance (or risk) that estimates made concerning the future will not occur. Risk is particularly important in the context of investment decisions.

Activity 5.7

Why should this be the case? Try to think of at least one reason.

Risk is particularly important because of:

■ the relatively long time scales involved – there may be a lot of time for things to go wrong between the decision being made and the end of the project
■ the size of the investment – if things do go wrong, the impact can be both significant and lasting.

Sometimes a distinction is made in the literature between risk and uncertainty. However, this distinction is not useful for our purposes and in this chapter the two words are used interchangeably.

Real World 5.3 looks at one of the world's biggest investment projects. The long timesscales involved with this project offered plenty of opportunities for things to go wrong – and they did. It proved to be a commercial disaster, despite being a technological success.

Real World 5.3

Wealth lost in the Chunnel

The Channel Tunnel, which runs for 31 miles between Folkestone in the UK and Sangatte in Northern France, was started in 1986 and opened for public use in 1994. From a techno-logical and social perspective it has been a success, but from a financial point of view it has been a disaster. The tunnel was purely a private sector venture for which a new business, Eurotunnel plc, was created. Relatively little public money was involved. To be a commercial success the tunnel needed to cover all of its costs, including interest charges, and leave sufficient to enhance the shareholders' wealth. In fact, the providers of long-term finance (lenders and shareholders) have lost virtually all of their investment. Though the main losers were banks and institutional investors, many individuals, particularly in France, bought shares in Eurotunnel.

Since the accounting year ended 31 December 2007, the business has made a profit, and in 2009 it paid its first dividend. However, this was achieved only as a result of the busi-ness forcing lenders, who would expect to be paid interest, to convert their investment to ordinary shares. This meant that the business eliminated the cost of financing some of the cost of building the tunnel.

Key inputs to the pre-1986 assessment of the project were the cost of construction and creating the infrastructure, the length of time required to complete construction and the level of revenue that the tunnel would generate when it became operational.

In the event:

■ construction cost was £10 billion – it was originally planned to cost £5.6 billion
■ construction time was seven years – it was planned to be six years
■ revenues from passengers and freight have been well below those projected – for example, 21 million annual passenger journeys on Eurostar trains were projected; the numbers have consistently remained at around 7 million.

The failure to generate revenues at the projected levels has probably been the biggest contributor to the problem. When preparing the projection pre 1986, planners failed to take adequate account of two crucial factors:

1 Fierce competition from the ferry operators. At the time many thought that the ferries would roll over and die.
2 The rise of no-frills, cheap air travel between the UK and the continent.

The commercial failure of the tunnel means that it will be very difficult in future for projects of this nature to be financed from private sector funds.

Sources: Annual Reports of Eurotunnel plc; J. Randall, 'How Eurotunnel went so wrong', BBC News, www.news.bbc.co.uk, 13 June 2005.

In the sections that follow, we examine various methods that can be used to help managers deal with the problem of risk. While these methods cannot insure businesses against the sort of disaster described in Real World 5.3, they can help to reduce their incidence and severity. Our examination will focus on the more useful and systematic approaches to dealing with risk that have been proposed. In practice, crude methods of dealing with risk are sometimes used, such as shortening the required payback period and employing conservative cash flows. However, these methods rely on arbitrary assumptions and have little to commend them. They have therefore been excluded from our examination.

The first two methods of dealing with risk that we consider were discussed briefly in Chapter 2 during our examination of projected financial statements. We now consider them in more detail as they are also relevant to investment decisions.

SENSITIVITY ANALYSIS

A popular way of assessing the level of risk is to carry out *sensitivity analysis*. We may recall from Chapter 2 that it involves an examination of key input values in order to see how changes in each input might influence the likely outcomes. One form of sensitivity analysis involves posing a series of 'what if?' questions. For example:

- What if sales volume is 5 per cent higher than expected?
- What if sales volume is 10 per cent lower than expected?

By answering these 'what if?' questions, managers will have a range of possible outcomes to consider. However, the changes to each input must be justified for them to be useful for decision making.

There is another form of sensitivity analysis that is particularly useful in the context of investment appraisal. Where the result from an appraisal, using the best estimates, is positive, the value for each key factor can be examined to see by how much it could be changed before the project became unprofitable for that reason alone.

Assume that the NPV for an investment in a machine to provide a particular service is estimated to be a positive value of £50,000. To carry out sensitivity analysis on this investment proposal, we must first identify each of the key input factors. Let us assume they are:

- initial cost of the machine
- sales volume and price
- relevant operating costs
- life of the machine
- financing cost.

We must then find the value that each factor could have before the NPV figure becomes negative (that is, the value at which NPV is zero). The difference between the value derived and the estimated value for that factor represents the 'margin of safety' for the particular factor.

The various elements considered in sensitivity analysis are set out in Figure 5.3.

In your previous studies of accounting, you may have studied break-even analysis. This form of sensitivity analysis is, in essence, a form of break-even analysis. The point at which the NPV is zero is the point at which the project breaks even (that is, makes neither profit nor loss). The 'margin of safety' for a particular factor associated with the project can be interpreted in the same way as the margin of safety is interpreted in break-even analysis.

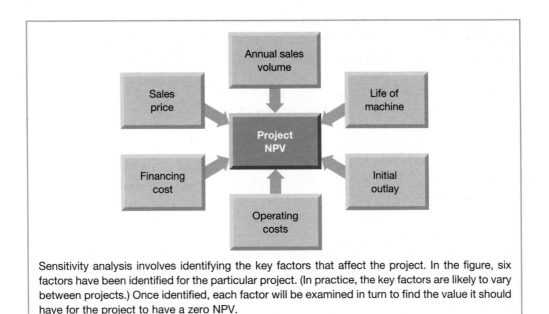

Sensitivity analysis involves identifying the key factors that affect the project. In the figure, six factors have been identified for the particular project. (In practice, the key factors are likely to vary between projects.) Once identified, each factor will be examined in turn to find the value it should have for the project to have a zero NPV.

Figure 5.3 Factors affecting the sensitivity of NPV calculations

A computer spreadsheet model of the project can be extremely valuable when undertaking sensitivity analysis because it then becomes a simple matter to try various values for the key factors and to calculate the effect of changes in each. Example 5.3, which illustrates sensitivity analysis, is straightforward and can be undertaken without recourse to a spreadsheet.

Example 5.3

S. Saluja (Property Developers) Ltd intends to bid at an auction, to be held today, for a manor house that has fallen into disrepair. The auctioneer believes that the manor house will be sold for about £450,000. The business wishes to renovate the property and divide it into flats to be sold for £150,000 each. The renovation will be in two stages and will cover a two-year period. Stage 1 will cover the first year of the project. It will cost £500,000 and the six flats completed during this stage are expected to be sold for a total of £900,000 at the end of the first year. Stage 2 will cover the second year of the project. It will cost £300,000 and the three remaining flats are expected to be sold at the end of the second year for a total of £450,000.

The cost of renovation is subject to a binding agreement with local builders if the manor house is acquired. There is, however, some uncertainty over the remaining input values. The business estimates its cost of capital at 12 per cent a year.

(a) What is the NPV of the proposed project?
(b) Assuming none of the other inputs deviates from the best estimates provided:
  (i) What auction price would have to be paid for the manor house to cause the project to have a zero NPV?
  (ii) What cost of capital would cause the project to have a zero NPV?
  (iii) What is the sale price of each of the flats that would cause the project to have a zero NPV? (Each flat will be sold for the same price: £150,000.)
(c) Comment on the calculations carried out in answering (b) above.

Solution

(a) The NPV of the proposed project is as follows:

	Cash flows £	Discount factor 12%	Present value £
Year 1 (£900,000 − £500,000)	400,000	0.893	357,200
Year 2 (£450,000 − £300,000)	150,000	0.797	119,550
Less Initial outlay			(450,000)
		NPV	26,750

(b) (i) To obtain a zero NPV, the auction price for the manor house would have to be £26,750 higher than the current estimate (that is, the amount of the estimated NPV). This would make a total price of £476,750, which is about 6 per cent above the current estimated price.

(ii) As there is a positive NPV, the cost of capital that would cause the project to have a zero NPV must be higher than 12 per cent. Let us try 20 per cent.

	Cash flows £	Discount factor 20%	Present value £
Year 1 (£900,000 − £500,000)	400,000	0.833	333,200
Year 2 (£450,000 − £300,000)	150,000	0.694	104,100
Less Initial outlay			(450,000)
		NPV	(12,700)

As the NPV, using a 20 per cent discount rate, is negative, the 'break-even' cost of capital must lie somewhere between 12 per cent and 20 per cent. A reasonable approximation is obtained as follows:

	Discount rate %	NPV £
	12	26,750
	20	(12,700)
Difference	8	Range 39,450

The change in NPV for every 1 per cent change in the discount rate will be:

$$\frac{39,450}{8} = 4,931$$

The reduction in the 20 per cent discount rate required to achieve a zero NPV would therefore be:

$$\frac{12,700}{4,931} = 2.6\%$$

The cost of capital (that is, the discount rate) would therefore have to be 17.4 (20.0 − 2.6) per cent for the project to have a zero NPV.

This calculation is, of course, the same as that used in the previous chapter when calculating the IRR of the project. In other words, 17.4 per cent is the IRR of the project.

(iii) To obtain a zero NPV, the sale price of each flat must be reduced so that the NPV is reduced by £26,750. In Year 1, six flats are sold, and in Year 2, three flats are sold. The discount factor for Year 1 is 0.893 and for Year 2 it is 0.797. We can derive the fall in value per flat (Y) to give a zero NPV by using the equation:

$$(6Y \times 0.893) + (3Y \times 0.797) = £26,750$$
$$Y = £3,452$$

The sale price of each flat necessary to obtain a zero NPV is therefore:

$$£150,000 - £3,452 = £146,548$$

This represents a fall in the estimated price of 2.3 per cent.

(c) These calculations indicate that the auction price would have to be about 6 per cent above the estimated price before a zero NPV is obtained. The margin of safety is therefore not very high for this factor. In practice, this should not represent a real risk because the business could withdraw from the bidding if the price rises to an unacceptable level.

The other two factors represent more real risks. Only after the project is at a very late stage can the business be sure as to what actual price per flat will prevail. It would be unusual to be able to have fixed contracts for sale of all of the flats before the auction. The calculations reveal that the price of the flats would have to fall only by 2.3 per cent from the estimated price before the NPV is reduced to zero. Hence, the margin of safety for this factor is very small.

The cost of capital is less sensitive to changes and there would have to be an increase from 12 per cent to 17.4 per cent before the project produced a zero NPV. It may be possible to raise finance for the project at a fixed rate before the auction of the house. However, even if the funding cost cannot be fixed in advance, the cost of capital does not seem to be a sensitive factor.

It appears from the calculations that the sale price of the flats is the key sensitive factor to consider. A careful re-examination of the market value of the flats seems appropriate before a final decision is made.

Real World 5.4 describes the evaluation of a mining project that incorporated sensitivity analysis to test the robustness of the findings.

Real World 5.4

Golden opportunity

In a news release, Hochschild Mining plc announced positive results from an independent study of the profitability of its Azuca project in southern Peru. The project involves drilling for gold and silver. The business provided calculations based on the most likely outcome (the base case) along with sensitivity analysis of key variables. These variables were the estimated prices for gold and silver and the discount rate to be applied. The following results were obtained:

Azuca project sensitivity analysis (base case in bold):

	Gold price/Silver price ($/ounce)			
	$1,000/$17.00	$1,100/$18.70	$1,200/$20.40	$1,300/$21.90
IRR	21%	30%	38%	46%
Cash flow	$107m	$155m	$204m	$247m
NPV (5% discount rate)	$61m	$97m	$133m	$165m
NPV (10% discount rate)	$32m	$60m	$87m	$112m

Source: 'Positive scoping study at 100% owned Azuca project in southern Peru', news release, Hochschild Mining plc, 30 September, http://www.hocplc.com/en/investors/news.

Activity 5.8 can also be attempted without recourse to a spreadsheet.

A business has the opportunity to invest £12 million immediately in new plant and equipment in order to produce a new product. The product will sell at £80 per unit and it is estimated that 200,000 units of the product can be sold in each of the next four years. Variable costs are £56 a unit and additional fixed costs (excluding depreciation) are £1.0 million in total. The residual value of the plant and machinery at the end of the life of the product is estimated to be £1.6 million.

The business has a cost of capital of 12 per cent.

(a) Calculate the NPV of the investment proposal.
(b) Carry out separate sensitivity analysis to indicate by how much the following factors would have to change in order to produce an NPV of zero:
   (i)   initial outlay on plant and machinery
   (ii) discount rate
   (iii) residual value of the plant and machinery.

(a) Annual operating cash flows are as follows:

	£m	£m
Sales (200,000 × £80)		16.0
Less		
Variable costs (200,000 × £56)	11.2	
Fixed costs	1.0	12.2
		3.8

Estimated cash flows are as follows:

	Year 0	Year 1	Year 2	Year 3	Year 4
	£m	£m	£m	£m	£m
Plant and equipment	(12.0)				1.6
Operating cash flows		3.8	3.8	3.8	3.8
	(12.0)	3.8	3.8	3.8	5.4

The NPV of the project is:

	Year 0	Year 1	Year 2	Year 3	Year 4
	£m	£m	£m	£m	£m
Cash flows	(12.0)	3.8	3.8	3.8	5.4
Discount rate (12%)	1.0	0.89	0.80	0.71	0.64
Present value	(12.0)	3.38	3.04	2.70	3.46
NPV	0.58				

(b) (i) The increase required in the initial outlay on plant and equipment to achieve an NPV of zero will be £0.58 million (as the plant and equipment are already expressed in present value terms). This represents a 4.8 per cent increase on the current estimated figure of £12 million ((0.58/12) × 100).

(ii) Using a discount rate of 14 per cent, the NPV of the project is:

	Year 0	Year 1	Year 2	Year 3	Year 4
	£m	£m	£m	£m	£m
Cash flows	(12.0)	3.8	3.8	3.8	5.4
Discount rate (14%)	1.0	0.88	0.77	0.68	0.59
Present value	(12.0)	3.34	2.93	2.58	3.19
NPV	0.04				

This is very close to an NPV of zero and so 14 per cent is the approximate figure. It is 16.7 per cent higher than the cost of capital (($14 - 12$)/12) × 100).

(iii) The fall in the residual value of the plant and equipment (R) that will lead to a zero NPV is:

$$(R \times \text{discount factor at the end of four years}) - \text{NPV of the project} = 0$$

By rearranging this equation, we have:

$$(R \times \text{discount factor at the end of four years}) = \text{NPV of the project}$$
$$R \times 0.64 = \text{£0.58 million}$$
$$R = \text{£0.58 million}/0.64$$
$$= \text{£0.9 million}$$

This represents a 43.8 per cent decrease in the current estimated residual value ((($1.6 - 0.9$)/1.6) × 100).

Sensitivity chart

It is possible to portray the effect of changes to key variables on the NPV of a project by preparing a sensitivity chart. To illustrate how this chart is prepared, we can use the following information from the answer to Activity 5.8:

■ The NPV of the project is estimated as £0.58m.
■ An NPV of zero will occur where there is a:
  ■ 4.8 per cent increase in initial outlay
  ■ 16.7 per cent increase in the cost of capital
  ■ 43.8 per cent decrease in the residual value of the plant and equipment.

In Figure 5.4, the NPV of the project is shown on the vertical axis and the percentage change in estimates on the horizontal axis. By using two coordinates – the estimated NPV without any change and the percentage change required to produce a zero NPV – a line can be drawn for each variable to show its sensitivity to change. The steeper the slope of the line, the more sensitive the particular variable is to change. The visual representation in Figure 5.4 can help managers to see more clearly the sensitivity of each variable.

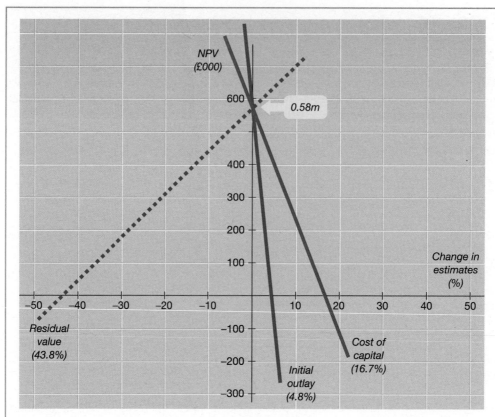

We can see that a 4.8 per cent increase in initial outlay, a 16.7 per cent increase in the cost of capital and a 43.8 per cent decrease in the residual value of plant and equipment will each result in a zero NPV. The slope of the line of each variable indicates sensitivity to change: the steeper the slope, the more sensitive the variable is to change.

Figure 5.4 Sensitivity chart

Strengths and weaknesses of sensitivity analysis

Sensitivity analysis should help in the following ways:

- Managers can see the margin of safety for each key factor. This should help them to identify highly sensitive factors that require more detailed information. The collection, reporting and evaluation of information can be costly and time-consuming. The more managers can focus their efforts on the critical aspects of a decision, the better.
- It can provide a basis for planning. Where a project outcome has been identified as highly sensitive to changes in a key factor, managers can formulate plans to deal with possible deviations from the estimated outcome.

Although sensitivity analysis is undoubtedly a useful tool, it has two major drawbacks:

- It does not give clear decision rules concerning acceptance or rejection of the project. There is no single-figure outcome to indicate whether a project is worth undertaking. This means that managers must rely on their own judgement.
- It is a static form of analysis. Only one factor is considered at a time while the rest are held constant. In practice, however, it is likely that more than one factor value will differ from the best estimates provided.

SCENARIO ANALYSIS

A slightly different approach, which overcomes the problem of dealing with a single variable at a time, is *scenario analysis*. This method was also briefly discussed in Chapter 2. We may recall that a number of variables are changed simultaneously so as to provide a particular 'state of the world', or scenario. A number of internally consistent 'states of the world' can be presented to managers, with each drawing attention to variables that are vital to a project's success. A popular form of scenario analysis is to provide:

- an optimistic view of likely future events
- a pessimistic view of likely future events
- a 'most likely' view of future events.

This approach has been criticised because it does not indicate the likelihood of each scenario occurring, nor does it identify other possible scenarios that might occur. Nevertheless, the portrayal of optimistic and pessimistic scenarios may be useful in providing managers with some feel for the 'downside' risk and 'upside' potential associated with a project.

SIMULATIONS

The **simulation** approach is really a development of sensitivity analysis. In this approach a distribution of possible values for key variables in the investment project is created and a probability of occurrence is attached to each value. A computer is used to select one of the possible values from each distribution on a random basis. It then generates outcomes on the basis of the selected values for each variable. This process represents a single trial. The process is then repeated using other values for each variable until many possible combinations of values for the key variables have been considered. In practice, this may mean that thousands of trials are carried out.

The starting point for carrying out a simulation exercise is to model the investment project. This involves identifying the key factors affecting the project and their interrelationships. Thus, the cash flows will have to be modelled to reveal the key factors influencing the cash receipts and the cash payments and their interrelationships. Let us illustrate this point using a simple example. The cash received from sales may be modelled by the following equation:

$$\text{Sales revenue} = \text{Selling price per unit} \times (\text{Market share} \times \text{Market size})$$

The modelling process will also require equations showing the factors determining the cash expenses and the interrelationships between these factors. The relationship between the cash inflows and outflows must also be modelled. As investment projects extend over more than one period, there may also be a need to model the relationship between the cash flows occurring in different periods. Thus, a fairly large number of equations may be required to model even a fairly simple investment project proposal.

Once the key factors have been identified and their relationships have been modelled, the next step is to specify the possible values for each of the factors within the model. As mentioned earlier, a computer is then used to select one of the possible values from each distribution on a random basis. It then generates projected cash flows using the selected values for each factor. This process represents a single trial. The process is then repeated using other values for each factor until many possible combinations of values for the key factors have been considered. The results of the repeated sampling allow us to obtain a probability distribution of the values of the cash flows for the project. The main steps in the simulation process are set out in Figure 5.5.

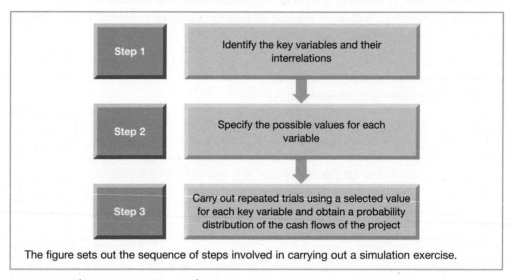

The figure sets out the sequence of steps involved in carrying out a simulation exercise.

Figure 5.5 The main steps in simulation

The use of simulations may provide two benefits. First, the process of modelling an investment project can help managers understand its nature and the key issues to be resolved. Second, it provides a distribution of outcomes that can help assess the riskiness of a project. These benefits, however, must be weighed against the problems involved.

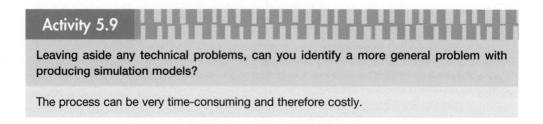

Activity 5.9

Leaving aside any technical problems, can you identify a more general problem with producing simulation models?

The process can be very time-consuming and therefore costly.

To save management time, the modelling may be undertaken by support staff. Where this task is delegated, the first benefit referred to above will often be lost. Furthermore, technical difficulties may undermine the second benefit mentioned. Problems are often encountered in modelling the relationship between key factors and also in establishing the distribution of outcomes for each factor. The more complex the project, the more complex these problems are likely to be. Finally, carrying out endless simulations can lead to a mechanical approach to dealing with risk. Emphasis may be placed on carrying out trials and producing the results, and insufficient attention may be given to a consideration of the underlying assumptions and issues.

RISK PREFERENCES OF INVESTORS

So far, the methods discussed have sought to identify the level of risk associated with a project. However, this is not, of itself, enough. The attitude of investors towards risk should also be determined. Unless we know how investors are likely to react to the presence of risk in investment opportunities, we cannot really make an informed decision.

In theory, investors fall into one of the following categories based on their attitude towards risk:

- **Risk-seeking investors**. Some investors enjoy a gamble. Given two projects with the same expected return but with different levels of risk, the risk-seeking investor would choose the project with the higher level of risk.
- **Risk-neutral investors**. Some investors are indifferent to risk. Thus, given two projects with the same expected return but with different levels of risk, the risk-neutral investor would have no preference. Both projects provide the same expected return and the fact that one project has a higher level of risk would not be an issue.
- **Risk-averse investors**. Some investors are averse to risk. Given two projects with the same expected return but with different levels of risk, a risk-averse investor would choose the project that has a lower level of risk.

Activity 5.10

In which of the above categories do you think most investors will fall?

While some investors may be risk seekers and some investors may be indifferent to risk, the evidence suggests that the vast majority of investors are risk-averse.

This does not mean, however, that most investors will not be prepared to take on risky investments. Rather, it means that they will require compensation in the form of higher returns from projects that have higher levels of risk. An explanation as to why this is the case can be found in utility theory.

Risk and utility theory

To describe utility theory, let us assume you can measure the satisfaction, or utility, you receive from money in the form of 'utils of satisfaction' and let us also assume that you are penniless. If a rich benefactor gives you £1,000, this may bring you a great deal of satisfaction as it would allow you to buy many things that you have yearned for. Let us say it provides you with 20 utils of satisfaction. If the benefactor gives you a further £1,000, this may also bring you a great deal of satisfaction, but not as much as the first £1,000 as your essential needs have now been met. Let us say, therefore, it provides you with 10 utils of satisfaction. If the benefactor then gives you a further £1,000, the additional satisfaction received from this additional sum may reduce to, say, 6 utils, and so on. (The expression *diminishing marginal utility of wealth* is often used to describe the situation where the additional satisfaction received from wealth declines with each additional amount of wealth received.)

The relationship between the level of satisfaction received and the amount of wealth received can be expressed in the form of a **utility function**. For a risk-averse individual, the utility function, when shown graphically, would take the shape of a curve such as that shown in Figure 5.6. We can see clearly from this graph that each increment in wealth provides a diminishing level of satisfaction for the individual. We can also see that the increase in satisfaction from gaining additional wealth is not the same as the decrease in satisfaction from losing the same amount of wealth.

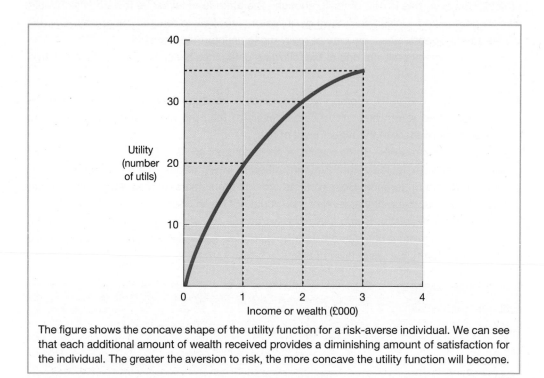

The figure shows the concave shape of the utility function for a risk-averse individual. We can see that each additional amount of wealth received provides a diminishing amount of satisfaction for the individual. The greater the aversion to risk, the more concave the utility function will become.

Figure 5.6 Utility function for a risk-averse individual

An individual with wealth of, say, £2,000 would receive satisfaction from this amount of 30 utils. If, however, the wealth of that individual fell by £1,000 for some reason, the loss of satisfaction would be greater than the satisfaction gained from receiving an additional £1,000. We can say that the loss of satisfaction from a fall in wealth of £1,000 would be 10 utils, whereas the gain in satisfaction from receiving an additional £1,000 would be only 6 utils. As the satisfaction, or happiness, lost from a fall in wealth is greater than the satisfaction, or happiness, gained from acquiring an equivalent amount of wealth, the individual will be averse to risk and will be prepared to undertake risk only in exchange for the prospect of higher returns.

The particular shape of the utility curve will vary between individuals. Some individuals are likely to be more risk averse than others. The more risk averse an individual is, the more concave the shape of the curve will become. However, this general concave curve shape will apply to all risk-averse individuals.

For an individual who is indifferent to risk, the marginal satisfaction, or utility, of wealth will not diminish as described above. Instead, the marginal utility of wealth will remain constant. This means the individual's utility function will look quite different from that of a risk-averse individual.

Try to draw a graph that plots the utility of wealth against wealth for an individual who is indifferent to risk. Explain the shape of the graph line.

An individual who is indifferent to risk would have a utility function that can be plotted in the form of a straight line, as shown in Figure 5.7.

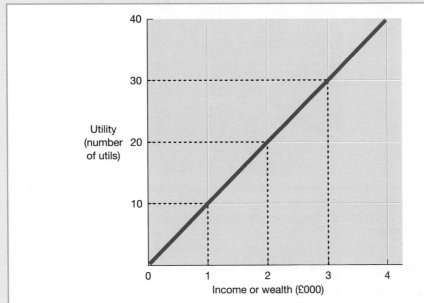

The figure shows the utility function for a risk-neutral individual. The straight line indicates that each additional util of wealth received will produce the same amount of satisfaction.

Figure 5.7 Utility function for a risk-neutral individual

This indicates that the satisfaction, or happiness, lost from a fall in wealth will be equal to the satisfaction, or happiness, gained from acquiring an equivalent amount of wealth.

For a risk-seeking individual, the marginal satisfaction, or utility, of wealth will increase rather than decrease or remain constant. This means that the shape of a risk-seeking individual's utility function, when displayed in the form of a graph, will be quite different from the two described above.

Draw a graph plotting the utility of wealth against wealth for an individual who is risk seeking, and explain the shape of the graph line.

The graph for a risk-seeking individual will be as shown in Figure 5.8. We can see from the graph that the curve is upwards-sloping. The satisfaction, or happiness, gained from an increase in wealth would be greater than the satisfaction, or happiness, lost from a decrease in wealth of an equivalent amount. This means the individual will be prepared to take on risks in order to obtain additional wealth.

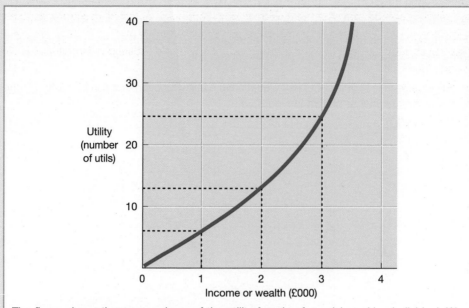

The figure shows the convex shape of the utility function for a risk-seeking individual. We can see that each additional amount of wealth received provides an increasing amount of satisfaction for the individual. The greater the attraction to risk, the more convex the utility function will become.

Figure 5.8 Utility function for a risk-seeking individual

Although utility theory helps us to understand why investors are risk averse, it would not be possible to identify the utility functions of individual investors and then combine these in some way so as to provide a guide for management decisions. The practical value of this theory is therefore limited. In the real world, managers may make decisions based on their own attitudes towards risk rather than those of investors, or may make assumptions about the risk preferences of investors.

RISK-ADJUSTED DISCOUNT RATE

We have seen from the section above that there is a relationship between risk and the rate of return required by investors. The reaction of a risk-averse individual will be to require a higher rate of return for risky projects. The higher the level of risk associated with a project, the higher the required rate of return. The **risk-adjusted discount rate** is based on this simple relationship between risk and return. Thus, when evaluating investment projects, managers will increase the NPV discount rate in the face of increased risk. In other words, a *risk premium* will be required for risky projects: the higher the level of risk, the higher the risk premium.

The risk premium is usually added to a 'risk-free' rate of return in order to derive the total return required. The risk-free rate is normally taken to be equivalent to the rate of return from long-term government loan notes. In practice, a business may divide projects into risk categories (for example, low, medium and high risk) and then assign a risk premium to each risk category. The cash flows from a particular project will then be discounted using a rate based on the risk-free rate plus the appropriate risk premium. Since all investments are risky to some extent, all projects will have a risk premium linked to them.

This relationship between risk and return, which we first discussed in Chapter 1, is illustrated in Figure 5.9.

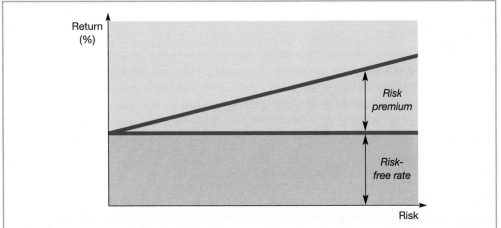

It is possible to take account of the riskiness of projects by changing the discount rate. A risk premium is added to the risk-free rate in order to derive the appropriate discount rate. A higher return will normally be expected from projects where the risks are higher. Thus, the more risky the project, the higher will be the risk premium.

Figure 5.9 Relationship between risk and return

The use of a risk-adjusted discount rate in investment appraisal provides a single-figure outcome that can be used to decide whether to accept or to reject a project. Often, managers have an intuitive grasp of the relationship between risk and return and so may feel comfortable with this technique. However, there are practical difficulties with implementing this approach.

Activity 5.13

Can you think what the practical problems with this approach might be?

Subjective judgement is required when assigning an investment project to a particular risk category and then in assigning a risk premium to each category. The choices made will reflect the personal views of the managers responsible and these may differ from the views of the shareholders they represent. Nevertheless, the choices made can make the difference between accepting and rejecting a particular project.

We shall see in Chapter 8 that there is a more sophisticated approach to deriving a risk premium that does not rely on subjective judgement.

EXPECTED NET PRESENT VALUE

Another means of assessing risk is through the use of statistical probabilities. It may be possible to identify a range of feasible values for a particular input, such as net cash flows, and to assign a probability of occurrence to each of these values. Using this information, we can derive an **expected value** which is a weighted average of the possible outcomes where the probabilities are used as weights. An **expected net present value (ENPV)** can then be derived using these expected values.

To illustrate this method in relation to an investment decision, let us consider Example 5.4.

Example 5.4

Patel Properties Ltd has the opportunity to acquire a lease on a block of flats that has only two years remaining before it expires. The cost of the lease would be £1,000,000. The occupancy rate of the block of flats is currently around 70 per cent and the flats are let almost exclusively to naval personnel. There is a large naval base located nearby and there is little other demand for the flats. The occupancy rate of the flats will change in the remaining two years of the lease depending on the outcome of a defence review.

The navy is considering three options for the naval base:

■ *Option 1*. Increase the size of the base by closing down a naval base in another region and transferring the naval personnel to the base located near to the flats.
■ *Option 2*. Close down the naval base near to the flats and leave only a skeleton staff there for maintenance purposes. The personnel would be moved to a base in another region.
■ *Option 3*. Leave the naval base open but reduce staffing levels by 20 per cent.

The directors of Patel Properties Ltd have estimated the following net cash flows for each of the two years under each option and the probability of their occurrence:

	£	Probability
Option 1	800,000	0.6
Option 2	120,000	0.1
Option 3	400,000	<u>0.3</u>
		<u>1.0</u>

Note: The sum of the probabilities is 1.0 (that is, it is certain that one of the possible options will arise).

The business has a cost of capital of 10 per cent.

Should the business purchase the lease on the block of flats?

Solution

To answer the question, the ENPV of the proposed investment can be calculated. To do this, the weighted average of the possible outcomes for each year must first be calculated. This involves multiplying each cash flow by its probability of occurrence (as the probabilities are used as weights). The expected annual net cash flows will be:

	Cash flows (a) £	Probability (b)	Expected cash flows (a × b) £
Option 1	800,000	0.6	480,000
Option 2	120,000	0.1	12,000
Option 3	400,000	0.3	<u>120,000</u>
Expected net cash flows in each year			<u>612,000</u>

Having derived the expected net cash flows in each year, they can be discounted using a rate of 10 per cent to reflect the cost of capital.

	Expected cash flows £	Discount rate 10%	Expected present value £
Year 1	612,000	0.909	556,308
Year 2	612,000	0.826	505,512
			1,061,820
Less Initial investment			(1,000,000)
Expected net present value (ENPV)			61,820

We can see that the ENPV is positive. Hence, the wealth of shareholders is expected to increase by purchasing the lease. (However, the size of the ENPV is small in relation to the initial investment and so the business may wish to check carefully the key assumptions used in the analysis before a final decision is made.)

The ENPV approach has the advantage of producing a single-figure outcome and of having a clear decision rule to apply (that is, if the ENPV is positive, the business should invest; if it is negative, it should not). However, this approach produces an average figure that may not be capable of actually occurring. This point was illustrated in Example 5.4 where the expected value of the net cash flows does not correspond to any of the stated options.

Using an average figure can also obscure the underlying risk associated with the project. Simply deriving the ENPV, as in Example 5.4, can be misleading. Without some idea of the individual possible outcomes and their probability of occurring, managers are in the dark. If either of Options 2 and 3 were to occur, the NPV of the investment would be negative (wealth destroying). It is 40 per cent probable that one of these options will occur, so this is a significant risk. Only if Option 1 were to occur (60 per cent probable) would investing in the flats represent a good decision. Of course, in advance of making the investment, which option will actually occur is not known.

None of the above should be taken to mean that the investment in the flats should not be made, simply that the managers are better placed to make a judgement where information on the possible outcomes is available. Thus, where the ENPV approach is being used, it is probably a good idea to reveal to managers the different possible outcomes and the probability attached to each outcome. By so doing, the managers will be able to gain an insight into the 'downside risk' attached to the project. This point is further illustrated by Activity 5.14.

Ukon Ltd is considering two competing projects. Details of each project are as follows:

- Project A has a 0.8 probability of producing a negative NPV of £500,000, a 0.1 probability of producing a positive NPV of £1.0 million, and a 0.1 probability of producing a positive NPV of £5.5 million.
- Project B has a 0.2 probability of producing a positive NPV of £125,000, a 0.3 probability of producing a positive NPV of £250,000, and a 0.5 probability of producing a positive NPV of £300,000.

What is the expected net present value of each project?

The ENPV of Project A is:

Probability	NPV	Expected value
	£	£
0.8	(500,000)	(400,000)
0.1	1,000,000	100,000
0.1	5,500,000	550,000
	ENPV	250,000

The ENPV of Project B is:

Probability	NPV	Expected value
	£	£
0.2	125,000	25,000
0.3	250,000	75,000
0.5	300,000	150,000
	ENPV	250,000

Although the ENPV of each project in Activity 5.14 is identical, this does not mean that the business will be indifferent about which project to undertake. Project A has a high probability of making a loss, whereas Project B is not expected to make a loss under any possible outcome. If we assume that investors are risk averse, they will prefer the business to take on Project B as this will provide the same level of expected return as Project A but has a lower level of risk.

It can be argued that the problem identified above may not be significant where the business is engaged in several similar projects. This is because a worse-than-expected outcome on one project may well be balanced by a better-than-expected outcome on another project. However, in practice, investment projects may be unique events and this argument will not then apply. Also, where the project is large in relation to other projects undertaken, the argument loses its force. There is also the problem that a factor that might cause one project to have an adverse outcome could also have adverse effects on other projects. For example, a large unexpected increase in the price of oil may have a simultaneous adverse effect on all of the investment projects of a particular business.

Where several possible outcomes arise from a particular investment opportunity, it is helpful to identify each of them by preparing an **event tree diagram**. This diagram, as the name implies, is shaped like a tree where each branch represents a possible event, or outcome. Probabilities may be assigned to each of the events, or outcomes, identified. Where individual outcomes could occur in different combinations, the probability of each combination can be derived by multiplying together the probabilities of each outcome.

Example 5.5 illustrates how a simple event tree may be prepared for an investment project with different possible outcomes that can combine in different ways.

Example 5.5

Zeta Computing Services Ltd has recently produced some software for a client organisation. The software has a life of two years and will then become obsolete. The cost of developing the software was £60,000. The client organisation has agreed to pay a licence fee of £80,000 a year for the software if it is used in only one of its two divisions and £120,000 a year if it is used in both of its divisions. The client may use the software for either one or two years in either division but will definitely use it in at least one division in each of the two years.

Zeta Computing Services Ltd believes there is a 0.6 chance that the licence fee received in any one year will be £80,000 and a 0.4 chance that it will be £120,000.

Produce an event tree diagram for the project.

Solution

The four possible outcomes attached to this project and their probability of occurrence (*p*) are as follows:

Outcome	Probability
1 Year 1 cash flow £80,000 (p = 0.6) and Year 2 cash flow £80,000 (p = 0.6). The probability of both years having cash flows of £80,000 will be (0.6 × 0.6).	0.36
2 Year 1 cash flow £120,000 (p = 0.4) and Year 2 cash flow £120,000 (p = 0.4). The probability of both years having cash flows of £120,000 will be (0.4 × 0.4).	0.16
3 Year 1 cash flow £120,000 (p = 0.4) and Year 2 cash flow £80,000 (p = 0.6). The probability of this sequence of cash flows occurring will be (0.4 × 0.6).	0.24
4 Year 1 cash flow £80,000 (p = 0.6) and Year 2 cash flow £120,000 (p = 0.4). The probability of this sequence of cash flows occurring will be (0.6 × 0.4).	0.24
	1.00

This information can be displayed in the form of an event tree diagram, as shown in Figure 5.10.

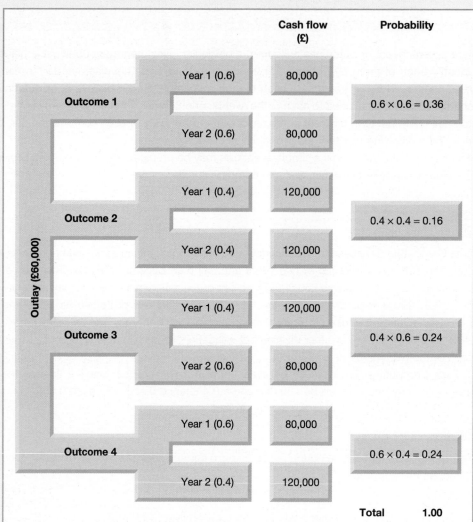

	Cash flow (£)	Probability

Outcome 1
- Year 1 (0.6) — 80,000
- Year 2 (0.6) — 80,000
- $0.6 \times 0.6 = 0.36$

Outcome 2
- Year 1 (0.4) — 120,000
- Year 2 (0.4) — 120,000
- $0.4 \times 0.4 = 0.16$

Outcome 3
- Year 1 (0.4) — 120,000
- Year 2 (0.6) — 80,000
- $0.4 \times 0.6 = 0.24$

Outcome 4
- Year 1 (0.6) — 80,000
- Year 2 (0.4) — 120,000
- $0.6 \times 0.4 = 0.24$

Outlay (£60,000)

Total   1.00

The event tree diagram sets out the different possible outcomes associated with a particular project and the probability of each outcome. We can see that each outcome is represented by a branch and that each branch has subsidiary branches. The sum of the probabilities attached to the outcomes must equal 1.00. In other words, it is certain that one of the possible outcomes will occur.

Figure 5.10 Event tree diagram showing different possible project outcomes

Kernow Ltd provides street-cleaning services for a small town. The work is currently labour intensive and few machines are employed. However, the business has recently been considering the purchase of a fleet of street-cleaning vehicles at a total cost of £540,000. The vehicles have a life of four years and are likely to result in a considerable saving of labour costs. Estimates of the likely labour savings and their probability of occurrence are set out below:

	Estimated savings £	Probability of occurrence
Year 1	80,000	0.3
	160,000	0.5
	200,000	0.2
Year 2	140,000	0.4
	220,000	0.4
	250,000	0.2
Year 3	140,000	0.4
	200,000	0.3
	230,000	0.3
Year 4	100,000	0.3
	170,000	0.6
	200,000	0.1

Estimates for each year are independent of other years. The business has a cost of capital of 10 per cent.

(a) Calculate the ENPV of the street-cleaning machines.
(b) Calculate the NPV of the worst possible outcome and the probability of its occurrence.

(a) The first step is to calculate the expected annual cash flows:

Year 1	£	Year 2	£
£80,000 × 0.3	24,000	£140,000 × 0.4	56,000
£160,000 × 0.5	80,000	£220,000 × 0.4	88,000
£200,000 × 0.2	40,000	£250,000 × 0.2	50,000
	144,000		194,000

Year 3	£	Year 4	£
£140,000 × 0.4	56,000	£100,000 × 0.3	30,000
£200,000 × 0.3	60,000	£170,000 × 0.6	102,000
£230,000 × 0.3	69,000	£200,000 × 0.1	20,000
	185,000		152,000

The ENPV can now be calculated as follows:

Year	Expected cash flow £	Discount rate 10%	Expected PV £
0	(540,000)	1.000	(540,000)
1	144,000	0.909	130,896
2	194,000	0.826	160,244
3	185,000	0.751	138,935
4	152,000	0.683	103,816
		ENPV	(6,109)

→

(b) The worst possible outcome can be calculated by taking the lowest values of savings each year, as follows:

Year	Cash flow	Discount rate	PV
	£	10%	£
0	(540,000)	1.000	(540,000)
1	80,000	0.909	72,720
2	140,000	0.826	115,640
3	140,000	0.751	105,140
4	100,000	0.683	68,300
			NPV (178,200)

The probability of occurrence can be obtained by multiplying together the probability of each of the worst outcomes above, that is, $(0.3 \times 0.4 \times 0.4 \times 0.3) = 0.014$ (or 1.4 per cent). Thus, the probability of occurrence is 1.4 per cent, which is very low.

RISK AND THE STANDARD DEVIATION

In the problems discussed so far, the number of possible outcomes relating to a particular project has been fairly small. Perhaps only two or three possible outcomes have been employed to illustrate particular principles. In reality, however, there may be a large number of outcomes that could occur. Indeed, a project may have thousands of possible outcomes, each with its own probability of occurrence. Although it would not be very realistic, let us suppose a particular project has a large number of possible outcomes and that we are able to identify each possible outcome and to assign a probability to it. This would mean that we could plot a probability distribution of the outcomes that could take the form of a continuous curve, such as the one shown in Figure 5.11.

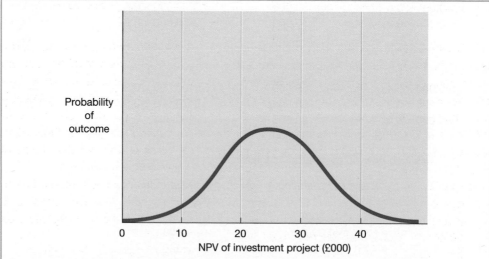

The figure shows the probability distribution of outcomes for a single investment project. We can see that the range of possible outcomes forms a continuous curve. The particular shape of the curve will vary according to the nature of the project.

Figure 5.11 Probability distribution of outcomes for a single investment project

The particular shape of the curve is likely to vary between investment projects. Variations in the shape of the curve can occur even where projects have identical expected values. To illustrate this point, the probability distribution for two separate projects that have the same expected value is shown in Figure 5.12. We can see, however, that Project A has a range of possible values that is much more tightly distributed around the expected value than Project B.

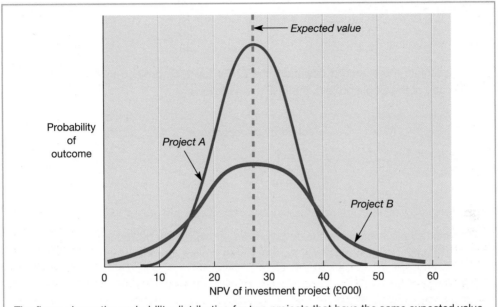

The figure shows the probability distribution for two projects that have the same expected value. We can see that the distribution for each project around the expected value is quite different. Project A has a much tighter distribution than Project B. This means that Project A has less 'downside' risk but also has less 'upside' potential.

Figure 5.12 Probability distribution of two projects with the same expected value

This difference in the shape of the two probability distributions can provide us with a useful indicator of risk. The graph shows that the tighter the distribution of possible future values, the greater the chance that the actual value will be close to the expected value. This means there is less 'downside' risk associated with the particular investment project (but also less 'upside' potential). We can say, therefore, that *the tighter the probability distribution of outcomes, the lower the risk associated with the investment project*. The graph in Figure 5.12 shows that the possible outcomes for Project A are much less spread out than those of Project B. Hence, Project A will be considered a less risky venture than Project B.

The variability of possible future values associated with a project can be measured using a statistical measure called the **standard deviation**. This is a measure of spread that is based on deviations from the mean, or expected value. To demonstrate how the standard deviation is calculated, let us consider Example 5.6.

Example 5.6

Telematix plc is considering two mutually exclusive projects: Cable and Satellite. The possible NPVs for each project and their associated probabilities are as follows:

Cable			Satellite	
NPV £m	Probability of occurrence		NPV £m	Probability of occurrence
10	0.1		15	0.6
20	0.5		20	0.2
25	0.4		40	0.2

To calculate the standard deviation, the ENPV for each project must be calculated. In the case of the Cable project, the ENPV is as follows:

(a) NPV £m	(b) Probability of occurrence	(a × b) ENPV £m
10	0.1	1.0
20	0.5	10.0
25	0.4	10.0
		21.0

The next step is to calculate the deviations around the ENPV by deducting the expected NPV from each possible outcome. For the Cable project, the following set of deviations will be obtained:

(a) Possible NPV £m	(b) ENPV £m	(a − b) Deviation £m
10	21	−11
20	21	−1
25	21	4

The calculations reveal that two of the deviations are negative and one is positive. To prevent the positive and negative deviations from cancelling each other out, we can eliminate the negative signs by squaring the deviations. The sum of the squared deviations is referred to as the variance. The variance for the Cable project will be:

Deviations £m	Squared deviations £m
−11	121
−1	1
4	16
	Variance 138

The problem with the variance is that it provides a unit of measurement that is the square of the NPV deviations. In this case, the variance is 138 $(£m)^2$ which is difficult to interpret. To make things easier, it is a good idea to take the square root of the variance. The final step in calculating the standard deviation is to do just that. The standard deviation is:

$$\text{Standard deviation} = \sqrt{\text{Variance}}$$

For the Cable project, the standard deviation is:

$$\text{Standard deviation} = \sqrt{138(\pounds m)^2} = \pounds 11.75m$$

It was mentioned earlier that the standard deviation is a measure of spread. Thus, we can say that the higher the standard deviation for a particular investment project, the greater the spread, or variability, of possible outcomes.

Activity 5.16

Calculate the standard deviation for the Satellite project. Which project has the higher level of risk?

To answer this activity, the steps outlined above must be followed. Thus:

Step 1. Calculate the ENPV:

(a) NPV £m	(b) Probability of occurrence	(a × b) ENPV £m
15	0.6	9.0
20	0.2	4.0
40	0.2	8.0
		21.0

Step 2. Calculate the deviations around the ENPV:

(a) Possible NPV £m	(b) ENPV £m	(a – b) Deviation £m
15	21	–6
20	21	–1
40	21	19

Step 3. Calculate the variance (that is, sum the squared deviations):

Deviations £m	Squared deviations £m
–6	36
–1	1
19	361
	Variance 398

Step 4. Find the square root of the variance (that is, the standard deviation):*

$$\text{Standard deviation} = \sqrt{398(\pounds m^2)} = \pounds 19.95m$$

The Satellite project has the higher standard deviation and therefore the greater variability of possible outcomes. Hence, it has the higher level of risk.

* Computer software or calculators with statistical functions can be used to calculate the standard deviation and so this manual approach need not be used in practice. It is shown here for illustrative purposes.

THE STANDARD DEVIATION AND THE NORMAL DISTRIBUTION

If the distribution of possible outcomes has a symmetrical bell shape when plotted on a graph, it is referred to as a **normal distribution**. In Figure 5.13 we can see an example of a normal distribution. Note that this kind of distribution has a single peak and that there is an equal tapering off from the peak to each tail. In practice, distributions of data often display this pattern. Where a normal distribution occurs, it is possible to identify the extent to which possible outcomes will deviate from the mean or expected value. The following rules will apply:

- Approximately 68 per cent of possible outcomes will fall within one standard deviation from the mean or expected value.
- Approximately 95 per cent of possible outcomes will fall within two standard deviations from the mean or expected value.
- Approximately 100 per cent of possible outcomes will fall within three standard deviations from the mean or expected value.

Even when the possible outcomes do not form a precise symmetrical bell shape, or normal distribution, these rules can still be reasonably accurate. We shall see below how these rules may be useful in interpreting the level of risk associated with a project.

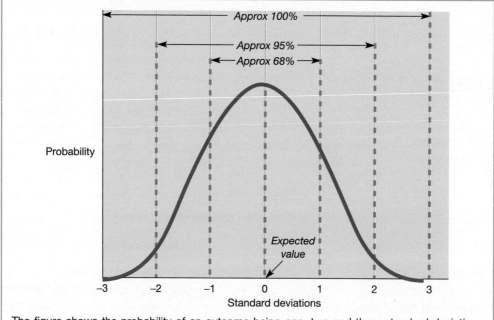

The figure shows the probability of an outcome being one, two and three standard deviations from the mean or expected value. Note that approximately 100 per cent of possible outcomes will fall within three standard deviations of the mean (assuming a normal distribution). There is only a very small probability of an outcome being more than three standard deviations from the mean.

Figure 5.13 Normal distribution and standard deviations

THE EXPECTED VALUE–STANDARD DEVIATION RULE

Where the expected value of the returns of investment opportunities and their standard deviation are known, we have both a measure of return and a measure of risk that can be used for making decisions. If investors are risk averse, they will be seeking the highest level of return for a given level of risk (or the lowest level of risk for a given level of return). The following decision rule can therefore be applied where the possible outcomes for investment projects are normally distributed.

Where there are two competing projects, X and Y, Project X should be chosen when:

■ *either* the expected return of Project X is equal to, or greater than, that of Project Y and the standard deviation of Project X is lower than that of Project Y

■ *or* the expected return of Project X is greater than that of Project Y and the standard deviation of Project X is equal to, or lower than, that of Project Y.

The expected value–standard deviation rule, as it is known, does not cover all possibilities. For example, the rule cannot help us discriminate between two projects where one has both a higher expected return and a higher standard deviation. Nevertheless, it provides some help for managers.

Activity 5.17

Refer back to Example 5.6. Which project should be chosen and why? (Assume the possible outcomes are normally distributed.)

We can see from our earlier calculations that the Cable and Satellite projects have an identical expected net present value. However, the Cable project has a much lower standard deviation, indicating less variability of possible outcomes. Applying the decision rule mentioned above, this means that the Cable project should be selected; or to put it another way, a risk-averse investor would prefer the Cable project as it provides the same expected return for a lower level of risk.

MEASURING PROBABILITIES

Probabilities may be derived using either an objective or a subjective approach. Objective probabilities are based on information gathered from experience. For example, the transport manager of a business operating a fleet of motor vans may be able to provide information concerning the possible life of a newly purchased van based on the record of similar vans acquired in the past. From the information available, probabilities may be developed for different possible life spans. However, past experience may not always be a reliable guide to the future, particularly during a period of rapid change. In the case of the motor vans, for example, changes in design and technology or changes in the purpose for which the vans are being used may undermine the validity of using past data.

Subjective probabilities are based on opinion and will be used where past data are either inappropriate or unavailable. The opinions of independent experts may provide a useful basis for developing subjective probabilities, though even these may contain bias, which will affect the reliability of the judgements made.

THE LIMITS OF PROBABILITY ANALYSIS

Probability analysis is now a widely accepted method of dealing with risk and uncertainty. It is worth striking a note of caution, however. Assigning probabilities to possible outcomes can be fraught with difficulties. There may be several possible outcomes arising from a particular event. To identify each outcome and then assign a probability to it may prove impossible.

Even so, we may still believe that a particular outcome, such as a 5 per cent rise in inflation, will occur. In developing our view, we often use a narrative rather than a probabilistic approach. That is, we either construct, or are persuaded by, a convincing story. In **Real World 5.5**, John Kay argues that this approach, which has long been used in reaching courtroom judgments, is highly relevant when dealing with complex business decisions.

Real World 5.5

Tell me a story

Narrative reasoning is the most effective means humans have developed of handling complex and ill-defined problems. A court can rarely establish a complete account of the probabilities of the events on which it is required to adjudicate. Similarly, an individual cannot know how career and relationships will evolve. A business must be steered into a future of unknown and unknowable dimensions.

So while probabilistic thinking is indispensable when dealing with recurrent events or histories that repeat themselves, it often fails when we try to apply it to idiosyncratic events and open-ended problems. We cope with these situations by telling stories, and we base decisions on their persuasiveness. Not because we are stupid, but because experience has told us it is the best way to cope. That is why novels sell better than statistics texts.

FT *Source*: Kay, J. (2013) 'A story can be more useful than maths', www.ft.com, 26 February.
© The Financial Times Limited 2012. All Rights Reserved.

Despite its limitations, we should not dismiss the use of probability analysis. It helps in the circumstances mentioned in **Real World 5.5**. It also helps to make explicit project risks so that managers can appreciate more fully the issues to be faced. **Real World 5.6** provides an example of how probabilities were used to assess the risks associated with an investment project.

Real World 5.6

Assigning probabilities

In 2005, the transport strategy for South Hampshire included a light rail transit route linking Fareham, Gosport and Portsmouth. The proposed route was 14.3 km long and contained 16 stops. A thorough appraisal of the proposed investment was undertaken, which estimated an NPV of £272 million for the scheme. An integral part of the investment appraisal involved assigning probabilities to various risks identified with the scheme, including risks relating to design, construction and development, performance, operating costs, revenue streams and technology.

During the period of construction and development, a number of risks were identified. One such risk related to cost overruns on the construction of a tunnel along part of the route.

The total cost of the tunnel was estimated at £42.2 million but the following probabilities were assigned to various possible cost overruns:

Probability of occurrence %	Cost overrun £000	Cost of risk £000	Expected cost £000
34	100	34	
46	1,000	460	
10	2,000	200	
5	4,000	200	
4	6,000	240	
1	10,000	100	
100			1,234

We can see from the table that it was estimated that there would be an 80 per cent chance of a cost overrun of £1.0 million or less and a 90 per cent chance that it would be £2.0 million or less.

Source: South Hampshire Rapid Transit Fareham–Gosport–Portsmouth Investment Appraisal, 2005, www.hants.gov.uk.

PORTFOLIO EFFECTS AND RISK REDUCTION

So far, our consideration of risk has looked at the problem from the viewpoint of an investment project being undertaken in isolation. However, in practice, a business will normally invest in a range, or *portfolio*, of investment projects rather than a single project. This approach to investment provides a potentially useful way of reducing risk. The problem with investing all available funds in a single project is, of course, that an unfavourable outcome could have disastrous consequences for the business. By investing in a spread of projects, an adverse outcome from a single project is less likely to have severe repercussions. The saying 'don't put all your eggs in one basket' neatly sums up the best advice concerning investment policy.

Investing in a range of different projects is referred to as **diversification**, and holding a diversified portfolio of investment projects can reduce the total risk associated with a business. Indeed, in theory, it is possible to combine two risky investment projects so as to create a portfolio of projects that is riskless. To illustrate this point let us consider Example 5.7.

Example 5.7

Frank N. Stein plc has the opportunity to invest in two investment projects in Transylvania. The possible outcomes from each project will depend on whether the ruling party of the country wins or loses the next election. (For the sake of simplicity, we shall assume the ruling party will either win or lose outright and there is no possibility of another outcome, such as a hung parliament.) The NPV from each project under each outcome is estimated as follows:

	Project 1 NPV £m	Project 2 NPV £m
Ruling party wins	(20)	30
Ruling party loses	40	(30)

What should the business do to manage the risks involved in each project?

Solution

If the business invests in *both* projects, the total NPV under each outcome will be as follows:

	Project 1 NPV	Project 2 NPV	Total returns
	£m	£m	£m
Ruling party wins	(20)	30	10
Ruling party loses	40	(30)	10

We can see that, whatever the outcome of the election, the total NPV for the business will be the same (that is, £10 million). Although the possible returns from each project vary according to the results of the election, they are inversely related and so the total returns will be stabilised. As risk can be diversified away in this manner, the relationship between the returns from individual investment projects is an important issue for managers.

The coefficient of correlation

A business may eliminate the variability in total returns by investing in projects whose returns are inversely related, such as in the example above. Ideally, a business should invest in a spread of investment projects so that when certain projects generate low (or negative) returns, other projects are generating high returns, and vice versa. It is possible to measure the degree to which the returns from individual projects are related by using the **coefficient of correlation**. This coefficient is an abstract measure that ranges along a continuum between +1 and −1.

When the coefficient for two projects, X and Y, is positive, it means that increases in the returns from Project X will be accompanied by increases in returns from Project Y: the higher the positive measure, the stronger the relationship between the returns of the two projects. A coefficient of +1 indicates a perfect positive correlation and this means that the returns are moving together in perfect step. In Figure 5.14, we see a graph showing the returns for two investment projects that have a perfect positive correlation.

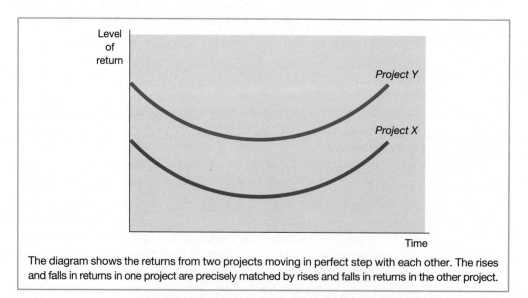

The diagram shows the returns from two projects moving in perfect step with each other. The rises and falls in returns in one project are precisely matched by rises and falls in returns in the other project.

Figure 5.14 Two projects whose returns have a perfect positive correlation

If the coefficient of correlation is negative, increases in the returns from Project X will be accompanied by decreases in the returns from Project Y. A coefficient of –1 indicates a perfect negative correlation between two projects. In other words, the projects' returns will move together in perfect step, but in *opposite directions*.

Activity 5.18

Suppose the returns from Project Y had a perfect negative correlation with those of Project X. Draw a graph depicting the relationship between the two projects.

The graph for two investment projects whose returns are perfectly negatively correlated is shown in Figure 5.15.

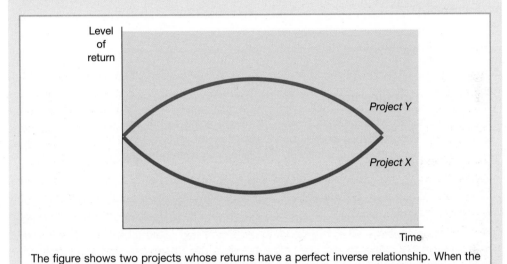

The figure shows two projects whose returns have a perfect inverse relationship. When the returns from Project Y are low, the returns from Project X are high, and vice versa.

Figure 5.15 Two projects whose returns have a perfect negative correlation

If the coefficient of correlation between the returns of two projects is 0, this means that the returns from Project X and Project Y move independently of one another and so there is no relationship between them.

To eliminate risk completely, a business should invest in projects whose returns are perfectly negatively correlated. This will mean that the variability in returns between projects will cancel each other out and so risk will be completely diversified away. So far, so good – unfortunately, however, it is rarely possible to do this. In the real world, projects whose returns are perfectly negatively correlated are extremely difficult to find. Nevertheless, risk can still be diversified away to some extent by investing in projects whose returns do not have a perfect positive correlation. Provided the correlation between projects is less than +1, some offsetting will occur. The further the coefficient of correlation moves away from +1 and towards –1 on the scale, the greater this offsetting effect will be.

Should the managers of a business seek project diversification as their main objective?

The answer is no. Even if two projects could be found whose returns had a perfect negative correlation, this does not necessarily mean that they should be pursued. The expected returns from the projects must also be considered when making any investment decision.

One potential problem of diversification is that a range of different projects can create greater project management problems. Managers will have to deal with a variety of projects with different technical and resource issues to resolve. The greater the number of projects, the greater the management problems are likely to be.

Real World 5.7 describes the benefits that one business received from diversifying its project portfolio.

Real World 5.7

Growing in all directions

Building the tallest skyscraper in Europe is always going to get you attention. Doing it during one of the continent's slowest periods of economic activity since the Second World War is going to guarantee you a lot of it. For Mace, the privately owned builder responsible for erecting the 1,000 ft Shard of Glass at London Bridge, however, the project is something of a mixed blessing.

The £400m contract, which Mace won back in 2009, has put it on the map as one of the UK's leading commercial property builders. But its management worries that it has also put the company's other projects into the shade and could give it a reputation for being a one-trick pony. In his site office between the Shard and the Guy's hospital tower, which is already dwarfed by its half-built neighbour, Mace's chairman and chief executive Stephen Pycroft explains: 'Although the Shard is the project that everyone knows about and wants to ask about, we've actually been more focused on moving into public works, school building and transport infrastructure projects and away from commercial construction.'

The decision to diversify out of being a specialist in building offices, and particularly tall ones – Mr Pycroft estimates Mace has been involved in about 60 per cent of all the skyscrapers which have gone up in London during the past decade – was taken four years ago. At the time the demand for new office space was booming in Europe and the notion of seeking to decrease risk through diversification could have seemed conservative. Then the financial crisis happened. Commercial construction work in Europe fell about 14 per cent to £46.2bn in 2009 and is expected to fall another 8 per cent this year, according to Euroconstruct, the research group. With projects being mothballed and cancelled, those too exposed to office developments were left with scant order books to support their workforces.

Source: Hammond, E. (2010) 'Mace set to grow in all directions', www.ft.com, 1 August.
© The Financial Times Limited 2012. All Rights Reserved.

Diversifiable and non-diversifiable risk

The benefits of risk diversification can be obtained by increasing the number of projects within the investment portfolio. As each investment project is added to the portfolio, the variability of total returns will diminish, provided that the projects are not perfectly correlated. However, there are limits to the benefits of diversification, due to the nature of the risks faced. The total risk relating to a particular project can be divided into two types: **diversifiable risk** and **non-diversifiable risk**. As the names suggest, it is only the former type of risk that can be eliminated through diversification.

The two types of risk can be described as follows:

- *Diversifiable risk* is that part of the total risk that is specific to the project, such as changes in key personnel, legal regulations, degree of competition and so on. By spreading available funds between investment projects, it is possible to offset adverse outcomes occurring in one project against beneficial outcomes in another. (Diversifiable risk is also referred to as avoidable risk, or unsystematic risk.)
- *Non-diversifiable risk* is that part of the total risk that is common to all projects and which, therefore, cannot be diversified away. This element of risk arises from general market conditions and will be affected by such factors as the rate of inflation, the general level of interest rates, exchange rate movements and the rate of growth within the economy. (Non-diversifiable risk is also referred to as unavoidable risk, or systematic risk.)

In Figure 5.16, the relationship between the level of portfolio risk and the size of the portfolio is shown. We can see that as the number of projects increases, the diversifiable element of total risk is reduced. This does not mean, necessarily, that a business should invest in a large number of projects. Most of the benefits from diversification can often be reaped from investing in a relatively small number of projects. In Figure 5.16, we can see the additional benefits from each investment project diminish quite sharply. This suggests that a business with a large portfolio of projects may gain very little from further diversification.

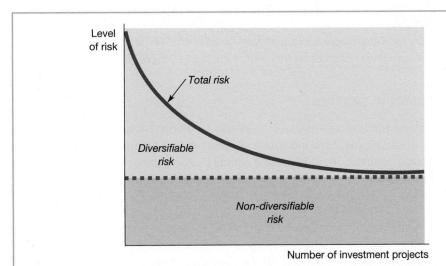

The figure shows that, as the size of the portfolio of projects is increased, the level of total risk is reduced. However, the rate of reduction in the level of total risk decreases quite sharply and soon reaches a point where investing in further projects to reduce risk is of little or no value.

Figure 5.16 Reducing risk through diversification

Non-diversifiable risk is based on general economic conditions and therefore all businesses will be affected. However, certain businesses are more sensitive to changes in economic conditions than others. For example, during a recession, some types of businesses will be seriously affected, whereas others will be only slightly affected.

Activity 5.20

Provide two examples of businesses that are likely to be:

(a) seriously affected by an economic recession
(b) slightly affected by an economic recession.

(a) Businesses that are likely to be badly hit by recession include those selling expensive or luxury goods and services such as:
- hotels and restaurants
- travel companies
- house builders and construction companies
- airlines
- jewellers.

(b) Businesses that are likely to be only slightly affected by recession include those selling essential goods and services such as:
- gas and electricity suppliers
- water suppliers
- basic food retailers and producers
- undertakers.

Businesses that are likely to be badly affected by an economic recession tend to have a cyclical pattern of profits. Thus, during a period of economic growth, they may make large profits, and during periods of recession they may make large losses. Businesses that are likely to be slightly affected by economic recession tend to have a fairly stable pattern of profits over the economic cycle.

The distinction between diversifiable and non-diversifiable risk is an important issue to which we shall return when considering the cost of capital in Chapter 8.

Risk assessment in practice

Surveys of UK businesses indicate that risk assessment methods have become more widely used over time. These surveys also indicate that sensitivity analysis and scenario analysis are the most popular methods. **Real World 5.8** sets out evidence from a survey of large UK manufacturing businesses that is consistent with these general findings.

Assessing risk

The survey of 83 large UK manufacturing businesses by Alkaraan and Northcott (see **Real World 4.9**) asked respondents to reveal their usage of risk analysis techniques when assessing investment projects. The following table sets out the results.

Method	Non-strategic investment projects Mean score	Strategic investment projects Mean score
1 Adjust required payback period to allow for risk	2.2892	2.6867
2 Adjust required return on investment to allow for risk	2.5181	3.1084
3 Adjust discount rate to allow for risk	2.6747	3.0723
4 Adjust forecast cash flows to allow for risk	2.8193	3.2169
5 Probability analysis	2.4337	2.6867
6 Computer simulation	1.8434	2.0000
7 Beta analysis (capital asset pricing model)*	1.7108	1.7590
8 Sensitivity/scenario analysis	3.1928	3.4699

Response scale: 1 = never, 2 = rarely, 3 = often, 4 = mostly, 5 = always.
* This method will be discussed in Chapter 8.

The table shows that sensitivity/scenario analysis is the most popular way of dealing with risk. It also shows that some unsophisticated methods of dealing with risk, such as shortening the payback period and adjusting the cash flows, are more popular than sophisticated methods such as computer simulation. Statistical analysis showed that methods 1, 2 and 4 above were used significantly more for strategic investments than for non-strategic investments.

The survey also found that 89 per cent of businesses used sensitivity/scenario analysis, while 82 per cent raised the required rate of return, 77 per cent used probability analysis and 75 per cent shortened the payback period. Clearly, many businesses use more than one method of dealing with risk.

Source: F. Alkaraan and D. Northcott, 'Strategic capital investment decision-making: A role for emergent analysis tools? A study of practice in large UK manufacturing companies', *The British Accounting Review*, 38, 2006, 149–173.

Self-assessment question 5.1

The directors of Tocantins Co. are considering whether to invest in two separate projects: one is small while the other is large. They are also trying to decide between two other competing projects. Details of all four projects are set out below.

Project 1

The directors are considering buying a new photocopier, which should lead to cost savings. Two machines that are suitable for the business are on the market. These machines have the following outlays and expected cost savings:

	Lo-tek £	Hi-tek £
Initial outlay	(10,000)	(15,000)
Cost savings		
1 year's time	4,000	5,000
2 years' time	5,000	6,000
3 years' time	5,000	6,000
4 years' time	–	5,000

The business will have a continuing need for whichever machine is chosen.

$\rightarrow$

Project 2

The directors are also considering building a new factory in Qingdao, China to produce clothing for the Western European market. To date, the company has invested £500,000 in researching the proposal and in obtaining the licences necessary to build the factory. The factory will cost £16 million to build and will take one year to complete. Payments for building the factory will be paid in 12 monthly instalments during the first year of the investment project.

The factory will be operational in the second year and estimates of the likely cash flows from the factory and their probability of occurrence are as follows:

	Estimated net cash flows £m	Probability of occurrence
Year 2	4.5	0.2
	5.0	0.4
	6.0	0.4
Year 3	5.0	0.3
	6.5	0.4
	8.0	0.3
Year 4	5.0	0.2
	7.0	0.6
	9.0	0.2
Year 5	2.0	0.5
	2.5	0.4
	3.0	0.1

Estimates for each year are independent of each other.

Projects 3 and 4

The directors have to decide between two competing projects. Their details are as follows:

	Expected net present value £m	Standard deviation £m
Project 3	14.0	2.0
Project 4	14.0	2.8

The company has a cost of capital of 12 per cent.

Required:
Project 1

(a) Evaluate each photocopier using both the shortest-common-period-of-time approach and the equivalent-annual-annuity approach.
(b) Which machine would you recommend and why?

Project 2

(c) Calculate the expected net present value of the project.
(d) Calculate the net present value of the worst possible outcome and the probability of its occurrence.
(e) State, with reasons, whether or not the business should invest in the new factory.

Projects 3 and 4

(f) State, with reasons, which of the two projects should be accepted.

The answer to this question can be found at the back of the book on p. 562.

SUMMARY

The main points in this chapter may be summarised as follows:

Investment decisions when funds are limited

■ Where projects are divisible, managers should maximise the present value per £ of scarce finance.

■ The profitability index provides a measure of the present value per £ of scarce finance.

■ Where funding requirements extend beyond a single period, linear programming can be used to maximise NPV.

Comparing projects with unequal lives

■ Can be done by assuming each project forms part of a repeat chain of replacement and then by making comparisons using the shortest-common-period-of-time approach.

■ As an alternative, the equivalent-annual-annuity approach converts the NPV of a project into an annual annuity stream over its expected life.

The problem of inflation

■ Inflation may be included by adjusting the annual cash flows and the discount rate to take account of price increases.

■ Inflation may be excluded by adjusting the cash flow to real terms and by using a 'real' discount rate.

Risk

■ Is important because of the long timescales and amounts involved in investment decisions.

■ Various methods of dealing with risk are available, including sensitivity analysis, scenario analysis, simulation, risk-adjusted discount rate and the expected net present value method.

Sensitivity analysis

■ Provides an assessment, by taking each input factor in turn, of how much each one can vary from estimate before a project is not viable.

■ Is a static form of analysis that does not indicate the likelihood of each factor variation occurring.

■ Does not give a clear decision rule.

Scenario analysis

■ Changes a number of variables simultaneously to provide a particular 'state of the world'.

■ Often three different states – optimistic, pessimistic and most likely – are portrayed.

■ Does not indicate the likelihood of each state occurring or other possible states that may occur.

Simulations

■ Involve identifying the key variables of the project and their key relationships.

■ Possible values are attached to each factor and a computer is used to select one of the possible values on a random basis to produce a projected cash flow.

- The process is repeated many times to obtain a probability distribution of the values of the cash flows.
- Can be costly and time-consuming.

Risk preferences of investors

- Given a choice between two projects with the same expected return but with different levels of risk:
    - risk-seeking investors will choose the project with the higher level of risk
    - risk-neutral investors will have no preference
    - risk-averse investors will choose the project with the lower level of risk.
- Most investors appear to be risk averse.
- Risk-averse investors require higher returns from projects with higher risks. The explanation for this can be found in utility theory.

Risk-adjusted discount rate

- Risk-averse investors require a risk premium for risky projects.
- A risk-adjusted discount rate, where a risk premium is added to the risk-free rate, can be used for NPV calculations.
- Determining the appropriate risk premium is problematic.

Expected net present value (ENPV) approach

- Assigns probabilities to possible outcomes.
- Expected value is the weighted average of the possible outcomes where their probabilities are used as weights.
- Provides a single value outcome and a clear decision rule.
- Outcome may obscure the riskiness of a project and so additional information on the range of possible outcomes should be provided.
- Probabilities may be either subjective (based on opinion) or objective (based on evidence).

The standard deviation

- Is a measure of spread based on deviations from the mean (average).
- Provides a measure of risk.
- The expected value–standard deviation rule may be used when comparing projects where possible outcomes for each project are normally distributed.

Portfolio effect

- By holding a diversified portfolio of investment projects, a business can reduce the total risk associated with its projects.
- The coefficient of correlation measures the degree to which returns from individual projects are related.
- Ideally, a business should hold a spread of projects, such that when certain projects generate low returns, others generate high returns.
- Risk relating to a particular project can be divided into two categories: diversifiable risk and non-diversifiable risk.
- Only diversifiable risk can be eliminated through diversification.

Profitability index p. 175
Linear programming p. 176
Shortest-common-period-of-time approach p. 177
Annuity p. 179
Equivalent-annual-annuity approach p. 179
Sensitivity chart p. 189
Simulation p. 191
Risk-seeking investors p. 193
Risk-neutral investors p. 193
Risk-averse investors p. 193
Utility function p. 193
Risk-adjusted discount rate p. 196

Expected value p. 198
Expected net present value (ENPV) p. 198
Event tree diagram p. 201
Standard deviation p. 205
Normal distribution p. 208
Expected value–standard deviation rule p. 209
Objective probabilities p. 209
Subjective probabilities p. 209
Diversification p. 211
Coefficient of correlation p. 212
Diversifiable risk p. 215
Non-diversifiable risk p. 215

For definitions of these terms see the Glossary, pp. 605–613.

FURTHER READING

If you wish to explore the topics discussed in this chapter in more depth, try the following books:

Arnold, G. (2013) *Corporate Financial Management*, 5th edn, Pearson, Chapters 5, 6 and 7.

Brigham, E. and Ehrhardt, M. (2013) *Financial Management: Theory and Practice*, 14th edn, South-Western Cengage Learning, Chapter 11.

McLaney, E. (2011) *Business Finance: Theory and Practice*, 9th edn, Financial Times Prentice Hall, Chapters 5 and 6.

Pike, R., Neale, B. and Linsley, P. (2012) *Corporate Finance and Investment*, 7th edn, Pearson, Chapters 7 and 8.

REVIEW QUESTIONS

Answers to these questions can be found at the back of the book on pp. 000–000.

5.1 Some businesses fail to take account of inflation in investment decisions. Does it matter given that, in recent years, the level of inflation has been low? What would be the effect of dealing with inflation incorrectly on NPV calculations (that is, would NPV be overstated or understated) by (a) discounting cash flows that include inflation at real discount rates and (b) discounting real cash flows at market discount rates that include inflation?

5.2 What is risk and to what extent can it be diversified away when making investment decisions?

5.3 What practical problems arise when using the risk-adjusted discount rate to deal with the problem of risk?

5.4 Explain why the standard deviation may be useful in measuring risk.

Exercises 5.5 to 5.7 are more advanced than 5.1 to 5.4. Those with coloured numbers have solutions at the back of the book, starting on p. 588.

If you wish to try more exercises, visit the students' side of this book's companion website.

5.1 Lee Caterers Ltd is about to make an investment in new kitchen equipment. It is considering whether to replace its existing kitchen equipment with cook/freeze or cook/chill technology. The following cash flows are expected from each form of technology:

	Cook/chill £000	Cook/freeze £000
Initial outlay	(200)	(390)
1 year's time	85	88
2 years' time	94	102
3 years' time	86	110
4 years' time	62	110
5 years' time	–	110
6 years' time	–	90
7 years' time	–	85
8 years' time	–	60

The business would expect to replace the new equipment purchased with similar equipment at the end of its life. The cost of capital for the business is 10 per cent.

Required:

Which type of equipment should the business invest in? Use both approaches to dealing with this problem, which were described in the chapter, to support your conclusions.

5.2 D'Arcy (Builders) Ltd is considering three possible investment projects: A, B and C. The expected pattern of cash flows for each project is:

	Project cash flows		
	A £000	B £000	C £000
Initial outlay	(17)	(20)	(24)
1 year's time	11	12	9
2 years' time	5	7	9
3 years' time	7	7	11
4 years' time	6	6	13

The business has a cost of capital of 10 per cent and the investment budget for next year is £25 million.

Required:

Which investment project(s) should the business undertake assuming each project is:
(a) divisible
(b) indivisible?

5.3 Simonson Engineers plc is considering the building of a new plant in Indonesia to produce products for the South-East Asian market. To date, £450,000 has been invested in market research and site surveys. The cost of building the plant will be £9 million and it will be in operation and paid for in one year's time. Estimates of the likely cash flows from the plant and their probability of occurrence are set out as follows:

	Estimated cash flows £m	Probability of occurrence
Year 2	2.0	0.2
	3.5	0.6
	4.0	0.2
Year 3	2.5	0.2
	3.0	0.4
	5.0	0.4
Year 4	3.0	0.2
	4.0	0.7
	5.0	0.1
Year 5	2.5	0.2
	3.0	0.5
	6.0	0.3

Estimates for each year are independent of each other. The cost of capital for the business is 10 per cent.

Required:
(a) Calculate the expected net present value of the proposed plant.
(b) Calculate the net present value of the worst possible outcome and the probability of its occurrence.
(c) Should the business invest in the new plant? Why?

5.4 Helena Chocolate Products Ltd is considering the introduction of a new chocolate bar into its range of chocolate products. The new chocolate bar will require the purchase of a new piece of equipment costing £30,000 which will have no other use and no residual value on completion of the project. Financial data relating to the new product are as follows:

	Per bar (£)
Selling price	0.60
Variable costs	0.22

Fixed costs of £20,000 a year will be apportioned to the new product. These costs represent a 'fair share' of the total fixed costs of the business. The costs are unlikely to change as a result of any decision to introduce new products into the existing range. Other developments currently being finalised will mean that the new product will have a life of only three years and the level of expected demand for the new product is uncertain. The marketing department has produced the following levels of demand and the probability of each for all three years of the product's life.

Year 1		Year 2		Year 3	
Sales (units)	Probability	Sales (units)	Probability	Sales (units)	Probability
100,000	0.2	140,000	0.3	180,000	0.5
120,000	0.4	150,000	0.3	160,000	0.3
125,000	0.3	160,000	0.2	120,000	0.1
130,000	0.1	200,000	0.2	100,000	0.1

A rival business has offered to buy the right to produce and sell the new chocolate bar for £100,000.

The cost of capital is 10 per cent and interest charges on the money borrowed to finance the project are expected to be £3,000 per year.

Required:

(a) Compute the expected net present value of the product.

(b) Advise the directors on the appropriate course of action. Give reasons.

5.5 Devonia (Laboratories) Ltd has recently carried out successful clinical trials on a new type of skin cream, which has been developed to reduce the effects of ageing. Research and development costs incurred to date for the new product amount to £190,000. To gauge the market potential of the new product, an independent firm of market research consultants was hired at a cost of £35,000. The market research report submitted by the consultants indicates that the skin cream is likely to have a product life of four years and could be sold to retail chemists and large department stores at a price of £20 per 100 ml container. For each of the four years of the new product's life, sales demand has been estimated as follows:

Probability of occurrence	Number of 100 ml containers sold
0.3	11,000
0.6	14,000
0.1	16,000

If the business decides to launch the new product, it is possible for production to begin at once. The equipment necessary to produce the product is already owned by the business and originally cost £150,000. At the end of the new product's life it is estimated that the equipment could be sold for £35,000. If the business decides against launching the new product the equipment will be sold immediately for £85,000 as it will be of no further use to the business.

The new skin cream will require one hour's labour for each 100 ml container produced. The cost of labour for the new product is £8.00 an hour. Additional workers will have to be recruited to produce the new product. At the end of the product's life the workers are unlikely to be offered further work with the business and redundancy costs of £10,000 are expected. The cost of the ingredients for each 100 ml container is £6.00. Additional overheads arising from production of the product are expected to be £15,000 a year.

The new skin cream has attracted the interest of the business's competitors. If the business decides not to produce and sell the skin cream it can sell the patent rights to a major competitor immediately for £125,000.

Devonia (Laboratories) Ltd has a cost of capital of 12 per cent. Ignore taxation.

Required:

(a) Calculate the ENPV of the new product.

(b) State, with reasons, whether or not Devonia (Laboratories) Ltd should launch the new product.

(c) Discuss the strengths and weaknesses of the ENPV approach for making investment decisions.

5.6 Nimby plc is considering two mutually exclusive projects: Delphi and Oracle. The possible NPVs for each project and their associated probabilities are as follows:

Delphi		Oracle	
NPV	Probability of occurrence	NPV	Probability of occurrence
£m		£m	
20	0.2	30	0.5
40	0.6	40	0.3
60	0.2	65	0.2

Required:

(a) Calculate the expected net present value and the standard deviation associated with each project.

(b) Which project would you select and why? State any assumptions you have made in coming to your conclusions.

(c) Discuss the limitations of the standard deviation as a measure of project risk.

5.7 Plato Pharmaceuticals Ltd has invested £500,000 to date in developing a new type of insect repellent. The repellent is now ready for production and sale, and the marketing director estimates that the product will sell 150,000 bottles a year over the next five years. The selling price of the insect repellent will be £5 a bottle and variable costs are estimated to be £3 a bottle. Fixed costs (excluding depreciation) are expected to be £200,000 a year. This figure is made up of £160,000 additional fixed costs and £40,000 fixed costs relating to the existing business which will be apportioned to the new product.

In order to produce the repellent, machinery and equipment costing £520,000 will have to be purchased immediately. The estimated residual value of this machinery and equipment in five years' time is £100,000. The business calculates depreciation on a straight-line basis.

The business has a cost of capital of 12 per cent. Ignore taxation.

Required:

(a) Calculate the net present value of the product.

(b) Undertake sensitivity analysis to show by how much the following factors would have to change before the product ceased to be worthwhile:

(i)   the discount rate

(ii) the initial outlay on machinery and equipment

(iii) the net operating cash flows

(iv) the residual value of the machinery and equipment.

Chapter 6

FINANCING A BUSINESS 1: SOURCES OF FINANCE

INTRODUCTION

This is the first of two chapters that examine the financing of businesses. In this chapter, we identify the main sources of finance available to businesses and discuss the main features of each source. We also consider the factors to be taken into account when choosing between the various sources of finance available.

In the following chapter, we go on to examine capital markets, including the role and efficiency of the London Stock Exchange and the ways in which share capital can be issued. We shall also see how smaller businesses, which do not have access to the London Stock Exchange, may raise finance.

Learning outcomes

When you have completed this chapter, you should be able to:

- Identify the main sources of external and internal finance available to a business and explain their main features.

- Discuss the advantages and disadvantages of each source of finance.

- Discuss the factors to be taken into account when choosing an appropriate source of finance.

SOURCES OF FINANCE

When considering the various sources of finance available, it is useful to distinguish between *external* and *internal* sources of finance. By external sources we mean those that require the agreement of other parties beyond the directors of the business. Thus, finance from an issue of new shares is an external source because the agreement of potential shareholders is required. Internal sources of finance, meanwhile, arise from management decisions that do not require agreement from other parties. Thus, retained earnings are a source of internal finance because directors have the power to retain earnings without the agreement of shareholders, whose earnings they are.

Within each of these categories, we can further distinguish between *long-term* and *short-term* finance. There is no agreed definition concerning each of these terms, but for the purpose of this chapter, a source of long-term finance will be defined as one that is expected to provide finance for at least one year. Sources of short-term finance provide finance for a shorter period. As we shall see, sources that are seen as short term when first used by the business may end up being used for quite long periods.

We begin by considering the external sources of finance available and then go on to consider the internal sources.

EXTERNAL SOURCES OF FINANCE

Figure 6.1 summarises the main external sources of long-term and short-term finance.

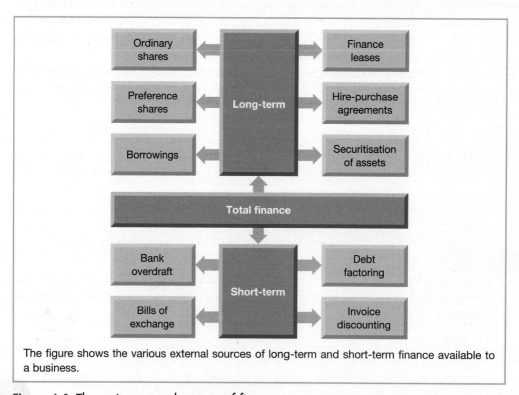

The figure shows the various external sources of long-term and short-term finance available to a business.

Figure 6.1 The major external sources of finance

EXTERNAL SOURCES OF LONG-TERM FINANCE

As Figure 6.1 reveals, the major external sources of long-term finance are:

- ordinary shares
- preference shares
- borrowings
- finance leases, including sale-and-leaseback arrangements
- hire purchase
- securitisation of assets.

We shall look at each of these sources in turn.

Ordinary shares

Ordinary (equity) shares represent the risk capital of a business and form the backbone of a business's financial structure. There is no fixed rate of dividend and ordinary shareholders will receive a dividend only if earnings available for distribution remain after other investors (preference shareholders and lenders) have received their dividend or interest payments. If the business is wound up, the ordinary shareholders will receive any proceeds from asset disposals only after lenders and creditors, and, in some cases, preference shareholders, have received their entitlements. Because of the high risks associated with this form of investment, ordinary shareholders will normally expect a relatively high rate of return.

Although ordinary shareholders' potential losses are limited to the amount that they have invested or agreed to invest, the potential returns from their investment are unlimited. After preference shareholders and lenders have received their returns, all the remaining earnings will accrue to the ordinary shareholders. Thus, while their 'downside' risk is limited, their 'upside' potential is not. Ordinary shareholders control the business through their voting rights, which give them the power to elect the directors and to remove them from office.

From the business's perspective, ordinary shares can be a valuable form of financing compared with borrowing. It may be possible to avoid paying a dividend, whereas it is not usually possible to avoid interest payments.

Activity 6.1

Under what circumstances might a business wish to avoid paying a dividend?

Two possible circumstances are where a business is:

- expanding and wishes to retain funds in order to fuel future growth
- in difficulties and needs the funds to meet its operating costs and debt obligations.

It is worth pointing out that the business does not obtain any tax relief on dividends paid to shareholders, whereas interest on borrowings is tax deductible. This makes it more expensive for the business to pay £1 of dividend than £1 of interest on borrowings.

Preference shares

Preference shares offer investors a lower level of risk than ordinary shares. Provided there are sufficient earnings available, preference shares will normally be given a fixed rate of dividend each year and preference dividends will be the first slice of any dividend paid. If the business is wound up, preference shareholders may be given priority over the claims of ordinary shareholders. (The business's own particular documents of incorporation will state the precise rights of preference shareholders in this respect.)

Activity 6.2

Would you expect the returns from preference shares to be higher or lower than those from ordinary shares?

Preference shareholders will be offered a lower level of return than ordinary shareholders. This is because of the lower level of risk associated with this form of investment (preference shareholders have priority over ordinary shareholders regarding dividends, and perhaps capital repayment).

Preference shareholders are not usually given voting rights, although these may be granted where the preference dividend is in arrears. Both preference shares and ordinary shares are, in effect, redeemable. The business is allowed to buy back the shares from shareholders at any time.

Activity 6.3

Would you expect the market price of ordinary shares or of preference shares to be the more volatile? Why?

The share price, which reflects the expected future returns from the share, will normally be less volatile for preference shares than for ordinary shares. The dividends of preference shares tend to be fairly stable over time, and there is usually an upper limit on the returns that can be received.

Preference shares are no longer an important source of new finance. A major reason for this is that dividends paid to preference shareholders, like those paid to ordinary shareholders, are not fully allowable against taxable profits, whereas loan interest is an allowable expense. From the business's point of view, preference shares and loans are quite similar, so the issue of the tax benefits of loan interest is an important one. Furthermore, in recent years, interest rates on borrowing have been at historically low levels.

Borrowings

Most businesses rely on borrowings as well as share capital to finance operations. Lenders enter into a contract with the business in which the interest (coupon) rate, dates of interest payments, capital repayments and security for the loan are clearly stated. If a business is successful, lenders will not benefit beyond the fact that their claim will become more secure. If, however, the business experiences financial difficulties, there is a risk that the agreed interest payments and capital repayments will not be paid. To protect themselves against this risk, lenders often seek some form of security from the business. This may take the form of assets pledged either by a fixed charge on particular assets held by the business, or by a floating charge, which 'floats' over the whole of the business's assets. A floating charge will only fix on particular assets in the event that the business defaults on its obligations.

What do you think is the advantage for the business of having a floating charge rather than a fixed charge on its assets?

A floating charge on assets will allow the managers of the business greater flexibility in their day-to-day operations than a fixed charge. Individual assets can be sold without reference to the lenders.

Not all assets are acceptable to lenders as security. They must normally be non-perishable, easy to sell and of high value relative to their size. (Property normally meets these criteria and so is often favoured by lenders.) In the event of default, lenders have the right to seize the assets pledged and to sell them. Any surplus from the sale, after lenders have been paid, will be passed to the business. In some cases, security offered may take the form of a personal guarantee by the owners of the business or, perhaps, some third party. This most often occurs with small businesses.

Lenders may seek further protection through the use of **loan covenants**. These are obligations, or restrictions, on the business that form part of the loan contract. Covenants may impose:

- the right of lenders to receive regular financial reports concerning the business
- an obligation to insure the assets being offered as security
- a restriction on the right to issue further loan capital without prior permission of the existing lenders
- a restriction on the right to sell certain assets held
- a restriction on dividend payments and/or payments made to directors
- minimum levels of liquidity and/or maximum levels of gearing.

Any breach of these covenants can have serious consequences. Lenders may demand immediate repayment of the loan in the event of a material breach.

Real World 6.1 describes the covenants relating to one bond loan issue.

Real World 6.1

Borrowing with strings attached

St Modwen, the property developer that owns the Elephant & Castle shopping centre in south east London, is aiming to raise £50–100m from an issue of unsecured bonds on the London Stock Exchange's retail bond market. The bonds will offer investors a 6.25 per cent coupon and mature in November 2019.

St Modwen has built covenants into the terms of its bonds to provide retail investors with some reassurance about the security. Interest cover – the number of times debt interest payments are covered by operating profit – will not fall below 1.5 times and the loan-to-value ratio of the property portfolio will not exceed 75 per cent. 'Our advisers believe that the covenants we've offered are becoming the norm for this kind of issue,' said chief executive Mr Oliver.

St Modwen operates primarily as a commercial property developer – specialising in brownfield and redevelopment sites such as MG Rover's former Longbridge car plant – rather than as a landlord. However, it also has a portfolio of income-generating assets that will underpin the coupons on the bond issue.

Loan covenants and the availability of security can significantly lower the risk to which lenders are exposed. They may make the difference between a successful and an unsuccessful issue of loan capital. They may also lower the cost of loan capital to the business, as the rate of return that lenders require will depend on the perceived level of risk to which they are exposed.

It is possible for a business to issue loan capital that is subordinated to (that is, ranked below) other loan capital already in issue. Holders of subordinated loan capital will not receive interest payments or capital repayments until the claims of more senior loan holders (that is, lenders ranked above them) are met. Any restrictive covenants imposed by senior loan holders concerning the issue of further loan capital often ignore the issue of subordinated loans as it poses no real threat to their claims. Subordinated loan holders normally expect to receive a higher return than senior loan holders because of the higher risks.

Activity 6.5

Would you expect the returns from loan capital to be higher or lower than those from preference shares?

Investors are usually prepared to accept a lower rate of return from loan capital. This is because they normally view loans as being less risky than preference shares. Lenders have priority over any claims from preference shareholders, and will usually have security for their loans.

The risk/return characteristics of loan, preference share and ordinary share finance, *from an investor's viewpoint*, are shown graphically in Figure 6.2. Note that from the viewpoint of the business (the existing shareholders), the level of risk associated with each form of finance is in reverse order. Thus, borrowing is the most risky because it exposes shareholders to the legally enforceable obligation to make regular interest payments and, usually, repayment of the amount borrowed.

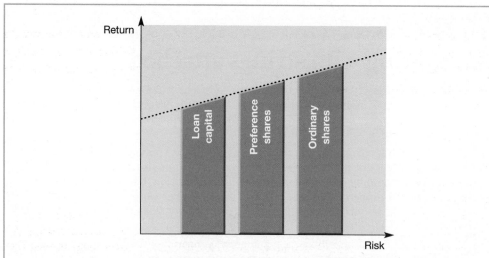

The higher the level of risk associated with a particular form of long-term finance, the higher will be the expected returns from investors. Ordinary shares are the most risky and have the highest expected return and, as a general rule, loan capital is the least risky and has the lowest expected return.

Figure 6.2 The risk/return characteristics of sources of long-term finance

What factors might a business take into account when deciding between preference shares and loan capital as a means of raising new finance?

The main factors are as follows:

- Preference shares have a higher rate of return than loan capital. From the investor's point of view, preference shares are more risky. The amount invested cannot be secured and the return is paid after the returns paid to lenders.
- A business has a legal obligation to pay interest and make capital repayments on loan capital at the agreed dates. It will usually make every effort to meet its obligations, as failure to do so can have serious consequences. Failure to pay a preference dividend, meanwhile, is less important. There is no legal obligation to pay if profits are not available for distribution. Failure to pay a preference dividend may therefore prove to be an embarrassment and nothing more. It may, however, make it difficult to persuade investors to take up future preference share issues.
- Interest on loan capital can be deducted from profits for taxation purposes, whereas preference dividends cannot. As a result, the cost of servicing loan capital is, £ for £, usually much less for a business than the cost of servicing preference shares.
- The issue of loan capital may result in managers having to accept some restrictions on their freedom of action. Loan agreements often contain covenants that can be onerous. However, no such restrictions can be imposed by preference shareholders.

A further point is that any preference shares issued form part of the permanent capital base of the business. If they are redeemed, UK law requires that they be replaced, either by a new issue of shares or by a transfer from revenue reserves, so that the business's capital base stays intact. Loan capital, however, is not viewed, in law, as part of the business's permanent capital base and therefore there is no legal requirement to replace any loan capital that has been redeemed.

Let us end this section by considering the wisdom of Warren Buffett, one of the world's richest individuals. He is chairman and chief executive officer of Berkshire Hathaway, a diversified business that has generated spectacular returns over many years. His warning on borrowing is set out in **Real World 6.2**.

Life and debt

Companies with large debts often assume that these obligations can be refinanced as they mature. That assumption is usually valid. Occasionally, though, either because of company-specific problems or a worldwide shortage of credit, maturities must actually be met by payment. For that, only cash will do the job. Borrowers then learn that credit is like oxygen. When either is abundant, its presence goes unnoticed. When either is missing, that's *all* that is noticed. Even a short absence of credit can bring a company to its knees.

Source: Shareholder letter, W. Buffett, Berkshire Hathaway Inc, www.berkshirehathaway.com, 26 February 2011, p. 22.

Forms of borrowing

Borrowings may take various forms and we shall now consider some of the more important of these.

Term loans

A **term loan** is a type of loan offered by banks and other financial institutions that can be tailored to the needs of the client business. The amount of the loan, time period, repayment terms and interest rate are all open to negotiation and agreement – which can be very useful. Where, for example, the whole amount borrowed is not required immediately, a business may agree with the lender that sums are drawn only when required. This means that interest will be paid only on amounts actually drawn and there is no need to pay interest on amounts borrowed that are not yet needed. Term loans tend to be cheap to set up (from the borrower's perspective) and can be quite flexible as to conditions. For these reasons, they tend to be popular in practice.

Loan notes (or loan stock)

Another form of long-term loan finance is the **loan note** (or *loan stock*). Loan notes are frequently divided into units (rather like share capital) and investors are invited to purchase the number of units they require. Loan notes may be redeemable or irredeemable. The loan notes of public limited companies are often traded on the Stock Exchange, and their listed value will fluctuate according to the fortunes of the business, movements in interest rates and so on.

Loan notes are usually referred to as **bonds** in the US and, increasingly, in the UK. **Real World 6.3** describes how Manchester United made a bond issue that, though fully taken up by investors, lost them money within the first two weeks. There are fears that this may make it difficult for the club to raise future funds through a bond issue.

Real World 6.3

Manchester United loses heavily

Manchester United may be battling to retain the Premier League title but success on the pitch has worked little magic in the City. The club's first bond issue, launched barely two weeks ago, has become one of the market's worst performers this year.

While the club has secured the £500m funding that it needs to refinance its bank debt, the paper losses suffered by investors could affect its ability to return to bond markets. If an investor had bought a £100,000 bond, he would have made a paper loss of £5,000. Analysts suggested the bonds had been priced too highly at launch and cited the lack of a credit rating.

Other recent issues that have fallen have not declined as heavily. 'In a benign credit market, Manchester United is one of the worst performing bonds since the beginning of 2009,' said Suki Mann, credit strategist at Société Générale.

While the club could issue more debt by increasing the size of the outstanding bond, people close to Manchester United said a return to the market was 'not on the agenda' and that the priority was to placate fans angered by the bond issue and plans by the Glazer family, United's US-based owners, to start paying down 'payment-in-kind' loans with club proceeds. The club declined to comment.

 Source: Extracts from Sakoui, A. and Blitz, R. (2010) 'Man Utd's first bond suffers from lack of support', www.ft.com, 3 February.
© The Financial Times Limited 2012. All Rights Reserved.

Would you expect the market price of ordinary shares or of loan notes to be the more volatile? Why?

Price movements will normally be much less volatile for loan notes than for ordinary shares. The price of loan notes and ordinary shares will reflect the expected future returns from each. Interest from loan notes is fixed by contract over time. Returns from ordinary shares, meanwhile, are more uncertain.

Eurobonds

Eurobonds are unsecured loan notes denominated in a currency other than the home currency of the business that issued them. They are issued by listed businesses (and other large organisations) in various countries and the finance is raised on an international basis. They are often denominated in US dollars, but many are issued in other major currencies. They are bearer bonds (that is, the owner of the bond is not registered and the holder of the bond certificate is regarded as the owner) and interest is normally paid, without deduction of tax, on an annual basis.

Eurobonds are part of an international capital market that is not restricted by regulations imposed by authorities in particular countries. This partly explains why the cost of servicing eurobonds is usually lower than the cost of similar domestic bonds. Eurobonds are made available to financial institutions, which may retain them as an investment or sell them to clients. Various banks and other financial institutions throughout the world have created a market for eurobonds. Nevertheless, some eurobonds are held for a long time and are not frequently traded.

The extent of borrowing by UK businesses in currencies other than sterling has expanded greatly in recent years. Businesses are often attracted to eurobonds because of the size of the international capital market. Access to a wider pool of potential investors can increase the chances of a successful issue.

Real World 6.4 provides an example of eurobond financing by a well-known business.

Real World 6.4

Something worth watching?

ITV plc, the broadcasting and online business, has various eurobonds in issue. As at 4 February 2013, eurobonds with the following maturity dates and interest (coupon) rates were outstanding:

	Coupon
€50.1m Euro bond due June 2014	10%
£78.4m Euro bond due October 2015	5.375%
£135m Convertible Euro bond due November 2016	4.0%
£160.6m Euro bond due January 2017	7.375%

Source: ITVplc.com/investors/debt_ir.

Deep discount bonds

A business may issue redeemable loan notes that offer a rate of interest below the market rate. In some cases, the loan notes may have a zero rate of interest. These loans are issued at a discount to their redeemable value and are referred to as deep discount bonds. Thus, loan notes may be issued at, say, £80 for every £100 of nominal value. Although lenders will receive little or no interest during the period of the loan, they will receive a £20 gain when it is finally redeemed at the full £100. The effective rate of return over the life of their loan (known as the redemption yield) can be quite high and often better than returns from other forms of lending with the same level of risk.

Deep discount bonds may have particular appeal to businesses with short-term cash flow problems. They receive an immediate injection of cash and there are no significant cash out-flows associated with the loan notes until the maturity date. From an investment perspective, the situation is reversed. Deep discount bonds are likely to appeal to investors that do not have short-term cash flow needs since a large part of the return is received on maturity of the loan. However, deep discount bonds can often be traded on the London Stock Exchange, which will not affect the borrower but will enable the lender to obtain cash.

Convertible loan notes

Convertible loan notes (or *convertible bonds*) give investors the right to convert loan notes into ordinary shares at a specified price at a given future date (or range of dates). The share price specified, which is known as the exercise price, will normally be higher than the market price of the ordinary shares at the time of the loan notes issue. In effect, the investor swaps the loan notes for a particular number of shares. The investor remains a lender to the business, and will receive interest on the amount of the loan notes, until such time as the conversion takes place. There is no obligation to convert to ordinary shares. This will be done only if the market price of the shares at the conversion date exceeds the agreed conversion price.

An investor may find this form of investment a useful 'hedge' against risk (that is, it can reduce the level of risk). It may be particularly useful when investment in a new business is being considered. Initially, the investment will be in the form of loan notes and regular interest payments will be received. If the business is successful, the investor can then convert the investment into ordinary shares.

A business may also find this form of financing useful. If the business is successful, the loan notes become self-liquidating (that is, no cash outlay is required to redeem them) as investors will exercise their option to convert. It may also be possible to offer a lower rate of interest on the loan notes because of the expected future benefits arising from conversion. However, there will be some dilution of control and possibly a dilution of earnings for existing shareholders if holders of convertible loan notes exercise their option to convert. (Dilution of earnings available to shareholders will not automatically occur as a result of the conversion of loan capital to share capital. There will be a saving in interest charges that will have an offsetting effect.)

Real World 6.5 outlines a recent convertible loan notes (bonds) issue. It was fairly unusual in that no interest was payable during the life of the bond. Investors therefore relied on the hope that the business's share price would rise adequately during the conversion period.

Real World 6.5

The name's Bond, convertible bond

Oh, James. Bonds of two kinds have produced good things for Sony. Mr Bond's latest outing in *Skyfall*, on course to be the most lucrative film in the spy franchise, will be a nice earner for Sony Pictures. And its parent's latest convertible bond, issued this week, netted the company Y150 billion, or $1.8 billion. But while *Skyfall*'s Japanese premiere in Tokyo next week will produce some good publicity, the financial kind of bond is sending very negative signals.

While 007 has never needed to do bond maths, Sony's shareholders do not get that luxury. Its zero-coupon convertible bonds were its first such debt in almost a decade. The bonds can be converted to shares at Y957, a 10 per cent premium to Wednesday's close, any time in the next five years from mid-December. Sony shares, however, fell almost 9 per cent on Thursday to Y793 in by far the heaviest day of trading the company has seen. But the fall should have been half as bad again, taking the shares to Y753 all else being equal, if it were to have fully reflected expectations that the bonds would be converted. The result instead suggests that investors are not very sure that Sony can even lift its shares to a point where it makes more sense to take a punt on future profitability than to hold an IOU that does not even offer interest.

Sony's troubles are well known, as are those of Sharp and Panasonic, its rivals. Its finances are at least on a somewhat sounder footing, thanks to its film, music, gaming and financial services units. But all the efforts of Mr Bond or even Sony's new film signing, the boy band One Direction, will not convince investors a corner has been turned until its electronics business produces its equivalent of a *Skyfall*-sized hit – a best-selling phone or tablet. Until then, Mr Bond will continue to make miraculous recoveries from disaster-laden scenarios but Sony's shares are unlikely to follow suit.

Source: Lex column (2012) 'Sony – group bonding', www.ft.com, 15 November.

Measuring the riskiness of loan capital

A number of credit-rating agencies, including Moody's Investor Services and Standard & Poor's Corporation (S&P), categorise loan capital issued by businesses according to their perceived default risk. The lower risk of default, the higher will be the rating category assigned to the loan. The ratings used by the two leading agencies are very similar and are set out below in **Real World 6.6**. To arrive at an appropriate loan rating, an agency may rely on various sources of information, including published and unpublished reports, interviews with directors and visits to the business's offices and factories.

Real World 6.6

The main debt-rating categories of two leading credit-rating agencies

Standard & Poor's	Moody's Investor Services	
AAA	Aaa	The lowest risk category. Lenders are well protected as the business has a strong capacity to pay the principal and interest.
AA	Aa	High-quality debt. Slightly smaller capacity to pay than the earlier category.
A	A	Good capacity to pay the principal and interest but the business may be more susceptible to adverse effects of changing circumstances and economic conditions.
BBB	Baa	Medium-quality debt. There is adequate capacity to pay the amounts due.
BB	Ba	Speculative aspects of the debt. Future capacity is not assured.
B	B	More speculative elements than the category above.
CCC	Caa	Poor-quality debt. Interest or capital may be at risk.
CC	Ca	Poorer-quality debt than the category above. The business is often in default.
C	C	Lowest-quality debt. No interest is being paid and the prospects for the future are poor.

These are the main categories of debt rating used; there are also sub-categories – for example, S&P uses BB–, BB+ and so on.

Source: Adapted from S.Z. Benninga and O.H. Sarig, *Corporate Finance: A valuation approach*, McGraw-Hill, 1997, p. 341. Copyright © 1997 The McGraw-Hill Companies, Inc.

Loan capital falling within any of the first four categories identified in Real World 6.6 is considered to be of high quality and is referred to as investment grade. Some institutional investors are restricted by their rules to investing only in investment-grade loans. For this reason, many businesses are concerned with maintaining investment-grade status.

Once loan capital has been assigned to a particular category, it will tend to remain in that category unless there is a significant change in circumstances.

Junk (high-yield) bonds

Loan notes rated below the first four categories identified in Real World 6.6 are often given the rather disparaging name of junk bonds. In some cases, loan notes with a junk bond rating began life with an investment-grade rating but, because of a decline in the business's fortunes, have been downgraded. (Such a bond is known as a 'fallen angel'.)

Activity 6.8

Does it really matter if the loan notes of a business are downgraded to a lower category?

A downgrade is usually regarded as serious as it will normally increase the cost of borrowing. Investors are likely to seek higher returns to compensate for the perceived increase in default risk.

In addition to increasing the cost of borrowing, a downgrade to junk bond status may cast doubt over the financial viability of the business. This may, in turn, affect its relationship with existing, or potential, customers. For example, a business that is bidding for a long-term government contract may find itself at a disadvantage when competing with other, better-capitalised businesses.

Not all junk bonds start life with an investment-grade rating. Since the 1980s, loan notes with an initial low rating have been issued by US businesses. This type of borrowing provides investors with high interest rates to compensate for the high level of default risk (hence their alternative name, high-yield bonds). Businesses that issue junk bonds, or high-yield bonds, are usually less financially stable than those offering investment-grade bonds. The junk bonds issued may also provide lower levels of security and weaker loan covenants than those normally associated with standard loan agreements.

Real World 6.7 describes recent plans for a junk bond issue.

Real World 6.7

Trash for cash?

Virgin Media is planning to issue one of the world's largest junk bonds since the end of the financial crisis to help fund its $23.3bn acquisition by John Malone's Liberty Global. The UK cable operator is set to borrow £2.3bn in bonds and another £2.3bn worth of loans in the coming weeks, loading more debt on to Virgin Media but reducing the financial burden of the deal on Liberty Global.

The high-yielding junk bonds – which are issued by companies seen to be at greater risk of default than investment-grade groups – are likely to receive attractive terms when they price this week. Strong risk appetite has pushed junk bond yields to all-time lows of below 6 per cent this year.

The bond is the largest non-investment grade issuance in Europe since Italy's Wind Telecomunicazioni in 2010 did a similar-sized deal, according to Dealogic.

FT *Source*: Adapted from Stothard, M. and Budden, R. (2013) 'Virgin Media prepares £2.3bn junk bond issue', www.ft.com, 6 February.
© The Financial Times Limited 2012. All Rights Reserved.

Junk bonds became popular in the US as they allowed some businesses to raise finance that was not available from other sources. Within a fairly short space of time, a market for this form of borrowing developed. Normally, businesses use junk bonds to finance everyday needs such as investment in inventories, receivables and non-current assets; however, they came to public attention through their use in financing hostile takeovers. There have been cases where a small business borrows heavily, through the use of junk bonds, to finance a takeover of a much larger business. Following the takeover, non-core assets of the larger business are then sold to repay the junk bond holders.

The junk bond market in the US has enjoyed a brief but turbulent history. It has suffered allegations of market manipulation, the collapse of a leading market maker and periods when default levels on junk bonds have been very high. While these events have shaken investor confidence, the market has proved more resilient than many had expected. Nevertheless, there is always the risk that, in a difficult economic climate, investors will make a 'flight to quality' and the junk bond market will become illiquid.

European investors show less interest in junk bonds than their US counterparts. Perhaps this is because they tend to view ordinary shares as a high-risk/high-return investment and view loan capital as a form of low-risk/low-return investment. Junk bonds are a hybrid form of investment lying somewhere between ordinary shares and conventional loan notes. It can be argued that the same results as from junk bonds can be achieved through holding a balanced portfolio of ordinary shares and conventional loan notes.

Mortgages

A mortgage is a form of loan that is secured on an asset, frequently property. Financial institutions such as banks, insurance businesses and pension funds are often prepared to lend to businesses on this basis. The mortgage may be over a long period (20 years or more).

Real World 6.8 describes the extent to which one well-known business uses mortgages to finance its main assets.

Real World 6.8

Flying with a heavy load

At 31 March 2012 Ryanair, the budget airline, reported aircraft held at a carrying amount (that is cost less depreciation) of €4882.4m. It also reported that aircraft with a carrying amount of €4,856.0m were mortgaged to lenders as security for loans.

Source: Ryanair Holdings plc, Annual Report 2012, www.ryanair.com, pp. 146–147.

Interest rates and interest rate risk

Interest rates on loan notes may be either floating or fixed. A floating interest rate means that the rate of return will rise and fall with market rates of interest. (But it is possible for a floating rate loan note to be issued that sets a maximum rate of interest and/or a minimum rate of interest payable.) The market value of the loan notes, however, is likely to remain fairly stable over time.

The converse will normally be true for loans with fixed interest rates. Interest payments will remain unchanged with rises and falls in market rates of interest, but the value of the loan notes will fall when interest rates rise, and will rise when interest rates fall.

Activity 6.9

Why do you think the value of fixed-interest loan notes will rise and fall with rises and falls in interest rates?

This is because investors will be prepared to pay less for loan notes that pay a rate of interest below the market rate of interest and will be prepared to pay more for loan notes that pay a rate of interest above the market rate of interest.

Movements in interest rates can be a significant issue for businesses that have high levels of borrowing. A business with a floating rate of interest may find that rate rises will place real strains on cash flows and profitability. Conversely, a business that has a fixed rate of interest will find that, when rates are falling, it will not enjoy the benefits of lower interest charges. To reduce or eliminate these risks, a business may enter into a hedging arrangement.

To hedge against the risk of interest rate movements, various devices may be employed. One popular device is the interest rate swap. This is an arrangement between two businesses whereby each business assumes responsibility for the other's interest payments. Typically, it involves a business with a floating-interest-rate loan note swapping interest payment obligations with a business with a fixed-interest-rate loan note. A swap agreement can be undertaken through direct negotiations with another business, but it is usually easier to negotiate through a bank or other financial intermediary. Although there is an agreement to swap interest payments, the legal responsibility for these payments will still rest with the business that entered into the original loan note agreement. Thus, the borrowing business may continue to make interest payments to the lender in line with the loan note agreement. However, at the end of an agreed period, a compensating cash adjustment between the two parties to the swap agreement will be made.

A swap agreement can be a useful hedging device where there are different views concerning future movements in interest rates. For example, a business with a floating rate agreement may believe that interest rates are going to rise, whereas a business with a fixed-rate agreement may believe that interest rates are going to fall.

Real World 6.9 sets out the policies of two large businesses for dealing with interest rate risk.

Real World 6.9

Managing interest rate risk

Wolseley plc, a major distributor of plumbing and heating products, states its hedging policy as follows:

> To manage the Group's exposure to interest rate fluctuations, the Group's policy is normally that between 0 per cent and 50 per cent of projected borrowings required during the next two years should be at fixed rates. However, this percentage is regularly reviewed by the Board and 72 per cent of loans were at fixed rates at 31 July 2012. Rates which reset at least every 12 months are regarded as floating rates, and the Group then uses interest rate swaps to generate the desired interest rate profile.[1]

Barratt Developments plc is a major UK builder. In its annual report for 2012, total loans and borrowings at the financial year end of £343.3 million were revealed. The annual report states:

> The majority of the Group's facilities are floating rate, which exposes the Group to increased interest rate risk. The Group has in place £192.0m (2011: £192.0m) of floating-to-fixed interest rate swaps.[2]

Sources: (1) Wolseley plc Annual Report 2012, p. 148, www.wolseley.com; (2) Barratt Developments plc, Annual Report and Accounts 2012, p. 86, www.barrattdevelopments.co.uk.

Swap agreements may also be used to exploit imperfections in the capital markets. It may be the case that one business has an advantage over another when negotiating interest rates for a fixed loan note agreement, but would prefer a floating loan note agreement, whereas the other business is in the opposite position. When this occurs, both businesses can benefit from a swap agreement.

Warrants

Holders of **warrants** have the right, but not the obligation, to buy ordinary shares in a business at a given price (the 'exercise' price). As with convertible loan notes, the price at which shares may eventually be bought is usually higher than the market price of those shares at the time of the issue of the warrants. The warrant will usually state the number of shares that the holder may buy and the time limit within which the option to buy them can be exercised. Occasionally, perpetual warrants are issued that have no set time limits. Warrants do not confer voting rights or entitle the holders to make any claims on the assets of the business.

Share warrants are often sold to investors by the business concerned. When this occurs, they can be a valuable source of finance. In some cases, however, they are given away 'free' as a 'sweetener' to accompany the issue of loan notes. That is, they are used as an incentive to potential lenders. The issue of warrants in this way may enable the business to offer lower rates of interest on the loan notes or to negotiate less restrictive loan conditions.

Warrants enable investors to benefit from any future increases in the business's ordinary share price, without having to buy the shares themselves. But if the share price remains below the exercise price, the warrant will not be used and the investor will lose out.

Activity 6.10

Under what circumstances will the holders of share warrants exercise their option to purchase?

Holders will exercise this option only if the market price of the shares exceeds the exercise price within the specified time period. If the exercise price is higher than the market price, it will be cheaper for the investor to buy the shares in the market.

Share warrants may be detachable, which means that they can be sold separately from the loan notes. The warrants of businesses whose shares are listed on the Stock Exchange are often also listed, providing a ready market for buying and selling the warrants.

Issuing warrants to lenders can be particularly useful for businesses investing in risky projects. Potential lenders may feel that such projects provide them with an opportunity for loss but no opportunity for gain. By attaching share warrants to the loan issue, they are given the opportunity to participate in future gains. This should increase their appetite for risk and, by doing so, make the issue more attractive.

Share warrants are a speculative form of investment. They have a gearing element, which means that changes in the value of the underlying shares can lead to a disproportionate change in value of the warrants. To illustrate this gearing element, let us suppose that a share has a current market price of £2.50 and that an investor is able to exercise an immediate option to purchase a single share for £2.00. In theory, the value of the warrant is £0.50 (that is, £2.50 – £2.00). Let us further suppose that the price of the share rises by 10 per cent, to £2.75, before the warrant option is exercised. The value of the warrant should now rise to £0.75 (that is, £2.75 – £2.00), which represents a 50 per cent increase in value. This gearing effect can, of course, operate in the opposite direction as well.

It is worth noting the difference in status within a business between holders of convertible loan notes and holders of loan notes with share warrants attached, where both groups decide to exercise their right to convert. Convertible loan note holders will become ordinary shareholders and will no longer be lenders to the business. The value of their loan notes will be converted into shares. Loan note holders with warrants attached will, by converting their warrants, also become shareholders. However, their status as lenders is unaffected. They will be both ordinary shareholders and lenders to the business.

Both convertible loans and warrants are examples of **financial derivatives**. These are any form of financial instrument, based on share or loan capital, which can be used by investors to increase their returns or reduce risk.

Finance leases

When a business needs a particular asset, such as a piece of equipment, instead of buying it direct from a supplier, the business may arrange for a bank (or other business) to buy it and then lease it to the business. The bank that owns the asset, and then leases it to the business, is known as a 'lessor'. The business that leases the asset from the bank and then uses it is known as the 'lessee'.

A **finance lease**, as such an arrangement is known, is in essence a form of lending. This is because, had the lessee borrowed the funds and then used them to buy the asset itself, the effect would be much the same. The lessee would have use of the asset but would also have a financial obligation to the lender – just as with a leasing arrangement.

With finance leasing, legal ownership of the asset remains with the lessor; however, the lease agreement transfers to the lessee virtually all the rewards and risks associated with the item being leased. The finance lease agreement will cover a substantial part of the life of the leased item, and often cannot be cancelled.

Real World 6.10 gives an example of the use of finance leasing by a large international business.

Real World 6.10

Leased assets take off

Many airline businesses use finance leasing as a means of acquiring new aeroplanes. This includes International Airlines Group (IAG), the business that owns British Airways and Iberia. At 31 December 2012, almost 40 per cent of the carrying amount of IAG's fleet of planes was leased.

Source: International Airlines Group, Annual Report and Accounts 2012, p. 110.

Over the years, some important benefits associated with finance leasing have disappeared. Changes in the tax laws make it no longer such a tax-efficient form of financing, and changes in accounting disclosure requirements make it no longer possible to conceal this form of 'borrowing' from investors. Nevertheless, the popularity of finance leases has continued. Other reasons must, therefore, exist for businesses to adopt this form of financing. These reasons are said to include the following:

■ *Ease of borrowing.* Leasing may be obtained more easily than other forms of long-term finance. Lenders normally require some form of security and a profitable track record before making advances to a business. However, a lessor may be prepared to lease assets to a new business without a track record and to use the leased assets as security for the amounts owing.

■ *Cost.* Leasing agreements may be offered at reasonable cost. As the asset leased is used as security, standard lease arrangements can be applied and detailed credit checking of lessees may be unnecessary. This can reduce administration costs for the lessor and thereby help in providing competitive lease rentals.

■ *Flexibility.* Leasing can help provide flexibility where there are rapid changes in technology. If an option to cancel can be incorporated into the lease, the business may be able to exercise this option and invest in new technology as it becomes available. This will help the business to avoid the risk of obsolescence. Avoiding this risk will come at a cost to the lessee, however, because the risk is passed to the lessor.

■ *Cash flows.* Leasing, rather than buying an asset outright, means that large cash outflows can be avoided. The leasing option allows cash outflows to be smoothed out over the asset's life. In some cases, it is possible to arrange for low lease payments to be made in the early years of the asset's life, when cash inflows may be low, and for these to increase over time as the asset generates positive cash flows.

These benefits are summarised in diagrammatic form in Figure 6.3.

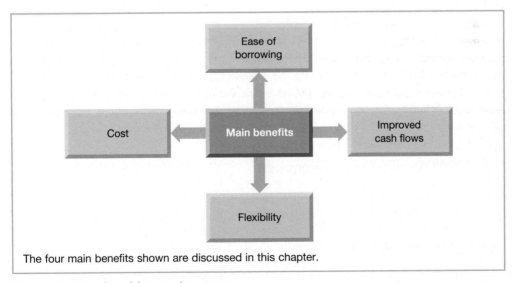

The four main benefits shown are discussed in this chapter.

Figure 6.3 Benefits of finance leasing

Real World 6.11 provides some impression of the importance of finance leasing over recent years.

Finance leasing in the UK

Figure 6.4 reveals the amount of new finance leasing employed by businesses to acquire core assets, such as plant and machinery and IT equipment, over the five-year period 2008 to 2012.

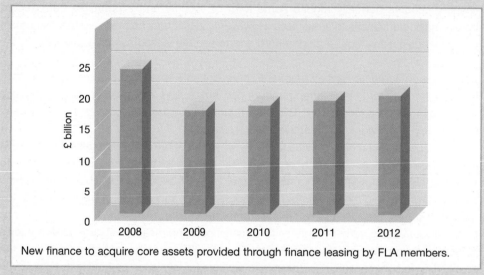

New finance to acquire core assets provided through finance leasing by FLA members.

Figure 6.4 Asset finance 2008–2012

Source: Annual Review 2013, Finance and Leasing Association, p. 16, www.fla.org.uk.

A finance lease should not be confused with an **operating lease**. The latter is a form of rental agreement rather than a form of lending. The rewards and risks of ownership stay with the owner and the lease period is shorter than the life of the asset. Operating leases can be found in many industries, including the airline industry. The operating lease period for an aircraft is often 3–5 years whereas the life of the leased aircraft may well be 25 years. An operating lease provides greater flexibility than a finance lease but is normally more expensive.

Sale-and-leaseback arrangements

A **sale-and-leaseback** arrangement involves a business raising finance by selling an asset to a financial institution. The sale is accompanied by an agreement to lease the asset back to the business to allow it to continue to use the asset. The lease rental payment is a business expense that is allowable against profits for taxation purposes.

There are usually rental reviews at regular intervals throughout the period of the lease, and the amounts payable in future years may be difficult to predict. At the end of the lease agreement, the business must either try to renew the lease or find an alternative asset. Although the sale of the asset will result in an immediate injection of cash for the business, it will lose benefits from any future capital appreciation on the asset. Where a capital gain arises on the sale of the asset to the financial institution, a liability for taxation may also arise.

Sale-and-leaseback arrangements can be used to help a business focus on its core areas of competence. In recent years, many hotel businesses have entered into sale-and-leaseback arrangements to enable them to become hotel operators rather than a combination of hotel operators and owners. Similarly, many UK high-street retailers (for example, Boots, Debenhams, Marks and Spencer, Tesco and Sainsbury) have sold off their store sites under sale-and-leaseback arrangements.

The terms of a sale-and-leaseback agreement may be vital to the future profitability and viability of a business. **Real World 6.12** explains how Woolworths' sale-and-leaseback arrangements contributed to the collapse of the business.

Real World 6.12

The wonder of Woolworths' sale and leaseback arrangements

This week the fight to save the much-loved but very under-shopped Woolworths chain finally drew to a close as the 800 stores and the wholesale distribution arm were placed into administration.

Having limped along for seven years, with the profit line gradually shifting from black to red, the directors finally called it a day after the retailer, labouring under £385 million ($591 million) of debt, succumbed to a cash crisis. But how did it come to pass that the near 100-year-old chain, which in its heyday was opening a store a week and was still selling £1.7 billion of goods a year through its stores at the time of its collapse, should end up in such a dire predicament?

Those close to Woolworths place this week's collapse firmly at the feet of those who demerged the retailer from Kingfisher in August 2001. They argue that the decision to carry out a sale-and-leaseback deal for 182 Woolworths' stores in return for £614 million of cash – paid back to Kingfisher shareholders – crippled the chain. For in return for the princely price tag, Woolworths was saddled with onerous leases that guaranteed the landlords a rising income stream.

One person who knows Woolworths well says: 'The rent bill rose from £70 million a decade ago to £160 million today. There is no doubt that back in 2001, with the de-merger and the sale of these stores, the company was saddled with a huge amount of quasi debt in terms of these leases.'

 Source: Rigby, E. (2008) 'Seeds of Woolworths' demise sown long ago', www.ft.com, 29 November.
© The Financial Times Limited 2012. All Rights Reserved.

Hire purchase

Hire purchase (HP) is a form of credit used to acquire an asset. Under the terms of a hire purchase agreement a customer pays for an asset by instalments over an agreed period. Normally, the customer will pay an initial deposit (down payment) and then make instalment payments at regular intervals, perhaps monthly, until the balance outstanding has been paid. The customer will usually take possession of the asset after payment of the initial deposit, although legal ownership of the asset will not be transferred until the final instalment has been paid.

HP agreements will often involve three parties:

- the supplier
- the customer
- a financial institution.

Although the supplier will deliver the asset to the customer, the financial institution will buy the asset from the supplier and then enter into an HP agreement with the customer. This intermediary role played by the financial institution enables the supplier to receive immediate payment for the asset but allows the customer a period of extended credit. Figure 6.5 sets out the main steps in the hire purchase process.

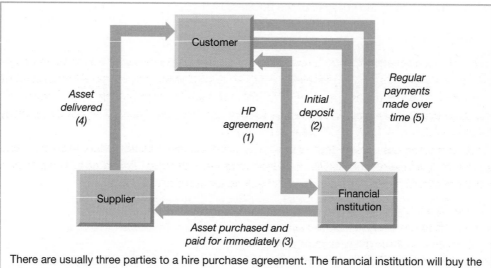

There are usually three parties to a hire purchase agreement. The financial institution will buy the asset from the supplier, who will then deliver it to the customer. The customer will pay an initial deposit and will agree to pay the balance to the financial institution through a series of regular instalments.

Figure 6.5 The hire purchase process

Real World 6.13 reveals the extent to which one large UK business depends on hire purchase to finance its main assets.

Getting there by instalments

HP agreements are, perhaps, most commonly associated with private consumers acquiring large household items or cars. It is also, however, a significant form of financing for businesses. Stagecoach Group plc, the transport business, reported in 2012 passenger service vehicles with a carrying value of £638.2 million. It also reported that £174.0 million of this figure related to assets purchased under HP agreements. This amounts to around 27 per cent of the total.

Source: Stagecoach Group plc, Annual Report 2012, p. 74.

Securitisation

Securitisation involves bundling together illiquid financial or physical assets of the same type so as to provide backing for an issue of bonds. This financing method was first used by US banks, which bundled together residential mortgage loans to provide asset backing for bonds issued to investors. (Mortgage loans held by a bank are financial assets that provide future cash flows in the form of interest receivable.)

Securitisation has spread beyond the banking industry and has now become an important source of finance for businesses in a wide range of industries. Future cash flows from a variety of illiquid assets are now used as backing for bond issues, including:

- credit card receipts
- water industry charges
- rental income from university accommodation
- ticket sales for football matches
- royalties from music copyright
- consumer instalment contracts
- beer sales to pub tenants.

The effect of securitisation is to capitalise future cash flows arising from illiquid assets. This capitalised amount is sold to investors, through the financial markets, to raise finance for the business holding these assets.

Securitisation usually involves setting up a special-purpose vehicle (SPV) to acquire the assets from the business wishing to raise finance. This SPV will then arrange the issue of bonds to investors. Income generated from the securitised assets is received by the SPV and used to meet the interest payable on the bonds. When the bonds mature, they may be repaid from receipts arising from one or more of the following:

- the securitised assets (so long as the maturity dates coincide)
- the issue of new bonds
- surplus income generated by the securitised assets.

To reassure investors about the quality of the bonds, the securitised assets may be of a higher value than the value of the bonds (this is known as *overcollateralisation*). Alternatively, some form of credit insurance can be available from a third party, such as a bank.

The main elements of the securitisation process are set out in Figure 6.6.

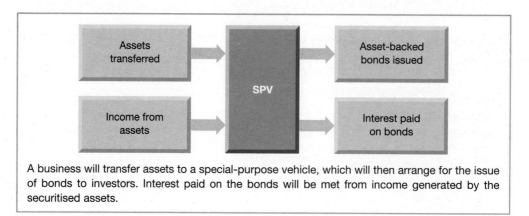

A business will transfer assets to a special-purpose vehicle, which will then arrange for the issue of bonds to investors. Interest paid on the bonds will be met from income generated by the securitised assets.

Figure 6.6 The securitisation process

Securitisation may also be used to help manage risk. Where, for example, a bank has lent heavily to a particular industry, its industry exposure can be reduced by bundling together some of the outstanding loan contracts and making a securitisation issue.

Securitisation and the financial crisis

Securitising mortgage loan repayments became popular among US mortgage lenders during the early 2000s. Monthly repayments due from mortgage borrowers were 'securitised' and sold to major banks. Unfortunately, many of the mortgage loans were made to people on low incomes who were not good credit risks (sub-prime loans). When they began to default on their obligations, it became clear that the securitised mortgages, now owned by the banks, were worth much less than they had paid to the mortgage lenders. This led to the so-called 'sub-prime' crisis, which then triggered the worldwide economic problems during 2008. There is, however, no inherent reason why securitisation should be a problem and it is unfortunate that it is linked to the sub-prime crisis. It can be a legitimate and practical method of raising finance.

Securitisation appears to be slowly regaining popularity. **Real World 6.14** describes a fairly recent securitisation issue by a UK business.

Real World 6.14

Like a Virgin

Virgin Money is set to launch its second securitisation issue of the year. It completed a £700m securitisation, its first since taking over Northern Rock in 2011, in June this year backed by a pool of UK prime, owner-occupied mortgages.

Virgin says its second securitisation will help to diversify both the source and term of its funding base, and support its business strategy including growing its lending.

Notes will be secured on Virgin Money prime UK residential mortgage assets. There is no information at the moment about how big this latest deal will be but sources close to it say it could exceed the £700m figure achieved in the first securitisation.

Source: Adapted from R. Thickett, 'Virgin Money set to launch second securitisation issue of the year', www.mortgagestrategy.co.uk, 5 November 2012.

EXTERNAL SOURCES OF SHORT-TERM FINANCE

Short term, in this context, is usually taken to mean up to one year. Figure 6.1 reveals that the major external sources of short-term finance are:

- bank overdrafts
- bills of exchange
- debt factoring
- invoice discounting.

Each of these sources is discussed below.

Bank overdrafts

A **bank overdraft** enables a business to maintain a negative balance on its bank account. It represents a very flexible form of borrowing as the size of an overdraft can (subject to bank approval) be increased or decreased more or less instantaneously. It is relatively inexpensive to arrange and interest rates are often very competitive, though normally higher than those for a term loan. As with all loans, the rate of interest charged will vary according to how creditworthy the customer is perceived to be by the bank. An overdraft is fairly easy to arrange – sometimes it can be agreed by a telephone call to the bank. In view of these advantages, it is not surprising that an overdraft is an extremely popular form of short-term finance.

Banks prefer to grant overdrafts that are self-liquidating, that is, the funds are used in such a way as to extinguish the overdraft balance by generating cash inflows. The banks may ask for projected cash flow statements from the business to see when the overdraft will be repaid and how much finance is required. They may also require some form of security on amounts advanced.

One potential drawback with this form of finance is that it is repayable on demand. This may pose problems for a business that is illiquid. However, many businesses operate for many years using an overdraft, simply because the bank remains confident of their ability to repay and the arrangement suits the business. Thus, bank overdrafts, though in theory regarded as short term, can, in practice, become a source of long-term finance.

Bills of exchange

A **bill of exchange** is similar, in some respects, to an IOU. It is a written agreement that is addressed by one person to another, requiring the person to whom it is addressed to pay a particular amount at some future date. Bills of exchange, which carry no interest, are used in trading transactions. They are offered by a buyer to a supplier in exchange for goods. The supplier who accepts the bill of exchange may either keep the bill until the date the payment is due (this is usually between 60 and 180 days after the bill is first drawn up) or present it to a bank for payment. The bank will often be prepared to pay the supplier the face value of the bill, less a discount, and will then collect the full amount of the bill from the buyer at the specified payment date.

What advantages do you see from a buyer drawing up a bill of exchange?

By drawing up a bill of exchange, a buyer is able to delay payment for goods purchased. It therefore provides a period of credit. The supplier, however, can receive immediate payment by discounting the bill with a bank.

Nowadays, bills of exchange are rarely used for trading transactions within the UK, but they are still used for international trading.

Debt factoring

Debt factoring is a service offered by a financial institution (known as a factor). Many of the large factors are subsidiaries of commercial banks. Debt factoring involves the factor taking over the trade receivables collection for a business. In addition to operating normal credit control procedures, a factor may offer to undertake credit investigations and advise on the creditworthiness of customers. It may also offer protection for approved credit sales. Two main forms of factoring agreement exist:

- *recourse factoring*, where the factor assumes no responsibility for bad debts arising from credit sales
- *non-recourse factoring*, where, for an additional fee, the factor assumes responsibility for bad debts up to an agreed amount.

The factor is usually prepared to make an advance to the business of up to around 80 per cent of approved trade receivables (although it can sometimes be as high as 90 per cent). This advance is usually paid immediately after the goods have been supplied to the customer. The balance of the debt, less any deductions for fees and interest, will be paid after an agreed period or when the debt is collected. The charge made for the factoring service is based on total sales revenue and is often around 2–3 per cent of sales revenue. Any advances made to the business by the factor will attract a rate of interest similar to the rate charged on bank overdrafts.

Debt factoring is, in effect, outsourcing trade receivables collection to a specialist sub-contractor. Many businesses find a factoring arrangement very convenient. It can result in savings in credit management and can create more certain cash flows. It can also release the time of key personnel for more profitable ends. This may be extremely important for smaller businesses that rely on the talent and skills of a few key individuals. In addition, the level of finance available will rise 'spontaneously' with the level of sales. The business can decide how much of the finance available is required and can use only that which it needs. However, there is a possibility that some will see a factoring arrangement as an indication that the business is experiencing financial difficulties. This may have an adverse effect on the confidence of customers, suppliers and staff. For this reason, some businesses try to conceal the factoring arrangement by collecting outstanding debts on behalf of the factor.

Not all businesses will find factoring arrangements the answer to their financing problems. Factoring agreements may not be possible to arrange for very small businesses (those with total sales revenue of, say, less than £100,000) because of the high set-up costs. In addition, businesses engaged in certain sectors where trade disputes are part of the business culture, such as building contractors, may find that factoring arrangements are simply not available. Figure 6.7 shows the factoring process diagrammatically.

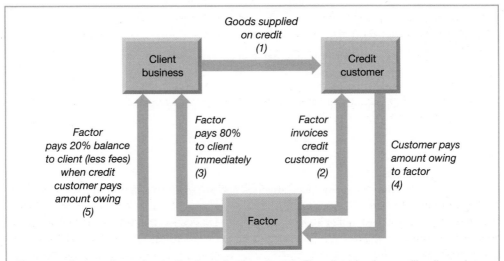

There are three main parties to the factoring agreement. The client business will sell goods on credit and the factor will take responsibility for invoicing the customer and collecting the amount owing. The factor will then pay the client business the invoice amount, less fees and interest, in two stages. The first stage typically represents 80 per cent of the invoice value and will be paid immediately after the goods have been delivered to the customer. The second stage will represent the balance outstanding and will usually be paid when the customer has paid the factor the amount owing.

Figure 6.7 The factoring process

When considering a factoring agreement, it is necessary to identify and carefully weigh the costs and likely benefits. Example 6.1 illustrates how this may be done.

Example 6.1

Balkan Ltd has annual credit sales revenue of £50 million, of which bad debts account for £0.2 million. The average settlement period for trade receivables is 80 days, which is causing some strain on the liquidity of the business.

Balkan Ltd is considering whether to use a factoring business to improve its liquidity position. The factor will advance an equivalent to 80 per cent of trade receivables (where the trade receivables figure is based on an average settlement period of 30 days) at an interest rate of 10 per cent. In addition, the factor will collect the trade receivables and will charge a fee of 3 per cent of total sales revenue for doing so. The remaining 20 per cent of the trade receivables will be paid to Balkan Ltd, when the factor receives the cash. If the factor service is used, it is expected that the average settlement period for trade receivables will be reduced to 30 days, bad debts will be eliminated and credit administration savings of £320,000 will be gained.

The business currently has an overdraft of £10.0 million at an interest rate of 11 per cent a year.

In evaluating the factoring arrangement, it is useful to begin by considering the cost of the existing arrangements:

Existing arrangements

	£000
Bad debts written off each year	200
Interest cost of average receivables outstanding [(£50m × 80/365) × 11%]	1,205
Total cost of existing arrangement	1,405

The cost of the factoring arrangement can now be compared with this:

Factoring arrangement

	£000
Factoring fee (£50m × 3%)	1,500
Interest on factor loan (assuming 80% advance and reduction in average credit period) [(£40m × 30/365) × 10%]	329
Interest on overdraft (remaining 20% of receivables financed in this way) [(£10m × 30/365) × 11%]	90
	1,919
Savings in credit administration	(320)
Total cost of factoring	1,599

The net additional cost for the business from factoring would be £194,000 (that is, £1,599,000 less £1,405,000). Obviously, all other things being equal, the business would continue with the existing arrangements.

Invoice discounting

Invoice discounting involves a factor or other financial institution providing a loan based on a proportion of the face value of a business's credit sales outstanding. The amount advanced is usually 75–80 per cent of the value of the approved sales invoices outstanding. The business must agree to repay the advance within a relatively short period – perhaps 60 or 90 days. Responsibility for collecting the trade receivables outstanding remains with the business and repayment of the advance is not dependent on the trade receivables being collected. Invoice discounting will not result in such a close relationship developing between the business and the financial institution as occurs with factoring. It may be a short-term arrangement, whereas debt factoring usually involves a longer-term arrangement.

Nowadays, invoice discounting is a much more important source of funds to businesses than factoring. There are three main reasons for this:

■ It is a confidential form of financing which the business's customers will know nothing about.
■ The service charge for invoice discounting is only about 0.2–0.3 per cent of sales revenue compared with 2.0–3.0 per cent for factoring.
■ A debt factor may upset customers when collecting the amount due, which may damage the relationship between the business and its customers.

Real World 6.15 shows the relative importance of invoice discounting and factoring.

The popularity of invoice discounting and factoring

Figure 6.8 charts the relative importance of invoice discounting and factoring in terms of the value of client sales revenue.

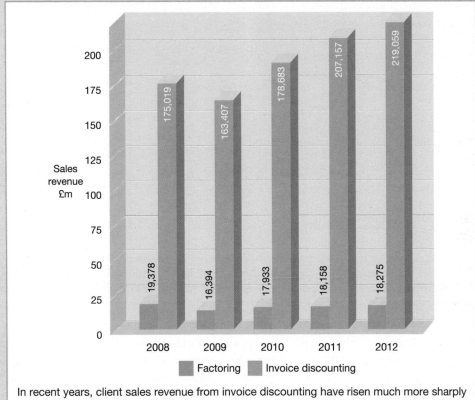

In recent years, client sales revenue from invoice discounting have risen much more sharply than client sales revenue for factoring.

Figure 6.8 Client sales revenue: invoice discounting and factoring, 2008–2012

Source: Chart constructed from data published by the Asset Based Finance Association, www.abfa.org.uk.

Factoring and invoice discounting are forms of **asset-based finance** as the assets of receivables are, in effect, used as security for the cash advances received by the business.

LONG-TERM VERSUS SHORT-TERM BORROWING

Where it is clear that some form of borrowing is required to finance the business, a decision must be made as to whether long-term or short-term borrowing is more appropriate. There are various issues to be taken into account, which include the following:

■ *Matching*. The business may attempt to match the type of borrowing with the nature of the assets held. Thus, long-term borrowing may be used to finance assets that form part of the permanent operating base of the business. These normally include non-current assets and a certain level of current assets. This leaves assets held for a short period, such as current assets used to meet seasonal increases in demand, to be financed by short-term borrowing, which tends to be more flexible in that funds can be raised and repaid at short notice. Figure 6.9 shows this funding division graphically. A business may wish to match the period of borrowing exactly with the asset life. This may not be possible, however, because of the difficulty of predicting the life of many assets.

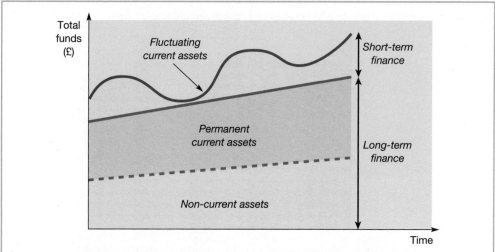

The broad consensus on financing seems to be that all of the permanent financial needs of the business should come from long-term sources. Only that part of current assets that fluctuates in the short term, probably on a seasonal basis, should be financed from short-term sources.

Figure 6.9 Short-term and long-term financing requirements

- *Flexibility.* Short-term borrowing may be used as a means of postponing a commitment to long-term borrowing. This may be desirable if interest rates are high but are forecast to fall in the future. Short-term borrowing does not usually incur a financial penalty for early repayment, whereas a penalty may arise if long-term borrowing is repaid early.
- *Refunding risk.* Short-term borrowing has to be renewed more frequently than long-term borrowing. This may create problems for the business if it is in financial difficulties or if there is a shortage of funds available for lending.
- *Interest rates.* Interest payable on long-term borrowing is often higher than that for short-term borrowing, as lenders require a higher return where their funds are locked up for a long period. This fact may make short-term borrowing a more attractive source of finance for a business. However, there may be other costs associated with borrowing (arrangement fees, for example) to be taken into account. The more frequently borrowings are renewed, the higher these costs will be.

Activity 6.14

Some businesses may take up a less cautious financing position than that shown in Figure 6.9 and others may take up a more cautious one. How would the diagram differ under each of these options?

A less cautious position would mean relying on short-term finance to help fund part of the permanent capital base. A more cautious position would mean relying on long-term finance to help finance the fluctuating assets of the business.

INTERNAL SOURCES OF FINANCE

In addition to external sources of finance there are certain internal sources of finance that a business may use to generate funds for particular activities. These sources usually have the advantage that they are flexible. They may also be obtained quickly – particularly working capital sources – and do not require the compliance of other parties. The main internal sources of funds are described below and summarised in Figure 6.10.

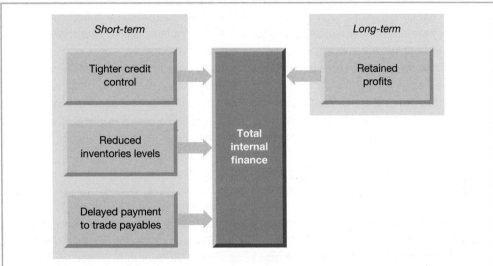

The major internal source of long-term finance is the profits that are retained rather than distributed to shareholders. The major internal sources of short-term finance involve reducing the level of trade receivables and inventories and increasing the level of trade payables.

Figure 6.10 The major internal sources of finance

INTERNAL SOURCES OF LONG-TERM FINANCE

Retained earnings

Earnings that are retained within the business, rather than distributed to shareholders in the form of dividends, represent by far the most important source of new finance for UK businesses in terms of value of funds raised.

Activity 6.15

Are retained earnings a free source of finance for the business? Explain.

No. This is because they have an opportunity cost to shareholders. If shareholders receive a dividend, they can use the cash to make other income-yielding investments. If the business retains the cash, shareholders are deprived of this potential income.

In view of the opportunity cost involved, shareholders will expect a rate of return from retained earnings that is equivalent to what they would receive had the funds been invested in another opportunity with the same level of risk.

The reinvestment of earnings, rather than the issue of new shares, can be a useful way of raising finance from equity (ordinary share) investors. No issue costs are incurred and the amount raised is certain once the earnings have been made. When new shares are issued, meanwhile, issue costs may be substantial and there may be uncertainty over the success of the issue. Where new shares are issued to outside investors, some dilution of control may also be suffered by existing shareholders.

Even though the reinvestment of earnings incurs a cost to the business, it may be preferable to raise finance from equity (ordinary share) investors in this way rather than by an issue of shares. No issue costs are incurred and the amount raised is certain, once the earnings have been generated. Where new shares are issued, issue costs may be substantial and the success of the issue may be uncertain. In addition, any new shares issued to outside investors will result in existing shareholders suffering some dilution of control.

Retaining earnings may be an easier option than asking investors to subscribe to a new share issue. These earnings are already held by the business and so there is no delay in receiving the funds. Moreover, there is often less scrutiny when earnings are retained for reinvestment purposes than when new shares are issued. Investors tend to examine closely the reasons for any new share issue. A problem with the use of earnings as a source of finance, however, is that their timing and future level cannot always be reliably determined.

It would be wrong to gain the impression that businesses either retain their entire earnings or pay them all out as dividends. Larger businesses, for example, tend to pay dividends but normally pay out no more than 50 per cent of their earnings.

Some shareholders may prefer earnings to be retained by the business rather than distributed in the form of dividends. If the business ploughs earnings back, it may be expected that it will expand and share values will increase as a result. An important reason for preferring earnings to be retained is the effect of taxation on the shareholder. In the UK, dividends are treated as income for tax purposes and therefore attract income tax. Gains on the sale of shares attract capital gains tax. Generally speaking, capital gains tax bites less hard than income tax. A further advantage of capital gains over dividends is that the shareholder has a choice as to when to sell the shares and realise the gain. In the UK, it is only when the gain is realised that capital gains tax comes into play. It is claimed that investors may be attracted to particular businesses according to the dividend/retention policies that they adopt. This point is considered in more detail in Chapter 9.

Retained earnings and 'pecking order' theory

It has been suggested that businesses have a 'pecking order' when taking on long-term finance. This pecking order can be summarised as follows:

- Retained earnings will be used to finance the business if possible.
- Where retained earnings are insufficient, or unavailable, loan capital will be used.
- Where loan capital is insufficient, or unavailable, share capital will be used.

One explanation for such a pecking order is that the managers of the business have access to information that investors do not. Let us suppose that the managers have reliable information indicating that the prospects for the business are better than that predicted by the market. This means that shares will be undervalued, and so to raise finance by an issue of shares under such circumstances would involve selling them at an undervalued price. This would, in effect, result in a transfer of wealth from existing shareholders to those investors who take up the new share issue. Hence, the managers, who are employed to act in the best interests of existing shareholders, will prefer to rely on retained earnings, followed by loan capital, instead.

Why shouldn't the managers simply release any inside information to the market to allow the share price to rise and so make it possible to issue shares at a fair price?

There are at least two reasons why this may not be a good idea:

■ It may be time-consuming and costly to persuade the market that the prospects of the business are better than current estimates. Investors may find it hard to believe what the managers tell them.
■ It may provide useful information to competitors about future developments.

Let us now suppose the managers of a business have access to bad news about the future. If the market knows that the business will rely on retained earnings and loan capital when in possession of good news, it will assume that the issue of share capital can be taken as an indication that the business is in possession of bad news. Investors are therefore likely to believe that the shares of the business are currently overvalued and will not be interested in subscribing to a new issue. (There is some evidence to show that the value of shares will fall when a share issue is announced.) Hence, this situation will again lead managers to favour retained earnings followed by loan capital, with share capital as a last resort.

The pecking order theory may help to explain the heavy reliance of businesses on retained earnings. It does not, however, provide a complete explanation of the way in which businesses behave. Why, for example, do some businesses issue new equity shares even though they have the opportunity to issue loan capital? Clearly, there are other influences that come into play when making a financing decision. We shall pursue this point further in Chapter 8.

INTERNAL SOURCES OF SHORT-TERM FINANCE

Figure 6.10 reveals that the major internal forms of short-term finance are:

■ tighter credit control
■ reducing inventories levels
■ delaying payments to trade payables.

We saw in Chapter 2, in the context of projected cash flow statements, that increases and decreases in these working capital items will have a direct and immediate effect on cash. This effectively raises finance that can be used elsewhere in the business.

Tighter credit control

By exerting tighter control over amounts owed by credit customers a business may be able to reduce the proportion of assets held in this form and so release funds for other purposes. Having funds tied up in trade receivables represents an opportunity cost in that those funds could be used for profit-generating activities. It is important, however, to weigh the benefits of tighter credit control against the likely costs in the form of lost customer goodwill and lost sales. To remain competitive, a business must take account of the needs of its customers and the credit policies adopted by rival businesses within the industry. We consider this further in Chapter 10.

Activity 6.17 involves weighing the costs of tighter credit control against the likely future benefits.

Activity 6.17

Rusli Ltd provides a car valet service for car hire businesses when their cars are returned from hire. Details of the service costs are as follows:

	Per car	
	£	£
Car valet charge		20
Less Variable costs	14	
Fixed costs	4	18
Profit		2

Sales revenue is £10 million a year and is all on credit. The average credit period taken by Rusli Ltd's customers is 45 days, although the terms of credit require payment within 30 days. Bad debts are currently £100,000 a year. Trade receivables are financed by a bank overdraft with an interest cost of 10 per cent a year.

The credit control department of Rusli Ltd believes it can eliminate bad debts and can reduce the average credit period to 30 days if new credit control procedures are implemented. These procedures will cost £50,000 a year and are likely to result in a reduction in sales of 5 per cent a year.

Should the business implement the new credit control procedures?

(*Hint*: To answer this activity it is useful to compare the current cost of trade credit with the costs under the proposed approach.)

The current cost of trade credit is:

	£
Bad debts	100,000
Overdraft interest ((£10m × 45/365) × 10%)	123,288
	223,288

The annual cost of trade credit under the new policy will be:

	£
Overdraft interest ((95% × £10m) × (30/365) × 10%)	78,082
Cost of control procedures	50,000
Net cost of lost sales ((£10m/£20 × 5%) × (20 – 14*))	150,000
	278,082

* The loss will be the contribution from valeting the car, that is, the difference between the valet charge and the variable costs. The fixed costs are ignored as they do not vary with the decision.

The above figures reveal that the business will be worse off if the new policies are adopted.

Reducing inventories levels

This internal source of funds may prove attractive to a business. As with trade receivables, holding inventories imposes an opportunity cost on a business as the funds tied up cannot be used for other purposes. If inventories are reduced, funds become available for those purposes. However, a business must ensure there are sufficient inventories available to meet likely future sales demand. Failure to do so will result in lost customer goodwill and lost sales revenue.

The nature and condition of the inventories held will determine whether it is possible to exploit this form of finance. A business may have excessive inventories as a result of poor buying decisions. This may mean that a significant proportion of inventories held is slow-moving or obsolete and therefore cannot be liquidated easily. These issues are picked up again in Chapter 10.

Delaying payment to trade payables

By providing a period of credit, suppliers are in effect offering a business an interest-free loan. If the business delays payment, the period of the 'loan' is extended and funds are retained within the business. This can be a cheap form of finance for a business, although this is not always the case. If a business fails to pay within the agreed credit period, there may be significant costs: for example, the business may find it difficult to buy on credit when it has a reputation as a slow payer.

Activity 6.18 concerns the cash flow benefit of more efficient management of the working capital elements.

Activity 6.18

Trader Ltd is a wholesaler of imported washing machines. The business is partly funded by a bank overdraft and the bank is putting pressure on Trader Ltd to reduce this as soon as possible.

Sales revenue is £14.6 million a year and is all on credit. Purchases and cost of sales are roughly equal at £7.3 million a year. Current investment in the relevant working capital elements are:

	£m
Inventories	1.5
Trade receivables	3.8
Trade payables	0.7

Trader Ltd's accountant believes that much of the overdraft could be eliminated through better control of working capital. As a result, she has investigated several successful businesses that are similar to Trader Ltd and found the following averages:

Average inventories turnover period	22
Average settlement period for trade receivables	57
Average settlement period for trade payables	55

How much cash could Trader Ltd generate if it were able to bring its ratios into line with those of similar businesses?

The cash that could be generated is as follows:

	£m	£m
Inventories		
Current level	1.5	
Target level: $^{7.3}/_{365} \times 22 =$	0.4	1.1
Trade receivables		
Current level	3.8	
Target level: $^{14.6}/_{365} \times 57 =$	2.3	1.5
Trade payables		
Current level	0.7	
Target level: $^{7.3}/_{365} \times 55 =$	1.1	0.4
Total		3.0

Some final points

The so-called short-term sources just described are short term to the extent that they can be reversed at short notice. For example, a reduction in the level of trade receivables can be reversed within a couple of weeks. Typically, however, once a business has established a reduced receivables collection period, a reduced inventories holding period and/or an expanded payables payment period, it will tend to maintain these new levels.

In Chapter 10, we shall see how these three elements of working capital may be managed. We shall also see that, for many businesses, the funds invested in working capital items are vast. By exercising tighter control of trade receivables and inventories and by exploiting opportunities to delay payment to trade payables, it may be possible to release substantial amounts for other purposes.

Self-assessment question 6.1

Helsim Ltd is a wholesaler and distributor of electrical components. The most recent draft financial statements of the business revealed the following:

Income statement for the year

	£m	£m
Sales revenue		14.2
Opening inventories	3.2	
Purchases	8.4	
	11.6	
Closing inventories	(3.8)	(7.8)
Gross profit		6.4
Administration expenses		(3.0)
Distribution expenses		(2.1)
Operating profit		1.3
Finance costs		(0.8)
Profit before taxation		0.5
Tax		(0.2)
Profit for the period		0.3

Statement of financial position as at the end of the year

	£m
ASSETS	
Non-current assets	
Property, plant and equipment	
Land and buildings	3.8
Equipment	0.9
Motor vehicles	0.5
	5.2
Current assets	
Inventories	3.8
Trade receivables	3.6
Cash at bank	0.1
	7.5
Total assets	12.7

	£m
EQUITY AND LIABILITIES	
Equity	
Share capital	2.0
Retained earnings	1.8
	3.8
Non-current liabilities	
Loan notes (secured on property)	3.5
Current liabilities	
Trade payables	1.8
Short-term borrowings	3.6
	5.4
Total equity and liabilities	12.7

Notes:
1 Land and buildings are shown at their current market value. Equipment and motor vehicles are shown at their written-down values (that is, cost less accumulated depreciation).
2 No dividends have been paid to ordinary shareholders for the past three years.

In recent months, trade payables have been pressing for payment. The managing director has therefore decided to reduce the level of trade payables to an average of 40 days outstanding. To achieve this, he has decided to approach the bank with a view to increasing the overdraft (the short-term borrowings comprise only a bank overdraft). The business is currently paying 10 per cent a year interest on the overdraft.

Required:
(a) Comment on the liquidity position of the business.
(b) Calculate the amount of finance required to reduce trade payables, from the level shown on the statement of financial position, to an average of 40 days outstanding.
(c) State, with reasons, how you consider the bank would react to the proposal to grant an additional overdraft facility.
(d) Identify four sources of finance (internal or external, but excluding a bank overdraft) that may be suitable to finance the reduction in trade payables and state, with reasons, which of these you consider the most appropriate.

The answer to this question can be found at the back of the book on 564–565.

SUMMARY

The main points in this chapter may be summarised as follows:

Sources of finance

- Long-term finance is for at least one year whereas short-term finance is for a shorter period.

- External sources of finance require the agreement of outside parties, whereas internal sources do not.

- The higher the risk associated with a source of finance, the higher the expected return from investors.

External sources of long-term finance

■ Include ordinary shares, preference shares, borrowings, leases, hire purchase agreements and securitisation.

■ From an investor's perspective, ordinary shares are normally the most risky form of investment and provide the highest expected returns to investors. Borrowings (loans) are normally the least risky and provide the lowest expected returns to investors.

■ Loans are relatively low risk because lenders usually have security for their loan. Loan covenants can further protect lenders.

■ Types of loan capital include convertible loan notes, term loans, mortgages, eurobonds, deep discount bonds and junk bonds.

■ Credit-rating agencies categorise loans issued by businesses according to estimated default risk.

■ Convertible loan notes offer the right of conversion to ordinary shares at a specified date and a specified price.

■ Junk bonds are relatively high risk and fall outside the investment-grade categories established by credit-rating agencies.

■ Warrants give holders the right, but not the obligation, to buy ordinary shares at a given price and are often used as a 'sweetener' to accompany a loan issue.

■ Interest rates may be floating or fixed.

■ Interest rate risk may be reduced, or eliminated, through the use of hedging arrangements such as interest rate swaps.

■ A finance lease is really a form of lending that gives the lessee the use of an asset over most of its useful life in return for regular payments.

■ A sale-and-leaseback arrangement involves the sale of an asset to a financial institution accompanied by an agreement to lease the asset back to the business.

■ Hire purchase is a form of credit used to acquire an asset. Under the terms of a hire purchase (HP) agreement a customer pays for an asset by instalments over an agreed period.

■ Securitisation involves bundling together similar, illiquid assets to provide backing for the issue of bonds.

External sources of short-term finance

■ Include bank overdrafts, bills of exchange, debt factoring and invoice discounting.

■ Bank overdrafts are flexible and cheap but are repayable on demand.

■ Bills of exchange are similar to IOUs.

■ Debt factoring and invoice discounting use trade receivables as a basis for borrowing, with the latter more popular because of cost and flexibility.

Choosing between long-term and short-term borrowing

■ Important factors include matching the type of borrowing to the type of assets, flexibility, refunding risk and interest rates.

Internal sources of finance

■ Include retained earnings, tighter control of trade receivables, reducing inventories levels and delaying payments to trade payables.

■ Retained earnings are by far the most important source of new long-term finance (internal or external) for UK businesses.

■ They are not a free source of finance, as investors will require returns similar to those from ordinary shares.

KEY TERMS

Security p. 230
Fixed charge p. 230
Floating charge p. 230
Loan covenants p. 231
Subordinated loans p. 232
Term loan p. 234
Loan note p. 234
Bonds p. 234
Eurobonds p. 235
Deep discount bonds p. 235
Convertible loan notes p. 236
Junk (high-yield) bonds p. 238
Mortgage p. 239
Floating interest rate p. 239
Fixed interest rate p. 240

Hedging arrangement p. 240
Interest rate swap p. 240
Warrant p. 241
Financial derivative p. 242
Finance lease p. 242
Operating lease p. 244
Sale and leaseback p. 244
Hire purchase p. 245
Securitisation p. 247
Bank overdraft p. 249
Bill of exchange p. 249
Debt factoring p. 250
Invoice discounting p. 252
Asset-based finance p. 253

For definitions of these terms see the Glossary, pp. 605–613.

FURTHER READING

If you wish to explore the topics discussed in this chapter in more depth, try the following books:

Arnold, G. (2013) *Corporate Financial Management*, 5th edn, Pearson, Chapters 11 and 12.

Brealey, R., Myers, S. and Allen, F. (2010) *Principles of Corporate Finance*, 10th edn, Irwin/McGraw-Hill, Chapters 14, 25 and 26.

Hillier, D., Ross, S., Westerfield, R., Jaffe, J. and Jordan, B. (2010) *Corporate Finance*, European edn, McGraw-Hill Higher Education, Chapters 19 to 21.

Pike, R., Neale, B. and Linsley, P. (2012) *Corporate Finance and Investment*, 7th edn, Pearson, Chapters 15 and 16.

Answers to these questions can be found at the back of the book on pp. 574–5.

6.1 What are share warrants and what are the benefits to a business of issuing share warrants?

6.2 'Convertible loan notes are really a form of delayed equity.' Do you agree? Discuss.

6.3 What are the benefits of an interest swap agreement and how does it work?

6.4 Distinguish between invoice discounting and debt factoring.

EXERCISES

Exercises 6.4 to 6.7 are more advanced than 6.1 to 6.3. Those with coloured numbers have solutions at the back of the book, starting on p. 264.

If you wish to try more exercises, visit the students' side of this book's companion website.

6.1 Answer *all* parts below.

Required:
Provide reasons why a business may decide to:

(a) lease rather than buy an asset which is to be held for long-term use
(b) use retained earnings to finance growth rather than issue new shares
(c) repay long-term loan capital earlier than the specified repayment date.

6.2 H. Brown (Portsmouth) Ltd produces a range of central heating systems for sale to builders' merchants. As a result of increasing demand for the business's products, the directors have decided to expand production. The cost of acquiring new plant and machinery and the increase in working capital requirements are planned to be financed by a mixture of long-term and short-term borrowing.

Required:
(a) Discuss the major factors that should be taken into account when deciding on the appropriate mix of long-term and short-term borrowing necessary to finance the expansion programme.
(b) Discuss the major factors that a lender should take into account when deciding whether to grant a long-term loan to the business.
(c) Identify three conditions that might be included in a long-term loan agreement and state the purpose of each.

6.3 Securitisation is now used in a variety of industries. In the music industry, for example, rock stars such as David Bowie and Iron Maiden have used this form of financing to their benefit.

Required:
(a) Explain the term 'securitisation'.
(b) Discuss the main features of this form of financing and the benefits of using securitisation.

6.4 Raphael Ltd is a small engineering business that has annual credit sales revenue of £2.4 million. In recent years, the business has experienced credit control problems. The average collection period for sales has risen to 50 days even though the stated policy of the business is for payment to be made within 30 days. In addition, 1.5 per cent of sales are written off as bad debts each year.

The business has recently been in talks with a factor that is prepared to make an advance to the business equivalent to 80 per cent of trade receivables, based on the assumption that customers will, in future, adhere to a 30-day payment period. The interest rate for the advance will be 11 per cent a year. The trade receivables are currently financed through a bank overdraft, which has an interest rate of 12 per cent a year. The factor will take over the credit control procedures of the business and this will result in a saving to the business of £18,000 a year; however, the factor will make a charge of 2 per cent of sales revenue for this service. The use of the factoring service is expected to eliminate the bad debts incurred by the business.

Required:
Calculate the net cost of the factor agreement to the business and state whether or not the business should take advantage of the opportunity to factor its trade receivables.

6.5 Cybele Technology Ltd is a software business that is owned and managed by two computer software specialists. Although sales have remained stable at £4 million per year in recent years, the level of trade receivables has increased significantly. A recent financial report submitted to the owners indicates an average settlement period for trade receivables of 60 days compared with an industry average of 40 days. The level of bad debts has also increased in recent years and the business now writes off approximately £20,000 of bad debts each year.

The recent problems experienced in controlling credit have led to a liquidity crisis for the business. At present, the business finances its trade receivables by a bank overdraft bearing an interest rate of 14 per cent a year. However, the overdraft limit has been exceeded on several occasions in recent months and the bank is now demanding a significant decrease in the size of the overdraft. To comply with this demand, the owners of the business have approached a factor who has offered to make an advance equivalent to 85 per cent of trade receivables, based on the assumption that the level of receivables will be in line with the industry average. The factor will charge a rate of interest of 12 per cent a year for this advance. The factor will take over the sales records of the business and, for this service, will charge a fee based on 2 per cent of sales. The business believes that the services offered by the factor should eliminate bad debts and should lead to administrative cost savings of £26,000 per year.

Required:
(a) Calculate the effect on the profit of Cybele Technology Ltd of employing a debt factor. Discuss your findings.
(b) Discuss the potential advantages and disadvantages for a business that employs the services of a debt factor.

6.6 Telford Engineers plc, a medium-sized manufacturer of automobile components, has decided to modernise its factory by introducing a number of robots. These will cost £20 million and will reduce operating costs by £6 million a year for their estimated useful life of 10 years starting next year (Year 10). To finance this scheme, the business can raise £20 million either by issuing:

1 20 million ordinary shares at 100p, or
2 loan notes at 7 per cent interest a year with capital repayments of £3 million a year commencing at the end of Year 11.

Telford Engineers' summarised financial statements appear below.

Summary of statements of financial position at 31 December

	Year 6 £m	Year 7 £m	Year 8 £m	Year 9 £m
ASSETS				
Non-current assets	48	51	65	64
Current assets	55	67	57	55
Total assets	103	118	122	119
EQUITY AND LIABILITIES				
Equity	48	61	61	63
Non-current liabilities	30	30	30	30
Current liabilities				
Trade payables	20	27	25	18
Short-term borrowings	5	–	6	8
	25	27	31	26
Total equity and liabilities	103	118	122	119
Number of issued 25p shares	80m	80m	80m	80m
Share price	150p	200p	100p	145p

Note that the short-term borrowings consisted entirely of bank overdrafts.

Summary of income statements for years ended 31 December

	Year 6 £m	Year 7 £m	Year 8 £m	Year 9 £m
Sales revenue	152	170	110	145
Operating profit	28	40	7	15
Interest payable	(4)	(3)	(4)	(5)
Profit before taxation	24	37	3	10
Tax	(12)	(16)	(0)	(4)
Profit for the year	12	21	3	6
Dividends paid during each year	6	8	3	4

You should assume that the tax rate for Year 10 is 30 per cent, that sales revenue and operating profit will be unchanged except for the £6 million cost saving arising from the introduction of the robots, and that Telford Engineers will pay the same dividend per share in Year 10 as in Year 9.

Required:
(a) Prepare, for each financing arrangement, Telford Engineers' projected income statement for the year ending 31 December Year 10 and a statement of its share capital, reserves and loans on that date.

(b) Calculate Telford's projected earnings per share for Year 10 for both schemes.

(c) Which scheme would you advise the business to adopt? You should give your reasons and state what additional information you would require.

6.7 Gainsborough Fashions Ltd operates a small chain of fashion shops. In recent months the business has been under pressure from its suppliers to reduce the average credit period taken from three months to one month. As a result, the directors have approached the bank to ask for an increase in the existing overdraft for one year to be able to comply with the suppliers' demands. The most recent financial statements of the business are as follows:

Statement of financial position as at 31 May

	£
ASSETS	
Non-current assets	
Property, plant and equipment at cost less depreciation	
Fixtures and fittings	67,000
Motor vehicles	7,000
	74,000
Current assets	
Inventories	198,000
Trade receivables	3,000
	201,000
Total assets	275,000
EQUITY AND LIABILITIES	
Equity	
£1 ordinary shares	20,000
General reserve	4,000
Retained earnings	17,000
	41,000
Non-current liabilities	
Borrowings – loan notes repayable in just over one year's time	40,000
Current liabilities	
Trade payables	162,000
Accrued expenses	10,000
Borrowings – bank overdraft	17,000
Tax due	5,000
	194,000
Total equity and liabilities	275,000

Abbreviated income statement for the year ended 31 May

	£
Sales revenue	740,000
Operating profit	38,000
Interest charges	(5,000)
Profit before taxation	33,000
Tax	(10,000)
Profit for the year	23,000

A dividend of £23,000 was paid for the year.

Notes:

1 The loan notes are secured by personal guarantees from the directors.

2 The current overdraft bears an interest rate of 12 per cent a year.

Required:

(a) Identify and discuss the major factors that a bank would take into account before deciding whether or not to grant an increase in the overdraft of a business.

(b) State whether, in your opinion, the bank should grant the required increase in the overdraft for Gainsborough Fashions Ltd. You should provide reasoned arguments and supporting calculations where necessary.

Chapter 7

FINANCING A BUSINESS 2: RAISING LONG-TERM FINANCE

INTRODUCTION

We begin this chapter by looking at the role of the London Stock Exchange (which we shall refer to as simply the Stock Exchange) in raising finance for large businesses. We then go on to consider whether shares listed on the Stock Exchange are efficiently priced. If so, this has important implications for both managers and investors.

Share capital may be issued in various ways and the most important of these will be explored in the chapter. We shall see that some involve direct appeals to investors, whereas others involve the use of financial intermediaries. Smaller businesses do not have access to the Stock Exchange and so must look elsewhere to raise long-term finance. We end this chapter by considering some of the main providers of long-term finance for these businesses.

Learning outcomes

When you have completed this chapter, you should be able to:

- Discuss the role and nature of the Stock Exchange.

- Discuss the nature and implications of stock market efficiency.

- Outline the methods by which share capital may be issued.

- Identify the problems that smaller businesses experience in raising finance and describe the ways in which they may gain access to long-term finance.

THE STOCK EXCHANGE

The **Stock Exchange** acts as an important *primary* and *secondary* capital market for businesses. As a primary market, its main function is to enable businesses to raise new capital. Thus, businesses may use the Stock Exchange to raise capital by issuing shares or loan notes. To issue either through the Stock Exchange, however, a business must be 'listed'. This means that it must meet fairly stringent Stock Exchange requirements concerning size, profit history, information disclosure and so on. Share issues arising from the initial listing of the business on the Stock Exchange are known as *initial public offerings* (IPOs). Share issues undertaken by businesses that are already listed and seeking additional finance are known as *seasoned equity offerings* (SEOs). IPOs are very popular, but SEOs rather less so.

Real World 7.1 suggests that IPOs may be a good investment for those taking up the shares.

Real World 7.1

Issues are not problems

It seems that taking up IPOs is profitable, relative to the returns available from investing in Stock Exchange listed shares generally. This emerged from a research exercise that examined 1,735 separate IPOs that took place through the London Stock Exchange during the period 1995 to 2006.

Among other things, the research looked at the performance (increase in share price and dividends, if any) during the 12 months following the date of the new issue. IPO shares fared about 13 per cent better than did the average Stock Exchange equity investment. In other words, an investor who took up all of the IPOs between 1995 and 2006 and held them for one year would be 13 per cent better off than one who bought shares in a range of other businesses listed on the Stock Exchange and held them for a year. This is not to say that all IPOs represented a profitable one-year investment. It simply means that the IPO investor would have lost less in those cases than the other investor.

FT *Source*: M. Levis, 'The London markets and private equity-backed IPOs', Cass Business School, April 2008.

The function of the Stock Exchange as a secondary market is to enable investors to transfer their securities (that is, shares and loan notes) with ease. It provides a 'second-hand' market where shares and loan notes already in issue may be bought and sold.

Activity 7.1

Could the fact that investors are able to transfer shares with ease also be of benefit to listed businesses?

Investors are more likely to invest if they know their investment can be turned into cash whenever required. Listed businesses are, therefore, likely to find it easier to raise long-term finance and to do so at lower cost.

Although investors are not obliged to use the Stock Exchange as the means of transferring shares in a listed business, it is usually the most convenient way of buying or selling shares.

Listed businesses

Businesses listed on the Stock Exchange vary considerably in size, with market capitalisations ranging from below £2 million to more than £2,000 million. **Real World 7.2** provides some idea of the distribution of businesses across this wide range.

UK listed businesses by equity market value

The distribution of UK listed businesses by equity market value at the end of April 2013 is shown in Figure 7.1.

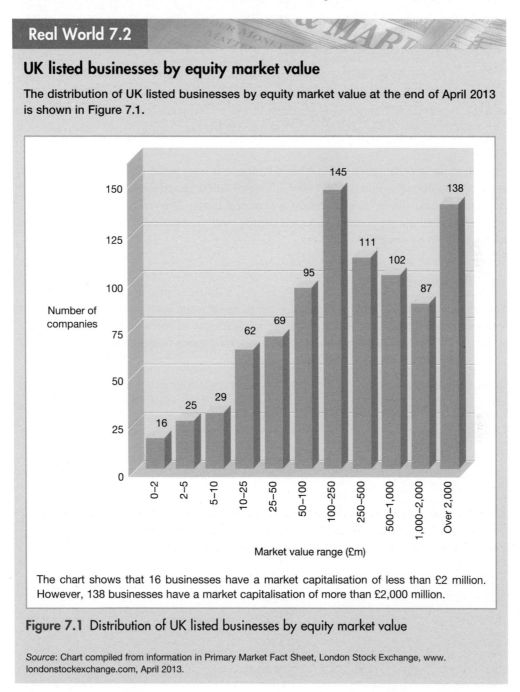

The chart shows that 16 businesses have a market capitalisation of less than £2 million. However, 138 businesses have a market capitalisation of more than £2,000 million.

Figure 7.1 Distribution of UK listed businesses by equity market value

Source: Chart compiled from information in Primary Market Fact Sheet, London Stock Exchange, www. londonstockexchange.com, April 2013.

Share price indices

There are various indices available to help monitor trends in overall share price movements of Stock Exchange listed businesses. **FTSE (Footsie) indices**, as they are called, derive their name from the organisations behind them: the *Financial Times* (FT) and the Stock Exchange (SE). The most common indices are:

- *FTSE 100*. This is probably the best-known share price index. It is based on the share price movements of the 100 largest businesses, by market capitalisation, listed on the Stock Exchange. (Market capitalisation is the total market value of the shares issued by a business.) Businesses within this index are often referred to as 'large cap' businesses.
- *FTSE Mid 250*. An index based on the share price movements of the next 250 largest businesses, by market capitalisation, listed on the Stock Exchange.
- *FTSE A 350*. This index combines businesses in the FTSE 100 and FTSE Mid 250 indices.
- *FTSE Actuaries All Share Index*. An index based on the share price movements of more than 800 shares, which account for more than 90 per cent of the market capitalisation of all listed businesses.

Each index is constructed using a base date and a base value (the FTSE 100 index, for example, was constructed in 1984 with a base of 1,000). Each index is updated throughout each trading day and reviewed on a quarterly basis. Changes in the relative size of businesses during a particular quarter will usually lead to some businesses within an index being replaced by others.

Raising finance

The amount of finance raised by Stock Exchange businesses each year varies according to economic conditions. **Real World 7.3** gives an indication of the amounts raised in recent years from equity issues by listed businesses (including those that are newly listed).

Real World 7.3

Equity issues

The following amounts were raised from new equity issues by listed businesses through the main market of the London Stock Exchange over the eight years 2005–2012.

	Number of businesses	Total amount raised (£m)
2012	532	11,449
2011	688	17,790
2010	510	23,915
2009	454	77,047
2008	527	66,472
2007	653	28,494
2006	822	33,448
2005	928	19,220

We can see that, in the last few years, the amounts raised have fallen significantly.

Source: Compiled from Main Market Fact Sheets, December 2005 to December 2012, London Stock Exchange, www.londonstockexchange.com.

The Stock Exchange can be a useful vehicle for entrepreneurs to realise value from their business.

How can the Stock Exchange help entrepreneurs to do this?

By floating their businesses on the Stock Exchange, and thereby making shares available to other investors, they can convert the value of their stake in the business into cash by selling shares.

Real World 7.4 describes how one entrepreneur was poised to benefit from an IPO.

Real World 7.4

Sure of cashing in

The prospect of the entrepreneur Peter Wood securing a bumper valuation for Esure has strengthened after the motor and home insurer found indicative buyers for its initial public offering. Investment banks handling the offer received enough orders from prospective institutional investors to float more than a third of the equity, giving the business a market capitalisation of at least £1bn, people with knowledge of the situation said. They said the development on Monday, the first working day after Esure issued its prospectus on Friday, was a sign of strong demand and a good indication for the final price of the IPO.

The order books being filled relatively early in the process will give a boost to Mr Wood, who is set to net as much as £152m by selling down his 49 per cent stake to about a third.

Esure, known for television adverts that feature the late Michael Winner, is aiming to float between 35 per cent and 50 per cent of its equity, priced at between 240p and 310p a share. This would put the company into the FTSE 250 with a market capitalisation of between £1bn and £1.3bn and make the IPO London's biggest so far this year.

 Source: A. Grey, 'Esure moves closer to bumper valuation', www.ft.com, 13 March 2013.

Advantages and disadvantages of a listing

In addition to the advantages already mentioned, it is claimed that a Stock Exchange listing can help a business by:

- raising its profile, which may be useful in dealings with customers and suppliers
- ensuring that its shares are valued in an efficient manner (a point to which we return later)
- broadening its investor base
- acquiring other businesses by using its own shares as payment rather than cash
- attracting and retaining employees by offering incentives based on share ownership schemes.

Before a decision is made to float (that is, to list), however, these advantages must be weighed against the possible disadvantages of a listing.

Raising finance through the Stock Exchange can be a costly process. To make an initial public offering, a business will rely on the help of various specialists such as lawyers, accountants and bankers. Their services, however, do not come cheap. Typically, between 4 per cent and 8 per cent of the total proceeds from a sale will be absorbed in professional fees. (See reference 1 at the end of the chapter.) In addition to these out-of-pocket expenses, a huge amount of management time is usually required, which can result in missed business opportunities.

Another important disadvantage is the regulatory burden placed on listed businesses. Once a business is listed, there are continuing requirements to be met, covering issues such as:

- disclosure of financial information
- informing shareholders of significant developments
- the rights of shareholders and lenders
- the obligations of directors.

These requirements can be onerous and can also involve substantial costs for the business.

The activities of listed businesses are closely monitored by financial analysts, financial journalists and other businesses. Such scrutiny can be unwelcome, particularly if the business is dealing with sensitive issues or is experiencing operational problems. Furthermore, if investors become disenchanted with the business and the price of its shares falls, this may make it vulnerable to a takeover bid from another business. **Real World 7.5** describes plans for one well-known business to avoid the spotlight and to protect itself by de-listing and then turning into a private company.

Real World 7.5

It's a private matter

American entrepreneur Michael Dell is taking the PC maker he founded private for $24.4bn (£15.6bn), in a deal that marks the end of an era for the computer industry. The billionaire, who already owns about 16 pc of the company, is combining with private-equity firm Silver Lake and Microsoft to buy the company he founded as a student. Having floated in New York in 1988 as PCs were becoming a staple in homes, Dell has struggled to adapt as consumers increasingly prefer tablet devices such as Apple's iPad.

Taking the company private will allow Mr Dell to more easily alter the company's direction as he will no longer face shareholder scrutiny. 'Under a new private company structure, we will have the time and flexibility to really pursue and realise [our strategy],' said Brian Gladden, Dell's chief financial officer.

Dell shareholders will receive $13.65 a share in cash, just over a 25 pc premium to the share price before rumours about the acquisition surfaced last month.

Source: R. Blackden, 'Dell to go private in $24.4bn deal', *Daily Telegraph*, 6 February 2013.

There is a risk that smaller listed businesses will be overlooked by investors. Institutional investors, which dominate the ownership of listed shares, usually buy shares in large tranches. As they do not normally wish to own a large proportion of a business's issued shares, they tend to focus on larger businesses. Smaller businesses may therefore find it difficult to raise fresh capital unless investors can be persuaded of their growth potential. They may also find that their shares suffer from poor liquidity as there are fewer buyers and sellers.

Stock Exchange investors are often accused of taking a short-term view, which puts pressure on managers to produce quick results. If managers judge that shareholders are focused on the forthcoming quarterly, or half-yearly, profit announcements, they may strive to produce results that meet expectations. This may prevent managers from undertaking projects that are likely to only yield benefits over the longer term. Instead, they will opt for investments that perform well over the short term, even though the long-term prospects may be poor. This is a serious criticism of the way in which the Stock Exchange operates, which we shall explore a little later in the chapter.

STOCK MARKET EFFICIENCY

We mentioned above that the Stock Exchange helps share prices to be efficiently priced. The term 'efficiency' in this context does not relate to the way in which the Stock Exchange is administered but rather to the way in which information is processed. An **efficient stock market** is one in which information is processed quickly and accurately and so share prices faithfully reflect all relevant information available. In other words, prices are determined in a rational manner and represent the best estimate of the 'true worth' of the shares.

The term 'efficiency' does not imply that investors have perfect knowledge concerning a business and its future prospects and that this knowledge is reflected in the share price. Information may come to light concerning the business that investors did not previously know about and which may indicate that the current share price is higher or lower than its 'true worth'. However, in an efficient market, new information will be quickly absorbed by investors and this will lead to an appropriate share price adjustment.

We can see that the term 'efficiency' in relation to the Stock Exchange is not the same as the economists' concept of perfect markets, which you may have come across in your previous studies. The definition of an efficient capital market does not rest on a set of restrictive assumptions regarding the operation of the market (for example, no taxes, no transaction costs, no entry or exit barriers and so on). In reality, such assumptions will not hold. The term 'efficient market' is a narrower concept that has been developed by studying how stock markets behave in the real world. It simply describes the situation where relevant information is *quickly* and *accurately* reflected in share prices. The speed at which new information is absorbed in share prices will mean that not even nimble-footed investors will have time to make superior gains by buying or selling shares when new information becomes available.

To understand why the Stock Exchange may be efficient, it is important to bear in mind that shares listed on the Stock Exchange are scrutinised by many individuals, including skilled analysts, who are constantly seeking to make gains from identifying shares that are inefficiently priced. They are alert to new information and will react quickly when new opportunities arise. If, for example, shares can be identified as being below their 'true worth', investors would immediately exploit this information by buying those shares. When this is done on a large scale, the effect will be to drive up the price of the shares, thereby eliminating any inefficiency within the market. Thus, as a result of the efforts to make gains from inefficiently priced shares, investors will, paradoxically, promote the efficiency of the market.

Three levels of efficiency have been identified concerning the operation of stock markets. These are as follows.

Weak form of efficiency

The weak form reflects the situation where past market information, such as the sequence of share prices, rates of return and trading volumes and so on, is fully reflected in current share prices and so should have no bearing on future share prices. In other words, future share price movements are independent of past share price movements. Movements in share prices will follow a random path and, as a result, any attempt to study past prices in order to detect a pattern of price movements will fail. It is not possible, therefore, to make gains from simply studying past price movements. Investors and analysts who draw up charts of share price changes (this is known as technical analysis) in order to predict future price movements will thus be wasting their time.

Semi-strong form of efficiency

The semi-strong form takes the notion of efficiency a little further and describes the situation where all publicly available information, including past share prices, is fully reflected in the current share price. Other publicly available forms of information will include published financial statements, business announcements, newspaper reports, economic forecasts and so on. These forms of information, which become available at random intervals, are quickly absorbed by the market and so investors who study relevant reports and announcements (this is known as fundamental analysis), in an attempt to make above-average returns on a consistent basis, will be disappointed. The information will already be incorporated into share prices.

Strong form of efficiency

The strong form is the ultimate form of efficiency and describes the situation where share prices fully reflect all available information, whether public or private. This means that the share price will be a good approximation to the 'true' value of the share. As all relevant information is absorbed in share prices, even those who have 'inside' information concerning a business, such as unpublished reports or confidential management decisions, will not be able to make superior returns, on a consistent basis, from using this information.

The various forms of efficiency described above can be viewed as a progression where each higher form of efficiency incorporates the previous form(s). Thus, if a stock market is efficient in the semi-strong form it will also be efficient in the weak form. Similarly, if a stock market is efficient in the strong form, it will also be efficient in the semi-strong and weak forms (see Figure 7.2).

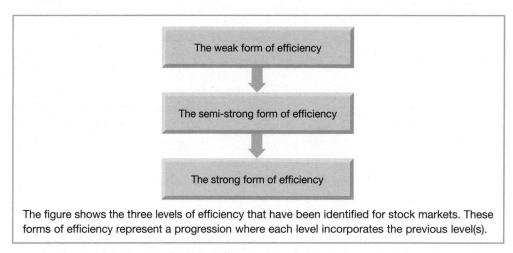

The figure shows the three levels of efficiency that have been identified for stock markets. These forms of efficiency represent a progression where each level incorporates the previous level(s).

Figure 7.2 The three levels of market efficiency

Activity 7.4 tests your understanding of how share prices might react to a public announcement under two different levels of market efficiency.

Evidence on stock market efficiency

You may wonder what evidence exists to support each of the above forms of efficiency. For the weak form there is now a large body of evidence that spans many countries and many time periods. Much of this evidence has involved checking to see whether share price movements follow a random pattern: that is, finding out whether successive price changes were independent of each other. The research evidence generally confirms the existence of a random pattern of share prices. Research has also been carried out to assess the value of trading rules used by some investors. These rules seek to achieve superior returns by identifying trend-like patterns to determine the point at which to buy or sell shares. The research has produced mixed results but tends to demonstrate that trading rules are not worthwhile. However, the value of these rules is difficult to assess, partly because of their sheer number and partly because of the subjective judgement involved in interpreting trends.

Although the weight of research evidence offers little support for the belief that share prices, or prices in other financial markets, exhibit repetitive patterns of behaviour, some analysts (known as technical analysts) continue to search for such patterns. **Real World 7.6** illustrates some of the techniques used by these analysts to help predict future price movements.

Reading the signs

The charts in Figure 7.3 are taken from the *Independent* and show the techniques used by technical analysts being applied to different markets: to the Dow Jones Index (a share price index of 30 industrial companies listed on the New York Stock Exchange), to the share price of Vodafone plc (a major mobile phone operator) and to currency markets.

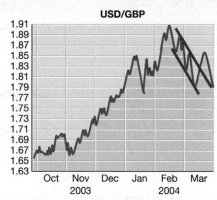

USD/GBP

The most basic tool of technical analysis is the trend line, which must go through at least three points on a chart. Markets frequently trade within a channel of two parallel lines: the top one is called the resistance line, the lower one the support line. A break-out of the channel can indicate the end of a market trend.

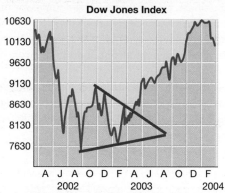

Dow Jones Index

The triangle is another popular trend indicator. Triangles show price convergence, and are formed during periods of consolidation in the markets, when the support and resistance lines converge, as shown here in the chart of the Dow Jones Index. A break-out from a triangle is seen as a strong indicator of market direction.

USD/EUR

The triangular formation in this recent chart of the US dollar/euro price also represents a period of consolidation in the market. However, the fact that this consolidation came after a price fall and the market then broke out of the triangle in the same downward direction makes this a particularly strong indicator.

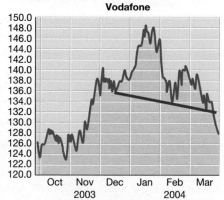

Vodafone

The chart of the Vodafone share price demonstrates a classic 'head and shoulders'. In this formation, the price reaches a peak and declines; rises above its former peak and declines; and rises a third time but not to the second peak, and then again declines. Chartists consider this formation a very negative market indicator.

The diagrams illustrate four techniques used by technical analysts to predict future market movements.

Figure 7.3 Reading the signs

Source: 'Reading the signs', *The Independent*, 27 March 2004.

Research to test the semi-strong form of efficiency has usually involved monitoring the reaction of the share price to new information, such as profit announcements. This is done to see whether the market reacts to new information in an appropriate manner. The results usually show that share prices readjust quickly and accurately to any new information that affects the value of the business. This implies that investors cannot make superior returns by reacting quickly to new information. The results also show that investors are able to distinguish between new information that affects the value of the underlying business and new information that does not.

Other semi-strong tests have assessed whether it is possible to predict future returns by using available public information. These tests have produced more mixed results. One test involves the use of P/E ratios. We saw in Chapter 3 that the P/E ratio reflects the market's view of the growth prospects of a particular share: the higher the P/E ratio, the greater the growth prospects. Tests have shown, however, that shares with low P/E ratios outperform those with high P/E ratios. The market overestimates the growth prospects of businesses with high P/E ratios and underestimates the growth prospects of those with low P/E ratios. In other words, the market gets it wrong. We shall return to this point a little later.

Research to test the strong form of efficiency has often involved an examination of the performance of investment fund managers. These managers are highly skilled and have access to a wide range of information, not all of which may be in the public domain. If, despite their advantage over private investors, fund managers were unable to generate consistently superior performance over time, it would provide support for the view that markets are strong-form efficient. The results, alas, are mixed. Although earlier studies often supported the view that fund managers cannot outperform the market, more recent studies have suggested that some can.

Implications for managers

If stock markets are efficient, what should managers do? It seems that they must learn six important lessons.

Lesson 1: Timing doesn't matter

Managers considering a new share issue may feel that timing is important. In an inefficient stock market, the share price may fall below its 'true worth' and making a new issue at this point could be costly. In an efficient stock market, however, the share price will faithfully reflect the available information. This implies that the timing of issues will not be critical as there is no optimal point for making a new issue. Even if the market is depressed and share prices are low, it cannot be assumed that things will improve. The prevailing share price still reflects the market's estimate of future returns from the share.

Activity 7.6

Why might managers who accept that the market is efficient, at least in the semi-strong form, be justified in delaying the issue of new shares until what they believe will be a more appropriate time?

They may believe the market has underpriced the shares because it does not have access to all relevant information. They may have access to inside information which, when made available to the market, will lead to an upwards adjustment in share prices.

Lesson 2: Don't search for undervalued businesses

If the stock market accurately absorbs publicly available information, share prices will represent the best estimates available of their 'true worth'. This means that investors should not spend time trying to find undervalued shares in order to make gains. Unless they have access to information which the market does not have, they will not be able to 'beat the market' on a consistent basis. To look for undervalued shares will only result in time being spent and transaction costs being incurred to no avail. Similarly, managers should not try to identify undervalued shares in other businesses with the intention of identifying possible takeover targets. While there may be a number of valid and compelling reasons for taking over another business, the argument that shares of the target business are undervalued by the stock market is not one of them.

Lesson 3: Take note of market reaction

The investment plans and decisions of managers will be quickly and accurately reflected in the share price. Where these plans and decisions result in a fall in share price, managers may find it useful to review them. In effect, the market provides managers with a 'second opinion', which is both objective and informed. This opinion should not go unheeded.

Lesson 4: You can't fool the market

Managers may believe that form is as important as substance when communicating information to investors. This may induce them to 'window dress' the financial statements to provide a better picture of financial health than is warranted by the facts. The evidence suggests, however, that the market will see through any cosmetic attempts to improve the financial picture. It quickly and accurately assesses the economic substance of a business and prices the shares accordingly. Thus, accounting policy changes (such as switching depreciation methods, or switching inventories valuation methods, to boost profits in the current year) will be a waste of time.

Lesson 5: The market, not the business, decides the level of risk

Investors will correctly assess the level of risk associated with an investment and will impose an appropriate rate of return. Moreover, this rate of return will apply to whichever business undertakes that investment. Managers will not be able to influence this rate of return by adopting particular financing strategies. This means, for example, that the issue of certain types of security, or combinations of securities, will not reduce investors' required rate of return.

Lesson 6: Champion the interests of shareholders

The primary objective of a business is the maximisation of shareholder wealth. If managers take decisions and actions that are consistent with this objective, it will be reflected in the share price. This is likely to benefit the managers of the business as well as the shareholders.

ARE THE STOCK MARKETS REALLY EFFICIENT?

The view that stock markets, at least in the major industrialised countries, are efficient has become widely accepted. However, there is a growing body of evidence that casts doubt on the efficiency of stock markets and has reopened the debate on this topic. Below we consider evidence concerning short-term behaviour by investors and other stock market 'anomalies' that challenge the notion of market efficiency.

The problem of short termism

We saw earlier that stock market investors are often accused of adopting a short-term focus. This is difficult to square with the efficient market hypothesis. The value of a share is represented by the future discounted cash flows that it generates. In a stock market where shares are efficiently priced, investors should therefore be concerned with the ability of a business to generate long-term cash flows rather than its ability to meet short-term profit targets. In other words, if a stock market is efficient, a critical mass of investors will not adopt a short-term view when making share investment decisions. The evidence on this issue, however, does not fully support this position.

The evidence

Early research found no evidence of investor short termism. Indeed, it provided compelling evidence to the contrary. The behaviour of share prices was found to be consistent with investors taking a long-term view when making decisions. The following examples provide illustrations:

- *Share price reaction to investment plans*. If investors took a short-term view, an announcement of long-term investment plans would be treated as bad news. Investors would sell their shares and this, in turn, would lead to a fall in share price. Conversely, any announcement that long-term investment plans are to be scrapped would be treated as good news and would result in a rise in share price. In fact, the opposite share price reaction to that stated was normally found to occur.
- *Dividend payments*. Investors demanding short-term returns would value businesses with a high dividend yield more highly than those with a low dividend yield. This would then allow an astute investor to buy shares in low-yielding businesses at a lower price than their 'true' value and so make higher returns over time. Research evidence suggested, however, that businesses with low dividend yields are more highly regarded by investors than those with high dividend yields (see reference 2 at the end of the chapter).

More recent research has provided ammunition for those who have been critical of short-term behaviour among investors. One important study examined 624 businesses listed on the UK FTSE and US S&P indices over the period 1980–2009 to see whether the pricing of shares was affected by short termism. If so, it should be apparent by the excessive discounting of future cash flows from shares over and above the risk-free rate. The findings of the study suggest that short termism does exist and that it is prevalent across all industry sectors. According to the study:

> In the UK and US, cash-flows five years ahead are discounted at rates more appropriate eight or more years hence; ten-year ahead cash-flows are valued as if sixteen or more years ahead; and cash-flows more than thirty years ahead are scarcely valued at all. (See reference 3 at the end of the chapter.)

Interestingly, there was much greater evidence of short termism among the sample businesses in the final decade of the study. It seems, therefore, that short termism is on the rise.

The behaviour of investors does appear to have changed over time. In the UK, shares of listed businesses are now held for around six months compared with eight years in 1960. (See reference 4 at the end of the chapter.) It seems that investors are acting increasingly like share traders and less like owners. Investors may, therefore, become less concerned with the future stream of dividends and more concerned with short-term share price movements (which, in turn, may be influenced by short-term profit performance). Some believe that such behaviour can be traced back to the short-term focus of institutional investors. The performance of fund managers is often subject to quarterly review, which, so it is argued, increases pressure to produce short-term returns.

Other stock market anomalies

Researchers have unearthed other 'anomalies' in major stock markets. Once again, these may be exploited by investors to achieve superior returns. Some of the more important are:

- *Business size.* A substantial body of evidence suggests that, other things being equal, small businesses yield higher returns than large businesses. It is not clear why this should be the case and various explanations exist. Some argue that it is because institutional investors tend to shun small businesses even though they may offer high returns. For such large investors, the size of the investment would be fairly modest and any benefits would be outweighed by the costs of evaluation and monitoring.
- *Price/earnings (P/E) ratio.* We mentioned earlier that research has shown that a portfolio of shares held in businesses with a low P/E ratio will outperform a portfolio of shares held in businesses with a high P/E ratio. This suggests that investors can make superior returns from investing in businesses with low P/E ratios.
- *Market overreaction.* Studies have shown that stock markets often overreact to new information. Where, for example, a business announces bad news, the fall in share price can be excessive and some time can elapse before the share price adjusts correctly to the news. In other words, the market does not react both quickly and accurately to new information. An investor could, therefore, make an abnormal gain by buying shares immediately after the announcement and then selling them when their price has correctly adjusted.
- *Investment timing.* Various studies indicate that superior returns may be gained by timing investment decisions appropriately. There is evidence, for example, that higher returns can be achieved by buying shares at the beginning of April, in the UK, and then selling them later in the month, than similar trading in other months. There is also evidence that on Mondays there is an above-average fall in share prices. This may be because investors review their share portfolio at the weekend and sell unwanted shares when the market opens on Monday, thereby depressing prices. This means it is better to buy rather than sell shares on a Monday. There is also evidence that the particular time of the day in which shares are traded can lead to superior returns.

Activity 7.7

Can you suggest why, in the UK, April may provide better returns than other months of the year?

A new tax year begins in April. Investors may sell loss-making shares in March to offset any capital gains tax on shares sold at a profit during the tax year. As a result, share prices will become depressed. At the start of the new tax year, however, investors will start to buy shares again and so share prices will rise.

The key question is whether these anomalies seriously undermine the idea of market efficiency. Many believe that they are of only minor importance and that, on the whole, the markets are efficient for most of the time. The view taken is that, in the real world, there are always likely to be inefficiencies. Furthermore, if investors discover share price anomalies, they will try to exploit them in order to make gains. By so doing, they will eliminate the anomalies and so make the markets more efficient. Others believe, however, that these anomalies confirm that stock markets cannot be viewed simply through the lens of efficient markets.

Bubbles, bull markets and behavioural finance

In recent years, a new discipline called **behavioural finance** has emerged, which tries to provide a more complete understanding of the way in which stock markets behave. This new discipline takes account of the psychological traits of individuals when seeking to explain market behaviour. It does not accept that individuals always behave in a rational manner, and there is a plethora of research evidence in psychology to support this view. Many studies have shown that individuals make systematic errors when processing information, for example.

Activity 7.8

What could be the effect of investors making systematic errors when buying and selling shares?

It could result in the mispricing of shares. Where this occurs, profitable opportunities can be exploited.

A detailed study of these systematic errors, or biases, is beyond the scope of this book. However, it is worth providing an example to illustrate the challenge they pose to the notion of efficient markets.

One well-documented bias is the overconfidence that individuals place in their own information-processing skills and judgement. Overconfidence may lead to various errors when making investment decisions, including:

- an under-reaction to new share price information, which arises from a tendency to place more emphasis on new information confirming an original share valuation than new information challenging this valuation
- a reluctance to sell shares that have incurred losses because this involves admitting to past mistakes
- incorrectly assessing the riskiness of future returns
- a tendency to buy and sell shares more frequently than is prudent.

These errors help to explain share price 'bubbles' and overextended 'bull' markets, where investor demand keeps share prices buoyant despite evidence suggesting that share prices are too high.

Share price bubbles, which inflate and then burst, appear in stock markets from time to time. When they inflate there is a period of high prices and high trading volumes, which is sustained by the enthusiasm of investors rather than by the fundamentals affecting the shares. During a bubble, investors appear to place too much faith in their optimistic views of future share price movements and, for a while at least, ignore warning signals concerning future growth prospects. However, as the warning signals become stronger, the disparity between investors' views and reality eventually becomes too great and a correction occurs, bringing investors' views more into line with fundamental values. This realignment of investors' views, leading to a large correction in share prices, means that the bubble has burst.

Share price bubbles are unusual and are often limited to particular industries or even particular businesses. **Real World 7.7** tells the story of a bubble concerning a particular business.

How should managers act?

The debate over the efficiency of stock markets rumbles on and further research is needed before a clear picture emerges. Although this situation may be fine for researchers, it may not be so fine for managers confronted with an increasingly mixed set of messages concerning stock market behaviour. Probably the best thing for managers to do is to assume that well-developed markets, such as those in the UK and the US, tend to be efficient, at least in the semi-strong form. The weight of evidence still supports this view, and failure to make this assumption could prove very costly. Where it is clear, however, that market inefficiency exists, managers should make the most of available opportunities.

SHARE ISSUES

A business may issue shares in a number of ways. These may involve direct appeals to investors or may involve financial intermediaries. The most common methods of share issue are set out in Figure 7.4 and considered in turn.

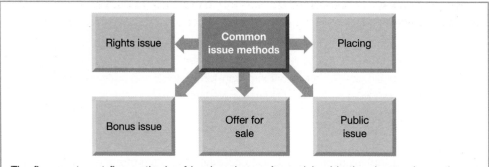

The figure sets out five methods of issuing shares. As explained in the chapter, bonus issues differ from the other methods in that they do not lead to an injection of cash for the business.

Figure 7.4 Common methods of share issue

Rights issues

Rights issues can be made by established businesses seeking to raise finance by issuing additional shares for cash. UK company law gives existing shareholders the right of first refusal on these new shares, which are offered to them in proportion to their existing shareholding. Only where they waive their right would the shares then be offered to the investing public.

The business (in effect, the existing shareholders) would typically prefer that existing shareholders buy the shares through a rights issue, irrespective of the legal position. This is for two reasons:

■ Ownership (and, therefore, control) of the business remains in the same hands; there is no 'dilution' of control.
■ The costs of making the issue (advertising; complying with various company law requirements) tend to be less if the shares are to be offered to existing shareholders.

Rights issues are a fairly common form of share issue. During 2012, they accounted for approximately 29 per cent of all finance raised from shares issued by Stock Exchange listed businesses. (See reference 5 at the end of the chapter.)

To encourage existing shareholders to take up their 'rights' to buy new shares, they are always offered at a price below the current market price of the existing ones. The evidence shows that shares are offered at an average 31 per cent below the current pre-rights price (see reference 6 at the end of the chapter).

As shareholders can acquire shares at a price below the current market price, the entitlement to participate in a rights offer has a cash value. Those shareholders not wishing to take up the rights offer can sell their rights to others. Calculating the cash value of the rights entitlement is quite straightforward. Example 7.1 can be used to illustrate how this is done.

Example 7.1

Shaw Holdings plc has 20 million ordinary shares of 50p in issue. These shares are currently valued on the Stock Exchange at £1.60 per share. The directors of Shaw Holdings plc believe the business requires additional long-term capital and have decided to make a one-for-four issue (that is, one new share for every four shares held) at £1.30 per share. What is the value of the rights per new share?

Solution

The first step in the valuation process is to calculate the price of a share following the rights issue. This is known as the *ex-rights price* and is simply a weighted average of the price of shares before the issue of rights and the price of the rights shares. In the above example we have a one-for-four rights issue. The theoretical ex-rights price is therefore calculated as follows:

		£
Price of four shares before the rights issue (4 × £1.60)		6.40
Price of taking up one rights share		1.30
		7.70
Theoretical ex-rights price	(£7.70/5)	£1.54

As the price of each share, in theory, should be £1.54 following the rights issue and the price of a rights share is £1.30, the value of the rights offer will be the difference between the two:

£1.54 – £1.30 = £0.24 per new share

Market forces will usually ensure that the actual price of rights and the theoretical price will be fairly close.

An investor with 2,000 shares in Shaw Holdings plc (see Example 7.1) has contacted you for investment advice. She is undecided whether to take up the rights issue, sell the rights or allow the rights offer to lapse.

Calculate the effect on the net wealth of the investor of each of the options being considered.

Before the rights issue, the position of the investor was:

	£
Value of shares (2,000 × £1.60)	3,200

If she takes up the rights issue, she will be in the following position:

	£
Value of holding after rights issue ((2,000 + 500) × £1.54)	3,850
Less Cost of buying the rights shares (500 × £1.30)	(650)
	3,200

If she sells the rights, she will be in the following position:

	£
Value of holding after rights issue (2,000 × £1.54)	3,080
Sale of rights (500 × £0.24)	120
	3,200

If she lets the rights offer lapse, she will be in the following position:

	£
Value of holding after rights issue (2,000 × £1.54)	3,080

As we can see, the first two options should leave her in the same position concerning net wealth as she was in before the rights issue. Before the rights issue she had 2,000 shares worth £1.60 each, or £3,200. However, she will be worse off if she allows the rights offer to lapse than under the other two options. In practice, the business may sell the rights offer on behalf of the investor and pass on the proceeds in order to ensure that she is not worse off as a result of the issue.

When making a rights issue, the total funds needed must first be determined. This will depend on the future plans of the business. A decision on the issue price of the rights shares must then be made. Generally speaking, this decision is not critical. In the example above, the business made a one-for-four issue with the price of the rights shares set at £1.30. However, it could have raised the same amount by making a one-for-two issue and setting the rights price at £0.65, or a one-for-one issue and setting the price at £0.325, and so on. The issue price that is finally decided upon will not affect the value of the underlying assets of the business or the proportion of the underlying assets and earnings of the business to which the shareholder is entitled. Nevertheless, it is important to ensure that the issue price is not *above* the current market price of the shares.

Activity 7.10

Why is this important?

If the issue price is above the current market price, it would be cheaper for the investor to buy shares in the open market (assuming transaction costs are not significant) than to take up the rights offer. This would mean that the share issue would fail.

It was mentioned earlier that rights shares will usually be priced at a discount to the market price of shares at the date of the rights announcement. By the date that the rights shares have to be taken up, there is a risk that the market price will have fallen below the rights price. If this occurs, the rights issue will fail for the same reasons as mentioned in Activity 7.10. The higher the discount offered, the lower the risk of such failure. Not surprisingly, discounts tend to be higher when markets are either volatile or falling. There is a danger, however, that offering a very high discount will convey the impression that there is little enthusiasm for the issue among shareholders.

Despite the benefits of giving pre-emptive rights to shareholders, it does result in less competition for new shares. This may increase the costs of raising finance, as other forms of share issue may be able to raise the amount more cheaply.

Real World 7.8 describes how a Spanish bank has used a rights issue to help to refinance its business. We can see that the discount offered was pretty high.

Money in the Banco

Banco Popular Espanol SA, the Spanish bank, made a three-for-one rights issue to raise €2.5 billion in November 2012. The shares were offered at €0.401, which was at a discount of 64 per cent on the price of the shares immediately before the issue.

The new funds were needed to help avoid the bank having to ask for aid from the Spanish government.

 Source: Based on information contained in 'Banco Popular shares gain on rights issue debut', www.reuters. com, 14 November 2012.

Bonus issues

A **bonus issue** should not be confused with a rights issue of shares. A bonus, or **scrip**, issue also involves the issue of new shares to existing shareholders in proportion to their existing shareholdings. However, shareholders do not have to pay for the new shares issued. The bonus issue is achieved by transferring a sum from the reserves to the paid-up share capital of the business and then issuing shares, equivalent in value to the sum transferred, to existing shareholders. As the reserves are already owned by the shareholders, they do not have to pay for the shares issued. In effect, a bonus issue will simply convert reserves into paid-up capital. To understand this conversion process, and its effect on the financial position of the business, let us consider Example 7.2.

Example 7.2

Wickham plc has the following abbreviated statement of financial position as at 31 March:

	£m
Net assets	<u>20</u>
Financed by	
Share capital (£1 ordinary shares)	10
Reserves	<u>10</u>
	<u>20</u>

The directors decide to convert £5 million of the reserves to paid-up capital. As a result, it was decided that a one-for-two bonus issue should be made. Following the bonus issue, the statement of financial position of Wickham plc will be as follows:

	£m
Net assets	<u>20</u>
Financed by	
Share capital (£1 ordinary shares)	15
Reserves	<u>5</u>
	<u>20</u>

We can see in Example 7.2 that, following the bonus issue, share capital has increased but there has also been a corresponding decrease in reserves. Net assets of the business remain unchanged. More shares are now in issue but the proportion of the total number of shares held by each shareholder will remain unchanged. Thus, bonus issues do not, of themselves, result in an increase in shareholder wealth. They will simply switch part of the owners' claim from reserves to share capital.

Assume that the market price per share in Wickham plc (see Example 7.2) before the bonus issue was £2.10. What will be the market price per share following the share issue?

The business has made a one-for-two issue. A holder of two shares would therefore be in the following position before the bonus issue:

2 shares held at £2.10 market price = £4.20

As the wealth of the shareholder has not increased as a result of the issue, the total value of the shareholding will remain the same. This means that, as the shareholder holds one more share following the issue, the market value per share will now be:

$$\frac{£4.20}{3} = £1.40$$

You may wonder from the calculations above why bonus issues are made. Various reasons have been put forward to explain this type of share issue, which include:

- *Share price*. The share price may be very high and, as a result, shares of a business may become difficult to trade on the Stock Exchange. It seems that shares trading within a certain price range generate more investor interest. If the number of shares in issue is increased, the market price of each share will be reduced, which may make the shares more marketable.
- *Lender confidence*. Making a transfer from distributable reserves to paid-up share capital will increase the permanent capital base of the business. This may increase confidence among lenders. In effect, it will lower the risk of ordinary shareholders withdrawing their investment through dividend distributions, thereby leaving lenders in an exposed position.
- *Market signals*. A bonus issue offers managers an opportunity to signal to shareholders their confidence in the future. The issue may be accompanied by the announcement of good news concerning the business (for example, securing a large contract or achieving an increase in profits). Under these circumstances, the share price may rise in the expectation that earnings/dividends per share will be maintained. Shareholders would, therefore, be better off following the issue. However, it is the *information content* of the bonus issue, rather than the issue itself, that will create this increase in wealth.

Offer for sale

An **offer for sale** may involve a public limited company selling a new issue of shares to a financial institution known as an issuing house. It may also involve shares already held by existing shareholders being sold to an issuing house. The issuing house will, in turn, sell the shares purchased from the business, or its shareholders, to the public. To do this, it will publish a prospectus setting out details of the business and the type of shares to be sold, and investors will be invited to apply for shares.

The advantage of this type of issue, from the business's viewpoint, is that the sale proceeds of the shares are certain. It is the issuing house that will take on the risk of selling the shares to investors. Any unsold shares will remain with the issuing house. An offer for sale is often used when a business seeks a listing on the Stock Exchange and wishes to raise a large amount of funds.

Public issue

A **public issue** involves a public limited company making a direct invitation to the public to buy its shares. Typically, this is done through a newspaper advertisement, and the invitation will be accompanied by the publication of a prospectus. The shares may, once again, be a new issue or shares already in issue. An issuing house may be asked by the business to help administer the issue of the shares to the public and to offer advice concerning an appropriate selling price. However, the business rather than the issuing house will take on the risk of selling the shares. Both an offer for sale and a public issue result in a widening of share ownership in the business.

Setting a share price

When making an issue, the business, or issuing house, will usually set a fixed price for the shares. However, establishing a price may not be an easy task, particularly where the market is volatile or where the business has unique characteristics.

Activity 7.12

What are the risks involved for the business of selling shares at a fixed price?

If the share price is set too high, the issue will be undersubscribed and the anticipated amount will not be received. If the share price is set too low, the issue will be oversubscribed and the amount received will be less than could have been achieved.

One way of dealing with the pricing problem is to make a **tender issue** of shares. This involves the investors determining the price at which the shares are issued. Although a reserve price may be set to help guide investors, it is up to each individual investor to decide on the number of shares to be purchased and the price to be paid. Once the offers from investors have been received, a price at which all the shares can be sold will be established (known as the striking price). Investors who have made offers at, or above, the striking price will be issued shares at the striking price and offers received below the striking price will be rejected. Note that all of the shares will be issued at the same price, irrespective of the prices actually offered by individual investors.

Example 7.3 illustrates the way in which a striking price is achieved.

Example 7.3

Celibes plc made a tender offer of shares and the following offers were received by investors:

Share price	Number of shares tendered at this particular price 000s	Cumulative number of shares tendered 000s
£2.80	300	300
£2.40	590	890
£1.90	780	1,670
£1.20	830	2,500

The directors of Celibes plc wish to issue 2,000,000 shares, at a minimum price of £1.20.

The striking price would have to be £1.20 as, above this price, there would be insufficient interest to issue 2,000,000 shares. At the price of £1.20, the total number of shares tendered exceeds the number of shares available and so a partial allotment would be made. Normally, each investor would receive 4 shares for every 5 shares tendered (that is 2,000/2,500).

Assume that, instead of issuing a fixed number of shares, the directors of Celibes plc (see Example 7.3) wish to maximise the amount raised from the share issue. What would be the appropriate striking price?

The price at which the amount raised from the issue can be maximised is calculated as follows:

Share price	Cumulative number of shares 000s	Share sale proceeds £000
£2.80	300	840
£2.40	890	2,136
£1.90	1,670	**3,173**
£1.20	2,500	3,000

The table shows that the striking price should be £1.90 to maximise the share sale proceeds.

Tender issues are not popular with investors and therefore are not in widespread use.

Placing

A placing does not involve an invitation to the public to subscribe to shares. Instead, the shares are 'placed' with selected investors, such as large financial institutions. These shares are normally offered at a small discount to the current market price. A placing can be a quick and relatively cheap method of raising funds because savings can be made in advertising and legal costs. It can, however, result in the ownership of the business being concentrated in a few hands and may prevent small investors from participating in the new issue of shares. Businesses seeking relatively small amounts of cash will often employ this form of issue.

Real World 7.9 describes how a placing was used by a high-technology business and how someone well known in the UK took up some of the shares.

Well placed

Roman Abramovich, the billionaire owner of Chelsea Football Club, has invested £5 million in a small UK technology company that specialises in turning natural gas into synthetic liquid fuels.

Mr Abramovich's Ervington Investments took part in a placing this week by Oxford Catalysts, which raised £30.6 million.

Oxford Catalysts' business is focused on a technology known as 'gas-to-liquids' or GTL, which uses chemical reactions to physically change the composition of gas molecules, yielding a high-quality liquid fuel. This can then be blended with crude oil or upgraded oil to produce diesel or jet fuel. Royal Dutch Shell has led the revival of global interest in GTL,

→

building a huge refinery in Qatar called Pearl which turns the emirate's abundant natural gas into an odourless, colourless fuel similar to diesel but without the sooty pollutants.

Oxford Catalysts is spearheading a different approach, focusing on the construction of small, modular GTL plants which can be deployed at remote oilfields. These convert gas that is extracted as a by-product of oil and would otherwise be simply burnt off or 'flared' into the atmosphere.

FT *Source*: Extracts from G. Chazan, 'Abramovich invests in "gas-to-liquids" in UK', www.ft.com, 4 January 2013.

A placing is sometimes used in conjunction with a rights issue. Where a planned rights issue is unlikely to raise all the funds needed, a placing may also be made to fill the funding gap.

LONG-TERM FINANCE FOR THE SMALLER BUSINESS

Although the Stock Exchange provides an important source of long-term finance for large businesses, it is not really suitable for smaller businesses. The total market value of shares to be listed on the Stock Exchange must be at least £700,000 and in practice the amounts are much higher because of the listing costs identified earlier. Thus, smaller businesses must look elsewhere for help in raising long-term finance. Reports and studies over several decades, however, have highlighted the problems that they encounter in doing so. These problems can be a major obstacle to growth and include:

- a lack of financial management skills (leading to difficulties in developing credible business plans that will satisfy lenders)
- a lack of knowledge concerning the availability of sources of long-term finance
- insufficient security for loan capital
- failure to meet rigorous assessment criteria (for example, a good financial track record over five years)
- an excessively bureaucratic screening process for loan applications (see reference 7 at the end of the chapter).

In addition, the cost of finance is often higher for smaller businesses than for larger businesses because of the higher risks involved.

Not all financing constraints are externally imposed. Small business owners often refuse to raise new finance through ordinary share issues if it involves a dilution of control. Some also refuse to consider loan finance as they do not believe in borrowing (see reference 8 at the end of the chapter).

Although obtaining long-term finance for smaller businesses is not always easy (and one consequence may be excessive reliance on short-term sources of finance, such as bank over-drafts), things have improved over recent years. Some important ways in which small businesses can gain access to long-term finance are set out in Figure 7.5 and considered below.

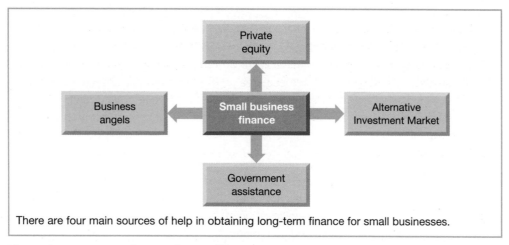

There are four main sources of help in obtaining long-term finance for small businesses.

Figure 7.5 Long-term finance for small businesses

Private-equity firms

Private-equity firms provide long-term capital to small and medium-sized businesses wishing to grow but that do not have ready access to stock markets. The supply of private equity has increased rapidly in the UK over recent years since both government and corporate financiers have shown greater commitment to entrepreneurial activity.

It is possible to distinguish between private equity and venture capital based on the investment focus. In broad terms, private equity focuses on investments in established businesses whereas venture capital focuses on investments in start-up, or early-stage, businesses. In the sections that follow, however, we shall treat private equity as encompassing investments that are sometimes described as being financed by venture capital.

Types of investment

Private-equity firms are interested in investing in small and medium-sized businesses with good growth potential. These businesses must also have owners with the ambition and determination to realise this potential. Although private-equity-backed businesses usually have higher levels of risk than would be acceptable to other providers of finance, they also have the potential for higher returns. An investment is often made for a period of five years or more, with the amount varying according to need.

Private equity is used to fund different types of business needs and provides:

- *Venture capital*. Start-up capital is provided to businesses that are still at the concept stage of development through to those that are ready to commence trading. It may be used to help design, develop and market new products and services. Venture capital is also available for businesses that have undertaken their development work and are ready to begin operations.
- *Expansion (development) capital*. This provides funding for established businesses needing additional working capital, new equipment, product development investment and so on.
- *Replacement capital*. This includes the refinancing of bank borrowings to reduce the level of gearing. It also includes capital for the buyout of part of the ownership of a business or the buyout of another private-equity firm.

- *Buyout and buyin capital*. This is capital available to finance the acquisition of an existing business. A *management buyout* (MBO) is where an existing management team acquires the business, and an *institutional buyout* (IBO) is where the private-equity firm acquires the business and instals a management team of its choice. A *management buyin* (MBI) is where an outside management team acquires an existing business. Buyouts and buyins often occur where a large business wishes to divest itself of one of its operating units or where the owners of a family business wish to sell because of succession problems.
- *Rescue capital*. This is used to turn around a business after a period of poor performance.

Venture capital investments can be particularly challenging for private-equity firms for two reasons. First, they are very high risk: investing in existing businesses with a good track record is a much safer bet. Second, start-ups and early-stage businesses often require fairly small amounts of finance. Unless a significant amount of finance is required, it is difficult to justify the high cost of investigating and monitoring the investment.

Real World 7.10 provides an impression of private-equity investment in UK businesses.

Real World 7.10

Nothing ventured, nothing gained

Figure 7.6 shows the main private-equity investments made in UK businesses during 2011 and 2012, according to financing stage.

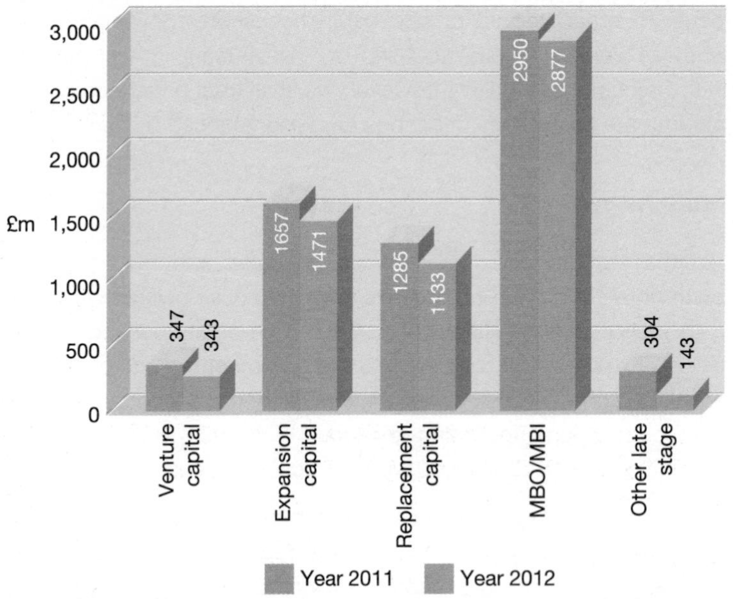

MBOs and MBIs were, by far, the most significant form of investment during 2011 and 2012.

Figure 7.6 Investment of private-equity firms in UK businesses by financing stage, 2011 and 2012

FT   *Source*: Chart compiled from information in British Private Equity and Venture Capital Association report on investment activity 2012, Table 4, p. 5, www.bvca.co.uk.

The private-equity investment process

Private-equity investment involves a five-step process that is similar to the investment process undertaken within a business. The five steps are set out in Figure 7.7 and below we consider each of these five steps.

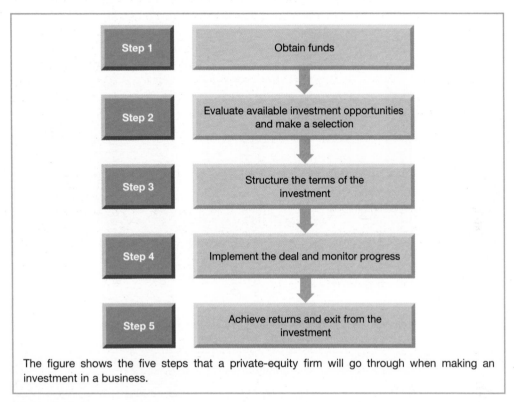

The figure shows the five steps that a private-equity firm will go through when making an investment in a business.

Figure 7.7 The investment process

Source: M. Van der Wayer, 'The venture capital vacuum', *Management Today*, July 1995, pp. 60–64, Figure 7.9.

Step 1: Obtaining the funds

Private-equity firms obtain their funds from various sources, including large financial institutions, government agencies and private investors. **Real World 7.11** provides an insight into the main sources of funds for private-equity firms.

Funding private equity

Figure 7.8 reveals the main UK sources of finance employed by private-equity firms during 2012 for investment purposes.

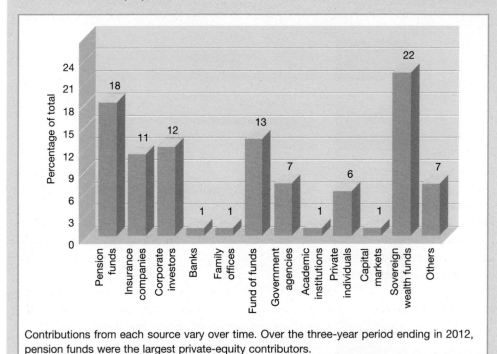

Contributions from each source vary over time. Over the three-year period ending in 2012, pension funds were the largest private-equity contributors.

Figure 7.8 Finance raised by private-equity firms by source, 2012

Source: Chart compiled from information in British Private Equity and Venture Capital Association report on investment activity 2012, Table 18, p. 12, www.bvca.co.uk.

Once obtained, there can be a two- or three-year time lag before the funds are invested in suitable businesses.

Activity 7.14

Can you think of reasons why there may be such a delay?

Suitable businesses take time to identify and, once found, they require careful investigation. There may also be lengthy negotiations with owners over the terms of the investment.

Step 2: Evaluating investment opportunities and making a selection

When a suitable business is identified, the management plans will be reviewed and an assessment made of the investment potential, including the potential for growth. This will involve an examination of:

- the market for the products
- the business processes and the ways in which they can be managed

- the ambition and quality of the management team
- the opportunities for improving performance
- the types of risks involved and the ways in which they can be managed
- the track record and future prospects of the business.

Private-equity firms will also be interested to see whether the likely financial returns are commensurate with the risks that have to be taken. The internal rate of return (IRR) method is often used in helping to make this assessment and an IRR in excess of 20 per cent is normally required (see reference 9 at the end of the chapter).

Step 3: Structuring the terms of the investment

When structuring the financing agreement, private-equity firms try to ensure that their own exposure to risk is properly managed. This will involve establishing control mechanisms within the financing agreements to protect their investment. One important control mechanism is the requirement to receive information on the progress of the business at regular intervals. The information provided, as well as information collected from other sources, will then be used as a basis for providing a staged injection of funds. In this way, progress is regularly reviewed and where serious problems arise, the option of abandoning further investments in order to contain any losses is retained.

In some cases, the private-equity firm may reduce the amount of finance at risk by establishing a financing syndicate with other private-equity firms. However, this will also reduce the potential returns and will increase the possibility of disputes between syndicate members, particularly when things do not go according to plan.

Private-equity firms will usually expect the owner/managers to demonstrate their commitment by investing in the business. Although the amounts they invest may be small in relation to the total investment, they should be large in relation to their personal wealth.

Step 4: Implementing the deal and monitoring progress

Private-equity firms usually work closely with client businesses throughout the period of the investment and it is quite common for them to have a representative on the board of directors to keep an eye on their investment. They may also provide a form of consultancy service by offering expert advice on technical and marketing matters.

Business plans that were prepared at the time of the initial investment will be monitored to see whether they are achieved. Those businesses that meet their key targets are likely to find the presence of the private-equity firms less intrusive than those that do not. Monitoring is likely to be much closer at the early stages of the investment until certain problems, such as the quality of management and cost overruns, become less of a risk (see reference 10 at the end of the chapter).

Step 5: Achieving returns and exiting from the investment

A major part of the total returns from the investment is usually achieved through the final sale of the investment. The particular method of divestment is therefore of great concern to the private-equity firm. The most common forms of divestment are through:

- a trade sale (that is, where the investment is sold to another business)
- flotation of the business on the Stock Exchange, or sale of the quoted equity
- sale of the investment to the management team (buyback)
- sale of the investment to another private-equity firm or financial institution.

In some cases, there will be an 'involuntary exit' when the business fails, in which case the investment must be written off.

Private equity and borrowing

A private-equity firm will often require a business to borrow a significant proportion of its needs from a bank or other financial institution, thereby reducing its own financing commitment. Cash flows generated by the business during the investment period are then used to reduce or eliminate the outstanding loan. Example 7.4 provides a simple illustration of this process.

Example 7.4

Ippo Ltd is a private-equity firm that has recently purchased Andante Ltd for £80 million. The business requires an immediate injection of £60 million to meet its needs and Ippo Ltd has insisted that this be raised by a 10 per cent bank loan. Ippo Ltd intends to float Andante Ltd in four years' time to exit from the investment and then expects to receive £160 million on the sale of its shares. During the next four years, the cash flows generated by Andante Ltd (after interest has been paid) will be used to eliminate the outstanding loan.

The net cash flows (before interest) of the business, over the four years leading up to the flotation, are predicted to be as follows:

Year 1	Year 2	Year 3	Year 4
£m	£m	£m	£m
20.0	20.0	20.1	15.0

Ippo Ltd has a cost of capital of 18 per cent and uses the IRR method to evaluate investment projects.

The following calculations reveal that the loan can be entirely repaid over the next four years.

	Year 1	Year 2	Year 3	Year 4
	£m	£m	£m	£m
Net cash flows	20.0	20.0	20.1	15.0
Loan interest (10%)	(6.0)	(4.6)	(3.1)	(1.4)
Cash available to repay loan	14.0	15.4	17.0	13.6
Loan at start of year	60.0	46.0	30.6	13.6
Cash available to repay loan	14.0	15.4	17.0	13.6
Loan at end of year	46.0	30.6	13.6	–

There are no cash flows remaining after the loan is repaid and so Ippo Ltd will receive nothing until the end of the fourth year, when the shares are sold.

The IRR of the investment will be the discount rate which, when applied to the net cash inflows, will provide an NPV of zero. Thus,

$$(£160m \times \text{discount factor}) - £80m = 0$$
$$\text{Discount factor} = 0.50$$

A discount rate of approximately 19 per cent will give a discount factor of 0.5 in four years' time.

Thus, the IRR of the investment is approximately 19 per cent. This is higher than the cost of capital of Ippo Ltd and so the investment will increase the wealth of its shareholders.

Taking on a large loan imposes a tight financial discipline on the managers of a business as there must always be enough cash to make interest payments and capital repayments. This should encourage them to be aggressive in chasing sales and to bear down on costs. Taking on a loan can also boost the returns to the private-equity firm.

Activity 7.15

Assume that:

(a) Ippo Ltd (see Example 7.4) provides additional ordinary share capital at the beginning of the investment period of £60 million, thereby eliminating the need for Andante Ltd to take on a bank loan

(b) any cash flows generated by Andante Ltd would be received by Ippo Ltd in the form of annual dividends.

What would be the IRR of the total investment in Andante Ltd for Ippo Ltd?

The IRR can be calculated using the trial and error method as follows. At discount rates of 10 per cent and 16 per cent, the NPV of the investment proposal is:

		Trial 1		Trial 2	
Year	Cash flows	Discount rate	Present value	Discount rate	Present value
	£m	10%	£m	16%	£m
0	(140.0)	1.00	(140.0)	1.00	(140.0)
1	20.0	0.91	18.2	0.86	17.2
2	20.0	0.83	16.6	0.74	14.8
3	20.1	0.75	15.1	0.64	12.9
4	175.0	0.68	119.0	0.55	96.3
			NPV 28.9		**NPV** 1.2

The calculations reveal that, at a discount rate of 16 per cent, the NPV is close to zero. Thus, the IRR of the investment is approximately 16 per cent, which is lower than the cost of capital. This means that the investment will reduce the wealth of the shareholders of Ippo Ltd.

The calculations in Example 7.4 and Activity 7.15 show that, by Andante Ltd taking on a bank loan, returns to the private-equity firm are increased. This 'gearing effect', as it is called, is discussed in more detail in the next chapter.

Self-assessment question 7.1

Ceres plc is a large conglomerate which, following a recent strategic review, has decided to sell its agricultural foodstuffs division. The managers of this operating division believe that it could be run as a separate business and are considering a management buyout. The division has made an operating profit of £10 million for the year to 31 May Year 6 and the board of Ceres plc has indicated that it would be prepared to sell the division to the managers for a price based on a multiple of 12 times the operating profit for the most recent year.

The managers of the operating division have £5 million of the finance necessary to acquire the division and have approached Vesta Ltd, a private-equity firm, to see whether it would be prepared to assist in financing the proposed management buyout. The divisional managers have produced the following forecast of operating profits for the next four years:

Year to 31 May	Year 7	Year 8	Year 9	Year 10
	£m	£m	£m	£m
Operating profit	10.0	11.0	10.5	13.5

To achieve the profit forecasts shown above, the division will have to invest a further £1 million in working capital during the year to 31 May Year 8. The division has premises costing £40 million and plant and machinery costing £20 million. In calculating operating profit for the division, these assets are depreciated, using the straight-line method, at the rate of 2.5 per cent on cost and 15 per cent on cost, respectively.

Vesta Ltd has been asked to invest £45 million in return for 90 per cent of the ordinary shares in a new business specifically created to run the operating division. The divisional managers would receive the remaining 10 per cent of the ordinary shares in return for their £5 million investment. The managers believe that a bank would be prepared to provide a 10 per cent loan for any additional finance necessary to acquire the division. (The properties of the division are currently valued at £80 million and so there would be adequate security for a loan up to this amount.) All net cash flows generated by the new business during each financial year will be applied to reducing the balance of the loan and no dividends will be paid to shareholders until the loan is repaid. (There are no other cash flows apart from those mentioned above.) The loan agreement will be for a period of eight years. However, if the business is sold during this period, the loan must be repaid in full by the shareholders.

Vesta Ltd intends to realise its investment after four years when the non-current assets and working capital (excluding the bank loan) of the business are expected to be sold to a rival at a price based on a multiple of 12 times the most recent annual operating profit. Out of these proceeds, the bank loan will have to be repaid by existing shareholders before they receive their returns. Vesta Ltd has a cost of capital of 25 per cent and employs the internal rate of return method to evaluate investment proposals.

Ignore taxation.

Workings should be in £ millions and should be made to one decimal place.

Required:

(a) Calculate:
  (i)   The amount of the loan outstanding at 31 May Year 10 immediately prior to the sale of the business.
  (ii) The approximate internal rate of return for Vesta Ltd of the investment proposal described above.

(b) State, with reasons, whether or not Vesta Ltd should invest in this proposal.

The answer to this question can be found at the back of the book on pp. 566.

Cause for concern?

In recent years, private-equity firms have extended their reach by acquiring listed businesses. Following acquisition, the business is usually de-listed and then restructured, perhaps with the intention of re-flotation at some future date. This has placed private-equity firms and their business methods in the spotlight. Critics have raised concerns over:

■ the job losses that usually accompany restructuring
■ the very high levels of gearing employed, which greatly increase financial risk

- the lack of transparency in business dealings
- the lack of accountability to employees and the communities in which they operate
- the adverse effect on the Stock Exchange's role, resulting from the acquisition and de-listing of large businesses
- the tax benefits received by private-equity firms.

Although some changes to levels of transparency and tax benefits have been made, the critics of private-equity firms remain largely unappeased.

It should be noted that the methods employed by private-equity firms have produced echoes elsewhere. Some businesses, particularly those vulnerable to a takeover from a private-equity firm, have adopted methods such as job losses and high gearing, to remain viable and independent.

BUSINESS ANGELS

Business angels are often wealthy individuals who have been successful in business. Most are entrepreneurs who have sold their businesses while others tend to be former senior executives of a large business, or business professionals such as accountants, lawyers and management consultants. They are usually willing to invest between £10,000 and £250,000 to acquire a minority equity stake in a business. Loan capital may also be provided as part of a financing package. Typically, business angels make one or two investments over a three-year period and will usually be prepared to invest for a period of between three and five years.

Business angels invest with the primary motive of making a financial return, but non-financial motives also play an important part. They often enjoy being involved in growing a business and may also harbour altruistic motives such as wishing to help budding entrepreneurs or to make a contribution to the local economy. (See reference 11 at the end of the chapter.)

Business angels play an important financing role because the size and/or nature of their investments rarely appeal to private-equity firms. They tend to invest in early-stage businesses, although they may also invest in more mature businesses. They are generally acknowledged to be a significant source of finance for small businesses; however, the exact scale of their investment is difficult to determine. This is because they are under no obligation to disclose how much they have invested. It has been estimated, however, that in the UK, business angels invest eight times as much in start-up businesses as do private-equity firms. (See reference 12 at the end of the chapter.)

Business angels can be an attractive source of finance because they are not encumbered by bureaucracy. They can make investment decisions quickly, particularly if they are familiar with the industry in which the business operates. They may also accept lower financial returns than are demanded by private-equity firms in order to have the opportunity to become involved in an interesting project.

Business angels often seek an active role within the business, which is usually welcomed by business owners as their skills, knowledge and experience can frequently be put to good use. The forms of involvement will typically include providing advice and moral support, providing business contacts and helping to make strategic decisions. However, the active involvement of a business angel may not simply be for the satisfaction gained from helping a business to grow.

Business angels tend to invest in businesses within their own locality. This may be because active involvement in the business may be feasible only if the business is within easy reach. Unsurprisingly, business angels also tend to invest in industries with which they have personal experience. One study revealed that around a third of business angels invest solely in industries with which they have had work experience. Around two-thirds of business angels, however, have made at least one investment within an industry with which they were unfamiliar. (See reference 11 at the end of the chapter.)

Angel syndicates

Where a large investment is required, a syndicate of business angels may be formed to raise the money. The syndicate may then take a majority equity stake in the business. Several advantages may spring from syndication.

Studies have shown that business angels are generally enthusiastic about syndication. There are, however, potential disadvantages, such as the greater complexity of deal structures, the potential for disputes within the syndicate and the need to comply with group decisions.

The investment process

It was mentioned earlier that business angels can make decisions quickly. This does not mean, however, that finance is made available to a business overnight. A period of 4–6 months may be needed between the initial introduction and the provision of the finance. There is usually a thorough review of the business plan and financial forecasts. This may be followed by a series of meetings to help the business angel gain a deeper insight into the business and to deal with any concerns and issues that may arise.

Assuming these meetings go well and the business angel wishes to proceed, negotiations over the terms of the investment will then be undertaken. This can be the trickiest part of the process as agreement has to be reached over key issues such as the value of the business, the equity stake to be offered to the business angel and the price to be paid. Failure to reach agreement with the owners over a suitable price, and the post-investment role to be played by a business angel, are the two most common 'deal killers'. One study revealed that business angels may make four offers for every offer that is finally accepted. (See reference 13 at the end of the chapter.)

If agreement can be reached between the parties, **due diligence** can then be carried out. This will involve an investigation of all material information relating to the financial, technical and legal aspects of the business. Even at this early stage, the business angel should be considering the likely exit route from the investment. The available routes are broadly the same as those identified earlier for private-equity firms.

Angel networks

Business angels offer an informal source of share finance and it is not always easy for owners of small businesses to identify a suitable angel. However, business angel networks have developed to help owners of small businesses find their 'perfect partner'. These networks will offer various services, including:

- publishing investor bulletins and organising meetings to promote the investment opportunities available
- registering the investment interests of business angels and matching them with emerging opportunities
- screening investment proposals and advising owners of small businesses on how to present their proposal to interested angels.

The British Business Angels Association (BBAA) is the trade association for the business angel networks. In addition to being a major source of information about the business angel industry, it can help direct small businesses to their local network.

The UK government has increased tax reliefs for business angels in the hope of encouraging greater investment from this source. **Real World 7.12**, however, which is written by a leading business angel researcher, argues that this is not what is needed.

Real World 7.12

Tempting angels

Tax is now the exclusive way in which government seeks to promote angel investing in the UK. Under the Seed Enterprise Investment Scheme (SEIS), which came into effect on April 6 2012, investors are given 50 per cent income tax relief on investments of up to £100,000 in young businesses, plus a one year capital gains tax holiday. At the same time, the limit for investments through the Enterprise Investment Scheme (EIS), upon which SEIS is based, was doubled and a wider range of companies became eligible. But are tax incentives for angel investors effective?

Proponents argue that it increases the amount of money that angels have available to invest, encourages new people to become business angels, and enables companies to attract investment to create new jobs. But critics say that tax incentives rarely, if ever, entice an investor to make an investment that they would otherwise not have made. There are also reasons to believe tax incentives are not enough to maintain a thriving business angel community.

→

First, the role of business angels is not simply to provide risk capital to businesses deemed too small or unattractive to attract venture capital or bank funding. Equally important is the hands-on role that angels play in their investee companies, by offering expertise to the entrepreneurs they back. Tax incentives arguably attract 'dumb' investors who cannot add any value. Second, angel investing has been described as 'a giant game of hide-and-seek with everyone blindfolded'. Potential investors need help to find entrepreneurs seeking finance and vice versa. Tax incentives do nothing to help with this. Third, tax incentives do not enhance the quality of the opportunities that angels come across. Indeed, the most frequent complaint of angels is that the businesses they see are not investment ready. Fourth, tax incentives put the emphasis on making the investment rather than enhancing returns. A tax incentive is ineffective if there is no 'harvest event'. Many business angels are stuck in investments that are unlikely to produce an exit but which need more money. Greater consideration of the exit at the time of the investment could have avoided some of these problems.

We used to have an effective infrastructure of business angel networks – mostly funded by the public sector, latterly regional development agencies – which addressed these issues. They enabled angels and entrepreneurs seeking finance to connect with one another. Several ran investment-ready courses for entrepreneurs. Some ran training programmes for angels. But, having lost their funding, most have now closed – and a huge amount of learning has been lost.

Some commercially orientated networks continue to operate, performing an important role. However, to be viable, they typically focus on larger deals of more than £500,000, and their geographical coverage is patchy. Angel networks supported by public sector funding focused on businesses seeking smaller amounts.

I believe the coalition government needs to move beyond its exclusive supply-side approach. Specifically, it should provide funding to recreate a network of regional business angel networks across the country. Research has shown that angel networks were effective in enabling investments to occur, their cost per job created was lower than other small business support measures, and they promoted an equity investment culture.

FT *Source*: C. Mason, 'Does tax relief tempt angels?' www.ft.com, 20 April 2012.

GOVERNMENT ASSISTANCE

One of the most effective ways in which the UK government assists small businesses is through the Enterprise Finance Guarantee Scheme (formerly the Small Firms Loan Guarantee Scheme). This aims to help small businesses that have viable business plans but lack the security to enable them to borrow. The scheme guarantees:

- 75 per cent of the amount borrowed, for which the borrower pays a premium of 2 per cent on the outstanding borrowing
- loans ranging from £1,000 to £1 million for a maximum period of 10 years.

The scheme is available for businesses that have annual sales revenue of up to £41 million.

More recently, in 2013, the UK government set up the British Business Bank. Its aim is to support economic growth by bringing together public and private funds so as to create a more effective and efficient finance market for small and medium size businesses. As well as taking new initiatives, the bank will also take over existing commitments of the UK government in the area of financing smaller businesses. The finance provided can be in the form of loans or equity.

In addition to other forms of financial assistance, such as government grants and tax incentives for investors to buy shares in small businesses, the government helps by providing information concerning the sources of finance available.

THE ALTERNATIVE INVESTMENT MARKET (AIM)

There are now a number of stock markets throughout the world that specialise in the shares of smaller businesses. These include the Alternative Investment Market (AIM), which is the largest and most successful. AIM is a second-tier market of the London Stock Exchange. It was created in 1995 and since then has achieved extraordinary growth. It includes a significant proportion of non-UK businesses, reflecting the international ambitions of the market. AIM offers smaller businesses a stepping stone to the main market – though not all AIM-listed businesses wish to make this step – and offers private-equity firms a useful exit route from their investments.

The regulatory framework

AIM provides businesses with many of the benefits of a listing on the main market without the cost or burdensome regulatory environment. Obtaining an AIM listing and raising funds costs the typical business about £500,000. Differences in the regulatory environment between the main market and AIM can be summarised as follows:

Main market	AIM
Minimum 25 per cent of shares in public hands	No minimum of shares to be in public hands
Normally, 3-year trading record required	No trading record requirement
Prior shareholder approval required for substantial acquisitions and disposals	No prior shareholder approval required for such transactions
Pre-vetting of admission documents by the UK Listing Authority	Admission documents not pre-vetted by the Stock Exchange or the UK Listing Authority
Minimum market capitalisation	No minimum market capitalisation

Source: Adapted from information on London Stock Exchange website, www.londonstockexchange.com.

A key element of the regulatory regime is that each business must appoint a Nominated Adviser (NOMAD) before joining AIM and then retain its services throughout the period of a listing. The NOMAD's role, which is undertaken by corporate financiers and investment bankers, involves the dual responsibilities of corporate adviser and regulator. It includes assessing the suitability of a business for joining AIM, bringing a business to market and monitoring its share trading. A NOMAD must also help AIM-listed businesses to strike the right balance between fostering an entrepreneurial culture and public accountability. It will therefore advise on matters such as corporate governance structures and the timing of public announcements.

To retain its role and status in the market, a NOMAD must jealously guard its reputation. It will, therefore, not act for businesses that it considers unsuitable for any reason. If a NOMAD ceases to act for a business, its shares are suspended until a new NOMAD is appointed. The continuing support of a NOMAD is therefore important, which helps it to wield influence over the business. This should help create a smooth functioning market and pre-empt the need for a large number of prescriptive rules.

This lighter regulatory touch has led some to accuse it of being little more than a casino. This criticism often emanates from competitor markets and reflects their discomfort over the growth of AIM. To date, the flexibility and cost-effectiveness of AIM have proved difficult to match.

AIM-listed businesses

AIM-listed businesses vary considerably in size, with equity market values ranging from less than £2 million to more than £1 billion. Most businesses, however, have an equity market value of less than £25 million. In recent years, the London Stock Exchange has tried to encourage larger AIM-listed businesses to transfer to the main market. However, as they can raise money easily and cheaply without enduring a heavy regulatory burden, there is little incentive to do so. AIM-listed businesses include Majestic Wine plc and Millwall Football Club.

Real World 7.13 shows the distribution of AIM-listed businesses by equity market value.

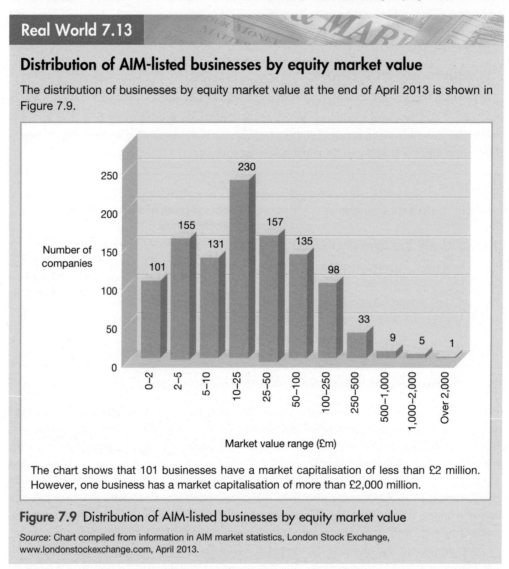

Real World 7.13

Distribution of AIM-listed businesses by equity market value

The distribution of businesses by equity market value at the end of April 2013 is shown in Figure 7.9.

The chart shows that 101 businesses have a market capitalisation of less than £2 million. However, one business has a market capitalisation of more than £2,000 million.

Figure 7.9 Distribution of AIM-listed businesses by equity market value

Source: Chart compiled from information in AIM market statistics, London Stock Exchange, www.londonstockexchange.com, April 2013.

Research shows that shares of smaller businesses are more actively traded on AIM than those of businesses of similar size on the main market (see reference 14 at the end of the chapter).

Investing in AIM-listed businesses

AIM has proved to be successful in attracting both private and institutional investors. Failure rates among AIM-listed businesses have been fairly low and share performance has been good compared with the main market. However, it has been pointed out that AIM-listed businesses are 'usually smaller, and younger, companies with less diversified businesses that are often heavily dependent on relatively small sectors of the economy. They are, therefore, more susceptible to economic shocks than larger, more established companies' (see reference 15 at the end of the chapter). Thus, there is always a concern that, during difficult economic times, share prices will be badly affected as investors make a 'flight to quality'. Share price weakness during periods of uncertainty may be increased by a lack of media coverage or analysts' reports to help investors understand what is going on.

Although market liquidity has improved in recent years, it can still be a problem. This is particularly true for businesses that are too small to attract institutional investors, or where the shares are tightly held by directors, or where investors lack confidence in the business. If, for whatever reason, shares are infrequently traded, market makers may significantly adjust buying and selling prices, leading to sharp price changes. This can also mean that relatively small share trades will lead to a huge change in share price.

A broad range of industry sectors are represented in the market. However, financial businesses and resource-based businesses, such as mining, oil and gas businesses, are easily the most important. The market might be more attractive to investors if a more balanced portfolio of businesses could be achieved.

AMAZON.COM: A CASE HISTORY

The internet retailer Amazon.com has grown considerably during its short life. In **Real World 7.14** we can see how growth was financed in the early years. To begin with, the business relied heavily on the founder and his family for finance. However, as the business grew, other ways of raising finance, as described in the chapter, have become more important. The table charts the progress of the business in its early years.

Real World 7.14

Financing Amazon.com – the early years

Financing of Amazon.com (1994–99)

Dates	Share price	Source of funds
1994: July to November	$0.0010	Founder: Jeff Bezos starts Amazon.com with $10,000; borrows $44,000
1995: February to July	$0.1717	Family: founder's father and mother invest $245,000
1995: August to December	$0.1287–0.3333	Business angels: 2 angels invest $54,408
1995/96: December to May	$0.3333	Business angels: 20 angels invest $937,000
1996: May	$0.3333	Family: founder's siblings invest $20,000
1996: June	$2.3417	Private equity firms: 2 private equity funds invest $8m
1997: May	$18.00	Initial public offering: 3m shares issued raising $49.1m
1997/98: December to May	$52.11	Bond issue: $326m bond issue

Source: Reproduced from M. Van Osnabrugge and R.J. Robinson, *Angel Investing: Matching start-up funds with start-up companies – a guide for entrepreneurs and individual investors*. Copyright © 2000 Jossey-Bass Inc. Reprinted with permission of John Wiley & Sons, Inc.

SUMMARY

The main points of this chapter may be summarised as follows:

The Stock Exchange

- Is an important primary and secondary market in capital for large businesses.
- Obtaining a Stock Exchange listing can help a business to raise finance and help to raise its profile, but obtaining a listing can be costly and the regulatory burden can be onerous.
- A stock market is efficient if information is processed by investors quickly and accurately so that prices faithfully reflect all relevant information.
- Three forms of efficiency have been suggested: the weak form, the semi-strong form and the strong form.
- If a stock market is efficient, managers of a listed business should learn six important lessons:
  - Timing doesn't matter.
  - Don't search for undervalued businesses.
  - Take note of market reaction.
  - You can't fool the market.
  - The market decides the level of risk.
  - Champion the interests of shareholders.
- Stock market anomalies and behavioural research provide a challenge to the notion of market efficiency.

Share issues

- Share issues that involve the payment of cash by investors include rights issues, public issues, offers for sale and placings.
- A rights issue is made to existing shareholders. The law requires that shares to be issued for cash must first be offered to existing shareholders.
- A public issue involves a direct issue to the public and an offer for sale involves an indirect issue to the public.
- A placing is an issue of shares to selected investors.
- A bonus (scrip) issue involves issuing shares to existing shareholders. No payment is required as the issue is achieved by transferring a sum from reserves to the share capital.
- A tender issue allows investors to determine the price at which the shares are issued.

Smaller businesses

- Do not have access to the Stock Exchange main market and so must look elsewhere for funds.
- Private equity (venture capital) is long-term capital for small or medium-sized businesses that are not listed on the Stock Exchange. These businesses often have higher levels of risk but provide the private-equity firm with the prospect of higher levels of return.

- Private-equity firms are interested in businesses with good growth prospects and offer finance for start-ups, business expansions and buyouts.

- The investment period is usually five years or more and the private-equity firms may exit by a trade sale, flotation, buyback or sale to another financial institution.

- Business angels are often wealthy individuals who are willing to invest in businesses at an early stage of development.

- They can usually make quick decisions and will often become actively involved in the business.

- Various business angel networks exist to help small business owners find an angel.

- The government assists small businesses through guaranteeing loans, creating the British Business Bank and by providing grants and tax incentives.

- The Alternative Investment Market (AIM) specialises in the shares of smaller businesses.

- AIM is a second-tier market of the Stock Exchange, which offers many of the benefits of a main market listing without the same cost or regulatory burden.

- AIM has proved popular with investors but could benefit from greater market liquidity and a more balanced portfolio of listed businesses.

KEY TERMS

Stock Exchange p. 270
FTSE (Footsie) indices p. 271
Market capitalisation p. 272
Efficient stock market p. 275
Behavioural finance p. 283
Rights issue p. 285
Bonus issue (scrip issue) p. 288
Offer for sale p. 289
Public issue p. 290

Tender issue p. 290
Placing p. 291
Private equity p. 293
Venture capital p. 293
Business angels p. 301
Due diligence p. 303
Alternative Investment Market (AIM)
    p. 305

For definitions of these terms see the Glossary, pp. 605–613.

REFERENCES

1 London Stock Exchange, *Practical Guide to Listing*, www.londonstockexchange.com, p. 24.

2 Marsh, P. (1998) 'Myths surrounding short-termism', *Mastering Finance*, Financial Times Pitman Publishing, pp. 168–174.

3 Haldane, A. and Davies, R. (2011) The short long Speech given at 29th Société Universitaire Européene de Recherches Financières Colloquium: New Paradigms in Money and Finance? Brussels, May, p. 1.

4 Wighton, D. (2011) 'We must end short termism. And it won't wait', *The Times*, 17 May, www.thetimes.co.uk.

5 London Stock Exchange, Market Statistics, December 2012, Table 3.

6 Armitage, S. (2000) 'The direct costs of UK rights issues and open offers', *European Financial Management*, March.

7 Institute of Chartered Accountants in England and Wales (2000) *SME Finance and Regulation*.

8 *Report of the Committee of Inquiry on Small Firms* (Bolton Committee), Cmnd 4811, HMSO, 1971.

9 British Private Equity and Venture Capital Association, *A Guide to Private Equity*, www.bvca.co.uk.

10 Norton, E. (1995) 'Venture capital as an alternative means to allocate capital: an agency-theoretic view', *Entrepreneurship*, Winter, 19–30.

11 Macht, S. (2007) 'The post-investment period of business angels: Impact and involvement', www.eban.org, July, pp. 14–15.

12 Mason, C.M. and Harrison, R.T. (2000) 'The size of the informal venture capital market in the United Kingdom', *Small Business Economics*, 15, 137–48.

13 Mason, C.M. and Harrison, R.T. (2002) quoted in Carriere, S. (2006) 'Best practice in angel groups and angel syndication', www.eban.org, January, p. 7.

14 'AIM makes its mark on the investment map', *Financial Times*, 9 February 2004.

15 Moore, J. (2008) 'The acid test – how the market has performed', *AIM: The growth market of the world*, London Stock Exchange, p. 93.

FURTHER READING

If you wish to explore the topics discussed in this chapter in more depth, try the following books:

Arnold, G. (2013) *Corporate Financial Management*, 5th edn, Pearson, Chapters 9 and 10.

Metrick, A. and Yasuda, A. (2010) *Venture Capital and the Finance of Innovation*, 2nd edn, John Wiley & Sons.

Pike, R. and Neale, B. (2012) *Corporate Finance and Investment*, 7th edn, Pearson, Chapters 2 and 16.

Sun, L. (2012) *Capital Market Efficiency and Stock Price Anomalies: Theories and evidence*, Lap Lambert Academic Publishing.

REVIEW QUESTIONS

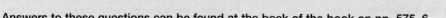

Answers to these questions can be found at the back of the book on pp. 575–6.

7.1 UK private-equity firms have been criticised for the low level of funding invested in business start-ups by comparison with the levels invested by their US counterparts. Can you think of possible reasons why such a difference may exist?

7.2 Why might a listed business revert to being an unlisted business?

7.3 Distinguish between an offer for sale and a public issue of shares.

7.4 What kind of attributes should the owners and managers of a business possess to attract private equity finance?

EXERCISES

Exercises 7.5 to 7.7 are more advanced than 7.1 to 7.4. Those with coloured numbers have answers at the back of the book, starting on p. 592.

If you wish to try more exercises, visit the students' side of this book's companion website.

7.1 Comment on each of the following statements.
  (a) A stock market that is efficient in the strong form is one in which investors cannot make any gains from their investment.
  (b) Private-equity firms are not interested in investing in business start-ups.
  (c) Short-term behaviour by investors is difficult to reconcile with the notion of stock market efficiency.

7.2 Consider each of the following.

1 An investor expects to make abnormal gains on her stock market investments by analysing published annual reports, relevant newspaper articles, industry reports and published share prices.

2 Dorsal plc, a business listed on the London Stock Exchange, received a confidential letter from a rival business on 30 July 2013 offering to buy all its shares at a premium of 20 per cent on their current market value. At a private meeting, convened on the same day, the directors of Dorsal plc agreed to accept the offer and made a public announcement of this decision on 3 August 2013.

3 Juniper plc is an airport operator that is listed on the London Stock Exchange. Recently, the board of directors agreed to change the company's depreciation policy concerning airport runways. In future, these assets will be written off over 100 years rather than 50 years. This change, which will reduce the annual depreciation charge over the next 50 years, is solely designed to increase reported profits over that period and thereby create a better impression to investors of business performance.

Required:

(a) What is the maximum level of market efficiency that the investor is assuming in (1) above? Briefly explain your answer.

(b) What would be the share price reaction to the announcement in (2) above under the strong form of market efficiency and why?

(c) What is the maximum level of market efficiency that the board of directors is assuming in (3) above that is consistent with such behaviour? Briefly explain your answer.

7.3 Provide *two* reasons why:

(a) Tax incentives may have only limited value in stimulating greater investment by business angels.

(b) Business angels can be an attractive source of finance to entrepreneurs.

(c) Business angels may find it difficult being part of an angel syndicate in order to finance a business.

7.4 Pizza Shack plc operates a chain of pizza restaurants. The business started operations five years ago and has enjoyed uninterrupted and rapid growth. The directors of the business, however, believe that future growth can be achieved only if the business seeks a listing on the London Stock Exchange. If the directors go ahead with a listing, the financial advisers to the business have suggested that an issue of ordinary shares by tender at a minimum price of £2.20 would be an appropriate method of floating the business. The advisers have suggested that 3 million ordinary shares should be issued in the first instance, although the directors of the business are keen to raise the maximum amount of funds possible.

Initial research carried out by the financial advisers suggests that the following demand for shares at different market prices is likely:

Share price £	Number of shares tendered at each share price 000s
3.60	850
3.20	1,190
2.80	1,380
2.40	1,490
2.00	1,540
1.60	1,560
	8,010

Required:

(a) Discuss the advantages and disadvantages of making a tender issue of shares.

(b) Calculate the expected proceeds from the tender issue, assuming the business

    (i)   issues 3 million shares

    (ii) wishes to raise the maximum amount of funds possible.

7.5 The board of directors of Wicklow plc is considering an expansion of production capacity following an increase in sales over the past two years. The most recent financial statements for the business are set out below.

Statement of financial position as at 30 November Year 5

	£m
ASSETS	
Non-current assets	
Property, plant and equipment	
Land and buildings	22.0
Machinery and equipment	11.0
Fixtures and fittings	8.0
	41.0
Current assets	
Inventories	14.0
Trade receivables	22.0
Cash at bank	2.0
	38.0
Total assets	79.0
EQUITY AND LIABILITIES	
Equity	
£0.50 ordinary shares	20.0
Retained earnings	19.0
	39.0
Non-current liabilities	
Borrowings – 12% loan	20.0
Current liabilities	
Trade payables	20.0
Total equity and liabilities	79.0

Income statement for the year ended 30 November Year 5

	£m
Sales revenue	95.0
Operating profit	8.0
Interest charges	(2.4)
Profit before taxation	5.6
Tax (30%)	(1.7)
Profit for the year	3.9

A dividend of £1.2 million was proposed and paid during the year.

    The business plans to invest a further £15 million in machinery and equipment and is considering two possible financing options. The first option is to make a one-for-four rights issue. The current market price per share is £2.00 and the rights shares would be issued at a discount of 25 per cent on this market price. The second option is to take a further loan that will have an initial annual rate of interest of 10 per cent. This is a variable rate and while interest rates have been stable for a number of years, there has been speculation recently that interest rates will begin to rise in the near future.

The outcome of the expansion is not certain. The management team involved in developing and implementing the expansion plans has provided three possible outcomes concerning profit before interest and tax for the following year:

	Change in profits before interest and tax from previous year
Optimistic	+30%
Most likely	+10%
Pessimistic	−20%

The dividend per share for the forthcoming year is expected to remain the same as for the year ended 30 November Year 5.

Wicklow plc has a lower level of gearing than most of its competitors. This has been in accordance with the wishes of the Wicklow family, which has a large shareholding in the business. The share price of the business has shown rapid growth in recent years and the P/E ratio for the business is 20.4 times, which is much higher than the industry average of 14.3 times.

Costs of raising finance should be ignored.

Required:

(a) Prepare calculations that show the effect of each of the possible outcomes of the expansion programme on:

(i) earnings per share

(ii) the gearing ratio (based on year-end figures), and

(iii) the interest cover ratio of Wicklow plc, under both of the financing options.

(b) Assess each of the financing options available to Wicklow plc from the point of view of an existing shareholder and compare the possible future outcomes with the existing situation.

7.6 Devonian plc has the following long-term capital structure as at 30 November Year 4:

	£m
Ordinary shares 25p fully paid	50.0
General reserve	22.5
Retained earnings	25.5
	98.0

The business has no long-term loans.

In the year to 30 November Year 4, the operating profit (profit before interest and taxation) was £40 million and it is expected that this will increase by 25 per cent during the forthcoming year. The business is listed on the London Stock Exchange and the share price as at 30 November Year 4 was £2.10.

The business wishes to raise £72 million in order to re-equip one of its factories and is considering two possible financing options. The first option is to make a one-for-five rights issue at a discount price of £1.80 per share. The second option is to take out a long-term loan at an interest rate of 10 per cent a year. If the first option is taken, it is expected that the price/earnings (P/E) ratio will remain the same for the forthcoming year. If the second option is taken, it is estimated that the P/E ratio will fall by 10 per cent by the end of the forthcoming year.

Assume a tax rate of 30 per cent.

Required:

(a) Assuming a rights issue of shares is made, calculate:
  (i)   the theoretical ex-rights price of an ordinary share in Devonian plc
  (ii) the value of the rights for each original ordinary share.
(b) Calculate the price of an ordinary share in Devonian plc in one year's time assuming:
  (i)   a rights issue is made
  (ii) a loan issue is made.
     Comment on your findings.
(c) Explain why rights issues are usually made at a discount.
(d) From the business's viewpoint, how critical is the pricing of a rights issue likely to be?

7.7   Carpets Direct plc wishes to increase the number of its retail outlets. The board of direc-tors has decided to finance this expansion programme by raising the funds from existing shareholders through a one-for-four rights issue. The most recent income statement of the business is as follows:

Income statement for the year ended 30 April

	£m
Sales revenue	164.5
Operating profit	12.6
Interest	(6.2)
Profit before taxation	6.4
Tax	(1.9)
Profit for the year	4.5

An ordinary dividend of £2.0 million was proposed and paid during the year.

The share capital of the business consists of 120 million ordinary shares with a nominal value of £0.50 per share. The shares of the business are currently being traded on the Stock Exchange at a price/earnings ratio of 22 times and the board of directors has decided to issue the new shares at a discount of 20 per cent on the current market value.

Required:

(a) Calculate the theoretical ex-rights price of an ordinary share in Carpets Direct plc.
(b) Calculate the price at which the rights in Carpets Direct plc are likely to be traded.
(c) Identify and evaluate, at the time of the rights issue, each of the options arising from the rights issue to an investor who holds 4,000 ordinary shares before the rights announcement.

Chapter 8

THE COST OF CAPITAL AND THE CAPITAL STRUCTURE DECISION

INTRODUCTION

We saw in Chapter 4 that the cost of capital has a vital role to play when using the NPV and IRR methods of investment appraisal. In this chapter, we examine how the cost of capital may be calculated. We first consider how to calculate the cost of each element of long-term capital and then how these costs can be combined so as to derive an overall cost of capital.

We shall also take a look at the factors to be taken into account when making capital structure decisions: in particular, the impact of gearing on the risks and returns to ordinary shareholders. We touched upon this area in Chapter 3 but now consider it in more detail. We end the chapter by considering whether there is an optimal capital structure for a business. This is an important topic, which has been the subject of much debate.

Learning outcomes

When you have completed this chapter, you should be able to:

■ Calculate the weighted average cost of capital for a business and assess its usefulness when making investment decisions.

■ Calculate the degree of financial gearing for a business and explain its significance.

■ Evaluate different capital structure options available to a business.

■ Discuss the key points in the debate over whether a business has an optimal capital structure.

COST OF CAPITAL

We saw in Chapter 4 that the *cost of capital* is used as the discount rate in NPV calculations and as the 'hurdle rate' when assessing IRR calculations. As investment projects are usually financed from long-term capital, the discount rate (or hurdle rate) applied to new projects should reflect the required returns from investors in long-term capital. From the business's viewpoint, these returns represent its cost of capital. It represents an *opportunity* cost as it will reflect the returns that investors require from investments of similar risk.

The cost of capital must be calculated with care as failure to do so could be damaging.

Activity 8.1

What adverse consequences might result from incorrectly calculating the cost of capital?

Where the NPV approach is used, an incorrect discount rate will be applied to the net cash flows of investment projects. If the cost of capital is understated, there is a risk that projects that reduce shareholder wealth will be accepted. This can occur when applying the understated cost of capital produces a positive NPV, whereas applying the correct cost of capital produces a negative NPV. If the cost of capital figure is overstated, projects that increase shareholder wealth may be rejected. This can occur when applying the overstated cost of capital produces a negative NPV, whereas applying the correct cost of capital produces a positive NPV.

Similar problems can occur with the IRR method where the cost of capital is used as the hurdle rate.

In Chapter 6, we saw that the main forms of *external* long-term capital for businesses include:

- ordinary shares
- preference shares
- loan capital.

In addition, an important form of *internal* long-term capital is:

- retained earnings.

In the sections that follow, we shall see how the cost of each element of long-term capital may be deduced. We shall also see that there is a strong link between the cost of each element and its value: both are determined by the level of return. As a result, our discussions concerning the cost of capital will also embrace the issue of value. For reasons that should soon become clear, we first consider how each element of capital is valued and then go on to deduce its cost to the business.

Ordinary (equity) shares

There are two major approaches to determining the cost of ordinary shares to a business: the dividend-based approach and the risk/return-based approach. Each approach is discussed below.

Dividend-based approach

Investors hold assets (including ordinary shares) in the expectation of receiving future benefits. In broad terms, the value of an asset can be defined in terms of the stream of future benefits that arises from holding the asset. When considering ordinary shares, the value of an ordinary share will be the future dividends that investors receive by holding the share. To be more precise, the value of an ordinary share will be the present value of the expected future dividends from the particular share.

In mathematical terms, the value of an ordinary share (P_0) can be expressed as follows:

$$P_0 = \frac{D_1}{(1 + K_0)} + \frac{D_2}{(1 + K_0)^2} + \frac{D_3}{(1 + K_0)^3} + \cdots + \frac{D_n}{(1 + K_0)^n}$$

where P_0 = the current market value of the share

D = the expected future dividend in years 1 to n

n = the number of years over which the business expects to issue dividends

K_0 = the cost of ordinary shares to the business (that is, the required return for investors).

Activity 8.2

The valuation approach above takes into account the expected dividend stream over the whole life of the business. Is this relevant for an investor who holds a share for a particular period of time (say five years) and then sells the share?

The valuation approach described is still relevant. The market value of the share at the time of sale should reflect the present value of the (remaining) future dividends. Thus, when determining an appropriate selling price, the expected dividend stream beyond the point at which the share is held should be highly relevant to the investor.

The valuation model above can be used to determine the *cost* of ordinary shares to the business (K_0). Assuming the value of an ordinary share and the expected future dividends are known, the cost of an ordinary share will be the discount rate that, when applied to the stream of expected future dividends, will produce a present value that is equal to the current market value of the share. Thus, the required rate of return for ordinary share investors (that is, the cost of ordinary shares to the business) is similar to the internal rate of return (IRR) used to evaluate investment projects.

To deduce the required rate of return for investors, we can use the same trial and error approach as that used to deduce the internal rate of return for investment projects. In practice, however, this trial and error approach is rarely used, as simplifying assumptions are normally employed concerning the pattern of dividends, which make the calculations easier. These simplifying assumptions help us to avoid some of the problems associated with predicting the future dividend stream from an ordinary share.

One of two simplifying assumptions concerning the pattern of future dividends will often be employed. The first assumption is that dividends will remain constant over time. Where dividends are expected to remain constant for an infinite period, the fairly complicated equation to deduce the current market value of a share stated above can be reduced to:

$$P_0 = \frac{D_1}{K_0}$$

where D_1 = the annual dividend per share in year 1 (which, assuming a constant dividend, will also be the annual dividend in perpetuity).

This equation (which is the equation for capitalising a perpetual annuity) can be rearranged to provide an equation for deducing the *cost* of ordinary shares to the business. Hence:

$$K_0 = \frac{D_1}{P_0}$$

Activity 8.3

Kowloon Investments plc has ordinary shares in issue with a current market value of £2.20. The annual dividend per share in future years is expected to be 40p. What is the cost of the ordinary shares to the business?

The cost will be:

$$K_0 = \frac{D_1}{P_0} = \frac{£0.40}{£2.20} = 0.182 \text{ or } 18.2\%$$

The second simplifying assumption that may be employed is that dividends will grow at a constant rate over time. Where dividends are expected to have a constant growth rate, the equation to deduce the current market value of a share can be reduced to:

$$P_0 = \frac{D_1}{K_0 - g}$$

where g is the expected annual growth rate. (The model assumes K_0 is greater than g.)

This equation can also be rearranged to provide an equation for deducing the *cost* of ordinary share capital. Hence:

$$K_0 = \frac{D_1}{P_0} + g$$

This is sometimes referred to as *Gordon's growth model* after the person credited with developing it.

Determining the future growth rate in dividends (g) can be a problem. One approach is to use the average past rate of growth in dividends (adjusted, perhaps, for any new information concerning future prospects). There are, however, several other approaches and a business must select whichever is likely to give the most accurate results.

Activity 8.4

Avalon plc has ordinary shares in issue that have a current market price of £1.50. The dividend expected for next year is 20p per share and future dividends are expected to grow at a constant rate of 3 per cent a year.

What is the cost of the ordinary shares to the business?

The cost is:

$$K_0 = \frac{D_1}{P_0} + g = \frac{0.20}{1.50} + 0.03 = 0.163 \text{ or } 16.3\%$$

It should now be clear why we began by looking at how a share is valued before going on to deduce its cost. We have now seen how the value of an ordinary share to an investor and the cost of capital for the business are linked and how valuation models can help in deriving the required returns from investors. This relationship between value and the cost of capital also applies to preference shares and to loan capital, as we shall see in later sections.

Risk/return-based approach

An alternative approach to deducing the returns required by ordinary shareholders is to use the **capital asset pricing model (CAPM)**. This approach builds on the ideas that we discussed in Chapter 5.

We may recall that, when discussing the attitude of investors towards risk and the risk-adjusted discount rate, the following points were made:

- Investors who are risk-averse will seek additional returns to compensate for the risks associated with a particular investment. These additional returns are referred to as the *risk premium*.
- The higher the level of risk, the higher the risk premium that will be demanded.
- The risk premium is an amount required by investors that is over and above the returns from investing in risk-free investments.
- The total returns required from a particular investment will therefore be made up of a risk-free rate plus any risk premium.

The relationship between risk and return is depicted in Figure 8.1.

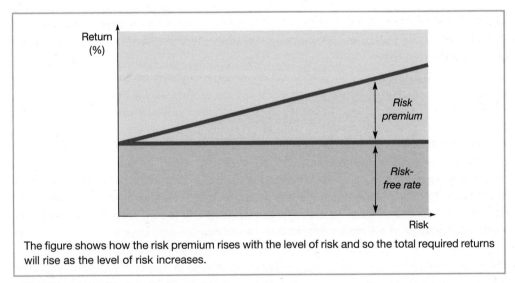

The figure shows how the risk premium rises with the level of risk and so the total required returns will rise as the level of risk increases.

Figure 8.1 The relationship between risk and return

Although the above ideas were discussed in respect of investment projects undertaken by a business, they are equally valid when considering investments in ordinary shares. CAPM (pronounced 'cap-M') is based on the above ideas and so the required rate of return to ordinary share investors (and, therefore, the cost of ordinary shares to the business) is viewed as being made up of a risk-free rate of return *plus* a risk premium. This means that to calculate the required return, we have to derive the risk-free rate of return and the risk premium associated with a particular share.

To derive the risk-free rate of return, the returns from government bonds are normally used as an approximation. Although not totally risk free, they offer the most secure return available. There is some debate in the literature as to whether short-term or long-term bonds should be used. The advantage of short-term bonds is that there is less uncertainty over the risk of default and interest rate changes.

To derive the risk premium for a particular share, CAPM adopts the following three-stage process:

1 Measure the risk premium for the stock market as a whole. This figure will be the difference between the returns from the stock market and the returns from risk-free investments.
2 Measure the returns from a particular share relative to the returns from the stock market as a whole.
3 Apply this relative measure of returns to the stock market risk premium (calculated in stage 1) to derive the risk premium for the particular share.

The second and third stages of the process require further explanation.

We may recall from Chapter 5 that total risk is made up of two elements: *diversifiable* and *non-diversifiable* risk. Diversifiable risk is that part of the risk that is specific to the investment project and which can be eliminated by spreading available funds among investment projects. Non-diversifiable risk is that part of total risk that is common to all projects and which therefore cannot be diversified away. It arises from general market conditions and can be avoided only by making risk-free investments.

This distinction between diversifiable and non-diversifiable risk is also relevant to investors. By holding a well-balanced portfolio of shares, an investor can eliminate diversifiable risk relating to a particular share, but not necessarily common to other shares, leaving only non-diversifiable risk, which is common to all shares. This is because, with a well-balanced portfolio, gains and losses arising from the diversifiable risk of different shares will tend to cancel each other out.

We know that risk-averse investors will be prepared to take on increased risk only if there is the expectation of increased returns. However, as diversifiable risk can be eliminated through holding a well-balanced portfolio, there is no reason why investors should receive additional returns for taking on this form of risk. It is, therefore, only the non-diversifiable risk element of total risk for which investors should expect additional returns.

The non-diversifiable risk element can be measured using **beta**. This measures the non-diversifiable risk of a particular share to the market as a whole. The higher the share's non-diversifiable risk relative to the market, the higher will be its beta value. A key feature of CAPM is that there is a linear relationship between risk and return. Thus, beta can also be seen as a measure of the responsiveness of returns from an individual share relative to the market as a whole. The higher the share's return relative to the market, the higher will be its beta value. Hence, a share that produces increased returns of 12 per cent when the market increases by 6 per cent will have a higher beta value than a share that produces increased returns of only 4 per cent in response to a 6 per cent market increase.

The CAPM equation

Using the above ideas, the required rate of return for investors for a particular share can be calculated as follows:

$$K_0 = K_{RF} + b(K_m - K_{RF})$$

where K_0 = the required return for investors for a particular share

K_{RF} = the risk-free rate

b = beta of the particular share

K_m = the expected returns to the market for the next period

$(K_m - K_{RF})$ = the expected market average risk premium for the next period.

This equation reflects the idea that the required return for a particular share is made up of two elements: the risk-free return plus a risk premium. We can see that the risk premium is equal to the expected risk premium for the market as a whole multiplied by the beta of the particular share. As explained earlier, beta measures are, in essence, a measure of responsiveness of changes in a particular share to changes in the market as a whole.

CAPM is a forward-looking model but information concerning the future is not available. This means that the expected risk premium for the market is derived by reference to past periods, on the assumption that they provide a good predictor of future periods. The CAPM equation shows that the expected risk premium can be deduced by subtracting the risk-free rate from the average returns to the market. Historical average market returns are usually calculated for a relatively long period, as returns çan fluctuate wildly over the short term. (Note that the returns to a share are made up of dividends plus any increase, or less any decrease, in the share price during a period.)

Real World 8.1 sets out the equity market risk premium for different countries.

Real World 8.1

Putting a premium on equities

Figure 8.2 is taken from *Credit Suisse Global Investment Returns Yearbook 2013*. It shows the equity risk premium for different countries calculated by using returns from very short-term government securities (bills) and also by using returns from long-term government securities (bonds). Both forms of government security may be used as a proxy for the risk-free rate of return. Annualised equity premia based on both are shown and are calculated using the period 1900–2012. These premia vary considerably, which may well reflect different levels of risk. However, the authors of the Yearbook conclude:

> The dominant factor is that some markets were blessed with good fortune, while others were cursed with bad luck.

→

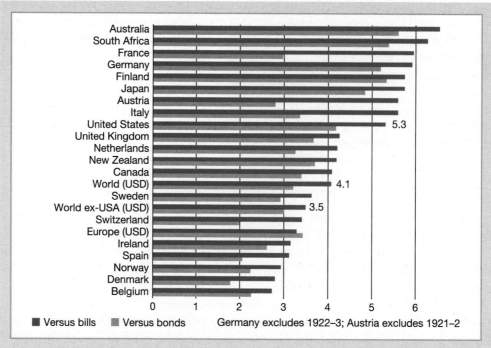

Figure 8.2 Annualised historical risk premia (%) 1900–2012

Source: E. Dimson, P. Marsh, M. Staunton (2002), *Triumph of the Optimists*, Princeton University Press.

The beta value for the market as a whole is set at 1.0. This provides a yardstick against which the risk premium of individual shares can be compared. Thus, where a share has the same expected risk premium as the market as a whole, it will have a beta value of 1.0. Where a share has an expected risk premium of half the expected market risk premium, it will have a beta of 0.5, and where a share has an expected risk premium that is twice the expected market risk premium, it will have a beta of 2.0. (Given a linear relationship between risk and return, it also means that a share with a beta of 2.0 has twice the expected return than the market as a whole.)

Activity 8.5

Would it be better to hold shares with a beta value of more than 1.0 or less than 1.0 when stock market prices are generally

(a) rising
(b) falling?

When stock market prices are rising, it is better to hold shares with a beta value of more than 1.0. Their returns are more responsive to market price changes and so when stock market prices are rising, their returns will be greater than for the market as a whole. Shares with a beta value of less than 1.0, meanwhile, are less responsive to market price changes. They will not, therefore, benefit so much from a rise in market prices. When stock market prices are falling, however, the position is reversed. It is better to hold shares with a beta value of less than 1.0 as their returns are less responsive to falls in market prices.

Shares with a beta value of more than 1.0 are often referred to as *aggressive shares*, whereas shares with a beta value of less than 1.0 are referred to as *defensive shares*. Shares with a beta of 1.0 are referred to as *neutral shares*. Bear in mind that while the points made in the solution to Activity 8.5 are generally true, factors specific to a particular business may cause its shares to move in a different manner.

Many shares have a beta that is fairly close to the market beta of 1.0, with most falling within the range 0.5 to 1.5. Generally speaking, the beta value for a share is largely determined by the nature of the industry in which the particular business operates. Beta values can change over time, particularly if the business changes its operating activities.

Measuring betas

Betas can be measured using regression analysis on past data, on the assumption that past periods provide a good predictor of future periods. The monthly returns from a particular share (that is, dividends plus any increase, or less any decrease, in share price) for a period are regressed against the returns from the market as a whole. A Stock Exchange index, such as the FTSE 100 or FTSE Actuaries All Share Index, is normally used as a proxy measure for returns from the market over time.

To illustrate this approach, let us assume that the monthly returns from a particular share and the returns to the market are plotted on a graph, as shown in Figure 8.3. A line of best fit can then be drawn, using regression analysis. Note the slope of this line (and the blue dotted lines to illustrate that slope). We can see that, for this particular share, the returns do not change as much as the returns for the market as a whole. In other words, the beta is less than 1.

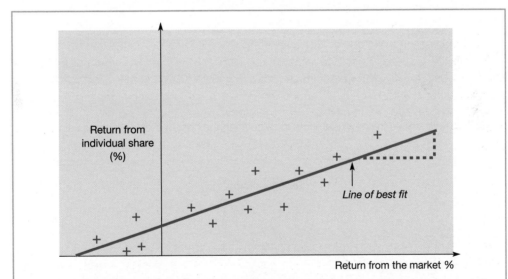

The figure shows the relationship between the returns from an individual share and the movements for the market. A linear relationship is assumed and linear regression analysis is used to establish a line of best fit.

Figure 8.3 The relationship between the returns from an individual share and returns from the market

Measures of beta for the shares of UK listed businesses are available from various information agencies such as the London Business School Risk Measurement Service and Reuters. Thus calculating beta is not usually necessary. **Real World 8.2** provides examples of betas of UK listed businesses operating in different industries.

Betas in practice

Betas for some well-known UK listed businesses are set out below.

Name	Industry	Beta
Royal Bank of Scotland	Banking	2.47
United Utilities	Utilities	0.32
Marks and Spencer	Retailer	0.73
easyJet	Airline	0.59
AstraZeneca	Pharmaceuticals	0.36
Premier Foods	Food producer	1.62
BP	Energy	1.16
Stagecoach	Passenger transport	0.88
GKN	Engineering	2.28
Tesco	Supermarket	0.64

Source: Compiled from information taken from www.reuters.com, accessed 4 March 2013.

Activity 8.6

Lansbury plc has recently obtained a measure of its beta from a business information agency. The beta value obtained is 1.2. The expected returns to the market for the next period is 10 per cent and the risk-free rate on government securities is 3 per cent. What is the cost of ordinary shares to the business?

Using the CAPM formula we have:

$$K_0 = K_{RF} + b(K_m - K_{RF}) = 3\% + 1.2(10\% - 3\%) = 11.4\%$$

Figure 8.4 illustrates the main elements in calculating the cost of ordinary shares using CAPM.

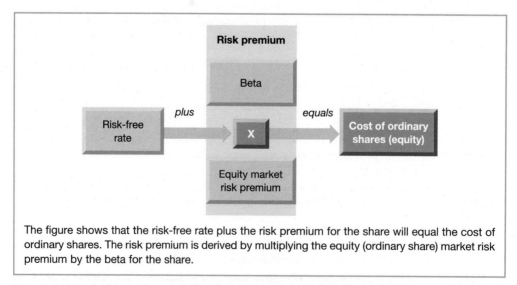

The figure shows that the risk-free rate plus the risk premium for the share will equal the cost of ordinary shares. The risk premium is derived by multiplying the equity (ordinary share) market risk premium by the beta for the share.

Figure 8.4 Calculating the cost of ordinary shares using CAPM

Criticisms of CAPM

CAPM has been subject to criticism, which will not be considered in detail as it is beyond the scope of this book. If you are interested in pursuing this issue, take a look at the further reading section at the end of this chapter. It is enough to say that there are various unrealistic assumptions underpinning the model. These include a world where there are no taxes and no transaction costs and where all investors have access to the same information and can borrow or lend at a risk-free interest rate. There are also technical problems concerning the measurement of key inputs to the model: beta values, returns to the market and the risk-free rate of return.

The key issue, however, is whether these unrealistic assumptions and measurement problems undermine CAPM's ability to explain stock market behaviour. Although early studies were broadly supportive of CAPM, more recent studies have cast doubt on the linear relationship between beta values and share returns. Researchers have found that beta values are not the only factor influencing average share returns. There is, for example, a 'size effect', which indicates that larger businesses tend to produce lower returns than smaller businesses.

Despite the weaknesses mentioned, a more complete model for estimating the cost of ordinary share capital has yet to be developed. We should not, therefore, be too eager to abandon CAPM (even though it may make life easier for students!).

CAPM and business practice

Having ploughed through the above sections on CAPM, you may be pleased to know that it is actually used in practice. **Real World 8.3** briefly sets out the findings of two surveys, which shed some light on how UK listed businesses compute their cost of ordinary share capital.

Real World 8.3

A beta way to do it

Two surveys have revealed that CAPM is the most popular way of computing the cost of ordinary share capital among UK listed businesses:

- A postal survey of 193 UK listed business revealed that CAPM was used by 47.2 per cent of the respondents. The dividend-based approach came a poor second, with only 27.5 per cent of respondents using it.[1]
- An interview-based survey of 18 UK listed businesses revealed that CAPM was used by 13 (78 per cent) of the respondents.[2]

Differences in usage of CAPM between these two surveys may be due to the fact that the first survey included businesses of all sizes whereas the second survey looked only at very large businesses. Larger businesses may adopt a more sophisticated approach to calculating the cost of ordinary shares than smaller businesses.

Sources: (1) E. McLaney, J. Pointon, M. Thomas and J. Tucker, 'Practitioners' perspectives on the UK cost of capital', *European Journal of Finance*, April 2004, pp. 123–138; (2) A. Gregory and J. Rutterford (with M. Zaman), *The Cost of Capital in the UK*, Chartered Institute of Management Accountants Research Monograph, 1999.

Some final points

To complete this topic, a few more points should be mentioned. First, CAPM cannot be directly applied to a business not listed on the Stock Exchange. In the absence of market information, a share beta value cannot be derived. However, the share beta value of a similar listed business can sometimes be used as a proxy measure.

Second, in a world where capital markets are perfectly competitive and where accurate measurements can be made, the CAPM and the dividend growth model will arrive at the same cost for an ordinary share. In the real world, however, we should expect the two models to produce different cost figures. It seems that the CAPM model is the more widely used of the two (see, for example, Real World 8.3). This suggests that the key inputs to CAPM (risk-free rate of return, share beta and risk premium) can be estimated more reliably than future dividend growth rates.

Retained earnings

Retained earnings are an important source of finance from ordinary shareholders and, as we saw in Chapter 6, cannot be regarded as 'cost free'. If earnings are reinvested by the business, the shareholders will expect to receive returns on these funds that are equivalent to the returns expected from investments in opportunities with similar levels of risk. The ordinary shareholders' stake in the business is made up of ordinary share capital plus any retained earnings, and the expected returns from each will, in theory, be the same. Hence, when we calculate the cost of ordinary share capital, we are also calculating the cost of any retained earnings.

Loan capital

We begin this section in the same way as we began the section relating to ordinary shares. We shall first consider the value of loan capital and then go on to consider its cost. It cannot be emphasised enough that these two aspects are really two sides of the same coin.

Loan capital may be irredeemable (that is, the principal sum is not expected to be repaid and so interest will be paid indefinitely). Where the rate of interest on the loan is fixed, the equation used to derive the value of irredeemable loan capital is similar to that used to derive the value of ordinary shares, where dividends remain constant over time. The value of irredeemable loan capital is:

$$P_d = \frac{I}{K_d}$$

where P_d = the current market value of the loan capital

K_d = the cost of loan capital to the business

I = the annual rate of interest on the loan capital.

This equation can be rearranged to provide an equation for deducing the *cost* of loan capital. Hence:

$$K_d = \frac{I}{P_d}$$

Interest on loan capital is a tax-deductible expense and so the net cost is the interest charge *after* tax. For investment appraisal purposes, we take the after-tax net cash flows resulting from a project. Thus, when calculating the appropriate discount rate, we should be consistent and use the after-tax rates for the cost of capital. The after-tax cost will be:

$$K_d = \frac{I(1-t)}{P_d}$$

where t is the rate of tax payable.

Tan and Co plc has irredeemable loan capital outstanding on which it pays an annual rate of interest of 10 per cent. The current market value of the loan capital is £88 per £100 nominal value and the tax rate is 20 per cent. What is the cost of the loan capital to the business?

Using the above formula, the cost is:

$$K_d = \frac{I(1-t)}{P_d} = \frac{10(1-0.20)}{88} = 9.1\%$$

Note that the rate of interest on the nominal value of the loan capital is not the relevant cost. Rather, we are concerned with the *opportunity* cost of the loan capital. This represents the return that can be earned by investing in an opportunity with the same level of risk. The *current market rate of interest* of the loan capital, as calculated above, provides us with a measure of opportunity cost.

Where the loan capital is redeemable, deriving the cost of capital figure is a little more complex. However, the principles and calculations required to derive the relevant figure have already been covered in Chapter 4. An investor who purchases redeemable loan capital will pay an initial outlay and then expect to receive annual interest plus a repayment of capital at the end of the loan period. The required rate of return for the investor will be the discount rate which, when applied to the future cash flows, will produce a present value that is equal to the current market value of the investment. Thus, the rate of return can be computed in the same way as the IRR is computed for other forms of investment opportunity. Let us consider Example 8.1.

Example 8.1

Lim Associates plc issues £20 million loan capital on which it pays an annual rate of interest of 10 per cent on the nominal value. The issue price of the loan capital is £88 per £100 nominal value and the tax rate is 20 per cent. The loan capital is due to be redeemed in four years' time at its nominal value.

What are the annual cash flows for this issue?

Solution

The cash flows for this issue of loan capital will be as follows:

		Cash flows £m
Year 0	Current market value (£20m × (88 ÷ 100))	17.6
Years 1–3	Interest payable (£20m × 10%)	(2.0)
Year 4	Redemption value (£20m) + Interest (£2m)	(22.0)

To derive the cost of loan capital to the business, the trial and error approach that is used in calculating the IRR can be used.

Calculate the pre-tax cost of loan capital for Lim Associates plc. (*Hint*: Start with a discount rate of 10 per cent.)

Using a discount rate of 10 per cent, the NPV is calculated as follows:

	Cash flows	Discount rate	PV of cash flows
	£m	10%	£m
Year 0	17.6	1.00	17.6
Year 1	(2.0)	0.91	(1.8)
Year 2	(2.0)	0.83	(1.7)
Year 3	(2.0)	0.75	(1.5)
Year 4	(22.0)	0.68	(15.0)
		NPV	(2.4)

The discounted future cash outflows exceed the issue price of the loan capital and so the NPV is negative. This means that the discount rate is too low. Let us try 15 per cent.

	Cash flows	Discount rate	PV of cash flows
	£m	15%	£m
Year 0	17.6	1.00	17.6
Year 1	(2.0)	0.87	(1.7)
Year 2	(2.0)	0.76	(1.5)
Year 3	(2.0)	0.66	(1.3)
Year 4	(22.0)	0.57	(12.5)
		NPV	0.6

This discount rate is a little too high as the discounted cash outflows are less than the issue price of the loan capital. Thus, the appropriate rate lies somewhere between 10 per cent and 15 per cent.

Trial	Discount factor	Net present value
		£m
1	10%	(2.4)
2	15%	0.6
Difference	5%	3.0

The change in NPV for every 1 per cent change in the discount rate will be:

$$£3.0m/5 = £0.6m$$

Thus, the reduction in the 15 per cent discount rate required to achieve a zero NPV will be 1 per cent as a 15 per cent discount rate produced an NPV of £0.6 million. In other words, the discount rate is 14 per cent.

The above figure of 14 per cent represents the *pre-tax* cost of loan capital. The tax rate is 20 per cent and so the after-tax cost of loan capital is 14 per cent $\times (1 - 0.2) = 11.2$ per cent.

As a footnote to this section, it is worth mentioning that not all loan notes are traded and so market values are not always available. To derive a proxy measure, the market value of similar traded loan notes of another business can sometimes be used.

Preference shares

Let us again begin by considering the value of this type of capital before moving on to calculate its cost. Preference shares may be redeemable or irredeemable. They are similar to loan capital in so far as the holders normally receive an agreed rate of return each year (which is expressed in terms of the nominal value of the shares). They differ, however, in that the annual dividend paid to preference shareholders is not a tax-deductible expense. Thus, the full cost of the dividend payments must be borne by the business (that is, the ordinary shareholders). As the rate of dividend on the preference shares is normally fixed, the equation used to derive the value of irredeemable preference shares is again similar to the equation used to derive the value of ordinary shares, where the dividends remain constant over time. The equation for irredeemable preference shares is:

$$P_p = \frac{D_p}{K_p}$$

where P_p = the current market price of the preference shares
K_p = the cost of preference shares to the business
D_p = the annual dividend payments.

This equation can be rearranged to provide an equation for deducing the *cost* of irredeemable preference shares. Hence:

$$K_p = \frac{D_p}{P_p}$$

Activity 8.9

Iordanova plc has 12 per cent irredeemable preference shares in issue with a nominal (par) value of £1. The shares have a current market price of £0.90 (excluding dividends).
   What is the cost of these shares?

The cost is:

$$K_p = \frac{D_p}{P_p} = \frac{12}{90} = 13.3\%$$

The cost of redeemable preference shares can be deduced using the IRR approach, which was used earlier to determine the cost of redeemable loan capital.

Activity 8.10

L.C. Conday plc has £50 million 10 per cent £1 preference shares in issue. The current market price is £0.92 and the shares are due to be redeemed in three years' time at their nominal value.
   What is the cost of these shares? (*Hint*: Start with a discount rate of 11 per cent.)

The annual cash flows are as follows:

		Cash flows £m
Year 0	Current market value (£50m × 0.92)	46.0
Years 1–2	Dividends (£50m × 10%)	(5.0)
Year 3	Redemption value (£50m) + Dividend (£5m)	(55.0)

Using a discount rate of 11 per cent, the NPV is as follows:

	Cash flows £m	Discount rate 11%	PV of cash flows £m
Year 0	46.0	1.00	46.0
Year 1	(5.0)	0.90	(4.5)
Year 2	(5.0)	0.81	(4.1)
Year 3	(55.0)	0.73	(40.2)
		NPV	(2.8)

This discount rate is too low as the discounted future cash outflows exceed the issue price of the preference share capital. Let us try 13 per cent:

	Cash flows £m	Discount rate 13%	PV of cash flows £m
Year 0	46.0	1.00	46.0
Year 1	(5.0)	0.89	(4.5)
Year 2	(5.0)	0.78	(3.9)
Year 3	(55.0)	0.69	(38.0)
		NPV	(0.4)

The discounted cash outflows are almost equal to the issue price of the preference share capital. Thus, the cost of preference shares is approximately 13 per cent.

WEIGHTED AVERAGE COST OF CAPITAL (WACC)

When making financing decisions, the managers of a business are assumed to have a target capital structure in mind. Although the relative proportions of equity, preference shares and loans may vary over the short term, these proportions are assumed to remain fairly stable when viewed over the medium to longer term. The existence of a fairly stable capital structure is consistent with the view that managers believe that a particular financing mix will minimise the cost of capital of the business, or, to put it another way, a particular financing mix provides an optimal capital structure for the business. (Whether or not there is such a thing as an optimal capital structure is discussed later in the chapter.) However, a target capital structure is unlikely to be set in stone. It may change from time to time in response to changes in the tax rates, interest rates and so on, which affect the cost of particular elements of the capital structure.

The existence of a stable capital structure (presumably reflecting the target capital structure) has important implications for the evaluation of investment projects. It has already been argued that the required rates of return from investors (that is, the costs of capital to the business) should provide the basis for determining an appropriate discount rate for investment projects. If we accept that a business will maintain a fairly stable capital structure over the period of the project, then the average cost of capital can provide an appropriate discount rate.

The average cost of capital can be calculated by taking the cost of the individual elements and then weighting each element in proportion to the target capital structure (by market value) of the business. Example 8.2 illustrates how the **weighted average cost of capital (WACC)** is calculated.

Example 8.2

Danton plc has 10 million ordinary shares in issue with a current market value of £2.00 per share. The expected dividend for next year is 16p per share and this is expected to grow each year at a constant rate of 4 per cent. The business also has:

- 10.0 million 9 per cent £1 irredeemable preference shares in issue with a market price of £0.90 per share
- £20 million of irredeemable loan capital in issue with a nominal rate of interest of 6 per cent and which is quoted at £80 per £100 nominal value.

Assume a tax rate of 20 per cent and that the current capital structure reflects the target capital structure of the business.

What is the weighted average cost of capital of the business?

Solution

The first step is to calculate the cost of the individual elements of capital. The cost of ordinary shares in Danton plc is calculated as follows:

$$K_0 = \frac{D_1}{P_0} + g \text{ (see note)} = \frac{16}{200} + 0.04 = 12\%$$

Note: The dividend valuation model has been used to calculate the cost of ordinary shares; however, the CAPM model could have been used instead if the relevant information had been available.

The cost of the preference share capital is as follows:

$$K_p = \frac{D_p}{P_p} = \frac{9}{90} = 10\%$$

The cost of loan capital is:

$$K_d = \frac{I(1-t)}{P_d} = \frac{6(1-0.2)}{80} = 6.0\%$$

Having derived the cost of the individual elements, we can now calculate the weighted average cost of these elements. The WACC will be:

	(a) Market value £m	(b) Proportion of total market value	(c) Cost %	(d) = (b × c) Contribution to WACC
Ordinary shares (10m × £2) (see note)	20	0.44	12	5.3
Preference shares (10m × £0.90)	9	0.20	10	2.0
Loan capital (£20m × 0.8)	16	0.36	6	2.2
	45	1.00		
WACC				9.5%

Note: The market value of the capital rather than the nominal value has been used in the calculations. This is because we are concerned with the opportunity cost of capital invested, as explained earlier.

Figure 8.5 sets out the approach used to calculate the WACC of a business.

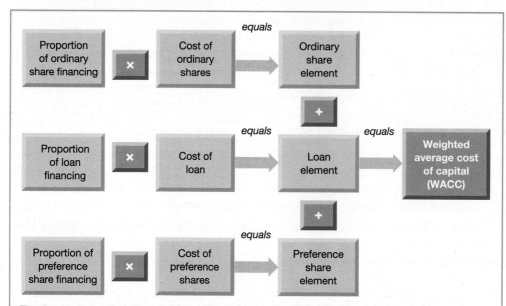

The figure shows that, for a business financed by a mixture of ordinary shares, loan capital and preference shares, the weighted average cost of capital (WACC) is calculated by first multiplying the proportion of each element by its cost. The WACC is the sum of the figures derived for each element.

Figure 8.5 Calculating WACC

Whether businesses maintain a target capital structure in practice has been the subject of some debate. **Real World 8.4** provides some evidence concerning this issue.

A mail survey of UK businesses revealed mixed support for the idea of a target capital structure. The surveyed businesses ranged in size (as measured by total assets) from more than £17 billion to less than £1 million. The extent to which respondents adopted a target capital structure was as follows:

	Company size			Total	
	Large >£140m	Medium £140m–£27.7m	Small <£27.7m	Number	%
No target	22	35	38	95	49
Target	43	30	28	101	51
	65	65	66	196	100

The results indicate that large businesses were more likely to have a target capital structure and small businesses were less likely to have one. The reasons for this are not clear but may be because large businesses have more control over their capital structure or have better access to finance.

Source: Adapted from V. Beattie, A. Goodacre and S.J. Thomson, 'Corporate financing decisions: UK survey vidence', *Journal of Business Finance and Accounting*, 33, 9–10, 2006, 1402–1434.

In practice, an investment project may be financed by raising funds from a particular source. It is tempting, therefore, to think that the appropriate cost of capital for the project will be the cost of the particular source of finance used. However, this is not the case. When new funds are needed for an investment project, it is not normally feasible to raise the funds in exactly the same proportions as in the existing capital structure. To minimise the cost of raising funds, it will usually make sense for a business to raise funds from one source and, later, to raise funds from another, even though this may lead to deviations in the required capital structure over the short term. The fact that a particular source of new funds is used for a project will be determined by the requirements for the long-term capital structure of the business rather than the requirements of the project.

Using the specific cost of funds raised for the project could lead to illogical decisions being made. Assume that a business is considering an investment in two identical machines and that each machine has an estimated IRR of 12 per cent. Let us further assume that the first machine will be financed using loan capital with an after-tax cost of 10 per cent. However, as debt capacity of the business will then be used up, the second machine must be financed by ordinary (equity) share capital at a cost of 14 per cent. If the specific cost of capital is used to evaluate investment decisions, the business would be in the peculiar position of accepting the investment in the first machine, because the IRR exceeds the cost of capital, and rejecting the second (identical) machine because the IRR is lower than the cost of capital! By using the WACC, we avoid this kind of problem. Each machine will be evaluated according to the average cost of capital, which should then result in consistent decisions being made.

Real World 8.5 reveals the weighted average cost of capital for some large businesses.

Real World 8.5

WACC in practice

Pre-tax WACC figures for a sample of large businesses, operating in different industrial sectors, are shown below. As mentioned earlier, tax should be deducted when using WACC to evaluate investment projects.

Name	Type of business	Pre-tax WACC (%)
J Sainsbury plc	Food retailer	10.0
GKN plc	Engineering	12.0
AstraZeneca plc	Pharmaceuticals	10.0
Go-Ahead Group plc	Transport services	10.0
Tui Travel plc	Travel operator	10.0
Premier Foods plc	Food producer	12.1
Rolls Royce plc	Engine manufacturer	13.0

Sources: 'GKN acquires Volvo aero for £633 million', www.gkn.com, 5 July 2012 and relevant annual reports for the years ended 2011 and 2012.

LIMITATIONS OF THE WACC APPROACH

The WACC approach has been criticised for failing to take risk into account. In practice, different investment opportunities are likely to have different levels of risk. Risk-averse investors will require higher returns to compensate for higher levels of risk. This means that the cost of capital for each project should reflect the particular level of risk undertaken.

Activity 8.11

Can you think of at least one situation where it would still be feasible for a business to use WACC when evaluating an investment project?

It is suitable where an investment project is:

■ expected to have the same level of risk as existing investments, or
■ fairly small and so will not significantly affect the overall risk level of the business.

We mentioned earlier that the WACC approach assumes that the capital structure of the business remains stable. In the real world, however, there will be changes in the market values and costs of various capital elements over time. To reflect these changes, businesses should therefore recalculate their WACC on a frequent basis.

Finally, measurement problems may conspire to make the WACC approach difficult to use. Some of these problems relate to the individual elements of capital. Not all shares and loan notes, for example, are frequently traded on well-regulated stock markets. This means that reliable market values may be unavailable. Other problems relate to the models used. We mentioned earlier that identifying dividend growth rates to use in the dividend growth model can be difficult.

COST OF CAPITAL – SOME EVIDENCE

Real World 8.6 provides some evidence on the frequency with which the cost of capital is reviewed in practice and the use of WACC as the appropriate discount rate in capital investment decisions.

Counting the cost

The survey of 193 UK listed businesses mentioned in Real World 8.3 revealed the frequency with which businesses reassess their cost of capital. As the financial environment continually changes, we should expect businesses to reassess their cost of capital in the light of these changes. The frequency with which the businesses surveyed reassess their cost of capital is shown in Figure 8.6. These findings indicate that an annual reassessment is preferred by more than half of respondents.

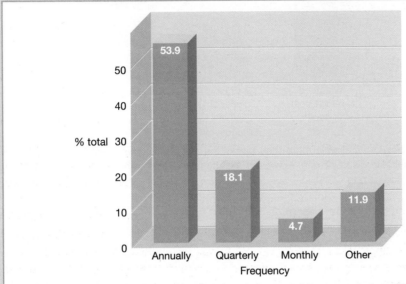

The figure shows that nearly all of the businesses surveyed reassess their cost of capital on at least an annual basis. Those falling into the 'other' category reassess every six months (2.6 per cent), when long-term interest rates change (3.1 per cent) and on a project-by-project basis (6.2 per cent).

Figure 8.6 Frequency with which businesses reassess their cost of capital

A further finding concerns the extent to which the weighted average cost of capital was used in evaluating investment decisions. Figure 8.7 shows the bases for the discount rates used for investment projects. We saw above that WACC is often the appropriate discount rate to use when evaluating investment projects. The reasons for using either the cost of ordinary shares or a long-term borrowing rate are not clear. The use of the ordinary share cost of capital would only be appropriate where the business was entirely financed by ordinary shares and the riskiness of the project was in line with that of the business as a whole. The use of a long-term borrowing rate is even more difficult to understand. It fails to take into account the required rate of return for equity investors.

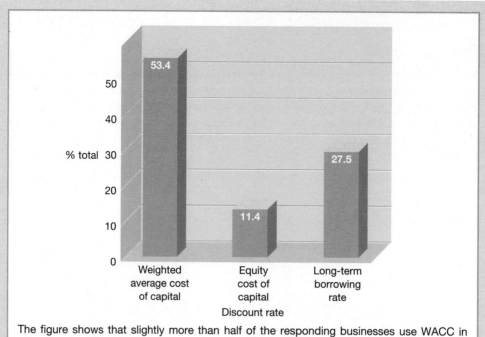

The figure shows that slightly more than half of the responding businesses use WACC in deriving a suitable discount rate. However, slightly fewer than half use other methods to derive the discount rate.

Figure 8.7 The discount rate used for investment projects

Source: Charts taken from E. McLaney, J. Pointon, M. Thomas and J. Tucker, 'Practitioners' perspectives on the UK cost of capital', *European Journal of Finance*, 10, April 2004, 123–138.

FINANCIAL GEARING

We have already seen that the presence of capital with a fixed rate of return, such as loans and preference shares, in the long-term capital structure of a business is referred to as 'gearing' (or, to be more precise, 'financial gearing'). The term 'gearing' is used because fixed-return capital can accentuate any changes in profit before interest and taxation (PBIT) on the returns to ordinary shareholders. The effect is similar to the effect of two intermeshing cog wheels of unequal size (see Figure 8.8). The movement in the larger cog wheel (profit before interest and taxation) causes a more than proportionate movement in the smaller cog wheel (returns to ordinary shareholders).

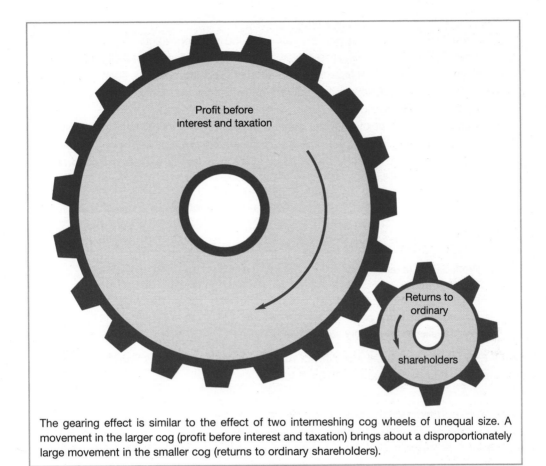

The gearing effect is similar to the effect of two intermeshing cog wheels of unequal size. A movement in the larger cog (profit before interest and taxation) brings about a disproportionately large movement in the smaller cog (returns to ordinary shareholders).

Figure 8.8 The effect of financial gearing

The effect of financial gearing on the returns to ordinary shareholders is demonstrated in Example 8.3.

Example 8.3

Alpha plc and Gamma plc have both been recently created and have identical operations. The long-term capital structure of each business is as follows:

	Alpha plc	Gamma plc
	£m	£m
£1 ordinary shares	200	340
12% preference shares	100	50
10% loan notes	100	10
	400	400

Although both businesses have the same total long-term capital, we can see that the level of financial gearing differs significantly between the two businesses.

A widely used measure of gearing, which we came across in Chapter 3, is as follows:

$$\text{Financial gearing ratio} = \frac{\text{Loan capital} + \text{Preference shares (if any)}}{\text{Total long-term capital}} \times 100\%$$

For Alpha plc and Gamma plc, the ratios are 50 per cent ((200/400) × 100%) and 15 per cent ((60/400) × 100%), respectively. These ratios indicate that Alpha has a high level of financial gearing, that is, a high proportion of fixed-return capital (loan capital plus preference shares) in relation to its total long-term capital, and Gamma has a relatively low level of financial gearing.

To consider the effect of financial gearing on the returns to ordinary shareholders, let us assume that, in Year 1, the businesses generated identical PBITs of £80 million. The earnings per share (EPS) for the ordinary share investors of each business for Year 1 can be calculated as follows:

	Alpha plc	Gamma plc
	£m	£m
PBIT	80.0	80.0
Loan interest	(10.0)	(1.0)
Profit before taxation	70.0	79.0
Tax (say, 30%)	(21.0)	(23.7)
Profit for the year	49.0	55.3
Preference dividend paid	(12.0)	(6.0)
Profit available to ordinary shareholders	37.0	49.3

The EPS for ordinary share investors of Alpha plc is 18.5p (that is, £37m/200m) and for Gamma plc it is 14.5p (that is, £49.3m/340m).

We can see that ordinary share investors in Alpha plc earn higher returns in Year 1 than those in Gamma plc. This arises from the use of a higher level of fixed-return capital (loan capital and preference share capital) in the capital structure. When additional profits generated from the use of fixed-return capital exceed the additional fixed payments (interest charges and preference dividends) incurred, the surplus will accrue to the ordinary shareholders. Alpha plc has a higher proportion of fixed-return capital and a lower proportion of ordinary share (equity) capital than Gamma plc. This means that, where a large surplus is available, ordinary shareholders in Alpha plc will receive higher earnings per share.

However, the financial gearing effect can operate in both directions. To illustrate this point, let us assume that the PBIT for Year 2 is much lower than for Year 1, say £40 million, for each business. The EPS for ordinary shareholders for Year 2 would then be as follows:

	Alpha plc	Gamma plc
	£m	£m
PBIT	40.0	40.0
Loan interest	(10.0)	(1.0)
Profit before taxation	30.0	39.0
Tax (say, 30%)	(9.0)	(11.7)
Profit for the year	21.0	27.3
Preference dividend	(12.0)	(6.0)
Profit available to ordinary shareholders	9.0	21.3
EPS	**4.5p**	**6.3p**

The cost of servicing the fixed-return capital in Year 2 is unchanged for both businesses, but Alpha plc has the higher costs to bear. The surplus available to ordinary shareholders of Alpha plc in Year 2 is therefore much lower. We can see that they suffer a greater decrease in earnings per share, and receive lower earnings per share in total, than shareholders in Gamma plc.

Managers must appreciate that gearing comes at a price – the loss of financial flexibility. Alpha Ltd is more highly geared than Gamma Ltd and, as a consequence, has a higher fixed cost burden. This means that it will be less able to cope with shocks, such as a sudden downturn in economic activity. Alpha Ltd also has less debt capacity (other things being equal), which may impose limits on future growth. Nevertheless, nearly all businesses rely on gearing to a greater or lesser extent.

In **Real World 8.7** Warren Buffett, chairman of Berkshire Hathaway Inc., warns that we should not be beguiled by the seemingly magical properties of gearing.

Real World 8.7

Wealth warning

Unquestionably, some people have become very rich through the use of borrowed money. However, that's also been a way to get very poor. When gearing works, it magnifies your gains. Your spouse thinks you're clever, and your neighbours get envious. But gearing is addictive. Once having profited from its wonders, very few people retreat to more conservative practices. And as we all learnt in third grade, any series of positive numbers, however impressive the numbers may be, evaporates when multiplied by a single zero. History tells us that gearing all too often produces zeroes, even when it is employed by very smart people.

Source: Adapted from Shareholder letter, Berkshire Hathaway Inc., www.berkshirehathaway.com, 26 February 2011, p. 22.

DEGREE OF FINANCIAL GEARING

We have just seen that, for a financially geared business, any change in profit before interest and taxation will result in a disproportionate change in earnings per share. The higher the level of financial gearing, the more sensitive earnings per share become to changes in profit before interest and taxation. The degree of financial gearing measures the sensitivity of earnings per share to changes in the level of profit before interest and taxation and is calculated as follows:

$$\text{Degree of financial gearing} = \frac{\text{PBIT}}{\text{PBIT} - I - [P \times 100/(100 - t)]}$$

where I = interest charges
P = preference dividend
t = tax rate.

(Note that the preference dividend is 'grossed up' to a pre-tax amount by multiplying the dividend by $100/(100 - t)$. This is done to ensure consistency with the other variables in the equation.)

For Alpha plc, the measure will be calculated as follows for Year 1:

$$\text{Degree of financial gearing} = \frac{80}{80 - 10 - [12 \times 100/(100 - 30)]} = \frac{80}{52.9} = 1.5$$

Activity 8.12

Using the above equation, calculate the degree of financial gearing for Gamma plc for Year 1.

The calculation is:

$$\text{Degree of financial gearing} = \frac{\text{PBIT}}{\text{PBIT} - I - [P \times 100/(100 - t)]}$$

$$= \frac{80}{80 - 1 - [6 \times 100/(100 - 30)]} = \frac{80}{70.4} = 1.1$$

This measure of financial gearing indicates that, in the case of Alpha plc, a 1.0 per cent change in profit before interest and taxation from the base level of £80 million will result in a 1.5 per cent change in earnings per share, whereas for Gamma plc, a 1.0 per cent change in profit before interest and taxation from the base level of £80 million will only result in a 1.1 per cent change in earnings per share. In both cases, the figure derived is greater than 1, which indicates the presence of financial gearing. The higher the figure derived, the greater the sensitivity of earnings per share to changes in profit before interest and taxation.

The impact of financial gearing will become less pronounced as the level of profit before interest and taxation increases in relation to fixed-return payments (interest charges and preference dividends). Where profit before interest and taxation barely covers the fixed-return payments, even small changes in the former figure can have a significant impact on earnings per share. This high degree of sensitivity will be reflected in the degree of financial gearing measure. However, as profit before interest and taxation increases in relation to fixed-return charges, earnings per share will become less sensitive to changes. As a result, the degree of financial gearing measure will be lower.

Activity 8.13

What is the degree of financial gearing for Alpha plc and Gamma plc for Year 2?

For Alpha plc, the degree of financial gearing in Year 2 (when profit before interest and taxation is much lower) will be:

$$\text{Degree of financial gearing} = \frac{\text{PBIT}}{\text{PBIT} - I - [P \times 100/(100 - t)]}$$

$$= \frac{40}{40 - 10 - [12 \times 100/(100 - 30)]} = 3.1$$

For Gamma plc, the degree of financial gearing in Year 2 will be:

$$\text{Degree of financial gearing} = \frac{\text{PBIT}}{\text{PBIT} - I - [P \times 100/(100 - t)]}$$

$$= \frac{40}{40 - 1 - [6 \times 100/(100 - 30)]} = 1.3$$

We can see that EPS for both businesses is now more sensitive to changes in the level of PBIT than in the previous year, when profits were higher. However, returns to ordinary shareholders in Alpha plc, which has a higher level of financial gearing, have become much more sensitive to change than returns to ordinary shareholders in Gamma plc.

GEARING AND CAPITAL STRUCTURE DECISIONS

When evaluating capital structure decisions, the likely impact of gearing on the expected risks and returns for ordinary shareholders should be taken into account. To do this, projected financial statements and gearing ratios, which we considered in earlier chapters, can be helpful. Example 8.4 illustrates the way in which a capital structure decision may be evaluated.

Example 8.4

Semplice Ltd manufactures catering equipment for restaurants and hotels. The statement of financial position of the business as at 31 May Year 4 is as follows:

Statement of financial position as at 31 May Year 4

	£m
ASSETS	
Non-current assets	
Premises	40.2
Machinery and equipment	17.4
	57.6
Current assets	
Inventories	22.5
Trade receivables	27.6
Cash at bank	1.3
	51.4
Total assets	109.0
EQUITY AND LIABILITIES	
Equity	
£0.25 ordinary shares	15.0
Retained earnings	46.2
	61.2
Non-current liabilities	
12% loan notes	20.0
Current liabilities	
Trade payables	25.2
Tax due	2.6
	27.8
Total equity and liabilities	109.0

An abridged income statement for the year ended 31 May Year 4 is as follows:

Income statement for the year ended 31 May Year 4

	£m
Sales revenue	137.4
Operating profit (profit before interest and taxation)	23.2
Interest payable	(2.4)
Profit before taxation	20.8
Tax	(5.2)
Profit for the year	15.6

A dividend of £6.0 million was paid and proposed during the year.

→

The board of directors of Semplice Ltd has decided to invest £20 million in new machinery and equipment to meet an expected increase in sales for the business's products. The expansion in production facilities is expected to result in an increase of £6 million in annual operating profit (profit before interest and taxation).

To finance the proposed investment, the board of directors is considering either:

1 a rights issue of 8 million ordinary shares at a premium of £2.25 per share, or
2 the issue of £20 million 10 per cent loan notes at nominal value.

The directors wish to increase the dividend per share by 10 per cent in the forthcoming year irrespective of the financing method chosen.

Assume a tax rate of 25 per cent.

Which financing option should be chosen?

Solution

A useful starting point in tackling this problem is to prepare a projected income statement for the year ended 31 May Year 5 under each financing option.

Projected income statement for the year ended 31 May Year 5

	Shares £m	Loan notes £m
Profit before interest and taxation (23.2 + 6.0)	29.2	29.2
Interest payable	(2.4)	(4.4)
Profit before taxation	26.8	24.8
Tax (25%)	(6.7)	(6.2)
Profit for the year	20.1	18.6

Having prepared these statements, we should consider the impact of each financing option on the overall capital structure of the business. The projected capital structure under each option will be:

	Shares £m	Loan notes £m
Equity		
Share capital – £0.25 ordinary shares (Note 1)	17.0	15.0
Share premium (Note 2)	18.0	
Retained earnings (Note 3)	58.8	58.2
	93.8	73.2
Loan capital	20.0	40.0

Notes:

1 The number of shares in issue (25p shares) for the share issue option is 68 million (£17m/£0.25) and for the loan note option is 60 million (£15m/£0.25).
2 The share premium account represents the amount received from the issue of shares that is above the nominal value of the shares. The amount is calculated as follows: 8 million × £2.25 = £18 million.
3 The retained earnings will be £58.8 (46.2 + 20.1 – 7.5 (dividends)) for the shares option and £58.2 (46.2 + 18.6 – 6.6 (dividends)) for the loan notes option.

To help us further, gearing ratios and profitability ratios may be calculated under each option.

Activity 8.14

Using the projected figures above, compute the return on ordinary shareholders' funds ratio, earnings per share, interest cover ratio, gearing ratio and degree of financial gearing, assuming the business issues:

(a) shares
(b) loan notes.

These ratios are as follows:

	Shares	Loan notes

Return on ordinary shareholders' funds (ROSF)

$$ROSF = \frac{\text{Earnings available to ordinary shareholders}}{\text{Ordinary shares plus reserves}}$$

	Shares	Loan notes
Share issue ROSF $= \dfrac{£12.6m}{£93.8m} \times 100\%$	13.4%	
Loan notes ROSF $= \dfrac{£12.0m}{£73.2m} \times 100\%$		16.4%

Earnings per share (EPS)

$$EPS = \frac{\text{Earnings available to ordinary shareholders}}{\text{No. of ordinary shares}}$$

	Shares	Loan notes
Share issue EPS $= \dfrac{£201.1m}{£68m} \times 100\%$	29.6p	
Loan notes EPS $= \dfrac{£18.6m}{£60m} \times 100\%$		31.0p

Interest cover ratio

$$\frac{\text{Profit before interest and taxation}}{\text{Interest payable}}$$

	Shares	Loan notes
Share issue interest cover ratio $= \dfrac{£29.2m}{£2.4m}$	12.2 times	
Loan notes interest cover ratio $= \dfrac{£29.2m}{£4.4m}$		6.6 times

Gearing ratio

$$= \frac{\text{Loan capital}}{\text{(Ordinary shares + Reserves + Loan capital)}} \times 100\%$$

	Shares	Loan notes
Share issue gearing ratio $= \dfrac{£20.0m}{(£93.8m + £20m)} \times 100\%$	17.6%	
Loan notes issue gearing ratio $= \dfrac{£40.0m}{(£73.2m + £40.0m)} \times 100\%$		35.3%

Degree of financial gearing

= PBIT/PBIT – I (there are no preference shares in issue)

	Shares	Loan notes
Share issue degree of financial gearing $= \dfrac{£29.2m}{(£29.2m - £2.4m)}$	1.1	
Loan note issue degree of financial gearing $= \dfrac{£29.2m}{(£29.2m - £4.4m)}$		1.2

The calculations undertaken in Activity 8.14 should help us assess the implications of each financing option.

Gearing and signalling

When a decision to change the existing level of gearing is announced, investors may interpret this as a signal concerning future prospects. For example, an increase in the level of gearing may be taken by investors to indicate management's confidence in future profitability and, as a result, share prices may rise. Managers must therefore be sensitive to the possible signals that are being transmitted to the market by their actions and, where necessary, provide further explanation.

CONSTRUCTING A PBIT–EPS INDIFFERENCE CHART

Managers may wish to know the returns to ordinary shareholders at different levels of PBIT for each of the financing options being considered. This can be presented in the form of a chart and, to show how this is done, we can use information contained in the answer to Example 8.4. The chart, which is referred to as a **PBIT–EPS indifference chart**, is set out in Figure 8.9. We can see that its vertical axis plots the earnings per share and its horizontal axis plots the profit before interest and taxation.

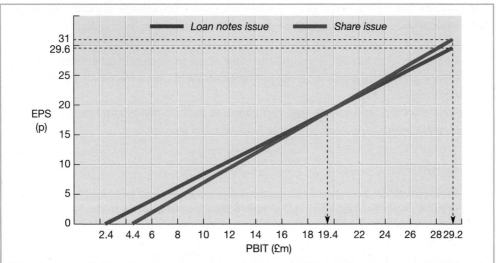

The chart reveals the returns to shareholders, as measured by earnings per share, for different levels of profit before interest and taxation of two financing options. The point at which the two lines intersect represents the level of profit before interest and tax at which both financing options provide the same rate of return to shareholders. This is referred to as the indifference point.

Figure 8.9 PBIT–EPS indifference chart for two financing options

To show the returns to shareholders at different levels of profit, we need two coordinates for each financing scheme. The first of these will be the profit before interest and taxation necessary to cover the fixed-return charges (the interest payable). For the loan notes issue, it is £4.4 million and for the ordinary share issue it is £2.4 million (see income statements above). At these points, there will be nothing available to the ordinary shareholders and so earnings per share will be zero. These points will be plotted on the vertical axis.

The second coordinate for each financing scheme will be the earnings per share at the expected PBIT. (However, an arbitrarily determined level of profit before interest and taxation could also be used.) For the loan notes issue, the earnings per share at the expected profit before interest and taxation is 31.0p, and for the ordinary share issue it is 29.6p (see earlier calculations). By joining the two coordinates relevant to each financing scheme, we have a straight line that reveals earnings per share at different levels of profit before interest and taxation.

We can see from the chart that, at lower levels of profit before interest and taxation, the ordinary share issue provides better returns to shareholders. However, the loan notes issue line has a steeper slope and returns to ordinary shareholders rise more quickly. Beyond a profit before interest and taxation of £19.4 million, ordinary shareholders begin to reap the benefits of gearing and their returns become higher under this alternative. The profit before interest and taxation of £19.4 million is referred to as the **indifference point** (that is, the point at which the two financing schemes provide the same level of return to ordinary shareholders).

The distance between the indifference point and the expected level of profit before interest and taxation provides us with a 'margin of safety'. The chart reveals a reasonable margin of safety for the loan notes option: there would have to be a fall in profit before interest and taxation of about 34 per cent before the ordinary share option became more attractive. Thus, provided the managers are confident that expected levels of profit can be maintained, the loan notes option is more attractive.

A business may consider issuing preference shares to finance a particular project. As preference dividends are paid out of profits *after taxation* this means that, when we are calculating the first coordinate for the chart, the profits *before* interest and taxation must be sufficient to cover both the dividends and the relevant tax payments. In other words, we must 'gross up' the preference dividend by the relevant tax rate to derive the profits before interest and taxation figure.

The indifference point between any two financing options can also be derived by using a simple mathematical approach. Example 8.5 illustrates the process.

Example 8.5

The information for Semplice Ltd in Example 8.4 can be used to illustrate how the indifference point is calculated.

Let x be the profit before interest and taxation (PBIT) at which the two financing options provide the same EPS.

	Shares £m	Loan notes £m
Profit before interest and taxation	x	x
Interest payable	(2.4)	(4.4)
Profit before taxation	$(x - 2.4)$	$(x - 4.4)$
Tax (25%)	$0.25(x - 2.4)$	$0.25(x - 4.4)$
Profit after taxation	$0.75(x - 2.4)$	$0.75(x - 4.4)$
EPS	$\dfrac{0.75(x - £2.4m)}{68m}$	$\dfrac{0.75(x - £4.4m)}{60m}$

Thus, the EPS of the two financing options will be equal when:

$$\frac{0.75(x - £2.4m)}{68m} = \frac{0.75(x - £4.4m)}{60m}$$

We can solve this equation as follows:

$$45x - £108m = 51x - £224.4m$$
$$6x = £116.4m$$
$$x = £19.4m$$

WHAT DETERMINES THE LEVEL OF GEARING?

In practice, the level of gearing adopted by a business is likely to be influenced by the attitude of owners, managers and lenders. The factors that each of these groups may bear in mind when making gearing decisions are considered below.

The attitude of the owners

The attitude of owners is likely to be influenced by the following:

- *Control.* Owners may be reluctant to issue more ordinary shares where it results in a dilution of control. Loan capital may therefore be viewed as a better option.
- *Flexibility.* Loan capital can often be raised more quickly than share capital, which can be important when a business operates in a fast-changing environment.
- *Debt capacity.* Too high a level of gearing may eliminate the capacity for future borrowing.
- *Risk.* Risk-averse investors will be prepared to take on more risk only where there is the opportunity for higher rates of return. Higher gearing must therefore offer the prospect of higher returns.
- *Returns.* Where shareholders are receiving relatively poor returns, they may be reluctant to provide additional share capital. Instead, they may encourage managers to try to increase their returns by exploiting the benefits of higher gearing.

These factors are summarised in Figure 8.10.

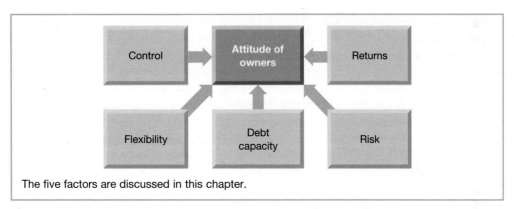

The five factors are discussed in this chapter.

Figure 8.10 Factors influencing owners' attitude to levels of gearing

The attitude of management

Although managers are meant to operate a business in the owners' best interests, they may nevertheless resist high levels of gearing if they feel that it places their income and jobs at risk. They make a big investment of 'human capital' in the business and become dependent on its continuing financial health. They cannot diversify this 'human capital' risk in the way that investors can diversify their financial capital risk.

Managers may also object to the tight financial discipline that loan capital imposes on them. They may be under constant pressure to ensure that sufficient cash is available to cover interest payments and capital repayments. Incentives may have to be offered to encourage them to take on these additional risks and pressures.

The attitude of lenders

When deciding whether to provide loan finance, lenders will be concerned with the ability of the business to repay the amount borrowed and to pay interest at the due dates. Various factors will have a bearing on these issues.

What factors are likely to influence the ability of a business to repay the amount borrowed and to pay interest at due dates?

The following factors are likely to be important:

- *Profitability*. Where a business has a stable level of profits, lenders may feel that there is less risk to their investment than where profits are volatile. Profit stability will depend on such factors as the nature of the products sold, the competitive structure of the industry and so on.
- *Cash-generating ability*. Where a business is able to generate strong, predictable cash flows, lenders may feel there is less risk to their investment.
- *Security for the loan*. The nature and quality of assets held by a business will determine whether there is adequate security for a loan. Generally speaking, lenders prefer assets that have a ready market value, which can be easily transferred and which will not deteriorate quickly (for example, property).
- *Fixed operating costs*. A business with high fixed operating costs, such as rents, has high operating risk. This is because these costs have to be paid irrespective of the profits earned. By taking on commitments to make interest payments, the business may increase its total risk to unacceptable levels.

This is not an exhaustive list: you may have thought of other factors.

Levels of gearing can vary significantly between industries. Generally speaking, gearing levels are higher in industries where profits are stable (which lenders tend to prefer). Thus, higher gearing is quite common in utilities such as electricity, gas and water businesses, which are less affected by economic recession, changes in consumer tastes and so forth.

THE CAPITAL STRUCTURE DEBATE

It may come as a surprise to discover that there is some debate in the finance literature over whether the capital structure decision really is important. There is controversy over whether the 'mix' of long-term funds employed can have an effect on the overall cost of capital of a business. If a particular mix of funds can produce a lower cost of capital, then the way in which the business is financed is important as it can affect its value. (In broad terms, the value of a business can be defined as the net present value of its future cash flows. Lowering the cost of capital, which is used as the discount rate, will increase the value of the business.)

There are two schools of thought concerning the capital structure decision, which we shall refer to as the traditional school and the modernist school. The position of each is described below.

The traditional view

According to the traditional school, the capital structure decision is very important. The traditionalists point out that the cost of loan capital is cheaper than the cost of ordinary (equity) share capital (see Chapter 6). This difference in the relative cost of finance suggests that, by increasing the level of borrowing (or gearing), the overall cost of capital of the business can be reduced. However, there are drawbacks to taking on additional borrowing. As the level of borrowing increases, ordinary shareholders will require higher levels of return on their investments to compensate for the higher levels of financial risk that they will have to bear. Existing lenders will also require higher levels of return.

The traditionalists argue, however, that at fairly low levels of borrowing, the benefits of raising finance through the use of loan capital will outweigh any costs that arise. This is because ordinary shareholders and lenders will not view low levels of borrowing as having a significant effect on the level of risk that they have to bear and so will not require a higher level of return in compensation. As the level of borrowing increases, however, things will start to change. Ordinary shareholders and existing lenders will become increasingly concerned with the higher interest charges that must be met and the risks this will pose to their own claims on the income and assets of the business. As a result, they will seek compensation for this higher level of risk in the form of higher expected returns.

The situation just described is set out in Figure 8.11. We can see that, where there are small increases in borrowing, ordinary shareholders and existing lenders do not require greatly increased returns. However, at significantly higher levels of borrowing, the risks involved take on greater importance for investors and this is reflected in the sharp rise in the returns required from each group. Note that the overall cost of capital (which is a weighted average of the cost of ordinary shares and loan capital) declines when small increases in the level of borrowing occur. However, at significantly increased levels of borrowing, the increase in required returns from ordinary (equity) shareholders and lenders will result in a sharp rise in the overall cost of capital.

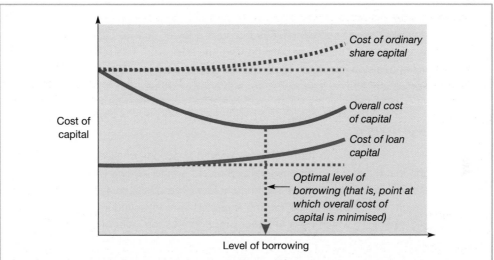

The figure assumes that at low levels of borrowing, ordinary (equity) shareholders will not require a higher level of return to compensate for the higher risk incurred. As loan finance is cheaper than ordinary share finance, this will lead to a fall in the overall cost of capital. However, this situation will change as the level of borrowing increases. At some point, the increased returns required by ordinary shareholders will begin to outweigh the benefits of cheap loan capital and so the overall cost of capital will start to rise. The implication is, therefore, that there is an optimal level of gearing for a business.

Figure 8.11 The traditional view of the relationship between levels of borrowing and expected returns

An important implication of the above analysis is that managers of the business should try to establish that mix of loan/equity finance that will minimise the overall cost of capital. At this point, the business will be said to achieve an **optimal capital structure**. Minimising the overall cost of capital in this way will maximise the value of the business (that is, the net present value of future cash flows). This relationship between the level of borrowing, the cost of capital and business value is illustrated in Figure 8.12.

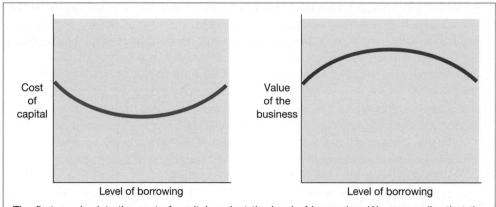

The first graph plots the cost of capital against the level of borrowing. We saw earlier that the traditionalist view suggests that, in the first instance, the cost of capital will fall as the level of borrowing increases. However, at higher levels of borrowing, the overall cost of capital will begin to increase. The second graph plots the level of borrowing against the value of the business. This is the inverse of the first graph. As the cost of capital decreases, so the value increases, and vice versa.

Figure 8.12 The relationship between the level of borrowing, the cost of capital and business value: the traditional view

We can see that the graph of the value of the business displays an inverse pattern to the graph of the overall cost of capital. (This is because a lower cost of capital will result in a higher net present value for the future cash flows of the business.) This relationship suggests that the financing decision is critical. Failure to identify and achieve the right financing 'mix' could have serious adverse consequences for shareholder wealth.

The modernist view

Modigliani and Miller (MM), who represent the modernist school, challenged the traditional view by arguing that the required returns to shareholders and to lenders would not follow the pattern as set out above. They argued that shareholders in a business with financial gearing will expect a return that is equal to the returns expected from investing in a similar ungeared business plus a premium, which rises in *direct proportion* to the level of gearing. Thus, the increase in returns required for ordinary shareholders as compensation for increased financial risk will rise in constant proportion to the increase in the level of borrowing over the *whole range of borrowing.* This pattern contrasts with the traditional view, of course, which displays an uneven change in the required rate of return over the range of borrowing.

The MM analysis also assumes that the returns required from borrowers would remain constant as the level of borrowing increases. This latter point may appear strange at first sight. However, if lenders have good security for the loans made to the business, they are unlikely to feel at risk from additional borrowing and therefore will not seek additional returns. This is provided, of course, that the business does not exceed its borrowing capacity.

The MM position is set out in Figure 8.13. As you can see, the overall cost of capital remains constant at varying levels of borrowing. This is because the benefits obtained from raising finance through borrowing, which is cheaper than share capital, are exactly offset by the increase in required returns from ordinary shareholders.

An important implication of the MM view is that the financing decision is not really important. Figure 8.13 shows that there is no optimal capital structure for a business, as suggested by the traditionalists, because the overall cost of capital remains constant. This means that one particular capital structure is no better or worse than any other and so managers should not spend time on evaluating different forms of financing 'mixes' for the business. Instead, they should concentrate their efforts on evaluating and managing the investments of the business.

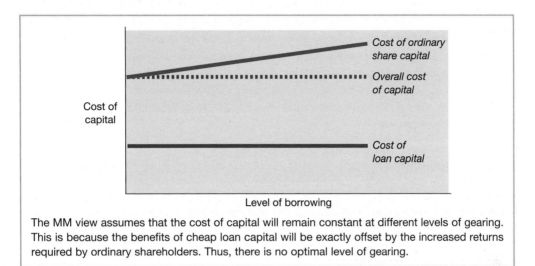

The MM view assumes that the cost of capital will remain constant at different levels of gearing. This is because the benefits of cheap loan capital will be exactly offset by the increased returns required by ordinary shareholders. Thus, there is no optimal level of gearing.

Figure 8.13 The MM view of the relationship between levels of borrowing and expected returns

Activity 8.17

In Figure 8.13 we saw the traditional view of the relationships between the cost of capital and the level of borrowing and the relationship between the value of the business and the level of borrowing. How would the MM view of these two relationships be shown in graphical form?

The relationship between (i) the level of borrowing and the cost of capital and (ii) the level of borrowing and the value of the business, as viewed by MM, is set out in Figure 8.14.

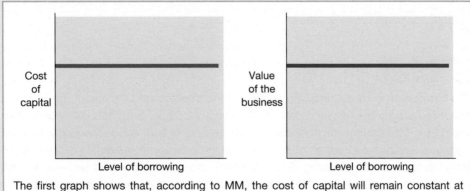

The first graph shows that, according to MM, the cost of capital will remain constant at different levels of borrowing. The second graph shows the implication of this for the value of the business. As the cost of capital is constant, the net present value of future cash flows from the business will not be affected by the level of borrowing. Hence, the value of the business will remain constant.

Figure 8.14 The relationship between the level of borrowing, the cost of capital and business value: the MM view

Although the views of Modigliani and Miller were first published in the late 1950s, they are described as modernists because they base their position on economic theory (unlike the traditional school). They argue that the value of a business is determined by the future income from its investments, and the risk associated with those investments, and not by the way in which this income is divided among the different providers of finance. In other words, it is not possible to increase the value of a business (that is, lower the overall cost of capital) simply by borrowing, as the traditionalists suggest. MM point out that borrowing is not something that only businesses are able to undertake; borrowing can also be undertaken by individual investors. As business borrowing can be replicated by individual investors, there is no reason why it should create additional value for the investor. **(Un)Real World 8.8** explains the theory from a lighter perspective.

(UN)Real World 8.8

To really understand MM . . . start with a pizza

We have just seen that it is the income-generating power and risks associated with the underlying investments of the business, rather than the different ways in which a business may be financed, that determine the value of a business. This point was once explained by Miller (of Modigliani and Miller fame) as follows:

> Think of the firm as a gigantic pizza, divided into quarters. If now, you cut each quarter in half into eighths, the M&M proposition says that you will have more pieces, but not more pizza.

In other words, different financing methods will have an effect on how the business investments and income stream will be divided up but will not affect the value of these.

Footnote: However, Miller's view of pizzas, like his view of capital structure, may be controversial. When Yogi Berra, a famous US baseball player, was asked whether he would like his pizza cut into six or eight pieces, he is reputed to have said, 'Better make it six, I don't think I can eat eight' (see reference 1 at the end of the chapter).

A simple example may help to illustrate the MM position that business borrowing should not create additional value for a business.

Example 8.6

Two businesses, Delta plc and Omega plc, are identical except for the fact that Delta plc is financed entirely by ordinary shares and Omega plc is 50 per cent financed by loans. The profit before interest for each business for the year is £2 million. The ordinary shareholders of Delta plc require a return of 12 per cent and the ordinary shareholders of Omega plc require a return of 14 per cent. Omega plc pays 10 per cent interest per year on the £10 million loans outstanding. (Tax is ignored for reasons that we shall discuss later.)

	Delta plc	Omega plc
	£m	£m
Profits before interest	2.0	2.0
Interest payable	–	(1.0)
Available to ordinary shareholders	2.0	1.0

The market value of the total ordinary shares of each business will be equivalent to the profits capitalised at the required rate of return. Thus, the market value of each business is as follows:

	Delta plc £m	Omega plc £m
Market value of ordinary (equity) shares:		
(£2m/0.12)	16.7	
(£1m/0.14)		7.1
Market value of loan capital	–	10.0
Market value of each business	16.7	17.1

MM argue that differences in the way in which each business is financed cannot result in a higher value for Omega plc as shown above. This is because an investor who owns, say, 10 per cent of the shares in Omega plc would be able to obtain the same level of income from investing in Delta plc, for the same level of risk as the investment in Omega plc and for a lower net investment. The investor, by borrowing an amount equivalent to 10 per cent of the loans of Omega plc (that is, an amount proportional to the ownership interest in Omega plc), and selling the shares held in Omega plc in order to finance the purchase of a 10 per cent equity stake in Delta plc, would be in the following position:

	£000
Return from 10% equity investment in Delta plc (£2m × 10%)	200
Interest on borrowing (£1,000 × 10%)	(100)
Net return	100
Purchase of shares (10% × £16.7m)	1,670
Amount borrowed	(1,000)
Net investment in Delta plc	670

The investor with a 10 per cent stake in the ordinary share capital of Omega plc is, currently, in the following position:

	£000
Return from 10% investment in Omega plc (£1m × 10%)	100
Net investment in Omega plc: existing shareholding (10% × £7.1m)	710

As we can see, the investor would be better off by taking on personal borrowing in order to acquire a 10 per cent share of the ordinary share capital of the ungeared business, Delta plc, than by continuing to invest in the geared business, Omega plc. The effect of a number of investors switching investments in this way would be to reduce the value of the shares in Omega plc (thereby increasing the returns to ordinary shareholders in Omega plc), and to increase the value of shares in Delta plc (thereby reducing the returns to equity in Delta plc). This switching from Omega plc to Delta plc (which is referred to as an arbitrage transaction) would continue until the returns from each investment were the same, and so no further gains could be made from such transactions. At this point, the value of each business would be identical.

The MM analysis, while extremely rigorous and logical, is based on a number of restrictive assumptions. These include the following.

Perfect capital markets

The assumption of perfect capital markets means that there are no share transaction costs and investors and businesses can borrow unlimited amounts at the same rates of interest. Although these assumptions may be unrealistic, they may not have a significant effect on the arguments made. Where the prospect of 'arbitrage' gains (that is, selling shares in an overvalued business and buying shares in an undervalued business) is substantial, share transaction costs are unlikely to be an important issue as the potential benefits will outweigh the costs. It is only at the margin that share transaction costs will take on significance.

Similarly, the assumption that investors can borrow unlimited amounts at the same rate of interest may only take on significance at the margin. We have seen that the UK stock market is dominated by large investment institutions such as pension funds, unit trusts and insurance businesses that hold a very large proportion of all shares issued by listed businesses. These institutions may well be able to borrow very large amounts at similar rates to those offered to a business.

No bankruptcy costs

Assuming that there are no bankruptcy costs means that, if a business were liquidated, no legal and administrative fees would be incurred and the business assets could be sold at a price that would enable shareholders to receive cash equal to the market value of their shareholding prior to the liquidation. This assumption will not hold true in the real world where bankruptcy costs can be very high.

However, it is only at high levels of gearing that bankruptcy costs are likely to be a real issue. We saw in Chapter 6 that borrowing leads to a commitment to pay interest and to repay capital: the higher the level of borrowing, the higher the level of commitment and the higher the risk that this commitment will not be met. In the case of a low-geared, or moderately geared, business it may be possible to take on additional borrowing, if necessary, to meet commitments, whereas a highly geared business may have no further debt capacity.

Risk

It is assumed that businesses exist that have identical operating risks but with different levels of borrowing. Although this is unlikely to be true, it does not affect the validity of MM's arguments.

No taxation

A world without corporate or personal income taxes is clearly an unrealistic assumption. The real issue, however, is whether this undermines the validity of MM's arguments. We shall therefore consider next the effect on the MM position of introducing taxes.

MM and the introduction of taxation

MM were subject to much criticism for not dealing with the problem of taxation in their analysis. This led them to revise their position so as to include taxation. They acknowledged in their revised analysis that the tax relief from interest payments on loans provides a real benefit to ordinary shareholders. The more the level of borrowing increases, the more tax relief the business receives and so the smaller the tax liability of the business will become.

We should recall that the original MM position was that the benefits of cheap loan capital will be exactly offset by increases in the required rate of return by ordinary share investors. Tax relief on loan interest should, therefore, represent an additional benefit to shareholders. As the amount of tax relief increases with the amount of borrowing, the overall cost of capital (after tax) will be lowered as the level of borrowing increases. The implication of this revised position is that there is an optimal level of gearing and it is at 100 per cent gearing. In Figure 8.15, we can see the MM position after taxation has been introduced.

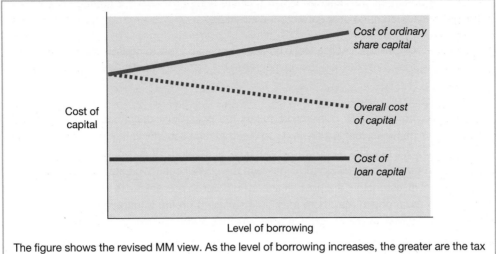

The figure shows the revised MM view. As the level of borrowing increases, the greater are the tax benefits to ordinary (equity) shareholders. These tax benefits will increase with the level of borrowing and so the overall cost of capital (after tax) will be lowered as the level of borrowing increases. This means that there is an optimal level of gearing and it is at the 100 per cent level of gearing.

Figure 8.15 The MM view of the relationship between levels of borrowing and expected returns (including tax effects)

Thus, the MM position moves closer to the traditional position in so far as it recognises a relationship between the value of the business and the way in which it is financed. It also recognises that there is an optimal level of gearing.

The relationship between (a) the level of borrowing and the cost of capital and (b) the level of borrowing and business value, after taking into account the tax effects, is set out in Figure 8.16.

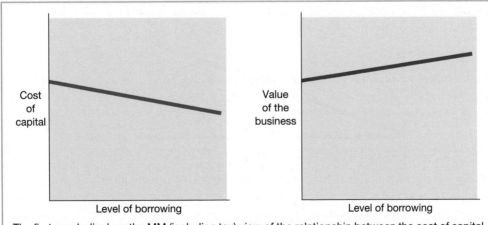

The first graph displays the MM (including tax) view of the relationship between the cost of capital and the level of borrowing. We can see that as the level of borrowing increases, the overall cost of capital decreases. The second graph shows the relationship between the value of the business and the level of borrowing. A decrease in the overall cost of capital results in a rise in the value of the business and so, as the level of borrowing increases, the value of the business increases.

Figure 8.16 The relationship between the level of borrowing, the cost of capital and business value: the MM view (including tax effects)

Activity 8.18

What do you think is the main implication of the above analysis for managers who are trying to decide on an appropriate capital structure?

This revised MM analysis implies that a business should borrow to capacity as this will lower the post-tax cost of capital and thereby increase the value of the business.

In practice, however, few businesses follow the policy just described. When borrowing reaches very high levels, lenders are likely to feel that their security is threatened and ordinary share investors will feel that bankruptcy risks have increased. Thus, both groups are likely to seek higher returns, which will, in turn, increase the overall cost of capital. (A business would have to attract investors that are not risk averse in order to prevent a rise in its cost of capital.) There is also the problem that there may be insufficient profits to exploit the benefits of tax relief on loan interest. In other words, a business may suffer **tax exhaustion** before reaching 100 per cent gearing.

The trade-off theory of capital structure

The **trade-off theory of capital structure** offers an explanation as to why many businesses settle for moderate levels of gearing. The theory takes into account the risk of bankruptcy mentioned above. It asserts that, when a business is deciding upon an appropriate level of gearing, it will weigh the benefits of taking on borrowing, in the form of tax benefits, against the costs involved, in the form of higher bankruptcy risk. The theory is set out in diagrammatic form in Figure 8.17.

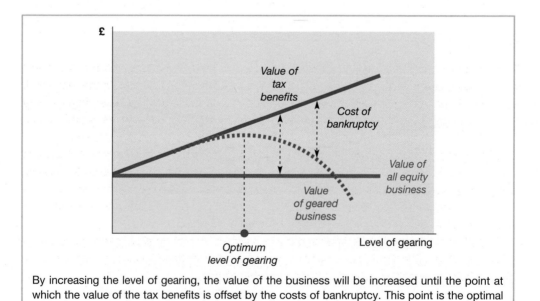

By increasing the level of gearing, the value of the business will be increased until the point at which the value of the tax benefits is offset by the costs of bankruptcy. This point is the optimal capital structure for the business.

Figure 8.17 The trade-off theory of capital structure

The horizontal line represents the value of the business when it is entirely financed by equity. By increasing the level of gearing, the value of tax benefits from borrowing increases. The business has an incentive to take on additional gearing as long as these tax benefits are greater than the bankruptcy costs. Figure 8.17 shows that the value of the geared business, as represented by the curved line, increases under these circumstances. When the point is reached where the tax benefits gained are just offset by the costs of bankruptcy, the optimal level of gearing has been achieved. Beyond this point, the tax benefits are outweighed by the costs of bankruptcy and the value of the geared business starts to fall.

Trade-off theory has undoubted appeal: it is quite true that taking on loan capital can be tax efficient but can also be risky. The problem is that, for many businesses, the tax benefits are substantial and certain, whereas bankruptcy risks are neither. If this theory provided the complete answer, we should expect much higher levels of gearing among businesses than those which actually exist. Weighing tax benefits against bankruptcy risk may, nevertheless, play some role in the capital structure decision.

Activity 8.19

In Chapter 6 we came across an alternative theory as to the way in which different sources of long-term capital are included in the capital structure of a business. Can you recall what it is and explain how it differs from the trade-off theory just described?

In Chapter 6 we examined pecking order theory. This theory does not focus on the balancing of the costs and benefits of borrowing in the way just described. Instead, it asserts that businesses have a hierarchy of preferences when raising long-term capital. They will first look to retained earnings, followed by borrowing and, finally, to the issue of new equity shares. This theory implies that there is no clearly defined optimal capital structure.

Some final points

The debate concerning capital structure rumbles on. The arguments of the traditional school have undoubtedly been undermined by the inexorable logic of MM. In the real world, however, it appears that businesses settle for moderate levels of gearing rather than the very high levels suggested by the MM (including tax) arguments. The trade-off theory offers some help in understanding why this may be so, but does not offer a complete explanation.

So far, no theory can fully explain why businesses adopt the particular capital structures that they do. We saw earlier that many factors can influence the capital structure decision. Furthermore, these factors can vary in intensity between businesses. (How else can we explain why there is such variation in gearing levels?) Thus, while a business may have an optimal capital structure, searching for it could well end in failure.

Real World 8.9 reveals how one large business takes on high levels of gearing in order to minimise its cost of capital. It is a utility business and, as mentioned earlier, greater certainty of cash flows probably enables it to become highly geared.

All geared up

Pennon Group plc is a large water, sewerage and waste management business. One of its main businesses is South West Water. In its 2012 annual report it states:

> The Group's objectives when managing capital are to safeguard the Group's ability to continue as a going concern in order to provide returns for shareholders and benefits for other stakeholders and to maintain an optimal capital structure to minimise the cost of capital.
>
> In order to maintain or adjust the capital structure the Group seeks to maintain a balance of returns to shareholders through dividends and an appropriate capital structure of debt and equity for each business segment and the Group.
>
> The Group monitors capital on the basis of the gearing ratio. This ratio is calculated as net borrowings divided by total capital. Net borrowings are . . . calculated as total borrowings less cash and cash deposits. Total capital is calculated as total shareholders' equity plus net borrowings.
>
> The gearing ratios at the balance sheet (statement of financial position) date were:

	2012	2011
	£m	£m
Net borrowings	2,104.6	1,933.8
Total shareholders' equity	822.1	779.5
Total capital	2,926.7	2,713.3
Gearing ratio	71.9%	71.3%

Source: Pennon Group plc Annual Report and Accounts 2012, p. 75.

Russell Ltd instals and services heating and ventilation systems for commercial premises. The most recent financial statements of the business are set out below:

Statement of financial position as at 31 May Year 4

	£000
ASSETS	
Non-current assets	
Machinery and equipment	555.2
Motor vehicles	186.6
	741.8
Current assets	
Inventories	293.2
Trade receivables	510.3
Cash at bank	18.4
	821.9
Total assets	1,563.7

	£000
EQUITY AND LIABILITIES	
Equity	
£1 ordinary shares	400.0
General reserve	52.2
Retained earnings	380.2
	832.4
Non-current liabilities	
12% loan notes (repayable Year 10/11)	250.0
Current liabilities	
Trade payables	417.3
Tax due	64.0
	481.3
Total equity and liabilities	1,563.7

Income statement for the year ended 31 May Year 4

	£000
Sales revenue	5,207.8
Operating profit (profit before interest and taxation)	542.0
Interest payable	(30.0)
Profit before taxation	512.0
Tax (25%)	(128.0)
Profit for the year	384.0

A dividend of £153,600 was proposed and paid during the year.

The business wishes to invest in more machinery and equipment in order to cope with an upsurge in demand for its services. Additional operating profit (profit before interest and taxation) of £120,000 per year is expected if an investment of £600,000 is made in plant and machinery.

The directors of the business are considering an offer from a private-equity firm to finance the expansion programme. The finance will be made available immediately through either:

(i)   an issue of £1 ordinary shares at a premium on nominal value of £3 per share, or
(ii) an issue of £600,000 10% loan notes at nominal value.

The directors of the business wish to maintain the same dividend payout ratio in future years as in past years, whichever method of finance is chosen.

Required:
(a) For each of the financing schemes:
   (i)   Prepare a projected income statement for the year ended 31 May Year 5.
   (ii) Calculate the projected earnings per share for the year ended 31 May Year 5.
   (iii) Calculate the projected level of gearing as at 31 May Year 5.
(b) Briefly assess both of the financing schemes under consideration from the viewpoint of the existing shareholders.
(c) Calculate the level of operating profit (profit before interest and taxation) at which the earnings per share under each of the financing options will be the same.

The answer to this question can be found at the back of the book on pp. 567–568.

SUMMARY

The main points in this chapter may be summarised as follows:

Cost of capital

■ The opportunity cost reflects the returns from investments with the same level of risk.

■ There are two major approaches to determining the cost of ordinary (equity) shares: the dividend-based approach and the risk/return (CAPM) approach.

■ The dividend-based approach values shares according to the future dividends received.

■ Dividend valuation models often assume constant dividends over time ($K_0 = D_1/P_0$) or that dividends will grow at a constant rate ($K_0 = (D_1/P_0) + g$).

■ The risk/return approach is based on the idea that the cost of an ordinary share is made up of a risk-free rate of return plus a risk premium.

■ The risk premium is calculated by measuring the risk premium for the market as a whole, then measuring the returns from a particular share relative to the market and applying this measure to the market risk premium ($K_0 = K_{RF} + b(K_m - K_{RF})$).

■ The cost of irredeemable loan capital can be derived in a similar way to that of ordinary shares where the dividend stays constant ($K_d = I(1 - t)/P_d$). However, taxation must also be taken into account.

■ The cost of redeemable loan capital can be computed using an IRR approach.

■ The cost of preference share capital can be derived in a similar way to that of ordinary shares where the dividend stays constant ($K_p = D_p/P_p$).

■ The weighted average cost of capital (WACC) is derived by taking the cost of each element of capital and weighting each element in proportion to the target capital structure.

Financial gearing

■ The effect of financial gearing is that changes in profit before interest and taxation (PBIT) result in disproportionate changes in the returns to ordinary shareholders.

■ Gearing results in a loss of financial flexibility.

■ The degree of financial gearing measures the sensitivity of changes in returns to ordinary shareholders to changes in PBIT.

■ A PBIT–EPS indifference chart can be constructed to reveal the returns to shareholders at different levels of PBIT for different financing options.

■ Gearing levels will be determined by the attitude of owners, managers and lenders.

The capital structure debate

■ There are two schools of thought.

■ The traditional view is that the capital structure decision is important whereas the modernist view (without taxes) is that it is not.

Traditional viewpoint

■ Traditionalists argue that, at lower levels of gearing, shareholders and lenders are unconcerned about risk; however, at higher levels they become concerned and demand higher returns.

- This leads to an increase in WACC.

- WACC decreases at lower levels of gearing (because investors do not demand increased returns) but then increases.

- This means that there is an optimal level of gearing.

Modernist viewpoint

- Modernists (MM) argue that shareholders are always concerned about the level of gearing.

- Cheaper loan finance is offset by increasing the cost of ordinary shares and so the cost of capital remains constant.

- This means that there is no optimal level of gearing.

- If tax is introduced, the modernist view is changed.

- Tax benefits arising from interest payments should be exploited by taking on loan capital up to 100 per cent gearing.

- In practice, bankruptcy risk, the risk to lenders' security and tax exhaustion may prevent a business taking on very high levels of gearing.

- The trade-off theory of capital structure suggests that a business will take on additional gearing until the point is reached where the tax benefits from loan interest are just offset by the bankruptcy costs.

KEY TERMS

Capital asset pricing model (CAPM)
   p. 319
Beta p. 320
**Weighted average cost of capital
   (WACC)** p. 331
Degree of financial gearing p. 339
PBIT–EPS indifference chart p. 344

Indifference point p. 345
Optimal capital structure p. 349
Arbitrage transaction p. 353
Tax exhaustion p. 356
Trade-off theory of capital structure
   p. 356

For definitions of these terms see the Glossary, pp. 605–613.

REFERENCES

1 Quoted in Hawawini, G. and Viallet, C. (2002) *Finance for Executives*, 2nd edn, South Western/Thomson Learning, p. 353.

2 Dimson, E., Marsh, P. and Staunton, M. (2002) Triumph of the Optimists: 101 years of global investment returns, Princeton University Press.

FURTHER READING

If you wish to explore the topics discussed in this chapter in more depth, try the following books:

Arnold, G. (2013) *Corporate Financial Management*, 5th edn, Pearson, Chapters 8, 16 and 18.

Brigham E. and Ehrhardt, M. (2010) *Financial Management: Theory and practice*, 13th edn, South-Western Cengage Learning, Chapter 15.

McLaney, E. (2012) *Business Finance: Theory and practice*, 9th edn, Financial Times Prentice Hall, Chapters 10 and 11.

Pike, R., Neale, B. and Linsley, P. (2012) *Corporate Finance and Investment*, 7th edn, Pearson, Chapters 18 and 19.

REVIEW QUESTIONS

Answers to these questions can be found at the back of the book on p. 576.

8.1 How might a business find out whether a particular planned level of gearing would be acceptable to investors?

8.2 What factors might a prospective lender take into account when deciding whether to make a long-term loan to a particular business?

8.3 Should the specific cost of raising finance for a particular project be used as the appropriate discount rate for investment appraisal purposes? Why?

8.4 What are the main implications for the financial manager who accepts the arguments of the following approaches concerning capital structure?

(a) Traditional approach.
(b) MM (excluding tax effects) approach.
(c) MM (including tax effects) approach.

EXERCISES

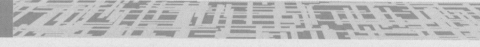

Exercises 8.5 to 8.7 are more advanced than 8.1 to 8.4. Those with coloured numbers have solutions at the back of the book, starting on p. 593.

If you wish to try more exercises, visit the students' side of this book's companion website.

8.1 Riphean plc and Silurian plc are two businesses operating in different industries. They are both financed by a mixture of ordinary share and loan capital and both are seeking to derive the cost of capital for investment decision-making purposes. The following information is available concerning the two businesses for the year to 30 November Year 8:

	Riphean plc	Silurian plc
Profit for the year	£3.0m	£4.0m
Gross dividends	£1.5m	£2.0m
Market value per ordinary share	£4.00	£1.60
Number of ordinary shares	5m	10m
Gross interest yield on loan capital	8%	12%
Market value of loan capital	£10m	£16m

The annual growth rate in dividends is 5 per cent for Riphean plc and 8 per cent for Silurian plc. Assume a 30 per cent tax rate.

Required:

(a) Calculate the weighted average cost of capital of Riphean plc and Silurian plc using the information provided.

(b) Discuss two possible reasons why the cost of ordinary share capital differs between the two businesses.

(c) Discuss two limitations of using the weighted average cost of capital when making investment decisions.

8.2 Celtor plc is a property development business operating in the London area. The business has the following capital structure as at 30 November Year 9:

	£000
£1 ordinary shares	10,000
Retained earnings	20,000
9% loan notes	12,000
	42,000

The ordinary shares have a current market value of £3.90 and the current level of dividend is 20p per share. The dividend has been growing at a compound rate of 4 per cent a year in recent years. The loan notes of the business are irredeemable and have a current market value of £80 per £100 nominal. Interest due on the loan notes at the year end has recently been paid.

The business has obtained planning permission to build a new office block in a redevelopment area. The business wishes to raise the whole of the finance necessary for the project by the issue of more irredeemable 9 per cent loan notes at £80 per £100 nominal. This is in line with a target capital structure set by the business where the amount of loan capital will increase to 70 per cent of ordinary share capital within the next two years. The tax rate is 25 per cent.

Required:

(a) Explain what is meant by the term 'cost of capital'. Why is it important for a business to calculate its cost of capital with care?

(b) Calculate the weighted average cost of capital of Celtor plc that should be used for future investment decisions.

8.3 Grenache plc operates a chain of sports shops throughout the UK. In recent years competition has been fierce and profits and sales have declined. The most recent financial statements of the business are as follows:

Statement of financial position as at 30 April Year 7

	£m
ASSETS	
Non-current assets	
Premises	46.3
Fixtures, fittings and equipment	16.1
	62.4
Current assets	
Inventories	52.4
Trade receivables	2.3
Cash	1.2
	55.9
Total assets	118.3

EQUITY AND LIABILITIES
Equity

£1 ordinary shares	25.0
Retained earnings	18.6
	43.6

Non-current liabilities

10% loan notes	25.0

Current liabilities

Trade payables	48.1
Tax due	1.6
	49.7
Total equity and liabilities	118.3

Income statement for the year ended 30 April Year 7

	£m
Sales revenue	148.8
Operating profit	15.7
Interest payable	(2.5)
Profit before taxation	13.2
Tax (25%)	(3.3)
Profit for the year	9.9

A dividend of £5.2 million was proposed and paid during the year.

A new chief executive was appointed during Year 7 to improve the performance of the business. She plans a 'sand and surf' image for the business in order to appeal to the younger market. This will require a large investment in new inventories and a complete redesign and refurbishment of the shops. The cost of implementing the plan is estimated to be £30 million.

The business is considering two possible financing options. The first option is to issue further 10 per cent loan notes at nominal value. The second option is to make a rights issue based on a 20 per cent discount on the current market value of the shares. The market capitalisation of the business is currently £187.5 million.

The future performance following the relaunch of the business is not certain. Three scenarios have been prepared concerning the possible effects on annual operating profits (profits before interest and taxation):

Scenario	Change in operating profits compared with most recent year %
Optimistic	+40
Most likely	+15
Pessimistic	−25

The dividend per share to be proposed and paid will increase by 10 per cent during the forthcoming year if there is an increase in profit but will decrease by 20 per cent if there is a reduction in profit.

The business has a current gearing ratio that is broadly in line with its competitors.

Required:

(a) Prepare, in so far as the information allows, a projected income statement for the forthcoming year for each scenario assuming:

(i)   a loan notes issue is made

(ii) a rights issue of shares is made.

Workings should be in £ million and to one decimal place.

(b) Calculate for each scenario:
  (i)   the earnings per share
  (ii) the gearing ratio for the forthcoming year
  both when a loan notes issue is made and when a rights issue of shares is made.
(c) Assess the future plans and financing options being considered from the perspective of a current shareholder and state what additional information, if any, you may require to make a more considered assessment.

8.4 Trexon plc is a major oil and gas exploration business that has most of its operations in the Middle East and South-East Asia. Recently, the business acquired rights to explore for oil and gas in the Gulf of Mexico. Trexon plc proposes to finance the new operations from the issue of ordinary shares. At present, the business is financed by a combination of ordinary share capital and loan capital. The ordinary shares have a nominal value of £0.50 and a current market value of £2.60. The current level of dividend is £0.16 per share and this has been growing at a compound rate of 6 per cent a year in recent years. The loan capital is irredeemable and has a current market value of £94 per £100 nominal. Interest on the loan capital is at the rate of 12 per cent and interest due at the year end has recently been paid. At present, the business expects 60 per cent of its finance to come from ordinary share capital and the rest from loan capital. In the future, however, the business will aim to finance 70 per cent of its operations from ordinary share capital.

When the proposal to finance the new operations via the rights issue of shares was announced at the annual general meeting of the business, objections were raised by two shareholders present, as follows:

■ *Shareholder A argued*: 'I fail to understand why the business has decided to issue shares to finance the new operation. Surely it would be better to reinvest profit, as this is, in effect, a free source of finance.'

■ *Shareholder B argued*: 'I also fail to understand why the business has decided to issue shares to finance the new operation. However, I do not agree with the suggestion made by Shareholder A. I do not believe that shareholder funds should be used at all to finance the new operation. Instead, the business should issue more loan capital, as it is cheap relative to ordinary share capital and would, therefore, reduce the overall cost of capital of the business.'

Tax is at the rate of 35 per cent.

Required:
(a) Calculate the weighted average cost of capital of Trexon plc that should be used in future investment decisions.
(b) Comment on the remarks made by:
  (i)   Shareholder A
  (ii) Shareholder B.

8.5 Ashcroft plc, a family-controlled business, is considering raising additional funds to modernise its factory. The scheme is expected to cost £2.34 million and will increase annual operating profits (profits before interest and tax) from 1 January Year 4 by £0.6 million. A summarised statement of financial position and an income statement are shown below. Currently the share price is 200p.

Two schemes have been suggested: (a) 1.3 million shares could be issued at 180p (net of issue costs); (b) a consortium of six City institutions has offered to buy loan notes from the business totalling £2.34 million. Interest would be at the rate of 13 per cent per year and capital repayments of equal annual instalments of £234,000 starting on 1 January Year 5 would be required.

Statement of financial position as at 31 December Year 3

	£m
ASSETS	
Non-current assets	1.4
Current assets	
Inventories	2.4
Trade receivables	2.2
	4.6
Total assets	6.0
EQUITY AND LIABILITIES	
Equity	
Share capital, 25p ordinary shares	1.0
Retained earnings	1.5
	2.5
Current liabilities	
Trade payables	3.2
Tax due	0.3
	3.5
Total equity and liabilities	6.0

Income statement for the year ended 31 December Year 3

	£m
Sales revenue	11.2
Operating profit	1.2
Tax	(0.6)
Profit for the year	0.6

Dividends of £0.3 million were proposed and paid during the year. Assume tax is charged at the rate of 50 per cent.

Required:

(a) Compute the earnings per share for Year 4 under the loan notes and the ordinary share alternatives.

(b) Compute the level of operating profit (profit before interest and taxation) at which the earnings per share under the two schemes will be equal.

(c) Discuss the considerations the directors should take into account before deciding between loan notes or ordinary share finance.

8.6 Hatleigh plc is a medium-sized engineering business. The financial statements for the year ended 30 April Year 8 are as follows:

Statement of financial position as at 30 April Year 8

	£000
ASSETS	
Non-current assets	
Property	3,885
Plant and machinery	2,520
Motor vehicles	1,470
	7,875
Current assets	
Inventories	8,380
Trade receivables	8,578
	16,958
Total assets	24,833
EQUITY AND LIABILITIES	
Equity	
Share capital (25p shares)	8,000
Retained earnings	5,034
	13,034
Non-current liabilities	
10% loan notes Years 13–14 (secured on property)	3,500
Current liabilities	
Trade payables	3,322
Bank overdraft	4,776
Tax due	201
	8,299
Total equity and liabilities	24,833

Income statement for the year ended 30 April Year 8

	£000
Sales revenue	34,246
Cost of sales	(24,540)
Gross profit	9,706
Expenses	(7,564)
Operating profit	2,142
Interest	(994)
Profit before taxation	1,148
Tax (35%)	(402)
Profit for the year	746

A dividend of £600,000 was proposed and paid during the year.

The business made a one-for-four rights issue of ordinary shares during the year. Sales for the forthcoming year are forecast to be the same as for the year to 30 April Year 8. The gross profit margin is likely to stay the same as in previous years but expenses (excluding interest payments) are likely to fall by 10 per cent as a result of economies.

The bank has been concerned that the business has persistently exceeded the agreed overdraft limits and, as a result, the business has now been asked to reduce its overdraft to £3 million over the next three months. The business has agreed to do this and has calculated that interest on the bank overdraft for the forthcoming year will be £440,000 (after taking account of the required reduction in the overdraft). In order to achieve the reduction in overdraft, the chairman of Hatleigh plc is considering either the issue of more ordinary shares for cash to existing shareholders at a discount of 20 per cent, or the issue of more 10 per cent loan notes redeemable Years 13–14 at the end of July Year 8. It is believed that the share price will be £1.50 and the 10 per cent loan notes will be quoted at £82 per £100 nominal value at the end of July Year 8. The bank overdraft is expected to remain at the amount shown in the statement of financial position until that date. Any issue costs relating to new shares or loan notes should be ignored.

Required:

(a) Calculate:
  (i) the total number of shares
  (ii) the total nominal value of loan notes
  that will have to be issued in order to raise the funds necessary to reduce the overdraft to the level required by the bank.

(b) Calculate the projected earnings per share for the year to 30 April Year 9 assuming:
  (i) the issue of shares
  (ii) the issue of loan notes
  are carried out to reduce the overdraft to the level required by the bank.

(c) Critically evaluate the proposal of the chairman to raise the necessary funds by the issue of:
  (i) shares
  (ii) loan notes.

8.7 Jubilee plc operates four wholesale food outlets. After several years of sales and profits growth the business has recently experienced some financial problems. The financial statements for the year ended 31 May Year 6 are shown below:

Statement of financial position as at 31 May Year 6

	£000
ASSETS	
Non-current assets	
Property	4,600
Fixtures and fittings	90
Motor vans	115
	4,805
Current assets	
Inventories	5,208
Trade receivables	5,240
Cash	6
	10,454
Total assets	15,259
EQUITY AND LIABILITIES	
Equity	
£1 ordinary shares	1,400
Retained earnings	2,706
	4,106
Non-current liabilities	
11% loan notes Years 10–11 (secured on property)	3,800
Current liabilities	
Trade payables	4,100
Tax due	53
Bank overdraft	3,200
	7,353
Total equity and liabilities	15,259

Income statement for the year ended 31 May Year 6

	£000
Sales revenue	45,000
Cost of sales	(36,000)
Gross profit	9,000
Expenses	(7,600)
Operating profit	1,400
Interest payable	(1,050)
Profit before taxation	350
Tax (30%)	(105)
Profit for the year	245

Dividends of £140,000 were proposed and paid during the year. Inventories levels remained constant throughout the year. All sales and purchases are on credit.

In recent months the business has failed to pay trade payables within the agreed credit periods. In order to restore its credit standing, the business wishes to reduce its trade payables to an average of 30 days' credit (all purchases are on credit). In addition, the business wishes to refurbish its outlets and to acquire a computerised accounting system at a total cost of £700,000. To finance these requirements, the business is considering making a rights issue of shares at a discount of 25 per cent on the market value. At present, shares are trading on the Stock Exchange at £1.60. Alternatively, the business may make an issue of 10 per cent loan notes at a price of £96 per £100 nominal value to be secured on the property.

In the forthcoming year, sales are expected to increase by 10 per cent and the gross profit margin is likely to remain the same as for the year ended 31 May Year 6. Expenses are likely to rise by 5 per cent during the forthcoming year. Interest charges on the overdraft are expected to be lower, due largely to falling interest rates, at £260,000. Dividends per share are planned to be the same as in the year to 31 May Year 6.

The raising of the necessary finance is expected to take place at the beginning of the year to 31 May Year 7. Issue costs relating to new shares and loan notes can be ignored.

Required:
(a) Treating separately each method of raising finance, calculate:
  (i)   the total number of shares
  (ii) the total nominal value of loan notes
  that have to be issued in order to raise the finance required.
(b) Calculate the forecast earnings per share for the year to 31 May Year 7 assuming:
  (i)   a rights issue of shares is made
  (ii) an issue of loan notes is made
  to raise the necessary finance.
(c) Calculate the gearing ratio as at 31 May Year 7 assuming:
  (i)   a rights issue of shares is made
  (ii) an issue of loan notes is made.
(d) Discuss the major factors to be considered by Jubilee plc when deciding between a rights issue of shares and an issue of loan notes to raise the necessary finance.
  Workings should be to the nearest £000.

Chapter 9

MAKING DISTRIBUTIONS TO SHAREHOLDERS

INTRODUCTION

Businesses normally make distributions to shareholders by paying cash dividends. Share buybacks, however, have become increasingly popular. In this chapter, we shall examine both of these forms of distribution.

The payment of dividends has provoked much debate over the years. At the centre of this debate is whether the pattern of dividends adopted by a business has any effect on shareholder wealth. We examine the arguments raised on each side of the debate and discuss the key assumptions employed. Although the importance of dividends to shareholders remains a moot point, there is evidence to suggest that managers perceive the dividend decision to be important. We consider the attitudes of managers towards dividends and discuss those factors likely to influence dividend policy in practice.

Dividends do not have to be paid in cash. Many businesses offer shareholders a scrip dividend as an alternative to a cash dividend. We shall consider the advantages and disadvantages of this type of distribution to shareholders.

Share buybacks provide an alternative way of distributing cash to shareholders. We end this chapter by considering why share buybacks may be preferred to cash dividends and how they may lead to a conflict of interest between managers and shareholders.

Learning outcomes

When you have completed this chapter, you should be able to:

■ Describe the nature of dividends and evaluate the arguments concerning their potential impact on shareholder wealth.

■ Identify and discuss the factors that influence dividend policy in practice.

■ Describe the nature of scrip dividends and discuss the case for and against this form of distribution.

■ Explain what share buybacks involve and discuss the main issues that they raise.

PAYING DIVIDENDS

It is probably a good idea to begin our examination of dividends and dividend policy by describing briefly what dividends are and how they are paid. Dividends represent a return by a business to its shareholders. This is normally paid in cash, although it could be paid with assets other than cash. There are legal limits on the amount that can be distributed in the form of dividend payments to shareholders.

Activity 9.1

Why do you think the law imposes limits on the amount that can be distributed as dividends?

If there were no legal limits, shareholders could withdraw their investment from the business and leave lenders and other creditors in an exposed financial position. The law therefore seeks to prevent excessive withdrawals of shareholder capital. One way of doing this is to restrict the amount that can be distributed through dividend payments.

The law states that dividends can be paid to shareholders only out of *accumulated realised profits less any accumulated realised losses*. This will generally mean that the maximum amount available will be the accumulated trading profits *plus* any accumulated profits on the sale of non-current assets. (Both types of profit are after deducting any losses incurred.) Accumulated profits arising from the revaluation of non-current assets are *unrealised profits* (as the asset is still held) and so cannot be distributed. Public companies are subject to the further restriction that, following a dividend payment, net assets must not be less than the issued share capital plus any non-distributable reserves.

Activity 9.2

Bio-tech Ltd, a private limited company, started trading in Year 1 and made a trading profit of £200,000 in this year. In Year 2, the business made a trading loss of £150,000 but made a profit on the sale of its office buildings of £30,000. Other non-current assets were revalued during the year, leading to a revaluation gain of £60,000. Assuming that no dividend was paid in Year 1, what is the maximum dividend that could be paid by Bio-tech Ltd in Year 2?

The revaluation gain, which is unrealised profit, cannot be taken into account when deciding the maximum dividend. This maximum is calculated as follows:

	£
Trading profit Year 1	200,000
Profit on sale of non-current asset Year 2	30,000
	230,000
Trading loss Year 2	(150,000)
Maximum amount available for distribution	80,000

Businesses rarely make a dividend payment based on the maximum amount available for distribution. The dividend payment is normally much lower than the trading profits for the particular year and so will be 'covered' by a comfortable margin.

Dividends are often paid twice yearly by listed businesses. The first dividend is paid after the interim (half-yearly) results have been announced and represents a 'payment on account'. The second and final dividend is paid after the year end. It is paid after the annual financial reports have been published, and after the shareholders have agreed, at the annual general meeting, to the dividend payment proposed by the directors.

As shares are bought and sold continuously, it is important to establish which shareholders have the right to receive any dividends declared. To do this, a record date is set by the business. Shareholders whose names appear in the share register on the record date will receive the dividends payable. When the share prices quoted on the Stock Exchange include accrued dividends payable, they are said to be quoted cum dividend. However, on a specified day before the record date, the quoted share prices will exclude the accrued dividend and so will become ex dividend. Assuming no other factors affect the share price, the ex-dividend price should be lower than the cum-dividend price by the amount of the dividend payable. This is because a new shareholder would not qualify for the dividend and so the share price can be expected to fall by the amount of the dividend.

Most listed businesses publish a financial calendar that sets out the key dates for shareholders for the forthcoming year. **Real World 9.1** provides an example of such a calendar for a large business.

Real World 9.1

Financial calendar

IMI plc, a global engineering business, has produced the following financial calendar for investors on its website.

Date	Title
15 Nov 2013	Interim management statement
22 Aug 2013	Interim results
09 May 2013	Interim management statement & AGM
07 Mar 2013	Preliminary results
16 Nov 2012	Interim management statement
12 Oct 2012	Interim dividend – payment date
07 Sep 2012	Interim dividend – record date
05 Sep 2012	Interim dividend – ex-dividend date
23 Aug 2012	Interim results
21 May 2012	Final dividend – payment date
04 May 2012	AGM
20 Apr 2012	Interim management statement
13 Apr 2012	Final dividend – record date
11 Apr 2012	Final dividend – ex-dividend date

Source: Financial calendar, IMI plc, www.Imiplc.com, accessed 13 March 2013.

DIVIDEND DISTRIBUTIONS IN PRACTICE

We mentioned above that dividends paid are normally lower than the profits available for this purpose. The extent to which profits for a period, which are available for dividend, cover the dividend payment can be expressed in the *dividend cover ratio*. This ratio is calculated as follows:

$$\text{Dividend cover} = \frac{\textbf{Earnings for the year available for dividends}}{\textbf{Dividends announced for the year}}$$

The dividend cover ratio has already been discussed in Chapter 3. We may recall that the higher the ratio, the lower the risk that dividends will be affected by adverse trading conditions. The inverse of this ratio is known as the *dividend payout ratio*, which was also discussed in Chapter 3. The lower this ratio, the lower the risk that dividends will be affected by adverse trading conditions.

Real World 9.2 provides an impression of average dividend coverage ratios for listed businesses in selected industries. Factors influencing the level of dividend cover are considered later in the chapter.

Real World 9.2

Dividend coverage

Figure 9.1 shows the average dividend coverage ratios for listed businesses in a range of industries.

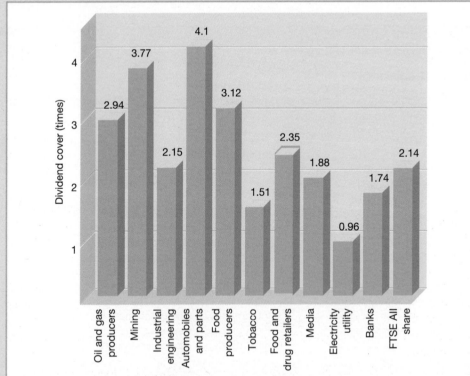

The figure reveals that the average dividend cover ratio for all listed businesses exceeds two times. The figure also reveals, however, that there are significant variations in this ratio between the selected industries.

Figure 9.1 Average dividend cover ratios for businesses in a range of industries

Source: Compiled from data in *Financial Times*, 11–12 May 2013, p. 22.

Dividend cover ratios may vary between countries according to the particular conditions that exist. Where there is easy access to capital markets, profit retention becomes less important and so dividend distributions can be higher. Other factors, such as the treatment of dividends for taxation purposes, can also exert an influence.

Setting dividend targets

Businesses will often set targets for dividend distributions. These may be expressed in various ways, such as a particular dividend payout ratio, an amount of dividend per share and a particular rate of growth in dividends. **Real World 9.3** provides some evidence of the dividend targets used by businesses.

Real World 9.3

Dividend targets

An international survey of 334 large businesses across a range of industries found that dividend targets varied. Figure 9.2 reveals the popularity of each type of target.

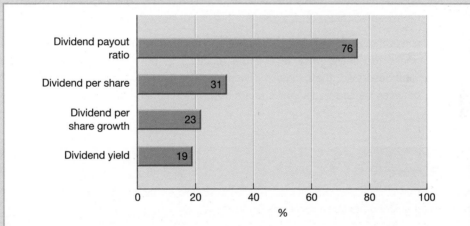

As the total percentage is greater than 100 per cent, some businesses clearly employ more than one target.

Figure 9.2 Dividend targets in practice

We can see that the dividend payout ratio (which presumably includes its variant, the dividend coverage ratio) is, by far, the most popular target. This applies to all geographical areas with the exception of Japan, where dividend per share is more popular. Dividends in Japan tend to be low, which may explain the focus on dividend level rather than the dividend payout ratio.

Source: H. Servaes and P. Tufano, *The Theory and Practice of Corporate Dividend and Share Repurchase Policy*, Deutsche Bank AG and Global Association of Risk Professionals, February 2006, p. 26.

DIVIDEND POLICY AND SHAREHOLDER WEALTH

Much of the interest surrounding dividend policy is concerned with the relationship between dividend policy and shareholder wealth. Put simply, the key question to be answered is: can the pattern of dividends adopted by a business influence shareholder wealth? (Note that it is the *pattern* of dividends rather than dividends themselves that is the issue. Shareholders must receive cash at some point in order for their shares to have any value.) While the question may be stated simply, the answer cannot. After more than three decades of research and debate, we have yet to solve this puzzle.

The notion that dividend policy is important may seem, on the face of it, to be obvious. In Chapter 8, for example, we considered various dividend valuation models, which suggest that dividends are important in determining share price. One such model, we may recall, was the dividend growth model, which is as follows:

$$P_0 = \frac{D_1}{K_0 - g}$$

where D_1 = expected dividend next year
g = a constant rate of growth
K_0 = the expected return on the share.

Looking at this model, it may appear that simply increasing the dividend (D_1) will automatically increase the share price (P_0). If the relationship between dividends and share price was as just described, then, clearly, dividend policy would be important. However, the relationship between these two variables is not likely to be as straightforward as this.

Activity 9.3

Why might an increase in the dividend (D_1) not lead to an increase in share price (P_0)? (*Hint*: Think of the other variables in the equation.)

An increase in dividend payments will result in an increase in share price only if there is no consequential effect on the dividend growth rate. It is quite possible, however, that an increase in dividend will result in a fall in this growth rate, as there will be less cash to invest in the business. Thus, the beneficial effect on share price arising from an increase in next year's dividend may be cancelled out by a decrease in future years' dividends.

The traditional view of dividends

The dividend policy issue, like the capital structure issue discussed in the previous chapter, has two main schools of thought: the traditional view and the modernist view. The early finance literature accepted the view that dividend policy was important for shareholders. It was argued that a shareholder would prefer to receive £1 today rather than to have £1 reinvested in the business, even though this might yield future dividends. The reasoning for this was that future dividends are less certain and so will be valued less highly. The saying 'a bird in the hand is worth two in the bush' is often used to describe this argument. Thus, if a business decides to replace an immediate and certain cash dividend with uncertain future dividends, shareholders will discount the future dividends at a higher rate in order to take account of this greater uncertainty. Referring back to the dividend growth model, the traditional view suggests that K_0 will rise if there is an increase in D_1, as dividends received later will not be valued so highly.

If this line of reasoning is correct, the effect of applying a higher discount rate to future dividends will be that the share price of a business intending to retain profits in order to pay dividends later will suffer. The implications for managers are therefore quite clear. They should adopt as generous a dividend distribution policy as possible, given the investment and financing policies of the business, as this will represent the optimal dividend policy. Furthermore, as the level of payout will affect shareholder wealth, the dividend decision is an important one.

The modernist (MM) view of dividends

Miller and Modigliani (MM) have challenged this view of dividend policy. They argue that, given perfect and efficient markets, the pattern of dividend payments adopted by a business has no effect on shareholder wealth. They make the point that shareholder wealth is affected only by the investment projects that the business undertakes. To maximise shareholder wealth, therefore, the business should take on all investment projects that have a positive NPV. The way in which returns from these investment projects are divided between dividends and retention is unimportant. Thus, a decision to pay a lower dividend will be compensated for by an increase in share price – and vice versa.

MM point out that it is possible for an individual shareholder to 'adjust' the dividend policy of a business to conform to his or her particular requirements. If a business does not pay a dividend, the shareholder can create 'home-made' dividends by selling a portion of the shares held. If, however, a business provides a dividend that the shareholder does not wish to receive, the amount can be reinvested in additional shares in the business. In view of this, there is no reason for a shareholder to value the shares of one business more highly than another simply because it adopts a particular dividend policy.

The implications of the MM position for managers are quite different from those of the traditional position described earlier. The MM view suggests that there is no such thing as an optimal dividend policy, and that one policy is as good as another (that is, the dividend decision is irrelevant to shareholder wealth). Thus managers should not spend time considering the most appropriate policy to adopt, but should, instead, devote their energies to finding and managing profitable investment opportunities.

The MM position explained

MM believe that dividends simply represent a movement of funds from inside the business to outside the business. This change in the location of funds should not have any effect on shareholder wealth. The MM position is set out in Example 9.1.

Example 9.1

Merton plc has the following statement of financial position as at 31 December Year 5:

Statement of financial position as at 31 December Year 5

	£000
Assets at market value (exc. cash)	60
Cash	30
Total assets	90
Ordinary (equity) share capital (30,000 shares) plus reserves	90

Suppose that the business decides to distribute all the cash available (that is, £30,000) to shareholders by making a 100p dividend per share. This will result in a fall in the value of assets to £60,000 (that is, £90,000 – £30,000) and a fall in the value of its shares from £3 (that is, £90,000/30,000) to £2 (that is, £60,000/30,000). The statement of financial position following the dividend payment will therefore be as follows:

Statement of financial position following the dividend payment

	£000
Assets at market value (exc. cash)	60
Cash	–
Total assets	60
Ordinary (equity) share capital (30,000 shares) plus reserves	60

Before the dividend distribution, a shareholder holding 10 per cent of the shares in Merton plc will have:

	£
3,000 shares at £3 per share	9,000

Following the distribution, the shareholder will have:

	£
3,000 shares at £2 per share	6,000
plus a cash dividend of 3,000 × £1.00	3,000
	9,000

In other words, the total wealth of the shareholder remains the same.

If the shareholder did not want to receive the dividends, the cash received could be used to purchase more shares in the business. Although the number of shares held by the shareholder will change as a result of this decision, his or her *total wealth* will remain the same. If, however, Merton plc did not issue a dividend and the shareholder wished to receive one, he or she could create the desired dividend by simply selling a portion of the shares held. Once again, this will change the number of shares held by the shareholder but will not change the total amount of wealth held.

What about the effect of a dividend payment on the amounts available for investment? We may feel that a high dividend payment will mean that less can be retained, which may, in turn, mean that the business cannot invest in all projects that have a positive NPV. If this occurs, then shareholder wealth will be adversely affected. However, if we assume that perfect and efficient capital markets exist, the business will be able to raise the finance required for investment purposes and will not have to rely on profit retention. In other words, dividend policy and investment policy can be regarded as quite separate issues.

The wealth of existing shareholders should not be affected by raising finance from new issues rather than retention. Activity 9.4 reinforces this point.

Activity 9.4

Suppose that Merton plc (see Example 9.1) replaces the £30,000 paid out as dividends by an issue of shares to new shareholders. Show the statement of financial position after the new issue and calculate the value of shares held by existing shareholders after the issue.

The statement of financial position following the new issue will be almost the same as before the dividend payment was made. However, the number of shares in issue will increase. If we assume that the new shares can be issued at a fair value (that is, current market value), the number of shares in issue will increase by 15,000 shares (£30,000/£2.00 = 15,000).

Statement of financial position following the issue of new shares

	£000
Assets at market value (exc. cash)	60
Cash	30
	90
Ordinary (equity) capital (45,000 shares) plus reserves	90

The existing shareholders will own 30,000 of the 45,000 shares in issue and will therefore own net assets worth £60,000 (30,000/45,000 × £90,000). In other words, their wealth will not be affected by the financing decision.

What about the traditional argument in support of dividend policy (that is, shareholders prefer 'a bird in the hand')? The answer is that they probably do not. The problem with this argument is that it is based on a misconception of the nature of risk. Risks borne by a shareholder will be determined by the nature of the business's operations and its level of borrowing. Risks do not necessarily increase over time, nor are they affected by the dividend policy of the business. Dividends will reduce risk for a shareholder only if the amount received is then placed in a less risky form of investment (with a lower level of return). This could equally be achieved, however, through the sale of the shares in the business.

Activity 9.5

There is one situation where even MM would accept that 'a bird in the hand is worth two in the bush' (that is, that immediate dividends are preferable). Can you think what it is? (*Hint*: Think of the way in which shareholder wealth is increased.)

Shareholder wealth is increased by the business accepting projects that have a positive NPV. If the business starts to accept projects with a negative NPV, this would decrease shareholder wealth. In such circumstances, a rational shareholder would prefer to receive a dividend rather than allow the business to reinvest any profits.

MM assumptions

The logic of the MM arguments has proved to be unassailable and it is now widely accepted that, in a world of perfect and efficient capital markets, dividend policy should have no effect on shareholder wealth. The burning issue, however, is whether or not the MM analysis can be applied to the real world of imperfect markets. There are three key assumptions on which the MM analysis rests, and these assumptions have aroused much debate. These assumptions are, in essence, that we live in a 'frictionless' world where there are:

■ no share issue costs
■ no share transaction costs
■ no taxation.

The first assumption means that money paid out in dividends can be replaced by the business through a new share issue without incurring additional costs. Thus, a business need not be deterred from paying a dividend simply because it needs cash to invest in a profitable project, as the amount can be costlessly replaced. In the real world, however, share issue costs can be significant.

The second assumption means that shareholders can make 'home-made' dividends or reinvest in the business at no extra cost. In other words, there are no barriers to shareholders pursuing their own dividend and investment strategies. Once again, in the real world, costs will be incurred when shares are purchased or sold. The creation of 'home-made' dividends as a substitute for business dividend policy may pose other practical problems for the shareholder, such as the indivisibility of shares, resulting in shareholders being unable to sell the exact amount of shares required, and the difficulty of selling shares in unlisted companies. These problems, it is argued, can lead to shareholders becoming reliant on the dividend policy of the business as a means of receiving cash income. It can also lead them to have a preference for one business rather than another, because of the dividend policies adopted.

The third assumption concerning taxation is unrealistic and in practice tax may be an important issue for shareholders. It has been argued that, in the UK, taxation rules have a significant influence on shareholders' preferences. It may be more tax-efficient for shareholders to receive benefits in the form of capital gains rather than dividends. This is partly because, below a certain threshold (£10,900 for 2013/14), capital gains arising during a particular financial year are not taxable. Shareholders can also influence the timing of capital gains by choosing when to sell shares.

Activity 9.6

How might the taxation rules, as described above, affect the way in which the shares of different businesses are valued?

They are likely to lead shareholders to prefer capital gains to dividends. As a result, the shares of a business with a high dividend payout ratio would be valued less highly than those of a similar business with a low payout ratio.

Although differences between the tax treatment of dividend income and capital gains still exist, changes in taxation policy have narrowed these differences in recent years. One important change has been the creation of tax shelters (for example, Individual Savings Accounts, or ISAs), which allow private shareholders to receive dividend income and capital gains free of taxation.

The three assumptions discussed undoubtedly weaken the MM analysis when applied to the real world. However, this does not necessarily mean that their analysis is destroyed. Indeed, the research evidence tends to support their position. One direct way to assess the validity of MM's arguments is to see whether, in the real world, there is a positive relationship between the dividends paid by businesses and their share price. If such a relationship exists then MM's arguments would lose their force. Most studies, however, have failed to find any significant correlation between dividends and share prices.

The thoughts of Chairman Buffett

Warren Buffett, chairman and chief executive officer of Berkshire Hathaway Inc., has consistently resisted calls for the business to pay dividends. He believes that it is better for shareholders to create 'home-made' dividends, despite the points made earlier. In **Real World 9.4**, he demonstrates the wealth-enhancing effects of taking this route.

Real World 9.4

Dividend lesson

We'll start by assuming that you and I are the equal owners of a business with $2 million of net worth. The business earns 12% on tangible net worth – $240,000 – and can reasonably expect to earn the same 12% on reinvested earnings. Furthermore, there are outsiders who always wish to buy into our business at 125% of net worth. Therefore, the value of what we each own is now $1.25 million.

You would like to have the two of us shareholders receive one-third of our company's annual earnings and have two-thirds be reinvested. That plan, you feel, will nicely balance your needs for both current income and capital growth. So you suggest that we pay out $80,000 of current earnings and retain $160,000 to increase the future earnings of the business. In the first year, your dividend would be $40,000, and as earnings grew and the one-third payout was maintained, so too would your dividend. In total, dividends and stock value would increase 8% each year (12% earned on net worth less 4% of net worth paid out).

After ten years our company would have a net worth of $4,317,850 (the original $2 million compounded at 8%) and your dividend in the forthcoming year would be $86,357. Each of us would have shares worth $2,698,656 (125% of our half of the company's net worth). And we would live happily ever after – with dividends and the value of our stock continuing to grow at 8% annually.

There is an alternative approach, however, that would leave us even happier. Under this scenario, we would leave *all* earnings in the company and each sell 3.2% of our shares annually. Since the shares would be sold at 125% of book value, this approach would produce the same $40,000 of cash initially, a sum that would grow annually. Call this option the 'sell-off' approach.

Under this 'sell-off' scenario, the net worth of our company increases to $6,211,696 after ten years ($2 million compounded at 12%). Because we would be selling shares each year, our *percentage* ownership would have declined, and, after ten years, we would each own 36.12% of the business. Even so, your share of the net worth of the company at that time would be $2,243,540. And, remember, every dollar of net worth attributable to each of us can be sold for $1.25. Therefore, the market value of your remaining shares would be $2,804,425, about 4% greater than the value of your shares if we had followed the dividend approach. Moreover, your annual cash receipts from the sell-off policy would now be running 4% more than you would have received under the dividend scenario. Voilà! – you would have both more cash to spend annually *and* more capital value.

→

This calculation, of course, assumes that our hypothetical company can earn an average of 12% annually on net worth and that its shareholders can sell their shares for an average of 125% of book value. To that point, the S&P 500 earns considerably more than 12% on net worth and sells at a price far above 125% of that net worth. Both assumptions also seem reasonable for Berkshire, though certainly not assured. Moreover, on the plus side, there also is a possibility that the assumptions will be exceeded. If they are, the argument for the sell-off policy becomes even stronger. Over Berkshire's history – admittedly one that won't come close to being repeated – the sell-off policy would have produced results for shareholders *dramatically* superior to the dividend policy.

Aside from the favourable maths, there are two further – *and important* – arguments for a sell-off policy. First, dividends impose a specific cash-out policy upon all shareholders. If, say, 40% of earnings is the policy, those who wish 30% or 50% will be thwarted. Our 600,000 shareholders cover the waterfront in their desires for cash. It is safe to say, however, that a great many of them – perhaps even most of them – are in a net-savings mode and logically should prefer no payment at all.

The sell-off alternative, on the other hand, lets each shareholder make his own choice between cash receipts and capital build-up. One shareholder can elect to cash out, say, 60% of annual earnings while other shareholders elect 20% or nothing at all. Of course, a shareholder in our dividend-paying scenario could turn around and use his dividends to purchase more shares. But he would take a beating in doing so: He would both incur taxes and also pay a 25% premium to get his dividend reinvested. (Keep remembering, open-market purchases of the stock take place at 125% of book value.)

The second disadvantage of the dividend approach is of equal importance: the tax consequences for *all* taxpaying shareholders are inferior – usually *far* inferior – to those under the sell-off program. Under the dividend program, all of the cash received by shareholders each year is taxed whereas the sell-off program results in tax on only the gain portion of the cash receipts.

Source: W. Buffett, Shareholder letter, www.berkshirehathaway.com, 1 March 2013, pp. 19–21.

THE IMPORTANCE OF DIVIDENDS

Whether or not we accept the MM analysis (or the points made by Warren Buffett), there is little doubt that, in practice, the pattern of dividends is usually seen by shareholders and managers to be important. It seems that there are three possible reasons to explain this phenomenon. These are:

■ the clientele effect
■ the information signalling effect
■ the need to reduce agency costs.

Each of these is considered below.

The clientele effect

We mentioned earlier that share transaction costs may result in shareholders becoming reliant on the dividend policies of businesses. It was also argued that the tax position of shareholders can exert an influence on whether dividends or capital gains are preferred. These factors may, in practice, mean that dividend policy will exercise an important influence on shareholder behaviour. Shareholders may seek out businesses whose dividend policies match closely their particular needs. Thus, individuals with high marginal tax rates may invest in businesses that retain their profits for future growth, whereas pension funds, which are tax exempt and require income to pay pensions, may invest in businesses with high dividend distributions. This phenomenon – that the particular dividend policies adopted by businesses tend to attract different types of shareholders – is referred to as the clientele effect.

The existence of a clientele effect has important implications for managers. First, dividend policy should be clearly set out and consistently applied. Shareholders attracted to a particular business because of its dividend policy will not welcome unexpected changes. Second, managers need not concern themselves with trying to accommodate the needs of different shareholders. The particular distribution policy adopted by the business will tend to attract a certain type of shareholder depending on his or her cash needs and tax position.

Shareholders should be wary, however, of making investment decisions primarily based on dividend policy for two reasons. First, minimising costs may not be so easy. Shareholders requiring a regular cash income may, for example, seek out businesses with high dividend payout ratios. By so doing, they may discover that savings in transaction costs are cancelled out by incurring other forms of cost.

Activity 9.7

What kind of costs may be borne by shareholders who invest in high dividend payout businesses?

Being committed to a high dividend payout may prevent a business from investing in profitable projects. Hence, there could be a loss of future benefits for shareholders. If, however, a business decides to raise finance to replace the amount distributed in dividends, the costs of raising the required finance will be borne by existing shareholders.

Second, it can result in an unbalanced portfolio of investments where certain types of businesses and industries are not represented. Shareholders seeking a regular cash income may, for example, ignore high-growth businesses, which do not pay dividends in order to conserve cash. It is, therefore, a good idea for shareholders to look beyond the dividend policy of a business when making investment decisions.

Evidence concerning the clientele effect is mixed. Some studies support the existence of a clientele effect whereas others do not. Overall, however, studies in the US and the UK provide broad support for the existence of the clientele effect.

Information signalling

In an imperfect world, managers have greater access to information regarding the profits and performance of the business than shareholders. This information asymmetry, as it is called, may lead to dividends being used by managers as a means of conveying information to shareholders. New information relating to future prospects may be signalled through changes in dividend policy. If, for example, managers are confident about future prospects, they may undertake information signalling by increasing dividends.

Real World 9.5 gives an example of the positive signal that one dividend payment was meant to convey.

Rescued from deep water

BP has increased its dividend payouts in a signal to investors of its greater optimism that it is finally bouncing back from the 2010 Deepwater Horizon disaster. Bob Dudley, chief executive, said BP's recent $27bn deal with Rosneft, its $35bn of divestments since 2010 and the suite of new high-margin projects it has in the pipeline had given it the confidence to reward its 'very patient shareholders'. He was speaking as BP posted adjusted third-quarter profit of $5.2bn, down 5 per cent from $5.5bn a year ago but well ahead of most analysts' estimates.

The decision on the BP dividend, which used to account for one-seventh of the total pay-outs by FTSE 100 companies before Deepwater Horizon, reflects a new, more upbeat mood at the UK oil group, driven by a deal that has finally resolved the lingering uncertainty over its future in Russia. Earlier this month, BP said it was selling its 50 per cent stake in its Russian joint venture TNK-BP to Rosneft in a deal that leaves it with $12.3bn in cash and a nearly 20 per cent stake in the Russian national oil champion.

FT   *Source*: Chazan, G. (2012) 'BP raises dividend after Russian deal', www.ft.com, 30 October.
© The Financial Times Limited 2012. All Rights Reserved.

Why would managers use dividends as a means of conveying information about the business's prospects? Why not simply issue a statement to shareholders? Try to think of at least one reason why managers may prefer a less direct approach.

At least three reasons have been put forward to explain why signalling through dividend payments may be preferred. First, it may be that the managers do not want to disclose the precise nature of the events that improve the business's prospects. Suppose, for example, that a business has signed a large government defence contract, which will be formally announced by the government at some time in the future. In the intervening period, however, the price of the shares in the business may be depressed and the managers may be concerned that the business is vulnerable to a takeover. The managers might, under the circumstances, wish to boost the share price without specifying the nature of the good news.

Second, issuing a statement about, say, improved future prospects may not be convincing, particularly if earlier statements by managers have proved incorrect. Statements are 'cheap' whereas an increase in dividends would be more substantial evidence of the managers' confidence in the future.

Third, managers may feel that an explicit statement concerning future prospects will attract criticism from shareholders if things do not work out as expected. They may, therefore, prefer more coded messages to avoid being held to account at a later date.

Sending a positive signal to the market by increasing dividends is an expensive way to send a message. It may also seem wasteful (particularly where shareholders do not wish to receive higher dividends for tax reasons). However, it may be the only feasible way of ensuring that shareholders take seriously the good news that managers wish to convey.

Real World 9.6 illustrates how it can sometimes be difficult to interpret the signal that businesses are sending when their dividend payout changes.

Various studies have been carried out to establish the 'information content' of dividends. Some of these have looked at the share price reaction to *unexpected* changes in dividends. If signalling exists, an unexpected dividend announcement should result in a significant share price reaction. The results suggest that signalling does exist; that is, a dividend increase (positive signal) results in an increase in share price, and a dividend decrease (negative signal) results in a decrease in share price. One interesting finding is that market reaction to dividend reductions tends to be much greater than market reaction to dividend increases. It seems that shareholders regard negative signals much more seriously. It is not surprising, therefore, that managers are normally reluctant to cut dividends. They may even forgo value-enhancing investment opportunities to avoid doing so.

Reducing agency costs

In recent years, *agency theory* has become increasingly influential in the financial management literature. Agency theory views a business as a coalition of different interest groups (managers, shareholders, lenders and so on) in which each group is seeking to maximise its own welfare. According to this theory, one group connected with the business may engage in behaviour that results in costs being borne by another group. However, the latter group may try to restrain the action of the former group, through contractual or other arrangements, so as to minimise these costs. Two examples of where a conflict of interest arises between groups, and the impact on dividend policy, are considered below.

The first example concerns a conflict of interest between shareholders and managers. If managers (who are agents of the shareholders) decide to invest in lavish offices, expensive cars and other 'perks', they will be pursuing their own interests at a cost to the shareholders.

(This point was discussed briefly in Chapter 1.) Shareholders may try to avoid incurring these costs by reducing the cash available for managers to spend. They may insist that surplus cash be distributed to them in the form of a dividend. It is often in the interests of managers to support this move as agency costs can prevent them from receiving full recognition for their achievements. Helping to reduce these costs could therefore be to their benefit.

The second example concerns a conflict between shareholders and lenders. Shareholders may try to reduce their stake in the business through withdrawals in the form of dividends. This may be done to reduce exposure to the risks associated with the business. Lenders, however, may seek to prevent this from happening as it would lead to them becoming more exposed to these risks. They may, therefore, impose restrictions on the dividends paid to shareholders.

Activity 9.9

How can lenders go about restricting shareholders' rights to dividends? (*Hint*: Think back to Chapter 6.)

Lenders can insist that loan covenants, which restrict the level of dividend payable, be included in the loan agreement.

Note that action taken by shareholders to avoid agency costs may lead to an increase in dividends, whereas action taken by lenders to avoid agency costs may lead to a reduction in dividends.

Figure 9.3 sets out the main reasons why dividends are important in the real world.

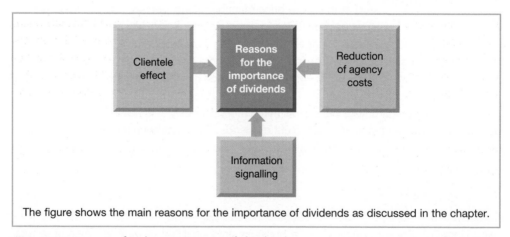

The figure shows the main reasons for the importance of dividends as discussed in the chapter.

Figure 9.3 Reasons for the importance of dividends

FACTORS DETERMINING THE LEVEL OF DIVIDENDS

We have now seen that there are three possible reasons why shareholders and managers regard dividends as being important. In addition, there are various factors that have a bearing on the level of dividends paid by a business. Managers must somehow weigh these factors to arrive at an appropriate dividend. These factors include the following.

Investment opportunities

Businesses with good investment opportunities may try to retain profits rather than distribute them. Investment opportunities may vary over the life cycle of a business and so its retention/dividend policies may also vary. At an early stage, when opportunities abound, a policy of low dividends or no dividends may be chosen in order to retain profits for reinvestment. At a more mature stage of the cycle, however, when investment opportunities are limited, a policy of higher dividends may be chosen.

Financing opportunities

Where raising external finance for new investment is a problem, profit retention may be the only option available. Under these circumstances, it may make sense for managers to regard dividends as simply a residual (assuming shareholders are indifferent towards dividends). Paying dividends would be appropriate only where the expected return from investment opportunities is below the required return for shareholders. This means that dividends may fluctuate each year according to the investment opportunities available. Where, however, a business can raise finance easily and cheaply from external sources, retained profits become less important and can be paid as dividends.

Legal requirements

UK company law restricts the amount that a business can distribute in the form of dividends. We saw earlier that the law states that dividends can only be paid to shareholders out of realised profits. In essence, the maximum amount available for distribution will be the accumulated trading profits (less any losses) plus any profits on the disposal of assets.

Loan commitments

Covenants included in a loan contract may restrict the dividends available to shareholders during the loan period. These covenants, as we saw in Chapter 6, are designed to protect the lenders' investment in the business. Even where a loan agreement does not impose any restriction on dividend payments, a business must retain its capacity to make interest and debt payments when they fall due. This may mean that dividends have to be restricted in order to conserve cash.

Profit stability

Businesses that have a stable pattern of profits over time are in a better position to make higher dividend payouts than those that have a volatile pattern of profits.

Activity 9.10

Why should this be the case?

Businesses with a stable pattern of profits are able to plan with greater certainty and are less likely to feel a need to retain profits for unexpected events.

Control

A high-profit-retention/low-dividend policy can help avoid the need to issue new shares, and so existing shareholders' control will not be diluted. (Even though existing shareholders may have pre-emptive rights, they may not always be in a position to buy new shares issued by the business.)

Threat of takeover

It has been suggested that a high-retention/low-dividend-distribution policy can increase the vulnerability of a business to takeover.

Activity 9.11

Can you figure out the possible reasoning behind this suggestion? Do you agree with such a suggestion?

A predator business may try to convince shareholders in the target business that the existing managers are not maximising their wealth. A record of low dividend payments may be cited as evidence. However, dividends represent only part of the total return from the shares. A record of low dividends is therefore not clear evidence of mismanagement. Shareholders will normally recognise this fact. (If profits are retained rather than distributed, however, they must be employed in a profitable manner. Failure to do this will increase the threat of takeover.)

Dividends are sometimes used to try to avert the threat of takeover. Managers may increase the dividend payout to signal to shareholders their confidence in the future prospects of the business. If shareholders interpret the dividend in this way, there may be an increase in share price and an increase in the cost of the takeover for the predator business. However, shareholders may not interpret a large dividend payment in this way. They may simply regard it as a desperate attempt by managers to gain their support and the share price will not respond to the news.

Real World 9.7 cites a dividend increase that seems to have been a defensive move.

Real World 9.7

On the defensive

Aer Lingus Group plc's annual profit fell 52 per cent, even as the Irish carrier boosted its dividend amidst a hostile takeover approach from discount rival and minority investor Ryanair Holdings plc.

Pre-tax profit slumped to €40.6 million ($55 million) from €84.4 million a year earlier, the Dublin-based carrier said in a statement today.

Aer Lingus, locked in a protracted battle to remain independent after Ryanair's renewed takeover interest, will lift its full-year dividend 25 per cent to 4 cents a share. Ryanair, Europe's largest low-cost carrier, already owns around 30 per cent of Aer Lingus and is seeking approval from European authorities to take majority control.

Source: R. Wall, 'Aer Lingus profit falls as dividend raised in Ryanair bid battle', www.bloomberg.com, 6 February 2013.

Market expectations

Shareholders may have developed certain expectations concerning the level of dividend to be paid. These expectations may be formed by various events such as earlier management announcements and past dividend payments. If these expectations are not met, there is likely to be a loss of shareholder confidence in the business. Where, for example, the market expects an increase in dividend payments and the actual increase is less than expected, the share price is likely to fall.

Inside information

Managers may have inside information concerning future prospects that cannot be published. However, this information may indicate that the shares are currently undervalued. To raise equity finance by an issue of shares under such circumstances would involve selling them at an undervalued price. This would, in effect, result in a transfer of wealth from existing shareholders to those investors who take up the new share issue. In such a situation, it would be more sensible to raise further equity finance by retaining profits rather than by issuing more shares.

Activity 9.12

With which theory would this behaviour be consistent? (Hint: think back to Chapter 6.)

Pecking order theory suggests that retained profits will be used by a business before the issue of new debt or equity finance.

Figure 9.4 sets out the main influences on the level of dividends declared by a business.

These factors influencing the level of dividends have been discussed in this section.

Figure 9.4 Factors influencing the level of dividends

The dividend policy of other businesses

It has been argued that shareholders make comparisons between businesses. Any significant deviation in dividend policy from the industry norm will, therefore, attract criticism. The implication seems to be that managers should shape the dividend policy of their business according to what comparable businesses are doing. This, however, may be neither practical nor desirable.

To begin with, there is the problem of identifying comparable businesses as a suitable benchmark. Significant differences often exist between businesses concerning risk characteristics and rates of growth as well as other key factors influencing dividend policy such as financing opportunities, loan covenants and so on. There is also the problem that, even if comparable businesses could be found, it cannot be automatically assumed that they adopt optimal dividend policies.

These problems suggest that dividend policy is best determined according to the particular requirements of the business. If the policy adopted differs from the norm, managers should be able to provide valid reasons.

DIVIDEND POLICY AND MANAGEMENT ATTITUDES: SOME EVIDENCE

An important aspect of the dividend policy debate is the attitudes and behaviour of managers. One of the earliest pieces of research on this topic was undertaken in the US by Lintner (see reference 1 at the end of the chapter), who carried out interviews with managers in 28 businesses. Although this research is now pretty old, it is still considered to be one of the most accurate descriptions of how managers set dividend policy in practice.

Lintner found that managers considered the dividend decision to be an important one and were committed to long-term target dividend payout ratios. He also found that managers were concerned more with variations in dividends than with the absolute amount of dividends paid. Managers took the view that shareholders preferred a smooth increase in dividend payments over time and were reluctant to increase the level of dividends in response to a short-term increase in profits. They wished to avoid a situation where dividends would have to be cut in the future, and so dividends were increased only when it was felt that the higher level of dividends could be sustained through a permanent increase in earnings. As a result, there was a time lag between dividend growth and earnings growth.

Activity 9.13

Are these attitudes of managers described above consistent with another view of dividends discussed earlier?

The attitudes of managers described by Lintner are consistent with more recent work concerning the use of dividends as a means of information signalling. The managers interviewed seem to be aware of the fact that a dividend cut would send negative signals to shareholders.

In a later study, Fama and Babiak (see reference 2 at the end of the chapter) found that businesses distributed about half of their profits in the form of dividends. However, significant increases in earnings would only be followed by a *partial adjustment* to dividends in the first year. On average, the increase in dividends in the first year was only about one-third of the increase that would have been consistent with maintaining the target payout ratio. The smooth and gradual adjustment of dividends to changes in profits revealed by this study is consistent with the earlier study by Lintner and confirms that managers wish to ensure a sustainable level of dividends.

Where a business experiences adverse trading conditions, DeAngelo and colleagues (see reference 3 at the end of the chapter) found that managers are often reluctant to reduce dividend payments immediately. Instead, they try to maintain the existing level of dividends until it becomes clear that former profit levels cannot be achieved. At this point, they will usually make a single large reduction, rather than a series of small reductions to a new level of dividends.

A study by Baker and others (see reference 4 at the end of the chapter) asked US managers to express their views concerning dividend policy. Some of the key findings regarding managers' attitudes are shown in **Real World 9.8**.

Managers' attitudes towards dividends

Baker and others surveyed 188 managers of US, dividend-paying, listed businesses. The researchers wished to establish the views of managers concerning dividend policies adopted, why dividends are important and whether dividends affected the value of the business. Figure 9.5 sets out some of the key statements that managers were asked to consider and their responses.

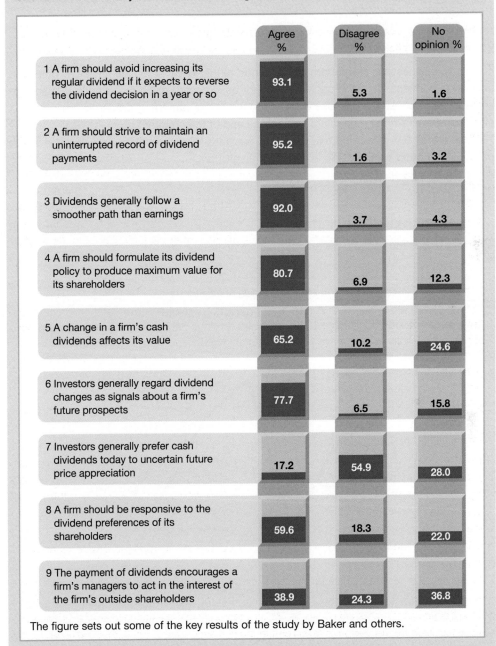

	Agree %	Disagree %	No opinion %
1 A firm should avoid increasing its regular dividend if it expects to reverse the dividend decision in a year or so	93.1	5.3	1.6
2 A firm should strive to maintain an uninterrupted record of dividend payments	95.2	1.6	3.2
3 Dividends generally follow a smoother path than earnings	92.0	3.7	4.3
4 A firm should formulate its dividend policy to produce maximum value for its shareholders	80.7	6.9	12.3
5 A change in a firm's cash dividends affects its value	65.2	10.2	24.6
6 Investors generally regard dividend changes as signals about a firm's future prospects	77.7	6.5	15.8
7 Investors generally prefer cash dividends today to uncertain future price appreciation	17.2	54.9	28.0
8 A firm should be responsive to the dividend preferences of its shareholders	59.6	18.3	22.0
9 The payment of dividends encourages a firm's managers to act in the interest of the firm's outside shareholders	38.9	24.3	36.8

The figure sets out some of the key results of the study by Baker and others.

Figure 9.5 The attitude of managers towards dividends

Source: Chart compiled from H. Baker, G. Powell and E. Theodor Veit, 'Revisiting managerial perspectives on dividend policy', *Journal of Economics and Finance*, Fall, 2002, pp. 267–283.

The study reveals that the majority of managers acknowledge the importance of a smooth, uninterrupted pattern of dividends. This is in line with the earlier findings of Lintner. The study also reveals that the majority of managers acknowledge the signalling effect and clientele effect but not the role of dividends in reducing agency costs. Their views, therefore, do not chime precisely with the theories concerning why dividends are important. Finally, the study reveals that the majority of managers do not support the bird-in-the-hand argument, and they therefore reject the traditional view. A more recent survey of the attitudes of managers of Canadian businesses, by Baker and others, found similar results to those above. (See reference 5 at the end of the chapter.)

DIVIDEND SMOOTHING IN PRACTICE

For many businesses, the pattern of dividends tends to be smoother than the pattern of underlying earnings. This is broadly what might be expected given the attitude of managers as described above. There is also evidence that a stable pattern of dividends has a positive effect on share returns. (See reference 6 at the end of the chapter.)

Real World 9.9 gives one example of a business where dividend smoothing is stated policy and another where dividend smoothing is evident.

Real World 9.9

Some real smoothies

Go-Ahead plc, the bus and rail operator, states on its website:

> We recognise that our dividend policy is a key part of the investment decision for many shareholders. Maintaining the amount of dividend per share throughout the economic cycle, including those times when earnings may reduce, is a high priority for us.

Mothercare plc is a specialist retailer of products for mothers-to-be and children. Over the six-year period to 31 March 2012, the basic earnings per share (EPS) and dividend per share (DPS) for the business were as set out in Figure 9.6.

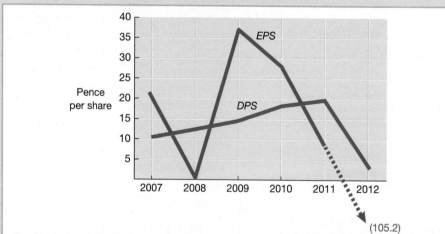

The figure shows that, whereas the basic earnings per share have been erratic, dividends per share have followed a smoother path over the six-year period. Although both measures decline in the most recent year, the decline in EPS is much more dramatic. A small dividend was still paid for this year.

Figure 9.6 Earnings and dividends per share for Mothercare plc over time

Sources: www.go-ahead.com, accessed 14 March 2013; chart compiled from information in Mothercare plc Annual Report and Accounts 2012, 2010 and 2008.

Sandarajan plc has recently obtained a listing on the Stock Exchange. The business operates a chain of supermarkets and was the subject of a management buyout five years ago. Since the buyout, the business has grown rapidly. The managers and a private equity firm owned 80 per cent of the shares prior to the Stock Exchange listing. However, this has now been reduced to 20 per cent. The record of the business over the past five years leading up to the listing is as follows:

Year	Profit for the year £000	Dividend £000	No. of shares issued 000s
1	420	220	1,000
2	530	140	1,000
3	650	260	1,500
4	740	110	1,500
5 (most recent)	880	460	1,500

Required:

(a) Comment on the dividend policy of the business leading up to the Stock Exchange listing.

(b) What advice would you give to the managers of the business concerning future dividend policy?

The answer to this question can be found at the back of the book on p. 568.

WHAT SHOULD MANAGERS DO?

Having read the above sections, you may be wondering what advice we should give to managers who are wrestling with the problem of dividend policy and who are looking for help. Probably the best advice is to make the dividend policy that is adopted clear to shareholders and then make every effort to keep to that policy. Shareholders are unlikely to welcome 'surprises' in dividend policy and may react by selling their shares and investing in businesses that have more stable and predictable dividend policies. Uncertainty over dividend policy will lower the value of the business's shares and will increase the cost of capital. If, for any reason, managers have to reduce the dividends for a particular year, they should prepare shareholders for the change and state clearly the reasons.

Dividends and financial policy

In this book we have dealt with three major areas of financial policy: the investment decision, the financing decision and the dividend decision. **Real World 9.10** provides some evidence concerning the importance of each to chief financial officers.

And the winner is . . .

A survey of investment and financing practices in five different countries was carried out by Cohen and Yagil (see Real World 4.10). This survey, based on a sample of the largest 300 businesses in each country, asked chief financial officers to rate the importance of the investment, financing and dividend decisions for their business using a scale from 1 (not important) through to 5 (very important). The survey results revealed the following scores:

	Mean score
Investment	4.23
Financing	3.90
Dividend	2.78

Although the dividend decision scored significantly lower than both the investment and financing decisions, there were significant differences in the importance assigned to the dividend decision between countries. It was considered more important in the UK (3.40) and Japan (3.57) than in the US (2.58) and Canada (2.06).

Source: G. Cohen and J. Yagil, 'A multinational survey of corporate financial policies', Working Paper, Haifa University, 2007.

ALTERNATIVES TO CASH DIVIDENDS

A business may make distributions to shareholders in a form different from a cash dividend. The two most important of these are scrip dividends and share buybacks. Below we consider each of these options.

Scrip dividends

A **scrip dividend** (or bonus share dividend) involves the issue of shares rather than the payment of cash to shareholders. The number of shares issued to each shareholder will be in proportion to the number of shares held. Thus, a 1-for-20 scrip dividend will mean that each shareholder will receive 1 new share for every 20 shares held. Making a scrip dividend simply involves the transfer of an amount from reserves to ordinary share capital. Total equity remains unchanged. Shares are then issued to shareholders that are equivalent in value to the amount transferred. Shareholder wealth should be unaffected by this procedure and so we might well ask why scrip dividends are made.

An important advantage for a business is that making a scrip dividend conserves the cash balance whereas a cash dividend does not. A scrip dividend also helps to keep total equity intact whereas a cash dividend will deplete total equity (by depleting reserves). For businesses struggling to keep within gearing limits demanded by lenders, this difference can be very important.

How will the gearing ratio of a business be affected by:

(a) a scrip dividend
(b) a cash dividend?

The gearing ratio (that is, long-term borrowing/(long-term borrowing + equity share capital and reserves)) will not be affected by a scrip dividend. We saw earlier that total equity is kept intact. A cash dividend, however, will deplete equity and shift the balance in favour of borrowings. This will increase the gearing ratio which, in turn, reflects an increase in financial risk.

Real World 9.11 provides an example of a business that paid a scrip dividend rather than a cash dividend to help strengthen its financial position.

Real World 9.11

Banking on a dividend

Millennium BCP, Portugal's largest listed bank by total assets, said on Wednesday it would pay a scrip dividend in shares instead of cash to strengthen the group's capital base and liquidity position. BCP is the third Portuguese lender within a week to announce plans to withhold or reduce cash dividends and increase capital because of funding difficulties caused by the eurozone debt crisis.

Carlos Santos Ferreira, chief executive, said that instead of cash, shareholders would receive new shares resulting from a €120m capital increase made through the incorporation of reserves.

This was the best way to 'find a balance between shareholder interests and the priority of preserving the group's capital and liquidity', he said.

Portugal's banks have been virtually frozen out of international capital markets since April when the country's sovereign debt rating was downgraded, forcing them to rely heavily on borrowing from the European Central Bank.

FT *Source*: Wise, P. (2011) 'Millennium BCP to pay scrip dividend', www.ft.com, 2 February.

A scrip dividend provides shareholders with the opportunity to increase their investment in the business without incurring share transaction costs. If the intention is to reinvest in the business, it would be preferable to a cash dividend. Often, shareholders are given the choice as to whether they wish to receive dividends in the form of cash or new shares. This may widen the appeal of the shares by making them attractive to both income-seeking and growth-seeking shareholders. Shareholders who elect to receive shares will increase their proportion of the total shares in issue compared with those taking the cash option. Taxation considerations are not an issue when deciding between cash dividends and scrip dividends as they are both treated as income for tax purposes.

Although a scrip issue will not, of itself, create value, shareholders may respond positively to a scrip dividend if it is interpreted as a sign of the managers' confidence in the future. They may believe that the managers will maintain the same dividend per share in the future, despite the increase in the number of shares in issue. Various studies have shown a positive market response to scrip dividend announcements. If a business does not maintain or increase its dividend per share in subsequent periods, however, the positive effect on share prices will be lost.

As scrip dividends increase the number of shares in issue, there is a risk that they will undermine the prospects of future rights issues. Shareholders may not wish to invest in the business beyond their scrip dividends. Some businesses have therefore abandoned scrip dividends and replaced them with a dividend re-investment plan (DRIP). Under such a plan, a business will buy shares in the open market on behalf of shareholders wishing to reinvest their cash dividends in the business. By operating a DRIP there is no increase in the number of shares in issue. However, cash will not be retained within the business and shareholders will incur (relatively small) transaction costs.

Share buybacks

A **share buyback** occurs when a business buys its own shares and then cancels them. To implement a share buyback, a business may acquire its shares:

1 in the open market in much the same way as any other shareholder, or
2 through a tender offer where a fixed number of shares is acquired at a particular price over a particular period or at a particular date, or
3 through an agreement with particular shareholders.

The law normally requires public companies to buy back shares from funds generated either from distributable profits or from the proceeds of a fresh issue of shares.

Buybacks or dividends?

Both share buybacks and cash dividends lead to funds being returned to shareholders. This raises the question as to which of the two methods shareholders would prefer. If we assume perfect capital markets, they should be indifferent between the two. A simple example should make this point clear.

Example 9.2

Chang plc has 1 million shares in issue and surplus cash of £2 million, which is to be distributed to shareholders. Following this distribution, earnings are expected to be £1 million per year and the price/earnings ratio is expected to be 8 times. The distribution will be made by either:

(i)   a dividend of £2.00 per share, or
(ii) a tender offer of 200,000 shares at £10 per share.

The risk and growth prospects of the business will be unaffected by the choice of distribution method and so the total market value (TMV) of the shares following distribution will be unaffected. The TMV (whichever distribution method is used) will therefore be:

$$\text{TMV} = \text{Earnings} \times \text{P/E ratio} = £1\ \text{million} \times 8 = \underline{£8\ \text{million}}.^*$$

Under the dividend option, however, there will be 1 million shares in issue and under the buyback option there will be 800,000 shares in issue. This means that the value per share will be £8 (£8m/1m) under the dividend option and £10 (£8m/800,000) under the buyback option.

Let us now consider the situation of a shareholder with 10,000 shares under both the dividend option and the buyback option – where there is a choice of either holding or selling the shares.

	Dividend option	Buyback option Hold	Sell
	£	£	£
10,000 shares held at £8 per share	80,000		
10,000 shares held at £10 per share		100,000	
10,000 shares sold at £10 per share			100,000
Dividend received (10,000 × £2)	20,000		
	100,000	100,000	100,000

We can see that total wealth is the same under each option and so the shareholder should be indifferent between them.

* We know from Chapter 3 that the price/earnings (P/E) ratio is MV/EPS. This can be rearranged so that MV = EPS × PE ratio (where MV = market value per share and EPS = earnings per share).

To find the TMV of the shares, rather than the value of a single share, it is therefore:

$$TMV = (Total)\ Earnings \times P/E\ ratio$$

Activity 9.15

Can you see any similarities between this line of argument and one that we considered earlier in the chapter?

The argument is similar to the MM argument concerning shareholder indifference between dividends and capital gains.

Share buybacks and imperfect markets

The above example relies on the assumptions underpinning perfect capital markets mentioned earlier such as no transaction costs, no taxation and so on. In our world of imperfect markets, however, managers may view share buybacks differently to dividends. We have seen that managers usually feel committed to maintaining a sustainable level of dividend payments. This means they will avoid increasing dividends, which then have to be decreased in subsequent periods.

Share buybacks, meanwhile, tend to be regarded as a residual. Thus, where there is a need to make exceptional distributions to shareholders, a buyback may be viewed as the better option. While the same effect may be achieved by a 'special' dividend to shareholders, a buyback focuses on those shareholders wishing to receive cash. There is also the advantage that payments to shareholders can be spread over a longer period.

The circumstances where a share buyback may be used include the following:

Undervalued shares. Share buybacks may be carried out where share values are temporarily depressed. In such circumstances, open market purchases can benefit shareholders who continue to hold. Buying back shares below their intrinsic value will transfer wealth from those shareholders that sell to those that hold. Thus, share buybacks can discriminate between shareholders. If, however, shareholders become aware that the buyback indicates that shares are undervalued, share prices are likely to rise quickly. Assuming they rise to their intrinsic value, the real wealth of shareholders will then be reflected in the market value of the shares. This will result in greater equity between those shareholders that hold and those that sell.

Activity 9.16

Why will it result in greater equity between the two shareholder groups?

Those that sell will receive a market price that reflects the intrinsic value of the shares. This means that there will be no transfer of wealth between those that hold and those that sell. Although those that hold will not increase their real wealth, it will now be reflected in the market price of the shares held.

To alter the capital structure. A business may use buybacks to achieve an optimal capital structure. A survey of finance directors of the top 200 UK businesses found that this was the main reason cited for share buybacks (see reference 7 at the end of the chapter). Buybacks reduce the amount of equity in relation to borrowings. By shifting the capital structure in favour of borrowings, the cost of capital may be lowered, which may, in turn, boost the share price. This will not, however, automatically occur: the additional benefits of higher gearing must outweigh the additional risks.

Returning surplus funds. Where a business has no profitable investment opportunities in which to invest, returning any surplus funds may be the best option for shareholders. More mature, low-growth businesses are more likely to find themselves in this position than younger, high-growth businesses.

It is worth pointing out that postponing, or even abandoning, a share buyback does not incur the kind of adverse reaction from shareholders that normally accompanies a cut in dividends. This may explain, at least in part, why managers do not always display the same commitment to carrying out buybacks as they do to paying dividends.

Real World 9.12 sets out the views of Warren Buffett, chairman, and Charlie Munger, vice-chairman, of Berkshire Hathaway Inc. towards share buybacks. (It should be mentioned that neither are great fans of the notion of efficient markets.) In this piece, Warren Buffett argues that shares must be undervalued by the market for buybacks to be worthwhile.

A guide to share buybacks

Charlie and I favour buybacks when two conditions are met: first, a company has ample funds to take care of the operational and liquidity needs of its business; second, its share is selling at a material discount to the company's intrinsic business value, conservatively calculated.

We have witnessed many bouts of buybacks that failed our second test. Sometimes, of course, infractions – even serious ones – are innocent; many CEOs never stop believing their share is cheap. In other instances, a less benign conclusion seems warranted. It doesn't suffice to say that buybacks are being made to offset the dilution from share issuances or simply because a company has excess cash. Continuing shareholders are *hurt* unless shares are purchased below intrinsic value. The first law of capital allocation – whether the money is slated for acquisitions or share buybacks – is that what is smart at one price is dumb at another.

Charlie and I have mixed emotions when Berkshire shares sell well below intrinsic value. We like making money for continuing shareholders, and there is no surer way to do that than by buying an asset – our own shares – that we know to be worth *at least* x for less than that – for 0.9x, 0.8x or even lower. (As one of our directors says, it's like shooting fish in a barrel, *after* the barrel has been drained and the fish have quit flopping.) Nevertheless, we don't enjoy cashing out partners at a discount, even though our doing so may give the selling shareholders a slightly higher price than they would receive if our bid was absent. When we are buying, therefore, we want those exiting partners to be fully informed about the value of the assets they are selling.

At our limit price of 110% of book value, repurchases clearly increase Berkshire's per-share intrinsic value. And the more and the cheaper we buy, the greater the gain for continuing shareholders. Therefore, if given the opportunity, we will likely repurchase shares aggressively at our price limit or lower. You should know, however, that we have no interest in supporting the share and that our bids will fade in particularly weak markets. Nor will we buy shares if our cash-equivalent holdings are below $20 billion. At Berkshire, financial strength that is unquestionable takes precedence over all else.

Source: Adapted from W. Buffett, Shareholder letter, www.berkshirehathaway.com, 26 February 2011, p. 6.

Some further issues

We saw earlier that the clientele effect, market signalling and reducing agency costs were important when considering dividends. Let us now consider these in the context of share buybacks.

Clientele effect

We have seen that the tax position of shareholders can exert an influence over whether capital gains or dividends are preferred. Any profits arising from the sale of shares are normally treated as capital gains and taxation rules tend to treat these more leniently than dividends. This means that share buybacks may be a more tax-efficient method of returning funds to shareholders. Where buybacks are made on a regular and frequent basis, however, the tax authorities may conclude that their purpose is simply to avoid taxation. This runs the risk that they will be treated as dividends for tax purposes.

Market signalling

In an imperfect world, managers may have access to information that shareholders do not have. Thus, if managers believe that the market undervalues the shares, they may wish to send a signal to the market concerning this fact. Whereas shareholders may discount bullish predictions, concrete actions such as share buybacks or increased dividends are usually taken more seriously.

A share buyback announcement may, however, send an ambiguous signal as buybacks may benefit managers rather than shareholders, as we shall see later. All relevant information will therefore be examined by shareholders to decide how the announcement should be interpreted. Thus, to establish whether a proposed buyback signals that shares are under-valued, shareholders may look for supporting evidence, such as a decision by managers to hold on to their shares.

Reducing agency costs

We saw earlier that managers may use business resources in ways that benefit themselves rather than shareholders. Where managers distribute any temporary cash surplus to share-holders through a share buyback, however, this risk can be reduced. If fresh capital is required at a later date, managers will then have to submit to the judgement of the market. When a buyback is used to alter the capital structure, agency costs may also be reduced. Where borrowings are substituted for equity capital, there will be an increase in interest pay-ments. This will subject managers to much tighter financial discipline as it will reduce the discretionary funds available.

Share buybacks and managers' incentives

There is a risk that poorly designed management incentive plans will encourage share buy-backs, even though they may not benefit shareholders. This can arise when incentive plans focus on achieving certain financial targets without sufficient regard to their nature or the ways in which they may be achieved. Two examples illustrate the problems that can arise.

Management share options

A common form of incentive plan is to give managers share options. These options give managers the right, but not the obligation, to purchase shares in the business at an agreed price at some future date. If the current market value exceeds the agreed price at that due date, they will make a gain by taking up the options. Managers are therefore given an incentive to increase share price in an attempt to align their interests with those of shareholders.

Excessive focus on share price, however, may not be in the best interests of share-holders. Share price represents only one part of the shareholders' total return: the other part is dividend payments. Undue concern for share price may lead managers to restrict dividend payments. We saw earlier that, following a dividend payment, share prices will be lower than if a share buyback for the same amount took place. Managers therefore have an incentive to employ buybacks rather than dividend payments as it can increase the value of their options.

Increasing earnings per share

Where a business has surplus funds, buying back shares will reduce the number of shares in issue but may have little or no effect on earnings. The result will be an increase in earnings per share. As this measure is often used in managers' long-term incentive plans, there is a risk that managers will try to improve this measure through a share buyback in order to boost their rewards. **Real World 9.13** cites an example where share buybacks have boosted EPS, leading to increased management rewards.

What Next?

The management of Next plc have been described as 'buyback junkies par excellence' by brokers Collins Stewart, which cites the retailer as an example where share buybacks can put the interests of shareholders and management in direct opposition.

Between 2000 and 2007, the company bought back one-third of its shares, creating considerable value for continuing shareholders. Between April and November 2007, however, the company spent £464m buying back around 10% of the shares as the price fell from its peak. As of the end of November, those shares would have had a market value of £374m – a notional loss of £70m for continuing shareholders, says Collins Stewart.

However, share buybacks in 2006–7 would have increased EPS by more than 4% than if cash had been returned via a special dividend, while buybacks in 2007–8 added 6.6% to EPS. But, as Collins Stewart points out, the board's annual performance bonus starts to pay out with EPS growth of 5%. 'The executives are in the money even if operating performance is flat,' says Collins Stewart, adding that the top four executives earned an extra £360,000 between them last year as a result of the buybacks.

Source: M. Goddard, 'The value of share buybacks', *Financial Director*, 28 February 2008. Copyright Inclusive Media Investments Limited 2008. Reproduced with permission.

It is worth making the point that increasing earnings per share is not the same as increasing shareholder value. This investment ratio is influenced by accounting policy choices and fails to take account of the cost of capital and future cash flows, which are the determinants of value. Thus, a change in this investment ratio may be of no real significance to shareholders.

Informing shareholders

As share buybacks may be for the benefit of managers rather than shareholders, there is a case for a much stronger light to be shone on them. There have been calls for buyback announcements to be accompanied by clear explanations as to why they are taking place as well as the likely effect on future profits, capital structure and dividends. There have also been calls for reporting the extent to which past share buybacks achieved their stated objectives.

SUMMARY

The main points in this chapter may be summarised as follows:

Dividends

■ Represent a return by a business to its shareholders.

■ There are legal limits on dividend distributions to protect lenders and creditors.

■ Are usually paid twice a year by large listed businesses.

■ Cum-dividend share prices include the accrued dividend; ex-dividend prices exclude the dividend.

■ Businesses often have a target dividend payout ratio or target dividend cover ratio.

Dividend policy and shareholder wealth

- There are two major schools of thought concerning the effect of dividends on shareholder wealth.
- The traditional school argues that shareholders prefer dividends now because the amounts are more certain.
- The implications for managers are that they should adopt as generous a dividend policy as possible.
- The modernists (MM) argue that, given perfect and efficient markets, the pattern of dividends has no effect on shareholder wealth.
- The implication for managers is that one dividend policy is as good as another and so they should not spend time considering which policy should be adopted.
- The MM position assumes no share issue costs, no share transaction costs and no taxation; these assumptions weaken (but do not necessarily destroy) their arguments.

Dividends in practice

- Appear to be important to shareholders.
- The clientele effect, the signalling effect and the need to reduce agency costs may explain this.
- The level of dividends distributed is dependent on various factors, including investment and financing opportunities, legal and loan requirements, profit stability, control issues (including takeover threats), market expectations and inside information.

Management attitudes

- Managers perceive dividends as being important for shareholders.
- They prefer a smooth increase in dividends and are reluctant to cut dividends.

Scrip dividends

- Do not, of themselves, create value, but may be interpreted as a sign of managers' confidence in the future and so share prices may rise.
- Allow shareholders to increase their investment in the business without incurring transaction costs.
- May undermine future rights issues as existing shareholders may not wish to invest in more shares.

Share buybacks

- Involve repurchasing and then cancelling shares.
- May be preferred to dividends for exceptional distributions to deal with undervalued shares, alter the capital structure and return surplus funds to shareholders.
- The clientele effect, reducing agency costs and the signalling effect are also relevant in share buybacks.
- Poorly designed management incentive plans may lead to share buybacks that do not benefit shareholders.

REFERENCES

1 Lintner, J. (1956) 'Distribution of incomes of corporations among dividends, retained earnings and taxes', *American Economic Review*, 46, May, 97–113.

2 Fama, E.F. and Babiak, H. (1968) 'Dividend policy: An empirical analysis', *Journal of the American Statistical Association*, December.

3 DeAngelo, H., DeAngelo, L. and Skinner, D. (1992) 'Dividends and losses', *Journal of Finance*, December, 281–9.

4 Baker, H., Powell, G. and Theodore Veit, E. (2002) 'Revisiting managerial perspectives on dividend policy', *Journal of Economics and Finance*, Fall, 267–83.

5 Baker, H., Saadi, S. and Dutta, S. (2007) 'The perception of dividends by Canadian managers: New survey evidence', *International Journal of Managerial Finance*, 3, 1, 70–91.

6 Ap Gwilym, O., Morgan, G. and Thomas, S. (2000) 'Dividend stability, dividend yield and stock returns: UK evidence', *Journal of Business Finance and Accounting*, 27, 261–81.

7 Dixon, R., Palmer, G., Stradling, B. and Woodhead, A. (2008) 'An empirical survey of the motivation for share repurchases in the UK', *Managerial Finance*, 34, 12, 886–906.

FURTHER READING

If you wish to explore the topics discussed in this chapter in more depth, try the following books:

Arnold, G. (2013) *Corporate Financial Management*, 5th edn, Pearson, Chapter 19.

Baker, H.K. (2009) *Dividends and Dividend Policy*, John Wiley & Sons, Chapters 1, 4, 5 and 6.

McLaney, E. (2012) *Business Finance: Theory and practice*, 9th edn, Financial Times Prentice Hall, Chapter 12.

Pike, R., Neale, B. and Linsley, P. (2012) *Corporate Finance and Investment*, 7th edn, Pearson, Chapter 17.

REVIEW QUESTIONS

Answers to these questions can be found in at the back of the book on p. 577.

9.1 Why should a business wish to buy back some of its shares?

9.2 'The business's dividend decision is really a by-product of its capital investment decision.' Discuss.

9.3 Is it really important for a business to try to meet the needs of different types of shareholders when formulating its dividend policy?

9.4 Describe how agency theory may help to explain the dividend policy of businesses.

Exercises 9.4 to 9.7 are more advanced than 9.1 to 9.3. Those with coloured numbers have answers at the back of the book, starting on p. 596.

If you wish to try more exercises, visit the students' side of this book's companion website.

9.1 What are the arguments for and against issuing a scrip dividend rather than a cash dividend?

9.2 The managers of Gripton plc are currently deciding between a dividend payment and a share buyback as a means of distributing funds to shareholders.

Required:
Which of the two do you think is more appropriate, assuming that the managers are concerned with:

(i)   flexibility regarding the level of distribution
(ii) ensuring equity between different shareholders
(iii) signalling information clearly to the markets?

Explain each of your answers.

9.3 The dividend policy of businesses has been the subject of much debate in the financial management literature.

Required:
Discuss the view that the pattern of dividend can increase the wealth of shareholders.

9.4 The following listed businesses each have different policies concerning distributions to shareholders:

- North plc pays all profits available for distribution to shareholders in the form of a cash dividend each year.
- South plc has yet to pay any cash dividends to shareholders and has no plans to make dividend payments in the foreseeable future.
- West plc buys back shares from shareholders as an alternative to a dividend payment.
- East plc offers shareholders the choice of either a small but stable cash dividend or a scrip dividend each year.

Required:
Discuss the advantages and disadvantages of each of the above policies.

9.5 Fellingham plc has 20 million ordinary £1 shares in issue. No shares have been issued during the past four years. The business's earnings and dividends record taken from the past financial statements showed:

	Year 1	Year 2	Year 3	Year 4 (most recent)
Earnings per share	11.00p	12.40p	10.90p	17.20p
Dividend per share	10.00p	10.90p	11.88p	12.95p

At the annual general meeting for Year 1, the chairman indicated that it was the intention to consistently increase annual dividends by 9 per cent, anticipating that, on average, this would maintain the spending power of shareholders and provide a modest growth in real income.

In the event, subsequent average annual inflation rates, measured by the general index of prices, have been:

Year 2	11%
Year 3	10%
Year 4	8%

The ordinary shares are currently selling for £3.44, excluding the Year 4 dividend.

Required:
Comment on the declared dividend policy of the business and its possible effects on both Fellingham plc and its shareholders, illustrating your answer with the information provided.

9.6 Mondrian plc is a new business that aims to maximise the wealth of its shareholders. The board of directors is currently trying to decide upon the most appropriate dividend policy to adopt for the business's shareholders. However, there is strong disagreement among three of the directors concerning the benefits of declaring cash dividends:

■ Director A argues that cash dividends would be welcomed by shareholders and that as high a dividend payout ratio as possible would reflect positively on the market value of the business's shares.

■ Director B argues that whether a cash dividend is paid or not is irrelevant in the context of shareholder wealth maximisation.

■ Director C takes an opposite view to Director A and argues that dividend payments should be avoided as they would lead to a decrease in shareholder wealth.

Required:
(a) Discuss the arguments for and against the position taken by each of the three directors.
(b) Assuming the board of directors decides to pay a dividend to shareholders, what factors should be taken into account when determining the level of dividend payment?

9.7 Traminer plc provides software solutions for the airline industry. At present, shares in the business are held by the senior managers and by a venture capital business. However, Traminer plc intends to seek a Stock Exchange listing and to make 75 per cent of the ordinary shares available to the investing public. The board of directors recently met to decide upon a dividend policy for the business once it has become listed. However, the meeting ended without agreement.

Information relating to the business over the past five years is set out below:

Year ended 30 April	Ordinary shares in issue 000	Profit for the year £000	Ordinary share dividends £000
2009	500	840	420
2010	500	1,190	580
2011	800	1,420	340
2012	1,000	1,940	450
2013	1,000	2,560	970

Required:
Evaluate the dividend policy pursued by Traminer plc over the past five years and discuss whether any changes to this policy are required.

Chapter 10

MANAGING WORKING CAPITAL

INTRODUCTION

This chapter considers the factors to be taken into account when managing the working capital of a business. Each element of working capital will be identified and the major issues surrounding them will be discussed. Working capital represents a significant investment for many businesses and so its proper management and control can be vital. We saw in Chapter 4 that an investment in working capital is typically an important aspect of many new investment proposals.

Learning outcomes

When you have completed this chapter, you should be able to:

■ Identify the main elements of working capital.

■ Discuss the purpose of working capital and the nature of the working capital cycle.

■ Explain the importance of establishing policies for the control of working capital.

■ Explain the factors that have to be taken into account when managing each element of working capital.

WHAT IS WORKING CAPITAL?

Working capital is usually defined as current assets less current liabilities. The major elements of current assets are:

- inventories
- trade receivables
- cash (in hand and at bank).

The major elements of current liabilities are:

- trade payables
- bank overdrafts.

The size and composition of working capital can vary between industries. For some types of business, the investment in working capital can be substantial. A manufacturing business, for example, will often invest heavily in raw material, work in progress and finished goods. It will also normally sell its goods on credit, giving rise to trade receivables. A retailer, meanwhile, holds only one form of inventories (finished goods) and will normally sell its goods for cash rather than on credit. Many service businesses hold no inventories.

Most businesses buy goods and/or services on credit, giving rise to trade payables. Few, if any, businesses operate without a cash balance. In some cases, however, it is a negative one (a bank overdraft).

Working capital represents a net investment in short-term assets. These assets are continually flowing into and out of the business and are essential for day-to-day operations. The various elements of working capital are interrelated and can be seen as part of a short-term cycle. For a manufacturing business, the working capital cycle can be depicted as shown in Figure 10.1.

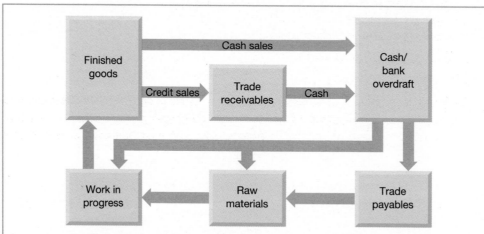

Cash is used to pay trade payables for raw materials, or raw materials are bought for immediate cash settlement. Cash is also spent on labour and other items that turn raw materials into work in progress and, finally, into finished goods. The finished goods are sold to customers either for cash or on credit. In the case of credit customers, there will be a delay before the cash is received from the sales. Receipt of cash completes the cycle.

Figure 10.1 The working capital cycle

For a retailer the situation would be as in Figure 10.1 except that there will be only inventories of finished goods. There will be no work in progress or raw materials. For a purely service business, the working capital cycle would also be similar to that depicted in Figure 10.1 except that there would be no inventories of finished goods or raw materials. There may well be work in progress, however, since many forms of service take time to complete. A case handled by a firm of solicitors, for example, may take several months. During this period, costs will build up before the client is billed for them.

Managing working capital

The management of working capital is an essential part of the business's short-term planning process. Management must decide how much of each element should be held. As we shall see later, there are costs associated with holding either too much or too little of each element. Management must be aware of these costs, which include opportunity costs, in order to manage working capital effectively. Potential benefits must then be weighed against likely costs in order to achieve the optimum investment.

The working capital needs of a business are likely to vary over time as a result of changes in the business environment. Managers must constantly monitor these changes to ensure that the business retains an appropriate level of investment in working capital.

Activity 10.1

What kinds of changes in the business environment might lead to a decision to change the level of investment in working capital? Try to identify four possible changes that could affect the working capital needs of a business.

These may include the following:

- changes in interest rates
- changes in market demand for the business's output
- changes in the seasons
- changes in the state of the economy.

You may have thought of others.

Changes arising within the business could also alter working capital needs. These internal changes might include using different production methods (resulting, perhaps, in a need to hold a lower level of inventories) and changes in the level of risk that managers are prepared to take.

THE SCALE OF WORKING CAPITAL

It is tempting to think that, compared with the scale of investment in non-current assets, the amounts invested in working capital are trivial. However, this is not the case. For many businesses, the scale of investment in working capital is vast.

Real World 10.1 gives some impression of the working capital investment for five UK businesses that either are very well known by name or whose products are everyday commodities for most of us. These businesses were randomly selected, except that each one is high profile and from a different industry. For each business, the major items appearing on the statement of financial position are expressed as a percentage of the total investment by the providers of long-term finance (equity and non-current liabilities).

A summary of the statements of financial position of five UK businesses

Business:	Next plc	easyJet plc	Babcock Int Group plc	Tesco plc	Severn Trent plc
Statement of financial position date:					
	28.1.12	30.9.12	31.3.12	25.2.12	31.3.12
Non-current assets	64	98	107	120	96
Current assets					
Inventories	34	–	9	11	1
Trade and other receivables	63	8	23	8	7
Other current assets	–	–	–	10	–
Cash and near cash	6	36	5	12	4
	103	44	37	41	12
Total assets	167	142	144	161	108
Equity and non-current liabilities	100	100	100	100	100
Current liabilities					
Trade and other payables	49	34	39	36	6
Taxation	9	1	1	1	1
Other short-term liabilities	–	2	4	18	–
Overdrafts and short-term borrowings	9	5	–	6	1
	67	42	44	61	8
Total equity and liabilities	167	142	144	161	108

The non-current assets, current assets and current liabilities are expressed as a percentage of the total net long-term investment (equity plus non-current liabilities) of the business concerned. Next plc is a major retail and home shopping business. easyJet is a leading airline. Babcock International Group plc is a large engineering and support business. Tesco plc is one of the UK's leading supermarkets. Severn Trent plc is an important supplier of water, sewerage services and waste management, mainly in the UK.

Source: Table constructed from information appearing in the financial statements for the year ended during 2012 for each of the five businesses concerned.

Real World 10.1 reveals quite striking differences in the make-up of the statement of financial position from one business to the next. Take, for example, the current assets and current liabilities. Although the totals for current assets are pretty large when compared with the total long-term investment, these percentages vary considerably between businesses. When looking at the mix of current assets, we can see that only Next, Babcock and Tesco, which produce and/or sell goods, hold significant amounts of inventories. The other two businesses are service providers and so inventories are not a significant item. We can also see that very few of Tesco's, easyJet's and Severn Trent's sales are on credit, as they have relatively little invested in trade receivables.

Note that Tesco's trade payables are much higher than its trade receivables. They are also high compared with its inventories. Since trade payables represent amounts due to suppliers of inventories, it means that Tesco receives the cash from a typical trolley load of groceries well in advance of paying for them.

In the sections that follow, we shall consider each element of working capital separately and how they might be properly managed. Before doing so, however, it is worth looking at

Real World 10.2, which suggests that there is scope for improving working capital management among European businesses.

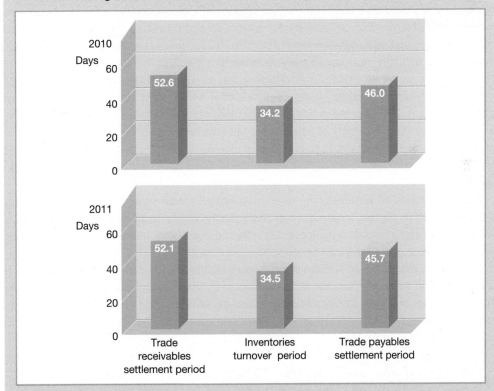

Real World 10.2 focuses on the working capital problems of large businesses. For smaller businesses, however, these problems may be even more acute.

MANAGING INVENTORIES

A business may hold inventories for various reasons, the most common of which is to meet the immediate day-to-day requirements of customers and production. However, a business may hold more than is necessary for this purpose where there is a risk that future supplies may be interrupted or scarce. Similarly, if there is a risk that the cost of inventories will increase in the future, a business may decide to buy in large quantities.

For some types of business, inventories held may represent a substantial proportion of total assets held. For example, a car dealership that rents its premises may have nearly all of its total assets in the form of inventories. Manufacturers also tend to invest heavily in inventories as they need to hold three kinds of inventories: raw materials, work in progress and finished goods. Each form of inventories represents a particular stage in the production cycle.

For some types of business, the level of inventories held may vary substantially over the year owing to the seasonal nature of the industry. A greetings card manufacturer may provide an example of such a business. For other businesses, inventories levels may remain fairly stable throughout the year.

Businesses that hold inventories simply to meet the day-to-day requirements of their customers, and for production, will normally seek to minimise the amount of inventories held. This is because there are significant costs associated with holding inventories. These costs include:

- storage and handling costs
- the cost of financing the inventories
- the cost of pilferage and obsolescence
- the cost of opportunities forgone in tying up funds in this form of asset.

To gain some impression of the cost involved in holding inventories, **Real World 10.3** estimates the *financing* cost of inventories for four large businesses.

Inventories financing cost

The financing cost of inventories for each of four large businesses, based on their respective opportunity costs of capital, is calculated below:

Business	Type of operations	Cost of capital (a) %	Average inventories held* (b)	Financing cost of holding inventories (a) × (b)	Operating profit	Financing cost as a % of operating profit/(loss) %
Associated British Foods	Food producer	10.4	£1,463m	£152m	£873m	17.4
International Airlines Group	Airline	10.0	€158m	€16m	€552m	2.9
Marks and Spencer	General retailer	16.5	£684m	£113m	£747m	15.1
J Sainsbury	Supermarket	10.0	£866m	£87m	£874m	10.0

* Based on opening and closing inventories for the relevant financial period.

We can see that for three of the four businesses, inventories financing costs are significant in relation to their operating profits. The nature of their businesses requires Associated British Foods, Marks and Spencer and J Sainsbury to invest heavily in inventories. (However, J Sainsbury is likely to move its inventories more quickly than the other two.) For International Airlines Group (BA and Iberia), inventories financing costs are not significant. This is because it is a service provider with a much lower investment in inventories.

These figures do not take account of other costs of inventories holding mentioned earlier, such as the cost of providing secure storage. As these costs may easily outweigh the costs of finance, the total cost of maintaining inventories may be very high in relation to operating profits.

The four businesses were not selected because they have particularly high inventories' costs but simply because they are among the relatively few that publish their costs of capital.

Source: Annual reports of the businesses for the years ended 2011 and 2012.

Given the potentially high cost of holding inventories, it may be tempting to think that a business should seek to hold few or no inventories. There are, however, costs that may arise when the level of inventories is too low.

What costs might a business incur as a result of holding too low a level of inventories? Try to jot down at least three types of cost.

In answering this activity you may have thought of the following costs:

- loss of sales, from being unable to provide the goods required immediately
- loss of customer goodwill, for being unable to satisfy customer demand
- purchasing inventories at a higher price than might otherwise have been necessary in order to replenish inventories quickly
- high transport costs incurred to ensure that inventories are replenished quickly
- lost production due to shortage of raw materials
- inefficient production scheduling due to shortages of raw materials.

Before dealing with the various approaches that can be taken to managing inventories, let us consider **Real World 10.4**. It describes how one large international business has sought to reduce its inventories level.

Back to basics

Wal-Mart has said it will seek further reductions in the levels of backroom inventory it holds at its US stores, in a drive to improve its performance . . . John Menzer, vice chairman and head of Wal-Mart's US operations, made the retailer's efforts to cut inventory one of the key elements of remarks to reporters this week when he outlined current strategy. Wal-Mart, he said, currently 'has a real focus on reducing our inventory. Inventory that's on trailers behind our stores, in backrooms and on shelves in our stores'. Cutting back on inventory, he said, reduced 'clutter' in the retailer's stores, gave a better return on invested capital, reduced the need to cut prices on old merchandise, and increased the velocity at which goods moved through the stores.

Eduardo Castro-Wright, chief executive of Wal-Mart's US store network, said the inventory reduction marked a return to basics for the retailer, which would be 'getting more disciplined'. Earlier this year, he said Wal-Mart would link inventory reduction to incentive payments to its officers and managers. Wal-Mart is already regarded as one of the most efficient logistical operations in US retailing. It is currently rolling out to all its US stores and distribution centres a new parallel distribution system that speeds the delivery to stores of 5,000 high turnover (sale revenue) items. It is also discussing with its suppliers how new RFID radio frequency tagging could be used to further reduce the volume of goods in transit to its stores. But further reductions in its inventory turnover would release working capital that could fund investment in its ongoing initiatives to improve its stores.

Adrienne Shapira, retail analyst at Goldman Sachs, has estimated that the retailer could reduce its annual inventory by 18 per cent, which would lead to a $6 billion reduction in working capital needs on a trailing 12-month basis.

FT   *Source*: Birchall, J. (2006) 'Wal-Mart aims for further inventory cuts', www.ft.com, 19 April.
© The Financial Times Limited 2012. All Rights Reserved.

To help manage inventories, a number of procedures and techniques may be employed. We shall now consider the more important of these.

Forecasting future demand

Preparing appropriate projections, or forecasts, is one of the best ways to ensure that inventories will be available to meet future production and sales requirements. These projections should deal with each product that the business makes and/or sells. It is important that they are realistic, as they will determine future ordering and production levels. The projections may be derived in various ways. We saw in Chapter 2 that they may be developed using statistical techniques, such as time series analysis, or may be based on the judgement of the sales and marketing staff.

Financial ratios

One ratio that can be used to help monitor inventories levels is the average inventories turnover period ratio, which we examined in Chapter 3. This ratio is calculated as follows:

$$\text{Dividend cover} = \frac{\text{Earnings for the year available for dividends}}{\text{Dividends announced for the year}}$$

The ratio provides a picture of the average period for which inventories are held. This can be useful as a basis for comparison. The average inventories turnover period can be calculated for individual product lines as well as for inventories as a whole.

Recording and reordering systems

A sound system of recording inventories movements is a key element in managing inventories. There should be proper procedures for recording inventories purchases and usages. Periodic checks should be made to ensure that the amount of physical inventories held corresponds with what is indicated by the inventories' records.

There should also be clear procedures for the reordering of inventories. Authorisation for both the purchase and the issue of inventories should be confined to a few nominated members of staff. This should avoid problems of duplication and lack of coordination. To determine the point at which inventories should be reordered, information will be required concerning the lead time (that is, the time between the placing of an order and the receipt of the goods) and the likely level of demand.

Activity 10.4

An electrical wholesaler sells a particular type of light switch. The annual demand for the light switch is 10,400 units and the lead time for orders is four weeks. Demand for the light switch is steady throughout the year. At what level of inventories of the light switch should the business reorder, assuming that it is confident of the information given above?

The average weekly demand for the switch is 10,400/52 = 200 units. During the time between ordering new switches and receiving them, the quantity sold will be 4×200 units = 800 units. So the business should reorder no later than when the level held reaches 800 units. This should avoid running out of inventories.

For most businesses, there will be some uncertainty surrounding the level of demand, pattern of demand and lead time. To avoid the risk of running out of inventories, a buffer, or safety, inventories level may be maintained. The amount of buffer inventories is a matter of judgement. In forming this judgement, the following should be taken into account:

■ the degree of uncertainty concerning the above factors
■ the likely costs of running out of the item concerned
■ the cost of holding the buffer inventories.

The effect of holding a buffer will be to raise the inventories level at which an order for new inventories is placed (the reorder point).

Activity 10.5

Assume the same facts as in Activity 10.4. However, we are also told that the business maintains buffer inventories of 300 units. At what level should the business reorder?

Reorder point = expected level of demand during the lead time *plus* the level of buffer inventories
= 800 + 300
= 1,100 units

Carrying buffer inventories will increase the cost of holding inventories. This must, however, be weighed against the cost of running out of inventories, in terms of lost sales, production problems and so on.

Activity 10.6

Hora plc holds inventories of a particular type of motor car tyre, which is ordered in batches of 1,200 units. The supply lead times and usage rates for the tyres are:

	Maximum	Most likely	Minimum
Supply lead times	25 days	15 days	8 days
Daily usage	30 units	20 units	12 units

The business wishes to avoid the risk of running out of inventories.

At what minimum level of inventories should Hora plc place a new order, such that it can guarantee not to run out?

What is the size of the buffer inventories based on the most likely lead times and usages?

If Hora plc were to place an order based on the maximum lead time and usage, but only the minimum lead time and usage were actually to occur, what would be the level of inventories immediately following the delivery of the new inventories? What does this inventories figure represent?

To be certain of avoiding running out of inventories, the business must assume a reorder point based on the maximum usage and lead time. This is 750 units (that is, 30×25).

The most likely usage during the lead time will be only 300 units (that is, 20×15). Thus, the buffer inventories based on most likely usage and lead time is 450 units (that is, $750 - 300$).

The level of inventories when a new order of 1,200 units is received, immediately following the minimum supply lead time and minimum daily usage during the lead time, is 1,854 units (that is, $1,200 + 750 - (8 \times 12)$). This represents the maximum inventories holding for the business.

Real World 10.5 is an extract from an article that discusses the problems of maintaining control over inventories in the modern retail environment.

Real World 10.5

Taking stock

As any successful shopkeeper will tell you, it is essential to know exactly what you have in stock (inventories) and where to find it. But the proliferation of sales channels and long-distance supply chains in today's retail environment are making this increasingly difficult.

Typically, there are loosely joined, but not integrated, inventory systems for stores, distribution centres and tracking, says Stephen Leng, retail merchandising and supply director for IBM Global Business Services. 'This is combined with inaccurate forecasting, poor promotional planning and little visibility on what is happening up and down the supply chain.'

The situation has been exacerbated in recent years, by the 'tsunami' of ecommerce, says Jonathan Bellwood, founder of PeopleVox, a retail inventory software company. Ideally, customers should be able to identify what they want on a website and swiftly take delivery, or collect it, at a convenient location. 'I might want to buy a Ted Baker shirt in the evening and pick it up on the way into the office next day,' says Mr Bellwood. To enable this, retailers need an integrated view of all products spanning stores, warehouses and goods in transit. They also need to know what has been returned by customers – up to 50 per cent for some internet shopping sites. Most inventory systems are not up to the task, Mr Bellwood says.

The result is frustration for customers when they visit shops that lack items they have seen online, or websites unable to specify which retail outlets have an item in stock.

Helen Slaven, vice-president of Torex, a retail consultancy and technology provider, agrees that retailers lack visibility of stock across multiple channels. 'Sometimes they are discounting in one channel while out of stock in another,' she says.

Creating a unified database meant having to be 'extremely brutal', she says. 'Retailers had to rip out existing systems and put in expensive upgrades, or lots of manual controls, both of which affect margins.'

FT *Source*: Extracts from Bird, J. (2012) 'Inventory control in retail', www.ft.com, 13 February.
© The Financial Times Limited 2012. All Rights Reserved.

Levels of control

Deciding on the appropriate level of inventories control to adopt requires a careful weighing of costs and benefits. This may lead to the implementation of different levels of control according to the nature of the inventories held. The **ABC system of inventories control** is based on the idea of selective levels of control. A business may find it possible to divide its inventories into three broad categories: A, B and C. Each category will be based on the value of inventories held, as illustrated in Example 10.1.

Example 10.1

Alascan Products plc makes door handles and door fittings. It makes them in brass, in steel and in plastic. The business finds that brass fittings account for 10 per cent of the physical volume of the finished inventories that it holds, but these represent 65 per cent of the total value. These are treated as Category A inventories. There are sophisticated recording procedures, tight control is exerted over inventories movements and there is a high level of security where the brass inventories are stored. This is economically viable because these inventories represent a relatively small proportion of the total volume.

The business finds that steel fittings account for 30 per cent of the total volume of finished inventories and represent 25 per cent of the total value. These are treated as Category B inventories, with a lower level of recording and management control being applied.

The remaining 60 per cent of the volume of inventories is plastic fittings, which represent the least valuable items, accounting for only 10 per cent of the total value of finished inventories held. These are treated as Category C inventories, so the level of recording and management control would be lower still. Applying to these inventories the level of control that is applied to Category A or even Category B inventories would be uneconomic.

Categorising inventories in this way helps to direct management effort to the most important areas. It also helps to ensure that the costs of controlling inventories are proportionate to their value.

Figure 10.3 provides a graphical depiction of the ABC approach to inventories control.

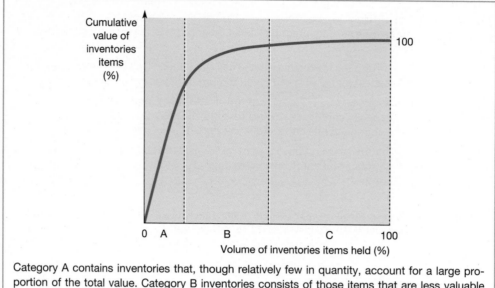

Category A contains inventories that, though relatively few in quantity, account for a large proportion of the total value. Category B inventories consists of those items that are less valuable but more numerous. Category C comprises those inventories items that are very numerous but relatively low in value. Different inventories' control rules would be applied to each category. For example, only Category A inventories would attract the more expensive and sophisticated controls.

Figure 10.3 ABC method of analysing and controlling inventories

INVENTORIES MANAGEMENT MODELS

Economic order quantity

Decision models may be used to help manage inventories. The **economic order quantity (EOQ)** model is concerned with determining the quantity of a particular inventories item that should be ordered each time. In its simplest form, the EOQ model assumes that demand is constant. This implies that inventories will be depleted evenly over time to be replenished just at the point that they run out. These assumptions would lead to a 'saw-tooth' pattern to represent inventories movements, as shown in Figure 10.4.

The EOQ model recognises that the key costs associated with inventories management are the cost of holding the inventories and the cost of ordering them. The model can be used to calculate the optimum size of a purchase order by taking account of both of these cost elements. The cost of holding inventories can be substantial. Management may, therefore, try to minimise the average amount of inventories held and with it, the holding cost. It will, however, increase the number of orders placed during the period and so ordering costs will rise.

Figure 10.5 shows how, as the level of inventories and the size of inventories orders increase, the annual costs of placing orders will decrease because fewer orders will be placed. However, the cost of holding inventories will increase, as there will be higher average inventories levels. The total costs curve, which is based on the sum of holding costs and ordering costs,

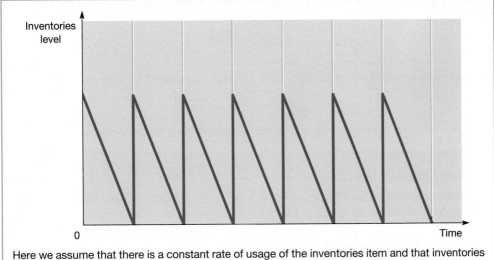

Here we assume that there is a constant rate of usage of the inventories item and that inventories are reduced to zero just as new inventories arrive. At time 0 there is a full level of inventories. This is steadily used as time passes and just as it falls to zero it is replaced. This pattern is then repeated.

Figure 10.4 Patterns of inventories movements over time

will fall until the point E, which represents the minimum total cost. Thereafter, total costs begin to rise. The EOQ model seeks to identify point E, at which total costs are minimised. This will represent half of the optimum amount that should be ordered on each occasion. Assuming, as we are doing, that inventories are used evenly over time and that they fall to zero before being replaced, the average inventories level equals half of the order size.

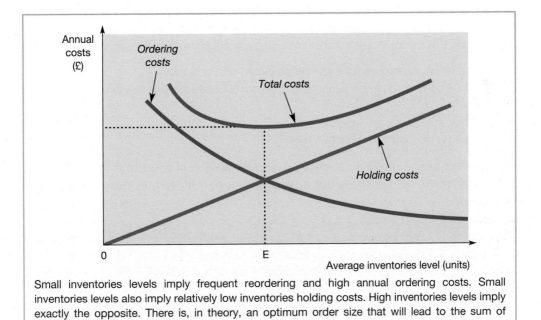

Small inventories levels imply frequent reordering and high annual ordering costs. Small inventories levels also imply relatively low inventories holding costs. High inventories levels imply exactly the opposite. There is, in theory, an optimum order size that will lead to the sum of ordering and holding costs (total costs) being at a minimum.

Figure 10.5 Inventories holding and order costs

The EOQ model, which can be used to derive the most economic order quantity, is:

$$EOQ = \sqrt{\frac{2DC}{H}}$$

where D = the annual demand for the inventories item (expressed in units of the inventories item)

C = the cost of placing an order

H = the cost of holding one unit of the inventories item for one year.

Activity 10.7

HLA Ltd sells 2,000 bags of cement each year. It has been estimated that the cost of holding one bag of cement for a year is £4. The cost of placing an order for new inventories is estimated at £250.

Calculate the EOQ for bags of cement.

Your answer to this activity should be as follows:

$$EOQ = \sqrt{\frac{2 \times 2,000 \times 250}{4}} = 500 \text{ bags}$$

This will mean that the business will have to order bags of cement four times each year (that is 2,000/500) in batches of 500 bags so that sales demand can be met.

Note that the cost of inventories, which is the price paid to the supplier, does not directly affect the EOQ model. It is concerned only with the administrative costs of placing and handling each order and the costs of holding the inventories. However, more expensive inventories items tend to have greater holding costs. This may be because an ABC system of inventories control is in place or because they tie up more finance than less expensive inventories, or both. Therefore the cost of inventories may have an indirect influence on the economic order size that is calculated.

The basic EOQ model has a number of limiting assumptions. In particular, it assumes that:

■ demand for an inventories item can be predicted with accuracy
■ demand is constant over the period and does not fluctuate through seasonality or for other reasons
■ no 'buffer' inventories are required
■ there are no discounts for bulk purchasing.

The model can be modified, however, to overcome each of these limiting assumptions. Many businesses use this model (or a development of it) to help in the management of inventories.

Activity 10.8

Petrov plc sells 10,000 tonnes of sand each year and demand is constant over time. The purchase cost of each tonne is £15 and the cost of placing and handling an order is estimated to be £32. The cost of holding 1 tonne of sand for one year is estimated to be £4. The business uses the EOQ model to determine the appropriate order quantity and holds no buffer inventories.

Calculate the total annual cost of trading in this product.

The total annual cost will be made up of three elements:

- the cost of purchases
- the cost of ordering
- the cost of holding this item in inventories.

The annual cost of purchases is $10,000 \times £15 = £150,000$.

The annual cost of ordering is calculated as follows:

The EOQ is:

$$EOQ = \sqrt{\frac{2 \times 10,000 \times 32}{4}} = 400 \text{ tonnes}$$

This will mean that $10,000/400 = 25$ orders will be placed each year. The annual cost of ordering is therefore $25 \times £32 = £800$.

The annual cost of holding inventories is calculated as follows:

The average quantity of inventories held will be half the optimum order size, as mentioned earlier. That is, $400/2 = 200$ tonnes.

The annual holding cost is therefore $200 \times £4 = £800$

The total annual cost of trading in this product is therefore:

$$£150,000 + £800 + £800 = £151,600*$$

* Note that the annual ordering cost and annual holding cost are the same. This is no coincidence. If we look back at Figure 10.5 we can see that the economic order quantity represents the point at which total costs are minimised. At this point, annual order costs and annual holding costs are equal.

Materials requirement planning systems

A materials requirement planning (MRP) system takes planned sales demand as its starting point. It then uses a computer package to help schedule the timing of deliveries of bought-in parts and materials to coincide with production requirements. It is a coordinated approach that links materials and parts deliveries to the scheduled time of their input to the production process. By ordering only those items that are necessary to ensure the flow of production, inventories levels are likely to be reduced. MRP is really a 'top-down' approach to inventories management, which recognises that inventories ordering decisions cannot be viewed as being independent of production decisions. The MRP approach can be extended to provide a fully integrated approach to production planning. This involves taking account of other manufacturing resources such as labour and machine capacity.

Just-in-time inventories management

In recent years, many businesses have tried to eliminate the need to hold inventories by adopting just-in-time (JIT) inventories management. This approach was originally used in the US defence industry during the Second World War, but was first used on a wide scale by Japanese manufacturing businesses. The essence of JIT is, as the name suggests, to have supplies delivered to the business just in time for them to be used in the production process or in a sale. By adopting this approach, the inventories holding cost rests with suppliers rather than with the business itself. A failure by a particular supplier to deliver on time, however, could cause enormous problems and costs to the business. Thus JIT may save cost, but it tends to increase risk.

For JIT to be successful, it is important that a business informs suppliers of its inventories requirements in advance. Suppliers must then deliver materials of the right quality at the agreed times. Any delivery failures could lead to a dislocation of production and could be very costly. This means a close relationship is required between a business and its suppliers. It may also mean that suppliers have to be physically close to the business. A close relationship should enable suppliers to schedule their own production to that of the business. This should result in a net saving, between supplier and business, in the amount of inventories that need to be held.

Adopting JIT may well require re-engineering a business's production process. To ensure that orders are quickly fulfilled, factory production must be flexible and responsive. This may require changes to both the production layout and working practices. Production flows may have to be redesigned and employees may have to be given greater responsibility to allow them to deal with unanticipated problems and to encourage greater commitment. Information systems must also be installed that facilitate an uninterrupted production flow.

Although a business that applies JIT will not have to hold inventories, there may be other costs associated with this approach. For example, the close relationship necessary between the business and its suppliers may prevent the business from taking advantage of cheaper sources of supply that become available. Furthermore, suppliers may need to hold inventories for the customer and so may try to recoup this additional cost through increased prices. The close relationship between customer and supplier, however, should enable the supplier to predict its customers' inventories needs. This means that suppliers can tailor their own production to that of the customer.

JIT is widely viewed as more than simply an inventories control system. The philosophy underpinning this approach is that of *total quality management*. This is concerned with eliminating waste and striving for excellence. There is an expectation that suppliers will always deliver inventories on time and that there will be no defects in the items supplied. There is also an expectation that, for manufacturers, the production process will operate at maximum efficiency. This means that there will be no production breakdowns and the queuing and storage times of products manufactured will be eliminated, as only time spent directly on processing the products is seen as adding value. While these expectations may be impossible to achieve, they can help to create a culture that is dedicated to the pursuit of excellence and quality.

Real World 10.6 and **Real World 10.7** show how two very well-known businesses operating in the UK (one a retailer, the other a manufacturer) use JIT to advantage.

Real World 10.6

JIT at Boots

Boots, the UK's largest health care retailer, has improved inventories management at its stores. The business is working towards a JIT system where delivery from its one central warehouse in Nottingham will be made every day to each retail branch, with nearly all of the inventories lines being placed directly on to the sales shelves, not into a store room at the branch. This is expected to bring major savings of stores' staff time and lead to significantly lower levels of inventories being held, without any lessening of the service offered to customers. In fact, the need to hold little or no inventories in the stores, except on the shelves, liberates more space that can be used for selling. The new system has led to major economic benefits for the business.

Sources: Information taken from 'Boots £60 million warehouse will improve supply chain', www.thisisnottingham.co.uk, 22 January 2009; 'Alliance Boots shortlisted for responsible business of the year 2012', Business in the Community, www.bitc.org.uk, 29 May 2012.

JIT at Nissan

Nissan Motors UK Ltd, the UK manufacturing arm of the world-famous Japanese car business, has a plant in Sunderland in the north east of England. Here it operates a fairly well-developed JIT system. For example, Calsonic Kansei supplies car exhausts from a factory close to the Nissan plant. It makes deliveries to Nissan once every 30 minutes on average, so as to arrive exactly as they are needed in production. This is fairly typical of all of the 200 suppliers of components and materials to the Nissan plant.

The business used to have a complete JIT system. More recently, however, Nissan has drawn back from its total adherence to JIT. By using only local suppliers it had cut itself off from the opportunity to exploit low-cost suppliers, particularly those located in China. A change in policy has led the business to hold buffer inventories for certain items to guard against disruption of supply arising from sourcing parts from the Far East.

Sources: Information taken from 'Planning for quality and productivity', *The Times* 100 Case Study, www.tt100.biz; C. Tighe, 'Nissan reviews just-in-time parts policy', *Financial Times*, 23 October 2006; Sunderland Automotive Conference 2010, www.automotiveinternational.co.uk; T. Rowley, 'Beaming North East business hails Nissan's growth', *The Journal*, www.journallive.co.uk.

MANAGING TRADE RECEIVABLES

Selling goods or services on credit will result in costs being incurred by a business. These costs include the costs of credit administration, of bad debts and of opportunities forgone to use the funds for other purposes. However, these costs must be weighed against the benefits of increased sales revenue resulting from the opportunity for customers to delay payment.

Selling on credit is very widespread and is the norm outside the retail industry. When a business offers to sell its goods or services on credit, it must have clear policies concerning:

■ which customers should receive credit
■ how much credit should be offered
■ what length of credit it is prepared to offer
■ whether discounts will be offered for prompt payment
■ what collection policies should be adopted
■ how the risk of non-payment can be reduced.

In this section, we shall consider each of these issues.

Which customers should receive credit and how much should they be offered?

A business offering credit runs the risk of not receiving payment for goods or services supplied. Therefore care must be taken over the type of customer to whom credit facilities are offered and how much credit is allowed. When considering a proposal from a customer for the supply of goods or services on credit, a business should take into account a number of factors. The following five Cs of credit provide a useful checklist:

■ *Capital.* The customer must appear to be financially sound before any credit is extended. Where the customer is a business, its financial statements should be examined. Particular regard should be given to the customer's likely future profitability and liquidity. In addition, any major financial commitments (such as outstanding borrowings, capital expenditure commitments and contracts with suppliers) should be taken into account.

- *Capacity.* The customer must appear to have the capacity to pay for the goods acquired on credit. The customer's payment record to date should be examined to provide important clues. To help further assess capacity, the type of business and the amount of credit required in relation to the customer's total financial resources should be taken into account.
- *Collateral.* On occasions, it may be necessary to ask for some kind of security for goods supplied on credit. When this occurs, the business must be convinced that the customer is able to offer a satisfactory form of security.
- *Conditions.* The state of the industry in which the customer operates, as well as the general economic conditions of the particular region or country, should be taken into account. The sensitivity of the customer's business to changes in economic conditions can also have an important influence on the ability of the customer to pay on time.
- *Character.* It is important to make some assessment of the customer's character. The willingness to pay will depend on the honesty and integrity of the individual with whom the business is dealing. Where the customer is a business, this will mean assessing the characters of its senior managers as well as their reputation within the industry. The selling business must feel confident that the customer will make every effort to pay any amounts owing.

To help assess the above factors, various sources of information are available. They include:

- *Trade references.* Some businesses ask potential customers to provide references from other suppliers that have extended credit to them. This can be extremely useful as long as the references provided are truly representative of the opinions of all the customer's suppliers. There is a danger that a potential customer will be selective when giving details of other suppliers, in an attempt to create a more favourable impression than is deserved.
- *Bank references.* It is possible to ask the potential customer for a bank reference. Although banks are usually prepared to supply references, their contents are not always very informative. The bank will usually charge a fee for providing a reference.
- *Published financial statements.* A limited company is obliged by law to file a copy of its annual financial statements with the Registrar of Companies. These are available for public inspection and can provide a useful insight into performance and financial position. Many companies also publish their annual financial statements on their websites or on computer-based information systems.
- *The customer.* Interviews with the directors of the customer business and visits to its premises may be carried out to gain an impression of the way that the customer conducts its business. Where a significant amount of credit is required, the business may ask the customer for access to internal forecasts and other unpublished financial information to help assess the level of risk involved.
- *Credit agencies.* Specialist agencies exist to provide information that can be used to assess the creditworthiness of a potential customer. The information that a credit agency supplies may be gleaned from various sources, including the customer's financial statements and news items relating to the customer from both published and unpublished sources. The credit agencies may also provide a credit rating for the business. Agencies will charge a fee for their services.
- *Register of County Court Judgments.* Any money judgments given against the business or an individual in a county court will be maintained on the register for six years. This register is available for inspection by any member of the public for a small fee.
- *Other suppliers.* Similar businesses will often be prepared to exchange information concerning slow payers or defaulting customers through an industry credit circle. This can be a reliable and relatively cheap way of obtaining information.

Activity 10.9

We mentioned above that although banks are usually prepared to supply references, their contents are not always very informative. Why might this be the case?

If a bank customer is in financial difficulties, the bank may be unwilling to add to its problems by supplying a poor reference. It is worth remembering that the bank's loyalty is likely to be with the customer rather than the enquirer.

Once a customer is considered creditworthy, credit limits should be established. When doing so, the business must take account of its own financial resources and risk appetite. Unfortunately, there are no theories or models to guide a business when deciding on the appropriate credit limit to adopt; it is really a matter of judgement. Some businesses adopt simple 'rule of thumb' methods based on the amount of sales made to the customer (say, twice the monthly sales figure for the customer) or the maximum the business is prepared to be owed (say, a maximum of 20 per cent of its working capital) by all of its customers.

Length of credit period

A business must determine what credit terms it is prepared to offer its customers. The length of credit offered to customers can vary significantly between businesses. It may be influenced by such factors as:

- the typical credit terms operating within the industry
- the degree of competition within the industry
- the bargaining power of particular customers
- the risk of non-payment
- the capacity of the business to offer credit
- the marketing strategy of the business.

The last point may require some explanation. If, for example, a business wishes to increase its market share, it may decide to be more generous in its credit policy in an attempt to stimulate sales. Potential customers may be attracted by the offer of a longer credit period. However, any such change in policy must take account of the likely costs and benefits arising. To illustrate this point, consider Example 10.2.

Example 10.2

Torrance Ltd produces a new type of golf putter. The business sells the putter to wholesalers and retailers and has an annual sales revenue of £600,000. The following data relate to each putter produced:

	£
Selling price	40
Variable cost	(20)
Fixed cost apportionment	(6)
Profit	14

The business's cost of capital is estimated at 10 per cent a year.

Torrance Ltd wishes to expand the sales volume of the new putter. It believes that offering a longer credit period can achieve this. The business's average trade receivables settlement period is currently 30 days. It is considering three options in an attempt to increase sales revenue. These are as follows:

	Option		
	1	2	3
Increase in average settlement period (days)	10	20	30
Increase in sales revenue (£)	30,000	45,000	50,000

To help the business to decide on the best option, the benefits of the various options should be weighed against their respective costs. Benefits will be represented by the increase in profit from the sale of additional putters. From the information supplied we can see that the contribution to profit (that is, selling price (£40) less variable costs (£20)) is £20 a putter. This represents 50 per cent of the selling price. So, whatever increase occurs in sales revenue, the additional contribution to profit will be half of that figure. The fixed cost can be ignored in our calculations, as it will remain the same whichever option is chosen.

The increase in contribution under each option will therefore be:

	Option		
	1	2	3
50% of the increase in sales revenue (£)	15,000	22,500	25,000

The increase in trade receivables under each option will be as follows:

	Option		
	1	2	3
	£	£	£
Projected level of trade receivables:			
40 × £630,000/365 (Note 1)	69,041		
50 × £645,000/365 (Note 2)		88,356	
60 × £650,000/365			106,849
Current level of trade receivables:			
30 × £600,000/365	(49,315)	(49,315)	(49,315)
Increase in trade receivables	19,726	39,041	57,534

The increase in receivables that results from each option will mean an additional finance cost to the business.

The net increase in the business's profit arising from the projected change is:

	Option		
	1	2	3
	£	£	£
Increase in contribution (see above)	15,000	22,500	25,000
Increase in finance cost (Note 3)	(1,973)	(3,904)	(5,753)
Net increase in profits	13,027	18,596	19,247

The calculations show that Option 3 will be the most profitable one.

Notes:

1 If the annual sales revenue totals £630,000 and 40 days' credit is allowed (both of which will apply under Option 1), the average amount that will be owed to the business by its customers, at any point during the year, will be the daily sales revenue (that is, £630,000/365) multiplied by the number of days that the customers take to pay (that is 40).

2 Exactly the same logic applies to Options 2 and 3 and to the current level of trade receivables.

3 The increase in the finance cost for Option 1 will be the increase in trade receivables (£19,726) × 10 per cent. The equivalent figures for the other options are derived in a similar way.

Example 10.2 illustrates the broad approach that a business should take when assessing changes in credit terms. However, by extending the length of credit, other costs may be incurred. These may include bad debts and additional collections costs, which should also be taken into account in the calculations.

Real World 10.8 shows how the length of credit taken varies greatly from one well-known UK business to the next.

Real World 10.8

Credit where it's due

The following are the lengths of time taken, on average, for each business to pay its credit suppliers (trade payables):

	Days taken
British Sky Broadcasting plc (satellite TV)	Fewer than 45
British Telecommunications Group plc (telecommunications)	61
easyJet plc (airline)	10
Greene King plc (brewer and hotel and pub operator)	62
JD Wetherspoon (pub operator)	58
Kingfisher plc (DIY retailer)	45
Marks and Spencer Group plc (retail)	26
Severn Trent Water plc (water)	21
Tate and Lyle plc (sugar)	53
Vodafone Group plc (telecommunications)	43
WH Smith plc (retail)	59
Wm Morrison Supermarkets plc (retail)	30

It is striking how much the days taken to pay suppliers vary from one business to another. Industry differences do not seem to explain this. BT takes around 50 per cent longer to pay than Vodafone. WH Smith takes more than twice the time that Marks and Spencer takes to pay.

Source: Based on information in the financial statements of the businesses concerned for the financial year ended during 2012.

An alternative approach to evaluating the credit decision

It is possible to view the credit decision as a capital investment decision. Granting trade credit involves an opportunity outlay of resources in the form of cash (which has been temporarily forgone) in the expectation that future cash flows will be increased (through higher sales) as a result. A business will usually have choices concerning the level of investment to be made in credit sales and the period over which credit is granted. These choices will result in different returns and different levels of risk. There is no reason in principle why the NPV investment appraisal method, which we considered in Chapter 4, should not be used to evaluate these choices. The NPV method takes into account both the time value of money and the level of risk involved.

Approaching the problem as an NPV assessment is not different in principle from the way that we dealt with the decision in Example 10.2. In both approaches the time value of money is considered, but in Example 10.2 we did it by charging a financing cost on the outstanding trade receivables.

Cash discounts

To encourage prompt payment from its credit customers, a business may offer a **cash discount** (or discount for prompt payment). The size of any discount will be an important influence on whether a customer decides to pay promptly.

From the business's viewpoint, the cost of offering discounts must be weighed against the likely benefits in the form of a reduction both in the cost of financing trade receivables and in the amount of bad debts. Example 10.3 shows how this may be done.

Example 10.3

Williams Wholesalers Ltd currently asks its credit customers to pay by the end of the month after the month of delivery. In practice, customers take rather longer to pay – on average 70 days. Sales revenue amounts to £4 million a year and bad debts to £20,000 a year.

It is planned to offer customers a cash discount of 2 per cent for payment within 30 days. Williams estimates that 50 per cent of customers will accept this facility but that the remaining customers, who tend to be slow payers, will not pay until 80 days after the sale. At present the business has an overdraft facility at an interest rate of 13 per cent a year. If the plan goes ahead, bad debts will be reduced to £10,000 a year and there will be savings in credit administration expenses of £6,000 a year.

Should Williams Wholesalers Ltd offer the new credit terms to customers?

Solution

The first step is to determine the reduction in trade receivables arising from the new policy.

		£	£
Existing level of trade receivables	(£4m × 70/365)		767,123
New level of trade receivables:	£2m × 80/365	438,356	
	£2m × 30/365	164,384	(602,740)
Reduction in trade receivables			164,383

The costs and benefits of offering the discount can be set out as follows:

	£	£
Cost and benefits of policy		
Cost of discount (£2m × 2%)		40,000
Less		
Interest saved on the reduction in trade receivables		
(£164,383* × 13%)	21,370	
Administration cost saving	6,000	
Cost of bad debts saved (20,000 – 10,000)	10,000	(37,370)
Net cost of policy		2,630

These calculations show that the business will be worse off by offering the new credit terms.

* It could be argued that the interest should be based on the amount expected to be received; that is the value of the trade receivables *after* taking account of the discount. Basing it on the expected receipt figure would not, however, alter the conclusion that the business should not offer the new credit terms.

In practice, there is always the danger that a customer may be slow to pay and yet may still take the discount offered. Where the customer is important to the business, it may be difficult to insist on full payment. How might a business overcome this problem?

Instead of allowing customers to deduct a discount, customers who pay promptly can be rewarded separately, say on a three-monthly basis. The reward could be a cash payment to the customer or, perhaps, a credit note. The value of the reward would be equal to the cash discounts earned by each customer during the three months.

Debt factoring and invoice discounting

Trade receivables can, in effect, be turned into cash by either factoring them or having sales invoices discounted. Both are forms of asset-based finance, which involves a financial institution providing a business with an advance up to 80 per cent of the value of the trade receivables outstanding. These methods, which are popular approaches to managing receivables, were discussed in Chapter 6.

Credit insurance

It is often possible for a supplier to insure its entire trade receivables, individual customer accounts or the outstanding balance relating to a particular transaction.

Collection policies

A business offering credit must ensure that receivables are collected as quickly as possible so that non-payment risk is minimised and operating cash flows are maximised. Various steps can be taken to achieve this, including the following.

Develop customer relationships

For major customers it is often useful to cultivate a relationship with the key staff responsible for paying sales invoices. By so doing, the chances of prompt payment may be increased. For less important customers, the business should at least identify the key members of staff responsible for paying invoices, who can be contacted in the event of a payment problem.

Publicise credit terms

The credit terms of the business should be made clear in all relevant correspondence, such as order acknowledgements, invoices and statements. In early negotiations with the prospective customer, credit terms should be openly discussed and an agreement reached.

Issue invoices promptly

An efficient collection policy requires an efficient accounting system. Invoices (bills) must be sent out promptly to customers, as must monthly statements. Reminders must also be despatched promptly to customers who are late in paying. If a customer fails to respond to a reminder, the accounting system should alert managers so that a stop can be placed on further deliveries.

Monitor outstanding receivables

Management can monitor the effectiveness of collection policies in a number of ways. One method is to calculate the average settlement period for trade receivables ratio, which we met in Chapter 3. This ratio is calculated as follows:

$$\text{Average settlement period for trade receivables} = \frac{\text{Average trade receivables}}{\text{Credit sales}} \times 365$$

Although this ratio can be useful, it is important to remember that it produces an *average* figure for the number of days for which debts are outstanding. This average may be badly distorted by a few large customers who are very slow, or very fast, payers.

Produce an ageing schedule of trade receivables

A more detailed and informative approach to monitoring receivables may be to produce an ageing schedule of trade receivables. Receivables are divided into categories according to the length of time they have been outstanding. An ageing schedule can be produced, on a regular basis, to help managers see the pattern of outstanding receivables. An example of an ageing schedule is set out in Example 10.4.

Example 10.4

Ageing schedule of trade receivables at 31 December

Customer	Days outstanding				Total
	1 to 30 days	31 to 60 days	61 to 90 days	More than 90 days	
	£	£	£	£	£
A Ltd	12,000	13,000	14,000	18,000	57,000
B Ltd	20,000	10,000	–	–	30,000
C Ltd	–	24,000	–	–	24,000
Total	32,000	47,000	14,000	18,000	111,000

This shows a business's trade receivables figure at 31 December, which totals £111,000. Each customer's balance is analysed according to how long the amount has been outstanding. (This business has just three credit customers.) To help focus management attention, accounts may be listed in order of size, with the largest debts first.

We can see from the schedule, for example, that A Ltd still has £14,000 outstanding for between 61 and 90 days (that is, arising from sales during October) and £18,000 outstanding for more than 90 days (that is, arising from sales during September or even before). This information can be very useful for credit control purposes.

Many accounting software packages now include this ageing schedule as one of the routine reports available to managers. Such packages often have the facility to put customers 'on hold' when they reach their credit limits. Putting a customer on hold means that no further credit sales will be made to that customer until amounts owing from past sales have been settled.

Identify the pattern of receipts

A slightly different approach to exercising control over receivables is to identify the pattern of receipts from credit sales on a monthly basis. This involves monitoring the percentage of credit sales that are paid in the month of sale and the percentage that is paid in subsequent months. To do this, credit sales for each month must be examined separately. Example 10.5 illustrates this.

A business made credit sales of £250,000 in June. It received 30 per cent of that amount during June, 40 per cent during July, 20 per cent during August and 10 per cent during September. The pattern of credit sales receipts and amounts owing is:

Pattern of credit sales receipts

	Receipts from June credit sales £	Amounts received %	Amount outstanding from June sales at month end £	Amount outstanding %
June	75,000	30	175,000	70
July	100,000	40	75,000	30
August	50,000	20	25,000	10
September	25,000	10	0	0

This information can be used as a basis for control. Targets may be established for the pattern of cash received from credit sales. The actual pattern can then be compared with the target pattern of receipts to see whether there is any significant deviation (see Figure 10.6). Where this is the case, managers should consider corrective action.

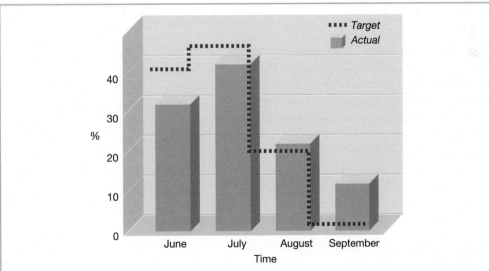

It can be seen that 30 per cent of the sales income for June is received in that month; the remainder is received in the following three months. The expected (target) pattern of cash receipts for June sales, which has been assumed, is also depicted. By comparing the actual and expected pattern of receipts, it is possible to see whether credit sales are being properly controlled and to decide whether corrective action is required.

Figure 10.6 Comparison of actual and expected (target) receipts over time for Example 10.5

Answer queries quickly

It is important for relevant staff to deal with customer queries on goods and services supplied quickly and efficiently. Payment is unlikely to be made by customers until their queries have been dealt with.

Deal with slow payers

A business making significant sales on credit will, almost inevitably, be faced with customers who do not pay. When this occurs, there should be established procedures for dealing with the problem. There should be a timetable for sending out reminders and for adding customers to a 'stop list' for future supplies. The timetable may also specify the point at which the unpaid amount is passed to a collection agency for recovery. These agencies often work on a 'no collection – no fee' basis. Charges for their services vary but can be up to 15 per cent of the amounts collected.

Legal action may also be considered against delinquent credit customers. The cost of such action, however, must be weighed against likely returns. There is little point, for example, in incurring large legal expenses to try to recoup amounts owing if there is evidence that the customer has no money. Where possible, an estimate of the cost of bad debts should be taken into account when setting prices for products or services.

As a footnote to our consideration of managing receivables, **Real World 10.9** outlines some of the excuses that long-suffering credit managers must listen to when chasing payment for outstanding debts.

Real World 10.9

It's in the post

The Atradius Group provides trade credit insurance and trade receivables collections services worldwide. It has a presence in 40 countries. Its products and services aim to reduce its customers' exposure to buyers who cannot pay for the products and services customers purchase. In a press release, Atradius stated:

> Although it happens rarely, some debtors (credit customers) still manage to surprise even us. These excuses have actually been used by credit customers:
>
> - It's not a valid debt as my vindictive ex-wife ran off with the company credit card.
> - I just got back from my luxury holiday, it cost more than I thought so I no longer have the funds to pay.
> - I wanted to pay but all the invoices were in my briefcase, which was stolen on the street.
> - My wife has been kidnapped and I need the money to get her back.

Source: www.atradius.uk/news/press-releases, 13 August 2008.

Reducing the risk of non-payment

Efficient collection policies are important in reducing the risk of non-payment. There are, however, other ways in which a business can reduce this type of risk. Possibilities include:

- requiring customers to pay part of their sale value in advance of the goods being sent
- agreeing to offset amounts owed for the purchase of goods against amounts due for goods supplied to the same business

- requiring a third-party guarantee from a financially sound business such as a bank or parent company
- making it a condition of sale that the legal title to the goods is not passed to the customer until the goods are paid for
- taking out insurance to cover the cost of any legal expenses incurred in recovering the amount owed. (Some customers may refuse to pay if they feel the business does not have the resources to pursue the debt through the courts.)

MANAGING CASH

Why hold cash?

Most businesses hold a certain amount of cash. There are broadly three reasons why they do so.

Activity 10.11

Can you think what these reasons may be?

The three reasons are:

1 *To meet day-to-day commitments*. A business needs a certain amount of cash to pay for wages, overhead expenses, goods purchased and so on, when they fall due. Cash has been described as the lifeblood of a business. Unless it circulates through the business and is available to meet maturing obligations, the survival of the business will be put at risk. Simply being profitable is not enough to ensure survival.

2 *For precautionary purposes*. If future cash flows are uncertain, it would be prudent to hold a balance of cash. For example, a major customer that owes a large sum to the business may be in financial difficulties. This could lead to an expected large receipt not arriving. By holding cash, the business could retain its capacity to meet its obligations. Similarly, if there is some uncertainty concerning future outlays, a cash balance will be needed.

3 *To exploit opportunities*. A business may decide to hold cash to put itself in a position to exploit profitable opportunities as and when they arise. For example, it may enable the acquisition of a competitor business that suddenly becomes available at an attractive price.

How much cash should be held?

The amount of cash held tends to vary considerably between businesses. The decision as to how much cash a business should hold is a difficult one. Various factors can influence the final decision.

Try to think of four possible factors that might influence the amount of cash that a business holds.

You may have thought of the following:

■ *The nature of the business*. Some businesses, such as utilities (for example, water, electricity and gas suppliers), have cash flows that are both predictable and reasonably certain. This will enable them to hold lower cash balances. For some businesses, cash balances may vary greatly according to the time of year. A seasonal business may accumulate cash during the high season to enable it to meet commitments during the low season.

■ *The opportunity cost of holding cash*. Where there are profitable opportunities in which to invest, it may not be wise to hold a large cash balance.

■ *The level of inflation*. Holding cash during a period of rising prices will lead to a loss of purchasing power. The higher the level of inflation, the greater will be this loss.

■ *The availability of near-liquid assets*. If a business has marketable securities or inventories that may easily be liquidated, high cash balances may not be necessary.

■ *The availability of borrowing*. If a business can borrow easily (and quickly) there is less need to hold cash.

■ *The cost of borrowing*. When interest rates are high, the option of borrowing becomes less attractive.

■ *Economic conditions*. When the economy is in recession, businesses may prefer to hold cash so that they can be well placed to invest when the economy improves. In addition, during a recession, businesses may experience difficulties in collecting trade receivables. They may therefore hold higher cash balances than usual in order to meet commitments.

■ *Relationships with suppliers*. Too little cash may hinder the ability of the business to pay suppliers promptly. This can lead to a loss of goodwill. It may also lead to discounts being forgone.

Controlling the cash balance

Several models have been developed to help control the cash balance of the business. One such model proposes the use of upper and lower control limits for cash balances and the use of a target cash balance. The model assumes that the business will invest in marketable investments that can easily be liquidated. These investments will be purchased or sold, as necessary, in order to keep the cash balance within the control limits.

The model proposes two upper and two lower control limits (see Figure 10.7). If the business exceeds either of the *outer* limits, the managers must decide whether, over the next few days, the cash balance is likely to return to a point within the *inner* control limits set. If this seems likely, then no action is required. If, however, it does not seem likely, managers should change the cash position by either buying or selling marketable investments. In Figure 10.7 we can see that the lower outer control limit has been breached for four days. If a four-day period is unacceptable, managers should sell marketable investments to replenish the cash balance.

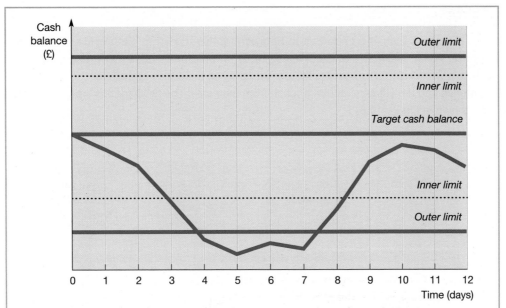

Management sets the upper and lower limits for the business's cash balance. When the balance goes beyond either of these limits, unless it is clear that the balance will return fairly quickly to within the limit, action will need to be taken. If the upper limit is breached, some cash will be placed on deposit or used to buy some marketable securities. If the lower limit is breached, the business will need to borrow some cash or sell some securities.

Figure 10.7 Controlling the cash balance

The model relies heavily on management judgement to determine where the control limits are set and the length of the period within which breaches of the control limits are acceptable. Past experience may be useful in helping managers decide on these issues. There are other models, however, that do not rely on management judgement. Instead, these use quantitative techniques to determine an optimal cash policy. One model proposed is the cash equivalent of the inventories economic order quantity model, discussed earlier in the chapter.

Projected cash flow statements and managing cash

To manage cash effectively, it is useful for a business to prepare a projected cash flow statement. This is a very important tool for both planning and control purposes. Projected cash flow statements were considered in Chapter 2 and so we shall not consider them again in detail. However, it is worth repeating that these statements enable managers to see how planned events are expected to affect the cash balance. The projected cash flow statements will identify periods when cash surpluses and cash deficits are expected.

When a cash surplus is expected to arise, managers must decide on the best use of the surplus funds. When a cash deficit is expected, managers must make adequate provision by borrowing, liquidating assets or rescheduling cash payments or receipts to deal with this. Projected cash flow statements can help to control the cash held. Actual cash flows can be compared with the projected cash flows for the period. If there is a significant divergence between the projected cash flows and the actual cash flows, explanations must be sought and corrective action taken where necessary.

To refresh your memory on projected cash flow statements it would probably be worth looking back at Chapter 2, pp. 36–40.

Operating cash cycle

When managing cash, it is important to be aware of the operating cash cycle (OCC) of the business. For a business that purchases goods on credit for subsequent resale on credit, such as a wholesaler, it represents the period between the outlay of cash for the purchase of inventories and the ultimate receipt of cash from their sale. The OCC for this type of business is as shown in Figure 10.8.

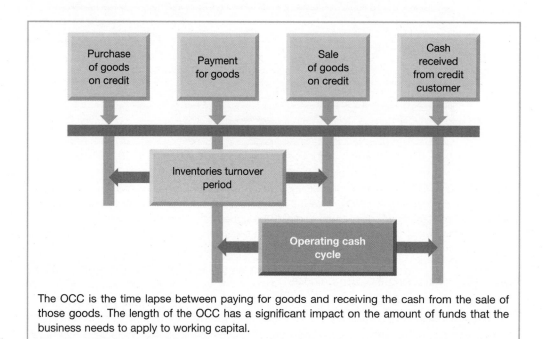

The OCC is the time lapse between paying for goods and receiving the cash from the sale of those goods. The length of the OCC has a significant impact on the amount of funds that the business needs to apply to working capital.

Figure 10.8 The operating cash cycle

Figure 10.8 shows that payment for inventories acquired on credit occurs some time after those inventories have been purchased. Therefore, no immediate cash outflow arises from the purchase. Similarly, cash receipts from credit customers will occur some time after the sale is made. There will be no immediate cash inflow as a result of the sale. The OCC is the period between the payment made to the supplier, for the goods concerned, and the cash received from the credit customer. Although Figure 10.8 depicts the position for a wholesaling business, the precise definition of the OCC can easily be adapted for other types of business.

The OCC is important because it has a significant influence on the financing requirements of the business. Broadly, the longer the cycle, the greater will be the financing requirements and the greater the financial risks. The business may therefore wish to reduce the OCC to the minimum period possible.

For businesses that buy and sell goods on credit, the OCC can be deduced from their financial statements through the use of certain ratios. The calculations required are as shown in Figure 10.9.

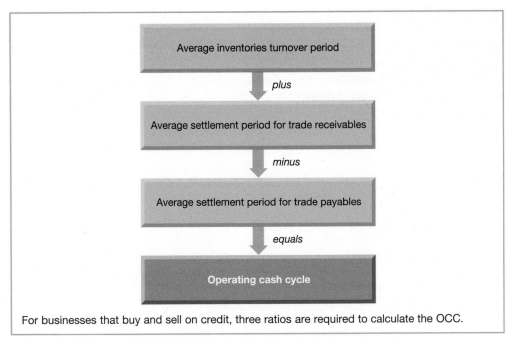

For businesses that buy and sell on credit, three ratios are required to calculate the OCC.

Figure 10.9 Calculating the operating cash cycle

Statement of financial position as at 31 December last year

	£000
ASSETS	
Non-current assets	
Property, plant and equipment	364
Current assets	
Inventories	166
Trade receivables	264
Cash	24
	454
Total assets	818
EQUITY AND LIABILITIES	
Equity	
Ordinary share capital	300
Retained earnings	352
	652
Current liabilities	
Trade payables	159
Taxation	7
	166
Total equity and liabilities	818

All purchases and sales are on credit. There has been no change in the level of trade receivables or payables over the period.

Calculate the length of the OCC for the business.

The OCC may be calculated as follows:

	Number of days
Average inventories turnover period:	
$\dfrac{\text{(Opening inventories + Closing inventories)}/2}{\text{Cost of sales}} \times 365 = \dfrac{(142 + 166)/2}{544} \times 365$	103
Average settlement period for trade receivables:	
$\dfrac{\text{Trade receivables}}{\text{Credit sales}} \times 365 = \dfrac{264}{820} \times 365$	118
Average settlement period for trade payables:	
$\dfrac{\text{Trade payables}}{\text{Credit purchases}} \times 365 = \dfrac{159}{568} \times 365$	(102)
OCC	119

We can see from the formula above that if a business wishes to reduce the OCC, it should do one or more of the following:

- reduce the average inventories turnover period
- reduce the average settlement period for trade receivables
- increase the average settlement period for trade payables.

Activity 10.14

Assume that Freezeqwik Ltd (Activity 10.13) wishes to reduce its OCC by 30 days. Evaluate each of the options available to this business.

The average inventories turnover period for the business represents more than three months' sales requirements. Similarly, the average settlement period for trade receivables represent nearly four months' sales. Both periods seem quite long. It is possible that both could be reduced through greater operating efficiency. Improving inventories control and credit control procedures may achieve the required reduction in OCC without any adverse effect on future sales. If so, this may offer the best way forward.

The average settlement period for trade payables represents more than three months' purchases. Any decision to extend this period, however, must be given very careful consideration. It is quite long and may already be breaching the payment terms required by suppliers.

Before a final decision is made, full account must be taken of current trading conditions.

It may be that a business wishes to maintain the OCC at a particular target level. However, not all days in the OCC are of equal value. In Activity 10.13, for example, the operating cycle is 119 days. If the average settlement period for both trade receivables and trade payables were increased by seven days, the OCC would remain at 119 days. The amount tied up in working capital, however, would not remain the same. Trade receivables would increase by £15,726 (that is, 7 × £820,000/365) and trade payables would increase by £10,893 (that is, 7 × £568,000/365). This means that there would be a net increase of £4,833 in working capital.

Real World 10.10 shows the average operating cash cycle for large European businesses.

Real World 10.10

Cycling along

The survey of working capital by Ernst and Young (see Real World 10.2, p. 411) calculates the average operating cash cycle for the top 1,000 European businesses (excluding financial and auto manufacturing businesses).

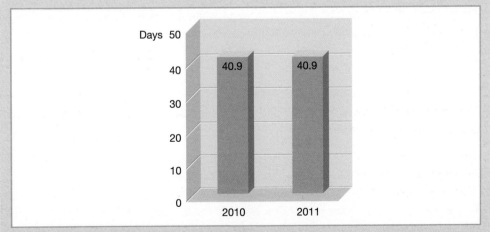

Figure 10.10 The average OCC of large European businesses for 2010 and 2011

The average operating cash cycle has reduced by 16 per cent since 2002, with each element of working capital making a contribution to this improvement. Inventories have fallen by 4 per cent, trade receivables by 10 per cent, while trade payables increased by 7 per cent over the period.

Source: Adapted from figure in 'All Tied Up: Working Capital Management Survey 2012', Ernst and Young, p. 5, www.ey.com.

Cash transmission

A business will normally wish to benefit from receipts from customers at the earliest opportunity. Where cash is received, the benefit is immediate. Where payment is made by cheque, however, there may be a delay before it is cleared through the banking system. The business must therefore wait before it can benefit from the amount paid in. In recent years, the CHAPS (Clearing House Automated Payments) system has helped to reduce the time that cheques spend in the banking system. It is now possible for cheques to be fast tracked so that they reach the recipient's bank account on the same day.

Another way for a business to receive money promptly is for the customer to pay by standing order or by direct debit. Both of these involve the transfer of an agreed sum from the customer's bank account to the business's bank account on an agreed date. Businesses providing services over time, such as insurance, satellite television and mobile phone services, often rely on this method of payment.

A final way in which a business may be paid promptly is through the use of a debit card. This allows the customer's bank account to be charged (debited) and the seller's bank account to be simultaneously increased (credited) with the sale price of the item. Many types of business, including retailers and restaurants, use this method. It is operated through computerised cash tills and is referred to as electronic funds transfer at point of sale (EFTPOS).

Bank overdrafts

Bank overdrafts are simply bank current accounts that have a negative balance. They are a type of bank loan and can be a useful tool in managing the business's cash flow requirements.

Real World 10.11 shows how Indesit, a large white-goods manufacturer, managed to improve its cash flows through better working capital management.

Real World 10.11

Dash for cash

Despite an impressive working capital track record, a 50% plunge in profit at Indesit in 2005 led to the creation of a new three-year plan that meant an even stronger emphasis on cash generation. Operating cash flow was added to the incentive scheme for senior and middle managers, who subsequently released more cash from Indesit's already lean processes by 'attacking the areas that were somehow neglected', Crenna (the chief financial officer) says.

Hidden in the dark corners of the accounts-receivable department in the UK's after-sales service operation, for example, were a host of delinquent, albeit small, payments – in some cases overdue by a year or more. 'If you don't put a specific focus on these receivables, it's very easy for them to become neglected,' Crenna says. 'In theory, nobody worries about collecting £20. In reality, we were sitting on a huge amount of receivables, though each individual bill was for a small amount.'

More trapped cash was found in the company's spare-parts inventory. The inventory is worth around €30 million today compared with around €40 million three years ago. 'This was a good result that came just from paying the same level of attention to spare parts as to finished products,' Crenna says. In general, Indesit has been able to improve working capital performance through 'fine-tuning rather than launching epic projects' over the past two years. According to REL, a research and consulting firm, Indesit has released €115 million from its working capital processes.

Source: J. Karaian, 'Dash for cash', *CFO Europe Magazine,* 8 July 2008, www.cfo.com.

MANAGING TRADE PAYABLES

Most businesses buy their goods and services on credit. Trade payables are the other side of the coin from trade receivables. In a trade credit transaction, one business's trade payable is another one's trade receivable. Trade payables are an important source of finance for most businesses. They have been described as a 'spontaneous' source, as they tend to increase in line with the increase in the level of activity achieved by a business.

There are potential costs associated with taking trade credit. A business that buys supplies on credit may incur additional administration and accounting costs resulting from the scrutiny and payment of invoices, maintaining and updating payables accounts, and so on. Furthermore, customers who take credit may not be as well treated as those who pay immediately. When goods are in short supply, they may be given lower priority. They may also be less favoured in terms of delivery dates or in gaining access to technical support. Where credit is required, customers may even have to pay more. In most industries, however, trade credit is the norm. As a result, these disadvantages do not normally apply unless, perhaps, the credit facilities are being abused.

The benefits to be gained from taking credit usually outweigh any costs involved. In effect, it is an interest-free loan from suppliers. It can also provide a more convenient way of paying for goods and services than paying by cash. Furthermore, during a period of inflation, there is an economic gain from paying later rather than sooner for goods and services supplied.

Activity 10.15

Why might a supplier prefer a customer to take a period of credit rather than pay for the goods or services on delivery? (There are probably two reasons.)

1 Paying on delivery may not be administratively convenient for the seller. Most customers will take a period of credit, so the systems of the seller will be geared up to receive payment after a reasonable period of credit.
2 A credit period can allow any problems with the goods or service supplied to be resolved before payment is made. This might avoid the seller having to make refunds.

Delaying payment to suppliers may be a sign of financial problems. However, it may also reflect an imbalance in bargaining power. It is not unusual for large businesses to delay payment to small suppliers, which are reliant on them for continuing trade. The UK government has encouraged large businesses to sign up to a 'Prompt Payment Code' to help small suppliers. **Real World 10.12** suggests that the response has been less than enthusiastic.

Real World 10.12

Taking on the big boys

Fewer than a fifth of Britain's biggest listed companies have pledged to pay suppliers promptly, despite a Whitehall push to cajole big business into improving the lot of smaller companies.

Michael Fallon, business and enterprise minister, wrote to companies in November asking them to sign up to a new prompt payment code, a voluntary agreement to promote good payment practices. He is now gearing up to 'name and shame' bigger companies which have failed to sign the code after his efforts to cajole them into doing so failed.

'Big companies are sitting on big piles of cash at the moment and life is difficult for subcontractors and suppliers if they're not paid promptly,' Mr Fallon told the *Financial Times*. 'I warned each of the FTSE 350 companies I will name those companies that aren't even prepared to sign up to the code. It's not good enough.'

Timely payment on goods and services is crucial for small businesses trying to grow but some big companies have lengthened payment terms in recent years to improve their own cash position. The government would like to see all suppliers paid within 30 days, although some small and medium enterprises have complained of having to wait up to 180 days to receive payment from large companies in return for goods and services. Whitehall pays its suppliers within five days.

Since Mr Fallon wrote to companies, nearly a third of the FTSE 100 have agreed to adopt the code. But the wider FTSE 250 has dragged its heels, with just 67 of the FTSE 350 companies signed up to the scheme.

Mr Fallon admitted that some public bodies including NHS trusts, police authorities and councils were among those not paying promptly, although he said the record of central government departments was better.

 Source: Rigby, E. and Parker, G. (2013) 'Big companies resist prompt payment code', www.ft.com, 9 January. © The Financial Times Limited 2012. All Rights Reserved.

Taking advantage of cash discounts

Where a supplier offers a discount for prompt payment, the business should give careful consideration to the possibility of paying within the discount period. The following example illustrates the cost of forgoing possible discounts.

Example 10.6

Hassan Ltd takes 70 days to pay for goods from its supplier. To encourage prompt payment, the supplier has offered the business a 2 per cent discount if payment for goods is made within 30 days. Hassan Ltd is not sure, however, whether it is worth taking the discount offered.

If the discount is taken, payment could be made on the last day of the discount period (that is, the 30th day). However, if the discount is not taken, payment will be made after

70 days. This means that, by not taking the discount, the business will receive an extra 40 days' (that is, 70 − 30) credit. The cost of this extra credit to the business will be the 2 per cent discount forgone. If we annualise the cost of this discount forgone, we have:

$$365/40 \times 2\% = 18.3\%^*$$

We can see that the annual cost of forgoing the discount is very high. It may, therefore, be profitable for the business to pay the supplier within the discount period, even if it means that it will have to borrow to enable it to do so.

* This is an approximate annual rate. For the more mathematically minded, the precise rate is:

$$\{[(1 + 2/98)^{9.125}] - 1\} \times 100\% = 20.2\%$$

The key difference is that, in this calculation, compound interest is used, whereas in the first calculation, simple interest is used, which is not strictly correct.

Controlling trade payables

To help monitor the level of trade credit taken, management can calculate the average settlement period for trade payables ratio. As we saw in Chapter 3, this ratio is:

$$\text{Average settlement period for trade payables} = \frac{\text{Average trade payables}}{\text{Credit purchases}} \times 365$$

Once again, this provides an average figure, which could be misleading. A more informative approach would be to produce an ageing schedule for payables. This would look much the same as the ageing schedule for receivables described earlier in Example 10.4.

We saw earlier that delaying payment to suppliers may create problems for a business. **Real World 10.13** describes how cash-strapped businesses may delay payments and yet retain the support of their suppliers.

Real World 10.13

Credit stretch

According to Gavin Swindell, European managing director of REL, a research and consulting firm, there are 'win-win' ways of extending credit terms. He states: 'A lot of businesses aren't worried about getting paid in 40 or 45 days, but are more interested in the certainty of payment on a specific date.'

Jas Sahota, a partner in Deloitte's UK restructuring practice, says that three-month extensions are common, 'as long as the supplier can see that there is a plan'. In times of stress, he says, it's important to negotiate with only a handful of the most important partners – squeezing suppliers large and small only generates grief and distracts employees with lots of calls.

More fundamentally, the benefits of pulling the payables lever in isolation is 'questionable', notes Andrew Ashby, director of the working capital practice at KPMG in London, 'especially as the impact on the receivables balance is typically a lot more than the payables balance'.

Improving collections, such as achieving longer payment terms, relies on the strength of relationships built over time, notes Robert Hecht, a London-based managing director of turnaround consultancy AlixPartners. 'You can't wait for a crisis and then expect suppliers to step up and be your best friends.'

Source: J. Karaian, 'Dash for cash', *CFO Europe Magazine*, 8 July 2008, www.CFO.com.

Town Mills Ltd is a wholesale business. Extracts from the business's most recent financial statements are as follows:

Income statement for the year ended 31 May

	£000
Sales	903
Cost of sales	(652)
Gross profit	251
Other operating expenses	(109)
Operating profit	142
Interest	(11)
Profit before taxation	131
Taxation	(38)
Profit for the year	93

Statement of financial position as at 31 May

	£000
ASSETS	
Non-current assets	
Property, plant and equipment at cost	714
Accumulated depreciation	(295)
	419
Current assets	
Inventories	192
Trade receivables	202
	394
Total assets	813
EQUITY AND LIABILITIES	
Equity	
Ordinary share capital	200
Retained earnings	246
	446
Current liabilities	
Trade payables	260
Borrowings (all bank overdraft)	107
	367
Total equity and liabilities	813

The levels of trade receivables and trade payables increased by 10 per cent, by value, during the year ended 31 May. Inventories levels remained the same. The finance director believes that inventories levels are too high and should be reduced.

Required:

(a) Calculate the average operating cash operating cycle (in days) during the year ended 31 May and explain to what use this value can be put and what limitations it has.

(b) Discuss whether there is evidence that the business has a liquidity problem.

(c) Explain the types of risk and cost that might be reduced by following the finance director's proposal to reduce inventories levels.

The answer to this question can be found at the back of the book on p. 568.

SUMMARY

The main points of this chapter may be summarised as follows.

Working capital

- Is the difference between current assets and current liabilities.
- That is, working capital = inventories + trade receivables + cash − trade payables − bank overdrafts.
- An investment in working capital cannot be avoided in practice – typically large amounts are involved.

Inventories

- There are costs of holding inventories, which include:
  - lost interest
  - storage cost
  - insurance cost
  - obsolescence.
- There are also costs of not holding sufficient inventories, which include:
  - loss of sales and customer goodwill
  - production dislocation
  - loss of flexibility – cannot take advantage of opportunities
  - reorder costs – low inventories imply more frequent ordering.
- Practical points on inventories management include:
  - identify optimum order size – models can help with this
  - set inventories reorder levels
  - use forecasts
  - keep reliable inventories records
  - use accounting ratios (for example, inventories turnover period ratio)
  - establish systems for security of inventories and authorisation
  - implement just-in-time (JIT) inventories management.

Trade receivables

- When assessing which customers should receive credit, the five Cs of credit can be used:
  - capital
  - capacity
  - collateral
  - condition
  - character
- The costs of allowing credit include:
  - lost interest
  - lost purchasing power
  - costs of assessing customer creditworthiness
  - administration cost
  - bad debts
  - cash discounts (for prompt payment).

- The costs of denying credit include loss of customer goodwill.
- Practical points on receivables management:
  - establish a policy
  - assess and monitor customer creditworthiness
  - establish effective administration of receivables
  - establish a policy on bad debts
  - consider cash discounts
  - use financial ratios (for example, average settlement period for trade receivables ratio)
  - use ageing summaries.

Cash

- The costs of holding cash include:
  - lost interest
  - lost purchasing power.
- The costs of holding insufficient cash include:
  - loss of supplier goodwill if unable to meet commitments on time
  - loss of opportunities
  - inability to claim cash discounts
  - costs of borrowing (should an obligation need to be met at short notice).
- Practical points on cash management:
  - establish a policy
  - plan cash flows
  - make judicious use of bank overdraft finance – it can be cheap and flexible
  - use short-term cash surpluses profitably
  - bank frequently
  - operating cash cycle (for a wholesaler) = Average inventories' turnover period + average settlement period for trade receivables – average settlement period for trade payables
  - transmit cash promptly.
- An objective of working capital management is to limit the length of the operating cash cycle (OCC), subject to any risks that this may cause.

Trade payables

- The costs of taking credit include:
  - higher price than purchases for immediate cash settlement
  - administrative costs
  - restrictions imposed by seller.
- The costs of not taking credit include:
  - lost interest-free borrowing
  - lost purchasing power
  - inconvenience – paying at the time of purchase can be inconvenient.
- Practical points on payables management:
  - establish a policy
  - exploit free credit as far as possible
  - use accounting ratios (for example, average settlement period for trade payables ratio).

working capital p. 408

average inventories turnover period ratio
    p. 414

lead time p. 415

ABC system of inventories control p. 417

economic order quantity (EOQ) p. 418

materials requirement planning (MRP)
    system p. 421

just-in-time (JIT) inventories
    management p. 421

five Cs of credit p. 423

cash discount p. 428

average settlement period for trade
    receivables p. 430

ageing schedule of trade receivables
    p. 430

operating cash cycle (OCC)
    p. 436

average settlement period for trade
    payables ratio p. 443

For definitions of these terms, see the Glossary, pp. 605–613.

FURTHER READING

If you would like to explore the topics covered in this chapter in more depth, try the following books:

Arnold, G. (2013) *Corporate Financial Management*, 5th edn, Pearson, Chapter 13.

Brealey, R., Myers, S. and Allen, F. (2010) *Corporate Finance*, 10th edn, McGraw-Hill International, Chapters 14, 25 and 26.

Hillier, D., Ross, S., Westerfield, R., Jaffe, J. and Jordan, B. (2010) *Corporate Finance*, European edn, McGraw-Hill Higher Education, Chapters 19 to 21.

McLaney E. (2012) *Business Finance: Theory and Practice*, 9th edn, Financial Times Prentice Hall, Chapters 8, 9, 11 and 12.

Pike, R., Neale, B. and Linsley, P. (2012) *Corporate Finance and Investment*, 7th edn, Pearson, Chapters 13 and 14.

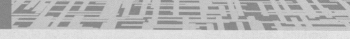

Solutions to these questions can be found at the back of the book on pp. 577–8.

10.1 Tariq is the credit manager of Heltex plc. He is concerned that the pattern of monthly cash receipts from credit sales shows that credit collection is poor compared with budget. Heltex's sales director believes that Tariq is to blame for this situation, but Tariq insists that he is not. Why might Tariq not be to blame for the deterioration in the credit collection period?

10.2 How might each of the following affect the level of inventories held by a business?

(a) An increase in the number of production bottlenecks experienced by the business.
(b) A rise in the business's cost of capital.
(c) A decision to offer customers a narrower range of products in the future.
(d) A switch of suppliers from an overseas business to a local business.
(e) A deterioration in the quality and reliability of bought-in components.

10.3 What are the reasons for holding inventories? Are these reasons different from the reasons for holding cash?

10.4 Identify the costs of holding:

(a) too little cash
(b) too much cash.

EXERCISES

Exercises 10.4 to 10.7 are more advanced than 10.1 to 10.3. Those with coloured numbers have solutions at the back of the book starting on p. 597.
   If you wish to try more exercises, visit the students' side of the companion website.

10.1 The chief executive officer of Sparkrite Ltd, a trading business, has just received summary sets of financial statements for last year and this year:

Income statements for years ended 30 September

	Last year £000	Last year £000	This year £000	This year £000
Sales revenue		1,800		1,920
Cost of sales				
Opening inventories	160		200	
Purchases	1,120		1,175	
	1,280		1,375	
Closing inventories	(200)	(1,080)	(250)	(1,125)
Gross profit		720		795
Expenses		(680)		(750)
Profit for the year		40		45

Statements of financial position as at 30 September

	Last year £000	This year £000
ASSETS		
Non-current assets	950	930
Current assets		
Inventories	200	250
Trade receivables	375	480
Cash at bank	4	2
	579	732
Total assets	1,529	1,662
EQUITY AND LIABILITIES		
Equity		
Fully paid £1 ordinary shares	825	883
Retained earnings	509	554
	1,334	1,437
Current liabilities	195	225
Total equity and liabilities	1,529	1,662

The chief financial officer has expressed concern at the increase in inventories and trade receivables levels.

Required:

(a) Show, by using the data given, how you would calculate ratios that could be used to measure inventories and trade receivables levels during last year and this year.

(b) Discuss the ways in which the management of Sparkrite Ltd could exercise control over the levels of:
   (i)   inventories
   (ii) trade receivables.

10.2 Hercules Wholesalers Ltd has been particularly concerned with its liquidity position in recent months. The most recent income statement and statement of financial position of the business are as follows:

Income statement for the year ended 31 December last year

	£000	£000
Sales revenue		452
Cost of sales		
Opening inventories	125	
Purchases	341	
	466	
Closing inventories	(143)	(323)
Gross profit		129
Expenses		(132)
Loss for the year		(3)

Statement of financial position as at 31 December last year

	£000
ASSETS	
Non-current assets	
Property, plant and equipment	357
Current assets	
Inventories	143
Trade receivables	163
	306
Total assets	663
EQUITY AND LIABILITIES	
Equity	
Ordinary share capital	100
Retained earnings	158
	258
Non-current liabilities	
Borrowings – loans	120
Current liabilities	
Trade payables	145
Borrowings – bank overdraft	140
	285
Total equity and liabilities	663

The trade receivables and payables were maintained at a constant level throughout the year.

Required:

(a) Explain why Hercules Wholesalers Ltd is concerned about its liquidity position.

(b) Calculate the operating cash cycle for Hercules Wholesalers Ltd.

(c) State what steps may be taken to improve the operating cash cycle of the business.

10.3 International Electric plc at present offers its customers 30 days' credit. Half of the customers, by value, pay on time. The other half takes an average of 70 days to pay. The business is considering offering a cash discount of 2 per cent to its customers for payment within 30 days.

The credit controller anticipates that half of the customers who now take an average of 70 days to pay (that is, a quarter of all customers) will pay in 30 days. The other half (the final quarter) will still take an average of 70 days to pay. The scheme will also reduce bad debts by £300,000 a year.

Annual sales revenue of £365 million is made evenly throughout the year. At present the business has a large overdraft (£60 million) with its bank at an interest cost of 12 per cent a year.

Required:

(a) Calculate the approximate equivalent annual percentage cost of a discount of 2 per cent, which reduces the time taken by credit customers to pay from 70 days to 30 days. (*Hint*: This part can be answered without reference to the narrative above.)

(b) Calculate the value of trade receivables outstanding under both the old and new schemes.

(c) How much will the scheme cost the business in discounts?

(d) Should the business go ahead with the scheme? State what other factors, if any, should be taken into account.

10.4 Your superior, the general manager of Plastics Manufacturers Limited, has recently been talking to the chief buyer of Plastic Toys Limited, which manufactures a wide range of toys for young children. At present, Plastic Toys is considering changing its supplier of plastic granules and has offered to buy its entire requirement of 2,000 kg a month from you at the going market rate, provided that you will grant it three months' credit on its purchases. The following information is available:

1 Plastic granules sell for £10 a kg, variable costs are £7 a kg and fixed costs £2 a kg.
2 Your own business is financially strong and has sales revenue of £15 million a year. For the foreseeable future it will have surplus capacity and it is actively looking for new outlets.
3 Extracts from Plastic Toys' financial statements:

	Year 1	Year 2	Year 3
	£000	£000	£000
Sales revenue	800	980	640
Profit loss before interest and tax	100	110	(150)
Capital employed	600	650	575
Current assets			
Inventories	200	220	320
Trade receivables	140	160	160
	340	380	480
Current liabilities			
Trade payables	180	190	220
Overdraft	100	150	310
	280	340	530
Working capital	60	40	(50)

Required:
Advise your general manager on the acceptability of the proposal. You should give your reasons and do any calculations you consider necessary.

10.5 Mayo Computers Ltd has annual sales of £20 million. Bad debts amount to £100,000 a year. All sales made by the business are on credit and, at present, credit terms are negotiable by the customer. On average, the settlement period for trade receivables is 60 days. Trade receivables are financed by an overdraft bearing a 14 per cent rate of interest per year. The business is currently reviewing its credit policies to see whether more efficient and profitable methods could be employed. Only one proposal has so far been put forward concerning the management of trade credit.

The credit control department has proposed that customers should be given a 2.5 per cent discount if they pay within 30 days. For those who do not pay within this period, a maximum of 50 days' credit should be given. The credit department believes that 60 per cent of customers will take advantage of the discount by paying at the end of the discount period. The remainder will pay at the end of 50 days. The credit department believes that bad debts can be effectively eliminated by adopting the proposed policies and by employing stricter credit investigation procedures, which will cost an additional £20,000 a year. The credit department is confident that these new policies will not result in any reduction in sales revenue.

Required:
Calculate the net annual cost (savings) to the business of abandoning its existing credit policies and adopting the proposals of the credit control department. (*Hint*: To answer this question you must weigh the costs of administration and cash discounts against the savings in bad debts and interest charges.)

10.6 Boswell Enterprises Ltd is reviewing its trade credit policy. The business, which sells all of its goods on credit, has estimated that sales revenue for the forthcoming year will be £3 million under the existing policy. Credit customers representing 30 per cent of trade receivables are expected to pay one month after being invoiced and 70 per cent are expected to pay two months after being invoiced. These estimates are in line with previous years' figures.

At present, no cash discounts are offered to customers. However, to encourage prompt payment, the business is considering giving a 2.5 per cent cash discount to credit customers who pay in one month or less. Given this incentive, the business expects credit customers accounting for 60 per cent of trade receivables to pay one month after being invoiced and those accounting for 40 per cent of trade receivables to pay two months after being invoiced. The business believes that the introduction of a cash discount policy will prove attractive to some customers and will lead to a 5 per cent increase in total sales revenue.

Irrespective of the trade credit policy adopted, the gross profit margin of the business will be 20 per cent for the forthcoming year and three months' inventories will be held. Fixed monthly expenses of £15,000 and variable expenses (excluding discounts), equivalent to 10 per cent of sales revenue, will be incurred and will be paid one month in arrears. Trade payables will be paid in arrears and will be equal to two months' cost of sales. The business will hold a fixed cash balance of £140,000 throughout the year, whichever trade credit policy is adopted. Ignore taxation.

Required:

(a) Calculate the investment in working capital at the end of the forthcoming year under:
(i)   the existing policy
(ii) the proposed policy.

(b) Calculate the expected profit for the forthcoming year under:
(i)   the existing policy
(ii) the proposed policy.

(c) Advise the business as to whether it should implement the proposed policy.

(*Hint*: The investment in working capital will be made up of inventories, trade receivables and cash, *less* trade payables and any unpaid expenses at the year end.)

10.7 Goliath plc is a food wholesaler. The most recent financial statements of the business are as follows:

Income statement for the year to 31 May

	£000	£000
Sales revenue		2,400.0
Cost of sales		
Opening inventories	550.0	
Purchases	1,450.0	
	2,000.0	
Closing inventories	(560.0)	(1,440.0)
Gross profit		960.0
Administration expenses		(300.0)
Selling expenses		(436.0)
Operating profit		224.0
Interest payable		(40.0)
Profit before taxation		184.0
Taxation (25%)		(46.0)
Profit for the period		138.0

Statement of financial position as at 31 May

	£000
Non-current assets	
Property, plant and equipment	456.4
Current assets	
Inventories	560.0
Trade receivables	565.0
Cash at bank	36.4
	1,161.4
Total assets	1,617.8
Equity	
£1 ordinary shares	200.0
Retained earnings	520.8
	720.8
Non-current liabilities	
Borrowings – loan notes	400.0
Current liabilities	
Trade payables	451.0
Taxation	46.0
	497.0
Total equity and liabilities	1,617.8

All sales and purchases are made on credit.

The business is considering whether to grant extended credit facilities to its customers. It has been estimated that increasing the settlement period for trade receivables by a further 20 days will increase the sales revenue of the business by 10 per cent. However, inventories will have to be increased by 15 per cent to cope with the increased demand. It is estimated that purchases will have to rise to £1,668,000 during the next year as a result of these changes. To finance the increase in inventories and trade receivables, the business will increase the settlement period taken from suppliers by 15 days and use a loan facility bearing a 10 per cent rate of interest for the remaining balance.

If the policy is implemented, bad debts are likely to increase by £120,000 a year and administration costs will rise by 15 per cent.

Required:
(a) Calculate the increase or decrease to each of the following that will occur in the forth-coming year if the proposed policy is implemented:
  (i)   operating cash cycle (based on year-end figures)
  (ii) net investment in inventories, trade receivables and trade payables
  (iii) profit for the period.
(b) Should the business implement the proposed policy? Give reasons for your conclusion.

Chapter 11

MEASURING AND MANAGING FOR SHAREHOLDER VALUE

INTRODUCTION

For some years, shareholder value has been a 'hot' issue among managers. Many leading businesses now claim that the quest for shareholder value is the driving force behind their strategic and operational decisions. In this chapter, we begin by considering what is meant by the term 'shareholder value' and then go on to look at some of the main approaches to measuring shareholder value.

We end the chapter by considering the role of share options as a means of promoting shareholder value. Although share options are often offered to senior managers as an incentive, they have been subject to much criticism. We consider the arguments for and against their use and see how share option schemes may be open to abuse.

Learning outcomes

When you have completed this chapter, you should be able to:

■ Describe the shareholder value approach and explain its implications for the management of a business.

■ Explain shareholder value analysis (SVA) and economic value added (EVA®) and discuss their role in measuring and delivering shareholder value.

■ Explain market value added (MVA) and total shareholder return (TSR) and evaluate their usefulness for investors.

■ Discuss the advantages and disadvantages of awarding share options to senior managers as a means of promoting shareholder value.

THE QUEST FOR SHAREHOLDER VALUE

Let us start by considering what the term shareholder value means. In simple terms, it is about putting the needs of shareholders at the heart of management decisions. It is argued that shareholders invest in a business with a view to maximising their financial returns in relation to the risks that they are prepared to take. As managers are appointed by the shareholders to act on their behalf, management decisions and actions should reflect a concern for maximising shareholder returns. Although the business may have other 'stakeholder' groups, such as employees, customers and suppliers, it is the shareholders that should be seen as the most important group.

This, of course, is not a new idea. Take a look at most books on finance or economics, including this one, and you will see that maximising shareholder returns is assumed to be the key objective of a business. Not everyone, however, accepts this idea. Some believe that a balance must be struck between the competing claims of the various stakeholders. The relative merits of each viewpoint were debated in Chapter 1 and we shall not retread this path. What we can say, however, is that changes in the economic environment over recent years have often forced managers to focus their attention on the needs of shareholders.

In the past, shareholders have been accused of being too passive and of accepting too readily the profits and dividends that managers have delivered. However, this has changed. Nowadays, shareholders are much more assertive and as owners of the business are in a position to insist that their needs are given priority. Since the 1980s we have witnessed the deregulation and globalisation of business as well as enormous changes in technology. The effect has been to create a much more competitive world. This has meant not only competition for products and services but also competition for funds. Businesses must now compete more strongly for shareholder funds and so must offer competitive rates of return.

Thus, self-interest may be the most powerful reason for managers to commit themselves to maximising shareholder returns. If they do not do this, there is a real risk either that shareholders will replace them with managers who will, or that shareholders will allow the business to be taken over by another business, with managers who are dedicated to maximising shareholder returns.

CREATING SHAREHOLDER VALUE

Creating shareholder value can be viewed as a four-stage process. The first stage is to set objectives that recognise the central importance of maximising shareholder returns. This should provide a clear direction for the business. The second stage is to establish an appropriate means of measuring the returns, or value, generated for shareholders. For reasons to be discussed later, the traditional methods of measuring returns to shareholders are inadequate for this purpose. The third stage is to manage the business so that shareholder returns are maximised. This means setting demanding targets and then achieving them through the best possible use of resources, the use of incentive systems and the embedding of a shareholder value culture throughout the business. The final stage is to measure shareholder returns over a period of time to see whether the objectives set have been achieved. These stages are set out in Figure 11.1.

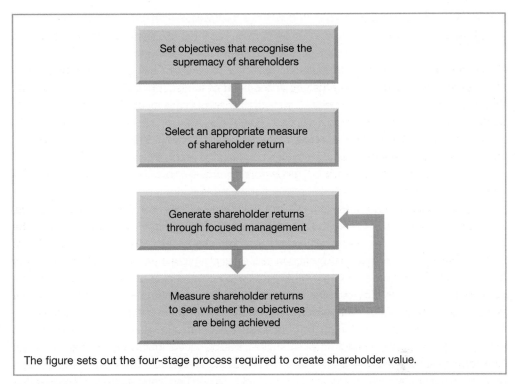

The figure sets out the four-stage process required to create shareholder value.

Figure 11.1 Creating shareholder value

THE NEED FOR NEW FORMS OF MEASUREMENT

Once a commitment is made to maximising shareholder returns, an appropriate measure is then needed to help assess the returns to shareholders over time. Many argue that conventional methods for measuring shareholder returns are seriously flawed and so should not be used.

Activity 11.1

What are the conventional methods of measuring shareholder returns?

Managers normally use accounting profit or some ratio that is based on accounting profit, such as return on shareholders' funds or earnings per share.

One problem with using accounting profit, or a ratio based on profit, is that profit is measured over a relatively short period of time (usually one year). When we talk about maximising shareholder returns, however, we are concerned with the long term. Using profit as a key measure runs the risk that actions taken by managers to improve short-term performance will have an adverse effect on long-term performance. For example, short-term profits may be improved by cutting back on staff training and research, even though these areas may be vital to long-term prosperity.

A second problem that arises with conventional methods of measuring shareholder returns is that risk is ignored. We saw in previous chapters that there is a linear relationship between the level of returns achieved and the level of risk that must be taken to achieve those returns. The higher the level of returns required, the higher the level of risk that must be taken to achieve those returns. A strategy that increases profits can also reduce shareholder returns if the increase in profits is not commensurate with the increased level of risk. Thus, profit alone is not enough.

A third problem with the use of profit, or a ratio based on profit, is that it does not take full account of the costs of capital invested. When measuring profit, the cost of loan capital (that is, interest charges) is deducted but there is no similar deduction for the cost of shareholder funds. (Dividends are not deducted in arriving at the profit figure and, anyway, represent only part of total shareholder returns.) Critics point out that a business will not make a profit, in an economic sense, unless it covers the cost of all capital invested, including shareholder funds. Unless this is done, the business will make a loss and shareholder value will be reduced.

A final problem is that reported profit can vary according to the particular policies adopted. Some businesses may adopt conservative accounting policies such as the immediate writing off of intangible assets (for example, research and development), the use of the reducing balance method of depreciation (which favours high depreciation charges in the early years) and so on. Businesses that adopt less conservative accounting policies would report profits more quickly. Thus, the writing off of intangible assets over a long period (or perhaps not writing off intangible assets at all), the use of the straight-line method of depreciation, and so forth, will mean that profits are reported more quickly. In addition, some businesses may adopt particular accounting policies, or structure transactions in a particular way, to portray a picture of financial health that accords with what preparers of the financial statements would like investors to see rather than what is a fair representation of financial performance and position. This practice, which we discussed in Chapter 3, is referred to as 'creative accounting' and has been a major problem for accounting rule makers.

The above points are summarised in Figure 11.2.

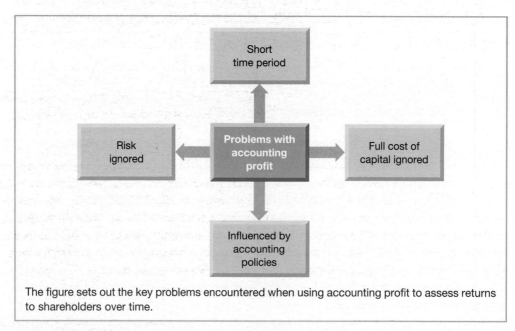

The figure sets out the key problems encountered when using accounting profit to assess returns to shareholders over time.

Figure 11.2 Problems with using accounting profit

NET PRESENT VALUE (NPV) ANALYSIS

To summarise the points made above, we can say that to measure changes in shareholder value, what we really need is a measure that will consider the long term, will take account of risk and of the cost of shareholders' funds, and will not be affected by accounting policy choices. Fortunately, we have a measure that can, in theory, do just this.

Net present value analysis was discussed in Chapter 4. We saw that if we want to know the NPV of an asset (whether this is a physical asset such as a machine or a financial asset such as a share), we should discount future cash flows generated by the asset over its life. Thus:

$$NPV = C_1\frac{1}{(1+r)^1} + C_2\frac{1}{(1+r)^2} + C_3\frac{1}{(1+r)^3} + \ldots$$

Where C = cash flows at time t (1, 2, 3, . . .)

r = the required rate of return.

Shareholders have a required rate of return and managers should strive to generate long-term cash flows for shares (in the form of dividends or proceeds that investors receive from the sale of the shares) that meet this rate of return. A negative present value will indicate that the cash flows generated do not meet the minimum required rate of return. If a business is to create value for its shareholders, it must generate cash flows that exceed the required returns of shareholders. In other words, the cash flows generated must produce a positive present value.

The NPV method fulfils the criteria that we mentioned earlier for the following reasons:

- It considers the long term. The returns from an investment, such as shares, are considered over the whole of the investment's life.
- It takes account of the cost of capital and risk. Future cash flows are discounted using the required rates of returns from investors (that is, both long-term lenders and shareholders). Moreover, this required rate of return will reflect the level of risk associated with the investment. The higher the level of risk, the higher the required level of return.
- It is not sensitive to the choice of accounting policies. Cash, rather than profit, is used in the calculations and is a more objective measure of return.

Extending NPV analysis: shareholder value analysis

We know from our earlier study of NPV that when evaluating an investment project, shareholder wealth will be maximised when the net present value of cash flows generated by the project is maximised. It can be argued that the business is simply a portfolio of investment projects and so the same principles should apply when considering the business as a whole. Shareholder value analysis (SVA) is founded on this basic idea.

The SVA approach involves evaluating strategic decisions according to their ability to maximise value, or wealth, for shareholders. To undertake this evaluation, conventional measures are discarded and replaced by discounted cash flows. We have seen that the net present value of a project represents the value of that particular project. Given that the business can be viewed as a portfolio of projects, the value of the business as a whole can therefore be viewed as the net present value of the cash flows that it generates. SVA seeks to measure the discounted cash flows of the business as a whole and then seeks to identify that part which is available to the shareholders.

If the net present value of future cash flows generated by the business represents the value of the business as a whole, how can we derive that part of the value of the business that is available to shareholders?

A business will normally be financed by a combination of loan capital and ordinary shareholders' funds. Thus, holders of loan capital will also have a claim on the total value of the business. That part of the total business value that is available to ordinary shareholders can therefore be derived by deducting the market value of any loans outstanding from the total value of the business (total NPV). Hence:

Shareholder value = Total business value − Market value of outstanding loans

Measuring free cash flows

The cash flows used to measure total business value are the **free cash flows**. These are the cash flows generated that are available to ordinary shareholders and long-term lenders. In other words, they are equivalent to the net cash flows from operations after deducting tax paid and cash for additional investment. These free cash flows can be deduced from information within the income statement and statement of financial position of a business. It is probably worth going through a simple example to illustrate how the free cash flows can be calculated in practice.

Example 11.1

Sagittarius plc generated sales of £220 million during the year and has an operating profit margin of 25 per cent of sales. Depreciation charges for the year were £8.0 million and the cash tax rate for the year was 20 per cent of operating profit. During the year, £11.3 million was invested in additional working capital and £15.2 million was invested in additional non-current assets. A further £8.0 million was invested in the replacement of existing non-current assets.

The free cash flows are calculated as follows:

	£m	£m
Sales revenue		220.0
Operating profit (25% × £220m)		55.0
Add Depreciation charge		8.0
Operating cash flows		63.0
Less Cash tax (20% × £55m)		(11.0)
Operating cash flows after tax		52.0
Less Additional working capital	(11.3)	
Additional non-current assets	(15.2)	
Replacement non-current assets	(8.0)	(34.5)
Free cash flows		17.5

We can see from Example 11.1 that to derive the operating cash flows, we add the depreciation charge to the operating profit figure. We can also see that the cost of replacement of existing non-current assets is deducted from the operating cash flows in order to deduce the free cash flows. When we are trying to predict future free cash flows, one way of arriving at an approximate figure for the cost of replacing existing assets is to assume that the depreciation charge for the year is equivalent to the replacement charge for non-current assets. This would mean that the two adjustments mentioned cancel each other out and the calculation above could be shortened to:

	£m	£m
Sales revenue		220.0
Operating profit (25% × £220m)		55.0
Less Cash tax (20% × £55m)		(11.0)
		44.0
Less: Additional working capital	(11.3)	
Additional non-current assets	(15.2)	(26.5)
Free cash flows		17.5

This shortened approach enables us to identify the key variables in determining free cash flows as being:

- sales
- operating profit margin
- **cash tax rate**
- additional investment in working capital
- additional investment in non-current assets (NCA).

Figure 11.3 sets out the process in the form of a flow chart.

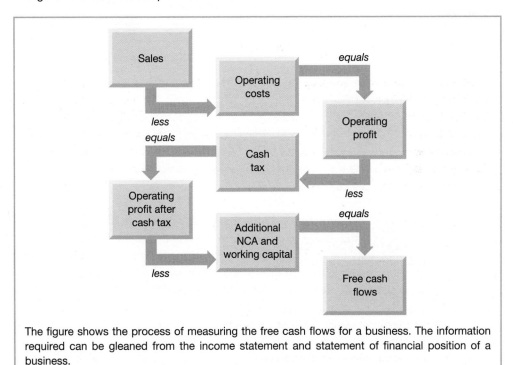

The figure shows the process of measuring the free cash flows for a business. The information required can be gleaned from the income statement and statement of financial position of a business.

Figure 11.3 Measuring free cash flows

The five variables identified are **value drivers** of the business that reflect key business decisions. These decisions convert into free cash flows and finally into total business value. To determine total business value we measure the free cash flows over time and discount them by the cost of capital.

The free cash flows should be measured over the life of the business. However, this is usually a difficult task. To overcome the problem, it is helpful to divide the future cash flows into two elements:

- cash flows over the planning horizon and which may be forecast with a reasonable level of reliability
- cash flows occurring beyond the planning horizon, which will be represented by a terminal value.

It is a good idea to make the planning horizon as long as possible. This is because the discounting process ensures that values beyond the planning horizon are given little weight. As can be imagined, cash flows in the distant future can be extremely difficult to forecast and so the less weight given to them, the better.

Activity 11.3

Libra plc has an estimated terminal value (representing cash flows beyond the planning horizon) of £100 million. What is the present value of this figure assuming a discount rate of 12 per cent and a planning horizon of:

(a) 5 years
(b) 10 years
(c) 15 years?

(*Hint*: You may find it helpful to refer to the present value table in Appendix A at the end of the book.)

The answers are:

(a) £100m × 0.567 = £56.7 million
(b) £100m × 0.322 = £32.2 million
(c) £100m × 0.183 = £18.3 million

We can see that there is a dramatic difference in the present value of the terminal calculation between the three time horizons, given a 12 per cent discount rate.

To calculate the terminal value of a business, it is usually necessary to make simplifying assumptions. It is beyond the scope of this book to discuss this topic in detail. However, one common assumption is that returns beyond the planning horizon will remain constant (perhaps at the level achieved in the last year of the planning period). Using the formula for a perpetuity, the calculation for determining the terminal value (TV) will be:

$$TV = C_1/r$$

Where C_1 = the free cash flows in the following year
r = the required rate of return from investors (that is, the weighted average cost of capital).

This formula provides a capitalised value for future cash flows. Thus, if an investor receives a constant cash flow of £100 per year and has a required rate of return of 10 per cent, the capitalised value of these cash flows will be £100/0.1 = £1,000. In other words, the future cash flows are worth £1,000, when invested at the required rate of return, to the investor. This formula is similar to the dividend formula, where dividends are assumed to be constant, that we covered in Chapter 8.

Activity 11.4

Can you think of another simplifying assumption that may be used to help calculate the terminal value? (*Hint*: Think back to the dividend valuation models in Chapter 8.)

A constant growth rate beyond the planning horizon may be assumed. In this case the formula will be $TV = C_1/(r - g)$ where g is the expected annual growth rate. Deriving an appropriate growth rate can be a difficult problem, however.

Let us go through an example to illustrate the way in which shareholder value can be calculated.

Example 11.2

The directors of United Pharmaceuticals plc are considering the purchase of all the shares in Bortex plc, which produces vitamins and health foods. Bortex plc has a strong presence in the UK and it is expected that the directors of the business will reject any bids that value the shares of the business at less than £11.00 per share.

Bortex plc generated sales for the most recent year of £3,000 million. Extracts from the statement of financial position of the business at the end of the most recent year are as follows:

	£m
Equity	
Share capital (£1 ordinary shares)	400.0
Retained earnings	380.0
	780.0
Non-current liabilities	
Loan notes	120.0

Forecasts that have been prepared by the business planning department of Bortex plc are as follows:

■ Sales revenue will grow at 10 per cent a year for the next five years.
■ The operating profit margin is currently 15 per cent and is likely to be maintained at this rate in the future.
■ The cash tax rate is 25 per cent.
■ Replacement non-current asset investment (RNCAI) will be in line with the annual depreciation charge each year.
■ Additional non-current asset investment (ANCAI) over the next five years will be 10 per cent of sales growth.
■ Additional working capital investment (AWCI) over the next five years will be 5 per cent of sales growth.

After five years, the sales of the business will stabilise at their Year 5 level.
The business has a cost of capital of 10 per cent and the loan notes figure in the statement of financial position reflects their current market value.

The free cash flow calculation will be as follows:

	Year 1	Year 2	Year 3	Year 4	Year 5	After Year 5
	£m	£m	£m	£m	£m	£m
Sales	3,300.0	3,630.0	3,993.0	4,392.3	4,831.5	4,831.5
Operating profit (15%)	495.0	544.5	599.0	658.8	724.7	724.7
Less Cash tax (25%)	(123.8)	(136.1)	(149.8)	(164.7)	(181.2)	(181.2)
Operating profit after cash tax	371.2	408.4	449.2	494.1	543.5	543.5
Less						
ANCAI (Note 1)	(30.0)	(33.0)	(36.3)	(39.9)	(43.9)	–
AWCI (Note 2)	(15.0)	(16.5)	(18.2)	(20.0)	(22.0)	–
Free cash flows	326.2	358.9	394.7	434.2	477.6	543.5

Notes:

1   The additional non-current asset investment is 10 per cent of sales growth. In the first year, sales growth is £300m (that is, £3,300m – £3,000m). Thus, the investment will be 10% × £300m = £30m. Similar calculations are carried out for the following years.

2   The additional working capital investment is 5 per cent of sales growth. In the first year the investment will be 5% × £300m = £15m. Similar calculations are carried out in following years.

Having derived the free cash flows (FCF), we can calculate the total business value as follows:

Year	FCF	Discount rate	Present value
	£m	10.0%	£m
1	326.2	0.91	296.8
2	358.9	0.83	297.9
3	394.7	0.75	296.0
4	434.2	0.68	295.3
5	477.6	0.62	296.1
Terminal value (543.5/0.10)	5,435.0	0.62	3,369.7
Total business value			4,851.8

Activity 11.5

What is the shareholder value figure for the business in Example 11.2? Would the sale of the shares at £11 per share really add value for the shareholders of Bortex plc?

Shareholder value will be the total business value less the market value of the loan notes. Hence, shareholder value is £4,851.8m – £120m = £4,731.8m.

The proceeds from the sale of the shares to United Pharmaceuticals would yield 400m × £11 = £4,400.0m.

Thus, from the point of view of the shareholders of Bortex plc, the sale of the business at the share price mentioned would not increase shareholder value.

Figure 11.4 sets out the key steps in calculating SVA.

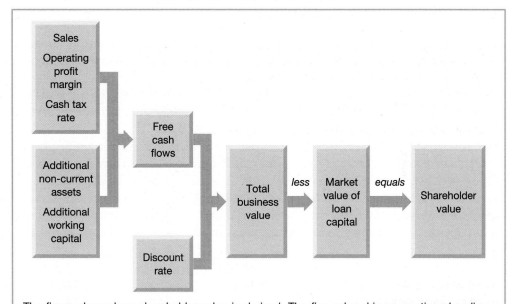

The figure shows how shareholder value is derived. The five value drivers mentioned earlier – sales, operating profit, cash tax, additional non-current assets and additional working capital – will determine the free cash flows. These cash flows will be discounted using the required rate of return from investors to determine the total value of the business. If we deduct the market value of any loan capital from this figure, we are left with a measure of shareholder value.

Figure 11.4 Deriving shareholder value

Non-operating income

In some cases, a business will also have non-operating income from marketable investments. As, by definition, this will not form part of the operating profits, its value must be separately determined. To do this, there is no need to forecast, and then discount, future non-operating cash inflows. Instead, we simply take the market value of the investments that give rise to these cash inflows. In theory, this should reflect the discounted value of the future cash inflows. Total business value, as shown in Figure 11.4, will then equal the sum of the discounted free cash flows *plus* the value of marketable investments.

MANAGING THE BUSINESS WITH SHAREHOLDER VALUE ANALYSIS

We saw earlier that the adoption of SVA indicates a commitment to managing the business in a way that maximises shareholder returns. Those who support this approach argue that SVA can be a powerful tool for strategic planning. For example, SVA can be extremely useful when considering major shifts of direction such as:

- acquiring new businesses
- selling existing businesses
- developing new products or markets
- reorganising or restructuring the business.

This is because SVA takes account of all the elements that determine shareholder value.

To illustrate this point let us suppose that a business develops a new product that is quite different from those within its existing range of products and appeals to a quite different market. Profit forecasts may indicate that the product is likely to be profitable and so a decision to launch the product may be made. This decision, however, may increase the level of risk for the business and, if so, investors will demand higher levels of return. In addition, there may have to be a significant investment in additional non-current assets and working capital in order to undertake the venture. When these factors are taken into account, using the type of analysis shown above, the present value of the venture may prove to be negative. In other words, shareholder value will be destroyed. When applying the SVA approach, scenario analysis and sensitivity analysis can be used to help gain an insight into the risks involved.

SVA is useful in focusing attention on the value drivers that create shareholder wealth. We saw earlier that the key variables in determining free cash flows were:

- sales
- operating profit margin
- cash tax rate
- additional investment in working capital
- additional investment in non-current assets.

To improve free cash flows and, in turn, shareholder value, targets can be set for improving performance relating to each value driver, with managers given responsibility for achieving particular targets.

Activity 11.7

Can you think of at least one practical problem of adopting an SVA approach?

Two practical problems spring to mind:

- Forecasting future cash flows lies at the heart of this approach. In practice, forecasting can be difficult and simplifying assumptions will usually have to be made.
- SVA requires more comprehensive information (for example, information concerning the value drivers) than the traditional measures discussed earlier.

You may have thought of other problems.

IMPLICATIONS OF SVA

Supporters of SVA believe that this measure should replace the traditional accounting measures of value creation such as profit, earnings per share and return on ordinary shareholders' funds. To check whether shareholder value has increased or decreased, a comparison of shareholder value at the beginning and the end of a period can be made.

SVA is a radical departure from the conventional approach to managing a business. It requires different performance indicators, different financial reporting systems and different management incentives. It may also require a cultural change within a business to embed the shareholder value philosophy. Not all may be committed to maximising shareholder wealth.

ECONOMIC VALUE ADDED (EVA®)

Economic value added has been developed and trademarked by a US management consultancy firm, Stern Stewart. However, it is based on the idea of economic profit, which has been around for many years. The measure reflects the point made earlier that for a business to be profitable in an economic sense, it must generate returns that exceed the required returns from investors. It is not enough simply to make an accounting profit as this measure does not take full account of the returns required from investors.

EVA® indicates whether the returns generated exceed the required returns from investors and is measured as follows:

$$\text{EVA}^{®} = \text{NOPAT} - (\text{R} \times \text{C})$$

where

   NOPAT = net operating profit after tax

   R = required returns from investors (that is, the weighted average cost of capital)

   C = capital invested (that is, the net assets of the business).

Only when EVA® is positive can we say that the business is increasing shareholder wealth. To maximise shareholder wealth, managers must increase EVA® by as much as possible.

Activity 11.8

What can managers do in order to increase EVA®? (*Hint*: Use the formula shown above as your starting point.)

The formula suggests that to increase EVA®, managers should try to:

- increase NOPAT – this may be done by either reducing expenses or increasing sales
- use capital invested more efficiently – this means selling off assets that are not generating returns which exceed their cost and investing in assets that do
- reduce the required rates of return for investors – this may be achieved by changing the capital structure in favour of borrowing (which is cheaper to service than share capital). This strategy can create problems, however, as discussed in Chapter 8.

Calculating EVA®

EVA® relies on conventional financial statements to measure the wealth created for shareholders. However, the NOPAT and capital invested figures shown on these statements are only taken as a starting point. They are adjusted because of the problems and limitations of conventional measures. According to Stern Stewart, the major problem is that profit and capital invested are understated because of the conservative bias in accounting measurement. Profit is understated as a result of arbitrary write-offs such as research and development expenditure and also as a result of excessive provisions being created (such as allowances for trade receivables). Capital invested is also understated because assets are often reported at their original cost (less amounts written off), which can produce figures considerably below current market values. In addition, certain assets, such as internally generated goodwill and brand names, are omitted from the financial statements because no external transactions have occurred.

Stern Stewart has identified more than 100 adjustments that could be made to the conventional financial statements to eliminate the conservative bias. However, it believes that, in practice, only a handful of adjustments to the accounting figures of any particular business is probably needed. Unless an adjustment has a significant effect on the calculation of EVA®, it is really not worth making. The adjustments made should reflect the nature of the particular business. Each business is unique and so must customise the calculation of EVA® to its particular circumstances. (Depending on your viewpoint, this aspect of EVA® can be seen either as indicating flexibility or as being open to manipulation.)

Common adjustments that have to be made include:

- *Research and development (R&D) costs and marketing costs.* These costs should be written off over the period that they benefit. In practice, however, they are often written off in the period in which they are incurred. This means that any amounts written off immediately should be added back to the assets on the statement of financial position, thereby increasing capital invested, and then written off over time.
- *Restructuring costs.* This item can be viewed as an investment in the future rather than an expense to be written off. Supporters of EVA® argue that by restructuring, the business is better placed to meet future challenges and so any amounts incurred should be added back to capital invested.
- *Marketable investments.* Investment in shares and loan notes are not included as part of the capital invested in the business. This is because the income from marketable investments is not included in the calculation of operating profit. (As mentioned earlier, income from this source will be added to the income statement *after* operating profit has been calculated.)

In addition to these accounting adjustments, the tax charge must be adjusted so that it is based on the operating profits for the year. This means that it should not take account of the tax charge on non-operating income, such as income from investments, or the tax allowance on interest payable.

Let us now consider a simple example to show how EVA® may be calculated.

Example 11.3

Scorpio plc was established two years ago and has produced the following statement of financial position and income statement at the end of the second year of trading.

Statement of financial position as at the end of the second year

	£m
ASSETS	
Non-current assets	
Plant and equipment	80.0
Motor vehicles	12.4
Marketable investments	6.6
	99.0
Current assets	
Inventories	34.5
Receivables	29.3
Cash	2.1
	65.9
Total assets	164.9
EQUITY AND LIABILITIES	
Equity	
Share capital	60.0
Retained earnings	23.7
	83.7
Non-current liabilities	
Loan notes	50.0
Current liabilities	
Trade payables	30.3
Taxation	0.9
	31.2
Total equity and liabilities	164.9

Income statement for the second year

	£m
Sales revenue	148.6
Cost of sales	(76.2)
Gross profit	72.4
Wages	(24.6)
Depreciation of plant and equipment	(12.8)
Marketing costs	(22.5)
Allowances for trade receivables	(4.5)
Operating profit	8.0
Income from investments	0.4
	8.4
Interest payable	(0.5)
Ordinary profit before taxation	7.9
Restructuring costs	(1.9)
Profit before taxation	6.0
Tax	(1.5)
Profit for the year	4.5

Discussions with the finance director reveal the following:

1 Marketing costs relate to the launch of a new product. The benefits of the marketing campaign are expected to last for three years (including this most recent year).
2 The allowance for trade receivables was created this year and the amount is considered to be very high. A more realistic figure for the allowance would be £2.0 million.
3 Restructuring costs were incurred as a result of a collapse in a particular product market. As a result of the restructuring, benefits are expected to flow for an infinite period.
4 The business has a 10 per cent required rate of return for investors.
5 The rate of tax on profits is 25 per cent.
6 The capital invested at the end of the year fairly reflects the average capital invested during the year.

The first step in calculating EVA® is to adjust the net operating profit after tax to take account of the various points revealed from the discussion with the finance director. The revised figure is calculated as follows:

NOPAT adjustment

	£m	£m
Operating profit		8.0
Tax (Note 1)		(2.0)
		6.0
EVA® adjustments (added back to profit)		
Marketing costs (2/3 × 22.5)	15.0	
Excess allowance	2.5	17.5
Adjusted NOPAT		23.5

The next step is to adjust the net assets (as represented by equity and loan notes) to take account of the points revealed.

Adjusted net assets (or capital invested)

	£m	£m
Net assets (from statement of financial position)		133.7
Marketing costs (Note 2)	15.0	
Allowance for trade receivables	2.5	
Restructuring costs (Note 3)	1.9	19.4
		153.1
Marketable investments (Note 4)		(6.6)
Adjusted net assets		146.5

Notes:

1 Tax is based on 25 per cent of the operating profits and is therefore £2 million (25% × £8.0m). (Tax complications, such as the difference between the tax allowance for non-current assets and the accounting charge for depreciation, have been ignored.)
2 The marketing costs represent two years' benefits added back (2/3 × £22.5m).
3 The restructuring costs are added back to the net assets as they provide benefits over an infinite period. (Note that they were not added back to the operating profit as these costs were deducted after arriving at operating profit in the income statement.)
4 The marketable investments do not form part of the operating assets of the business and the income from these investments is not part of the operating profit.

We are told in Note 6 that the capital invested at the end of the year reflects the average capital invested for the year. Where this is not the case, an average may be calculated by taking the opening and closing figures and dividing by two. (This, of course, is the same approach used in Chapter 3 to derive average capital employed when calculating the return on capital employed ratio.)

Managing resources with EVA®

A key advantage of this measure is the discipline to which managers are subjected. Before any increase in shareholder wealth can be recognised, an appropriate charge is made for the use of business resources. EVA® should therefore encourage managers to use these resources efficiently. Where managers are focused simply on increasing profit, there is a risk that resources used to achieve any increase will not be taken into account.

The benefits of EVA® may be undermined, however, if a short-term perspective is adopted. **Real World 11.1** describes how, in one large engineering business, using EVA® may have distorted management behaviour.

Real World 11.1

Hard times

Klaus Kleinfeld, Siemens' chief executive, is stuck in an unfortunate position after a deeply testing period at the helm of Europe's largest engineering group.

On the one side he is receiving pressure from investors fed up with a stagnating share price and profitability that continues to lag behind most of the German group's main competitors. But from the other he is under attack from the powerful IG Metall union aimed at holding him back from doing any serious restructuring. 'He is having to walk a tightrope,' says a former senior Siemens director. 'His focus right now has to be on fixing the problem areas and very quickly.'

Ben Uglow, an analyst at Morgan Stanley, says: 'I think the real question now in Siemens is one of management incentivisation. I think Kleinfeld has done a good job in the last year of refocusing the portfolio but some of his big chiefs have let him down.' Many investors are concerned that the margin targets that Mr Kleinfeld set last year for all his divisions to reach by April 2007 are distorting matters by making managers relax if they have already exceeded them.

Mr Kleinfeld and other directors disagree vehemently. Management pay is based on the 'economic value added' each division provides against each year's budget, not on specific margin targets. But a former senior director says this has led to a lack of investment in some parts of the business as managers look to earn as much as possible.

EVA®-BASED RATIOS

It is possible to produce financial ratios based on EVA®. One such ratio is the **EVA margin**, which is calculated as follows:

$$\text{EVA margin} = \frac{\text{EVA}^{\circledR} \text{ for the period}}{\text{Sales revenue for the period}} \times 100\%$$

This is a profitability ratio, which is similar to the operating profit margin discussed in Chapter 3. The EVA margin is claimed to be superior, however, because EVA® reflects the ability of a business to manage its resources efficiently.

Activity 11.10

Calculate the EVA margin for the second year of Scorpio plc in Example 11.3.

The ratio is:

$$\text{EVA margin} = \frac{\pounds 8.9\text{m}}{\pounds 148.6\text{m}} \times 100\%$$

$$= \underline{6.0\%}$$

Like all ratios, a suitable benchmark, such as the performance in past periods, or of other businesses, should be employed to evaluate this figure.

A further EVA®-based ratio is **EVA momentum**. This ratio is considered by Stern Stewart to be of primary importance. It is calculated as follows:

$$\text{EVA momentum} = \frac{\text{Change in EVA}^{\circledR} \text{ from the previous period}}{\text{Sales revenue for the previous period}} \times 100\%$$

Thus, if a business reported an increase of EVA of £3 million, when compared to the previous period, and the sales revenue in the previous period was £100 million, the EVA momentum would be 3 per cent. The ratio measures the growth rate of EVA® and can be used to identify trends, or turning points, in the fortunes of a business.

EVA momentum highlights the 'direction of travel' in financial performance. Where, for example, a distressed business is being successfully turned around, it will show positive EVA momentum even though it may report a negative EVA® for a period. Where a business is in decline, it will show negative EVA momentum even though it may still report positive EVA®.

The bigger this ratio, the better, as it is directly linked to shareholder wealth enhancement. Stern Stewart argues, therefore, that it should be adopted as the key financial target for a business.

Note that both ratios discussed incorporate the sales revenue of the business. This helps to eliminate the problems of scale. Comparisons between operating divisions, or businesses, of different size can then be made more easily.

Real World 11.2 reveals these EVA®-based ratios for some well-known US businesses.

Real World 11.2

Gathering momentum

CFO, in association with EVA Dimensions LLC, provides rankings of large US businesses according to their EVA® momentum. Other EVA®-based information for each business is also provided. Below are extracts, taken from the 2011 rankings list, for a selection of well-known businesses.

Ranking	Business	Industry	EVA momentum	5-year average EVA momentum	Current EVA®	Current EVA margin
			%	%	$m	%
11	Xerox Corp	Electronics and office equipment	13.4	2.8	1,444	6.5
17	Intel Corp	Semiconductors and semiconductor equipment	10.7	2.2	7,842	17.0
19	Apple Inc	Computers and peripherals	10.1	14.5	13,822	15.8
25	Motorola Solutions Inc	Communications equipment	8.6	−1.5	2,279	11.7
34	Google Inc	Internet software and services	7.2	13.4	6,229	20.0
59	Microsoft Corp	Software	5.1	2.7	16,618	24.2
65	eBay Inc	Internet software and services	4.7	0.5	421	4.4
74	Chevron Corp	Oil, gas and consumable fuels	4.1	0.2	14,068	7.0

Source: Extracts from Eva momentum 2011 rankings list at www3.cfo.com/eva-momentum-rankings, accessed 17 May 2013.

EVA® IN PRACTICE

In this short section, we provide some insights concerning how EVA® is reported and used and how widely it is implemented in practice. EVA® tends to be used by businesses for management purposes only. Few businesses report this measure to shareholders. **Real World 11.3** reveals one business, however that does so.

Reporting EVA®

IMI plc is a large engineering business that reported the following EVA® results in its 2012 Annual Report.

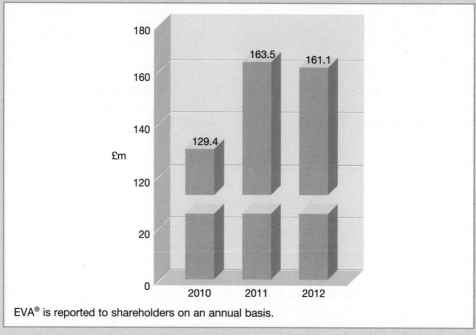

EVA® is reported to shareholders on an annual basis.

Figure 11.5 IMI plc economic value added

The 2012 EVA® figure shown was calculated by using a net operating profit after tax of £276 million, average capital invested of £1,435.9 million and a cost of capital of 8 per cent. Thus:

$$EVA = £276m - (£1,435.9m \times 8\%) = \underline{£161.1m}$$

Source: IMI plc Annual Report, 2012, p. 3.

Real World 11.4 indicates how one business uses EVA® for capital investment decisions.

The whole picture

Whole Foods Market is a leading retailer of natural and organic foods, which operates in the US and the UK. It uses EVA® to evaluate capital investment decisions such as the acquisition of new stores. A new store is normally expected to achieve a cumulative positive EVA® after five years or less.

Source: Based on information in Whole Foods Market, Annual Report 2012, www.wholefoodsmarket.com.

One often-mentioned limitation of EVA® is that it can be difficult to allocate revenues, costs and capital easily between different business units (such as individual stores in the case of Whole Foods Market). As a result, this technique cannot always be applied to individual business units. We have just seen, however, that Whole Foods Market seems able to do this.

Real World 11.5 provides an impression of the extent to which EVA® is used by UK businesses.

EVA® in practice

The Chartered Institute of Management Accountants (CIMA) carried out a survey of current accounting and finance practice in 2009 and received 439 responses. Part of the survey was concerned with the extent to which EVA® is used within different business sectors. The survey results are set out in Figure 11.6.

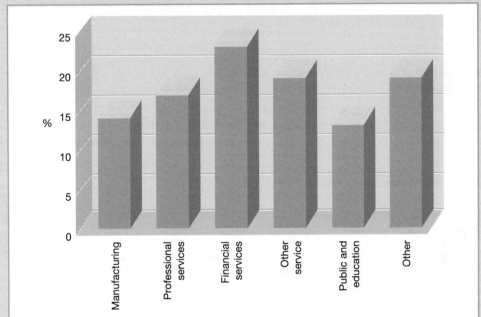

The figure indicates that EVA® is not in widespread use. It appears to be most popular in financial services businesses.

Figure 11.6 Use of economic value added

Source: Adapted from figure in 'Management accounting tools for today and tomorrow', CIMA, 2009, p. 20.

Finally, **Real World 11.6** contains some advice on how to implement EVA®.

The thoughts of Robert Goizueto

Robert Goizueto was the chief executive of Coca-Cola Co. for many years and was an ardent supporter of EVA®. He offered two pieces of advice for those wishing to implement this technique:

■ *Keep it simple*. By this he meant that EVA® should be the only method of value measurement used by managers. To do otherwise would lessen the impact of EVA® and would also make the management of the business unnecessarily complicated.
■ *Make it accountable*. By this he meant that managers should be rewarded for increasing EVA®. In this way, the managers' own interests become indistinguishable from those of the owners of the business.

Source: A. Ehrbar, *EVA: The real key to creating wealth*, John Wiley & Sons, 1998.

EVA® AND SVA COMPARED

Although at first glance it may appear that EVA® and SVA are worlds apart, this is not the case. In fact, the opposite is true. EVA® and SVA are closely related and, in theory at least, should produce the same figure for shareholder value. The way in which shareholder value is calculated using SVA has already been described. The EVA® approach to calculating shareholder value adds the capital invested to the present value of future EVA® flows and then deducts the market value of any loan capital. Figure 11.7 illustrates the two approaches to determining shareholder value.

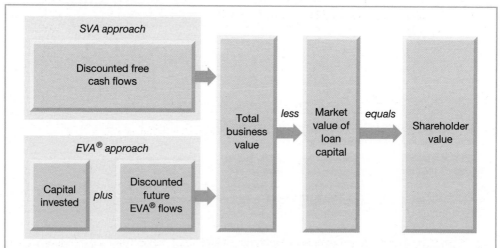

The figure shows how EVA® and SVA can both provide a measure of shareholder value. Total business value can be derived either by discounting the free cash flows over time or by discounting the EVA® flows over time and adding the capital invested. Whichever approach is used, the market value of loan capital must then be deducted to derive shareholder value.

Figure 11.7 Two approaches to determining shareholder value

Let us go through a simple example to illustrate this point.

Leo Ltd has just been formed and has been financed by a £20 million issue of share capital and a £10 million issue of loan notes. The proceeds of the issue have been invested in non-current assets with a life of three years and during this period these assets will depreciate by £10 million per year. The operating profit after tax is expected to be £15 million each year. There will be no replacement of non-current assets during the three-year period and no investment in working capital. At the end of the three years, the business will be wound up and the non-current assets will have no residual value.

The required rate of return by investors is 10 per cent.

The SVA approach to determining shareholder value will be as follows:

Year	FCF	Discount rate	Present value
	£m	10%	£m
1	25.0*	0.91	22.8
2	25.0	0.83	20.7
3	25.0	0.75	18.7
		Total business value	62.2
		Less Loan notes	(10.0)
		Shareholder value	52.2

* The free cash flows will be the operating profit after tax *plus* the depreciation charge (that is, £15m £10m). In this case, there are no replacement non-current assets against which the depreciation charge can be netted off. It must therefore be added back.

The EVA® approach to determining shareholder value will be as follows:

Year	Opening capital invested (C)	Capital charge (10% × C)	Operating profit after tax	EVA®	Discount rate 10%	Present value of EVA®
	£m	£m	£m	£m		£m
1	30.0*	3.0	15.0	12.0	0.91	10.9
2	20.0	2.0	15.0	13.0	0.83	10.8
3	10.0	1.0	15.0	14.0	0.75	10.5
						32.2
					Opening capital	30.0
						62.2
					Less Loan notes	(10.0)
					Shareholder value	52.2

* The capital invested decreases each year by the depreciation charge (that is, £10 million).

EVA® OR SVA?

While both EVA® and SVA are consistent with the objective of maximising shareholder wealth and, in theory, should produce the same decisions and results, EVA® has a number of practical advantages over SVA. One advantage is that EVA® sits more comfortably with the conventional financial reporting systems and financial reports. There is no need to develop entirely new systems to implement EVA® as it can be calculated by making a few adjustments to the conventional income statement and statement of financial position. (We should not, however, underestimate the problems of deciding on an appropriate period over which to write off research and development costs, restructuring costs and so on when making these adjustments.)

Another advantage is that EVA® is more useful as a basis for rewarding managers. Supporters of both EVA® and SVA believe that management rewards should be linked to increases in shareholder value. This should ensure that the interests of managers are closely aligned to the interests of shareholders. Under the SVA approach, management rewards will be determined on the basis of the contribution made to the generation of long-term cash flows. However, there are practical problems in using SVA for this purpose.

Activity 11.11

Try to identify at least one practical problem that may arise when using SVA calculations to reward managers. (*Hint*: Think about how SVA is calculated.)

The SVA approach measures changes in shareholder value by reference to predicted changes in future cash flows. It is unwise, however, to pay managers on the basis of predicted rather than actual achievements. If the predictions are optimistic, the effect will be that the business rewards optimism rather than real achievement. There is also a risk that unscrupulous managers will manipulate predicted future cash flows in order to increase their rewards.

Under EVA®, managers may receive bonuses based on actual achievement during a particular period. However, it is important to strike a note of caution. If bonuses are linked to a single period, there is a danger that managers will place undue attention on increasing EVA® during this period. The objective should be to maximise EVA® over the longer term. An appropriate balance must therefore be struck between the short-term and long-term rewards offered to managers.

Real World 11.7 reveals how two businesses use EVA® to reward their managers.

Real World 11.7

Rewarding managers

IMI plc, the engineering business (see Real World 11.3), provides share incentives to executive directors and senior managers based on improvements in EVA® over a three-year period.

Halma plc, a producer of health and safety products, offers its senior executives an annual performance-related bonus tied to increases in economic value added. The remuneration report states that the bonus is 'based 100% on growth in the Economic Value Added (EVA®) compared with a target based on a weighted average of the previous three financial years. There are no individual objectives'. The bonus is worth up to 100 per cent of the annual salary.

Sources: IMI plc Annual Report, p. 55; Halma plc, Remuneration Report, Annual Report and Accounts 2012, www.halmareports.com.

An EVA®-based bonus system should encompass as many managers as possible to encourage widespread commitment. It is worth noting that Stern Stewart believes that bonuses, calculated as a percentage of EVA®, should form a large part of the total remuneration for managers. Thus, the higher the EVA® figure, the higher the rewards to managers – with no upper limits. The philosophy is that EVA® should make managers wealthy provided it makes shareholders extremely wealthy. One drawback of using this approach, however, is that the EVA® generated during a period is rarely reported to shareholders. This means that they will be unable to check whether the rewards given to managers are appropriate.

MARKET VALUE ADDED (MVA)

EVA® is designed to motivate managers to achieve shareholder value. It is really for internal reporting purposes. A further measure has been developed by Stern Stewart to complement EVA® and to provide shareholders with a way of tracking changes in shareholder value over time. **Market value added (MVA)** attempts to measure the gains or losses in shareholder value by measuring the difference between the market value of the business and the total investment that has been made in it over the years. The market value of the business is usually taken to be the market value of shares and loan capital. The total investment is the long-term capital invested, which is made up of equity (share capital plus retained earnings) and loan capital. Figure 11.8 illustrates the derivation of MVA.

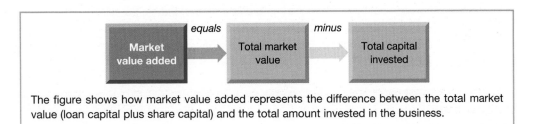

The figure shows how market value added represents the difference between the total market value (loan capital plus share capital) and the total amount invested in the business.

Figure 11.8 Market value added (MVA)

It is worth going through a simple example to show how market value can be calculated.

Example 11.5

Cosmo plc began trading ten years ago. It has 2 million £1 ordinary shares in issue that have a current market value of £5 per share. These shares were issued at their nominal value when the business was founded. The business also has £6 million 10 per cent loan notes. The book value of the loan notes is the same as their current market value. In addition, the business has retained earnings of £3 million.

The market value added can be calculated as follows:

	£m	£m
Market value of investments		
Ordinary shares (2m × £5)		10
Loan notes		<u>6</u>
		16
Total amount invested		
Ordinary shares (2m × £1)	2	
Retained earnings	3	
Loan notes	<u>6</u>	(11)
Market value added		<u>5</u>

We can see that market valued added is, in essence, a very simple idea. The cash value of the investment is compared with the cash invested. If the cash value of the investment is more than the cash invested, there has been an increase in shareholder value. If the cash value of the investment is less than the cash invested, there has been a decrease in shareholder value. There are, however, complications in measuring the figure for cash invested, which arise because of the conservative bias in accounting measurement. Thus, the adjustments to the statement of financial position that are necessary for the proper calculation of EVA® are also required when measuring MVA.

The measurement of the cash value of capital invested is straightforward. The market value of each share is simply multiplied by the number of shares in issue in order to derive the total market value of the shares. If shares are not listed on the Stock Exchange it is not really possible to measure MVA, unless perhaps a bid for the business has been received from a possible buyer.

In Example 11.5, it was assumed that the market value and book value of loan notes are the same. This is a common assumption used in practice, and where this assumption is made, the calculation of MVA reduces to the difference between the market value of shares and the sum of the nominal value of those shares and retained earnings. Thus, in the example, MVA is simply the difference between £10m and £5m (£2m + £3m), that is, £5 million.

In the example, we calculated MVA over the whole life of the business. The problem with doing this, in the case of an established business, is that it would not be clear when the value was actually created.

Activity 11.12

Why is it important to identify when the value was created and how could this be done?

The pattern of value creation over time may be useful in the assessment of past and likely future performance. It is perfectly feasible, however, to measure the change in MVA over any period by comparing the opening and closing positions for that period.

THE LINK BETWEEN MVA AND EVA®

Stern Stewart argues that there is a strong relationship between MVA and EVA®. The theoretical underpinning of this relationship is clear. We saw earlier that the value of a business is equal to the present value of future expected EVA® plus the capital invested. Thus:

$$\text{Business value} = \text{Capital invested} + \text{PV of future EVA}®$$

This equation could be rearranged so that:

$$\text{PV of future EVA}® = \text{Business value} - \text{Capital invested}$$

We have also seen that market value added is the difference between the value of the business and the capital invested. Thus:

$$\text{MVA} = \text{Business value} - \text{Capital invested}$$

By comparing the above equations, we can see that:

$$\text{PV of future EVA}® = \text{MVA}$$

Stern Stewart states that the relationship described holds in practice as well as in theory. The firm has produced evidence to show that the correlation between MVA and EVA® is much stronger than the correlation between MVA and other measures of performance such as earnings per share, return on shareholders' funds, or cash flows.

Given that MVA reflects the expected future EVA® of a business, it follows that an investor using this measure will be able to see whether a business generates returns above the cost of capital invested. If a business only manages to provide returns in line with the cost of capital, the EVA® will be zero and so there will be no MVA. Thus, MVA can be used to impose a capital discipline on managers in the same way that EVA® does.

LIMITATIONS OF MVA

MVA has a number of limitations as a tool for investors. To begin with, it has a fairly narrow scope. As mentioned earlier, MVA relies on market share prices and so it can be calculated only for businesses listed on a stock exchange. Furthermore, MVA can only be used to assess the business as a whole as there are no separate market share prices available for strategic business units.

The interpretation of MVA can also be a problem. It is a measure of the absolute change occurring over time and so its significance is difficult to assess when deciding among competing investment opportunities involving businesses of different size or trading over different periods. Consider the following financial information relating to three separate businesses:

Business	Total marke value (a) £m	Total capital invested (b) £m	Market value added (a) – (b) £m	No. of years trading
Alpha	250	120	130	18
Beta	480	350	130	16
Gamma	800	670	130	15

The table shows that each business has an identical MVA, but does this mean that each business has performed equally well? We can see that they operate with different amounts of capital invested and have operated over different periods.

The problems identified are not insurmountable but they reveal the difficulties of relying on an absolute measure when making investment decisions.

Activity 11.13

How could the problems of interpretation mentioned above be overcome?

The problem of the different time periods is probably best dealt with by comparing the businesses over the same time period. The problem of scale is probably best dealt with by comparing the MVA for each business with the capital invested in the business. (MVA/Capital provides a relative measure of wealth creation for investors.)

The businesses that are most successful at generating MVA are also the largest. Because MVA is an absolute measure of performance, large businesses have a greater potential to generate MVA. However, they also have a greater potential to destroy MVA.

Romeo plc produced the following statement of financial position at the end of the third year of trading:

Statement of financial position as at the end of the third year

	£m
ASSETS	
Non-current assets	
Property	60.0
Computing equipment	90.0
Motor vehicles	22.0
	172.0
Current assets	
Inventories	39.0
Trade receivables	53.0
Cash	12.0
	104.0
Total assets	276.0
EQUITY AND LIABILITIES	
Equity	
£1 ordinary shares	60.0
Retained earnings	81.0
	141.0
Non-current liabilities	
Loan notes	90.0
Current liabilities	
Trade payables	45.0
Total equity and liabilities	276.0

An analysis of the underlying records reveals the following:

1 R&D costs relating to the development of a new product in the current year had been written off at a cost of £10 million. However, this is a prudent approach and the benefits are expected to last for ten years.
2 Property has a current value of £200 million.
3 The current market value of an ordinary share is £8.50.
4 The book value of the loan notes reflects their current market value.

Required:
Calculate the MVA for the business over its period of trading.

The answer to this question can be found at the back of the book on p. 569.

TOTAL SHAREHOLDER RETURN

Total shareholder return (TSR) has been used for many years by investors as a means of assessing value created and is often used as a basis for management reward systems. The total return from a share is made up as follows:

1 The increase (or decrease) in share value over a period plus (minus)
2 Any dividends paid during the period.

To illustrate how total shareholder return is calculated, let us assume that a business commenced trading by issuing shares of £0.50 each at their nominal value (P_0) and by the end of the first year of trading the shares had increased in value to £0.55 (P_1). Furthermore, the business paid a dividend of £0.06 (D_1) per share during the period. We can calculate the total shareholder return as follows:

$$\text{Total shareholder return} = \frac{D_1 + (P_1 - P_0)}{P_0} \times 100\%$$

$$= \frac{0.06 + (0.55 - 0.50)}{0.50} \times 100\% = 22\%$$

The figure calculated has little information value when taken alone. It can only really be used to assess performance when compared with some benchmark.

Activity 11.14

What benchmark would be most suitable?

Perhaps the best benchmark to use would be the returns made by similar businesses operating in the same industry over the same period of time.

Where such a benchmark is used, returns generated will be compared with those generated from other investment opportunities with the same level of risk. We have seen in earlier chapters that the level of return from an investment should always be related to the level of risk that has to be taken.

TSR in practice

Many large businesses now publish total shareholder returns in their annual reports. **Real World 11.8** gives an example.

Tesco's TSR

Tesco plc, a major food retailer, publishes its TSR for a five-year period, along with movements in the FTSE 100 index for the same period. The TSR for the business is displayed graphically in Figure 11.9.

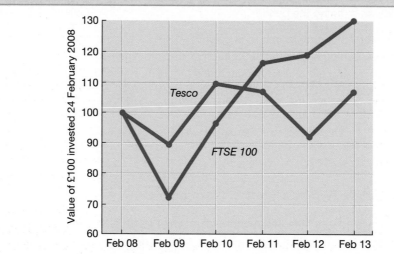

The figure shows that shareholder returns vary over time and so a measure of total shareholder return is likely to be sensitive to the particular time period chosen.

Figure 11.9 Tesco plc: total shareholder returns, February 2008 to February 2013

Source: Tesco plc, Annual Report and Financial Statements 2013, p. 55.

Real World 11.9 shows international TSR rankings for large businesses based on their performance over a five-year period.

Sustainable development

The Boston Consulting Group publishes global rankings of large businesses based on TSR. All businesses included in the rankings have a market capitalisation of at least $35 billion. The top ten rankings for the five-year period to 2011 are set out below.

Ranking	Business	Location	Industry	TSR%	Market cap. $bn
1	Baidu	China	Media and publishing	59.5	40.7
2	Tencent	Hong Kong	Media and publishing	41.8	36.6
3	Apple	United States	Technology	36.7	376.4
4	Amazon.com	United States	Retail	34.4	78.8
5	AmBev	Brazil	Consumer non-durables	31.1	119.8
6	Novo Nordisk	Denmark	Pharmaceuticals	25.0	64.3
7	British American Tobacco	United Kingdom	Consumer non-durables	21.6	96.4
8	McDonald's	United States	Retail	21.4	102.5
9	Novatek	Russia	Oil and gas	20.8	38.2
10	Union Pacific	United States	Transportation and logistics	20.2	50.8

Although the top spot is occupied by a business from a developing economy, six out of the top ten are from developed economies. More traditional industries such as media and publishing, retailing and consumer goods feature strongly. Surprisingly, perhaps, high-growth industries, such as technology and telecommunications, do not dominate the rankings.

Source: Boston Consulting Group, 'The 2012 Value Creators Rankings', www.bcgperspectives.com.

Applying TSR

TSR is also a fairly robust measure that can accommodate different operating and financing arrangements. However, there are various drawbacks to adopting this measure. They include:

- *Restricted application*. To calculate TSR, share price information must be available. This means it can be applied only to businesses listed on a stock exchange. Listed businesses represent a very small percentage of the total number of businesses in existence and so its potential application is severely restricted.
- *Share values*. Prices quoted for the shares of a listed business may not provide a reliable guide to their intrinsic value. There are times, for example, when investors' perceptions about the value of shares become detached from underlying reality. This can lead to share price 'bubbles' as described in Chapter 7.
- *Performance comparison*. It may be difficult to find similar businesses against which to assess relative performance. There is also the potential problem that unsuitable businesses will be deliberately selected by managers to make their performance appear better than it is.

TSR and management incentives

TSR is widely used by large listed businesses as a basis for management incentives (see reference 1 at the end of the chapter). The use of TSR for this purpose has sparked much criticism, however. It raises a number of problems, including the following:

- Share prices reflect investors' views concerning future returns. As a result, managers may receive rewards based on expected future performance rather than on actual performance.
- Managers may achieve higher share returns by simply taking on higher-risk projects. However, this policy shift may not align with the risk appetite of investors.
- Share price movements may be beyond the control of managers. (For this reason, TSR-based incentives have been described as a lottery for managers.)
- The contribution of individual managers to overall business performance cannot normally be determined.
- TSR can be manipulated over the short term (by, for example, the timing of important announcements).

Thus, TSR-based incentives awarded to managers may neither reflect their actual effort nor encourage long-term shareholder value creation.

Real World 11.10 reveals how TSR is used by Unilever, a leading provider of food, beverages and household products, to reward its directors.

Peer group pressure

Unilever awards shares in the business to executive directors under a share incentive plan. The number of shares awarded depends on performance over a three-year period. The maximum grant levels are 200 per cent of salary for the chief executive and 175 per cent of salary for the chief financial officer. The vesting range (that is the amount awarded) is from 0 per cent to 200 per cent of the maximum grant levels. This means that the chief executive could receive a maximum of 400 per cent of salary in the form of shares and the chief financial officer 350 per cent.

TSR is one of four measures used by the business to execute the incentive plan, with each given equal weighting. The TSR of the business is compared against a peer group of 19 other businesses, which includes Coca-Cola, Heinz and Kellogg. Shares are then vested according to how well the business performs in relation to its peer group over a three-year period.

Unilever's 2012 Directors' Remuneration Report states that no awards of shares will be made if the business is ranked below tenth position in the peer group at the end of the three-year period. 60 per cent of the shares will be vested if the business is ranked 10th, 100 per cent if it is ranked 7th and 200 per cent if it is ranked third or above. Rewards are vested on a straight-line basis between these points.

Source: Based on information in Unilever Annual Report and Accounts 2012, pp. 72–73.

Figure 11.10 sets out the main value measures that we have discussed in this chapter.

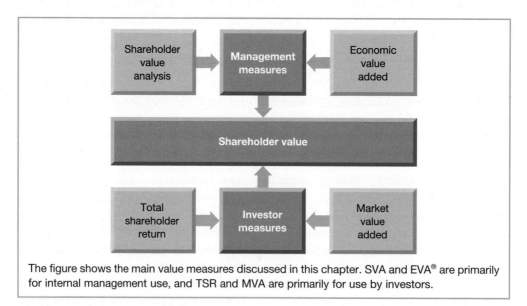

The figure shows the main value measures discussed in this chapter. SVA and EVA® are primarily for internal management use, and TSR and MVA are primarily for use by investors.

Figure 11.10 The main value measures

CRITICISMS OF THE SHAREHOLDER VALUE APPROACH

In recent years, there has been growing criticism of the shareholder value approach. It is claimed that the pursuit of shareholder value has resulted in conflicts between shareholders and other stakeholders and has created a crisis for the world of business. There is no reason in theory, however, why such problems should occur. We have seen that shareholder value reflects a concern for long-term value creation, and to achieve this, the interests of other stakeholders cannot be trampled over. Nevertheless, it is easy to see how, in practice, the notion of shareholder value may be corrupted.

The quest for shareholder value implies a concern for improving the efficiency of current operations and for exploiting future growth opportunities. The latter of these is by far the more difficult task. The future is unpredictable and risks abound. Managers must therefore tread carefully. They must be painstaking in their analysis of future opportunities and in developing appropriate strategies. However, this is not always done. **Real World 11.11** describes the issues encountered by mobile phone operators in pursuit of growth and why things went horribly wrong.

Real World 11.11

Future imperfect

Telecommunication businesses became convinced that their future lay in G3 technology. They believed that there would be huge demand for the new technology from customers who were desperate to use their mobile phones for music downloads, picture and video exchange and for internet access. As a result they paid huge sums to acquire G3 operating licences. These costly investments, however, were an act of faith rather than a result of rigorous planning. There was no detailed analysis of who would use the new technology, how it would be paid for and when it would be required.

As the future unfolded, it became clear that the existing technology would not fade as quickly as predicted and that far too much had been paid for the G3 licences. The end result was a massive loss of shareholder value.

Source: Based on 'Companies must achieve the right balance for a successful strategy', *Financial News*, 22 February 2004.

Given the problems of exploiting future growth opportunities, managers may prefer to focus on improving efficiency. This is usually achieved by bearing down on costs through working assets harder, shedding staff and putting pressure on suppliers to lower prices. If, however, these cost-reduction measures are taken too far, the result will be an emaciated business that is unable to take advantage of future growth opportunities and has its major stakeholder groups locked in conflict.

To be successful, the shareholder value approach must strike the right balance between a concern for efficiency and a concern for future growth; a concern for efficiency alone is not enough. In order to achieve this balance, the way in which managers are assessed and rewarded must reflect the importance of both.

MEASURING THE VALUE OF FUTURE GROWTH

If managers are to be assessed and rewarded, at least in part, on the basis of developing growth potential, a suitable measure of this potential is required. According to Stern Stewart, the EVA® approach can provide such a measure.

We saw earlier that the value of a business can be described as:

$$\text{Business value} = \text{Capital invested} + \text{PV of future EVA}^{\circledR}$$

If a business has no growth potential and EVA® remains constant, we can use the formula for a perpetuity, so that the present value of future EVA® is:

$$\text{PV of future EVA}^{\circledR} = \frac{\text{EVA}^{\circledR}}{r}$$

where r = required returns from investors (that is, the weighted average cost of capital).

Thus, the value of a business with no growth potential is:

$$\text{Business value} = \text{Capital invested} + \frac{\text{EVA}^{\circledR}}{r}$$

Where the business has growth potential (as measured by growth in EVA®), business value (as measured by the market value of share and loan capital) will be greater than this. The value placed on future growth potential by investors is, therefore:

$$\text{Value of future growth potential} = \text{Business value} - \left(\text{Capital invested} + \frac{\text{EVA}^{\circledR}}{r} \right)$$

Stern Stewart refers to the above value as **future growth value (FGV®)** and by using this measure periodically we can see whether managers are creating or destroying future value.

The percentage contribution to the value of the business arising from investor expectations concerning future growth in EVA® is:

$$\text{Percentage contribution to business value} = \left(\frac{\text{FGV}^{\circledR}}{\text{Business value}} \right) \times 100\%$$

This measure can be used to see whether managers are striking the right balance between efficiency and future growth.

Centaur plc has 5 million shares in issue with a market value of £8.40 per share. The business has £14.2 million capital invested and EVA® for the most recent year was £1.8 million. The required return from investors is 10 per cent a year.

What is the percentage contribution to the market value of the business arising from future growth?

$$\text{Assuming no growth, PV of future EVA}^® = \frac{\text{EVA}^®}{r} = \frac{£1.8m}{0.10} = £18.0m$$

$$\text{Future growth value (FGV}^®) = \text{Business value} - \left(\text{Capital invested} + \frac{\text{EVA}^®}{r}\right)$$

$$= (5m \times £8.40) - (£14.2m + £18.0m) = £9.8m$$

$$\text{Percentage contribution to business value} = \left(\frac{\text{EVA}^®}{\text{Business value}}\right) \times 100\%$$

$$= \frac{£9.8m}{(5m \times £8.40)} \times 100\% = 23.3\%$$

IMPLEMENTING THE SHAREHOLDER VALUE APPROACH

We have seen above that shareholder value may not always be implemented properly within a business. **Real World 11.12** sets out four different levels of implementation of shareholder value that may be found in practice.

Real World 11.12

Walking the talk

The extent to which a shareholder value philosophy is adopted within businesses varies. It has been suggested that four distinct levels can be identified.

Level 1

At this base level, the term 'shareholder value' is employed only as a business mantra and no real effort is made to implement shareholder value policies or techniques. Existing policies and techniques, however, may be re-labelled to give the impression that a shareholder value approach is being actively pursued. While the term 'shareholder value' may be used in published financial statements, websites and other forms of communications, it is simply to impress investors and others.

Level 2

At this level, shareholder value is seen in fairly narrow terms as being concerned with greater efficiency. The business will, however, demonstrate serious intent by reorganising to reflect a concern for shareholder value, by, for example, setting up shareholder value committees. It will also introduce shareholder value measures, such as EVA®, and use these measures as a means of incentivising and rewarding senior managers.

Level 3

This level of adoption recognises that shareholder value must be concerned with long-term growth as well as greater efficiency. These twin concerns will, furthermore, be proclaimed in communications with managers and investors. A concern for long-term growth, however, is not deeply rooted within the culture of the business. An emphasis will remain on short-term growth and managers are aware that they will be judged and rewarded on this basis. The lack of commitment to long-term growth strategies means these will be abandoned without much struggle in the face of outside pressures.

Level 4

At this final level, long-term growth and efficiency are fully recognised within the business and will inform all major decisions. Policies, measures and managerial rewards will all be attuned to the successful pursuit of both. The business will communicate its growth vision to investors and will not be easily deflected from its long-term strategies. What is being said and what is being done will be in harmony.

Source: Based on 'Companies must achieve the right balance for a successful strategy', *Financial News*, 22 February 2004.

DIRECTORS' SHARE OPTIONS AND SHAREHOLDER VALUE

Directors' share options are often used to encourage greater focus on increasing shareholder value. For years, however, a debate has raged over whether this form of incentive is consistent with good corporate governance. Peter Drucker, an eminent management thinker, has been a vociferous critic of this practice and has condemned it as 'an encouragement to loot the corporation'. In this final section, we consider the main features of directors' share options and then go on to explore the case for and against their use in rewarding directors.

What are directors' share options?

A directors' share option scheme gives directors the right, but not the obligation, to buy equity shares in their business at an agreed price. The conditions of the scheme will usually stipulate that the option to buy must be exercised either on, or after, a specified future date. A final date for exercising the option will also usually be specified. Share options are normally awarded only to executive directors (that is, those involved in the day-to-day management of the business). The UK Corporate Governance Code states that non-executive directors should not be rewarded in this way.

Directors' share options will be exercised only if the market value of the shares exceeds the option price. Where the option is exercised, the business must issue the agreed number of shares to the director, who will make a profit from the transaction. The option differs from most financial options in that a director will not normally be required to pay for the option rights: they are granted at no cost to the directors concerned. Directors' share options, however, cannot be traded and will usually be forfeited if the person leaves the business before the option can be exercised.

In the UK, directors' share options are normally issued at the current market price of the underlying shares. In the past, share options were sometimes issued at a discount to the market price; however, the UK Corporate Governance Code has discouraged this practice. The terms of a share option scheme often allow the directors to exercise their option no earlier than three years, but no later than ten years, after the option has been granted. Inland Revenue rules and best practice guidelines from institutional investors limit the value of options to £100,000 or four times current salary (see reference 2 at the end of the chapter). The exercise of the option may be subject to certain performance targets, such as growth in earnings per share, being met (see reference 3 at the end of the chapter).

What are the benefits of granting options?

Directors' share option schemes have been a popular method of rewarding the directors of large listed companies and various arguments have been put forward to support their use. It is often suggested, for example, that a well-designed scheme will benefit shareholders as it will help to align the interests of directors with those of shareholders.

Activity 11.16

How might this alignment of interests occur?

It is argued that share options give directors an incentive to increase the value of the business's shares and, thereby, to increase the wealth of shareholders.

Some argue that share options may even help to strengthen the psychological bond that a director has with the business. Through exercising an option and acquiring shares, the directors may identify more closely with the business and feel a sense of shared purpose with other shareholders. However, this argument does depend on the directors retaining, rather than selling, the shares acquired under the option agreement.

It has also been suggested that share options may help to retain board members. The fact that a director's share options are normally forfeited if a director leaves the business can provide a strong incentive to stay. Options can, therefore, provide a set of 'golden handcuffs' for talented directors who have other employment opportunities.

Unlike other forms of directors' remuneration, share options involve no financial outlay for the business at the time that they are granted. If the share price does not perform well over the option period, the option will be allowed to lapse and the business will incur no cost. If the shares perform well and the options are exercised, they represent a form of deferred payment to the directors. This deferral of rewards may be particularly attractive to a growing business that is short of cash.

Where directors exercise their options and the business, therefore, issues shares at below their current market value, there is a very real cost to the business. If the business were to issue those same shares to an ordinary investor, it would receive the current market price for them.

What are the problems of options?

Many see share options as a poor means of rewarding directors. Warren Buffett, chairman of Berkshire Hathaway, has made clear his opposition to their use. One problem that concerns him is that share option schemes cannot differentiate between the performances achieved by individual directors. He argues:

> Of course stock (share) options often go to talented, value-adding managers and sometimes deliver them rewards that are perfectly appropriate. (Indeed, managers who are really exceptional almost always get far less than they should.) But when the result is equitable, it is accidental. Once granted, the option is blind to individual performance. Because it is irrevocable and unconditional (so long as a manager stays in the company), the sluggard receives rewards from his options precisely as does the star. A managerial Rip Van Winkle, ready to doze for ten years, could not wish for a better 'incentive' system. (See reference 4 at the end of the chapter.)

A further problem concerning the incentive value of share options, to which Buffett refers, is that, where the share price falls significantly below the exercise price, the prospects of receiving benefits from the share options may become remote and any incentive value will be lost.

Both rises and falls in share price may be beyond the control of the directors and may simply reflect changes in economy-wide or industry-wide factors. Any incentive scheme that is subject to the vagaries of the stock market is, therefore, likely to present problems. There is always a risk that directors will either be undercompensated or overcompensated for their achievements.

Buffett's criticism of share options is not confined to their dubious incentive value. He also challenges the view that share options place directors in the same position as that of shareholders. He argues:

> The rhetoric about options frequently describes them as desirable because they put owners and managers in the same financial boat. In reality, the boats are far different. No owner has ever escaped the burden of capital costs, whereas a holder of a fixed-price option bears no capital costs at all. An owner must weigh upside potential against downside risk; an option holder has no downside. In fact, the business project in which you would wish to have an option frequently is a project in which you would reject ownership. (I'll be happy to accept a lottery ticket as a gift – but I'll never buy one.) (See reference 4 at the end of the chapter.)

This latter point, concerning the lack of 'downside' risk associated with the acquisition of options, may have an impact on the directors' risk-taking behaviour.

Activity 11.17

How might this affect the risk-taking behaviour of directors?

As options are granted to directors at no cost to them, the directors have an incentive to take risks when these options are 'underwater' (that is, when they cannot be exercised at a profit). By taking risks, there is a prospect of a rise in share prices and resulting benefits. If, on the other hand, by taking risks there is a fall in share prices, the directors will incur no financial loss.

Where share options are exercised, the directors may find themselves holding a large proportion of their total wealth in the form of equity in the business. The concentration of wealth in this form may have a number of unintended consequences. For example, it may lead to risk-averse behaviour as directors may be concerned with maintaining their wealth intact. This behaviour may not, however, find favour with the shareholders, who are likely to have a more diversified portfolio of investments and so may be more willing to take risks.

Share option schemes are based on the assumption that shareholders are concerned with share price increases and that directors' behaviour and incentives should reflect this concern. An excessive focus on share price, however, may not be in the best interests of shareholders. Share price represents only one part of the shareholders' total return from the business: the other part is dividend income.

Activity 11.18

How might directors behave as a result of this focus on share price increases rather than dividends?

There is a risk that this may lead the directors to restrict dividend payments so that profits are retained to fuel share price growth. Indeed, as directors are rewarded on the basis of share price growth rather than dividend growth, they have an incentive to act in this way. (This potential problem has led some businesses to incorporate dividend-protection conditions in the share option schemes offered to directors.)

Using similar reasoning, it can be argued that directors also have an incentive to have the business re-purchase its own shares as this, too, may lead to increases in share price.

In the UK, directors' share options have declined in popularity, which is partly due to the changes in the corporate governance environment. An influential report on directors' remuneration discouraged the use of share option schemes and a number of large institutional investors have voiced their concerns over their cost and effectiveness. Furthermore, international accounting standards now require the 'fair value' of share option schemes to be included in the financial statements. Shareholders can now see more clearly the cost incurred by granting share options as it is shown as a charge against profits.

Share option schemes are open to abuse. The particular forms of abuse that have been identified usually relate to the conditions of the share option scheme and to the pricing of options. A share option scheme will often include a condition that certain performance targets, such as earnings per share, must be met before the directors can exercise their options. There have been allegations, however, that some companies have set performance targets too low for them to have any real incentive effect.

The pricing of options has often been a target for manipulation by unscrupulous individuals and, in the US, several scandals have been unearthed. Some high-profile US businesses have been found to have reissued share options to directors at a lower price when the share price of the business fell below the option price. This practice effectively eliminates any risks for directors and may also eliminate any incentive effect that share options may have. (See reference 5 at the end of the chapter.)

Activity 11.19

Can you think of any circumstances under which reissuing share options at a lower price to directors might be justified?

It is sometimes argued that by 're-pricing' options in this way, it may re-incentivise directors, particularly when stock market prices are falling.

Real World 11.13 describes one high-profile case concerning the re-pricing of options.

Buy now at eBay

In a move likely to rekindle the debate over controversial pay practices in Silicon Valley, eBay yesterday asked its shareholders for permission to reset the terms of its employee stock (share) options. The plan would allow employees whose options are 'underwater', or have exercise prices that are significantly higher than the current share price, to exchange them for restricted stock (share) units.

Re-pricing stock (share) options is controversial because it benefits employees even as shareholders suffer from a depressed share price. Despite its unpopularity on Wall Street, it became common during the technology bust earlier this decade. Now, with the share prices of technology companies down because of the recession, options re-pricing may become common once again.

In January, Google unveiled a similar plan, responding to its own devalued share price. Sandeep Aggarwal, an analyst with Collins Stewart, said he believed additional companies would follow suit. 'I think there will be several more technology companies to do this,' he said. The window of opportunity to exchange under the Google plan ran out yesterday and the company said employees exchanged about 93 per cent for new options with a lower exercise price.

Stock [share] options, a common part of Silicon Valley pay packages, are meant to encourage employees to work hard, stay with a company, and share in its profits. But when the market price of the share dips below the exercise price, the options lose their value.

In a filing with the US Securities Exchange Commission, eBay said the plan would help boost morale in the company: 'Because of the continued challenging economic environment and the uncertain impact of our efforts to change our business, we believe these underwater stock options are no longer effective as incentives to motivate and retain our employees.'

An even more controversial practice is when directors benefit from the backdating of options. One study found that 1,400 directors of 460 US businesses benefited from the backdating of share options to the lowest price in a monthly period (see reference 6 at the end of the chapter).

SUMMARY

The main points in this chapter may be summarised as follows:

Shareholder value

- Means putting shareholders' interests at the heart of management decisions.

- To create shareholder value, the objectives of the business must reflect a concern for shareholder value, there must be appropriate methods of measurement, the business must be managed to create shareholder value and there must be periodic assessment of whether shareholder value has been achieved.

Measuring shareholder value – internal (management) measures

- Conventional forms of accounting measurement are inadequate – they focus on the short term, ignore risk, fail to take proper account of the cost of capital invested and are influenced by accounting methods employed.

- Two main approaches are used to measure shareholder value: shareholder value analysis (SVA) and economic value added (EVA®).
- SVA is based on the concept of net present value analysis.
- It identifies key value drivers for generating shareholder value.
- EVA® provides a means of measuring whether the returns generated by the business exceed the required returns from investors.
- EVA® = NOPAT − ($R \times C$).
- EVA® relies on conventional financial statements, which are adjusted because of their limitations.
- Two financial ratios based on EVA® – EVA margin and EVA momentum – can be calculated.
- In theory, EVA® and SVA should produce the same decisions and results.

Measuring shareholder value – external (investor) measures

- There are two main approaches: market value added (MVA) and total shareholder return (TSR).
- MVA measures the difference between the market value of the business and the investment made in the business.
- MVA = present value of EVA®.
- MVA is suitable only for listed businesses.
- Interpreting MVA can be a problem.
- TSR measures the total return to shareholders over a period.
- TSR is made up of the increase (decrease) in share value and the dividends paid.
- TSR can be sensitive to the time period chosen and it can be difficult to find similar businesses for comparison purposes.
- It is suitable only for listed business and where market prices reflect the intrinsic value of the shares.
- It has a number of drawbacks when used as a basis for management incentives.

Criticisms of the shareholder value approach

- There are two elements to shareholder value: efficiency of current operations and future growth.
- Undue emphasis on efficiency can undermine the prospects for future growth.

Measuring the value of future growth

- One approach is to use the EVA® methodology.
- Value of future growth potential = Market value of the business − (Capital invested + EVA®/r).
- To check whether managers strike the right balance between efficiency and future growth, the future growth potential can be compared with the market value of the business.

Directors' share options

- May be used to promote shareholder value. However, they have been criticised for failing to align the interests of directors with those of shareholders and for their openness to abuse.
- Most listed businesses use a variety of measures and incentives to reward executive directors rather than relying on a single measure.

REFERENCES

1 Kay, J., *The Kay Review of UK Equity Markets and Long-term Decision Making*, Interim Report February 2012, Department for Business Innovation and Skills, p. 25.

2 Pope, P. and Young, S., 'Executive remuneration: an investor's guide', www.manifest.co.uk, 2002.

3 Bender, R. (2005) 'Just rewards for a new approach to pay', *Financial Times*, 2 June.

4 Buffett, W. (1985) *Annual Report to Shareholders*, Berkshire Hathaway, Inc., p. 12.

5 Monks, R. and Minow, N. (2001) *Corporate Governance*, 2nd edn, Blackwell, p. 226.

6 Quoted in Guerrera, F. (2006) 'Study links directors to options scandal', *Financial Times*, 18 December.

FURTHER READING

If you wish to explore the topic of shareholder value in more depth, try the following books:

Arnold, G. (2013) *Corporate Financial Management*, 5th edn, Pearson, Chapters 14 and 15.

Asaf, S. (2004) *Executive Corporate Finance: The Business of Enhancing Shareholder Value*, Financial Times Prentice Hall.

Institute of Chartered Accountants in England and Wales Faculty of Finance and Management (2001) *Measuring Value for Shareholders*, Good Practice Guideline No. 33, March.

Stewart, B. (2013) *Best-practice EVA: The Definitive Guide to Measuring and Maximising Shareholder Value*, Wiley Finance.

REVIEW QUESTIONS

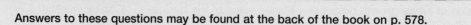

Answers to these questions may be found at the back of the book on p. 578.

11.1 How might the directors' attitude towards risk be affected by the business offering them share options?

11.2 Why is MVA not really suitable as a tool for internal management purposes?

11.3 Should managers take changes in the total market value of the shares (that is, share price × number of shares issued) over time as an indicator of shareholder value created (or lost)?

11.4 It has been argued that many businesses are overcapitalised. If this is true, what may be the reasons for businesses having too much capital and how can EVA® help avoid this problem?

Questions 11.4 to 11.6 are more advanced than 11.1 to 11.3. Those with coloured numbers have solutions at the back of the book, starting on p. 600.

If you wish to try more exercises, visit the students' side of this book's companion website.

11.1 Advocates of the shareholder value approach argue that, by delivering consistent and sustainable improvements in shareholder value, a business will benefit several stake-holder groups. The performance of a business such as the Stagecoach Group plc, which is committed to maximising shareholder value, may be used to support their arguments. Key elements of the income statement for the Stagecoach Group for the year to 30 April 2012 are set out below.

Required:

Fill out the right-hand column below to show how advocates of the shareholder value approach might seek to identify the stakeholder groups that benefit from the business's operations.

	£m	Stakeholders that benefit
Revenue	2,590.7	
Operating costs	2,352.2	
Finance costs	38.2	
Taxation	51.5	
Profit for the year	188.3	

Source: Stagecoach Group plc, Group Income Statement, Annual Report 2012, www.stagecoach.com.

11.2 Aquarius plc has estimated the following free cash flows for its five-year planning period:

Year	Free cash flows
	£m
1	35.0
2	38.0
3	45.0
4	49.0
5	53.0

Required:

How might it be possible to check the accuracy of these figures? What internal and external sources of information might be used to see whether the figures are realistic?

11.3 Aries plc was recently formed and issued 80 million £0.50 shares at nominal value and loan capital of £24 million. The business used the proceeds from the capital issues to purchase the remaining lease on some commercial properties that are rented out to small businesses. The lease will expire in four years' time and during that period the annual operating profits are expected to be £12 million each year. At the end of the three years, the business will be wound up and the lease will have no residual value.

The required rate of return by investors is 12 per cent.

Required:

Calculate the expected shareholder value generated by the business over the four years, using:

(a) the SVA approach

(b) the EVA® approach.

11.4 Virgo plc is considering introducing a system of EVA® and wants its managers to focus on the longer term rather than simply focus on the year-to-year EVA® results. The business is seeking your advice on how a management bonus system could be arranged so as to ensure that the longer term is taken into account. The business is also unclear as to how much of the managers' pay should be paid in the form of a bonus and when such bonuses should be paid. Finally, the business is unclear as to where the balance between individual performance and corporate performance should be struck within any bonus system.

The finance director has recently produced figures that show that if Virgo plc had used EVA® over the past three years, the results would have been as follows:

	£m
2011	25
2012	(20)
2013	10

Required:
Set out your recommendations for a suitable bonus system for the divisional managers of the business.

11.5 Leo plc is considering entering a new market. A new product has been developed at a cost of £5 million and is now ready for production. The market is growing and estimates from the finance department concerning future sales of the new product are as follows:

Year	Sales
	£m
1	30.0
2	36.0
3	40.0
4	48.0
5	60.0

After Year 5, sales are expected to stabilise at the Year 5 level.
You are informed that:

- the operating profit margin from sales in the new market is likely to be a constant 20 per cent of sales revenue
- the cash tax rate is 25 per cent of operating profit
- replacement non-current asset investment (RNCAI) will be in line with the annual depreciation charge each year
- additional non-current asset investment (ANCAI) over the next five years will be 15 per cent of sales growth
- additional working capital investment (AWCI) over the next five years will be 10 per cent of sales growth.

The business has a cost of capital of 12 per cent. The new market is considered to be no more risky than the markets in which the business already has a presence.

Required:
Using an SVA approach, indicate the effect of entering the new market on shareholder value.

11.6 Pisces plc produced the following statement of financial position and income statement at the end of the third year of trading:

Statement of financial position as at the end of the third year

	£m
ASSETS	
Non-current assets	
Property	40.0
Machinery and equipment	80.0
Motor vans	18.6
Marketable investments	9.0
	147.6
Current assets	
Inventories	45.8
Receivables	64.6
Cash	1.0
	111.4
Total assets	259.0
EQUITY AND LIABILITIES	
Equity	
Share capital	80.0
Retained earnings	36.5
	116.5
Non-current liabilities	
Loan notes	80.0
Current liabilities	
Trade payables	62.5
Total equity and liabilities	259.0

Income statement for the third year

	£m
Sales revenue	231.5
Cost of sales	(143.2)
Gross profit	88.3
Wages	(43.5)
Depreciation of machinery and equipment	(14.8)
R&D costs	(40.0)
Allowance for trade receivables	(10.5)
Operating loss	(20.5)
Income from investments	0.6
	(19.9)
Interest payable	(0.8)
Ordinary loss before taxation	(20.7)
Restructuring costs	(6.0)
Loss before taxation	(26.7)
Tax	–
Loss for the year	(26.7)

An analysis of the underlying records reveals the following:

1 R&D costs relate to the development of a new product in the previous year. These costs are written off over a two-year period (starting last year). However, this is a prudent approach and the benefits are expected to last for 16 years.
2 The allowance for trade receivables was created this year and the amount is very high. A more realistic figure for the allowance would be £4 million.
3 Restructuring costs were incurred at the beginning of the year and are expected to provide benefits for an infinite period.
4 The business has a 7 per cent required rate of return for investors.
5 The capital employed at the end of the year fairly reflects the average capital employed during the year.

Required:
Calculate the EVA® for the business for the third year of trading.

Chapter 12

BUSINESS MERGERS AND SHARE VALUATION

INTRODUCTION

This chapter examines various aspects of mergers and takeovers. We begin by looking at possible reasons for mergers and takeovers and how they may be financed. We then go on to identify the likely winners and losers in a takeover as well as the defences available to a business seeking to fend off a hostile bid.

In the final part of this chapter, we consider how the shares of a business can be valued. This is relevant to a range of financial decisions, including mergers and takeovers.

Learning outcomes

When you have completed this chapter, you should be able to:

- Identify and discuss the main reasons for mergers and takeovers.

- Discuss the advantages and disadvantages of each of the main forms of purchase consideration used in a takeover.

- Identify the likely winners and losers from takeover activity.

- Outline the tactics that may be used to defend against a hostile takeover bid.

- Identify and discuss the main methods of valuing the shares of a business.

MERGERS AND TAKEOVERS

When two (or possibly more) businesses combine, this can take the form of either a **merger** or a **takeover**. The term 'merger' is normally used to describe a situation where the two businesses are of roughly equal size and there is agreement among the managers and owners of each business on the desirability of combining them. A merger is usually effected by creating an entirely new business from the assets of the two existing businesses, with both shareholder groups receiving a substantial ownership stake in the new business.

The term 'takeover' is normally used to describe a situation where a larger business acquires control of a smaller business, which is then absorbed by the larger business. When a takeover occurs, shareholders of the target business may cease to have any financial interest in the business and the resources of the business may come under entirely new ownership. (The particular form of consideration used to acquire the shares in the target business will determine whether the shareholders continue to have a financial interest in the business.) Although the vast majority of takeovers are not contested, there are occasions when the management of the target business will fight to retain its separate identity.

In practice, however, many business combinations do not fit into these neat categories and it may be difficult to decide whether a merger or a takeover has occurred. The distinction between the two forms of combination used to be important in the context of financial reporting, as different accounting rules existed for each type of combination. However, changes to these rules have meant that the distinction is really no longer an issue. In this chapter, no distinction will be made between 'merger' and 'takeover' and we shall use the terms interchangeably.

Mergers and takeovers can be classified according to the relationship between the businesses being merged:

- A **horizontal merger** occurs when two businesses in the same industry, and at the same point in the production/distribution process, decide to combine.
- A **vertical merger** occurs when two businesses in the same industry, but at different points in the same production/distribution process, decide to combine.
- A **conglomerate merger** occurs when two businesses in unrelated industries decide to combine.

Activity 12.1

Can you think of an example of each type of merger for a tyre retailer?

An example of a horizontal merger would be where a tyre retailer merges with another tyre retailer to form a larger retail business. An example of a vertical merger would be where a tyre retailer merges with a manufacturer of tyres. This would mean that the combined business operates at different points in the production/distribution chain. An example of a conglomerate merger would be where a tyre retailer merges with an ice cream manufacturer.

MERGER AND TAKEOVER ACTIVITY

Although mergers and takeovers are a normal part of the business landscape, there are surges in merger and takeover activity from time to time. Each surge will have its own particular combination of economic, political and technological factors to create the required environment. Important economic factors usually include rising share prices, the availability of credit and low interest rates, which make financing mergers and takeovers much easier.

Real World 12.1 provides some impression of the pattern of merger and takeover activity over recent times.

Real World 12.1

The urge to merge

	Acquisitions abroad by UK companies		Acquisitions in the UK by foreign companies		Acquisitions in the UK by other UK companies	
	Number	Value £bn	Number	Value £bn	Number	Value £bn
2007	441	57.8	269	82.1	869	26.8
2008	298	29.7	252	52.6	558	36.5
2009	118	10.1	112	32.0	286	12.2
2010	199	12.4	212	36.6	325	12.6
2011	286	50.2	237	33.0	373	8.1
2012	107	16.4	155	16.7	255	3.3

There has been a slowdown in merger activity in recent years. This may well be due to the poor economic outlook and the lack of availability of credit due to the financial crisis.

Source: 'Mergers and acquisitions involving UK companies, Q4 2012', www.statistics.gov.uk, p. 2.

THE RATIONALE FOR MERGERS

In economic terms, a merger will be worthwhile for shareholders only if combining the two businesses will lead to gains that would not arise if the two businesses had stayed apart. We saw in the previous chapter that the value of a business can be defined in terms of the *present value of its future cash flows*. Thus, if a merger is to make economic sense, the present value of the combined business should be equal to the present value of future cash flows of the bidding and target businesses *plus* a gain from the merger. Figure 12.1 illustrates this point.

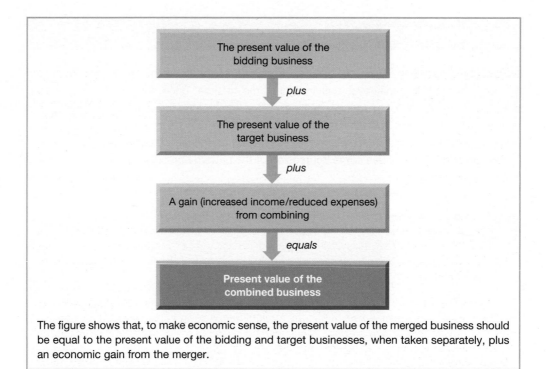

The figure shows that, to make economic sense, the present value of the merged business should be equal to the present value of the bidding and target businesses, when taken separately, plus an economic gain from the merger.

Figure 12.1 The rationale for mergers

WEALTH-ENHANCING MOTIVES FOR MERGERS

There are various ways in which an economic gain for shareholders may be achieved through a merger or takeover. The more important of these are described below.

Benefits of scale

A merger or takeover will result in a larger business being created that may enable certain benefits of scale to be achieved. For example, a larger business may be able to negotiate lower prices with suppliers in exchange for larger orders. It may also be able to lower the cost of finance when larger sums are being raised. A merger or takeover may also provide the potential for savings, as some operating costs may be duplicated (for example, administrative costs, IT costs, marketing costs, research and development costs). These benefits are more likely to be gained from horizontal and vertical mergers than from conglomerate mergers; it is more difficult to achieve economies where the businesses are unrelated. However, the benefits outlined must be weighed against the increased costs of organising and controlling a larger business.

Real World 12.2 describes the anticipated benefits of scale arising from a merger between a software giant and a large internet business.

Searching for a partner

In 2008 a software giant made an abortive attempt to merge with a multinational business operating an internet search engine. The management of the software giant believed that, by combining, a more efficient business could be created that would improve services to customers and add value for shareholders. The arguments put forward in support of a merger largely centred round the benefits of scale that could be reaped.

In a letter to the board of the internet business, the chief executive of the software giant outlined four main advantages of combining:

1. *Advertising growth*. It was argued that synergies were possible in advertising that related to both search-related and non-search-related advertising. It was felt that the benefits of these synergies would be appealing to advertisers and to publishers. It was also argued that capital spending on developing new software, such as a search index, could be consolidated.
2. *R&D capacity*. Both businesses employ highly skilled software engineers and it was argued that these could be brought together to focus on building a single advertising platform and a single search index. It was also argued that much new development and innovation relied on engineering scale, which the businesses did not have as separate entities but which would be available through combining.
3. *Operational efficiencies*. By removing operating activities that were currently being duplicated and unnecessary elements of business infrastructure, the combined entity would benefit from significant savings. This, in turn, would improve financial performance.
4. *Emerging technology*. It was argued that emerging opportunities such as online commerce, social media, mobile services and video services could be developed more successfully by using the combined engineering capability of the two businesses.

Although the letter stressed that the industry was moving towards greater consolidation and the time was therefore right for such a merger, the board of the internet business rejected the overtures. The software giant had spent a considerable amount of time and resources in developing its merger proposals and so was left nursing its losses.

As a footnote to this failed merger attempt, it is worth mentioning that not all financial analysts and commentators were convinced that the benefits of a merger between the two businesses were as potent as suggested in the letter. Although many recognised the need for the software giant to increase its scale in order to combat its loss of market share in internet search queries and to improve its relatively poor internet advertising revenues, some felt that the merger was unlikely to seriously threaten the dominance of Google in these markets. Search engine users had demonstrated a clear preference for Google over time and so it was believed that advertisers were unlikely to switch from Google as a result of the merger.

FT *Source*: adapted from 'Letter from Steve Ballmer to Yahoo!', www.ft.com, 1 February 2008, and C. Nuttall and R. Waters, 'Computing the future for Yahoo and Microsoft', www.ft.com, 4 May 2007.

Eliminating competition

A business may combine with, or take over, another business in order to eliminate competition and to increase its market share. The resulting increase in market power may enable the business to raise prices and thereby increase profits.

Eliminating weak and inefficient management

A weak management team may prevent the full potential of a business being achieved. In this case, a takeover may offer the chance to install a stronger management team that could do better. This argument is linked to what is referred to as the 'market for corporate control'. The term is used to describe the idea that mergers and takeovers are motivated by teams of managers that compete for the right to control business resources. The market for corporate control ensures that weak management teams will not survive and that, sooner or later, they will be succeeded by stronger management teams.

A merger or takeover can also be the solution to the agency problem. Where managers are not acting in the interests of shareholders but are busy pursuing their own interests, the effect is likely to be a decline in business performance and share price. The market for corporate control may lead to a takeover by another business whose managers are committed to serving the interests of shareholders.

The threat of takeover, however, may motivate managers to improve their performance. This suggests that mergers and takeovers are good for the economy as they help ensure that resources are fully utilised and that shareholder wealth maximisation remains the top priority.

Complementary resources

Two businesses may have complementary resources which, when combined, will allow higher profits to be made than if the businesses remain separate. By combining the two businesses, the relative strengths of each business will be brought together, which may lead to additional profits being generated. It may be possible, of course, for each business to overcome its particular deficiency and continue as a separate entity. Even so, it may still make sense to combine.

Activity 12.4

Why might there still be an argument in favour of a merger, even though a business could overcome any deficiency on its own?

Combining the resources of two businesses may lead to a quicker exploitation of the strengths of each business than if the businesses remained separate.

Real World 12.3 sets out the overtures made by the chief executive of Comcast, a major cable networks business, to Michael Eisner, chief executive of the Walt Disney Company, for a merger of the two businesses. These overtures, which were made in an open letter, pointed to the complementary resources of each business.

Real World 12.3

Dear Mickey

Dear Michael,

I am writing following our conversation earlier this week in which I proposed that we enter into discussions to merge Disney and Comcast to create a premier entertainment and communications company. It is unfortunate that you are not willing to do so. Given this, the only way for us to proceed is to make a public proposal directly to you and your Board.

We have a wonderful opportunity to create a company that combines distribution and content in a way that is far stronger and more valuable than either Disney or Comcast can be standing alone ... Under our proposal, your shareholders would own approximately 42% of the combined company. The combined company would be uniquely positioned to take advantage of an extraordinary collection of assets. Together, we would unite the country's premier cable provider with Disney's leading filmed entertainment, media networks and theme park properties.

In addition to serving over 21 million cable subscribers, Comcast is also the country's largest high speed internet service provider with over 5 million subscribers. As you have expressed on several occasions, one of Disney's top priorities involves the aggressive pursuit of technological innovation that enhances how Disney's content is created and delivered.

We believe this combination helps accelerate the realisation of that goal – whether through existing distribution channels and technologies such as video-on-demand and broadband video streaming or through emerging technologies still in development – to the benefit of all our shareholders, customers and employees.

We believe that improvements in operating performance, business creation opportunities and other combination benefits will generate enormous value for the shareholders of both companies. Together, as an integrated distribution and content company, we will be best positioned to meet our respective competitive challenges. We have a stable and respected management team with a great track record for creating shareholder value . . . Very truly yours,

Brian L. Roberts

FT *Source*: 'Dear Mickey: open letter to Disney', www.ft.com, 11 February 2004.
Footnote: Alas, Mickey did not write back and so the merger proposal was withdrawn.
© The Financial Times Limited 2012. All Rights Reserved.

Protecting sources of supply or revenue

A business may buy an important product or service from a particular supplier. There may be a risk, however, that the supplier will switch its output to a competitor business. In this kind of situation, the business may decide to acquire the supplier's business in order to protect its continuing operations. For similar reasons, a business may decide to acquire the business of an important customer where there is a risk that the customer will switch allegiance to a competitor. Although future cash flows may not be increased by such acquisitions, the risk of losing those cash flows may be greatly reduced.

The main shareholder wealth-enhancing motives for mergers and takeovers are shown in Figure 12.2.

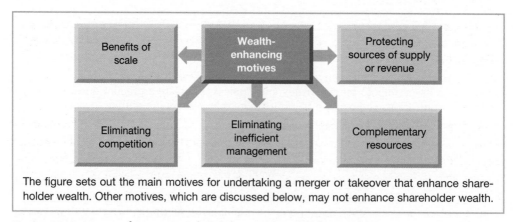

The figure sets out the main motives for undertaking a merger or takeover that enhance share-holder wealth. Other motives, which are discussed below, may not enhance shareholder wealth.

Figure 12.2 Motives for mergers that enhance shareholder wealth

OTHER MOTIVES FOR MERGERS

The motives for mergers and takeovers discussed so far are consistent with the objective of enhancing shareholder wealth. Other motives, which are more problematic, can also provide the driving force for business combinations. The following are examples.

Diversification

A business may invest in another business, operating in a different industry, in order to reduce risk. By having income streams from different industries, a more stable pattern of overall profit may be created. At first sight, such a policy may seem appealing. However, we must ask ourselves whether diversification by *management* will provide any benefits to shareholders that the *shareholders themselves* cannot provide more cheaply. It is often easier and cheaper for a shareholder to deal with the problem of risk by holding a diversified portfolio of shares than for the business to acquire another. It is quite likely that the latter approach will be expensive, as a premium may have to be paid to acquire the shares, and external investment advisers and consultants may have to be hired at substantial cost.

Activity 12.5

Who do you think might benefit most from diversification?

Diversification may well benefit the managers of the bidding business most. Managers cannot diversify their investment of time and effort in the business easily. Managing a more diversified business reduces the risks of unemployment and increases the prospects of increased income.

Diversification may also benefit lenders by making their investment more secure. As a result, they may be prepared to lend at a lower cost. (Where this occurs, shareholders will benefit indirectly from diversification.)

There are some circumstances where diversification can make sense for shareholders. Owner-managers, for example, may find it difficult to diversify their time and wealth because they are fully committed to the business. By diversifying the business's operations, they may be able to improve their financial stability. Another example is where a business is in difficulties and a merger or takeover would help it to avoid the costs of financial distress.

In recent years, questions have been raised about the future of diversified businesses. **Real World 12.4** describes the difficulties that US conglomerates are facing.

Decline sets in at the conglomerate

For nearly half a century the diversified business group was a cornerstone of American capitalism, but now many are either disappearing or struggling to justify their existence. Their predicament is made all the more serious by the rise of nimbler predators – private-equity groups betting that the old business-guru mantra got it backwards: the parts of a conglomerate are actually worth more than the whole.

Last week Altria put an end to a 20-year marriage of convenience between its tobacco and food businesses by spinning off Kraft from Philip Morris. A day later, American Standard split its $10bn-a-year toilets, brakes and air conditioning business. It will soon be followed by Tyco, which is poised to ask investors to forgive and forget its recent scandals by breaking itself in three.

Other once-mighty groups such as Cendant, the property-to-travel giant, and Viacom, Sumner Redstone's media powerhouse, have already unravelled decades of acquisitions to split into their component parts. Those that remain, like GE and its rival Honeywell, are reshaping their portfolio in an effort to convince sceptical investors of their worth. So far, their calls have gone unheeded, with share prices in both languishing below their historic highs. 'The conglomerates are dead,' says Chris Zook, head of the global strategy practice at Bain, the management consultancy. 'With some rare exceptions, the conglomerates' business model belongs to the past and is unlikely to reappear.'

The struggles of some of the oldest names in US business raise the prospect of a fundamental shift in corporate America's make-up. Supporters of conglomerates argue that their diversified structure has enabled them to safeguard industries, and their millions of employees, that would have struggled on their own. Leaving such businesses to private-equity groups, whose focus is on asset trades and cost-cutting, or turning them into stand-alone operations exposed to the whims of the equity market might lead to further dramatic reductions in the US industrial base.

Lewis Campbell, chief executive of Textron, widely regarded as America's first conglomerate, recalls that when its Cessna aircraft unit was hit by a downturn in 2001–03, the investment needed to turn it around came from other parts of the helicopters-to-lawnmowers group. 'Where would Cessna's employment level and profitability be now if we were not a diversified, multi-industry company?' he asks.

To be sure, conglomerates are alive and kicking in Asian economies, from Japan to India, and even in the US not all diversified groups are gasping for air. Companies such as Warren Buffett's Berkshire Hathaway – with interests ranging from car insurance to Fruit of the Loom apparel – and, to a lesser extent, Rupert Murdoch's multimedia News Corporation have reaped rewards from operating across several industries. But the rare successes highlight the problems of the rapidly shrinking US conglomerate sector. Indeed, the strategy of a renowned investor such as Mr Buffett is remarkably similar to the leaders of the conglomerates of old: buying companies whose diverse dynamics together cushion the whole group from the vagaries of business cycles.

'Conglomerates were the most exciting corporate form to appear in more than a generation,' wrote the late Robert Sobel in his 1984 *The Rise and Fall of the Conglomerate Kings*. 'They shook up the business scene as no other phenomenon had since the era of trust creation at the turn of the century.' A bespectacled First World War veteran called Royal Little is credited with starting the trend in 1953 when his Textron, then a maker of rayon, bought a car upholstery supplier. The acquisition helped the company to weather a downturn in textile supplies and the recession of the late 1950s, emboldening Mr Little to go for an even more extravagant move: the purchase of Bell Aerospace, the helicopter manufacturer.

Companies such as Litton Industries, International Telephone & Telegraph and Gulf + Western followed suit, acquiring many unrelated businesses in a quest to expand earnings and revenues. The success of the early conglomerates was predicated on the simple tenet that businesses find strength in numbers. This strategy of harvesting synergies between businesses, or simply cross-subsidising weaker operations with revenues generated by the more profitable ones, was warmly received by investors looking for safe, reliable earnings streams. That, in turn, gave conglomerates a powerful weapon: highly-rated stock that could be used to acquire even more companies, further expanding earnings power.

Over the past few decades, this virtuous circle has been progressively undone by profound changes in the US financial and business world. On the financial front, Wall Street has grown to dislike the 'one-stop shop' nature of the conglomerate. As capital markets have become more global and liquid, fund managers believe that they can diversify risk, and gain better returns, by buying shares across several sectors rather than by delegating that choice to a conglomerate's chief executive.

At the same time, academic and empirical evidence began to show that, far from delivering the promised synergies, conglomerates' bias towards ploughing surplus resources back into their weaker businesses led to waste and inefficiency. 'Conglomerates that engage in "winner picking" find it optimal to allocate scarce capital internally to mediocre projects,' say Heitor Almeida and Daniel Wolfenzon, two New York University academics, in a recent study. Indeed, academic studies dispelled the theory that acquisitions and cross-subsidies boost earnings and share prices, calculating that conglomerates are valued at average discounts of 10–12 per cent to the rest of the stock market. Henry Silverman, who built Cendant through an acquisition spree in the 1990s and then disbanded it in 2005, summed up the conglomerates' plight when he said the company had been a 'financial success but a stock market failure'. 'This is a classic case of the sum of the parts is worth more than the whole,' he said in announcing the break-up.

Sluggish share prices have been mirrored by financial performance. Looking at data from the past decade, Bain found that conglomerates have 50 per cent less chance of achieving sustained earnings growth than more focussed groups. Klaus Kleinfeld, chief executive of Siemens, the German conglomerate, rejects this view, arguing that the ability of diversified groups to cross-fertilise ideas, products and talent gives them an inherent advantage over focussed companies. 'Customers want a stable partner that can offer a variety of services. Customers do rely on us being around for a long time,' he says. If he is right, conglomerates should come back in favour during an economic slowdown, when investors flee to the relative safety of broad-based companies whose earnings are less sensitive to a downturn.

But investment professionals argue that a cyclical return in the favour of conglomerates is unlikely because today's financial markets offer investors more sophisticated risk management tools. 'Investing in a conglomerate is not the only way to diversify your risk, as it perhaps was 30 years ago,' says one. 'The financial instruments we have today mean anyone can diversify risk effectively by going on [the broking site] E*Trade.'

The space in the business landscape left by the slow unwinding of the conglomerates is likely to be taken over by aggressive private-equity groups. Armed with cash raised from indulgent lenders, the buyout groups are assembling large collections of varied businesses. Even Jeffrey Immelt, Mr Welch's successor at the helm of GE, arguably the quintessential modern conglomerate, acknowledges private equity's coming of age. 'Private-equity funds are the conglomerates of this era,' he recently told the FT. '[Trade buyers] have not seized the moment in terms of doing deals they could have done to build their companies for the long term.'

It is perhaps ironic that private equity should fatten its portfolios with businesses hived off from old-style conglomerates, such as Cendant's Travelport and GE's speciality materials unit. The crucial difference between the new hoarders of businesses and their predecessors, however, is that the former have it in mind to sell them again within years. But that comes after private equity applies, and extracts benefits from, another lesson learnt from the conglomerates of old: that diffuse businesses can be held together by a common set of managerial skills and processes.

Experts argue the conglomerates that will survive and prosper are the ones that succeed in linking their disparate operations through a common denominator of management and business principles. It is no coincidence that two surviving conglomerates, GE and Washington-based Danaher, have each created management 'playbooks' to remind their employees of their shared business goals and values. 'I am not prepared to bury the conglomerate just yet,' says Cynthia Montgomery, professor of management at Harvard Business School. 'There will always be a role for them because they bring managerial expertise and discipline.'

Perhaps the longer-lasting heirs to the conglomerates will be companies that spread themselves across more than one industry but do not overstretch into wildly different sectors. Bain's Mr Zook points to Apple as a company that branched out of its traditional computer business by harnessing a neighbouring technology with the iPod. Google is following a similar path, building on its dominance of online search to expand into the global advertising market.

'It is not a matter of being diversified or not, it is the degree of diversification,' says Michael Patsalos-Fox, chairman of the Americas region for McKinsey, the management consultancy. 'A modest degree of diversification can lead to superior shareholder returns because companies that only do one thing eventually run out of rope.'

 Source: Guerrera, F. (2007) 'Decline of the conglomerates', www.ft.com, 4 February.

Undervalued shares

Another possible motive for a takeover is where managers of a bidding business believe that the market undervalues the shares of a target business. As a result there is a profitable opportunity to be exploited. If we accept that the market is efficient, at least in the semi-strong form, this motive is difficult to justify. Close monitoring of the market by investors will ensure that share prices reflect all publicly available information. It is possible, however, that managers of the bidding business have access to information that the market does not have. It is also possible that the market, perhaps for a short period, fails to price the shares in an efficient manner. However, such situations are relatively rare.

Management interests and goals

A merger or takeover may be undertaken to fulfil the personal interests and goals of managers. Managers may acquire another business to reduce the risks they face (for example, from a takeover by another business) or to increase the amount of resources under their control. The ultimate prize will be increased job security and/or increased remuneration. In some cases, managers are directly rewarded on the basis of growth in sales or profits, thereby providing them with a greater incentive for making acquisitions. In the end, however, takeovers motivated by the interests of managers may result in a destruction of shareholder value.

Real World 12.5 also points out that managers may enjoy the excitement of mergers and takeovers.

The personal interests and goals of managers may also explain why some proposed takeovers are fiercely contested by them.

FORMS OF PURCHASE CONSIDERATION

When a business takes over another business, payment for the shares acquired may be made in different forms.

Activity 12.6

What different forms of payment do you think may be used?

The main methods of payment are:

- cash
- shares in the bidding business
- loan capital in the bidding business.

Below we consider the advantages and disadvantages of each form of payment from the point of view of both the bidding business's shareholders and the target business's shareholders.

Cash

Payment by cash means the amount of the purchase consideration will be both certain and clearly understood by the target business's shareholders. This may improve the chances of a successful bid. It will also mean that shareholder control of the bidding business will not be diluted as no additional shares will be issued.

Raising the necessary cash, however, can create problems for the bidding business, particularly when the target business is large. It may only be possible to raise the amount required by a loan or share issue or by selling off assets, which the bidding business's shareholders may not like. On occasions, it may be possible to spread the cash payments over a period. However, deferred payments are likely to weaken the attraction of the bid to the target business's shareholders.

The receipt of cash will allow the target business's shareholders to adjust their share portfolios without incurring transaction costs on disposal. Transaction costs will be incurred, however, when new shares or loan capital are acquired to replace the shares sold. Moreover, the receipt of cash may result in a liability to capital gains tax (which arises on gains from the disposal of certain assets, including shares).

Shares

The issue of ordinary shares in the bidding business as purchase consideration avoids any strain on its cash position. However, some dilution of existing shareholder control will occur and there may also be a risk of dilution in earnings per share. (Dilution will occur if the additional earnings from the merger divided by the number of new shares issued is lower than the existing earnings per share.) The directors must ensure that the authorised share capital of the business is sufficient to make a new issue and, more importantly, that the market value of the business's shares does not fall during the course of the takeover. A substantial fall in share price will reduce the value of the bid and could undermine the chances of acceptance. To avoid this risk, the bidding business may well make a more generous offer where the bid is in the form of shares rather than cash. The cost of this form of financing must also be taken into account. We saw in Chapter 8 that the cost of servicing ordinary shares is relatively expensive.

The target business's shareholders may find a share-for-share exchange attractive. As they currently hold shares, they may wish to continue with this form of investment rather than receive cash or other forms of security. A share-for-share exchange does not result in a liability for capital gains tax. (For capital gains tax purposes, no disposal is deemed to have occurred when this type of transaction takes place.) The target shareholders will also have a continuing ownership link with the original business, although it will now be part of a larger business. However, the precise value of the offer may be difficult to calculate owing to movements in the share prices of the two businesses. There is also the risk that share prices do not reflect their intrinsic value.

Real World 12.6 contains a warning from Warren Buffett about share-for-share bids where share prices do not reflect their intrinsic value.

Real World 12.6

Mergers can be costly

In evaluating a share-for-share offer, shareholders of the target company quite understandably focus on the market price of the acquirer's shares that are to be given them. But they also expect the transaction to deliver them the *intrinsic* value of their own shares – the ones they are giving up. If shares of a prospective acquirer are selling below their intrinsic value, it's impossible for that buyer to make a sensible deal in an all-share deal. You simply can't exchange an undervalued share for a fully-valued one without hurting your shareholders.

Imagine, if you will, Company A and Company B, of equal size and both with businesses intrinsically worth $100 per share. Both of their shares, however, sell for $80 per share. The CEO of A, long on confidence and short on smarts, offers $1^1/_4$ shares of A for each share of B, correctly telling his directors that B is worth $100 per share. He will neglect to explain, though, that what he is giving will cost his shareholders $125 in intrinsic value. If the directors are mathematically challenged as well, and a deal is therefore completed, the shareholders of B will end up owning 55.6% of A and B's combined assets and A's shareholders will own 44.4%.

Not everyone at A, it should be noted, is a loser from this nonsensical transaction. Its CEO now runs a company twice as large as his original domain, in a world where size tends to correlate with both prestige and compensation.

Source: Adapted from shareholder's letter, Berkshire Hathaway Inc, www.berkshirehathaway.com, 26 February 2010, p. 16.

Loan capital

Like the issue of shares, the issue of loan capital is simply an exchange of paper and so it avoids any strain on the cash resources of the bidding business. However, it has certain advantages over shares in that the issue of loan capital involves no dilution of shareholder control and the service costs will be lower. A disadvantage of a loan-capital-for-share exchange is that it will increase the gearing of the bidding business and therefore the level of financial risk. The directors of the bidding business must ensure that the issue of loan capital is within its borrowing limits.

Loan capital may be acceptable to shareholders in the target business if they have doubts over the future performance of the combined business. Loan capital provides investors with both a fixed level of return and security for their investment. When a takeover bid is being made, convertible loan notes may be offered as purchase consideration.

Activity 12.7

What is the attraction of this form of loan capital from the point of view of the target business's shareholders?

The issue of convertible loan notes would give target business shareholders a useful hedge against uncertainty. This type of loan capital will provide relative security in the early years, with an option to convert to ordinary shares at a later date. Investors will, of course, exercise this option only if things go well for the combined business.

Various factors may influence the form of payment used by bidding businesses. Market conditions may be critical. It seems that ordinary shares are more likely to be used following a period of strong stock market performance. Recent high returns from shares make them more attractive to investors. Businesses with good growth opportunities often favour ordinary shares when financing acquisitions. It is seen as less constraining than issuing loan capital or paying cash. Businesses with poor growth opportunities, however, may not be able to offer ordinary shares as payment.

To make a bid more attractive, a choice of payment method may be offered to shareholders in the target business. Often, the choice is between shares in the bidding business and cash. This allows shareholders an opportunity to adjust their portfolios in a way that suits them.

Real World 12.7 reveals the ways in which mergers have been financed in recent years.

How mergers are financed

The popularity of each form of bid consideration varies over time. Figure 12.3 shows that, in recent years, cash has usually been the most popular.

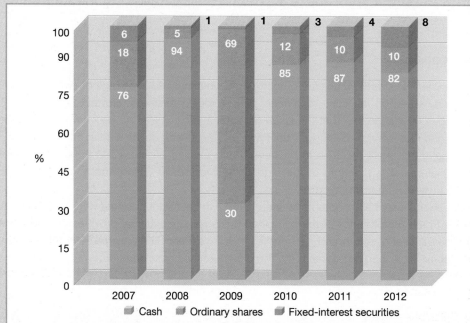

The figure shows that, with the exception of 2009, cash has been the most important form of bid consideration. Fixed-interest securities, such as preference shares and loan notes, have been fairly insignificant forms of bid consideration.

Figure 12.3 Bid consideration in mergers and acquisitions in the UK by other UK businesses, 2007–2012

Source: Based on information from 'Mergers and acquisitions involving UK companies, Q4 2012', www.statistics.gov.uk, Table 9.

It is interesting to note that research in the UK and the US suggests that businesses using ordinary shares as a means of acquisition achieve significantly poorer returns following the acquisition than those using cash (see reference 1 at the end of the chapter). The reasons for this are not entirely clear. Perhaps the relatively poor performance of share-for-share deals indicates that the bidding businesses' shares were too highly valued to begin with.

MERGERS AND FINANCIAL PERFORMANCE

A proposed merger can be evaluated in terms of its effect on the wealth of both groups of shareholders. This is considered in Example 12.1.

Example 12.1

Ixus plc is a large sugar-refining business that is currently considering the takeover of Decet plc, an engineering business. Financial information concerning each business is as follows:

Income statements for the year ended 30 June 2014

	Ixus plc £m	Decet plc £m
Sales revenue	432.5	242.6
Operating profit	64.8	35.0
Interest payable	(20.6)	(13.2)
Profit before taxation	44.2	21.8
Taxation	(10.6)	(7.4)
Profit for the period	33.6	14.4
Other financial information		
Ordinary shares (£1.00 nominal)	£120.0m	£48.0m
Dividend payout ratio	50%	25%
Price/earnings ratio	20	16

The board of directors of Ixus plc has offered shareholders of Decet plc 5 shares in Ixus plc for every 4 shares held. If the takeover is successful, the price/earnings ratio of the enlarged business is expected to be 19 times. The dividend payout ratio will remain unchanged.

As a result of the takeover, after-tax savings in head office costs of £9.6 million per year are expected.

(a) Calculate:
  (i) the total value of the proposed bid
  (ii) the expected earnings per share and share price of Ixus plc following the takeover.
(b) Evaluate the proposed takeover from the viewpoint of an investor holding 20,000 shares in:
  (i) Ixus plc
  (ii) Decet plc.

Solution

Before we consider this problem in detail we should recall from Chapter 3 that the P/E ratio is calculated as follows:

$$\text{P/E ratio} = \frac{\text{Market value per share}}{\text{Earnings per share}}$$

The P/E ratio reflects the market's view of the likely future growth in earnings. The higher the P/E ratio, the more highly regarded are the future growth prospects. The equation above can be rearranged so that:

$$\text{Market value per share } (P_0) = \text{P/E ratio} \times \text{Earnings per share}$$

We shall use this rearranged formula to value the shares of both businesses.

(a) (i)   Five shares in Ixus plc are offered for every four shares in Decet plc. The total number of shares offered is, therefore:

$$5/4 \times 48.0m = 60.0m$$

$$\text{EPS of Ixus plc} = \text{Earnings available to shareholders/No. of shares in issue}$$
$$= \pounds33.6m/120.0m$$
$$= \underline{\pounds0.28}$$
$$\text{Value of share in Ixus plc} = \text{P/E ratio} \times \text{EPS}$$
$$= \pounds0.28 \times 20$$
$$= \pounds5.60$$
$$\text{Total bid value} = \pounds5.60 \times 60.0$$
$$= \pounds336.0m$$

(ii)   Following the takeover, the EPS of Ixus plc would be:

	£m
Earnings of Ixus plc	33.6
Earnings of Decet plc	14.4
After-tax savings	9.6
Total earnings	57.6

$$\text{No. of shares following the takeover} = 180m \text{ (that is, } 120m + 60m)$$
$$\text{EPS after the takeover} = \pounds57.6m/180m = \pounds0.32$$
$$\text{Value of a share following the takeover} = \text{P/E ratio} \times \text{EPS}$$
$$= 19 \times \pounds0.32 = \underline{\pounds6.08}$$

(b) (i)   *Ixus plc investor*

$$\text{Value of shares before the takeover} = 20{,}000 \times \pounds5.60 = \pounds112{,}000$$
$$\text{Value of 20,000 shares after the takeover} = \pounds121{,}600 \text{ (that is, } 20{,}000 \times \pounds6.08)$$
$$\text{Increase in value of shares} = \underline{\pounds9{,}600}$$

(ii)   *Decet plc investor*

$$\text{EPS of Decet plc before the takeover} = \pounds14.4m/48.0m = \pounds0.30$$
$$\text{Value of a share in Decet plc} = 16 \times \pounds0.30 = \underline{\pounds4.80}$$
$$\text{Shares held in Ixus plc} = 5/4 \times 20{,}000 = \underline{25{,}000}$$
$$\text{Value of 20,000 shares before the takeover} = 20{,}000 \times \pounds4.80 = \pounds96{,}000$$
$$\text{Value of 25,000 shares after the takeover} = 25{,}000 \times \pounds6.08 = \pounds152{,}000$$
$$\text{Increase in value of shares held} = \underline{\pounds56{,}000}$$

We can see that the gain arising from the takeover is not shared equally between the two shareholder groups. The investor in Decet plc will receive a 58 per cent increase in the value of shares held whereas the investor in Ixus plc will receive only a 9 per cent increase. The annual dividends received by each investor will be:

	Ixus plc investor £	Decet plc investor £
Dividend received before the takeover		
((£33.6m × 50%)/120m) × 20,000	2,800	
((£14.4m × 25%)/48.0m) × 20,000		1,500
Dividend received after the takeover		
((£57.6m × 50%)/180m) × 20,000	3,200	
((£57.6m × 50%)/180m) × 25,000		4,000

The investor in Decet plc is again the winner. The increase in dividend payout is 167 per cent compared with 14 per cent for the investor in Ixus plc.

The investor in Ixus plc may insist on a more equal division of the gains from the takeover. The fairly modest gains predicted for the investor in Ixus plc will depend partly on achieving substantial cost savings. These savings, however, may be difficult to achieve given that the two businesses operate in quite different industries. The gains also rely on achieving a P/E ratio of 19 times after the takeover. However, there may be problems in combining the two businesses because of differences in culture, operating systems, management conflict and so on. As a result, the predicted P/E ratio may also not be achieved.

WHO BENEFITS?

In this section, we shall try to identify the likely winners and losers in a merger. We begin by considering the shareholders, as the pursuit of shareholder value is usually claimed to be the driving force behind merger activity. It is worth asking, however, whether the reality matches the rhetoric. The answer, it seems, will depend on whether the bidding shareholders or the target shareholders are being discussed. Where mergers create value, it is often unevenly allocated. (See reference 2 at the end of the chapter.)

Shareholders in the target business

Studies in both the UK and the US show that shareholders in the target business are the main beneficiaries. They are normally rewarded through a substantial premium on the share price.

Activity 12.8

Why might a bidding business be prepared to pay a premium above the market price for the shares of a business? Try to think of at least two reasons.

Various reasons have been put forward to explain this phenomenon. They include the following:

- The managers of the bidding business have access to information that is not available to the market and which is not, therefore, reflected in the share price. (This assumes that the market is not efficient in the strong form.)
- The managers of the bidding business may simply misjudge the value of the target business.
- The managers may feel that there will be significant gains arising from combining the two businesses that are worth paying for. In theory, the maximum price a buyer will be prepared to pay will be equivalent to the present value of the business plus any gains from the merger.
- Management hubris. Where there is more than one bidder or where the takeover is being resisted, the managers of a bidding business may fail to act rationally and may raise the bid price above an economically justifiable level. This may be done in order to salvage management pride as they may feel humiliated by defeat.

The size of bid premia tends to be inversely related to the size of the target business. One study of 3,691 US businesses acquired over the period 1990–2007 found that bid premia for the top third, in terms of size, averaged 38 per cent compared with 54 per cent for the bottom third. (See reference 3 at the end of the chapter). There could be various reasons for this. The bigger the target business, the bigger the investment required. This may prompt the bidding business to act with more care and to employ specialists with expertise in negotiation and valuation. Furthermore, the bigger the target business, the smaller will be the pool of potential buyers. The resulting lack of competition may also help to keep bid premia lower.

Bid premia also tend to be significantly higher when a hostile bid is launched.

Activity 12.9

Why should we expect this to be the case?

A higher premium will often be needed to overcome resistance to the bid.

There are also other, less obvious, reasons why a higher premium may be paid under these circumstances. A hostile bid may attract greater competition among buyers, which is likely to push up the bid premium. Where a friendly merger is under way, other suitors may see little point in launching a bid. A hostile bid often indicates that managers of the bidding business believe the target business is badly run. They may, therefore, be prepared to offer a high bid premium in the expectation that large gains can be made through better management.

Share prices in the target business will usually reflect the bid premium for as long as the bid is in progress. Where a takeover bid is unsuccessful and the bid is withdrawn, the share price of the target business will usually return to its pre-offer level. However, shares may fall below their pre-bid prices if investors believe that the managers have failed to exploit a profitable opportunity. The same fate may be experienced by shares in the bidding business.

Shareholders in the bidding business

Shareholders of the bidding business usually have little to celebrate. Although early studies offered some evidence that a merger provided them with either a small increase or no increase in the value of their investment, more recent studies suggest that, over the long run, takeovers produce a significant decrease in shareholder value (see, for example, reference 4 at the end of the chapter). Some studies also suggest that cross-border mergers are particularly poor performers (see, for example, reference 5 at the end of the chapter). This may be partly due to cultural differences resulting in poor integration of the combined businesses.

Why might shares in the bidding business lose value as a result of a takeover of a target business? Try to think of two reasons why this may be so.

Various reasons have been suggested. These include:

- *Overpayment*. The bidding business may pay too much to acquire the target business. We saw earlier that large premia are often paid to acquire another business, which may result in a transfer of wealth from the bidding business shareholders to the target business shareholders. Hostile bids usually lead to bigger premia being paid and so may be particularly bad news for shareholders of the bidding business.
- *Integration problems*. Following a successful bid, it may be difficult to integrate the target business's operations. Problems relating to organisational structure, management style, management rivalries and so on may work against successful integration. Such problems are most likely to arise in horizontal mergers where an attempt is made to fuse the systems and operations of the two separate businesses into a seamless whole. There are likely to be fewer problems where a conglomerate merger is undertaken and where there is no real attempt to adopt common systems or operations.
- *Management neglect*. There is a risk that, following the takeover, managers may relax and expect the combined business to operate smoothly. If the takeover has been bitterly contested, the temptation for management to ease back after the struggle may be very strong.
- *Hidden problems*. Problems relating to the target business may be unearthed following the takeover. This is most likely to arise where a thorough investigation was not carried out prior to the takeover.

Managers

Any discussion concerning winners and losers in a merger should include the senior managers of the bidding business and the target business. They are important stakeholders in their respective businesses and play an important role in takeover negotiations.

Following a successful bid, what is the likelihood of the senior managers in (a) the bidding business, and (b) the target business benefiting from the merger?

(a) The managers of the bidding business are usually beneficiaries as they will manage an enlarged business, which will, in turn, result in greater status, income and security.
(b) The position of senior managers in the acquired business is less certain. In some cases, they may be retained and may even become directors of the enlarged business. In other cases, however, the managers may lose their jobs.

A study by Franks and Mayer found that nearly 80 per cent of executive directors in a target business either resign or lose their job within two years of a successful takeover. As might be expected, a higher proportion lost their jobs following a hostile bid than following a friendly bid. (See reference 6 at the end of the chapter.)

Where senior managers in the target business lose their jobs, generous severance packages may be available. Furthermore, highly paid management jobs in other businesses may await them. This can often help to soften the blow.

Advisers

Mergers and takeovers can be very rewarding for investment advisers and lawyers employed by each business during the bid period. Whatever the outcome of the bid, it seems that they are winners. **Real World 12.8** describes a particularly rewarding merger for advisers between Glencore International plc, a large commodities business, and Xstrata plc, a large mining business.

Real World 12.8

Nice work (if you can get it)

The potential merger between Glencore and Xstrata is likely to give a more than $100m boost to the advisers involved. Deutsche Bank, Goldman Sachs, JPMorgan and Nomura are advising Xstrata on the deal, while Citigroup and Morgan Stanley are advising Glencore. Other banks could still be added to the register, people familiar with the situation said. The merger, if completed, would be the biggest in any sector globally since September 2010.

Even though the merger would be the largest mining deal ever by value according to Dealogic, the fees are unlikely to break records in M&A. As an all-share deal, expensive financing fees will not need to be paid, bringing down the cost, said the people familiar with the situation. Thomson Reuters and Freeman Consulting estimate the deal value is $42bn, based on Xstrata's enterprise value. Freeman estimates that Xstrata and Glencore could each pay up to $70m in fees, a total of $140m. Some of the people familiar with the situation estimate the banks could be paid about $15m each, leading to an estimated $100m total fee pay-out.

Lawyers will also share in the fees, with Linklaters advising Glencore and Freshfields advising Xstrata. Including payments for Xstrata's accountants, Ernst & Young, and Glencore's accountants, Deloitte, the fee haul would be about $150m, said one of the people familiar with the situation.

The biggest M&A fees ever paid were by RBS for its $98.2bn acquisition of ABN Amro, which came to $299m, according to Thomson Reuters. The advisers all declined to comment.

 Source: Sakoui, A. and Blas, J. (2012) 'Merger to provide $100m boost for advisers', www.ft.com, 2 February.
© The Financial Times Limited 2012. All Rights Reserved.

In recent years, concern has been expressed over the influence of advisers in stimulating merger activity. There can be a conflict between the short-term financial incentives available to advisers for promoting merger activity and the long-term economic consequences of mergers.

THE MERGER PUZZLE

A substantial body of evidence now exists, covering different time periods and across several different countries, indicating the dubious value of takeovers for bidding business shareholders. This raises the question of why businesses persist in acquiring other businesses. The answer is still unclear. Perhaps it is because takeovers satisfy the interests of managers, or perhaps it reflects Samuel Johnson's view of remarriage – the triumph of hope over experience.

Real World 12.9 sets out the thoughts of Warren Buffett on why mergers occur.

Real World 12.9

A modern fairy tale

Many managements apparently were overexposed in impressionable childhood years to the story in which the imprisoned handsome prince is released from a toad's body by a kiss from a beautiful princess. Consequently, they are certain their managerial kiss will do wonders for the profitability of Company T[arget] . . . Investors can always buy toads at the going price for toads. If investors instead bankroll princesses who wish to pay double for the right to kiss the toad, those kisses had better pack some real dynamite. We've observed many kisses but very few miracles. Nevertheless, many managerial princesses remain serenely confident about the future potency of their kisses – even after their corporate back-yards are knee-deep in unresponsive toads . . .

We have tried occasionally to buy toads at bargain prices with results that have been chronicled in past reports. Clearly our kisses fell flat. We have done well with a couple of princes – but they were princes when purchased. At least our kisses didn't turn them into toads. And, finally, we have occasionally been quite successful in purchasing fractional interests in easily identifiable princes at toad-like prices.

Source: Warren Buffett's letter to Berkshire Hathaway Inc. shareholders, 1981, www.berkshirehathaway.com.

INGREDIENTS FOR SUCCESSFUL MERGERS

Although many mergers and takeovers do not add value for the bidding business's share-holders, not all are unsuccessful. Why do some succeed? What are the magic ingredients for success? Business consultancy firms often try to answer these questions, mainly through surveys of business executives that have gone through the merger process. One extensive review of the consultancy literature (see reference 7 at the end of the chapter) found that, to be successful, a merger should normally have strategic fit. In other words, it should align with the overall aims and objectives of the business. Even where this is the case, however, it seems that a merger involving businesses of equal size, or with different cultures, can be extremely difficult to implement. The review also found that mergers between businesses in the same, or related, industries that exploit existing business strengths tend to be more successful. No real surprises here then.

Perhaps more interestingly, the literature review found that the following may help to tip the balance in favour of successfully implementing a merger:

- early planning to ensure proper integration of the physical and human resources of the combined entity
- rapid integration, along with early action to secure cost savings
- identifying and incentivising managers to lead the integration process
- being aware of cultural issues and keeping the various stakeholders, such as employees and customers, fully informed
- retaining customers by ensuring that the sales force remain fully engaged
- retaining talented employees, particularly where the business is technology or human resource based.

While the importance of most of these factors will vary from merger to merger, the import-ance of early planning is paramount. It is seen as vital in achieving rapid gains and in building commitment to the merger.

REJECTING A TAKEOVER BID

A takeover bid may be rejected, of course. This need not imply that the bid is unwelcome and that shareholders are committed to maintaining the business as an independent entity. It may simply be a tactic to increase the bid premium and thereby increase shareholder wealth. If, however, it is not a negotiating tactic but a genuine attempt to remain independent, there is no certainty that rejection will be the end of the story. The spurned business may decide to press ahead with a hostile bid. Some of the defensive tactics that can be used against such a bid are considered below.

Defensive tactics

Various tactics may be used to fend off a hostile bid. Some of these must be put in place before a hostile bid is received, whereas others can be deployed when the bid has been made. Defensive tactics to be used before a bid has been received include:

- *Conversion to private company status*. By converting to private limited company status, the business makes its shares more difficult to acquire.
- *Employee share option schemes.* Encouraging employees to acquire shares in the business is likely to increase the proportion of shareholders willing to resist a bid.
- *Maintaining good investor relations*. All shareholders should be kept fully informed of the strengths, opportunities and potential of the business, and good relations with major shareholders should be cultivated.
- *Share repurchase*. By reducing the numbers of shares in issue, it may be possible to make it more difficult for a bidder to acquire a controlling interest in the business.
- *Increasing gearing*. By the judicious use of gearing, returns to shareholders may be enhanced, which may, in turn, make a takeover more expensive. It may also make it more difficult for a predator business that is already highly geared to launch a takeover.
- *Increasing operating efficiency*. Every effort should be made to ensure that the business is operating at a high level of efficiency and profitability. This may help to ward off interest from predator businesses seeking to exploit underutilised resources.

Activity 12.12

How might the managers of a business seek to increase efficiency and profitability?

Managers may impose tight discipline through cost savings, asset disposals, productivity improvements and sales campaigns.

Once a bid has been made, defensive tactics may include:

- *Presenting the case to shareholders*. When an offer has been received, the directors of the target business will normally notify the shareholders in a circular letter. In this letter the case for rejection may be set out. It might be argued, for example, that it is not in the long-term interests of the shareholders to accept the offer, or that the price offered is too low. In support of such arguments, the managers may disclose hitherto confidential information such as profit forecasts, asset valuations, details of new contracts and so on. The circular may also try to attack the record of the bidding business in creating value for its shareholders. At the very least, this may boost share price, thereby making the takeover more expensive (and therefore less attractive).

- *Increasing dividend payouts*. The aim of this tactic is to signal to shareholders the directors' confidence in the future prospects of the business. It was mentioned in Chapter 9, however, that it may simply be seen by shareholders as a desperate attempt by the directors to gain their support and so may be discounted.
- *Finding a white knight*. A target business may avoid the attentions of an unwelcome bidder by seeking out another business (a white knight) with which to combine. This tactic will normally be used only as a last resort, however, as it will result in the loss of independence. There is also a risk that the white knight will be less gallant after the merger than was hoped.
- *Finding a white squire*. This is a variation of the white knight tactic. In this case, a supportive business will purchase a block of shares in the target business. This will be big enough to prevent any real prospect of a takeover but will not provide a controlling interest. The white squire will usually be given some incentive to 'ride to the rescue', which may take the form of a seat on the board or a discount on the purchase price of the shares.

There are other defensive tactics, which are acceptable in some countries, but which are not normally acceptable to regulatory authorities in the UK. These include:

- *Making the business unattractive*. Managers may take steps to make the business unattractive to a bidder. In the colourful language of mergers, this may involve taking a poison pill through the sale of prized assets of the business (the crown jewels). Other tactics include agreements to pay large sums to directors for loss of office resulting from a takeover (golden parachutes) and the purchase of certain assets that the bidding business does not want.
- *Making a counterbid.* The target business may launch a counterbid for the bidding business. However, this tactic is difficult to carry out where the target business is much smaller than the bidding business. (This is often referred to as the pac-man defence and derives its name from a well-known computer game.)

Real World 12.10 shows that modern tactics used to resist takeover attempts are pretty tame when compared with those used in the US during the 19th century.

Real World 12.10

Defensive tactics – Western style

The following is a brief description of a 'Wild West' style takeover battle that involved an attempt to take control of the Erie Railway in 1868:

> The takeover attempt pitted Cornelius Vanderbilt against Daniel Drew, Jim Fisk and Jay Gould. As one of the major takeover defences, the defenders of the Erie Railway issued themselves large quantities of stock (that is, shares), even though they lacked the authorisation to do so. At that time, bribery of judges and elected officials was common, and so legal remedies for violating corporate laws were particularly weak. The battle for control of the railway took a violent turn when the target corporation hired guards, equipped with firearms and cannons, to guard their headquarters. The takeover attempt ended when Vanderbilt abandoned his assault on the Erie Railway and turned his attention to weaker targets.

Source: P. Gaughan, *Mergers and Acquisitions*, HarperCollins, 1991, p. 13.

Overcoming resistance to a bid

Managers of the bidding business may try to overcome resistance to the bid by circularising shareholders of the target business with information that counters any claims made against the commercial logic of the bid or the offer price. They may also increase the offer price for the shares in the target business. In some cases, the original offer price may be pitched at a fairly low level as a negotiating ploy. The offer price will then be increased at a later date, thereby allowing the target business's managers and shareholders to feel that they have won some sort of victory.

Protecting the interests of shareholders and the public

To protect the interests of shareholders of both the bidding business and the target business, there is the City Code on Takeovers and Mergers. The Code sets out rules for conducting takeover activity in an orderly manner and has statutory underpinning. It seeks to ensure that all shareholders are treated equally when a takeover is being negotiated. The Code requires shareholders to be supplied with the information needed to make a proper decision. Forecasts provided by both parties to the bid must be carefully prepared and key assumptions underlying the forecast figures must be stated. Furthermore, time limits must be set for each stage of a takeover bid. The Code is issued and administered by the Panel on Takeovers and Mergers. This is an independent body that draws its membership from major business and financial institutions.

Protecting the interests of the public also becomes a consideration when larger businesses combine. Where a business with UK sales revenue in excess of £70 million is being taken over, or where the combined business has a 25 per cent share of a particular market, the proposed merger can be referred to the Competition Commission. Referrals are usually made by the Office of Fair Trading, which investigates proposed mergers to see whether they could have an adverse effect on competition.

The Competition Commission is an independent public body that considers the effect of mergers and takeovers on the level of competition operating within particular markets. If the Commission believes a merger would result in a substantial lessening of competition within a market, it has the power to take action. This may involve imposing conditions on the merger or preventing the merger from taking place.

Where a merger is referred to the Commission, detailed inquiries are carried out, which can take some time. A large business that becomes the target of a hostile bid may therefore seek a referral as a defensive ploy. The delay and trouble caused by a Commission inquiry may make the bid less attractive to the bidding business.

In addition to national rules, the European Union has competition rules to eliminate restrictive practices that may affect trade between EU member states. These rules can restrict mergers that could distort competition or could lead to an abuse of a dominant market position. EU member states will normally enforce EU competition rules.

RESTRUCTURING A BUSINESS: DIVESTMENTS AND DEMERGERS

A business may seek to decrease, rather than increase, its scale of operations. Restructuring a business in this way can be achieved through either a divestment or a demerger. Each of these is discussed below.

Divestment

A divestment involves selling off part of the business's operations to a third party. This kind of restructuring may be undertaken for various reasons, including:

- *Financial problems*. A business that is short of cash or too highly geared may sell off certain operations to improve its financial position.
- *Defensive tactics*. A business that is vulnerable to a takeover may take pre-emptive action by selling its 'crown jewels'. This would be a fairly drastic step for a business but may be necessary in order to retain its independence.
- *Strategic focus*. A business may wish to focus exclusively on 'core' operations. That is, those operations which align with its strategic objectives. As a consequence, non-core operations will be sold off.
- *Poor performance*. Where the performance of a particular business operation is disappointing, it may be sold off to enable more profitable use of resources.
- *Reverse synergy*. The value of the sum of the individual parts of a business may be greater than the whole. This may happen with a diversified business where shareholders find it difficult to value the whole and/or where senior managers struggle to control its different operations.

In such circumstances, selling off individual business operations may unlock shareholder value. The above reasons are summarised in Figure 12.4.

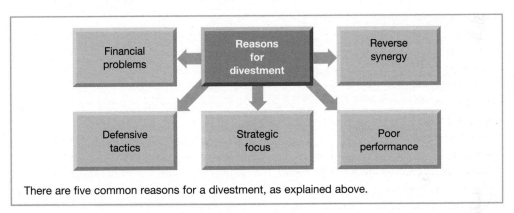

There are five common reasons for a divestment, as explained above.

Figure 12.4 Common reasons for divestment

Divestment and the agency problem

When a sell-off is undertaken, the managers of the particular business operations may bid to become the new owners. However, this may give rise to an agency problem for the shareholders.

Activity 12.13

Why might an agency problem arise?

The managers have a duty to act in the interests of the shareholders. However, when a management buyout is in prospect, the managers have a conflict of interest. On the one hand, they have a duty to ensure that the sale of the business will maximise the wealth of the owners, and on the other, they will be keen to acquire the business for as low a price as possible. There is a risk, therefore, that unscrupulous managers will suppress important information or will fail to exploit profitable opportunities in the period leading up to a buyout in order to obtain the business operations at a cheap price.

Shareholders must be aware of this potential problem and should seek independent advice concerning the value and potential of the business operations for which the managers are bidding. If the bid by managers is successful, the purchase arrangement is referred to as a *management buyout*. We saw in Chapter 7 that management buyouts are often financed by private-equity firms, which usually acquire a shareholding in the business.

Demerger

Rather than business operations being sold off to a third party, they may be transferred to a newly created business. This kind of restructuring is referred to as a demerger or spin-off. In this case, ownership of the business operations remains unchanged as the current owners will be given shares in the new business. The allocation of shares to the owners is usually made in proportion to their shareholdings in the existing business.

The reasons for a demerger overlap with those for a divestment. Thus, a demerger may be used as a defensive tactic in a takeover bid and/or may help to provide greater strategic focus to the business. It may also help to unlock shareholder value. This may be the result from the effects of reverse synergy, mentioned earlier, or because managers of the newly created business perform more effectively when given greater autonomy.

Real World 12.11 considers some further issues concerning divestments.

Real World 12.11

Thinking about shrinking

The slimming of big business proceeds apace. We have already been treated to big spinoffs by the likes of Kraft and ConocoPhillips. More modestly, Tesco said last week it will sell its Japanese business, while GlaxoSmithKline pursued the sale of a £1.5bn ($2.4bn) assortment of over-the-counter medicines. The vogue for spinoffs and disposals is no doubt partly cyclical. The corporate urge to grow is intimately connected with so-called animal spirits. In times of doubt and depression, the underlying logic of getting smaller is more likely to assert itself.

That logic seems to hold, by and large, in both good times and bad.

A recent paper from McKinsey calculates that in a sample of almost 60 large spinoffs since 1992, average operating margins rose markedly over the following five years – both in the spinoff and the parent. In one sense, this is what we should expect. The growth gene in successful companies means their boards have a bias towards acquisition, which tends on average to destroy value. Reducing the scale of the corporation goes against the grain – particularly for executives whose remuneration is tied to size. The case for a big disposal or demerger must therefore be the more compelling.

There are other deterrents to getting smaller. Disposing of a business may be seen as strategic weakness – consider how commentators have leapt swiftly from Tesco's minor exit from Japan to speculating about a bigger one from the US. Boards may also worry about losing economies of scale. But logic also points the opposite way.

Corporations, like states, have a natural tendency towards bureaucracy. And while growth in scale economies – purchasing power, for instance – tends to be linear, that in bureaucracy tends to be exponential. Thus, as a corporation moves from small to medium size its operating staff – in manufacturing, in sales, in accounts – will grow in parallel. But as it gets bigger again, whole new functions sprout up – treasury, legal, investor relations and so forth. All those are costs that must be pushed down to the divisions. But suppose a given division already has the necessary scale within its own market. Hive it off, and it will retain scale economies while shedding the bureaucratic overhead. Hive off enough divisions, and the parent can shed the overhead as well.

A poorly performing division will be unloved. Fixing it properly would mean more immediate damage to the bottom line than leaving it alone. It would also draw attention to the division's underperformance, and carry the risky promise of improvement. Alternatively, the division may be in an industry which needs consolidation. It might be qualified to lead that process. Getting the board to put cash behind it might be another question.

Does that mean small is necessarily beautiful? Not so fast.

Big companies, if properly run, can allocate cash to advantage across their divisions. The purist might say that is unnecessary; any spare cash should be returned to shareholders, who will allocate it themselves. But that presupposes the corporation has no particular skills that the shareholders lack. The whole premise of investing in Berkshire Hathaway over the years has been that Warren Buffett is better at spending his cash flow than outsiders would be.

Big corporations also have the edge in raising debt capital. Banks will lend to them below cost in hopes of corporate and advisory business. Bond markets are open to them when they are closed to smaller and less liquid borrowers.

And big corporations play an important role in buying out entrepreneurs who – as very often happens – have reached their personal wealth targets and would rather quit the game than double up. If the function of entrepreneurs is to take the initial risk, it is usually that of big business to carry it forward and diversify it.

Horses for courses, then. But the general case is clear. If I were a portfolio manager, I would sooner back divesters than acquirers any day.

FT *Source:* Jackson, T. (2011) 'Logic of corporate shrinkage asserts itself', www.ft.com, 4 September.
© The Financial Times Limited 2012. All Rights Reserved.

Finally, it is worth emphasising a point made in Real World 12.11. Both forms of restructuring will result in a smaller business. Thus, any benefits arising from size, such as economies of scale and greater protection from takeover, will be lost.

THE VALUATION OF SHARES

An important aspect of any merger or takeover negotiation is the value to be placed on the shares of the businesses to be merged or acquired. In this section, we explore various methods that can be used to derive an appropriate share value for a business. Share valuation methods are not, of course, used only in the context of merger or takeover negotiations; they will also be required in other circumstances such as business flotations and liquidations. Nevertheless, mergers and takeovers are an important area for their application.

In theory, the value of a share can be defined in terms of either the current value of the assets held or the future cash flows generated from those assets. In a world of perfect information and perfect certainty, share valuation would pose few problems. However, in the real world, measurement and forecasting problems conspire to make the valuation process difficult. Various valuation methods have emerged to deal with these problems, but they often produce quite different results.

The main methods employed to value a share can be divided into three broad categories:

- methods based on the value of a business's net assets
- methods that use stock market information
- methods based on future cash flows.

To examine the more important methods falling within each of these categories, we shall use Example 12.2.

CDC Ltd owns a chain of tyre- and exhaust-fitting garages. The business has been approached by ATD plc, which owns a large chain of motor service stations, with a view to a takeover of CDC Ltd. ATD plc is prepared to make an offer in cash or a share-for-share exchange. The most recent financial statements of CDC Ltd are summarised below.

Income statement for the year ended 30 November Year 8

	£m
Sales revenue	18.7
Profit before interest and tax	6.4
Interest	(1.6)
Profit before taxation	4.8
Tax	(1.2)
Profit for the year	3.6

Statement of financial position as at 30 November Year 8

	£m
ASSETS	
Non-current assets (cost less depreciation)	
Property	4.0
Plant and machinery	5.9
	9.9
Current assets	
Inventories	2.8
Trade receivables	0.4
Bank	2.6
	5.8
Total assets	15.7
EQUITY AND LIABILITIES	
Equity	
£1 ordinary shares	2.0
Retained earnings	3.6
	5.6
Non-current liabilities	
Loan notes	3.6
Current liabilities	
Trade payables	5.9
Tax	0.6
	6.5
Total equity and liabilities	15.7

The accountant for CDC Ltd has estimated the future free cash flow of the business to be as follows:

Year 9	Year 10	Year 11	Year 12	Year 13
£4.4m	£4.6m	£4.9m	£5.0m	£5.4m

After Year 13, the free cash flows are expected to remain constant at £5.4 million for the following 12 years.

The business has a cost of capital of 10 per cent.

CDC Ltd has recently had a professional valuer establish the current resale value of its assets. The current resale value of each asset group was as follows:

	£m
Property	18.2
Plant and machinery	4.2
Inventories	3.4

The current resale values of the remaining assets are considered to be in line with their values as shown on the statement of financial position.

A business listed on the Stock Exchange, which is in the same business as CDC Ltd, has a gross dividend yield of 5 per cent and a price/earnings ratio of 11 times.

The financial director believes that replacement costs are £1 million higher than the resale values for both property and plant and machinery, and £0.5 million higher than the resale value of the inventories. The replacement costs of the remaining assets are considered to be in line with their statement of financial position values. In addition, the financial director believes that brands held by the business, which are not shown on the statement of financial position, have a replacement value of £10 million. The values of liabilities, as shown on the statement of financial position, reflects their current values.

Asset-based methods

Asset-based methods attempt to value a share by reference to the value of the net assets held by the business. Shareholders own the business and therefore own the underlying net assets (total assets less liabilities) of the business. This means that a single share can be valued by dividing the value of the net assets of the business by the number of shares in issue.

Net assets (book value) method

The simplest method is to use the statement of financial position (book) values of the assets held. The net assets (book value) method will determine the value of an ordinary share (P_0) as follows:

$$P_0 = \frac{\textbf{Net assets at statement of financial position values}}{\textbf{Number of ordinary shares issued}}$$

Where preference shares are in issue, they must also be deducted (at their statement of financial position value) from total assets to obtain the value of an ordinary share.

Activity 12.14

Calculate the net assets (book value) of an ordinary share in CDC Ltd.

The value of an ordinary share (P_0) will be:

$$P_0 = \frac{(15.7 - (3.6 + 6.5))}{2.0}$$

$$= £2.80$$

This method has the advantage that the valuation process is straightforward and the data are easy to obtain. The share value derived, however, usually provides a conservative figure. Certain intangible assets, such as internally generated goodwill and brand names, may not be reported on the statement of financial position and will, therefore, be ignored for the purposes of valuation. In addition, assets shown on the statement of financial position are often reported at their original cost (less any depreciation to date, where relevant), which may be below their current market value. During a period of inflation, the current market values of certain assets held, such as property, normally exceed their original cost.

For businesses listed on the Stock Exchange it is possible to compare the current market price of a share with its net asset (book) value. The **price/book value (P/B) ratio**, which is expressed as a number of time**s**, is calculated as follows:

$$\text{P/B ratio} = \frac{\text{Market value per share}}{\text{Net asset (book) value per share}}$$

Real World 12.12 sets out the price/book value ratios of some selected listed businesses. Assuming that the market price of a share is a reasonable guide to its intrinsic value, this ratio highlights the conservative nature of the net asset (book) value figure for valuation purposes.

Real World 12.12

Going by the book

The price/book value ratio of seven large listed businesses operating in different industries is shown in Figure 12.5.

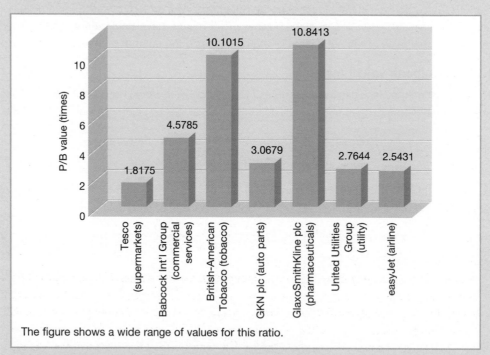

The figure shows a wide range of values for this ratio.

Figure 12.5 Price/book value ratios for selected businesses

We can see that, for each business, the market price of a share is considerably higher than its net asset (book) value. For British-American Tobacco plc and GlaxoSmithKline plc, the market price is more than 10 times higher.

Source: Based on market statistics quoted on www.bloomberg.com, accessed 11 May 2013.

In the context of takeovers, the net asset (book) value figure may be used to measure 'downside' risk. Where the bid price is close to this figure, the level of investment risk is likely to be small. The market price of a share in a listed business will rarely dip below the net asset (book) value figure.

Current market value methods

The current market value of net assets may also be used as a basis for valuation. In economic theory, the value of an asset (such as a share in a business) should reflect the present value of future benefits generated. Furthermore, the current market value of an asset should reflect the market's view of the present value of these future benefits as investors will be prepared to pay up to this amount to acquire the asset. Current market values can be expressed in terms of either:

1 net realisable values, which reflect the price obtained from the resale of the assets, less any selling costs, or
2 replacement costs, which reflect the cost of replacing the assets with identical assets in the same condition.

The net assets (liquidation) method values the assets held according to their net realisable values that could be obtained in an orderly liquidation of the business. It adopts the same basic equation as before, but uses net realisable values instead of statement of financial position values for assets and liabilities. Thus, the value for an ordinary share is calculated as follows:

$$P_0 = \frac{\text{Net assets at net realisable values}}{\text{Number of ordinary shares issued}}$$

Activity 12.15

Calculate the value of an ordinary share in CDC Ltd using the net assets (liquidation) method.

The value for an ordinary share will be:

$$P_0 = \frac{((18.2 + 4.2 + 3.4 + 0.4 + 2.6) - (6.5 + 3.6))}{2.0}$$

$$= £9.35$$

Although an improvement on the previous method, the net assets (liquidation) method is also likely to provide a conservative share value. This is because it fails to take account of the value of the business as a going concern. Normally, this is higher than the sum of the individual values of assets, when sold piecemeal, because of the benefits from combining them. Net realisable value represents a lower limit for the current market value of an asset. The value of an asset *in use* is normally greater than its net realisable value. If this were not the case, the asset would be sold rather than held.

Using net realisable values may present practical difficulties. Where, for example, the asset is unique, such as a custom-built piece of equipment, it may be impossible to obtain a reliable figure. Furthermore, any goodwill, which normally exists only when the business is a going concern, will not be included in the calculations. Finally, net realisable values may vary according to the circumstances of the sale. The amount obtained in a hurried sale may be considerably below that which could be obtained in an orderly, managed sale.

The **net assets (replacement cost) method** can also be used to derive a share value. Once again the basic equation of the net assets (book value) method is tweaked so that it now becomes:

$$P_0 = \frac{\text{Net assets at replacement cost}}{\text{Number of ordinary shares issued}}$$

This approach takes account of the brand values of CDC Ltd as well as the other assets held. The amount derived represents an upper limit for the market value of assets held.

Activity 12.16

Calculate the value of an ordinary share in CDC Ltd using the net assets (replacement cost) method.

This will yield the following value for an ordinary share:

$$P_0 = \frac{(19.2 + 5.2 + 3.9 + 0.4 + 2.6 + 10.0) - (3.6 + 6.5)}{2.0}$$

$$= £15.6$$

Using replacement costs may also present practical difficulties. Where there is no active market for assets, such as brand values, or where major technological changes occur, such as with computers, deriving accurate replacement costs can be a problem.

Stock market methods

Where a business is listed on the Stock Exchange, the quoted share price usually provides a reliable guide to its economic value. We saw in Chapter 7 that the efficiency of stock markets means that share prices tend to react quickly and in an unbiased manner to new information. As information is fully absorbed in share prices it implies that, until new information becomes available, share prices reflect the market's view of its true worth.

It is possible to use stock market information and ratios to help value the shares of an unlisted business. The first step in this process is to find a listed business within the same industry that has similar risk and growth characteristics. Stock market ratios relating to the listed business can then be applied to the unlisted business in order to derive a share value. Two ratios that can be used in this way are the price/earnings ratio and the dividend yield ratio.

Price/earnings ratio method

We saw earlier that the equation for the P/E ratio can be rearranged so that:

$$\text{Market value per share } (P_0) = \text{P/E ratio} \times \text{Earnings per share}$$

Using this equation, the market value is a multiple of the current earnings per share. It is forward looking as the P/E ratio reflects the market's view of the prospects for the business: the higher the P/E ratio, the better the prospects.

To derive a share value, the P/E ratio of a listed business can be applied to the earnings per share of a similar unlisted business. The value of an ordinary share of an unlisted business is therefore:

$$P_0 = \text{P/E ratio of similarlisted business} \times \text{Earnings per share (of unlisted business)}$$

Activity 12.17

Calculate the value of an ordinary share in CDC Ltd, using the P/E ratio method.

The value of an ordinary share using the P/E ratio method will be:

$$P_0 = 11 \times \frac{\text{£3.6 (earnings available to shareholders)}}{2.0 \text{ (number of ordinary shares)}}$$

$$= \text{£19.80}$$

Although the calculations are fairly simple, this valuation approach is fraught with problems. An obvious problem is finding a listed business with similar risk and growth characteristics. Even if one can be found, we must assume that the market price of its shares provides a good indicator of their intrinsic value. To add to our problems, differences in accounting policies and accounting year ends between the two businesses can undermine the valuation process. Finally, an unlisted business may also have different operational policies on such matters as directors' remuneration, which may have to be adjusted before applying the P/E ratio.

Shares in unlisted businesses are less marketable than those of similar listed businesses. To take account of this difference, a discount may be applied to the share value derived by using the above equation. A discount of 30 per cent is not uncommon, and if applied to CDC Ltd would mean that the share value reduces to £13.86. However, determining an appropriate discount is more art than science.

Dividend yield ratio method

The *dividend yield ratio*, which was discussed in Chapter 3, relates the cash return from dividends to the current market value per share. It is calculated as follows:

$$\text{Dividend yield} = \frac{\text{Gross dividend per share}}{\text{Market value per share}} \times 100$$

The dividend yield can be calculated for shares listed on the Stock Exchange as both the market value per share and the gross dividend per share will normally be known. However, for unlisted businesses, the market value per share is not normally known and therefore this ratio cannot normally be applied.

The above equation can be expressed in terms of the market value per share by rearranging as follows:

$$\text{Market value per share } (P_0) = \frac{\text{Gross dividend per share}}{\text{Dividend yield}} \times 100$$

This rearranged equation can be used to value the shares of an unlisted business. For this purpose, the gross dividend per share of the unlisted business, whose shares are to be valued, and the dividend yield of a similar listed business are used in the equation.

Calculate the value of an ordinary share in CDC Ltd using the dividend yield method. (Assume a lower rate of tax of 10 per cent.)

The value of an ordinary share using the dividend yield method will be:

$$P_0 = \frac{0.5 \times 100/90^*}{5} \times 100$$

$$= £11.11$$

* We may recall from Chapter 3 that the dividend as shown in the financial statements must be 'grossed up' in order to obtain the gross dividend required for the equation.

This approach to share valuation has a number of weaknesses. Once again, there is the problem of finding a similar listed business as a basis for the valuation. Furthermore, dividend policies may vary considerably between businesses in the same industry, and may also vary between listed and unlisted businesses. Unlisted businesses, for example, are usually under less pressure to pay dividends than listed businesses.

Dividends represent only part of the earnings stream of a business, and to value shares on this basis may be misleading. The valuation obtained will be largely a function of the dividend policy adopted (which is at the discretion of management) rather than the earnings generated. Where a business does not make dividend distributions, this method cannot be applied.

Cash flow methods

We have already seen that the value of an asset is equivalent to the present value of the future cash flows that it generates. The most direct, and theoretically appealing, approach is, therefore, to value a share on this basis. The dividend valuation method and free cash flow method adopt this approach and both are discussed below.

Dividend valuation method

The cash returns from holding a share take the form of dividends received. It is possible, therefore, to view the value of a share in terms of the stream of future dividends received. We have already seen in Chapter 8 that the value of a share will be the *discounted value of the future dividends received* and can be shown as:

$$P_0 = \frac{D_1}{(1 + K_0)} + \frac{D_2}{(1 + K_0)^2} + \ldots + \frac{D_n}{(1 + K_0)^n}$$

where $D_{1,2\ldots,n}$ = the dividend received in periods 1, 2 . . . , n

K_0 = required rate of return on the share.

Although this model is theoretically appealing, there are practical problems in forecasting future dividend payments and in calculating the required rate of return on the share. The first problem arises because dividends tend to fluctuate over time. If, however, dividends can be assumed to remain constant over time, we have already seen that the discounted dividend model can be reduced to:

$$P_0 = \frac{D_1}{K_0}$$

where D_1 = the annual dividend per share in Year 1.

Activity 12.19

Assume that CDC Ltd has a constant dividend payout and the cost of ordinary share capital is estimated at 12 per cent. Calculate the value of an ordinary share in the business using the discounted dividend approach.

The value of an ordinary share using the discounted dividend approach will be:

$$P_0 = \frac{0.5 \text{ (that is, } 1.0\text{m}/2.0\text{m)}}{0.12}$$

$$= £4.17$$

The assumption of constant dividends may not be very realistic, however, as many businesses attempt to increase their dividends to shareholders over time.

We saw in Chapter 8 that where businesses increase their dividends at a constant rate of growth, the discounted dividend model can be revised to:

$$P_0 = \frac{D_1}{K_0 - g}$$

where g = the constant growth rate in dividends (the model assumes K_0 is greater than g).

In practice, an attempt may be made to estimate dividend payments for a particular forecast horizon (say, five years). After this period, accurate forecasting may become too difficult, and so a constant growth rate may be assumed for dividends received beyond the forecast horizon. Thus, the future dividend stream is divided into two separate elements: the first element based on dividend estimates over a particular forecast horizon, and the second representing dividends beyond the forecast horizon (and involving the use of a simplifying assumption). Although avoiding one problem, this approach creates another: deciding on an appropriate growth rate to use. Figure 12.6 illustrates this process.

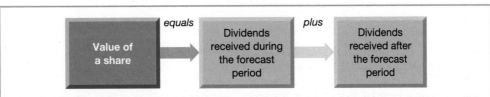

The figure shows how the future dividend stream is divided into two elements in order to provide a value for a share. In the previous chapter a similar approach was used when making SVA calculations beyond the planning horizon.

Figure 12.6 Dividend valuation method

As mentioned earlier, the use of dividends as a basis for valuation can create difficulties because of their discretionary nature. Different businesses will adopt different dividend payout policies and this can affect the calculation of share values. In some cases, no dividends may be declared by a business for a considerable period. There are, for example, high-growth businesses that prefer to plough back profits into the business rather than make dividend payments.

Free cash flow method

Another approach to share valuation is to value the free cash flows generated over time. Free cash flows were considered in Chapter 11. They represent the cash flows available to lenders and shareholders after any new investments in assets. In other words, they are equivalent to the net cash flows from operations after deducting tax paid and cash for investment.

The valuation process is the same as the process that we looked at in Chapter 11. To value shares using free cash flows, we have to discount the future free cash flows over time, using the cost of capital. The present value of the free cash flows, after deducting amounts owing to long-term lenders at current market values, will represent that portion of the free cash flows that accrues to the ordinary shareholders. If this amount is divided by the number of ordinary shares in issue, we have a figure for the value of an ordinary share. Hence, the value of an ordinary share will be:

$$P_0 = \frac{\text{Present value of future free cash flows} - \text{Long-term loans at current market values}}{\text{Number of ordinary shares issued}}$$

Activity 12.20

Calculate the value of an ordinary share in CDC Ltd using the free cash flow method.

The value of an ordinary share will be calculated as follows:

	Cash flow £m	Discount rate 10%	Present value £m
Year 9	4.4	0.91	4.00
Year 10	4.6	0.83	3.82
Year 11	4.9	0.75	3.68
Year 12	5.0	0.68	3.40
Next 13 years	5.4	4.90*	26.46
Total present value			41.36

$$P_0 = \frac{\text{Total present value} - \text{Long-term loans at current market value}^\dagger}{\text{Number of ordinary shares}}$$

$$= \frac{41.36 - 3.6^\dagger}{2.0} = £18.88$$

* This is the total of the individual discount rates for the 13-year period. This shortcut can be adopted where cash flows are constant. For the sake of simplicity, it is assumed that there are no cash flows after the 13-year period.

† This method, unlike the net asset methods discussed earlier, does not deduct short-term liabilities in arriving at a value per share. This is because they are dealt with in the calculation of free cash flows.

‡ We are told in the example that the statement of financial position value of liabilities reflects their current market values.

We saw in Chapter 11 that a major problem with this method is that of accurate forecasting. However, this can be tackled in the same way as described above. Free cash flows may be estimated over a particular forecast horizon (say, five years) and then a terminal value substituted for free cash flows arising beyond that period. Determining the terminal value is, of course, a problem – and an important one – as it may be a significant proportion of the total cash flows.

In the previous chapter we used an example to illustrate the valuation of a business where it was assumed that returns remained constant after the forecast horizon and used the following formula for a perpetuity in order to determine the terminal value (TV):

$$TV = \frac{C_1}{r}$$

where C_1 = the free cash flows in the following year
r = the required rate of return from investors.

However, another approach would be to assume a constant growth rate over time, just as we did with dividends earlier. The terminal value would then be:

$$TV = \frac{C_1}{(r - g)}$$

where C_1 = free cash flows in the following year
r = the required rate of return from investors (cost of capital)
g = the constant rate of growth in free cash flows.

Although free cash flows may appear to be clearly defined, in practice there may be problems. The discretionary policies of management concerning new investments will have a significant influence on the figure calculated. Free cash flows are likely to fluctuate considerably between periods. Unlike earnings, management has no incentive to smooth out cash flows over time. However, for valuation purposes, it may be useful to smooth out cash flow fluctuations between periods in order to establish trends over time.

As a final point, it is worth emphasising the importance of checking carefully the underlying assumptions, when using cash flow-based methods of valuation. The share value figure derived using both the dividend valuation method and free cash flow method can be very sensitive to small changes to inputs. Sensitivity analysis may therefore be carried out to help gain a feel for the range of possible values.

The various share valuation methods discussed are summarised in Figure 12.7.

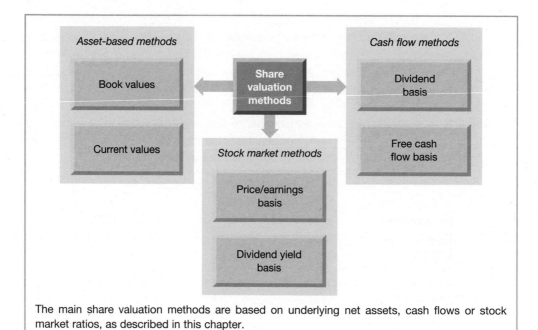

The main share valuation methods are based on underlying net assets, cash flows or stock market ratios, as described in this chapter.

Figure 12.7 Share valuation methods

Self-assessment question 12.1

Permian Holdings plc is a large conglomerate that is listed on the London Stock Exchange. The board of directors of Permian Holdings plc has decided to restructure the business and, as part of the restructuring plan, it has been agreed to spin off one of its largest subsidiaries, Miocene plc, as a separate business. Miocene plc will not seek an immediate Stock Exchange listing.

The most recent financial statements of Miocene plc are set out below.

Statement of financial position as at 30 November Year 10

	£m
ASSETS	
Non-current assets (cost less depreciation)	
Property	33.2
Plant and equipment at cost	24.3
Fixtures and fittings at cost	10.4
	67.9
Current assets	
Inventories	34.8
Trade receivables	29.6
	64.4
Total assets	132.3
EQUITY AND LIABILITIES	
Equity	
£0.25 ordinary shares	10.0
Share premium account	5.0
Retained earnings	45.1
	60.1

Non-current liabilities

10% loan notes	21.0

Current liabilities

Trade payables	35.9
Tax	3.9
Bank overdraft	11.4
	51.2
Total equity and liabilities	132.3

Income statement for the year ended 30 November Year 10

	£m
Sales revenue	153.6
Cost of sales	(102.4)
Gross profit	51.2
Selling and distribution expenses	(12.3)
Administrative expenses	(10.2)
Operating profit	28.7
Finance expenses	(3.6)
Profit before taxation	25.1
Tax	(7.9)
Profit for the year	17.2

The following additional information has been gathered concerning Miocene plc:

1 A firm of independent valuers has recently established the current realisable value of the business's assets as:

	£m
Property	65.4
Plant and equipment	18.8
Fixtures and fittings	4.6
Inventories	38.9

The statement of financial position value of trade receivables reflects their current realisable values.

2 A similar business to Miocene plc is listed on the London Stock Exchange and has a P/E ratio of 11.

3 The profit for Miocene plc for the forthcoming year is expected to be the same as for the year to 30 November Year 10. The dividend payout ratio is expected to be 40 per cent and dividends are expected to grow at 4 per cent per year for the foreseeable future.

4 The business has an estimated cost of ordinary shares (equity) of 10 per cent.

Required:

Calculate the value of a share in Miocene plc using the following valuation methods:

(i)   net assets (book value) basis
(ii) net assets (liquidation) basis
(iii) P/E basis
(iv) dividend growth basis.

The answer to this question can be found at the end of the book on p. 570.

CHOOSING A VALUATION MODEL

When deciding on an appropriate valuation model, we should consider the purpose for which the shares are being valued. Different valuation models may be appropriate for different circumstances. For example:

- An 'asset stripper' (that is, someone who wishes to acquire a business with a view to selling off its individual assets) may find the net assets (liquidation) basis of valuation most appropriate.
- A potential buyer of a property business may find the net assets (replacement cost) basis of valuation most appropriate as replacement values will tend to reflect future cash flows from rentals.
- A potential buyer of a minority interest in a business may find dividend-based approaches most appropriate as there would be no control over future dividend policy.
- Managers of a new business being floated on the stock market may find the P/E ratio method or the free cash flow method most appropriate. (We saw earlier that the former approach takes account of share values of similar businesses already listed on the Stock Exchange.)

During a merger or takeover, valuations derived from the models discussed may be used as a basis for negotiation. They may help to set boundaries within which a final share value will be determined. The final figure, however, is likely to be influenced by various factors, including the negotiating skills and the relative bargaining position of the parties.

SUMMARY

The main points in this chapter may be summarised as follows:

Mergers and takeovers

- A merger is when two businesses of roughly equal size combine; a takeover is when a larger business absorbs a smaller business.
- Mergers can be achieved through horizontal or vertical integration or by combining with unrelated businesses.
- Surges in merger activity occur from time to time, often as a result of a combination of political, economic and technological factors.
- To make economic sense, the merged business should generate greater cash flows than if the two businesses remained apart.

Rationale for mergers

- There are various reasons for a merger, which include:
  - benefits of scale
  - eliminating competition
  - eliminating weak and inefficient management
  - combining complementary resources
  - protecting sources of supply or revenue

- diversification
- shares in the target business being undervalued
- pursuing managers' interests.
- The last three of these may not be consistent with the objective of maximising shareholder wealth.

Forms of purchase consideration

- Payment for the shares in an acquired business may take the form of:
  - cash
  - shares
  - loan capital
  - some combination of the above.

Who benefits?

- Shareholders in the target business usually see an increase in the value of their investment.
- Shareholders in the bidding business often see a decrease or, at best, a very modest increase in the value of their investment.
- Managers of the bidding business may gain through an increase in status, income and security.
- Managers of the target business often leave within a few years of the takeover.
- Financial advisers and lawyers usually benefit from a merger.

Ingredients for successful mergers

- Should be in line with the strategy of the business.
- Work best between businesses in the same, or related, industries.
- Early planning to ensure proper integration is essential.

Resisting a takeover bid

- Various defensive tactics may be employed before a bid is received, including:
  - conversion to private company status
  - employee share option schemes
  - maintaining good investor relations
  - share repurchases
  - increasing efficiency and profitability.
- Defensive tactics after a bid is received include:
  - presenting a case to shareholders
  - increasing dividend payouts
  - white knight defence
  - white squire defence.
- Other tactics that are acceptable in some countries include:
  - making the business unattractive
  - pac-man defence.
- Managers of the bidding business may try to overcome resistance by circularising shareholders to explain the logic of the case or by increasing the bid price.

Protecting shareholders and the public

- The City Code on Takeovers and Mergers aims to ensure that shareholders are given every opportunity to evaluate a merger on its merits.
- The Competition Commission has the power to investigate mergers where a weakening of competition may occur.
- In the case of cross-border mergers, the EU has rules to protect competition.

Restructuring the business

- A divestment involves selling off part of the business operations.
- A demerger, or spin-off, involves transferring business operations to a new business that is owned by the current shareholders.

Valuing shares in a business

- Shares may be valued on the following bases:
  - methods based on the value of the net assets (book value, liquidation value and replacement cost methods)
  - methods based on stock market ratios (P/E ratio method and dividend yield method)
  - methods based on future cash flows (dividend valuation method and free cash flow method).
- The choice of valuation methods will depend on the reasons for the valuation.

KEY TERMS

Merger p. 502	Competition Commission p. 526
Takeover p. 502	Office of Fair Trading p. 526
Horizontal merger p. 502	Divestment p. 527
Vertical merger p. 502	Demerger (spin-off) p. 528
Conglomerate merger p. 502	Net assets (book value) method p. 531
White knight p. 525	
White squire p. 525	Price/book value (P/B) ratio p. 532
Poison pill p. 525	Net realisable value p. 533
Crown jewels p. 525	Net assets (liquidation) method p. 533
Golden parachute p. 525	Net assets (replacement cost) method p. 534
Pac-man defence p. 525	

For definitions of these terms see the Glossary, pp. 605–613.

REFERENCES

1 Gregory, A. (1998) 'The long-run performance of UK acquirers: motives underlying the method of payment and their influence on subsequent performance', University of Exeter Discussion Paper.

2 Weston, F., Siu, J. and Johnson, B. (2001) *Takeovers, Restructuring and Corporate Governance*, 3rd edn, Prentice Hall, Chapter 8.

3 Alexandridis, G., Fuller, K., Terhaar, L. and Travlos, N. (2013) 'Deal size, acquisition premia and shareholder gains', *Journal of Corporate Finance*, April, 20, 1–13.

4 Gregory, A. (2005) 'The long run abnormal performance of UK acquiring firms and the free cash flow hypothesis', *Journal of Business Finance and Accounting*, June/July, 777–814.

5 Conn, R., Cosh, A., Guest, P. and Hughes, A. (2005) 'The impact of UK acquirers of domestic, cross-border, public and private acquisitions', *Journal of Business Finance and Accounting*, June/July, 815–70.

6 Franks, J. and Mayer, C. (1994) 'Corporate ownership and corporate control: A study of France, Germany and the UK', *Economic Policy*, No. 10.

7 Pautler, P. (2003) 'The effects of mergers and post-merger integration: A review of the business consulting literature', Bureau of Economics, Federal Trade Commission.

FURTHER READING

If you wish to explore the topics discussed in this chapter in more depth, try the following books:

Arnold, G. (2013) *Corporate Financial Management*, 5th edn, Financial Times Prentice Hall, Chapters 17 and 20.

Damodaran, A. (2010) *Applied Corporate Finance*, 3rd edn, John Wiley & Sons, Chapter 12.

Gaughan, P. (2011) *Mergers, Acquisitions and Corporate Restructurings*, 5th edn, John Wiley & Sons, Chapters 1–2 and 4–6.

Peek, E., Palepu, K. and Healy, P. (2013) *Business Analysis and Valuation: Text and Cases*, 3rd edn, Cengage Learning, Chapters 6–8 and 11.

REVIEW QUESTIONS

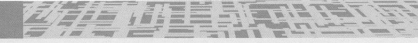

Answers to these questions can be found at the back of the book on pp. 578–579.

12.1 Distinguish between a merger and a takeover.

12.2 Identify and discuss four reasons why a business may undertake divestment of part of its operations.

12.3 Identify four reasons why a business seeking to maximise the wealth of its shareholders may wish to take over another business.

12.4 Identify four tactics the directors of a target business might employ to resist an unwelcome bid after the bid has been received.

Exercises 12.4 to 12.7 are more advanced than 12.1 to 12.3. Those with coloured numbers have solutions at the back of the book, starting on p. 601.

If you wish to try more exercises, visit the students' side of this book's companion website.

12.1 When a business wishes to acquire another, it may make a bid in the form of cash, a share-for-share exchange, or loan capital-for-share exchange.

Required:
Discuss the advantages and disadvantages of each form of consideration from the viewpoint of:

(a) the bidding business's shareholders
(b) the target business's shareholders.

12.2 Dawn Raider plc has just offered one of its shares for two shares in Sleepy Giant plc, a business in the same industry as itself. Extracts from the financial statements of each business for the year ended 31 May Year 8 appear below:

	Dawn Raider £m	Sleepy Giant £m
Income statements		
Sales revenue	150	360
Profit for the year	18	16
Statement of financial position data		
Non-current assets	150	304
Net current assets (Note 1)	48	182
	198	486
Loans	(80)	(40)
	118	446
Share capital (Note 2)	50	100
Reserves	68	346
	118	446

Notes:

	Dawn Raider	Sleepy Giant
1 Includes cash/(overdrafts):	(£60m)	£90m
2 Shares	25p	50p
3 Dividends paid and proposed	4	14

Stock market data for each business is as follows:

	31 May Year 6	31 May Year 7	31 May Year 8
Dawn Raider plc			
Share price (pence)	120.0	144.0	198.0
Earnings per share (pence)	5.3	6.9	9.0
Dividends per share (pence)	2.0	2.0	2.0
Sleepy Giant plc			
Share price (pence)	45.0	43.0	72.0
Earnings per share (pence)	8.4	7.4	8.0
Dividends per share (pence)	8.0	7.0	7.0

If the takeover succeeds, Dawn Raider plans to combine Sleepy Giant's marketing and distribution channels with its own, with a post-tax saving of £1 million a year. In addition, it expects to be able to increase Sleepy Giant's profits after tax by at least £5 million a year by better management. Dawn Raider's own profits after tax are expected to be £23 million (excluding the £1 million saving already mentioned) in the year ended 31 May Year 9.

One of the shareholders of Sleepy Giant has written to its chairman arguing that the bid should not be accepted. The following is an extract from his letter: 'The bid considerably undervalues Sleepy Giant since it is below Sleepy Giant's net assets per share. Furthermore, if Dawn Raider continues its existing policy of paying only 2p a share as a dividend, Sleepy Giant's shareholders will be considerably worse off.'

Required:

(a) Calculate:

(i)   The total value of the bid and the bid premium.

(ii) Sleepy Giant's net assets per share at 31 May Year 8.

(iii) The dividends the holder of 100 shares in Sleepy Giant would receive in the year before and the year after the takeover.

(iv) The earnings per share for Dawn Raider in the year after the takeover.

(v)   The share price of Dawn Raider after the takeover assuming that it maintains its existing price/earnings ratio.

(b) Comment on:

(i)   the points that the shareholder in Sleepy Giant raises in his letter

(ii) the amount of the bid consideration.

12.3 An investment business is considering taking a minority stake in two businesses, Monaghan plc and Cavan plc. Both are in the same line of business and both are listed on the London Stock Exchange. Monaghan plc has had a stable dividend policy over the years. In the financial reports for the current year, the chairman stated that a dividend of 30p a share would be paid in one year's time and financial analysts employed by the investment business expect dividends to grow at an annual compound rate of 10 per cent for the indefinite future.

Cavan plc has had an erratic dividend pattern over the years and future dividends have been difficult to predict. However, to defend itself successfully against an unwelcome takeover, the business recently announced that dividends for the next three years were expected to be as follows:

Year	Dividend per share (pence)
1	20
2	32
3	36

Financial analysts working for the investment business believe that, after Year 3, Cavan plc will enjoy a smooth pattern of growth, and dividends will be expected to grow at a compound rate of 8 per cent for the indefinite future.

The investment business believes that a return of 14 per cent is required to compensate for the risks associated with the type of business in which the two businesses are engaged. Ignore taxation.

Required:

(a) State the arguments for and against valuing a share on the basis of its future dividends.

(b) Calculate the value of a share in:

(i)   Monaghan plc

(ii) Cavan plc

based on the expected future dividends of each business.

12.4 The directors of Simat plc have adopted a policy of expansion based on the acquisition of other businesses. The special projects division of Simat has been given the task of identifying suitable businesses for takeover.

Stidwell Ltd has been identified as being a suitable business and negotiations between the board of directors of each business have begun. Information relating to Stidwell Ltd is set out below:

Statement of financial position as at 31 May Year 9

	£
ASSETS	
Non-current assets (at cost less depreciation)	
Property	180,000
Plant and machinery	90,000
Motor vehicles	19,000
	289,000
Current assets	
Inventories	84,000
Receivables	49,000
Cash	24,000
	157,000
Total assets	446,000
EQUITY AND LIABILITIES	
Equity	
Ordinary £0.50 shares	150,000
Retained earnings	114,000
	264,000
Non-current liabilities	
10% loan notes	140,000
Current liabilities	
Payables and accruals	42,000
Total equity and liabilities	446,000

Stidwell Ltd's profit for the year ended 31 May Year 9 was £48,500 and the dividend paid for the year was £18,000. Profits and dividends of the business have shown little change over the past five years.

The realisable values of the assets of Stidwell Ltd, at the end of the year, were estimated to be as follows:

	£
Property	285,000
Plant and machinery	72,000
Motor vehicles	15,000

For the remaining assets, the values as per the statement of financial position were considered to reflect current realisable values.

The special projects division of Simat plc has also identified another business, Asgard plc, which is listed on the Stock Exchange and is broadly similar to Stidwell Ltd. The following details were taken from a recent copy of a financial newspaper:

Years 8–9 High	Low	Stock	Price	± or	Dividend (net)	Cover (times)	Yield (gross %)	P/E (times)
560p	480p	Asgard plc	500p	+4p	10.33p	4.4	2.76	11

Required:
Calculate the value of an ordinary share of Stidwell Ltd using each of the following valuation methods:

(a) net assets (liquidation) basis
(b) dividend yield
(c) price/earnings ratio.
   Assume a lower rate of tax of 10 per cent.

12.5 Alpha plc, a dynamic, fast-growing business in microelectronics, has just made a bid of 17 of its own shares for every 20 shares of Beta plc, which manufactures a range of electric motors.
   Financial statements for the two businesses are as follows:

Income statements for the year ended 31 March Year 9

	Alpha plc £000	Beta plc £000
Sales revenue	3,000	2,000
Operating profit	300	140
Interest	(100)	(10)
Profit before tax	200	130
Tax	(100)	(65)
Profit for the year	100	65

Other information:

	Alpha plc	Beta plc
Number of issued shares (million)	1.0	0.5
Earnings per share	10p	13p
Price/earnings ratio	20	10
Market price per share	200p	130p
Capitalisation (that is, market price per share × number of shares)	£2m	£0.65m
Dividend per share	2p	6p
Dividends paid and proposed	20,000	30,000

Historical share prices (in pence) at 31 March each year have been:

	Year 4	Year 5	Year 6	Year 7	Year 8
Alpha plc	60	90	150	160	200
Beta plc	90	80	120	140	130

Statements of financial position at 31 March Year 9

	Alpha plc £000	Beta plc £000
ASSETS		
Non-current assets	1,200	900
Current assets	900	700
Total assets	2,100	1,600
EQUITY AND LIABILITIES		
Equity		
Share capital £0.25 ordinary shares	250	125
Retained earnings	750	755
	1,000	880
Non-current liabilities – loans	800	120
Current liabilities	300	600
Total equity and liabilities	2,100	1,600

The merger of the two businesses will result in post-tax savings of £15,000 per year to be made in the distribution system of Alpha.

One of the shareholders of Beta has queried the bid and has raised the following points. First, he understands that Alpha normally pays only small dividends and that his dividend per share will decrease. Second, he is concerned that the bid undervalues Beta since the current value of the bid is less than the figure for shareholders' funds in Beta's statement of financial position.

Required:

(a) Calculate the bid consideration.

(b) Calculate the earnings per share for the combined group.

(c) Calculate the theoretical post-acquisition price of Alpha shares assuming that the price/earnings ratio stays the same.

(d) Comment on the shareholder's two points.

12.6 Larkin Conglomerates plc owns a subsidiary, Hughes Ltd, which sells office equipment. Recently, Larkin Conglomerates plc has been reconsidering its future strategy and has decided that Hughes Ltd should be sold off. The proposed divestment of Hughes Ltd has attracted considerable interest from other businesses wishing to acquire this type of business. The most recent financial statements of Hughes Ltd are as follows:

Statement of financial position as at 31 May Year 5

	£000
ASSETS	
Non-current assets (cost less depreciation)	
Property	200
Motor vans	11
Fixtures and fittings	8
	219
Current assets	
Inventories	34
Trade receivables	22
Cash at bank	20
	76
Total assets	295

	£000
EQUITY AND LIABILITIES	
Equity	
£1 ordinary shares	60
General reserve	14
Retained earnings	55
	129
Non-current liabilities	
12% loan: Cirencester bank	100
Current liabilities	
Trade payables	52
Tax and accruals	14
	66
Total equity and liabilities	295

Income statement for the year ended 31 May Year 5

	£000
Sales revenue	352.0
Profit before interest and taxation	34.8
Interest charges	(12.0)
Profit before taxation	22.8
Tax	(6.4)
Profit for the year	16.4

A dividend of £4,000 was proposed and paid during the year.

The subsidiary has shown a stable level of sales and profits over the past three years. An independent valuer has estimated the current realisable values of the assets of the business as follows:

	£000
Property	235
Motor vans	8
Fixtures and fittings	5
Inventories	36

For the remaining assets, the statement of financial position values are considered to reflect their current realisable values.

Another business in the same industry, which is listed on the Stock Exchange, has a gross dividend yield of 5 per cent and a price/earnings ratio of 12. Assume a tax rate of 25 per cent.

Required:

(a) Calculate the value of an ordinary share in Hughes Ltd using the following methods:
   (i)   net assets (liquidation) basis
   (ii) dividend yield
   (iii) price/earnings ratio.

(b) Briefly state what other information, besides the information provided above, would be useful to prospective buyers in deciding on a suitable value to place on the shares of Hughes Ltd.

12.7 The senior management of Galbraith Ltd is negotiating a management buyout of the business from the existing shareholders. The most recent financial statements of Galbraith Ltd are as follows:

Statement of financial position as at 30 November Year 6

	£
ASSETS	
Non-current assets (cost less depreciation)	
Property	292,000
Plant and machinery	145,000
Motor vehicles	42,000
	479,000
Current assets	
Inventories	128,000
Trade receivables	146,000
	274,000
Total assets	753,000
EQUITY AND LIABILITIES	
Equity	
£0.50 ordinary shares	100,000
General reserve	85,000
Retained earnings	169,000
	354,000
Non-current liabilities	
13% loan notes (secured)	180,000
Current liabilities	
Trade payables	147,000
Tax	19,000
Bank overdraft	53,000
	219,000
Total equity and liabilities	753,000

Income statement for the year ended 30 November Year 6

	£
Sales revenue	1,430,000
Cost of sales	(870,000)
Gross profit	560,000
Selling and distribution expenses	(253,000)
Administration expenses	(167,000)
Operating profit	140,000
Finance expenses	(35,000)
Profit before taxation	105,000
Tax	(38,000)
Profit for the year	67,000

The following additional information is available:

1 Dividends of £5,000 were proposed and paid during the year.
2 A professional surveyor has recently established the current realisable value of the business's assets as being:

	£
Property	365,000
Plant and machinery	84,000
Motor vehicles	32,000
Inventories	145,000

The current realisable value of trade receivables was considered to be the same as their statement of financial position (balance sheet) values.

3 The free cash flows of the business over the next ten years are estimated as follows:

	£
Year 7	97,000
Year 8	105,000
Years 9–16	150,000

4 The cost of capital for the business is 10 per cent.
5 A similar business which is listed on the Stock Exchange has a price/earnings ratio of 8 and a gross dividend yield of 2.2 per cent.

Assume a 20 per cent rate of tax.

Required:

(a) Calculate the value of a share in Galbraith Ltd using the following valuation methods:
   (i)   net assets (liquidation) basis
   (ii) price/earnings basis
   (iii) dividend yield basis
   (iv) free cash flow basis (assuming a ten-year life for the business).
(b) Briefly evaluate each of the share valuation methods set out in (a).
(c) Which share valuation method, if any, do you consider most appropriate as a basis for negotiation and why?
(d) What potential problems will a management buyout proposal pose for the shareholders of Galbraith Ltd?

Appendix A

PRESENT VALUE TABLE

Present value of 1, that is, $(1 + r)^{-n}$

where: r = discount rate

n = number of periods until payment.

Discount rate (r)

Period (n)	1%	2%	3%	4%	5%	6%	7%	8%	9%	10%	Period (n)
1	0.990	0.980	0.971	0.962	0.952	0.943	0.935	0.926	0.917	0.909	1
2	0.980	0.961	0.943	0.925	0.907	0.890	0.873	0.857	0.842	0.826	2
3	0.971	0.942	0.915	0.889	0.864	0.840	0.816	0.794	0.772	0.751	3
4	0.961	0.924	0.888	0.855	0.823	0.792	0.763	0.735	0.708	0.683	4
5	0.951	0.906	0.863	0.822	0.784	0.747	0.713	0.681	0.650	0.621	5
6	0.942	0.888	0.837	0.790	0.746	0.705	0.666	0.630	0.596	0.564	6
7	0.933	0.871	0.813	0.760	0.711	0.665	0.623	0.583	0.547	0.513	7
8	0.923	0.853	0.789	0.731	0.677	0.627	0.582	0.540	0.502	0.467	8
9	0.914	0.837	0.766	0.703	0.645	0.592	0.544	0.500	0.460	0.424	9
10	0.905	0.820	0.744	0.676	0.614	0.558	0.508	0.463	0.422	0.386	10
11	0.896	0.804	0.722	0.650	0.585	0.527	0.475	0.429	0.388	0.350	11
12	0.887	0.788	0.701	0.625	0.557	0.497	0.444	0.397	0.356	0.319	12
13	0.879	0.773	0.681	0.601	0.530	0.469	0.415	0.368	0.326	0.290	13
14	0.870	0.758	0.661	0.577	0.505	0.442	0.388	0.340	0.299	0.263	14
15	0.861	0.743	0.642	0.555	0.481	0.417	0.362	0.315	0.275	0.239	15

Period	11%	12%	13%	14%	15%	16%	17%	18%	19%	20%	Period
1	0.901	0.893	0.885	0.877	0.870	0.862	0.855	0.847	0.840	0.833	1
2	0.812	0.797	0.783	0.769	0.756	0.743	0.731	0.718	0.706	0.694	2
3	0.731	0.712	0.693	0.675	0.658	0.641	0.624	0.609	0.593	0.579	3
4	0.659	0.636	0.613	0.592	0.572	0.552	0.534	0.516	0.499	0.482	4
5	0.593	0.567	0.543	0.519	0.497	0.476	0.456	0.437	0.419	0.402	5
6	0.535	0.507	0.480	0.456	0.432	0.410	0.390	0.370	0.352	0.335	6
7	0.482	0.452	0.425	0.400	0.376	0.354	0.333	0.314	0.296	0.279	7
8	0.434	0.404	0.376	0.351	0.327	0.305	0.285	0.266	0.249	0.233	8
9	0.391	0.361	0.333	0.308	0.284	0.263	0.243	0.225	0.209	0.194	9
10	0.352	0.322	0.295	0.270	0.247	0.227	0.208	0.191	0.176	0.162	10
11	0.317	0.287	0.261	0.237	0.215	0.195	0.178	0.162	0.148	0.135	11
12	0.286	0.257	0.231	0.208	0.187	0.168	0.152	0.137	0.124	0.112	12
13	0.258	0.229	0.204	0.182	0.163	0.145	0.130	0.116	0.104	0.093	13
14	0.232	0.205	0.181	0.160	0.141	0.125	0.111	0.099	0.088	0.078	14
15	0.209	0.183	0.160	0.140	0.123	0.108	0.095	0.084	0.074	0.065	15

Period

(n)	16%	17%	18%	19%	20%	21%	22%	23%	24%	25%	26%	27%	28%	29%	30%
1	0.862	0.855	0.847	0.840	0.833	0.826	0.820	0.813	0.806	0.800	0.794	0.787	0.781	0.775	0.769
2	0.743	0.731	0.718	0.706	0.694	0.683	0.672	0.661	0.650	0.640	0.630	0.620	0.610	0.601	0.592
3	0.641	0.624	0.609	0.593	0.579	0.564	0.551	0.537	0.524	0.512	0.500	0.488	0.477	0.466	0.455
4	0.552	0.534	0.516	0.499	0.482	0.467	0.451	0.437	0.423	0.410	0.397	0.384	0.373	0.361	0.350
5	0.476	0.456	0.437	0.419	0.402	0.386	0.370	0.355	0.341	0.328	0.315	0.303	0.291	0.280	0.269
6	0.410	0.390	0.370	0.352	0.335	0.319	0.303	0.289	0.275	0.262	0.250	0.238	0.227	0.217	0.207
7	0.354	0.333	0.314	0.296	0.279	0.263	0.249	0.235	0.222	0.210	0.198	0.188	0.178	0.168	0.159
8	0.305	0.285	0.266	0.249	0.233	0.218	0.204	0.191	0.179	0.168	0.157	0.148	0.139	0.130	0.123
9	0.263	0.243	0.225	0.209	0.194	0.180	0.167	0.155	0.144	0.134	0.125	0.116	0.108	0.101	0.094
10	0.227	0.208	0.191	0.176	0.162	0.149	0.137	0.126	0.116	0.107	0.099	0.092	0.085	0.078	0.073
11	0.195	0.178	0.162	0.148	0.135	0.123	0.112	0.103	0.094	0.086	0.079	0.072	0.066	0.061	0.056
12	0.168	0.152	0.137	0.124	0.112	0.102	0.092	0.083	0.076	0.069	0.062	0.057	0.052	0.047	0.043
13	0.145	0.130	0.116	0.104	0.093	0.084	0.075	0.068	0.061	0.055	0.050	0.045	0.040	0.037	0.033
14	0.125	0.111	0.099	0.088	0.078	0.069	0.062	0.055	0.049	0.044	0.039	0.035	0.032	0.028	0.025
15	0.108	0.095	0.084	0.074	0.065	0.057	0.051	0.045	0.040	0.035	0.031	0.028	0.025	0.022	0.020
16	0.093	0.081	0.071	0.062	0.054	0.047	0.042	0.036	0.032	0.028	0.025	0.022	0.019	0.017	0.015
17	0.080	0.069	0.060	0.052	0.045	0.039	0.034	0.030	0.026	0.023	0.020	0.017	0.015	0.013	0.012
18	0.069	0.059	0.051	0.044	0.038	0.032	0.028	0.024	0.021	0.018	0.016	0.014	0.012	0.010	0.009
19	0.060	0.051	0.043	0.037	0.031	0.027	0.023	0.020	0.017	0.014	0.012	0.011	0.009	0.008	0.007
20	0.051	0.043	0.037	0.031	0.026	0.022	0.019	0.016	0.014	0.012	0.010	0.008	0.007	0.006	0.005

Appendix B
ANNUAL EQUIVALENT FACTOR TABLE

Annual equivalent factor $A_{N,i}^{-1}$

	i	0.04	0.06	0.08	0.10	0.12	0.14	0.16	0.18	0.20
N	1	1.0400	1.0600	1.0800	1.1000	1.1200	1.1400	1.1600	1.1800	1.2000
	2	0.5302	0.5454	0.5608	0.5762	0.5917	0.6073	0.6230	0.6387	0.6545
	3	0.3603	0.3741	0.3880	0.4021	0.4163	0.4307	0.4453	0.4599	0.4747
	4	0.2755	0.2886	0.3019	0.3155	0.3292	0.3432	0.3574	0.3717	0.3863
	5	0.2246	0.2374	0.2505	0.2638	0.2774	0.2913	0.3054	0.3198	0.3344
	6	0.1908	0.2034	0.2163	0.2296	0.2432	0.2572	0.2714	0.2859	0.3007
	7	0.1666	0.1791	0.1921	0.2054	0.2191	0.2332	0.2476	0.2624	0.2774
	8	0.1485	0.1610	0.1740	0.1874	0.2013	0.2156	0.2302	0.2452	0.2606
	9	0.1345	0.1470	0.1601	0.1736	0.1877	0.2022	0.2171	0.2324	0.2481
	10	0.1233	0.1359	0.1490	0.1627	0.1770	0.1917	0.2069	0.2225	0.2385
	11	0.1141	0.1268	0.1401	0.1540	0.1684	0.1834	0.1989	0.2148	0.2311
	12	0.1066	0.1193	0.1327	0.1468	0.1614	0.1767	0.1924	0.2086	0.2253
	13	0.1001	0.1130	0.1265	0.1408	0.1557	0.1712	0.1872	0.2037	0.2206
	14	0.0947	0.1076	0.1213	0.1357	0.1509	0.1666	0.1829	0.1997	0.2169
	15	0.0899	0.1030	0.1168	0.1315	0.1468	0.1628	0.1794	0.1964	0.2139

Chapter 2

2.1 Quardis Ltd

(a) The projected income statement for the year ended 31 May Year 9 is:

	£000	£000
Sales revenue		280
Cost of sales		
Opening inventories	24	
Purchases	186	
	210	
Closing inventories	(30)	(180)
Gross profit		100
Wages		(34)
Other overhead expenses		(21)
Depreciation – Property		(9)
Fixtures		(6)
Operating profit		30
Interest payable		(12)
Profit before tax		18
Tax (35%)		(6)
Profit for the year		12

(b) Projected statement of financial position as at 31 May Year 9:

	£000	£000
ASSETS		
Non-current assets		
Property	460	
Accumulated depreciation	(39)	421
Fixtures and fittings	60	
Accumulated depreciation	(16)	44
		465
Current assets		
Inventories		30
Trade receivables (60% × 280 × 3/12)		42
		72
Total assets		537
EQUITY AND LIABILITIES		
Equity		
£1 ordinary shares		200
Retained earnings [144 + (12 − 10)]		146
		346

	£000	£000
Non-current liabilities		
Borrowings – loan		95
Current liabilities		
Trade payables (186 × 2/12)	31	
Accrued expenses (3 + 4)	7	
Bank overdraft (balancing figure)	55	
Tax due (50% × 6)	3	
	96	
Total equity and liabilities		537

(c) The projected statements reveal a poor profitability and liquidity position for the business. The liquidity position at 31 May Year 9 reveals a serious deterioration when compared with the previous year.

As a result of preparing these projected statements the management of Quardis Ltd may wish to make certain changes to their original plans. For example, the repayment of part of the loan may be deferred or the dividend may be reduced in order to improve liquidity. Similarly, the pricing policy of the business and the level of expenses proposed may be reviewed in order to improve profitability.

Chapter 3

3.1 Ali plc and Bhaskar plc

(a) To answer this question, you may have used the following ratios:

	Ali plc	Bhaskar plc
Return on ordinary shareholders' funds ratio	99.9/687.6 × 100 = 14.5%	104.6/874.6 × 100 = 12.0%
Operating profit margin ratio	151.3/1,478.1 × 100 = 10.2%	166.9/1,790.4 × 100 = 9.3%
Inventories turnover period ratio	592.0/1,018.3 × 12 = 7.0 months	403.0/1,214.9 × 12 = 4.0 months
Settlement period for trade receivables ratio	176.4/1,478.1 × 12 = 1.4 months	321.9/1,790.4 × 12 = 2.2 months
Current ratio	$\dfrac{853.0}{422.4} = 2.0$	$\dfrac{816.5}{293.1} = 2.8$
Acid test ratio	$\dfrac{(853.0 - 592.0)}{422.4} = 0.6$	$\dfrac{(816.5 - 403.0)}{293.1} = 1.4$
Gearing ratio	$\dfrac{190}{(687.6 + 190)} \times 100 = 21.6\%$	$\dfrac{250}{(874.6 + 250)} \times 100 = 22.2\%$
Interest cover ratio	$\dfrac{151.3}{19.4} = 7.8$ times	$\dfrac{166.9}{27.5} = 6.1$ times
Earnings per share	99.9/320 = 31.2p	104.6/250 = 41.8p
Price/earnings ratio	650/31.2 = 20.8 times	820/41.8 = 19.6 times

(Note: It is not possible to use any average ratios because only the end-of-year figures are provided for each business.)

Ali plc seems more effective than Bhaskar plc at generating returns for shareholders indicated by the higher ROSF ratio. This may be partly caused by Ali plc's higher operating profit margin.

Both businesses have a very high inventories turnover period; this probably needs to be investigated. This ratio is particularly high for Ali plc. Both may suffer from poor inventories management.

Ali plc has a lower settlement period for trade receivables than Bhaskar plc. This may suggest that Bhaskar plc needs to exert greater control over trade receivables.

Ali plc has a much lower current ratio and acid test ratio than Bhaskar plc. The acid test ratio of Ali plc is substantially below 1.0: this may suggest a liquidity problem.

The gearing ratio of each business is quite similar. Neither business seems to have excessive borrowing. The interest cover ratio for each business is also similar. The ratios indicate that both businesses have good profit coverage for their interest charges.

Earnings per share is significantly higher for Bhaskar plc than for Ali plc. However, the P/E ratio for Bhaskar plc is slightly lower. This latter ratio suggests that the market considers Ali plc has slightly better prospects than Bhaskar plc.

To draw better comparisons between the two businesses, it would be useful to calculate other ratios from the financial statements. It would also be helpful to calculate ratios for both businesses over (say) five years as well as key ratios of other businesses operating in the same industry.

(b) The Altman Z-score model is as follows:

$$Z = 0.717a + 0.847b + 3.107c + 0.420d + 0.998e$$

where a = Working capital/Total assets
b = Accumulated retained profits/Total assets
c = Operating profit/Total assets
d = Book (statement of financial position) value of ordinary and preference shares/
   Total liabilities at book (statement of financial position) value
e = Sales revenue/Total assets

For Ali plc, the Z-score is:

$$0.717[(853.0 - 422.4)/1{,}300.0] + 0.847(367.6/1{,}300.0) + 3.107(151.3/1{,}300.0)$$
$$+ 0.420[320.0/(190.0 + 422.4)] + 0.998(1{,}478.1/1{,}300.0) = \underline{2.193}$$

For Bhaskar plc, the Z-score is:

$$0.717[(816.5 - 293.1)/1{,}417.7] + 0.847(624.6/1{,}417.7) + 3.107(166.9/1{,}417.7)$$
$$+ 0.420[250.0/(250.0 + 293.1)] + 0.998(1{,}790.4/1{,}417.7) = \underline{2.457}$$

(c) The Z-scores for these two businesses are quite close, with Bhaskar looking slightly safer. They are both in the category of businesses in the 'zone of ignorance' and therefore difficult to classify (a Z-score between 1.23 and 4.14). This is quite unusual in that the Altman model is able confidently to classify 91 per cent of businesses. Clearly, these two businesses fall into the remaining 9 per cent.

It is questionable whether the Altman model is strictly applicable to UK businesses, since it was derived from data relating to US businesses that had failed. Nevertheless, it probably provides a useful insight.

Chapter 4

4.1 Beacon Chemicals plc

(a) Relevant cash flows are as follows:

	Year 0 £m	Year 1 £m	Year 2 £m	Year 3 £m	Year 4 £m	Year 5 £m
Sales revenue	—	80	120	144	100	64
Loss of contribution		(15)	(15)	(15)	(15)	(15)
Variable cost		(40)	(50)	(48)	(30)	(32)
Fixed cost (Note 1)		(8)	(8)	(8)	(8)	(8)
Operating cash flows		17	47	73	47	9
Working capital	(30)					30
Capital cost	(100)					
Net relevant cash flows	(130)	17	47	73	47	39

Notes:

1. Only the elements of fixed cost that are incremental to the project (existing only because of the project) are relevant. Depreciation is irrelevant because it is not a cash flow.
2. The research and development cost is irrelevant since it has been spent irrespective of the decision on X14 production.

(b) The payback period is as follows:

	Year 0 £m	Year 1 £m	Year 2 £m	Year 3 £m
Cumulative cash flows	(130)	(113)	(66)	7

Thus the equipment will have repaid the initial investment by the end of the third year of operations. Therefore, the payback period is three years.

(c) The net present value is as follows:

	Year 0 £m	Year 1 £m	Year 2 £m	Year 3 £m	Year 4 £m	Year 5 £m
Discount factor	1.00	0.926	0.857	0.794	0.735	0.681
Present value	(130)	15.74	40.28	57.96	34.55	26.56
Net present value	45.09 (that is, the sum of the present values for years 0 to 5)					

Chapter 5

5.1 Tocantins Co.

Project 1

(a) In evaluating the two machines, the first step is to calculate the NPV of each project over their respective time periods:

Lo-tek

	Cash flows £	Discount rate 12%	Present value £
Initial outlay	(10,000)	1.00	(10,000)
1 year's time	4,000	0.89	3,560
2 years' time	5,000	0.80	4,000
3 years' time	5,000	0.71	3,550
NPV			1,110

Hi-tek

	Cash flows £	Discount rate 12%	Present value £
Initial outlay	(15,000)	1.00	(15,000)
1 year's time	5,000	0.89	4,450
2 years' time	6,000	0.80	4,800
3 years' time	6,000	0.71	4,260
4 years' time	5,000	0.64	3,200
		NPV	1,710

The shortest common period of time over which the machines can be compared is 12 (that is, 3 × 4) years. This means that Lo-tek will be repeated four times and Hi-tek will be repeated three times during the 12-year period.

The NPV for Lo-tek will be:

$$\text{Total NPV} = £1{,}110 + \frac{£1{,}110}{(1+0.12)^6} + \frac{£1{,}110}{(1+0.12)^9} + \frac{£1{,}110}{(1+0.12)^{12}}$$

$$= £2{,}358.8$$

The NPV for Hi-tek will be:

$$\text{Total NPV} = £1{,}710 + \frac{£1{,}710}{(1+0.12)^8} + \frac{£1{,}710}{(1+0.12)^{12}}$$

$$= £2{,}840.3$$

The equivalent-annual-annuity approach will provide the following results for Lo-tek:

$$£1{,}110 \times 0.4163 = £462.09$$

and the following results for Hi-tek:

$$£1{,}710 \times 0.3292 = £562.93$$

(b) Hi-tek is the better buy because calculations show that it has the higher NPV over the shortest common period of time and provides the higher equivalent-annual-annuity value.

Project 2

(c) Expected net cash flows

	Net cash flows (a) £m	Probability of occurrence (b)	Expected cash flows (a × b) £m
Year 2	4.5	0.2	0.9
	5.0	0.4	2.0
	6.0	0.4	2.4
Expected net cash flow			5.3
Year 3	5.0	0.3	1.5
	6.5	0.4	2.6
	8.0	0.3	2.4
Expected net cash flow			6.5
Year 4	5.0	0.2	1.0
	7.0	0.6	4.2
	9.0	0.2	1.8
Expected net cash flow			7.0
Year 5	2.0	0.5	1.0
	2.5	0.4	1.0
	3.0	0.1	0.3
Expected net cash flow			2.3

Expected net present value

Year	Expected net cash flow £m	Discount rate 12%	Expected present value £m
1	(16.0)	1.00	(16.0)
2	5.3	0.89	4.7
3	6.5	0.80	5.2
4	7.0	0.71	5.0
5	2.3	0.64	1.5
		ENPV	0.4

(d) Worst possible outcome

Year	Estimated cash flow £m	Discount rate 12%	Present value £m
1	(16.0)	1.00	(16.0)
2	4.5	0.89	4.0
3	5.0	0.80	4.0
4	5.0	0.71	3.6
5	2.0	0.64	1.3
		ENPV	(3.1)

The probability of occurrence is $(0.2 \times 0.3 \times 0.2 \times 0.5) = 0.006$.

(e) The ENPV of the investment is positive (£0.4 million). The decision rule is to accept projects with a positive ENPV as this will shareholder wealth. However, the investment outcome is only just in positive territory. A thorough review of critical assumptions, as well as the gathering of further information, should be undertaken before a final decision is made.

Projects 3 and 4

(f) Project 4 has the higher standard deviation and therefore the greater variability of possible outcomes. Hence, it has the higher level of risk. Using the expected value-standard deviation rule, we should accept Project 3. This is because the expected return of Project 3 is equal to that of Project 4 but the standard deviation of Project 3 is lower than that of Project 4.

Chapter 6

6.1 Helsim Ltd

(a) The liquidity position may be assessed by using the liquidity ratios discussed in Chapter 3:

$$\text{Current ratio} = \frac{\text{Current assets}}{\text{Current liabilities}} = \frac{£7.5m}{£5.4m} = 1.4$$

$$\text{Acid test ratio} = \frac{\text{Current assets (excluding inventories)}}{\text{Current liabilities}} = \frac{£3.7m}{£5.4m} = 0.7$$

These ratios reveal a fairly weak liquidity position. The current ratio seems quite low and the acid test ratio very low. This latter ratio suggests that the business does not have sufficient liquid assets to meet its maturing obligations. It would be useful, however, to have details of the liquidity ratios of similar businesses in the same industry in order to make a more informed judgement. The bank overdraft represents 67 per cent of the current liabilities and 40 per cent of the total liabilities of the business. The continuing support of the bank is therefore important to the ability of the business to meet its commitments.

(b) The finance required to reduce trade payables to an average of 40 days outstanding is calculated as follows:

	£m
Trade payables at the date of the statement of financial position	1.80
Trade payables outstanding based on 40 days' credit	
(40/365 × £8.4m (that is, credit purchases))	(0.92)
Finance required	0.88 (say £0.9m)

(c) The bank may not wish to provide further finance to the business. The increase in overdraft will reduce the level of trade payables but will increase the risk exposure of the bank. The additional finance invested by the bank will not generate further funds (it will not increase profit) and will not therefore be self-liquidating. The question does not make it clear whether the business has sufficient security to offer the bank for the increase in overdraft facility. The profits of the business will be reduced and the interest cover ratio, based on the profits generated last year, would reduce to about 1.6* times if the additional overdraft were granted (based on interest charged at 10 per cent each year). This is very low and means that only a small decline in profits would leave interest charges uncovered.

* Existing bank overdraft (3.6) + extension of overdraft to cover reduction in trade payables (0.9) + loan notes (3.5) = £8.0m. Assuming a 10 per cent interest rate means a yearly interest payment of £0.8 million. The operating profit was £1.3 million. Interest cover would be 1.63 (that is, 1.3/0.8).

(d) A number of possible sources of finance might be considered. Four possible sources are as follows:

■ *Issue ordinary (equity) shares*. This option may be unattractive to investors. The return on equity is fairly low at 7.9 per cent (that is, profit for the year (0.3)/equity (3.8)) and there is no evidence that the profitability of the business will improve. If profits remain at their current level, the effect of issuing more equity will be to reduce further the returns to equity.

■ *Make other borrowings*. This option may also prove unattractive to investors. The effect of making further borrowings will have a similar effect to that of increasing the overdraft. The profits of the business will be reduced and the interest cover ratio will decrease to a low level. The gearing ratio of the business is already quite high at 48 per cent (that is, loan notes (3.5)/(loan notes + equity (3.5 + 3.8)) and it is not clear what security would be available for the loan. The gearing ratio would be much higher if the overdraft were to be included.

■ *Chase trade receivables*. It may be possible to improve cash flows by reducing the level of credit outstanding from customers. At present, the average settlement period is 93 days (that is, (trade receivables (3.6)/sales revenue (14.2)) × 365), which seems quite high. A reduction in the average settlement period by approximately one-quarter would generate the funds required. However, it is not clear what effect this would have on sales.

■ *Reduce inventories*. This appears to be the most attractive of the four options. At present, the average inventories turnover period is 178 days (that is, (closing inventories (3.8)/cost of sales (7.8)) × 365), which seems very high. A reduction in this period by less than one-quarter would generate the funds required. However, if the business holds a large amount of slow-moving and obsolete items, it may be difficult to reduce inventories levels.

Chapter 7

7.1 Ceres plc

(a) (i) Preliminary calculations

Annual depreciation is £4 million [that is, property (£40m × 2½%) and plant (£20m × 15%)].
Cost of acquiring the business is £120 million (that is, £10m × 12).
Loan finance required is £70 million (that is, £120m – £50m).

Loan outstanding at 31 May Year 10

Year to 31 May	Year 7	Year 8	Year 9	Year 10
	£m	£m	£m	£m
Operating profit	10.0	11.0	10.5	13.5
Add Annual depr'n	4.0	4.0	4.0	4.0
	14.0	15.0	14.5	17.5
Less Working capital	–	(1.0)	–	–
Loan interest	(7.0)	(6.3)	(5.5)	(4.6)
Cash to repay loan	7.0	7.7	9.0	12.9
Loan at start of year	70.0	63.0	55.3	46.3
Cash to repay loan	(7.0)	(7.7)	(9.0)	(12.9)
Loan at end of year	63.0	55.3	46.3	33.4

(ii) Internal rate of return (IRR)

The net amount to be received in Year 10 by the private-equity firm is calculated as follows:

	£m
Sale proceeds (12 × £13.5m)	162.0
Loan repayment	(33.4)
Proceeds to shareholders	128.6
Less	
Amount to shareholder/managers (10%)	(12.9)
For private-equity firm	115.7

Trial 1 – Discount rate 24%
NPV is:

$$(£115.7m \times 0.42) - £45m = £3.6m$$

As it is positive, the IRR is higher.

Trial 2 – Discount rate 28%
NPV is:

$$(£115.7m \times 0.37) - £45m = (2.2m)$$

As it is negative, the IRR is lower.

A 4 per cent change in the discount rate leads to a £5.8m (£3.6m + £2.2m) change in the NPV. Thus, a 1 per cent change in the discount rate results in a £1.45m change in NPV. The IRR is:

$$24\% + \left(\frac{£3.6m}{1.45}\right)\% = 26.5\%$$

(b) The IRR exceeds the cost of capital and so the investment should go ahead. However, the calculations are likely to be sensitive to forecast inaccuracies. The forecast inputs should be re-examined, particularly the anticipated profit in the year of sale. It is much higher than in previous years and forms the basis for calculating the sale price.

Chapter 8

8.1 Russell Ltd

(a) (i) The projected income statements are:

Projected income statements for the year ended 31 May Year 5

	Shares £000	Loan notes £000
Profit before interest and tax	662.0	662.0
Interest	(30.0)	(90.0)
Profit before taxation	632.0	572.0
Tax (25%)	(158.0)	(143.0)
Profit for the year	474.0	429.0

(ii) The earnings per share (EPS) are:

	Shares	Loan notes
$\text{EPS} = \dfrac{\text{Profit available to ordinary shareholders}}{\text{No. of ordinary shares}}$	$\dfrac{474}{(400 + 150)}$	$\dfrac{429}{400}$
	£0.86	£1.07

(iii) Gearing ratio

	Shares	Loan notes
$\dfrac{\text{Loan capital}}{\text{Share capital} + \text{Reserves} + \text{Loan capital}} \times 100\%$ (See note below)	$\dfrac{250}{(832.4 + 284.4 + 600.0 + 250)} \times 100\%$	$\dfrac{850}{(832.4 + 257.4 + 850)} \times 100\%$
	12.7%	43.8%

Note: The retained earnings for the year are calculated as follows:

	Shares £000	Loan notes £000
Profit for the year (see above)	474.0	429.0
Dividend proposed and paid (40% payout ratio)	(189.6)	(171.6)
Retained earnings	284.4	257.4

(b) The loan notes option provides a significantly higher EPS figure than the share option. The EPS for the most recent year is £0.96 (384/400) and this lies between the two options being considered. On the basis of the EPS figures, it seems that the loan notes option is the more attractive. Pursuing the share option will lower EPS compared with the current year, and will result in a single shareholder obtaining 25 per cent of the voting share capital. As a result, this option is unlikely to be attractive. However, the gearing ratio under the loan notes option is significantly higher than under the share option. This ratio is also much higher than the current gearing ratio of the business of 23.1 per cent (250/1,082.4). The investor must balance the significant increase in financial risk with the additional returns that are generated.

(c) The level of operating profit (profit before interest and taxation) at which EPS under each option is the same will be:

$$\underset{\text{Ordinary shares}}{\dfrac{(x - 30.0)(1 - 0.25)}{(400.0 + 150.0)}} = \underset{\text{Ordinary shares plus loan notes}}{\dfrac{(x - 90.0)(1 - 0.25)}{400.0}}$$

$$400(0.75x - 22.5) = 550(0.75x - 67.5)$$
$$300x - 9{,}000 = 412.5x - 37{,}125$$
$$112.5x = 28{,}125$$
$$x = \underline{250}(000)$$

The above figure could also have been calculated using a PBIT–EPS indifference chart as shown in the chapter.

Chapter 9

9.1 Sandarajan plc

(a) The dividend per share and dividend payout ratio over the five-year period under review are as follows:

Year	Dividend per share	Dividend payout %
1	22.0p	52.4
2	14.0p	26.4
3	17.3p	40.0
4	7.3p	14.9
5	30.7p	52.3

The figures above show an erratic pattern of dividends over the five years. Such a pattern is unlikely to be welcomed by investors. In an imperfect market, dividends may be important to investors because of the clientele effect, the need to reduce agency costs and information signalling.

(b) Managers should, therefore, decide on a payout policy and then make every effort to stick with this policy. This will help ensure that dividends are predictable and contain no 'surprises' for investors. Any reduction in the dividend is likely to be seen as a sign of financial weakness and the share price is likely to fall. If a reduction in dividends cannot be avoided, the managers should make clear the change in policy and the reasons for the change.

Chapter 10

10.1 Town Mills Ltd

(a) Operating cash cycle

	days
Inventories turnover period	
$(192/652) \times 365$	107
Trade receivables settlement period	
$202 \times (105/110)/903 \times 365$ (Note 1)	78
	185
Trade payables settlement period	
$260 \times (105/110)/652 \times 365$ (Notes 1 and 2)	(139)
	46

Notes:

1 Since the closing level of trade receivables/payables was 10 per cent higher at the end of the year than at the start, the average balance would be 105/110 of the end-of-year balance.

2 Since inventories were the same at both ends of the year, purchases equal cost of sales.

Knowledge of the length of the operating cash cycle (OCC) allows the business to monitor it over time, perhaps relative to other businesses or to some target. It is not possible to draw any helpful conclusions from looking at just one figure; there needs to be a basis of comparison.

A problem with using the 'bottom line' figure for the OCC is that values within it are not equivalent. In the case of Town Mills, one day's sales are worth £2,474, whereas one day's purchases or inventories holding are worth £1,786. So, while an extra day of trade receivables period coupled with an extra day of trade payables period would leave the OCC unchanged at 46 days, it would involve an additional £700 or so of investment in working capital.

(b) As mentioned in (a) above, knowing the number of days of the OCC tells us little without some basis of comparison.

The acid test ratio for this company is very low at 0.55:1. If inventories were fairly fast moving with a short trade receivables period, this might not be a worry, but this is not the case.

The current ratio is close to 1:1, which seems low. It is not possible, however, to say too much without making a comparison with similar businesses or with this business over time.

The level of the overdraft is a cause for concern. It represents almost 20 per cent of the total financing of the business, according to statement of financial position values. This represents a lot of short-term finance that could be recalled instantly, or at very short notice. A term loan may be a better arrangement than an overdraft.

The level of trade payables also seems high, compared with trade receivables. This too could be a problem. It depends on the relative bargaining positions of Town Mills and its suppliers.

Overall, liquidity does not seem strong and probably needs to be reviewed. It is not possible to be too emphatic on this point, however, given such limited bases for comparison.

(c) The types of risk and cost that might be associated with high inventories levels of a wholesaler include:

- *Financing cost*. Inventories need to be financed. Buying on trade credit, which is free, normally covers at least some of this. In the case of Town Mills, trade payables are currently greater than the value of inventories. Trade credit is linked to purchases, not to inventories levels. If inventories levels were to be reduced, the level of trade payables would not follow suit.
- *Storage costs*. These are likely to be lower where inventories are lower. How significant these costs are will depend on the nature of the inventories. Those which are high value and/or need special treatment are typically more expensive to store than other inventories.
- *Insurance cost*. This is likely to be subject to the same considerations as storage cost, of which it may be seen as forming part.
- *Obsolescence cost*. The more inventories held, the greater the risk that they will lose value through physical deterioration or obsolescence. A spare part for a machine may be in perfect condition and, in principle, capable of being used. If the machine is no longer being used, however, the spare part may be worthless.

Chapter 11

11.1 Romeo plc

Adjusted net assets (capital invested)

	£m	£m
Total assets less current liabilities as per the statement of financial position		231.0
Add Property (£200m – £60m)	140.0	
R&D (9/10 × £10m)	9.0	149.0
Adjusted total assets less current liabilities		380.0*

* This figure represents the adjusted figure for share and loan capital.

Market value added calculation

	£m
Market value of shares (60m × £8.50)	510.0
Less Capital invested (see above)	(380.0)
MVA	130.0

Chapter 12

12.1 Miocene plc

(i) Net assets (book value) basis:

$$\text{Price of an ordinary share } (P_0) = \frac{\text{Net assets at statement of financial position values}}{\text{Number of ordinary shares}}$$

$$= \frac{£60.1m}{40m}$$

$$= £1.50$$

(ii) Net assets (liquidation) basis:

$$P_0 = \frac{\text{Net assets* at current realisable values}}{\text{Number of ordinary shares}}$$

$$= \frac{£85.1m}{40m}$$

$$= £2.13$$

* The net assets figure is derived as follows:

	£m	£m
Assets		
Property		65.4
Plant and equipment		18.8
Fixtures and fittings		4.6
Inventories		38.9
Trade receivables		29.6
		157.3
Less **Liabilities**		
Current	(51.2)	
Non-current	(21.0)	(72.2)
Net assets		85.1

(iii) Price/earnings basis:

$$P_0 = \frac{\text{Price/earnings ratio} \times \text{Profit for the year}}{\text{Number of ordinary shares}}$$

$$= \frac{11 \times £17.2m}{40m}$$

$$= \frac{£189.2m}{40m}$$

$$= £4.73$$

(iv) Dividend growth basis:

$$P_0 = \frac{D_1}{K_0 - g}$$

$$= \frac{((£17.2m \times 40\%)/40m)}{(0.10 - 0.04)}$$

$$= £2.87$$

Chapter 1

1.1 The key tasks of the finance function are:

- financial planning and forecasting
- investment appraisal
- financing decisions
- capital market operations
- financial control.

1.2 Wealth maximisation is considered to be superior to profit maximisation for the following reasons:

- The term 'profit' is ambiguous. Different measures of profit can lead to different decisions being made.
- Profit measures are influenced by the accounting policies and estimates employed.
- There is a lack of clarity over the time period over which profit should be maximised. There is a potential conflict between short-term and long-term profit.
- Profit maximisation ignores the issue of risk. This may lead to investments in risky projects in order to gain higher returns. However, this may not align with shareholders' needs.
- Profit maximisation fails to take account of the opportunity cost of shareholders' funds.

Wealth maximisation takes into account risk, the opportunity cost of shareholders' funds and long-run returns. It is also a more objective measure of performance.

1.3 Survival may be a basic objective for a business. However, shareholders will expect to receive returns from their investment and will not be interested in businesses that simply see this as their primary objective. Nevertheless, there may be times when survival has to become the main objective.

In a highly competitive economy, a business has to pursue shareholder wealth maximisation in order to survive. Under such circumstances, shareholder wealth maximisation and survival become inextricably linked.

1.4 The stakeholder approach raises various difficult issues, including:

- who the stakeholders are and their relative importance
- the extent to which each stakeholder group should benefit from the business and the ways in which managers should mediate between the conflicting interests of the various groups
- how accountability can be achieved where multiple objectives are being pursued. In particular, how performance can be measured and how managers can be prevented from pursuing their own interests behind a screen of multiple objectives.

Chapter 2

2.1 When a business is growing fast, it is vital that managers maintain a balance between increases in the level of sales and the finance available to sustain this increase. The business must not pursue sales growth to the point where it becomes financially overstretched and then collapses. Projected financial statements will show the impact of future changes in sales on the profitability, liquidity and financing requirements of the business. If the business shows signs of being unable to sustain the required level of sales growth in the future, corrective action can be taken.

2.2 It is true that the future is uncertain. It is also probably true that projected financial statements will prove to be inaccurate. However, most businesses find that, despite the inaccuracies inherent in forecasting, it is better to produce these statements than not to do so. The question to be asked is: can a business function if no projections are made available to managers? The problem of uncertainty should not prevent some form of financial planning. It is far better to deal with uncertainty through such techniques as sensitivity analysis and scenario analysis.

2.3 An existing business may find it easier than a new business to prepare projected financial statements for several reasons. These include:

- past data concerning sales, overheads and so on for a number of years which may be used for comparison and extrapolation
- close links with customers, suppliers and so on which will help to identify likely future changes within the industry and future price changes
- a management team that is experienced in producing forecasts and that has an understanding of the impact of competition on the business.

2.4 The sales forecast is critical because it will determine the overall level of operations of the business. Thus, the future levels of investment, financing and overheads will be influenced by the level of sales. The cash received from sales will be an important factor in deriving the projected cash flows, and the sales revenue will be an important factor in deriving the projected profits. The projected cash flows and profits, in turn, will be important factors in preparing the projected statement of financial position (balance sheet). For these reasons, care must be taken in deriving a sales forecast for the business.

Chapter 3

3.1 The fact that a business operates on a low operating profit margin indicates that only a small operating profit is being produced for each £1 of sales revenue generated. However, this does not necessarily mean that the ROCE will be low. If the business is able to generate sufficient sales revenue during a period, the operating profit may be very high even though the operating profit per £1 of sales revenue is low. If the overall operating profit is high, this can lead, in turn, to a high ROCE, since it is the total operating profit that is used as the numerator (top part of the fraction) in this ratio. Many businesses (including supermarkets) pursue a strategy of 'low margin, high sales revenue'.

3.2 The statement of financial position is drawn up at a single point in time – the end of the financial period. As a result, the figures shown on the statement represent the position at that single point in time and may not be representative of the position during the period. Wherever possible, average figures (perhaps based on monthly figures) should be used. However, an external user may only have access to the opening and closing statements of financial position for the year and so a simple average based on these figures may be all that it is possible to calculate. Where a business is seasonal in nature or is subject to cyclical changes, this simple averaging may not be sufficient.

3.3 In view of the fact that Z-scores are derived from information that is published by the businesses themselves, it is difficult to say that Z-scores should not be made publicly available. Indeed, many of those connected with a business – shareholders, lenders, employees and so on – may find this information extremely valuable for decision making. However, there is a risk that a poor Z-score will lead to a loss of confidence in the business among investors and suppliers, which will, in turn, prevent the business from taking corrective action as lines of credit and investment will be withdrawn.

3.4 The P/E ratio may vary between businesses within the same industry for the following reasons:

- *Accounting policies.* Differences in the methods used to compute profit (for example, inventories valuation and depreciation) can lead to different profit figures and therefore different P/E ratios.
- *Different prospects.* One business may be regarded as having a much brighter future due to factors such as the quality of management, the quality of products, location and so on. This

will affect the market price investors are prepared to pay for the share and, hence, it will also affect the P/E ratio.

■ *Different asset structure*. One business's underlying asset base may be much higher and this may affect the market price of the shares.

Chapter 4

4.1 NPV is usually considered the best method of assessing investment opportunities because it takes account of:

■ *The timing of the cash flows*. By discounting the various cash flows associated with each project according to when they are expected to arise, it recognises the fact that cash flows do not all occur simultaneously. Associated with this is the fact that, by discounting, using the opportunity cost of capital (that is, the return which the next best alternative opportunity would generate), the net benefit after the financing cost has been met is identified (as the NPV).

■ *The whole of the relevant cash flows*. NPV includes all of the relevant cash flows irrespective of when they are expected to occur. It treats them differently according to their date of occurrence, but they are all taken account of in the NPV and they all have, or can have, an influence on the decision.

■ *The objectives of the business*. NPV is the only method of appraisal where the output of the analysis has a direct bearing on the wealth of the business. (Positive NPVs enhance wealth; negative ones reduce it). Since most private sector businesses seek to increase their value and wealth, NPV clearly is the best approach to use.

NPV provides clear decision rules concerning acceptance/rejection of projects and the ranking of projects. It is fairly simple to use, particularly with the availability of modern computer software that takes away the need for routine calculations to be done manually.

4.2 The payback method, in its original form, does not take account of the time value of money. However, it would be possible to modify the payback method to accommodate this requirement. Cash flows arising from a project could be discounted, using the cost of capital as the appropriate discount rate, in the same way as the NPV method. The discounted payback approach is used by some businesses and represents an improvement on the original approach described in the chapter. However, it retains the other flaws of the original payback approach that were discussed. For example, it ignores relevant data after the payback period. Thus, even in its modified form, the PP method cannot be regarded as superior to NPV.

4.3 The IRR method does appear to be preferred to the NPV method among many practising managers. The main reasons for this appear to be as follows:

■ A preference for a percentage return ratio rather than an absolute figure as a means of expressing the outcome of a project. This preference for a ratio may reflect the fact that other financial goals of the business are often set in terms of ratios, an example being return on capital employed.

■ A preference for ranking projects in terms of their percentage return. Managers may feel it is easier to rank projects on the basis of percentage returns (though NPV outcomes should be just as easy for them). We saw in the chapter that the IRR method could provide misleading advice on the ranking of projects and the NPV method was preferable for this purpose.

4.4 Cash flows are preferred to profit flows because cash is the ultimate measure of economic wealth. Cash is used to acquire resources and for distribution to shareholders. When cash is invested in an investment project an opportunity cost is incurred, as the cash cannot be used in other investment projects. Similarly, when positive cash flows are generated by the project, the cash can be used to reinvest in other investment projects.

Profit, meanwhile, is relevant to reporting the productive effort for a period. This measure of effort may have only a tenuous relationship to cash flows for a period. The conventions of accounting may lead to the recognition of gains and losses in one period and the relevant cash inflows and outflows occurring in another period.

Chapter 5

5.1 Although inflation rates have been quite low in recent years, the effect of inflation on investments should be taken into account. Investments are often made over a long time period and even quite low rates of inflation can have a significant effect on cash flows over time.

(a) The effect of discounting cash flows that include inflation at real discount rates will be to overstate NPV, as the cash flows will be increased in line with inflation whereas the discount rate will not.

(b) The effect of discounting real cash flows at a market discount rate will be to understate NPV, as the discount rate will be increased in line with inflation whereas the cash flows will not.

5.2 It has been suggested that risk arises when more things can happen than will happen. In other words, the future is unclear and there is a chance that estimates made concerning the future may not necessarily occur. Risk can be divided into two types: diversifiable and non-diversifiable risk. It is only the former that can be diversified away by investing in a spread of projects whose returns are not positively correlated. Non-diversifiable risk is, however, common to all projects and cannot be diversified away.

5.3 The risk-adjusted discount rate suffers from three major problems:

■ Subjective judgement is required in assigning projects to particular risk categories.
■ The risk premium will reflect the views of the managers rather than those of the investors. Any difference between the attitudes of investors and the interpretation of these attitudes by managers can have an effect on the accept/reject decision.
■ It assumes that risk increases over time. The further into the future the cash flows arise, the more heavily they are discounted. However, risk may not necessarily increase with time. It may be determined by the nature of the product or service being offered, and so on.

5.4 Risk arises when there is more than one possible outcome for a project. The standard deviation measures the variability of returns and can provide a useful measure of risk. Generally speaking, the higher the standard deviation, the higher the level of risk associated with a project. However, when the distribution of possible outcomes is skewed, the standard deviation may not provide a reliable measure of risk as it fails to distinguish between 'downside' and 'upside' risk.

Chapter 6

6.1 Share warrants may be particularly useful for young, expanding businesses wishing to attract new investors. They can help provide a 'sweetener' for the issue of loan notes. Attaching warrants may make it possible to agree a lower rate of interest and/or less restrictive loan covenants. If the business is successful, the warrants will provide a further source of finance. Investors will exercise their option to acquire shares if the market price of the shares exceeds the exercise price of the warrant. However, this will have the effect of diluting the control of existing shareholders.

6.2 Convertible loan notes are not necessarily a form of delayed equity. Although they give an investor the right to convert them into ordinary shares at a given future date, there is no obligation to convert. This will be done only if the market price of the shares at the conversion date exceeds the agreed conversion price. The conversion price is usually higher than the market price at the time the convertible loan notes are issued and so the market price of the shares will usually have to rise over time in order for the lender to exercise the option to convert. During a period of stagnant or falling market prices, the lender is unlikely to exercise the option and so no conversion will take place. Hence, it cannot be assumed that there is an automatic conversion from loan notes to ordinary (equity) share capital.

6.3 A swap agreement can be a useful hedging device. A business with a floating rate loan agreement, for example, may believe that interest rates are going to rise, whereas a business with a fixed-rate agreement may believe that interest rates are going to fall. By entering into a swap agreement, they can both hedge against risk. Swap agreements may also be used to exploit capital market imperfections, such as where one business has an advantage over another when negotiating interest rates.

A swap arrangement involves two businesses agreeing to assume responsibility for the other's interest payments (although, in some cases, a bank may act as counterparty to a swap agreement). Typically, a business with a floating-interest-rate loan will swap interest payment obligations with a business with a fixed-interest-rate loan. The arrangement is usually negotiated through a bank. Legal responsibility for interest payments still rests with the business that entered into the original loan agreement. Thus, the borrowing business may continue to make interest payments to the lender in line with the loan agreement. However, at the end of an agreed period, a compensating cash adjustment between the two swap parties will be made.

6.4 Invoice discounting is a service offered to businesses whereby a financial institution is prepared to advance a sum up to 80 per cent of outstanding trade receivables. The amount advanced is usually payable within 60 to 90 days. The business will retain responsibility for collecting the amounts owing from customers and the advance must be repaid irrespective of whether the receivables have been collected. Factoring is a service whereby a financial institution (factor) takes over the sales and trade receivables records and will undertake to collect trade receivables on behalf of the client business. The factor will also be prepared to make an advance of 80 per cent (or perhaps more) of approved trade receivables, which is repayable from the amounts received from customers. The service charge for invoice discounting is up to 0.5 per cent of sales revenue, whereas the service charge for factoring is up to 3 per cent of sales revenue. This difference explains, in part, why businesses have shown a preference for invoice discounting rather than factoring in recent years. However, the factor provides additional services, as explained.

Chapter 7

7.1 Various reasons have been put forward to explain the difference in the proportion of total investment made in business start-ups by UK and US private-equity firms. These include:

- UK firms are more cautious than their US counterparts. Start-ups are more risky and UK private-equity firms may be less willing to take on these risks.
- UK firms have a shorter-term investment perspective that makes them prefer financing existing businesses.
- There is greater competition for good investment opportunities among US private-equity firms, which leads them to invest in business start-ups to achieve the required returns.

7.2 A listed business may wish to revert to unlisted status for a number of possible reasons. These include:

- *Cost*. A Stock Exchange listing can be costly as the business must adhere to certain administrative regulations and requirements for financial disclosures.
- *Scrutiny*. Listed businesses are subject to close scrutiny by analysts and this may not be welcome if the business is engaged in sensitive negotiations or controversial activities.
- *Takeover risk*. The shares of the business may be purchased by an unwelcome bidder and this may result in a takeover.
- *Investor profile*. If the business is dominated by a few investors who wish to retain their interest in the business and do not wish to raise further capital by public issues, the benefits of a listing are few.

7.3 An offer for sale involves an issuing house buying the shares in the business and then, in turn, selling the shares to the public. The issue will be advertised by the publication of a prospectus that will set out details of the business and the issue price of the shares (or reserve price if a tender issue is being made). The shares issued by the issuing house may be either new shares or shares that have been purchased from existing shareholders.

A public issue is one where the business undertakes direct responsibility for issuing shares to the public. If an issuing house is employed it will usually be in the role of adviser and administrator of the issue. However, the issuing house may also underwrite the issue. A public issue runs the risk that the shares will not be taken up and is a less popular form of issue for businesses.

7.4 A business should have owners who are:

- committed to realising the growth potential of the business
- prepared to sell some of the ordinary shares in the business
- comfortable with the financing arrangements that private-equity firms usually employ.

It should have a management team that is:

- ambitious
- experienced
- capable
- well balanced.

Chapter 8

8.1 To find out whether or not a planned level of gearing is likely to be acceptable to investors, the managers of a business could look at the levels of gearing in similar businesses operating within the same industry. If the business adopts a much higher level of gearing than these businesses, there may be problems in raising long-term funds. The managers could also discuss the proposed level of gearing with prospective investors such as banks and financial institutions to see whether they regard the level of gearing as acceptable.

8.2 The lender may consider the following factors:

- security for the loan
- the performance record of the business
- likely future prospects of the business and the industry
- the existing level of gearing for the business
- likely interest cover for the loan
- the purpose of the loan
- the expected level of return compared with other investment opportunities of the same level of risk
- restrictive loan covenants in place from existing lenders.

8.3 It would not be appropriate to employ the specific cost of raising capital for an investment project as the appropriate discount rate. The use of such an approach could result in bizarre decisions being made. Projects with an identical return may be treated differently according to the particular cost of raising finance for each project. It is better to view the individual elements of capital as entering a pool of funds and thereby losing their separate identity. The cost of capital used for investment decisions will represent the average cost of the pool of funds. It should also be remembered that individual elements of capital are interrelated. It would not be possible, for example, to raise debt unless the business had a reasonable level of ordinary share capital. To treat each source of capital as being quite separate is therefore incorrect.

8.4 An important implication of (a), the traditional approach, is that financial managers should try to establish the mix of loan/share finance that will minimise the overall cost of capital. At this point, the business will be said to achieve an optimal capital structure. Minimising the overall cost of capital in this way will maximise the value of the business. An important implication of (b), the MM (excluding tax effects) approach, is that the financing decision is not really important. As the overall cost of capital remains constant, a business does not have an optimal capital structure as suggested by the traditionalists. This means that one particular capital structure is no better or worse than any other and so managers should not spend time evaluating different forms of financing the business. Instead, they should concentrate their efforts on evaluating and managing the investments of the business. However, (c), the MM (including tax effects) approach, recognises that the tax shield on loan capital benefits the ordinary shareholders and the higher the level of interest payments, the greater the benefits. The implications of this approach are that there is an optimal capital structure (and in that sense it is similar to the traditional approach) and that the optimal structure is a gearing ratio of 100 per cent.

Chapter 9

9.1 Where it is appropriate to make an extraordinary distribution to shareholders, buybacks may be preferable to dividends. Managers are usually reluctant to increase dividends in one period and then decrease them in a subsequent period. Such extraordinary distributions include:

- dealing with undervalued shares
- returning surplus cash to shareholders
- adjusting the capital structure.

9.2 The residual theory of dividends states that dividends should be regarded as a residual amount arising when the business does not have enough profitable opportunities in which to invest. The argument assumes that shareholders will prefer the business to reinvest earnings rather than pay dividends, as long as the returns earned by the business exceed the returns that could be achieved by shareholders investing in similar projects. However, when all the profitable projects that meet this criterion have been taken up, any surplus remaining should be distributed to shareholders. Thus, dividends will be, in effect, a by-product of the investment decision, as stated.

9.3 The type of distribution policy adopted may not be critical because of the clientele effect. The particular distribution policy will attract a certain type of investor depending on his or her cash needs and taxation position. Thus, investors who rely on dividend income to meet living expenses may prefer a high payout policy whereas investors with high marginal tax rates may prefer a low (or zero) payout policy.

9.4 Agency theory is based on the idea that the business is a coalition of interest groups, with each group seeking to maximise its own welfare. This behaviour is often at the expense of the other groups, and so 'agency costs' arise. In order to minimise these agency costs, the particular group bearing the costs may seek to restrain the actions of others through contractual or other arrangements. Thus, in order to prevent managers from awarding themselves various perks, the shareholders may insist that all surplus cash is returned to them in the form of a dividend. Similarly, in order to prevent shareholders from withdrawing their investment in the business and allowing lenders to bear all, or the majority of, the risks of the business, the lenders may seek to limit the amount that can be declared in the form of a dividend.

Chapter 10

10.1 Although the credit manager is responsible for ensuring that receivables pay on time, Tariq may be right in denying blame. Various factors may be responsible for the situation described which are beyond the control of the credit manager. These include:

- a downturn in the economy leading to financial difficulties among credit customers
- decisions by other managers within the business to liberalise credit policy in order to stimulate sales
- an increase in competition among suppliers offering credit, which is being exploited by customers
- disputes with customers over the quality of goods or services supplied
- problems in the delivery of goods leading to delays.

   You may have thought of others.

10.2 The level of inventories held will be affected in the following ways:

   (a) An increase in production bottlenecks is likely to result in an increase in raw materials and work in progress being processed within the plant. Therefore, inventories levels should rise.

   (b) A rise in the cost of capital will make holding inventories more expensive. This may, in turn, lead to a decision to reduce inventories levels.

   (c) The decision to reduce the range of products should result in a lower level of inventories being held. It would no longer be necessary to hold certain items in order to meet customer demand.

   (d) Switching to a local supplier may reduce the lead time between ordering an item and receiving it. This should, in turn, reduce the need to carry such high levels of the particular item.

(e) A deterioration in the quality of bought-in items may result in the purchase of higher quantities of inventories in order to take account of the defective element in inventories acquired. It may also lead to an increase in the inspection time for items received. This too would lead to a rise in inventories levels.

10.3 Inventories are held to:

- meet customer demand
- avoid the problems of running out of inventories
- take advantage of profitable opportunities (for example, buying a product that is expected to rise steeply in price in the future).

The first reason may be described as transactionary, the second precautionary and the third speculative. They are, in essence, the same reasons why a business holds cash.

10.4 (a) The costs of holding too little cash are:

- failure to meet obligations when they fall due, which can damage the reputation of the business and may, in the extreme, lead to the business being wound up
- having to borrow and thereby incur interest charges
- an inability to take advantage of profitable opportunities.

(b) The costs of holding too much cash are:

- failure to use the funds available for more profitable purposes
- loss of value during a period of inflation.

Chapter 11

11.1 The directors' attitude towards risk may be affected by the availability of share options in different ways. Where, for example, the options are 'underwater', the directors may engage in risky behaviour in order to increase the price of the shares. Where, however, the directors are holding much of their personal wealth in the form of share options, they may seek to avoid risk. In both examples, the directors' personal interests would prevail over the interests of shareholders.

11.2 Two problems with the use of MVA as a tool for internal management purposes were identified in the text. First, MVA depends on establishing a market price for shares and so only businesses listed on the Stock Exchange can use this technique. Second, MVA cannot be used to evaluate the performance of strategic business units as there is no market share price for each unit. However, there is also a third reason why it is inappropriate for management purposes: share prices may fluctuate significantly over the short term and this could obscure the performance of managers.

11.3 The problem with taking changes in the market value of the shares as an indicator of shareholder value created (or lost) is that it does not take account of capital required to generate that market value. Let us assume there are two companies, A and B, which each start with £100 million capital invested. After two years, let us assume that the market value of A is £250 million and the market value of B is £300 million. However, B raised £80 million in additional capital to finance the business. Although B has a higher market value after two years, it has been achieved through a much higher level of capital invested. MVA takes the difference between the market value and the capital invested and so avoids this problem.

11.4 If businesses are overcapitalised it is probably because insufficient attention is given to the amount of capital that is required. Management incentive schemes that are geared towards generating a particular level of profits or achieving a particular market share without specifying the level of capital invested can help create such a problem. EVA® can help avoid the problem by focusing on the need to obtain a profitable return on capital invested.

Chapter 12

12.1 A merger involves a combination of two (or more) businesses of roughly equal size. This results in the creation of a new business and does not involve the purchase of the shares of one of the existing businesses by the other business. A merger is undertaken with the agreement of the managers and shareholders of each business and there is continuity of ownership of the resources. A takeover involves one business acquiring the shares of another business in order to gain control of the resources of that business. This may lead to a change of ownership and the takeover may be resisted by the managers of the target business.

12.2 Reasons for divestment may include the following:

■ A business may decide to focus on its core activities. Any activities that are not regarded as core activities may be sold following such a review. In recent years, a number of businesses have decided, often as a result of bitter experience, that it is better for them to 'stick to their knitting'.

■ A business may receive an unwelcome takeover bid because it has particular operations that are of interest to the predator business. The target business may, therefore, try to sell off these operations in order to protect the rest of its operations from takeover.

■ A business may decide that in order to improve its overall profitability, poorly performing operations should be sold. The business may not feel it is worth investing time and resources in trying to improve the level of performance achieved by these poorly performing operations.

■ A business may require funds for investment purposes or to deal with cash flow problems. The disposal of certain business operations may be the most feasible solution to these problems.

12.3 Four reasons for taking over another business are to:

■ exploit underutilised resources
■ acquire complementary resources
■ achieve benefits of scale
■ eliminate competition and increase market share.

12.4 Four methods of resisting a takeover bid, once a bid has been received, are:

■ find a white knight to take over the business instead
■ put a case to shareholders arguing that it is not in their long-term interests to support the takeover
■ increase dividend payouts
■ find a white squire to purchase a significant block of shares in the business.

Other reasons could have been cited.

Appendix E
SOLUTIONS TO SELECTED EXERCISES

Chapter 2

2.1 *Choice Designs Ltd*

(a) The projected income statement is:

Projected income statement for the year to 31 May Year 9

	£000
Sales revenue	1,400
Cost of sales (70%)	(980)
Gross profit (30%)	420
Admin. expenses	(225)
Selling expenses	(85)
Profit before taxation	110
Tax	(34)
Profit for the year	76

(b) The projected statement of financial position is:

Projected statement of financial position as at 31 May Year 9

	£000	£000
ASSETS		
Non-current assets		
Property	600	
Depreciation	(112)	488
Fixtures and fittings	140	
Depreciation	(118)	22
Motor vehicles	40	
Depreciation	(10)	30
		540
Current assets		
Inventories (240 + (25% × 240))		300
Trade receivables (8/52 × (80% × 1,400))		172
Bank (balancing figure)		42
		514
Total assets		1,054
EQUITY AND LIABILITIES		
Equity		
Ordinary £1 shares		500
Retained earnings		297
		797
Current liabilities		
Trade payables (12/52 × 1,040*)		240
Tax due (50% × 34)		17
		257
Total equity and liabilities		1,054

* Purchases = (Cost of sales + Closing inventories − Opening inventories)
= (980 + 300 − 240) = 1,040

2.2 *Saturn plc*

Projected net cash inflows from operating activities:

		£m
Projected profit before taxation (after interest)		165
Depreciation		41
Interest expense		21
		227
Increase in working capital		
Increase in inventories (23 – 22)	(1)	
Increase in trade receivables (21 – 18)	(3)	
Increase in trade payables (17 – 15)	2	(2)
Projected cash generated from operations		225
Interest paid		(25)
Taxation paid		(49)
Dividends paid		(28)
Projected net cash from operating activities		123

2.5 *Danube Engineering plc*

Projected income statement for the year ended 31 December Year 6

	£m
Sales revenue (500 + (20% × 500))	600
Cost of sales (70% of sales)	(420)
Gross profit (30% of sales)	180
Selling expenses (6% of sales)	(36)
Distribution expenses (8% of sales)	(48)
Other expenses (5% of sales)	(30)
Profit before taxation (11% of sales)	66
Tax (20% of profit before tax)	(13)
Profit for the year	53

Projected statement of financial position as at 31 December Year 6

	£m
ASSETS	
Non-current assets	700
Current assets	
Inventories (35% of sales)	210
Trade receivables (25% of sales)	150
Cash (8% of sales)	48
	408
Total assets	1,108
EQUITY AND LIABILITIES	
Equity	
Share capital – 50p ordinary shares (balancing figure)	316
Retained earnings [249 + (53 – 13*)]	289
	605
Non-current liabilities	
Loan notes (500 – 250)	250
Current liabilities	
Trade payables (40% of sales)	240
Tax due (Year 7 tax)	13
	253
Total equity and liabilities	1,108

* The dividend is 25 per cent of the profit for the year (as in previous years) and is deducted in deriving the retained profit for the year.

Chapter 3

3.1 Three businesses

A plc operates a supermarket chain. The grocery business is highly competitive and to generate high sales volumes it is usually necessary to accept low operating profit margins. Thus, we can see that the operating profit margin of A plc is the lowest of the three businesses. The inventories turnover period of supermarket chains also tends to be quite low. They are often efficient in managing inventories and most supermarket chains have invested heavily in inventories control and logistical systems over the years. The average settlement period for receivables is very low as most sales are for cash, although where a customer pays by credit card there is usually a small delay before the supermarket receives the amount due. A low inventories turnover period and a low average settlement period for receivables usually mean that the investment in current assets is low. Hence, the current ratio (current assets/current liabilities) is also low.

B plc is the holiday tour operator. We can see that the sales to capital employed ratio is the highest of the three businesses. This is because tour operators do not usually require a large investment of capital: they do not need a large asset base in order to conduct their operations. The inventories turnover period ratio does not apply to B plc. It is a service business, which does not hold inventories for resale. We can see that the average settlement period for receivables is low. This may be because customers are invoiced near to the holiday date for any amounts outstanding and must pay before going on holiday. The lack of inventories held and low average settlement period for receivables leads to a very low current ratio.

C plc is the food manufacturing business. We can see that the sales to capital employed ratio is the lowest of the three businesses. This is because manufacturers tend to invest heavily in both current and non-current assets. The inventories turnover period is the highest of the three businesses. Three different kinds of inventories – raw materials, work-in-progress and finished goods – are held by manufacturers. The average receivables settlement period is also the highest of the three businesses. Manufacturers tend to sell to other businesses rather than to the public and their customers will normally demand credit. A one-month credit period for customers is fairly common for manufacturing businesses, although customers may receive a discount for prompt payment. The relatively high investment in inventories and receivables usually results in a high current ratio.

3.2 Amsterdam Ltd and Berlin Ltd

The ratios for Amsterdam Ltd and Berlin Ltd reveal that the trade receivables settlement ratio for Amsterdam Ltd is three times that for Berlin Ltd. Berlin Ltd is therefore much quicker in collecting amounts outstanding from customers. There is not much difference, however, between the two businesses in the time taken to pay trade payables.

It is interesting to compare the difference in the trade receivables and payables settlement periods for each business. As Amsterdam Ltd allows an average of 63 days' credit to its customers, yet pays suppliers within 50 days, it will require greater investment in working capital than Berlin Ltd, which allows an average of only 21 days to its customers but takes 45 days to pay its suppliers.

Amsterdam Ltd has a much higher gross profit margin than Berlin Ltd. However, the operating profit margin for the two businesses is identical. This suggests that Amsterdam Ltd has much higher overheads (as a percentage of sales revenue) than Berlin Ltd. The inventories turnover period for Amsterdam Ltd is more than twice that of Berlin Ltd. This may be due to the fact that Amsterdam Ltd maintains a wider range of inventories in an attempt to meet customer requirements. The evidence therefore suggests that Amsterdam Ltd is the one that prides itself on personal service. The higher average settlement period for trade receivables is consistent with a more relaxed attitude to credit collection (thereby maintaining customer goodwill) and the high overheads are consistent with incurring the additional costs of satisfying customers' requirements. Amsterdam Ltd's high inventories levels are consistent with maintaining a wide range of inventories, with the aim of satisfying a range of customer needs.

Berlin Ltd has the characteristics of a more price-competitive business. Its gross profit margin is much lower than that of Amsterdam Ltd; that is, a much lower gross profit for each £1 of sales revenue. However, overheads have been kept low, the effect being that the operating profit margin is the same as Amsterdam Ltd's. The low inventories turnover period and average settlement period for trade receivables are consistent with a business that wishes to minimise investment in current assets, thereby reducing costs.

3.7 Clarrods Ltd

(a)

	2013	2014
ROCE	$\dfrac{310}{1,600} = 19.4\%$	$\dfrac{350}{1,700} = 20.6\%$
ROSF	$\dfrac{155}{1,100} = 14.1\%$	$\dfrac{175}{1,200} = 14.6\%$
Gross profit margin	$\dfrac{1,040}{2,600} = 40\%$	$\dfrac{1,150}{3,500} = 32.9\%$
Operating profit margin	$\dfrac{310}{2,600} = 11.9\%$	$\dfrac{350}{3,500} = 10\%$
Current ratio	$\dfrac{735}{400} = 1.8$	$\dfrac{660}{485} = 1.4$
Acid test ratio	$\dfrac{485}{400} = 1.2$	$\dfrac{260}{485} = 0.5$
Trade receivables settlement period	$\dfrac{105}{2,600} \times 365 = 15 \text{ days}$	$\dfrac{145}{3,500} \times 365 = 15 \text{ days}$
Trade payables settlement period	$\dfrac{300}{1,560^*} \times 365 = 70 \text{ days}$	$\dfrac{375}{2,350^*} \times 365 = 58 \text{ days}$
Inventories turnover period	$\dfrac{250}{1,560} \times 365 = 58 \text{ days}$	$\dfrac{400}{2,350} \times 365 = 62 \text{ days}$
Gearing ratio	$\dfrac{500}{1,600} = 31.3\%$	$\dfrac{500}{1,700} = 29.4\%$

* Used because the credit purchases figure is not available.

(b) There has been a considerable decline in the gross profit margin during 2014. This fact, combined with the increase in sales revenue by more than one-third, suggests that a price-cutting policy has been adopted in an attempt to stimulate sales. However, the resulting increase in sales revenue has led to only a small improvement in ROCE and ROSF.

Despite a large cut in the gross profit margin, the operating profit margin has fallen by less than 2 percentage points. This suggests that overheads have been tightly controlled during 2014. Certainly, overheads have not risen in proportion to sales revenue.

The current ratio has fallen and the acid test ratio has fallen by more than half. Even though liquidity ratios are lower in retailing than in manufacturing, the liquidity of the business should now be a cause for concern. However, this may be a passing problem. The business is investing heavily in non-current assets and is relying on internal funds to finance this growth. When this investment ends, the liquidity position may improve quickly.

The trade receivables settlement period has remained unchanged over the two years, and there has been no significant change in the inventories turnover period in 2014. The gearing ratio seems quite low and provides no cause for concern given the profitability of the business.

Overall, the business appears to be financially sound. Although there has been rapid growth during 2014, there is no real cause for alarm provided that the liquidity of the business can be improved in the near future. In the absence of information concerning share price, it is not possible to say whether an investment should be made.

Chapter 4

4.1 *Mylo Ltd*

(a) The annual depreciation of the two projects is:

$$\text{Project 1: } \frac{(£100,000 - £7,000)}{3} = £31,000$$

$$\text{Project 2: } \frac{(£60,000 - £6,000)}{3} = £18,000$$

Project 1

(i) Net present value

	Year 0 £000	Year 1 £000	Year 2 £000	Year 3 £000
Operating profit (loss)		29	(1)	2
Depreciation		31	31	31
Capital cost	(100)			
Residual value				7
Net cash flows	(100)	60	30	40
10% discount factor	1.000	0.909	0.826	0.751
Present value	(100.00)	54.54	24.78	30.04
Net present value	(9.36)			

(ii) Internal rate of return

Clearly the IRR lies above 10 per cent; try 15 per cent:

15% discount factor	1.000	0.870	0.756	0.658
Present value	(100.00)	52.20	22.68	26.32
Net present value	1.20			

Thus the IRR lies a little above 15 per cent, perhaps around 16 per cent.

(iii) Payback period

To find the payback period, the cumulative cash flows are calculated:

Cumulative cash flows	(100)	(40)	(10)	30

Thus the payback will occur after 3 years if we assume year-end cash flows.

Project 2

(i) Net present value

	Year 0 £000	Year 1 £000	Year 2 £000	Year 3 £000
Operating profit (loss)		18	(2)	4
Depreciation		18	18	18
Capital cost	(60)			
Residual value				6
Net cash flows	(60)	36	16	28
10% discount factor	1.000	0.909	0.826	0.751
Present value	(60.00)	32.72	13.22	21.03
Net present value	6.97			

(ii) Internal rate of return

Clearly the IRR lies above 10 per cent; try 15 per cent:

15% discount factor	1.000	0.870	0.756	0.658
Present value	(60.00)	31.32	12.10	18.42
Net present value	1.84			

Thus the IRR lies a little above 15 per cent; perhaps around 17 per cent.

(iii) Payback period

The cumulative cash flows are:

Cumulative cash flows	(60)	(24)	(8)	20

Thus, the payback will occur after 3 years (assuming year-end cash flows).

(b) Presuming that Mylo Ltd is pursuing a wealth-enhancement objective, Project 1 is preferable since it has the higher NPV. The difference between the two NPVs is not significant, however.

4.5 *Newton Electronics Ltd*

(a) **Option 1**

	Year 0 £m	Year 1 £m	Year 2 £m	Year 3 £m	Year 4 £m	Year 5 £m
Plant and equipment	(9.0)					1.0
Sales revenue		24.0	30.8	39.6	26.4	10.0
Variable cost		(11.2)	(19.6)	(25.2)	(16.8)	(7.0)
Fixed cost (ex. dep'n)		(0.8)	(0.8)	(0.8)	(0.8)	(0.8)
Working capital	(3.0)					3.0
Marketing cost		(2.0)	(2.0)	(2.0)	(2.0)	(2.0)
Opportunity cost		(0.1)	(0.1)	(0.1)	(0.1)	(0.1)
	(12.0)	9.9	8.3	11.5	6.7	4.1
Discount factor 10%	1.000	0.909	0.826	0.751	0.683	0.621
Present value	(12.0)	9.0	6.9	8.6	4.6	2.5
NPV	19.6					

Option 2

	Year 0 £m	Year 1 £m	Year 2 £m	Year 3 £m	Year 4 £m	Year 5 £m
Royalties	–	4.4	7.7	9.9	6.6	2.8
Discount factor 10%	1.000	0.909	0.826	0.751	0.683	0.621
Present value	–	4.0	6.4	7.4	4.5	1.7
NPV	24.0					

Option 3

	Year 0	Year 2
Instalments	12.0	12.0
Discount factor 10%	1.000	0.826
Present value	12.0	9.9
NPV	21.9	

(b) Before making a final decision, the board should consider the following factors:

(i) The long-term competitiveness of the business may be affected by the sale of the patents.

(ii) At present, the business is not involved in manufacturing and marketing products. Would a change in direction be desirable?

(iii) The business will probably have to buy in the skills necessary to produce the product itself. This will involve cost, and problems could arise. Has this been taken into account?

(iv) How accurate are the forecasts made and how valid are the assumptions on which they are based?

(c) Option 2 has the highest NPV and is therefore the most attractive to shareholders. However, the accuracy of the forecasts should be checked before a final decision is made.

4.6 *Chesterfield Wanderers*

(a) Player option

Years	0	1	2	3	4	5
	£000	£000	£000	£000	£000	£000
Sale of player	2,200					1,000
Purchase of Bazza	(10,000)					
Sponsorship and so on		1,200	1,200	1,200	1,200	1,200
Gate receipts		2,500	1,300	1,300	1,300	1,300
Salaries paid		(800)	(800)	(800)	(800)	(1,200)
Salaries saved		400	400	400	400	600
	(7,800)	3,300	2,100	2,100	2,100	2,900
Discount factor 10%	1.000	0.909	0.826	0.751	0.683	0.621
Present values	(7,800)	3,000	1,735	1,577	1,434	1,801
NPV	1,747					

Ground improvement option

Years	1	2	3	4	5
	£000	£000	£000	£000	£000
Ground improvements	(10,000)				
Increased gate receipts	(1,800)	4,400	4,400	4,400	4,400
	(11,800)	4,400	4,400	4,400	4,400
Discount factor 10%	0.909	0.826	0.751	0.683	0.621
Present values	(10,726)	3,634	3,304	3,005	2,732
NPV	1,949				

(b) The ground improvement option provides the higher NPV and is therefore the preferable option, based on the objective of shareholder wealth maximisation.

(c) A professional football club may not wish to pursue an objective of shareholder wealth maximisation. It may prefer to invest in quality players in an attempt to enjoy future sporting success. If this is the case, the NPV approach will be less appropriate because the club is not pursuing a strict wealth-related objective.

Chapter 5

5.1 Lee Caterers Ltd

The first step is to establish the NPV for each project:

(a) Cook/chill project

	Cash flows £000	Discount rate 10%	Present value £000
Initial outlay	(200)	1.00	(200)
1 year's time	85	0.91	77.4
2 years' time	94	0.83	78.0
3 years' time	86	0.75	64.5
4 years' time	62	0.68	42.2
		NPV	62.1

(b) Cook/freeze project

	Cash flows £000	Discount rate 10%	Present value £000
Initial outlay	(390)	1.00	(390)
1 year's time	88	0.91	80.1
2 years' time	102	0.83	84.7
3 years' time	110	0.75	82.5
4 years' time	110	0.68	74.8
5 years' time	110	0.62	68.2
6 years' time	90	0.56	50.4
7 years' time	85	0.51	43.4
8 years' time	60	0.47	28.2
		NPV	122.3

Eight years is the minimum period over which the two projects can be compared. The cook/chill will provide the following NPV over this period:

$$\text{NPV} = £62.1 + \frac{£62.1}{(1 + 0.1)^4} = £104.6$$

This NPV of £104,600 is lower than the NPV for the cook/freeze project of £122,300 (see above). Hence, the cook/freeze project should be accepted.

Using the equivalent-annual-annuity approach we derive the following:

$$\text{Cook/chill: } £62.1 \times 0.3155 = £19.59$$

$$\text{Cook/freeze: } £122.3 \times 0.1874 = £22.92$$

This approach leads to the same conclusion as the earlier approach.

5.3 Simonson Engineers plc

(a) The steps in calculating the expected net present value of the proposed plant are as follows:

	(a) Estimated cash flows £m	(b) Probability of occurrence	(a) × (b) Expected value £m
Year 2	2.0	0.2	0.4
	3.5	0.6	2.1
	4.0	0.2	0.8
			3.3
Year 3	2.5	0.2	0.5
	3.0	0.4	1.2
	5.0	0.4	2.0
			3.7

	(a) Estimated cash flows £m	(b) Probability of occurrence	(a) × (b) Expected value £m
Year 4	3.0	0.2	0.6
	4.0	0.7	2.8
	5.0	0.1	0.5
			3.9
Year 5	2.5	0.2	0.5
	3.0	0.5	1.5
	6.0	0.3	1.8
			3.8

Taking into account the expected cash flows for each year:

	Year 1 £m	Year 2 £m	Year 3 £m	Year 4 £m	Year 5 £m
Expected cash flows	(9.0)	3.3	3.7	3.9	3.8
Discount factor	0.909	0.826	0.751	0.683	0.621
Expected present values	(8.18)	2.73	2.78	2.66	2.36
ENPV 2.35					

The expected net present value is £2.35 million.

(b) To find the NPV of the worst possible outcome and the probability of its occurrence:

	Year 1 £m	Year 2 £m	Year 3 £m	Year 4 £m	Year 5 £m
Cash flows	(9.0)	2.0	2.5	3.0	2.5
Discount factor	0.909	0.826	0.751	0.683	0.621
Present values	(8.18)	1.65	1.88	2.05	1.55
NPV (1.05)					

Probability of occurrence $0.2 \times 0.2 \times 0.2 \times 0.2 = \underline{0.0016}$.

(c) The ENPV of the project is positive and so acceptance will increase the wealth of shareholders.

5.4 Helena Chocolate Products Ltd

(a) The first step is to calculate expected sales (units) for each year:

	Sales (units)	Probability	Expected sales
Year 1	100,000	0.2	20,000
	120,000	0.4	48,000
	125,000	0.3	37,500
	130,000	0.1	13,000
			118,500
Year 2	140,000	0.3	42,000
	150,000	0.3	45,000
	160,000	0.2	32,000
	200,000	0.2	40,000
			159,000
Year 3	180,000	0.5	90,000
	160,000	0.3	48,000
	120,000	0.1	12,000
	100,000	0.1	10,000
			160,000

Then the expected net present value can be arrived at:

Expected demand (units)	Incremental cash flow per unit	Total cash flow	Discount rate	ENPV
	£	£	10%	£
118,500	0.38	45,030	0.909	40,932
159,000	0.38	60,420	0.826	49,907
160,000	0.38	60,800	0.751	45,661
				136,500

Less	
Initial outlay	(30,000)
Opportunity costs	(100,000)
ENPV	6,500

Note: Interest charges should be ignored as the cost of capital is reflected in the discount factor.

The expected net present value is £6,500.

(b) As the ENPV is positive, the wealth of shareholders should be increased as a result of taking on the project. However, the ENPV is quite small and so careful checking of the underlying figures and assumptions is essential. The business has the option to sell the new product for an amount that is certain, but this option may have associated risks. The effect of selling the product on the long-term competitiveness of the business must be carefully considered.

Chapter 6

6.1 Financing issues

(a) This topic is dealt with in the chapter. The main benefits of leasing include ease of borrowing, reasonable cost, flexibility, and avoidance of large cash outflows (which normally occur where an asset is purchased).

(b) This topic is also dealt with in the chapter. The main benefits of using retained earnings include no dilution of control, no share issue costs, no delay in receiving funds and the tax benefits of capital appreciation over dividends.

(c) A business may decide to repay a loan earlier than required for various reasons including the following:

- A fall in interest rates may make the existing loan interest rates higher than current loan interest rates. Thus, the business may decide to repay the existing loan using finance from a cheaper loan.
- A rise in interest rates or changes in taxation policy may make loan financing more expensive than other forms of financing. This may make the business decide to repay the loan using another form of finance.
- The business may have surplus cash and may have no other profitable uses for the cash.
- The business may wish to reduce the level of financial risk by reducing the level of gearing.

6.5 Cybele Technology Ltd

(a) Cost of current policies

	£
Cost of financing receivables (60/365 × £4m × 14%)	92,055
Bad debts	20,000
	112,055
Cost of using a factor	
Factor service charge (2% × £4m)	80,000
Finance charges (40/365 × (85% × £4m) × 12%)	44,712
Bank overdraft charges (40/365 × (15% × £4m) × 14%)	9,205
	133,917
Less Administration cost savings	(26,000)
	107,917

The expected increase in profits arising from using a factor is:

$$£112,055 - £107,917 = \underline{£4,138}$$

Thus it would be more profitable to employ a factor. However, the difference between the two options is fairly small and other considerations, such as the need for the business to control all aspects of customer relationships, may have a decisive influence on the final outcome.

(b) This topic is dealt with in the chapter. The main benefits include savings in credit management, releasing key individuals for other tasks, cash advances linked to sales activity and greater certainty in cash flows.

6.6 *Telford Engineers plc*

(a) Projected income statements for the year ending 31 December Year 10:

	Loan notes		Shares
	£m		*£m*
Operating profit	21.00		21.00
Interest payable	(7.80)	((20 × 14%) + £5m)	(5.00)
Profit before taxation	13.20		16.00
Tax (30%)	(3.96)		(4.80)
Profit for the year	9.24		11.20
Dividends payable	4.00		5.00

Statements of share capital, reserves and loans:

	Loan notes	Shares
	£m	*£m*
Equity		
Share capital 25p shares	20.00	25.00 (20m + (20m × 0.25))
Share premium	–	15.00 (20 × (1.00 – 0.25))
Reserves*	48.24	49.20
	68.24	89.20
Non-current liabilities	50.00	30.00
	118.24	119.20

* The reserves figures are the Year 9 reserves *plus* the Year 10 (after taxation) profit *less* dividend paid. The Year 9 figure for share capital and reserves was 63, of which 20 (that is, 80 × 0.25) was share capital, leaving 43 as reserves. Add to that the retained profit for Year 10 (that is, 5.24 (loan) or 6.20 (shares)).

(b) The projected earnings per share are:

Loan notes (9.24/80)	11.55p	
Shares (11.20/100)		11.20p

(c) The loan notes option will raise the gearing ratio and lower the interest cover of the business. This should not provide any real problems for the business as long as profits reach the expected level for Year 9 and remain at that level. However, there is an increased financial risk as a result of higher gearing and shareholders must carefully consider the adequacy of the additional returns to compensate for this higher risk. This appears to be a particular problem since profit levels seem to have been variable over recent years. The figures above suggest only a marginal increase in EPS compared with the equity alternative at the expected level of profit for Year 9.

The share alternative will have the effect of reducing the gearing ratio and is less risky. However, there may be a danger of dilution of control by existing shareholders under this alternative and it may, therefore, prove unacceptable to them. An issue of equity shares may, however, provide greater opportunity for flexibility in financing future projects. Information concerning current loan repayment terms and the attitude of shareholders and existing lenders towards the alternative financing methods would be useful.

Chapter 7

7.1 **(a)** It is not true that the strong form of market efficiency means that investors cannot make a gain from their investment. It does mean, however, that it is not possible to make *abnormal* gains on a consistent basis. Under this form of efficiency, all relevant information is absorbed in share prices. Thus, even those who have 'inside' information concerning a business, such as unpublished reports or confidential management decisions, will be unable to make abnormal gains, on a consistent basis, from using this information.

(b) It is not true to say that private equity firms do not invest in business start-ups. They do however find them challenging for two reasons. First, they are very high-risk: investing in existing businesses with a good track record is a much safer bet. Second, start-ups and early-stage businesses often require fairly small amounts of finance. Unless a significant amount of finance is required, it is difficult to justify the high cost of investigating and monitoring the investment.

(c) This statement is true. The value of a share is represented by the future discounted cash flows that it generates. In a stock market where shares are efficiently priced, investors should therefore be concerned with the ability of a business to generate long-term cash flows rather than its ability to meet short-term profit targets. In other words, if a stock market is efficient, a critical mass of investors will not adopt a short-term view when making share investment decisions.

7.2 **(a)** The weak form of market efficiency is the maximum level of efficiency assumed. When a market shows efficiency beyond this form (that is, semi-strong or strong forms of efficiency) current share prices reflect all publicly available information. There would, therefore, be no point in examining the type of published information mentioned in order to achieve abnormal gains.

(b) There will be no share price reaction. Under the strong form of market efficiency, the share price will rise on 30 July 2013, when the decision to accept the offer is made. All information, whether or not it is formally put into the public domain, will be available to the market.

(c) The maximum level of efficiency assumed is the weak form. Under the semi-strong form of market efficiency, you cannot fool the market. Investors will 'see through' cosmetic changes in accounting policies. Thus, the lengthening of the depreciation period should not provoke a share price reaction.

7.7 *Carpets Direct plc*

(a) The stages in calculating the theoretical ex-rights price of an ordinary share are as follows:

(i) Earnings per share

$$\frac{\text{Profit for the year}}{\text{No. of ordinary shares}} = \frac{£4.5m}{120m} = \underline{£0.0375}$$

(ii) Market value per share

$$\text{Earnings per share} \times \text{P/E ratio} = £0.0375 \times 22 = \underline{£0.825}$$

(iii) For the theoretical ex-rights price:

	£
Original shares (4 × £0.825)	3.30
Rights share (80% × £0.825)	0.66
Value of five shares following rights issue	3.96
Value of one share following the rights issue	$\frac{£3.96}{5}$
Theoretical ex-rights price	= 79.2p

(b) The price at which the rights are likely to be traded is derived as below:

Value of one share after rights issue	79.2p
Less Cost of a rights share	(66.0p)
Value of rights to shareholder	13.2p

(c) Comparing the three options open to the investor:

(i) Option 1: Taking up rights issue

	£
Shareholding following rights issue $((4{,}000 + 1{,}000) \times 79.2p)$	3,960
Less Cost of rights shares $(1{,}000 \times 66p)$	(660)
Shareholder wealth	3,300

(ii) Option 2: Selling the rights

	£
Shareholding following rights issue $(4{,}000 \times 79.2p)$	3,168
Add Proceeds from sale of rights $(1{,}000 \times 13.2p)$	132
Shareholder wealth	3,300

(iii) Option 3: Doing nothing
As the rights are neither purchased nor sold, the shareholder wealth following the rights issue will be:

Shareholding $(4{,}000 \times 79.2p)$	£3,168

We can see that the investor will have the same wealth under the first two options. However, if the investor does nothing the rights issue will lapse and so the investor will lose the value of the rights and will be worse off.

Chapter 8

8.2 *Celtor plc*

(a) The cost of capital is important in the appraisal of investment projects as it represents the return required by investors. Incorrect calculation of the cost of capital can lead to incorrect investment decisions. Too high a cost of capital figure may lead to the rejection of profitable opportunities whereas too low a figure may lead to the acceptance of unprofitable opportunities.

(b) The first step in calculating the weighted average cost of capital is to arrive at the cost of ordinary shares:

$$K_0 = \frac{D_1}{P_0} = \frac{(20 \times 1.04)}{390} + 0.04 = 9.3\%$$

Then the cost of loan capital:

$$K_d = \frac{I(1 - t)}{P_d} = \frac{9(1 - 0.25)}{80} \times 100 = 8.4\%$$

The WACC can now be calculated:

	Cost	Target structure	Proportion (weights)	Contribution to WACC
	%		%	%
Cost of ordinary shares	9.3	100	58.8	5.5
Cost of loan capital	8.4	70	41.2	3.5
WACC				9.0

The weighted average cost of capital to use for future investment decisions is 9 per cent.

8.3 *Grenache plc*

(a) (i) Loan notes issue

Projected income statement for the year ended 30 April Year 8:

	Optimistic £m	Most likely £m	Pessimistic £m
Profit before interest and taxation	22.0	18.1	11.8
Interest payable (£55m × 10%)	(5.5)	(5.5)	(5.5)
Profit before taxation	16.5	12.6	6.3
Tax (25%)	(4.1)	(3.2)	(1.6)
Profit for the year	12.4	9.4	4.7

(ii) Rights issue

Projected income statement for the year ended 30 April Year 8:

	Optimistic £m	Most likely £m	Pessimistic £m
Profit before interest and taxation	22.0	18.1	11.8
Interest payable (10% × £25m)	(2.5)	(2.5)	(2.5)
Profit before taxation	19.5	15.6	9.3
Tax (25%)	(4.9)	(3.9)	(2.3)
Profit for the year	14.6	11.7	7.0

(b) (i) Earnings per share (EPS)
Loan notes option

$$EPS = \frac{\text{Profit available for ordinary shareholders}}{\text{No. of ordinary shares in issue}}$$

	Optimistic	Most likely	Pessimistic
EPS =	$\dfrac{£12.4m}{25m}$	$\dfrac{£9.4m}{25m}$	$\dfrac{£4.7m}{25m}$
=	£0.50	£0.38	£0.19

Rights option

	Optimistic	Most likely	Pessimistic
EPS =	$\dfrac{£14.6m}{30m}$	$\dfrac{£11.7m}{30m}$	$\dfrac{£7.0m}{30m}$
=	£0.49	£0.39	£0.23

(ii) Gearing ratio
Loan notes option

$$\text{Gearing ratio} = \frac{\text{Loan capital}}{\text{Ordinary share capital} + \text{Reserves} + \text{Loan}}$$

Optimistic	Most likely	Pessimistic
$\dfrac{£55m}{£(55.0 + 43.6 + 6.7)m} \times 100\%$	$\dfrac{£55m}{£(55.0 + 43.6 + 3.7)m} \times 100\%$	$\dfrac{£55m}{£(55.0 + 43.6 + 0.5)m} \times 100\%$
= 52.2%	= 53.8%	= 55.5%

Note: The retained profit for the year, which appears in the lower part of the fraction, is calculated as follows:

	Optimistic £m	Most likely £m	Pessimistic £m
Profit for the year	12.4	9.4	4.7
Dividends proposed and paid	(5.7)	(5.7)	(4.2)
Retained profit for the year	6.7	3.7	0.5

Rights option

$$\text{Optimistic} \quad \frac{£25m}{£(25.0+43.6+30.0+7.7)m} \times 100\% = \underline{23.5\%}$$

$$\text{Most likely} \quad \frac{£25m}{£(25.0+43.6+30.0+4.8)m} \times 100\% = \underline{24.2\%}$$

$$\text{Pessimistic} \quad \frac{£25m}{£(25.0+43.6+30.0+2.0)m} \times 100\% = \underline{24.9\%}$$

Note: The retained profit for the year, which appears in the lower part of the fraction, is calculated as follows:

	Optimistic £m	Most likely £m	Pessimistic £m
Profit for the year	14.6	11.7	7.0
Dividends proposed and paid	(6.9)	(6.9)	(5.0)
Retained profit	7.7	4.8	2.0

(c) The above calculations do not reveal any major differences in EPS between the two financing options. The optimistic and most likely options are almost identical. The pessimistic option favours the rights issue. The differences in the gearing ratios, however, are much more pronounced. Under each scenario the gearing ratio for the loan notes option is more than double that under the rights option. The loan notes option involves a significant increase in the level of financial risk for the business as the existing gearing ratio is 36.4 per cent (£25m/£68.6m).

The existing EPS is £0.40 (£9.9m/25m) and so the returns offered under the most likely and pessimistic scenarios do not compare favourably. This may make it difficult to persuade ordinary share investors that additional ordinary share finance should be provided. It may also mean that existing shareholders would resist any increase in gearing in order to finance the venture.

In order to produce a more considered assessment, it would be useful to attach probabilities to each of the three scenarios. An assessment of the likely implications of not undertaking a proposed change should also be provided. Finally, all investments undertaken by the business should be subject to proper investment appraisal using NPV analysis.

8.5 Ashcroft plc

(a) The earnings per share for Year 4 for the loan notes and ordinary share alternatives are computed as follows:

	Loan notes £m	Shares £m
Profit before interest and taxation	1.80	1.80
Interest payable	(0.30)	(–)
Profit before taxation	1.50	1.80
Tax	(0.75)	(0.90)
Profit for the year	0.75	0.90
Shares issued	4.0m	5.3m
EPS	18.75p	17.0p

(b) Let X = the operating profit (profit before interest and taxation) at which the two schemes have equal EPS.

$$\underset{\text{Loan note}}{\frac{(X - \pounds0.3m)(1 - 0.5)}{4.0m}} = \underset{\text{Shares}}{\frac{X(1 - 0.5)}{5.3m}}$$

$$(5.3m\, X - \pounds1.59m)(1 - 0.5) = 4.0m\, X(1 - 0.5)$$

$$0.65m\, X = \pounds0.795m$$

$$X = \underline{\pounds1.223m}$$

This could also be solved graphically as described in the chapter.

(c) The following factors should be taken into account:

- stability of sales and profits
- stability of cash flows
- interest cover and gearing levels
- ordinary share investors' attitude towards risk
- dilution of control caused by new share issue
- security available to offer lenders
- effect on earnings per share and future cash flows.

Chapter 9

9.1 *Scrip dividend*

A scrip dividend can help to maintain the total equity of the business as it simply involves a transfer from reserves to the ordinary share capital account. This means that there will be no increase in the gearing ratio as a result of a scrip dividend. Scrip dividends can also help to conserve cash. Some shareholders may, however, wish to receive cash rather than shares and so a business may offer shareholders the choice of a cash dividend or a scrip dividend. For those wishing to reinvest in the business, a scrip dividend offers the opportunity to acquire shares without incurring share transaction costs. Scrip dividends may undermine the prospects of making rights issues as existing shareholders may be reluctant to invest beyond the scrip dividends.

9.2 *Gripton plc*

(i) A share buyback is likely to offer greater flexibility. Dividends are normally distributed at regular intervals and shareholders will develop expectations concerning both the timing and amount of dividends to be received. Failure to meet these expectations could well provoke an adverse reaction among shareholders. Thus, managers usually feel committed to maintaining a sustainable level of dividend payments. This means they will avoid increasing dividends, which then have to be decreased in subsequent periods.

Share buybacks, meanwhile, tend to be regarded by shareholders as 'one off' events and so there is less expectation concerning their amount or the timing. Where a buyback has been announced, but is then postponed, or even abandoned, it does not incur the kind of adverse reaction from shareholders that would normally accompany a cut in dividends.

(ii) A dividend may offer greater equity between shareholders. Where a buyback is carried out when the share price is below its intrinsic value, it will lead to a transfer of wealth from those shareholders that sell to those that hold. A dividend, meanwhile, is paid to all shareholders and so does not discriminate between different groups of shareholders.

(iii) Dividends are likely to have a stronger signalling effect. A share buyback announcement can send an ambiguous signal to the market as buybacks may benefit managers rather than shareholders.

9.5 *Fellingham plc*

The dividends over the period indicate a 9 per cent compound growth rate and so the chairman has kept to his commitment made in Year 1. This has meant that there has been a predictable stream of income for shareholders. However, during the period, inflation reached quite high levels and in order to maintain purchasing power the shareholders would have had to receive dividends adjusted in line with the general price index. These dividends would be as follows:

$$
\begin{array}{lll}
\text{Year 2} & 10.00 \times 1.11 = 11.10\text{p} \\
\text{Year 3} & 11.10 \times 1.10 = 12.21\text{p} \\
\text{Year 4} & 12.21 \times 1.08 = 13.19\text{p}
\end{array}
$$

We can see that the actual dividends (Year 2, 10.90p; Year 3, 11.88p; Year 4, 12.95p) have fallen below these figures and so there has been a decline in real terms in the dividend income received by shareholders. Clearly, the 9 per cent growth rate did not achieve the anticipated maintenance of purchasing power plus a growth in real income that was anticipated.

However, the 9 per cent dividend growth rate is already high in relation to the earnings of the business, and a higher level of dividend to reflect changes in the general price index may have been impossible to achieve. The dividend coverage ratio for each year is:

Dividend coverage (EPS/DPS)

Year 1	1.1
Year 2	1.1
Year 3	0.9
Year 4	1.3

We can see that the earnings barely cover the dividend in the first two years and that in the third year, earnings fail to cover the dividend. The existing policy seems to be causing some difficulties for the business and can be maintained only if earnings grow at a satisfactory rate.

9.7 *Traminer plc*

The dividend payout ratio and dividend per share of the business over the past five years are:

Year	Dividend payout %	Dividend per share £
2009	50.0	0.84
2010	48.7	1.16
2011	23.9	0.43
2012	23.2	0.45
2013	37.9	0.97

We can see from this table that there is no stable dividend policy. The payout ratio fluctuated between 50 per cent and 23.2 per cent. The dividend per share has also fluctuated significantly over the period. This suggests that dividends are viewed simply as a residual; that is, dividends will be paid only when the business has no profitable opportunities in which to invest its earnings.

A fluctuating dividend policy is unlikely to be popular with shareholders. The evidence suggests that a policy that is predictable and contains no surprises is likely to be much more welcome. The signalling effect of dividends must also be borne in mind. Sudden changes in payout ratios may result in the market interpreting these changes incorrectly.

Chapter 10

10.2 *Hercules Wholesalers Ltd*

(a) The business is probably concerned about its liquidity position because:

- it has a substantial overdraft, which together with its non-current borrowings means that it has borrowed an amount roughly equal to its equity (according to statement of financial position values)

- it has increased its investment in inventories during the past year (as shown by the income statement)
- it has a low current ratio of 1.1:1 (that is, 306/285) and a low acid test ratio of 0.6:1 (that is, 162/285).

(b) The operating cash cycle can be calculated as follows:

Number of days

Average inventories turnover period:

$$\frac{[(\text{Opening inventories} + \text{Closing inventories})/2] \times 365}{\text{Cost of inventories}} = \frac{[(125 + 143)/2] \times 365}{323} \qquad = 151$$

Add Average settlement period for trade receivables:

$$\frac{\text{Trade receivables} \times 365}{\text{Credit sales revenue}} = \frac{163}{452} \times 365 \qquad\qquad = \underline{132}$$

$$283$$

Less Average settlement period for trade payables:

$$\frac{\text{Trade payables} \times 365}{\text{Credit purchases}} = \frac{145}{341} \times 365 \qquad\qquad = \underline{(155)}$$

Operating cash cycle $\qquad\qquad\qquad\qquad\qquad\qquad\qquad \underline{128}$

(c) The business can reduce the operating cash cycle in a number of ways. The average inventories turnover period seems quite long. At present, average inventories held represent about five months' inventories usage. Reducing the level of inventories held can reduce this period. Similarly, the average settlement period for receivables seems long at more than four months' sales revenue. Imposing tighter credit control, offering discounts, charging interest on overdue accounts and so on may reduce this. However, any policy decisions concerning inventories and receivables must take account of current trading conditions.

Extending the period of credit taken to pay suppliers would also reduce the operating cash cycle. For the reasons mentioned in the chapter, however, this option must be given careful consideration.

10.4 *Plastics Manufacturers Ltd*

Ratio analysis

Year	1	2	3
ROCE	16.7%	16.9%	(26.1%)
Operating profit margin	12.5%	11.2%	(23.4%)
Current ratio	1.2	1.1	0.9
Acid test ratio	0.5	0.5	0.3
Inventories turnover period*	91 days	82 days	183 days
Average settlement period for trade receivables	64 days	60 days	91 days

* Using sales revenue figure rather than cost of sales, which is unavailable.

The above figures reveal that Year 3 was a disastrous one for Plastic Toys Ltd (PT). Sales revenue and profitability fell dramatically. The fall in sales revenue does not appear to have been anticipated as inventories levels have risen dramatically in Year 3. The fall in profitability and increase in inventories have created a strain on liquidity that should cause acute concern. The liquidity ratios are very low and it seems the business is in a dangerous state. Extreme caution must therefore be exercised in any dealings with the business.

Before considering the proposal to supply, Plastics Manufacturers Ltd (PM) should establish why Plastic Toys Ltd wishes to change its suppliers. In view of the problems that it faces, there may well be problems with current suppliers. If three months' credit were to be granted, PM will be committed to supplying 6,000 kilos before payment is due. At a marginal cost of £7 a kilo, this means an exposure of £42,000. The risks of non-payment seem to be very high unless there is information concerning PT that indicates that its fortunes will improve in the near future. If PM is determined to supply the goods to PT then some kind of security should be required in order to reduce the risk to PM.

10.5 *Mayo Computers Ltd*

New proposals from credit control department

	£000	£000
Current level of investment in receivables		
(£20m × (60/365))		3,288
Proposed level of investment in receivables		
((£20m × 60%) × (30/365))	(986)	
((£20m × 40%) × (50/365))	(1,096)	(2,082)
Reduction in level of investment		1,206

The reduction in overdraft interest as a result of the reduction in the level of investment will be £1,206,000 × 14% = £169,000.

	£000	£000
Cost of cash discounts offered (£20m × 60% × 2.5%)		300
Additional cost of credit administration		20
		320
Bad debt savings	(100)	
Interest charge savings (see above)	(169)	(269)
Net cost of policy each year		51

These calculations show that the business would incur additional annual cost if it implemented this proposal. It would therefore be cheaper to stay with the existing credit policy.

10.6 *Boswell Enterprises Ltd*

(a)

	Current policy		New policy	
	£000	£000	£000	£000
Trade receivables				
[(£3m × 1/12 × 30%) + (£3m × 2/12 × 70%)]		425.0		
[(£3.15m × 1/12 × 60%) + (£3.15m × 2/12 × 40%)]				367.5
Inventories				
{[£3m − (£3m × 20%)] × 3/12}		600.0		630.0
{[£3.15m − (£3.15m × 20%)] × 3/12}				
Cash (fixed)		140.0		140.0
		1,165.0		1,137.5
Trade payables				
[£3m − (£3m × 20%)] × 2/12]	(400.0)			
{[£3.15m − (£3.15m × 20%)] × 2/12}			(420.0)	
Accrued variable expenses				
[£3m × 1/12 × 10%]	(25.0)			
[£3.15m × 1/12 × 10%]			(26.3)	
Accrued fixed expenses	(15.0)	(440.0)	(15.0)	(461.3)
Investment in working capital		725.0		676.2

(b) The expected profit for the year

	Current policy		New policy	
	£000	£000	£000	£000
Sales revenue		3,000.0		3,150.0
Cost of goods sold		(2,400.0)		(2,520.0)
Gross profit (20%)		600.0		630.0
Variable expenses (10%)	(300.0)		(315.0)	
Fixed expenses	(180.0)		(180.0)	
Discounts (£3.15m × 60% × 2.5%)	–	(480.0)	(47.3)	(542.3)
Profit for the year		120.0		87.7

(c) Under the proposed policy we can see that the investment in working capital will be slightly lower than under the current policy. However, profits will be substantially lower as a result of offering discounts. The increase in sales revenue resulting from the discounts will not be sufficient to offset the additional cost of making the discounts to customers. It seems that the business should, therefore, stick with its current policy.

Chapter 11

11.2 *Aquarius plc*

There are a number of ways in which the accuracy of the predicted free cash flow figures may be checked. These include:

- Internal

  - *Past results*. These may be used to see whether the future projections are in line with past achievements.

  - *Strategy*. The future free cash flows for the business should reflect the strategies that have been put in place over the planning period.

  - *Capacity*. The ability of the business to generate the free cash flows from the resources available over the planning period should be considered.

  - *Market research*. The evidence from any market research carried out by the business should be consistent with the estimates made.

- External

  - *Industry forecasts*. Forecasts for the industry as a whole may be examined to see whether the predicted sales and profits for the business are in line with industry forecasts.

  - *External commentators*. Stockbrokers and financial journalists may have made predictions about the likely future performance of the business and so may provide an external (and perhaps more objective) view of likely future prospects.

  - *Technology*. The likely impact of technological change on free cash flows may be assessed using technology forecasts.

  - *Competitor analysis*. The performance of competitors may be used to help assess likely future market share.

This is not an exhaustive list. You may have thought of other ways.

11.4 *Virgo plc*

There is no single correct answer to this problem. The suggestions set out below are based on experiences that some businesses have had in implementing a management bonus system based on EVA® performance.

In order to get the divisional managers to think and act like the owners of the business, it is recommended that divisional performance, as measured by EVA®, should form a significant part of their total rewards. Thus, around 50 per cent of the total rewards paid to managers could be related to the EVA® that has been generated for a period. (In the case of very senior managers it could be more, and for junior managers less.)

The target for managers to achieve could be a particular level of improvement in EVA® for their division over a year. A target bonus can then be set for achievement of the target level of improvement. If this target level of improvement is achieved, 100 per cent of the bonus should be paid. If the target is not achieved, an agreed percentage (below 100 per cent) could be paid according to the amount of shortfall. If, however, the target is exceeded, an agreed percentage (with no upper limits) may be paid.

The timing of the payment of management bonuses is important. In the question it was mentioned that Virgo plc wishes to encourage a longer-term view among its managers. One approach is to use a 'bonus bank' system whereby the bonus for a period is placed in a bank and a certain proportion (usually one-third) can be drawn in the period in which it is earned. If the target for the following period is not met, there can be a charge against the bonus bank and so the total amount available for withdrawal is reduced. This will ensure that the managers try to maintain improvements in EVA® consistently over the years.

In some cases, the amount of bonus is determined by three factors: the performance of the business as a whole (as measured by EVA®), the performance of the division (as measured by EVA®) and the performance of the particular manager (using agreed indicators of performance). Performance for the business as a whole is often given the highest weighting and individual performance the lowest weighting. Thus, 50 per cent of the bonus may be for corporate performance, 30 per cent for divisional performance and 20 per cent for individual performance.

11.6 *Pisces plc*

Adjusted NOPAT

	£m	£m
Operating loss		(20.5)
EVA® adjustments		
R&D costs (40 − (1/16 × 80)) (Note 1)	35.0	
Excess allowance	6.5	41.5
Adjusted NOPAT		21.0

Adjusted net assets (or capital invested)

	£m	£m
Net assets per statement of financial position		196.5
Add		
R&D costs (Note 1)	70.0	
Allowance for trade receivables	6.5	
Restructuring costs (Note 2)	6.0	82.5
		279.0
Less Marketable investments		(9.0)
Adjusted net assets		270.0

Notes:

1 The R&D costs represent a writing back of £40 million and a writing off of 1/16 of the total cost of the R&D as the benefits are expected to last 16 years.

2 The restructuring costs are added back to the net assets as they provide benefits over an infinite period.

EVA® can be calculated as follows:

$$EVA® = NOPAT - (R \times C)$$
$$= £21m - (7\% \times £270m)$$
$$= £2.1m$$

Thus, the EVA® for the period is positive even though an operating loss was recorded. This means that shareholder wealth increased during the third year.

Chapter 12

12.2 *Dawn Raider plc*

	£m
(a) (i) The bid consideration is ((200m shares/2) × 198p)	198
The market value of the shares in Sleepy Giant is (£100m × 2 × 72p)	(144)
The bid premium is therefore	54

(ii) Sleepy Giant's net assets per share are £446m/200m   = £2.23

(iii) Dividends from Sleepy Giant before the takeover are 100 × 7p = £7.00
Dividends from Dawn Raider after takeover are 50 × 2p   = £1.00

(iv) Earnings per share after takeover:

	£m
Expected post-tax profits of Dawn Raider	23
Current post-tax profits of Sleepy Giant	16
Post-tax savings	1
Improvements due to management	5
Total earnings	45
Expected EPS (£45m/(200m + 100m shares))	15p

(v) Expected share price following takeover will be calculated as follows:

P/E ratio × expected EPS.

$$\text{P/E ratio at 31 May Year 8} = \text{Share price/EPS}$$
$$= 198/9.0$$
$$= 22$$
$$\text{Expected share price} = 22 \times 15\text{p}$$
$$= \underline{£3.30}$$

(b) (i) The net assets per share of the business is irrelevant. This represents a past investment that is irrelevant to future decisions. The key comparison is between the current market value of the shares of Sleepy Giant and the bid price.

   The dividend received from Dawn Raider will be substantially lower than that received from Sleepy Giant. However, the share value of Dawn Raider has grown much faster than that of Sleepy Giant. The investor must consider the total returns from the investment rather than simply the dividends received.

(ii) We can see above that by accepting the bid, the shareholders of Sleepy Giant will make an immediate and substantial gain. The bid premium is more than 37 per cent higher than the current market value of the shares in Sleepy Giant. This could provide a sufficient incentive for the shareholders of Sleepy Giant to accept the offer. However, the shareholders of Dawn Raider must consider the bid carefully. Although the expected share price calculated above is much higher following the bid, it is based on the assumption that the P/E ratio of the business will not be affected by the takeover. However, this may not be the case. Sleepy Giant is a much larger business in terms of sales and net assets than Dawn Raider and has a much lower P/E ratio (nine times). The market would have to be convinced that Sleepy Giant's prospects will be substantially improved following the takeover.

12.4 *Simat plc*

(a) Calculating the value per share in the consideration of Stidwell Ltd on a net assets (liquidation) basis gives:

$$P_0 = \frac{\text{Total assets at realisable values} - \text{Total liabilities}}{\text{No. of shares in issue}}$$

$$= \frac{£347{,}000 \ (\text{that is } 285 + 72 + 15 + 157) - (42 + 140)}{300{,}000}$$

$$= £1.16$$

(b) The dividend yield method gives:

$$P_0 = \frac{\text{Gross dividend per share}}{\text{Gross dividend yield}} \times 100$$

$$= \frac{(18{,}000/300{,}000) \times 100/90}{2.76} \times 100$$

$$= £2.42$$

(c) The P/E ratio method gives:

$$P_0 = \text{P/E ratio} \times \text{earnings per share}$$
$$= 11 \times (\pounds 48,500/300,000)$$
$$= \pounds 1.78$$

12.6 *Larkin Conglomerates plc*

(a) The value of an ordinary share in Hughes Ltd according to the three methods is calculated as follows:

(i) Net assets (liquidation) basis:

$$P_0 = \frac{\text{Total assets at realisable values} - \text{Total liabilities}}{\text{No. of shares in issue}}$$

$$= \frac{\pounds(326 - 166)}{60}$$

$$= \frac{\pounds 160}{60}$$

$$= \pounds 2.67$$

(ii) Dividend yield method:

$$P_0 = \frac{(\text{Net dividend per share} \times 100/75)}{\text{Gross dividend yield}} \times 100$$

$$= \frac{(4.0/60.0) \times 100/75}{5} \times 100$$

$$= \pounds 1.78$$

(iii) Price/earnings ratio method:

$$P_0 = \text{P/E ratio} \times \text{earnings per share}$$
$$= 12 \times (\pounds 16.4/60)$$
$$= \pounds 3.28$$

(b) Other information might include:

■ Details of relations with suppliers, employees, the community and other stakeholders should be ascertained.

■ The nature and condition of the assets owned by the target business should be examined. The suitability of the assets and their ability to perform the tasks required will be vital.

■ Key personnel will need to be identified and their intentions with regard to the business following the takeover must be ascertained.

■ Onerous commitments entered into by the business (for example, capital expenditure decisions, contracts with suppliers) must be identified and evaluated.

■ Details of the state of the order book, the market share of the products or services provided by the business and the loyalty of its customers should be established.

■ Examination of the budgets which set out expected performance levels, output levels and future financing needs would be useful.

■ Information concerning the cost structure of the business would be useful.

Glossary of key terms

ABC system of inventories control A method of applying different levels of inventories control based on the value of each category of inventories. *p. 417*

accounting rate of return (ARR) The average profit from an investment, expressed as a percentage of the average investment made. *p. 128*

acid test ratio A liquidity ratio that relates the current assets (less inventories) to the current liabilities. *p. 91*

ageing schedule of trade receivables A report dividing receivables into categories, depending on the length of time outstanding. *p. 430*

agency problem The conflict of interest between shareholders (the principals) and the managers (agents) of a business which arises when the managers seek to maximise their own welfare. *p. 17*

Alternative Investment Market (AIM) Second-tier market of the London Stock Exchange that specialises in the securities of smaller businesses. *p. 305*

annuity An investment that pays a constant sum each year over a period of time. *p. 179*

arbitrage transaction A transaction that exploits differences in price between similar shares (or other assets) and which involves selling the overpriced shares and purchasing the under-priced shares. *p. 353*

asset-based finance A form of finance where assets are used as security for cash advances to a business. Factoring and invoice discounting, where the security is trade receivables, are examples of asset-based finance. *p. 253*

average inventories turnover period An efficiency ratio that measures the average period for which inventories are held by a business. *p. 83*

average settlement period for (trade) payables An efficiency ratio that measures the average time taken by a business to pay its payables. *p. 85*

average settlement period for (trade) receivables An efficiency ratio that measures the average time taken for credit customers to pay the amounts owing. *p. 84*

bank overdraft Amount owing to a bank that is repayable on demand. The amount borrowed and the rate of interest may fluctuate over time. *p. 249*

behavioural finance An approach to finance that rejects the notion that investors behave in a rational manner but rather make systematic errors when processing information. *p. 283*

beta (coefficient) A measure of the extent to which the returns on a particular share vary with the market as a whole. *p. 320*

bill of exchange A written agreement requiring one party to the agreement to pay a particular amount to the other party at some future date. *p. 249*

bonds See Loan notes. *p. 234*

bonus issue (scrip issue) Transfer of reserves to share capital requiring the issue of new shares to shareholders in proportion to existing shareholdings. *p. 288*

business angels Wealthy individuals willing to invest in businesses that are often at an early stage in their development. *p. 301*

capital asset pricing model (CAPM) A method of establishing the cost of share capital that identifies two forms of risk: diversifiable risk and non-diversifiable risk. *p. 319*

capital markets Financial markets for long-term loan capital and shares. *p. 5*

capital rationing Limiting the long-term funds available for investment during a period. Capital rationing may be imposed by managers or by investors. *p. 157*

cash discount A reduction in the amount due for goods or services sold on credit in return for prompt payment. *p. 428*

cash tax rate The percentage of profits that a business pays in cash taxes for a period. *p. 461*

clientele effect The phenomenon where investors seek out businesses whose dividend policies match their particular needs. *p. 383*

coefficient of correlation A statistical measure of association that can be used to measure the degree to which the returns from two separate projects are related. The measure ranges from +1 to −1. A measure of +1 indicates a perfect positive correlation and a measure of −1 indicates a perfect negative correlation. *p. 212*

Competition Commission (formerly Monopolies and Mergers Commission) A UK government regulatory body that seeks to prevent monopolies and mergers from occurring that are anti-competitive and not in the public interest. *p. 526*

conglomerate merger A merger between two businesses engaged in unrelated activities. *p. 502*

convertible loan notes Loan notes that can be converted into ordinary share capital at the option of the holders. *p. 236*

corporate governance Systems for directing and controlling a business. *p. 17*

cost of capital The rate of return required by investors in the business. The cost of capital is used as the criterion rate of return when evaluating investment proposals using the NPV and IRR methods of appraisal. *p. 144*

creative accounting Adopting accounting policies to achieve a particular view of performance and position that preparers would like users to see rather than what is a true and fair view. *p. 110*

crown jewels The most valued part of a business (which may be sold to fend off a hostile takeover bid). *p. 525*

cum dividend A term used to describe the price of a share that includes the right to receive a forthcoming dividend. *p. 373*

current ratio A liquidity ratio that relates the current assets of the business to the current liabilities. *p. 90*

debt factoring See Factoring. *p. 250*

deep discount bonds Redeemable bonds that are issued at a low or zero rate of interest and at a large discount to their redeemable value. *p. 235*

degree of financial gearing A measure of the sensitivity of earnings per share to changes in profit before interest and taxation. *p. 339*

demerger (spin-off) The transfer of part of the assets in an existing business to a new business. Shareholders in the existing business will be given shares, usually on a pro rata basis, in the new business. *p. 528*

directors' share options A directors' share option scheme gives directors the right, but not the obligation, to buy equity shares in their company at an agreed price. The conditions of the scheme will usually stipulate that the option to buy must be exercised either on, or after, a specified future date. *p. 490*

discount factor The rate used when making investment decisions to discount future cash flows in order to arrive at their present value. *p. 142*

discriminate function A boundary line, produced by multiple discriminate analysis, that identifies those businesses that are likely to suffer financial distress and those that are not. *p. 106*

diversifiable risk That part of the total risk that is specific to an investment and which can be diversified away through combining the investment with other investments. *p. 215*

diversification The process of reducing risk by investing in a variety of different projects or assets. *p. 211*

divestment The selling off of part of the operations of a business. *p. 527*

dividend A transfer of assets (usually cash) made by a business to its shareholders. *p. 372*

dividend cover ratio The reciprocal of the dividend payout ratio (see below). *p. 96*

dividend payout ratio An investment ratio that divides the dividends announced for the period by the profit generated during the period and available for dividends. *p. 95*

dividend per share An investment ratio that divides the dividends announced for a period by the number of shares in issue. *p. 96*

dividend yield ratio An investment ratio that relates the cash return from a share to its current market value. *p. 96*

due diligence An investigation of all material information relating to the financial, technical and legal aspects of a business prior to making an investment. *p. 303*

earnings per share An investment ratio that divides the earnings (profits) generated by a business, and available to ordinary shareholders, by the number of shares in issue. *p. 97*

economic order quantity (EOQ) The quantity of inventories that should be purchased in order to minimise total inventories costs. *p. 418*

economic value added (EVA®) The difference between the net operating profit after tax and the required returns from investors. *p. 467*

efficient stock market A stock market in which new information is quickly and accurately absorbed by investors, resulting in an appropriate share price adjustment. *p. 295*

equivalent-annual-annuity approach An approach to deciding among competing investment projects with unequal lives which involves converting the NPV of each project into an annual annuity stream over the project's expected life. *p. 179*

eurobonds Bearer bonds that are issued by listed businesses and other organisations in various countries with the finance being raised on an international basis. *p. 235*

EVA margin A ratio that divides EVA for the period by sales revenue for the period and expresses the answer as a percentage. *p. 472*

EVA momentum A ratio that divides the change in EVA from the previous period by the sales revenue for the previous period. The answer is expressed as a percentage. *p. 472*

event tree diagram A diagram that portrays the various events or outcomes associated with a particular course of action and the probabilities associated with each event or outcome. *p. 201*

ex dividend A term used to describe the price of a share that excludes any right to a forthcoming dividend. *p. 373*

expected net present value (ENPV) A method of dealing with risk that involves assigning a probability of occurrence to each possible outcome. The expected net present value of the project represents a weighted average of the possible NPVs where the probabilities are used as weights. *p. 198*

expected value A weighted average of a range of possible outcomes where the probabilities are used as weights. *p. 198*

expected value–standard deviation rule A decision rule that can be employed to discriminate among competing investments where the possible outcomes are known and are normally distributed. *p. 209*

factoring (debt factoring) A method of raising short-term finance. A financial institution ('factor') will manage the credit sales records of the business and will be prepared to advance sums to the business based on the amount of trade receivables outstanding. *p. 250*

finance lease Agreement that gives the lessee the right to use a particular asset for substantially the whole of its useful life in return for regular fixed payments. It represents an alternative to outright purchase. *p. 242*

financial derivative Any form of financial instrument, based on share or loan capital, which can be used by investors either to increase their returns or to decrease their exposure to risk. *p. 242*

financial gearing The existence of fixed-payment-bearing securities (for example, loans) in the capital structure of a business. *p. 92*

five Cs of credit A checklist of factors to be taken into account when assessing the credit-worthiness of a customer. *p. 423*

fixed charge Where a specific asset is offered as security for a loan. *p. 230*

fixed interest rate A rate of return payable to lenders that will remain unchanged with rises and falls in market interest rates. *p. 240*

floating charge Where the whole of the assets of the business is offered as security for a loan. The charge will 'crystallise' and fix on specific assets in the event of a default in loan obligations. *p. 230*

floating interest rate A rate of return payable to lenders that will rise and fall with market rates of interest. *p. 239*

free cash flows Cash flows available to long-term lenders and shareholders after any new investment in assets. *p. 460*

FTSE (Footsie) indices Indices available to help monitor trends in overall share price movements of Stock Exchange listed businesses. *p. 271*

future growth value (FGV®) Value placed on the future growth potential of a business by investors. Equal to the market value of the business minus (capital invested plus EVA®/r). *p. 488*

gearing ratio A ratio that relates the contribution of long-term lenders to the total long-term capital of the business. *p. 92*

golden parachute Substantial fee payable to a manager of a business in the event that the business is taken over. *p. 525*

gross profit margin A profitability ratio relating the gross profit for the period to the sales for that period. *p. 80*

hedging arrangement An attempt to reduce or eliminate the risk associated with a particular action by taking some form of counter-action. *p. 240*

hire purchase A method of acquiring an asset by paying the purchase price by instalments over a period. Normally, control of the asset will pass as soon as the hire purchase contract is signed and the first instalment is paid, whereas ownership will pass on payment of the final instalment. *p. 245*

horizontal merger A merger between two businesses in the same industry and at the same point in the production/distribution chain. *p. 502*

indifference point The level of profit and interest before taxation at which two, or more, financing schemes provide the same level of return to ordinary shareholders. *p. 345*

inflation A rise in the general price level. *p. 139*

information asymmetry Where the availability of information differs between groups (such as managers and shareholders). *p. 383*

information signalling Conveying information to shareholders through management actions (for example, increasing dividends to convey management optimism concerning the future). *p. 383*

interest cover ratio A gearing ratio that divides the profit before interest and taxation by the interest payable for a period. *p. 93*

interest rate swap An arrangement between two businesses whereby each business assumes responsibility for the other's interest payments. *p. 240*

internal rate of return (IRR) The discount rate for a project that has the effect of producing zero NPV. *p. 145*

invoice discounting A form of finance provided by a financial institution based on a proportion of the face value of the credit sales outstanding. *p. 252*

junk (high-yield) bonds Loan capital with a relatively high level of investment risk for which investors are compensated by relatively high levels of return. *p. 238*

just-in-time (JIT) inventories management A system of inventories management that aims to have supplies delivered to production just in time for their required use. *p. 421*

lead time The time lag between placing an order for goods or services and their delivery. *p. 415*

linear programming A mathematical technique for rationing limited resources in such a way as to optimise the benefits. *p. 176*

loan covenants Conditions contained within a loan agreement that are designed to protect the lenders. *p. 231*

loan notes Long-term borrowings usually made by limited companies. *p. 234*

market capitalisation Total market value of the shares of a business. *p. 272*

market value added (MVA) The difference between the market value of the business and the total investment that has been made in it. *p. 479*

materials requirement planning (MRP) system A computer-based system of inventories control that schedules the timing of deliveries of bought-in parts and materials to coincide with production requirements to meet demand. *p. 421*

merger When two or more businesses combine in order to form a single business. *p. 502*

mortgage A loan secured on property. *p. 239*

multiple discriminate analysis A statistical technique, used to predict financial distress, which involves using an index based on a combination of financial ratios. *p. 105*

net assets (book value) method A method of valuing the shares of a business by reference to the value of the net assets as shown in the statement of financial position. *p. 531*

net assets (liquidation) method A method of valuing the shares of a business by reference to the net realisable values of its net assets. *p. 533*

net assets (replacement cost) method A method of valuing the shares of a business by reference to the replacement cost of its net assets. *p. 534*

net present value (NPV) The net cash flows from a project that have been adjusted to take account of the time value of money. The NPV measure is used to evaluate investment projects. *p. 136*

net realisable value The selling price of an asset, less any costs incurred in selling the asset. *p. 533*

non-diversifiable risk That part of the total risk that is common to all investments and which cannot be diversified away by combining investments. *p. 215*

normal distribution The description applied to the distribution of a set of data which, when displayed graphically, forms a symmetrical bell-shaped curve. *p. 208*

objective probabilities Probabilities based on information gathered from past experience. *p. 209*

offer for sale Method of selling shares to the public through the use of an issuing house which acts as an intermediary. *p. 289*

Office of Fair Trading (OFT) A government department that seeks to improve the functioning of markets by ensuring competition and consumer choice. Where a takeover or merger is likely to adversely affect competition within a particular market, the OFT may refer it to the Competition Commission. *p. 526*

operating cash cycle The time period between the outlay of cash to purchase goods supplied and the ultimate receipt of cash from the sale of the goods. *p. 436*

operating lease A short-term lease where the rewards and risks of ownership stay with the owner. *p. 244*

operating profit margin A profitability ratio relating the operating profit for the period to the sales for that period. *p. 79*

opportunity cost The value in monetary terms of being deprived of the next best opportunity in order to pursue a particular objective. *p. 150*

optimal capital structure The particular mix of long-term funds employed by a business that minimises the cost of capital. *p. 349*

overtrading The situation arising when a business is operating at a level of activity that cannot be supported by the amount of finance which has been committed. *p. 101*

pac-man defence A means of defending against a hostile takeover bid, which involves launching a bid for the bidding company. *p. 525*

payback period (PP) The time taken for the initial investment in a project to be repaid from the net cash inflows of the project. *p. 133*

PBIT–EPS indifference chart A chart that plots the returns to shareholders at different levels of profit before interest and taxation for different financing schemes. *p. 344*

per-cent-of-sales method A method of financial planning that first estimates the sales for the planning period and then estimates other financial variables as a percentage of the sales figure. *p. 45*

placing An issue of shares to selected investors, such as financial institutions, rather than to the public. *p. 291*

plug The particular form of finance used to fill a financing gap. *p. 46*

poison pill A defensive measure taken by a business that is designed to make it unattractive to potential acquirers. *p. 525*

post-completion audit A review of the performance of an investment project to see whether actual performance matched planned performance and whether any lessons can be drawn from the way in which the investment was carried out. *p. 160*

price/book value ratio A ratio that relates the market price per share to the net assets (book value) per share. *p. 532*

price/earnings ratio An investment ratio that relates the market value of a share to the earnings per share. *p. 97*

private equity Equity finance primarily for small and medium-sized businesses wishing to grow but which do not have ready access to stock markets. *p. 293*

profitability index The present value of the future cash flows from a project divided by the present value of the outlay. *p. 175*

projected financial statements Financial statements such as the cash flow statement, income statement and statement of financial position that have been prepared on the basis of estimates and which relate to the future. *p. 33*

public issue Method of issuing shares that involves a direct invitation from the business to the public to subscribe for shares. *p. 290*

record date A date that is set by the directors of a business to establish who is eligible to receive dividends. Those shareholders registered with the company on this date will receive any dividends announced for the period. *p. 373*

relevant costs Costs that are relevant to a particular decision. *p. 150*

replacement cost The cost of replacing an asset with an identical asset. *p. 534*

return on capital employed (ROCE) A profitability ratio expressing the relationship between the operating profit and the long-term capital invested in the business. *p. 77*

return on ordinary shareholders' funds (ROSF) A profitability ratio expressing the relationship between the profit available for ordinary shareholders during the period and the ordinary shareholders' funds invested in the business. *p. 76*

rights issue An issue of shares to existing shareholders on the basis of the number of shares already held. *p. 285*

risk The likelihood that what is estimated to occur will not actually occur. *p. 54*

risk-adjusted discount rate A method of dealing with risk that involves adjusting the discount rate for projects according to the level of risk involved. The rate will be the risk-free rate plus an appropriate risk premium. *p. 196*

risk-averse investors Investors who select the investment with the lowest risk, where the returns from different investments are equal. *p. 193*

risk-neutral investors Investors who are indifferent to the level of risk associated with different investments. *p. 193*

risk premium An extra amount of return from an investment, owing to a perceived level of risk: the greater the perceived level of risk, the larger the risk premium. *p. 139*

risk-seeking investors Investors who select the investment with the highest risk where the returns from different investments are equal. *p. 193*

rolling cash flow projections The preparation of forecasts to compensate for time that has elapsed during the forecast period so that a complete forecast horizon is restored. *p. 39*

sale and leaseback An agreement to sell an asset (usually property) to another party and simultaneously lease the asset back in order to continue using the asset. *p. 244*

sales revenue per employee An efficiency ratio that relates the sales generated during a period to the average number of employees of the business. *p. 87*

sales revenue to capital employed An efficiency ratio that relates the sales generated during a period to the long-term capital employed. *p. 86*

scenario analysis A method of dealing with risk that involves changing a number of variables simultaneously so as to provide a particular future scenario for managers to consider. *p. 56*

scrip dividend A dividend to shareholders consisting of additional shares rather than cash. *p. 394*

scrip issue See Bonus issue. *p. 288*

securitisation Bundling together illiquid financial or physical assets of the same type in order to provide backing for issuing interest-bearing securities, such as bonds. *p. 247*

security An asset pledged or guarantee provided against a loan. *p. 230*

sensitivity analysis An examination of the key variables affecting a project to see how changes in each variable might influence the outcome. *p. 54*

sensitivity chart A chart that portrays the effect of changes to key variables on the NPV of a project. *p. 189*

share buyback Where a business buys its own shares and then cancels them. *p. 396*

share options A scheme that allows managers and employees the right, but not the obligation, to acquire shares in the business at some future date at an agreed price. *p. 400*

shareholder value Putting the needs of shareholders at the heart of management decisions. *p. 455*

shareholder value analysis (SVA) A method of measuring and managing business value based on the long-term cash flows generated. *p. 459*

shareholder wealth maximisation The idea that the main purpose of a business is to maximise the wealth of its owners (shareholders). This idea underpins modern financial management. *p. 6*

shortest-common-period-of-time approach A method of comparing the profitability of projects with unequal lives that establishes the shortest common period of time over which the projects can be compared. *p. 177*

simulation A method of dealing with risk that involves calculating probability distributions from a range of possible outcomes. *p. 191*

spin-off see Demerger. *p. 528*

stakeholder approach The view that each group with a legitimate stake in the business should have its interests reflected in the objectives that the business pursues. Managers then serve the interests of these groups and mediate between them. *p. 9*

standard deviation A measure of spread that is based on deviations from the mean or expected value. *p. 205*

Stock Exchange A primary and secondary market for business capital. *p. 270*

subjective probabilities Probabilities based on opinion rather than past data. *p. 209*

subordinated loan A loan that is ranked below other loan capital in the order of interest payment and capital repayment. *p. 232*

takeover Normally used to describe a situation where a larger business acquires control of a smaller business, which is then absorbed by the larger business. *p. 502*

tax exhaustion the situation arising where a business has insufficient profits to exploit the tax benefits of loan finance. *p. 356*

tender issue An issue of shares to investors that requires investors to state the amount they are prepared to pay for the shares. *p. 290*

term loan A loan, usually from a bank, which is tailored specifically to the needs of the borrower. The loan contract usually specifies the repayment date, interest rate and so on. *p. 234*

total shareholder return (TSR) The change in share value over a period plus any dividends paid during the period. *p. 483*

trade-off theory of capital structure This theory asserts that when a business is deciding upon an appropriate level of gearing, it will weigh the benefits of taking on debt, in the form of tax benefits, against the costs involved, in the form of higher bankruptcy risk. *p. 356*

UK Corporate Governance Code A code of practice for companies listed on the London Stock Exchange that deals with corporate governance matters. *p. 19*

UK Stewardship Code A code of practice that aims to improve the quality of engagement between financial institutions and investee companies. *p. 26*

univariate analysis A method, used to help predict financial distress, which involves the use of a single ratio as a predictor. *p. 104*

utility function A chart that portrays the level of satisfaction or pleasure obtained from receiving additional wealth at different levels of existing wealth. *p. 193*

value drivers Key variables that determine business performance. *p. 461*

venture capital Finance available for investment in start-up and early-stage businesses. *p. 293*

vertical merger A merger between a supplier of goods or services and its customer. *p. 502*

warrant A document giving the holder the right, but not the obligation, to acquire shares in a business at an agreed price at some future date. *p. 241*

weighted average cost of capital (WACC) A weighted average of the post-tax costs of the forms of long-term finance employed within a business where the market value of the particular forms of finance are used as weights. *p. 331*

white knight A bidder for a business that has been invited by the managers of that business to make a bid. The invitation is made to defend the business against a hostile bid from another business. *p. 525*

white squire A business that is approached by the managers of another business to purchase a large block of shares (but not a controlling interest) in that business with the object of rescuing the business from a hostile takeover. *p. 525*

working capital Current assets less current liabilities. *p. 52*

Index

Page numbers in **bold** refer to glossary entries.